A Programmer's Introduction to
Windows DNA

Christian Gross

apress

A Programmer's Introduction to Windows DNA

Library of Congress Catalog-in-Publication Data

[Insert CIP Data here]

ISBN 978-1-893115-17-0

Additional material to this book can be downloaded from http://extras.springer.com

10 9 8 7 6 5 4 3 2

Trademarked names may appear in this book. Rather than use a trademark symbol with every occurrence of a trademarked name, we use the names only in an editorial fashion and to the benefit of the trademark owner, with no intention of infringement of the trademark.

Project Coordinator: Grace Wong

Developmental Editor: Andy Carroll

Technical Reviewers: Isabelle Laurin

Production: TSI Graphics

Copyediting: Freelance Editorial Services

Indexing: Barbara Palumbo

Cover Design: Derek Yee Design

Distributed to the book trade worldwide by Springer-Verlag New York, Inc.
175 Fifth Avenue, New York, NY 10010

In the United States, phone 1-800-SPRINGER; orders@springer-ny.com
http://www.springer-ny.com

For information on translations, please contact APress directly:
APress, 6400 Hollis Street, Suite 9, Emeryville, CA 94608
Phone: (510) 595-3110; Fax: (510) 595-3122; info@apress.com; www.apress.com

TO MY WIFE:

Isabelle, it has been a long time, but here it is finally.

TO MY FATHER:

It hurts that you never saw the book, but with the passing of time,

I understand that experience and humility are the keys to understanding.

Contents

Introduction

This book is about building custom applications. It explains how to write optimal multitier applications using a variety of tools and services. Writing custom applications is very different from writing shrink-wrapped software.

Writing custom applications requires that you develop an application to solve a specific business problem. You do not try to solve the application in a generic context—you try to solve it for the specific situation because, when you are writing custom applications, there is always a time and cost factor. Also, each custom application is different and has its own quirks and tweaks.

The other major difference between writing custom applications and writing shrink-wrapped applications is that you have to be able to judge what solution is wanted. The best technical solution is not always the most appropriate solution. Custom applications are influenced by both politics and logic, which often conflict.

Writing good custom applications is an art, and it is learned by combining practice and some theory. In this book, I explain some of the art of building custom applications. Not all of what I will explain is "theoretically" correct, but it is all correct in practice. In other words, all the things I'll show you in this book have been tested in real-life situations and work well. So, if someone says that person X, Y, or Z has said that a particular technique is incorrect, my answer is that that's okay. There is more than one way to peel a banana. Use the method that works best for you.

Examples, Languages, and Source Code

Throughout the book I have tried very hard to use a variety of programming languages. When I use one language or another, it is because that language is better for that particular circumstance. To me a language is a tool for creating a program—no more and no less. Each language has its advantages and disadvantages. It is best to think in terms of components and concepts. Any language can then be related to those concepts.

The source code for the various examples is available in Visual Basic, Visual C++, and, when possible, Visual J++. The only place where I did not provide code in multiple languages is in the scripts. I am a die-hard JavaScript/JScript programmer.

I hope you enjoy the book. If you want to discuss anything, do not hesitate to send me e-mail at ChristianGross@yahoo.de or at ChristianGross@excite.com.

Acknowledgments

I need to give thanks to all of the people who helped me.

Lon Fisher: Dude, what can I say? Thanks...

Richard Hale Shaw: Richard, thanks for understanding my "sky is going to be falling" moments, and for believing in me.

Gary Cornell: Thank you for being a superb and understanding publisher. You are a publisher that stands above the rest, and I went through quite a few... a publisher that stood by me to the end.

Andy Carroll: I never knew developmental editors could be that fantastic. A great job.

Mary Kirtland: The wonder woman of Microsoft—you are probably the only person who actually understands all of the technologies that Microsoft develops. One of these days, I will stump you with a question.

Mathias Heffner and Arne Steingräber: Guys, thanks for not laughing too much when I kept saying, "Trust me, it is done." And thanks for giving me the support that I needed.

The Visual C++ team and some specific team members: Chris Hargarten, Jeff Ressler, Dean Rowe, Christian Beaumont, Mike Blaszack: I just have to say, thank you, thank you, thank you. You treated me like I was a member of your team, and I have always treasured that relationship. It has helped me understand that you guys are not the Microsoft Gorilla, but the hacks who just want to write cool code.

My wife Isabelle: My technical editor, the woman who does not shy away from telling me when I was full of it in the book. You are the person who stood by me time and time again.

And my two English Bulldogs: Patches and Bossy, who through thick and thin managed to put a smile on my face.

Chapter 1

Introduction to Windows DNA

If you are reading this book, you are probably a software developer who needs to understand Windows 2000 and Windows DNA. What you need is a solution that ties together all of the services and Component Object Model (COM) objects that you need to work with. And that is what you are going to learn. You are going to learn how to build distributed Windows 2000 applications. You are going to learn about Windows DNA and what it means.

Windows DNA is the Windows Distributed Internet Applications Architecture. Microsoft's marketing slogans have since changed, but Windows DNA is still what Microsoft originally described as a

> *blueprint that enables corporate developers and independent software vendors to design and build distributed business applications using technologies that are integral to the Windows platform.*

This means that Microsoft will be and is defining how to best build solutions using its technologies. The reason why Windows DNA and Windows 2000 solutions are synonymous is that Windows 2000 has all of the services that are needed in a full Windows DNA application.

I will be talking about the DNA model, but I will also be advocating the use of the technologies that best solve your client's problems. I have worked with Microsoft technologies for over ten years in a corporate setting, and the most important thing I have learned is that working with Microsoft technologies can produce good results, but you need to take things with a grain of salt.

The application of Windows DNA that I promote is what I found works best when applied to a client's problems. Many concepts that Windows DNA promotes are also available on other platforms, in the form of Java or Common Object Request Broker Architecture (CORBA). I am sure you are going to like it.

The Importance of Context

When I approach problems, I try to understand the context of the problem. The context includes and tries to make sense of the past and present of a current situation. When dealing with custom software, I often find that choices are made not only for technical reasons, but also for personal and other reasons. And the problem with personal reasons is that they are unpredictable. At times they are logical, and at times they are not logical. The decision is based on the context of the problem.

For this book, part of your context is to solve the problem using Windows DNA.

Let's establish the context of how Windows 2000 became the operating system it is. Consider this statement:

Windows 2000 is stable.

Did you laugh at that statement? I'll bet most of you did. We all have heard horror stories of the BSOD (blue screen of death) on Windows NT. You may think that Windows 2000 cannot ever be stable because of its track record. But if you inspect the past in detail and look at what Microsoft has attempted to achieve, you will see why certain things were done in certain ways. You will then understand how we came to Windows DNA.

Windows and Microsoft have been around for quite a few years. DOS was successful, but it was Windows 3 that started the Microsoft steamroller. Let's look at how Windows got to where it is now.

DOS—The First Era

When DOS first emerged, the context was the availability of an inexpensive computing device that could be programmed by a single person—it did not require the effort of large teams nor the budgets of multimillion-dollar corporations. DOS (disk operating system) ran on a device called the personal computer. Neither of these innovations were new. Apple developed its own personal computer and operating system, and Digital's CP/M was a type of disk operating system. What was new was that DOS could run on cheaper, generic hardware, and that DOS was cheap.

Windows 3.x—The Second Era

As the first era of personal computing grew, problems became apparent. Hardware was plentiful, but generic software with consistent drivers was not. Computer manufacturers made computers faster, and gave them bigger storage capacities and more RAM, but for software to take advantage of these new hardware innovations, the applications had to have custom drivers. Each application had its own drivers, which in most cases were incompatible with other applications.

Thus, the context was a growing amount of proprietary software that didn't interact well. The solution to this problem was Windows. Windows abstracted the concept of a device driver to be something that the operating system understood. This enabled people to buy software independently of hardware. Now anyone could run a piece of software, as long as there was a Windows driver for it. Hardware manufacturers only needed to write one driver to be used by all applications.

Windows 32-Bit—The Third Era

As the second era of computing grew, so did the problems associated with it. The second era of computing built on technological concepts introduced in the first era. For example, in the second era, applications used 16-bit processor commands, there was no multitasking, and there was no application fault protection.

Application faults caused the individual applications to crash, and often the entire Windows operating system would crash with the application.

This problem was a result of the driver model introduced in the second era. In the first era, every developer created their own systems. They had full control of the processor, hard disk, and screen. In the second era, applications had to share, but many people did not write applications or drivers that shared correctly. In fact, even Windows did not expose the interfaces properly, so the sharing caused faults. Writing systems that share is difficult because it requires a certain amount of trust that all other applications are doing their jobs properly.

The response to this context of bad sharing was to introduce multitasking and protected application space. The processor made the application believe that they were in the first era and that the application had exclusive control of the environment. The processor did this sharing at the chip level. This protected sharing made the operating system stable, as well as much more responsive and usable.

Windows DNA—The Fourth Era

So now we are at the fourth generation. Applications can now safely run in their protected space. What we still need is a way for applications to share a common plumbing without interfering with each other. The answer to this problem is the sharing of services. Sharing with other pieces in a system is extremely difficult to control because when a system has as widespread use as Windows, not everyone has the same idea of how things should function.

What has happened is that everyone developed their own version of various services. Some services were based on databases. Some services were based on the Web. Other services were based on transactions. And each of these services had its own interface. As users updated their shared versions of services, conflicts arose and systems started crashing. Users generally think that Windows is unstable because it is poorly written. In fact, Windows can be unstable because of the multitude of applications sharing the operating system and the compromises that are made. When applications share correctly, there is no problem.

To solve this problem, part of the Windows DNA strategy is to expose a set of common services and facilities that implement the "plumbing." The "plumbing" is the core services, such as transaction services, messaging services, and other components that can be reused in the various applications. This simplifies the concept of sharing, because there is only one set of services.

The goal of Windows DNA is to create a generic solution, which has these characteristics:

- Interacts with the user via a keyboard, screen, or mouse
- Potentially uses other input devices, such as touch screen, pen device, voice activation
- Connects to other machines using networking concepts
- Shares data with multiple machines in a reliable and consistent manner
- Manages itself and its environment easily

This type of solution calls for very different requirements than were considered in the Windows Application Programming Interface (API) era. Then, developers focused on their own specific applications. The focus has changed now, because the computer has become a part of our daily lives and, as such, it must solve more tasks and be able to interact with other machines and environments. People want computers to work easily and simply, like toasters or radios.

The Windows DNA Strategy

In words that I have adapted from Microsoft literature, Windows DNA is definable as:

> The combination of an operating system that has a consistent set of reusable services with a logical design process to build applications.

There are three important aspects to this definition. The first is that it is an operating system. The operating system is a fundamental aspect of the computer system; it provides the basis of your entire framework. This operating system should be fast, stable, and scalable. The second aspect is that this operating system has a series of services and facilities. These services make it possible to do certain tasks, such as transaction processing or messaging. And finally, the operating system and services should be combined such that applications can be logically developed and take advantage of those services and facilities.

A Windows DNA solution is typically used by companies that are delivering applications to solve specific business problems. Microsoft already provides the plumbing. The size of the company using the solution does not matter—small companies and large companies generally have the same problems, the only difference being the scale.

The Guiding Principles of Windows DNA

The guiding principles of Windows DNA are as follows:

- **Internet ready**: Internet technology such as TCP/IP, HTTP, FTP, and so on, are integrated into the operating system. This makes it possible for applications to assume Internet availability.
- **Shorter time to market**: The built-in services and facilities allow developers to focus on writing the applications and not on the basic "plumbing," which enables faster development cycles.
- **Interoperability**: Open protocols and open standards make it possible for applications on various platforms to communicate easily and interoperate, so that a solution works with multiple vendors.
- **Less complexity**: Shared services and facilities are integrated within the operating system, and new versions are released with operating system upgrades. This avoids having incompatible versions of the same services installed by different application installers, making operating system releases and program installations simpler.
- **Language independence**: A strength of the Windows platform is that it is possible for third-party developers to choose their own development environments. This means developers can choose the language that will best solve the problem at hand.

- **Lowering the total cost of ownership**: It should be simple to deploy, manage, and iterate the application over time. This can be achieved by simplifying installation and version-control processes.

The Architecture of Windows DNA

Windows DNA is a tiered architecture. A tier is a logical separation of functionality from another piece of functionality. The tier may be an abstract concept, or it may be reflected in the actual components of a project.

Figure 1–1 shows the Windows DNA architecture, which is used to build multitier applications. There are three tiers: presentation, business logic, and data. Between the presentation tier and the business logic tier, there is a firewall. This architecture doesn't represent a physical architecture; it represents an abstract concept. Multiple physical tiers can exist within one of the abstract tiers.

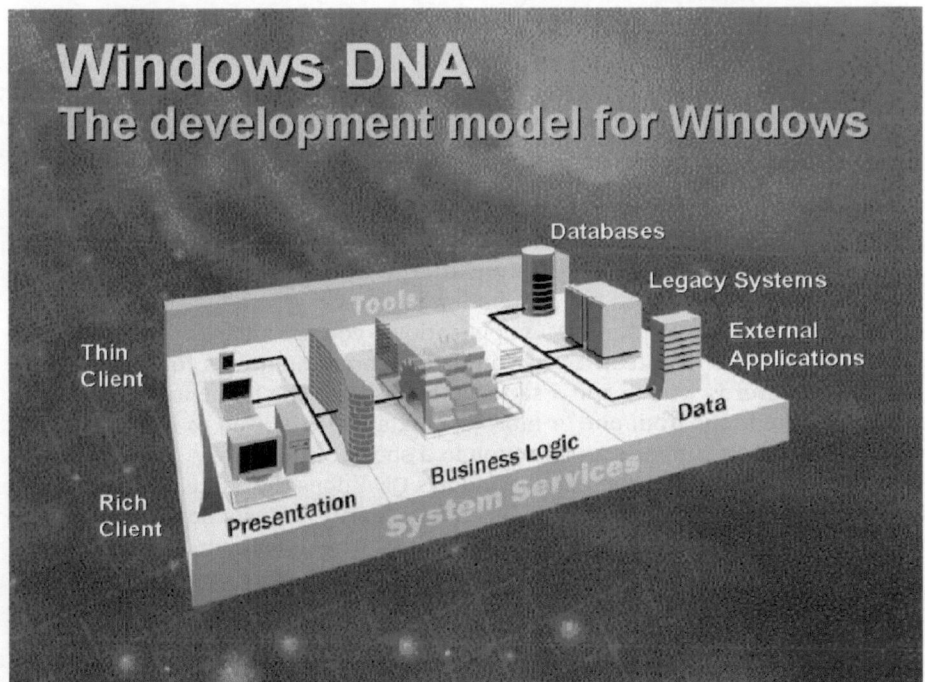

Figure 1–1: Windows DNA architecture

To make the entire architecture of a Windows DNA application work, the different tiers making up the application must be capable of communicating with each other without knowing their individual implementation details. This communication happens with a technology called COM.

COM Everywhere

The basis of COM is a binary standard that makes it possible for two pieces of code to exchange information. Figure 1–2 shows a vtable. The vtable is a series of function pointers to code implementations, and the vtable definition can exist on any platform—it is generated in a platform-neutral manner. Because the vtable is generic, it is called an interface. It simply defines specific intentions—the interface then points to implementations that actually perform the intended actions.

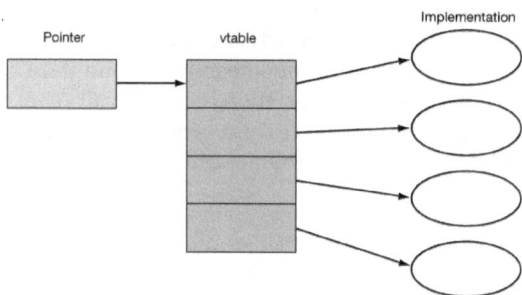

Figure 1–2: COM interface and implementation technique

The implementation has traditionally been binary and platform specific, but with the advent of Visual J++, this need not be the case. Visual J++ generates Java code, which can be executed on any platform. The only condition is that the COM run-time must exist on the destination platform.

When developing Windows DNA applications, you are likely to start by investigating the problem context. Then you define some intentions for the application. In other words, you define a series of interfaces. The implementations may implement intentions from one or more contexts. COM is used to query whether an implementation supports an intention in a specific context.

Windows 2000 in the context of Windows DNA does the same. The operating system exposes a number services, such as security, transactions, messaging, and hardware support, as a set of COM objects. This is in contrast to previous versions of Windows NT, where the majority of services were exposed as APIs.

So why COM? Besides the technical reasons, COM is currently the largest component strategy by far. By basing Windows DNA on COM, compatibility is improved. With COM it is possible to build software components that can be executed and deployed on any of the tiers. The COM run-time provides support for packaging, partitioning, and other multitier issues.

Presentation Tier

The presentation tier is the tier where the application interacts with the user. This is where the data is represented in a manner that we can understand. Currently this presentation is largely based on the keyboard, screen, and mouse, but this will change in the future to provide better facilities for voice and gesture communication.

In the current version of Windows DNA, the focus on the presentation tier is to promote anywhere, anyhow, anytime access. This is made possible with Internet integration, including a browser and dial-up and networking facilities. Designing this tier is a challenge, because the types of clients vary dramatically. In the Windows DNA architecture, the client is not necessarily Windows based, but may include UNIX, Mac OS, and other operating systems.

To be capable of supporting various platforms, the presentation tier is graded from a rich client to a thin client. Please do not think of a thin client in terms of bytes to download. A thin client may be several hundred megabytes. The varying parameter is the amount of functionality that can be executed on the client side.

Figure 1–3 is an abstraction of how the presentation tier is built. On the right side, represented by a series of cogs, are the various technologies. Using these technologies, we can build two types of clients—EXE-based and page-based clients. Those types of clients can be further subdivided into four types, ranging from a thin client to a rich client.

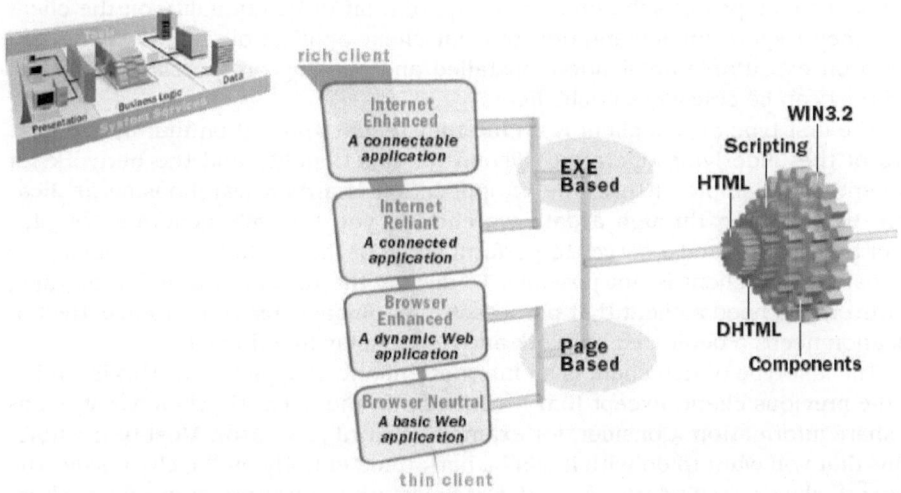

Figure 1–3: Presentation tier details

PAGE-BASED SOLUTIONS

The thin client is a type of page-based client. This means that the client machine is connected to the network and downloads content as it is required. The client application only displays and gathers information.

When a specific piece of content is downloaded, it is presented as static information. You can then fill out a few text boxes or set some checkboxes and submit it for processing. This type of functionality is very similar to batch-form processing in the mainframe days. The only difference is that the terminal can be anywhere on the Internet. Typically this type of client is a Web browser, and this type of application is called a browser-neutral application. A static Web-browser approach ensures that your application has the broadest support.

The functionality on the client side is determined by the richness of the run-time on the client machine. There are simple Web browsers, or to get more functionality, a more sophisticated Web browser can be used. The type of solution is still the same, in that the application is downloaded. This is the first rich client shown in Figure 1–3, the browser-enhanced client. The difference between this client and the browser-neutral thin client is that some processing is performed on the client machine.

Using a browser-enhanced client makes the application more interactive, but the cost of this interaction is that fewer Web browsers can decipher the content. For example, it is possible to develop content that will function only on Internet Explorer or only on Netscape Navigator. Typical applications are Web browser-based intranet or extranet applications. Usually in this situation, it is possible to know which browser will be used.

EXE-BASED SOLUTIONS

The next two types of solutions require quite a bit of functionality on the client side; they require implementation of a fat-client application. These clients are based on executable applications installed and residing on the client machine, and they can be considered rich clients.

The first type of rich client is an Internet-reliant application that uses a mixture of the underlying operating system for functionality and the network for content. An example of this type of application is a data-warehousing application. When sifting through a data warehouse, you typically generate complex pivot tables and need a server to perform some of the work, because moving all the data to the client is not possible. To display the results in terms of a graph, however, you need a client that possesses a graphical subsystem. Hence, the application needs a dedicated network and rich-display functionality.

The last type of rich client is an Internet-enhanced application. This is similar to the previous client, except that it connects to the network whenever it needs to share information. Consider, for example, a word processor. Most of the functions that you want to do with it can be performed entirely on the client side. The network plays a secondary role in that it helps other word-processor users share documents.

This type of client is also breeding the new hybrid client application, which uses the Internet when it needs to, but does so invisibly. The user does not notice the difference. An example of this type of application is Microsoft Money. This application is installed on the client machine and can, for the most part, live in isolation. But when you want to retrieve your statements from the bank, you must go online. An embedded browser starts up and connects to your bank. From there it downloads your statements and displays them. During this entire process, the user never types a URL (Uniform Resource Locator) or gives any network commands aside from connecting to the Internet. In other words, the hybrid client made seamless use of the Internet.

THE TECHNOLOGIES

To understand what is going on behind the various client types, the core technologies need to be outlined:

- **HTML**: Hypertext markup language, the user-interface language of the Web. When only the term *HTML* is mentioned, typically it refers to Version 3.2 or, more recently, Version 4.0 of the HTML specifications. Both of these versions are plain-vanilla HTML, which supports form-based processing. This technology has the broadest reach among all technologies and is typically used in the thin client.
- **DHTML**: Dynamic HTML is the more advanced Web-browser user interface. Dynamic HTML differs from HTML in that it supports a full-fledged object model. Every part of the user interface can be dynamically addressed, removed, or added. This makes the user interface incredibly powerful. However, there are few browsers that support this feature.
- **Scripting**: Within the DHTML object model, a scripting interface is defined. It is considered a separate technology because with scripting it is possible to control any type of client. For example, Microsoft Excel can be scripted to perform certain tasks. The major benefit of scripting is that it allows applications to be customized without requiring complex programming skills.
- **Components**: Components are compiled pieces of code that represent some functionality. The DHTML and scripting services are components. Using COM, it is possible for these environments to communicate with each other.
- **Win32**: The Win32 API is a way of interacting with the Windows operating system. This technology is appropriate for those clients that need special graphics or high performance. The Win32 API is specific to Windows. It is not a similar programming model to HTML or DHTML.

Firewall

The firewall is not a tier, but it needs to be mentioned. Between the presentation tier and the business logic tier the firewall is erected. A firewall is a security wall that ensures the data on the inside of the firewall is not compromised.

In the general architecture, a firewall is only a service within the overall framework, but this is not the case with Windows DNA. Windows DNA is different from most operating systems in that it moves the security to the business logic tier.

There are several advantages to doing this. The first is that there is a consistent security-verification mechanism. Imagine your private network as a castle. Using current security mechanisms, a rider could ride into the castle anonymously. Then, depending on the service accessed, security verification is required. The problem is that as the rider moves through the castle, repeated ID checks are needed. As well, if one service is not as secure, an evil rider could cause destruction. Finally, with each service asking for identification it is not easy to keep a consistent security policy. If the rider is kicked out of one pub, all pubs in the castle should refuse to admit the rider. Without a central security authority, this does not happen.

By making the firewall a central security authority, anyone accessing any service is known. They are assigned a specific set of rights and privileges. If they abuse those rights, the rights can be revoked in an easy and consistent manner. In the end, it makes for a faster and simpler security framework.

Business Logic Tier

The business logic tier is the heart of your application. It processes and manipulates the data. The business process rules and workflow procedures handle this. This tier requires the most programming effort. This tier handles high-volume processing, transaction support, large-scale deployment, messaging, and possibly the Web interface. As you can imagine, the business logic tier is very complex.

If you are using Windows 2000 as a business-logic-tier server, there are three major services: COM+, Microsoft Message Queue (MSMQ), and Internet Information Server (IIS) (see Figure 1–4). There are other services, such as Microsoft Exchange and Microsoft Structured Query Language (SQL) Server, but they are not part of the standard Windows 2000 distribution. They are purchased separately.

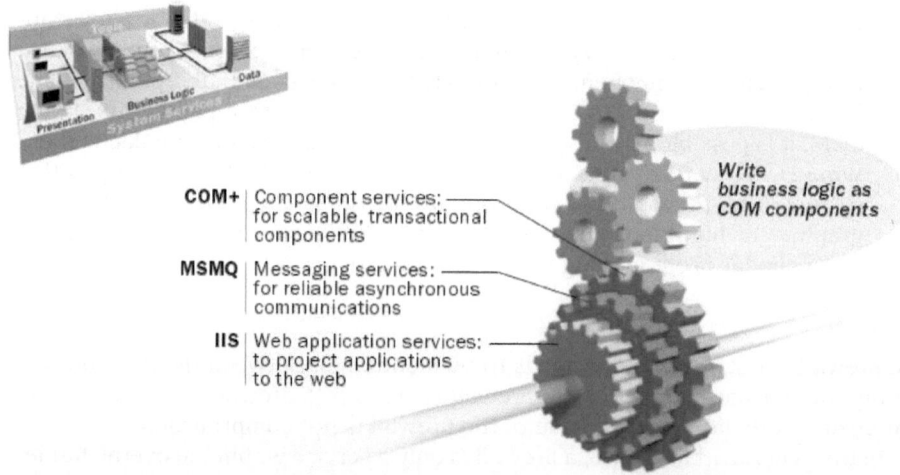

Figure 1–4: Architecture of the business logic tier

Each service performs a specific task. COM+ is responsible for the basic COM and transaction functionality. IIS is responsible for Internet services, such as SMTP (Simple Mail Transfer Protocol), FTP (File Transfer Protocol), and HTTP (Hypertext Transfer Protocol). MSMQ is responsible for messaging. Each of these services may use other services to create new services. For example, queued components uses both COM+ and MSMQ to create a new service.

COM+

The next generation of COM is COM+. It extends COM by adding services that make COM more useful for the enterprise. COM only provides the component framework; COM+ adds transaction capabilities to COM.

COM+ and transaction services first came to life in SQL Server 6.5, which distributed a service called the DTC (Distributed Transaction Coordinator). This service was responsible for SQL Server transaction management. Then the DTC was re-released with a simpler wrapper called MTS (Microsoft Transaction Server). MTS made it possible to write COM objects that performed business processes and that could control transactions. COM+ takes the transaction aspect and ingrains it in the COM run-time and the operating system. MTS was also embedded in the operating system, but an MTS object could bypass MTS. COM+ closes these loopholes, and it is more consistent and elegant. From a programming point of view, COM+ permits all server-side COM objects to take advantage of transactions and make their applications more reliable.

The business logic tier contains by far the largest number of COM objects that provide specific services. This flexibility is required to build world-class enterprise applications that can receive, process, and send back data from the data tier. There are a number of enhancements that are based on COM and COM+, such as TIP (Transaction Internet Protocol) integration, enhanced security, in-memory database (IMDB), and dynamic load balancing, which are discussed in the following sections.

TIP Integration

COM+ uses Object Linking and Embedding (OLE) Transactions to manage the transaction-processing environment. However, that is only specific to the Windows 2000 platform. TIP makes it possible for COM objects to participate in other transaction-processing (TP) environments. These transactions can be managed by the TP system, which is different from the previous version in MTS. In that version, the transaction had to be managed by MTS and the DTC.

Enhanced Security

In the previous firewall discussion, it was explained that Windows 2000 enhanced the security model. The COM+ environment does quite a bit of that work. In COM+, security is either role-based security or process access permissions. Role-based security is a mechanism by which a role is assigned a set of permissions needed to perform a type of task, and then that role is assigned to the users who perform that task. Roles could be managers, employees, order processing, and so on. Roles make it simpler to assign different security privileges to users depending on their domain. For example, an accounting employee may have high access to the accounting processes, but low access to the manufacturing processes. An extension of role-based security in COM+ is the ability to apply security at the method level for COM objects.

Centralized Administration

In the previous edition of Windows NT, COM components were managed using the MTS Explorer. To manage any DCOM settings, the DCOMCNFG utility was used. In Windows 2000, both of these tools are replaced with the Component Services Explorer. It combines and extends the administration of the COM+ objects. Tasks include deployment, management, and monitoring of the COM+ application.

IMDB

One service that is new in Windows 2000 is IMDB. IMDB is an in-memory database that keeps tables in RAM. IMDB works with an OLE DB provider, which means SQL Server and ORACLE are usable. Many applications today require high performance, and most of the data used by those applications is read-only. An example would be the retrieval of a product catalog—this table changes, but very slowly. Most of the time it is read, and it could be cached. This is where IMDB serves its purpose. With IMDB, you can cache the product catalog tables so that it becomes a high-speed access table.

Queued Components

DCOM enables a COM object to be called between two different machines. DCOM is a synchronous protocol—when a call originates from one machine, the receiver must be available. If that receiver is not available, the call fails and any operation it is part of also fails. If that operation was executing within the context of a transaction, then the transaction will also fail. You must then implement a fail-and-retry mechanism.

In Windows 2000, an easier solution is to use queued components. Queued components make it possible to call another component on another machine asynchronously. Queued components use MSMQ as the underlying messaging architecture. Therefore, if the connection or call fails, it can retry until it succeeds.

Event Services

In Windows NT 4.x, it was not possible to easily connect events to components. There was a technology called COM connection points, but it was very limiting. COM+ events is a technology that permits loosely coupled events, where the event receiver may be active or not active. Using COM+ events, it is possible to make unicast or multicast calls—unicast means one-to-one and multicast means one-to-many. The receiver of the event connects to the sender of events using a subscription technique.

The publish and subscribe mechanism enables the publisher to inform the COM+ event service that it has information it wants to distribute. A receiver that is interested in this information indicates its interest to the COM+ event service using a subscription. Then, when the publisher has any information that changes, COM+ event services will propagate the changes to the various subscribers.

Dynamic Load Balancing

With the release of Windows 2000, it has become possible to dynamically load-balance a COM+ object. Dynamic load balancing is the technique of evenly distributing the processing load over a set of machines. Load balancing is a server-oriented process and it occurs transparently with respect to the client making the server call.

INTERNET SERVICES

There are various Internet services that are provided by the IIS.

- **HTTP:** This is the protocol of the Web, and it serves up Web pages or any content that the Web browser requests.
- **FTP:** This is the protocol used on the Internet to transfer files. It is specifically geared toward file transfer and is therefore more efficient for that task.
- **SMTP:** This is the protocol used to transfer mail messages from one machine to another. It can be used in conjunction with POP.
- **Gopher:** This protocol existed in previous editions of IIS, but has become obsolete, since Gopher was superceded by HTTP.

What makes IIS special with respect to other Internet servers is its integration with transactions. When a request is made to IIS, it is a transaction request. By using transactions as a basis for handling requests, all of the benefits of COM+ can be realized. This also makes IIS more flexible when it needs to be dynamically load-balanced or optimized.

To build content for IIS, it is possible to use ISAPI (Internet Server API) or, more commonly, ASP (Active Server Pages). ASP is a scripting environment, where logic is executed from scripts. The script language is neutral and totally dynamic. It is used in conjunction with the COM+ object to provide a full-featured business application. ASP can be used to generate DHTML or XML (Extensible Markup Language). While not part of Windows 2000, the process of creating ASP, DHTML, and XML applications can be handled with Microsoft Visual InterDev.

MESSAGING SERVICES

Asynchronous messaging is handled by MSMQ. Messaging is a totally different way of writing code. It assumes that the connection between the client and server does not exist, but that eventually the operation will be carried out. The eventuality model makes it possible to write applications that function over unreliable networks or in unreliable conditions.

MSMQ is an event-driven architecture. The data is pushed to the server and then the server must react to the event being called. The event-driven model is nothing new, because Windows itself is event driven. However, it does mean application programming must be different from the usual norm, since an immediate reply is not to be expected.

INTEROPERATING WITH EXISTING SYSTEMS, APPLICATIONS, AND DATA

Making Windows 2000 Internet-ready was one task. But another very big task is to prepare it for the integration of legacy systems. Legacy systems are legacy because they work and do the task well enough. Therefore, replacing these systems is not an option. Instead, these systems must be integrated into the overall architecture.

Windows 2000 provides options for integrating various legacy technologies:

- **MSMQ Integration**: Messaging integration is provided for MSMQ using various products. To connect from the Windows platform to the MQSeries Product, SNA Server can be used. To connect from other platforms (UNIX, MVS, OS/2, and so on) to MSMQ, FalconMQ client from Level8 can be used.
- **COM Transaction Integrator**: Using this interface, it is possible to extend CICS and IMS transactions (messaging and transaction products offered by IBM) as a series of COM objects. In the COM Transaction Integrator, there is a series of development tools and business logic that wraps the IBM mainframe transaction. The communication with the IBM transaction is handled by Windows SNA server.
- **Universal Data Access**: This layer is the database-access layer. By using native drivers it is possible to connect to resources that reside on the other platform's side.
- **DCOM on UNIX and Mainframe**: This is a technology that makes it possible to write COM objects on platforms other than Windows. Software AG provided the first port to Solaris. That porting has been extended to include the mainframe platform and currently extends to a full architecture called EntireX iNTegrator.
- **TIP/XA-Transaction Integration**: There exist several transaction protocol standards. TIP has already been discussed, and another standard is the XA-Protocol. The integration is provided through a resource dispenser/manager.

Data Tier

The last tier is the data tier. It is the resource-management tier. In contrast to the business logic tier, this tier does no processing of data. Instead, the task of managing the huge amount of data is defined. Databases and resources are getting bigger every day and the task of managing the data is becoming more and more difficult.

Some data is in spreadsheets, some in word processing documents, and yet more in relational databases. There are two ways to store this variety and amount of data. The first way is to create a storage repository that can handle all of these different data types. In current-day practice, this way of storing data uses blobs (binary large objects).

However, blobs only manage data as binary images. They do not ensure relations. For example, if a stored blob referenced another document, an invalid reference would not be caught. At the data tier, this invalid reference means nothing, but it is important at the business logic tier. It could cause a transaction or multiple transactions to be aborted.

One solution is to ensure that the business logic tier writes a correct blob. However, this adds extra programming steps that should be part of the data tier—because reference management is a data operation. To add reference management, an external module must be added to the data repository. This is not the optimal solution.

A better solution is to decide that each resource handles its own data format, but that the resource must adhere to a common object model. This makes it possible to manipulate, copy, and reference data in a format-neutral manner. This is what the Universal Data Access (UDA) strategy offers.

The UDA object model is called the OLE DB object model (see Figure 1–5). It is a low-level format that includes the specification of how transactions and rowsets are defined. The OLE DB object is very high speed and low level. This means that writing to OLE DB requires quite a bit of work. While it is not part of the Windows 2000 distribution, Visual C++ has a thin template layer on top called OLE DB Consumer templates. It simplifies OLE DB, without making it slower or less efficient.

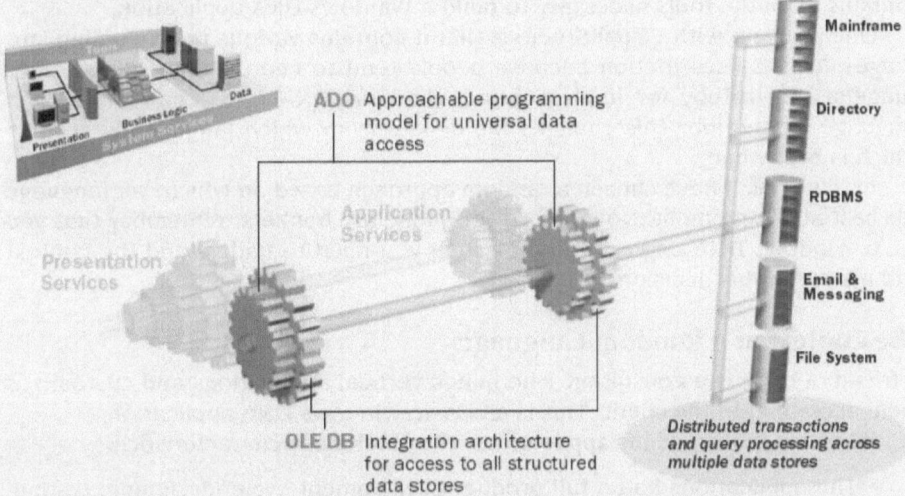

ADO Approachable programming model for universal data access

OLE DB Integration architecture for access to all structured data stores

Distributed transactions and query processing across multiple data stores

Mainframe

Directory

RDBMS

Email & Messaging

File System

Figure 1–5: Universal data access (UDA)

The advantage of the OLE DB object model is that it is not limited by a particular shape or format. For example, in a relational mode, the only resultset possible is rectangular. It must consist of a number of rows and columns. OLE DB has a minimum number of COM interfaces that must be implemented, but beyond that, it is up to the OLE DB provider. There are no limits other than that it must be a COM object.

OLE DB is a very low-level technology and only compiler-based development environments, such as Visual C++ or Delphi, can use it. For the Visual Basic programmer or the script writer, a simpler object model called Active Data Objects

(ADO) is made available. ADO is not less powerful, as it does enable access to most of the features of OLE DB.

One question that must be answered is this: How does OLE DB expose the functionality of relational database blobs? The answer is by using COM objects. This is why ADO does not need to handle all the various data formats. It is the responsibility of the provider to generate the COM objects that will provide the interface between the data and the ADO calls.

Writing Applications Using Visual Studio

The strategy of Windows DNA is not focused only on the services and facilities in Windows 2000. It also involves building applications using these services and facilities. This is what this book focuses on.

To build applications, a set of tools must be used, and Microsoft Visual Studio is a suite that contains all of the necessary tools. There are various versions of this suite. The one that you are interested in is Visual Studio Enterprise Edition, which could also be called Visual Studio DNA Edition. This is because it contains all of the tools necessary to build a Windows DNA application.

One problem with Visual Studio is that it contains various programming languages. This causes friction because people tend to choose their favorite language(s). A strategy for implementing Windows DNA is to choose the best language for the job. This changes the debate from which language is best, to which is best when.

In this book, I have chosen a random approach based on whichever language felt best at the moment. Now before you judge me bonkers, remember that you are a Windows DNA engineer, and as such you need to understand the context and history of this decision.

The Context of a Random Language

A friend of mine is a consultant who builds vertical applications and customizes them according to the client. This is a classic Windows DNA application.

When he developed his applications, they had these characteristics:

- The applications had a full product development cycle (designing, testing, documentation, etc.)
- The applications had a full lifetime cycle (bug fixing, versioning)
- Each step of the product development cycle was carried out in the most efficient manner possible

My friend had some very hard decisions to make when it came to choosing a language for his applications. In the first version of his application, he decided to write in C++, because some legacy applications were present. However, he wanted the optimal return on his investment. His team did an internal study focused on the entire product development cycle, looking at various projects that used various languages.

What were his conclusions? That the language does not matter. What matters is how good your team is. Experienced developers made all the difference. In the details of the study, though, there were some interesting findings to do with the specific languages.

Let's start with the initial productivity of the programmer. Visual Basic is an environment that makes it possible to quickly implement an application. Visual C++ was slower because it required some library and object development.

Another measure of productivity is how fast a programmer can learn the language. There, again, Visual Basic is superior, because learning it is simpler. Visual C++ is more difficult to learn and to program with.

Another measure of productivity is the number of bugs produced in the code written. This time Visual Basic fails miserably. For every bug in Visual C++, there were three bugs in Visual Basic.

So, which language is more productive? It would seem Visual Basic. Even though there are more bugs, fixing them is faster because the productivity is that much higher. Unfortunately, that answer is incorrect. The real answer is that Visual Basic is as difficult a language as Visual C++.

What tips the scale is the nature of the bugs in Visual Basic. In Visual Basic, the bugs are logical, whereas in Visual C++, the bugs are bad pointers or corrupted memory. Logical bugs are bad for the product development cycle because they require changes in documentation, design, and so on. All of these can require extra time and money. Bugs in Visual C++ are simpler because they generally only require changes to the code and not to the logic of the code.

Why is this the case? Visual C++ is a difficult language that requires a lot of learning. You are forced to ensure that you dot your *i*'s and cross your *t*'s. This means a beginner Visual C++ programmer has more experience than a beginner Visual Basic programmer. This experience ensures that the Visual C++ programmer has the ability to properly design classes and systems.

So what was my friend's decision in the end? Get the right programmer! When experienced Visual Basic programmers were used, the number of logical bugs dropped dramatically. This is why there is no right language for the job—there is only a right developer for the job. And this is why this book uses a variety of languages for the examples. Naturally, I do not use batch scripting to build logical components. But I do, at times, use Visual Basic, or Visual J++, or even Visual C++. But throughout this book, I always show you the correct technique of applying the technology. This is part of building Windows DNA applications using Windows 2000.

Programming Languages in Visual Studio

The basic edition of Visual Studio has five development language products.

VISUAL J++

Visual J++ is a development tool that is based on the Java language. Java is a language that takes source code and compiles it to an intermediary bytecode. The bytecode is then interpreted by a virtual machine. Using this approach it is possible to compile sources and then have them execute on any machine that has a Java virtual machine.

Sun Microsystems developed the original Java language and also defines Java's standard libraries. The Visual J++ product supports most Sun Java library calls, but is geared toward Windows development. This makes Visual J++ somewhat incompatible with the standard Java libraries. Also, at the time of this writing there is still an outstanding decision regarding Microsoft Java and Sun Java. This is causing Microsoft to delay the release of a new version of Visual J++.

Advantages

The Java language is simpler to use than C++, but it is more complicated than Visual Basic. It is a pure object-oriented language, which forces the developer to develop using objects. It does not understand the pointers that make C++ development very complex. The interface concept is integrated into the language, which makes component development a natural evolution. The Visual J++ development environment currently in the Visual Studio environment offers the most productive environment. It integrates documentation with the product.

Disadvantages

The biggest disadvantage is the speed and flexibility. Java can be viewed as being simple and yet expressive, or it can be viewed as complex and limiting. It really depends on whether you have a positive attitude about Java. The current implementation of Visual J++ does support the library set of Sun Java, but the productive aspects are not compatible with Sun Java. While cross-platform capabilities are one of Java's greatest features, this isn't well supported in the Visual J++ context.

VISUAL C++

This is a development tool that uses C++ as the development language. It is the development tool that is used most often for systems and software application development. This language has the capability to integrate C and COM, and there are no limitations.

Advantages

The C++ language is by far the most popular development language for systems or software applications. It supports all aspects of object-oriented development, while having the capability to integrate legacy C source code. It is a language that can do everything, and is a natural choice for building libraries, objects, and components. With an experienced developer, the code tends to be more reliable than other languages because of the capability to tie in debug libraries and objects. These objects can be used to focus in on run-time and compile-time inconsistencies.

Disadvantages

C++ may sound like a dream development language, but it does have its share of problems. C++ provides the ultimate development and design freedom and flexibility, but programming errors can produce disastrous results. It is also a difficult language to learn. With all this power, many C++ developers have their own development strategies, and these varying techniques can complicate team development.

VISUAL BASIC

This is one of the most popular development tools on the Windows platform. It is a language that is based on a Microsoft-specific version of Basic. The Visual Basic 6.0 edition supports object-oriented constructs, such as objects, but not inheritance. It masks the complexities of the operating system as a series of COM objects.

Advantages

The biggest advantage of Visual Basic is its popularity. It is very productive because components and applications are easily developed. The language and environment are simple and easy to learn.

Disadvantages

The biggest disadvantage of Visual Basic is its simplicity. It leads to design-and-code-as-you-go applications. While these applications will not have as many development errors as they would in Visual C++ (pointer errors), Visual Basic tends to produce more logical errors. This sort of error can be more expensive to fix, because logical errors require a redesign of the logic. Because Visual Basic tends to abstract the operating system and services as a series of COM objects, the distribution of a Visual Basic application is more challenging because of the size of the final application.

VISUAL FOXPRO

In the previous explanations of development environments, each of the tools represented a code-and-compile scenario. Visual FoxPro is different because it is a development environment integrated with a database environment. This makes developing database applications much simpler. It is object oriented and extremely fast when making database accesses.

Advantages

Visual FoxPro developers tend to be incredibly talented and to understand their development tool very well. This means FoxPro applications tend to be well designed and developed. FoxPro is an all-in-one environment that has full object-oriented capabilities.

Disadvantages

The developer pool, while constant, is smaller than that of the other tools. FoxPro is a classic client/server development tool. It is not the ideal component-development tool.

VISUAL INTERDEV

The last development tool in the Visual Studio development environment is the Dynamic HTML and ASP tool Visual InterDev. Visual InterDev does not attempt to be an all-in-one tool. It is a tool used to build Web applications and make use of components. While Dynamic HTML is a standard, Microsoft Internet Explorer is the only browser that supports it.

Advantages

Visual InterDev is the development tool for Dynamic HTML and ASP. It is well-suited for and makes it simple to build full-scale Web applications.

Disadvantages

Visual InterDev tends to overcomplicate something that could have been expressed more simply. While it does a good job of moving the classic programmer to a Web environment, for those developers who grew up with the Web, it is not rich enough or diverse enough. It can be used to build Web pages for Netscape Navigator or other browsers, but client-side scripting tends to be more suited for the Microsoft Internet Explorer browser.

Enterprise Features

In the Visual Studio 6.0 Enterprise edition, there are series of enterprise-development tools. These tools make it simpler to build Windows DNA applications. These tools are not development oriented, but support other aspects of the development process, such as versioning and performance.

VISUAL SOURCE SAFE

This is the version-control system for all of your development tasks. It is integrated into all of the development tools of the Microsoft platform. This tool makes it possible to work with your source code, documentation, and other development tools in a team environment.

APPLICATION PERFORMANCE EXPLORER

When developing an application you often need to know the ROI (return on investment). For example, is it better to get a server with 4 processors and 1 gigabyte of memory, or is it more cost effective to buy two 2-processor systems with 512MB of RAM? There is no easy answer, because it depends on the network connections, hard disk types, bus speeds, and processor speeds among other things. The number of parameters on the hardware level is enormous. And then it is possible to tune the services of the operating system to take advantage of the hardware. This adds even more parameters. Calculating the ROI becomes next to impossible.

One way of making the ROI calculation simpler is to use Application Performance Explorer. This is a tool that provides a series of distributed-application scenarios that can be used to test the efficiency of the hardware. These scenarios can then be moved from one machine to another and run again. Based on the results of these scenarios, mathematical calculations can be performed to calculate which hardware gives the best ROI.

VISUAL STUDIO ANALYZER

When testing distributed applications, it is necessary to understand where the bottlenecks are. This is not like using a profiler, because a profiler is specific to a language and requires source code access. Instead, unintrusive testing of the run-time system is accomplished using Visual Studio Analyzer. It can establish a series of counters that can be used to find the bottlenecks in the entire system.

VISUAL MODELER

Every architecture requires a way of designing the entire system. Visual Modeler is a tool that makes it possible to design the system using UML (Unified Modeling Language). UML is a notation used to define classes, methods, and parameters. UML is not specific to a language, and is purely intended for design purposes. Visual Modeler has the capability to generate the model from the source code, and the model can then be used in the implementation phase of the product cycle.

COMPONENT MANAGER

When developing many systems with components, you want to reuse components. These components could be source code, design concepts, or binary components. Component Manager helps manage this process. This tool makes it possible to publish a piece of information that can be reused by someone else.

Component Manager uses Microsoft's repository framework. With Microsoft Repository it is possible to query for specific components based on functionality and feature sets. The repository can be considered a database, but it is more than that, because it is geared toward the development cycle.

Putting It in Perspective

Windows DNA is a way of building applications that support various capabilities, such as transactions, messaging, and data services. Windows DNA and Windows 2000 are joined at the hip. Windows DNA is based on the services exposed by Windows 2000. From the Microsoft point of view, Windows DNA is a marketing tool that presents a way of building applications. However, I find that there are multiple messages and ways of building applications in Windows DNA.

To me, Windows DNA is a way of promoting good programming practices, and the first good programming practice is to define the context of the problem. We took a short look at the context of Windows, which gave us an understanding of why things are as they are on the Windows platform. Doing the same for your own problems explains their history and gives you an understanding of why things have happened the way they have. Based on that understanding, you can develop a sense of direction and better figure out how best to get to your goal.

Chapter 2

All About Patterns

In this chapter, we start looking at application development. One way to approach application development is to use patterns. We use many patterns in this book. You will find throughout your software development career that many problems appear repeatedly. In these situations, it makes sense to apply a solution, or pattern, that has proven effective in the past.

An Introduction to Patterns

What is a pattern? It is a solution to a problem in a particular context. Additionally, a pattern is identifiable because it repeats over and over. A solution can only be officially classified as a pattern if it has been used to solve a problem in at least three identifiable situations. As you can probably guess from this definition, patterns are not only found in computer application development. The architect Christopher Alexander defined patterns as follows: "Each pattern is a three-part rule, which expresses a relation between a certain context, a problem, and a solution."

The pattern associates a problem and solution with a context. This ties in with Chapter 1's discussion of context. A properly defined context is the basis of a good pattern. If there are loose ends in the context, then your understanding of the problem may be incorrect, and your solution may be inappropriate.

Now let's consider the situation of a problem for which the context has been defined, and a solution found. Does this mean the solution is finished? Unfortunately not, because a pattern can only solve a specific problem or problems, and that solution will have ramifications on other parts of the system. As a result, a new context with new problems will be created. There is never an absolutely correct answer that doesn't affect the system in some way. You can always apply a new context, which requires yet another pattern and another solution.

The ramifications of using a pattern are just as important as the context in which the pattern is used. If you have a clearly defined problem, context, and pattern, you can put your patterns together like puzzle pieces and possibly deduce the best solution for the application.

A Simple Pattern Example

The following real-life example does not involve computers but will aid your understanding of the concept of patterns:

The problem you need to solve is the building of a house. The context is that this house needs to be built in the woods, in California. As you might be aware, this means that fire is a big danger and that the building of the house will need to be optimized for the prevention of fire. However, this is not the first house that needs to be built under these circumstances. To help you in designing your house, you can look at what was done when other houses were built in the middle of the woods, where forest fires are likely. You would then learn that a lot of those homes followed certain patterns; for example, the area immediately surrounding the house was cleared of trees, and as much nonflammable material as possible was used in the construction of the house. So, by following this pattern for the construction of your house, you minimize your chances of losing it to fire.

To understand the pattern and apply it in the right situation, you need to understand the context, problem, and solution. In the house-building example, the context is the area in which you want to build your house—the woods. Next, the problem is stated: the region where you want to build your house is subject to forest fires. This means that your house could be in danger of burning down.

Finally, the solution to this problem is to clear the trees around your house and to use nonflammable material to build it. This way, you optimize your chances of surviving forest fires, and your problem is solved.

Where the Pattern Fails

Patterns are not always perfect. The most common problems are not understanding the context and making assumptions when using a pattern. Let's state again that the context says that the house is being built in a woody, dry area, and that the solution to this pattern is to clear the trees around the house and use nonflammable material. The assumption you are making is that you can select any material you like to build your house, and that you can cut the trees around it.

But suppose you are building your house in an area with strict rules regarding the look of the house: it needs to blend with nature. Furthermore, some of the trees around the house are protected and cannot be cut down. Now the existing pattern does not apply. The existing pattern makes the assumption that you have free reign over your land and the building of your house. This is a failing, and using this pattern in such a situation would lead to a partial failure of the project.

So, is the pattern incorrect? No—the pattern is correct in cases in which there are no protected trees and any material can be used for building a house. But the context must be properly stated and the pattern properly matched. This reinforces the importance of carefully defining the context.

Understanding Patterns

The main purpose of using patterns is to make it possible to develop a lingo. With a lingo it is possible to communicate with other system developers without having to explain the context each time. A pattern enables you to convert a context/problem/solution set into specifications that can be easily communicated.

Defining a Good Pattern

A good pattern solves the problem and provides a nonlinear solution based on experience. It meets these requirements:

Solves the problem: The pattern defines a solution and problem pair. This must be done clearly because multiple systems will depend on this solution and problem pair. The problem and solution pair must also be recurring, otherwise it would not be a pattern.

Is a nonlinear solution: Patterns are not entirely logical or rational. If the problem was logical, the solution would be simple and everyone would come to the same answer. For example, mathematics is logical. When two numbers are added, there is only one result. Adding numbers, whether you are in the forest or not, will always yield the same result. There is no context dependency and no need to define a pattern.

Is based on experience: Because patterns are nonlinear and partially irrational, they are heavily dependent on the experience of the pattern creator. A pattern can be good or it can be bad. Therefore, patterns should be based on multiple systems. Some references require at least three systems, and the more occurrences, the better.

With a good pattern, you acquire experience without doing an experiment. In engineering-speak, this is called making an intelligent guess. It is a guess because there is no real right or wrong answer, but it is intelligent because it is not a random guess—you are using a proven solution to solve your problem.

Types of Patterns

In the product-development process, there are several steps and different types of patterns for the different steps. There are three types of software patterns:

Conceptual patterns: In the initial product development, these patterns are used to describe the system as a group of entities. For example, when thinking about the initial architecture, specific problems appear. These problems are very abstract and deal with the application concept itself. These are not technological issues—they are issues at the conceptual level.

Design patterns: When the application-domain model is implemented, there is a series of general software constructs. For example, a model may demonstrate how to best access a database and generate dynamic objects. The patterns defined at this level tend to take abstract concepts and apply them to software constructs such as interfaces, objects, and the like. Typically design patterns do not include implementation details.

Programming patterns: When implementing the application interfaces and designs there is a specific way of writing some code segments. These patterns are very language-, platform-, and technology-specific. They try to show how best to write a programming construct using the technology at hand; for example, how to write a smart pointer in C++.

The three different patterns serve specific purposes. There is a clear progression from the conceptual level to the implementation level. However, through the various stages, the patterns are always kept abstract and they outline a principle. Patterns are not a cookbook recipe on how to implement an algorithm or a UML (Unified Modeling Language) diagram.

WHEN IS A PATTERN NOT A PATTERN?

The entire world is not a pattern. There are fundamental principles or rules that do not depend on context, such as the rules of mathematics, and these principles are not patterns. If the concept can be proven to be true in all cases, it is not a pattern.

Patterns are not theoretically thought out. It is not possible to go into a project and say, "I am going to design a pattern to solve my project." Patterns are evolutionary and reactionary evolving out of mistakes and projects that work. When mistakes are inevitably made, you learn and develop an understanding of the dynamics, modifying your pattern. Hence the inability to think out a pattern ahead of time.

Peer review is important to the evolution of patterns. Patterns have an intimate human tie, and without peer critique it is impossible to determine whether the pattern is correct. The peer critique will perform comparisons and assess the correctness of the pattern.

Template for Describing Patterns

Applying patterns requires that you understand patterns. Unfortunately, reading the definitions of patterns is very boring; it is like reading a standards book. Nevertheless, you can read all about various patterns and then solve problems using the patterns you have learned about. Or you can attempt to define the problem and context and then search for an appropriate pattern. I tend to lean toward the latter approach, but the downside is that before you develop a firm understanding of several common patterns, you are constantly searching the books for patterns that fit your situation.

When searching for a pattern you need to be able to categorize and compare it with your problem and context. This can be difficult because different pattern books use different notations. However, many of these notations do share common terminology. Some of those terms are described below.

GENERIC PATTERN TERMS

A pattern is identified by a *name*. The name can be a short phrase or a single word. In either case, it must be unique and meaningful. It is helpful, when naming a pattern, to have the name reference what the pattern does.

In many pattern definitions, the next item is the *problem*, also known as the *intent*. It defines the objectives of the pattern—what the pattern is designed to achieve. Typically, this description is a short paragraph.

The next step is to define the purpose of the design pattern. This can be called the *motivation* or *forces*, and it describes why the pattern was created. Many times a scenario is defined. If possible, the philosophical argument of the pattern should be outlined to let the reader understand what the developer of the pattern was thinking when the developer documented the pattern. Understanding this thinking makes it possible for the reader to correlate the reader's situation with the situation posed by the pattern. The different types of forces could be correctness, resources, structure, construction, or usage.

The *applicability* of a pattern defines the boundaries of the pattern. By looking at the intent and applicability, it is very easy to determine whether the pattern is appropriate for your situation. It defines a sort of checklist that should be used once the intent is determined to be a match.

The last point defines the *ramifications* or *consequences* of the pattern. Consider the poor developer who implements a pattern and then realizes that it is incompatible with another pattern. That developer will not be pleased because patterns were supposed to make life easier. Describing the consequences of using a pattern makes it possible for the developer to better judge whether the implementation will conflict with another goal. If the implementation does conflict with another pattern, then the pattern is impractical.

The other aspect of consequences is to highlight the positive aspects of the pattern. Consider the developer who wants to justify the use of the pattern. Using the positive aspects of the consequences, the developer has that needed ammunition to decide whether or not to use this pattern in the design. While they are not encouraged, it is okay to use buzzwords such as scalability, robust, extendable, and so on.

Finally, all patterns need an *implementation*. The implementation is simple, because it defines how to use the pattern. It may include code or UML diagrams, depending on the type of pattern that is being described.

READING PATTERNS IN THIS BOOK

Now that the terms are explained, you will be able to read a pattern. But how do you apply a pattern to a problem? The way to do that is to compare your context to the motivation or forces of the pattern. Once you have a pattern, make sure that the consequences do not create problems in other parts of the application.

This book applies patterns when the scenario requires it. For example, when describing the problems that COM (Component Object Model) solves, the bridge pattern applies. So, within the context of a chapter describing COM, the bridge pattern is referenced and explained. Simplified definitions of the patterns are given in Appendix B; they are described in these terms:

Name: This is the name of the design pattern.

Intent: This is like the generic intent as previously defined.

Starting and ending contexts: Using terms such as motivation, applicability, intent, and so on, the pattern definition becomes complicated. It is possible to define the same thing by using a starting context and an ending context. This is simpler because it is only necessary to define two elements. The starting context defines the problem being faced. The ending context defines the goals or aspirations of the system with simple parameters. You can compare this entire process to putting the starting context into a black box and then getting the ending context out of it.

Solution: This is an implementation of the black box that takes as input the starting context and produces the ending context.

Ramifications: With all solutions, there are consequences, which may be complicated or simple. They need to be defined, because they help establish the ending context.

This pattern definition is very simple, but it also lends itself to a component architecture. Components are like computer chips—there are some wires dangling out that get connected and activated. A component methodology and a pattern definition that supplement this approach to software development make everything easier to comprehend. Components are defined in the next set of chapters.

Relating Patterns to Other Concepts

Besides patterns there are frameworks, how-to guides, best practices, and so on. What makes a pattern different from these things? First, a pattern is a generic concept. It can define an implementation, but more importantly, it is a concept. Frameworks and how-to guides define specific solutions to specific problems. These concepts do not have a context. Instead they try to solve problems generically. Examples include the MFC (Microsoft Foundation Library used in C++) framework, which is used to build an object-oriented user interface. MFC is not a design pattern.

Best practices and patterns are similar. Best practices are not validated patterns—the why and context of a best practice have not been defined or validated. Patterns take best practices and organize them. For example, a best practice may be "Don't put your hand in boiling water." It sounds a like good best practice. But, in fact, it is limited. What happens if a gloved hand is put in boiling water? The best practice does not define the exact context, whereas a pattern defines a context and a solution.

Antipatterns

Patterns are designed to achieve positive goals. But sometimes projects fail. Sometimes applications are lackluster. When this happens, the concept of patterns can be applied, because very often the mistakes are repeated. However, it is a misnomer to call this analysis a pattern. Instead, it is called an antipattern.

Why Antipatterns Evolve

An antipattern is a pattern that repeats and generates negative consequences. An obvious question regarding antipatterns is why not avoid them in the first place? That would seem logical. The answer is that people make mistakes and do not always make logical decisions when building applications. Remember the context—compromises are often made because of politics, business processes, technical inexperience, limitation of the technology available at the time, and so on.

When applications are built within companies, we are dealing with a closed type of environment. Decisions on how to build an application are dictated by company policies, which do not always allow the best designs to be followed. The design is also influenced by the personal preferences of the architects, along with the political climate of the company and the personal goals of people involved. And, let's not forget those tight deadlines that must be met at all costs. Given this context, it is not surprising that antipatterns start populating our applications.

Another cause of antipatterns is corporations insisting on custom business processes. This itself is good, because it distinguishes the company from other companies. It gives the company a competitive advantage. However, because business processes do not evolve overnight, problems often occur. Compromises are made in the business process, and these compromises are often illogical. The software system has to reflect this illogical design and often results in bad software systems.

The counterpart to the bad business process is bad software. Often a company has one business process, but the software cannot cope with this process and the company is forced to adapt to the software page. The company goes through this process of integrating the software because it is perceived as beneficial to the company, which is not always true.

And the last cause of antipatterns is the inexperience of software developers. Building a competitive product means doing research and development work, and then using that work to build something that has not been built before. Mistakes will be made and, over time, patterns of bad behavior will evolve.

So, regardless of how hard you try, mistakes will always be made and antipatterns will develop. Your task is to minimize the number of antipatterns in your project and, whenever possible, to get rid of existing antipatterns. There will always be some projects that do not work out as they should. It hurts each time that happens, but the key is to learn from the experience.

Putting It in Perspective

Patterns are still very nebulous because not everyone thinks of them in the same way. However, I still believe in the concept of the pattern. Patterns are a practical way of tying together a context with a problem and then defining a solution. Try not to think of patterns as a cookbook recipe for solving a problem. Instead, think of patterns as a way of approaching a problem.

The advantage of using a pattern is that you do not need go through the same thought processes that others have tested and proven already. Instead, you evolve the development process because you apply some basic concepts and add your own twists. By documenting those twists in the design using a pattern-development cycle, you can further the development process. In the end, this makes the software more stable and understandable, even if it is complex.

Chapter 3
Designing Your Application

This chapter defines the process of developing applications. We begin by defining an application cycle and go on to define a practical development strategy called iterative contextual development. Then, the steps of defining an application are investigated using the application-development cycle.

Developing Applications

Developing applications has never been a simple task. Defining an application development model is at times like selling snake oil—many promise to make it simple in one way or another. However, my experience has taught me that if it were simple, everyone would do it. There is no simple answer because the process of developing applications is complex. Many trade-offs, compromises, and adjustments need to be made.

Does this mean that all application-development models are hopeless? No. It is possible to define various generic processes and then attempt to logically optimize them. For example, when developing an application, everyone goes through a common cycle—the application development cycle (ADC). It is a *cycle* because when it is complete, you are back at the starting point again.

The Application Development Cycle

The application development cycle follows this general sequence:

- **Defining the process**: The initial concept of the application is developed. Customer approval and motivation are investigated. In this phase, the client and the application developer come together and reach an agreement on what is the ideal business process.
- **Designing a model**: The technical details of the application concept and business process are defined, such as the details of the component model, how transactions will be manipulated, and which database will be used. Also important in this phase is the definition of terms and concepts. These terms will be used throughout the cycle to reference specific contexts. At this step the initial documentation is started.
- **Building a prototype**: Based on the design model, the first prototype is built. This model implements a core set of features and tests certain assumptions.
- **Implementing the business process**: Based on the design model and the prototype, a detailed implementation of the business process is done.

- **Testing the implementation**: The implementation needs to be tested to ensure that the business processes are implemented correctly and consistently.
- **Final documentation of code and application**: After testing, the source code and application must be documented. The documentation focuses on explaining what has been done and why.
- **Releasing the application**: Finally, the system is released to the client. The client can then use the system to simplify its own business. In time, this entire process is started again for the next version of the application.
- **Fixing bugs**: Because no system is bug-free bug fixes will be needed and the improved application will need to be redistributed.

The application development cycle defines the general sequence of the various steps, but it does not define how the steps are implemented. For example, are the steps following serially or in parallel? The waterfall model is one way to approach this cycle.

The Waterfall Model

The classic implementation of the ADC is the waterfall model, in which the steps are followed serially. Each step is accomplished before the next step is attempted. Figure 3–1 diagrams this model.

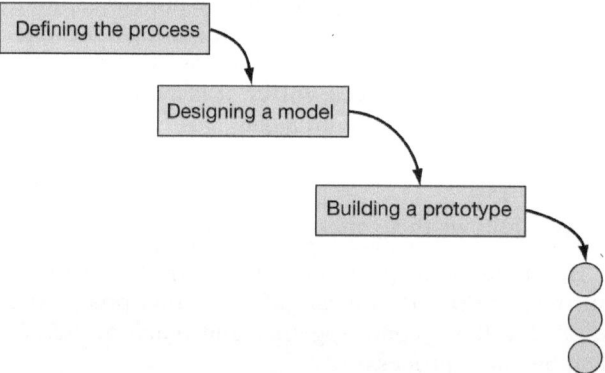

Figure 3–1: Waterfall development model

In the diagram, each bucket must be filled before the next one is filled, just as in the development cycle, each step must be completed before the next step is started. This type of development makes it simpler to control the project, because the steps serve as checkpoints where measurable quantities, such as cost, time, and other factors, can be tallied.

However, this is not the best model to follow because it does not make optimal use of resources. A typical development team has people that are specialists in specific techniques. For example, if the programmers wait for the design to become available, that results in idle time for the programmers. Another problem with the waterfall model is that it clearly segregates the designer from the developer from the programmer, which is not a good idea. Often, a programmer or developer may have insights that a designer does not and this lack of communication results in more money being spent on design changes.

Consider the situation when a decision needs to be reversed. Figure 3–2 shows the costs involved.

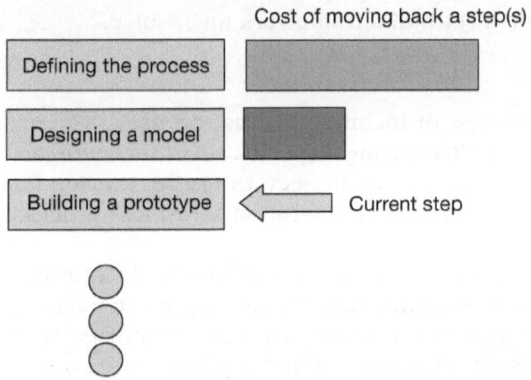

Figure 3–2: Cost of reversing a decision made previously

In this diagram of a decision that needs to be reversed, the cost increases incrementally with the number of steps that need to be backtracked. Consider the case of an error in the release step that causes a return to the design step. This means that five steps need to be repeated, and the costs of doing this are enormous, because everyone must be moved back to the design phase.

The waterfall model has not proven very effective in large-scale development, and in most cases, this model has been discarded.

Dangers in Implementing an Application

A fact of life in the computer industry is that its environment constantly changes. Less than ten years ago, DOS applications were considered "state of the art." Now anyone building a new application would never consider using DOS interrupts to build a user interface. The industry is in a constant state of change. The constant is that there is no constant. However, many developers attempt to ignore this changing environment and design for permanence.

FRAMEWORKS

A classic approach is to build an isolation layer in the application. When a change occurs, the isolation layer can be adapted to compensate for the changes. The isolation layer is often called a framework. A framework is defined as an attempt by an entity to build a set of meaningful utilities so that solving a specific set of problems is much easier. The utilities could be tools, libraries, or a combination of the two.

At the extreme, frameworks can be all encompassing and can give the impression that they are used to build isolation layers. This then brings the entire solution into a full circle. The solution becomes a problem, which then becomes a solution. Doing this doesn't usually make sense.

The key to designing and building a meaningful framework is understanding that the framework must solve a problem set. For example, in a conference business process environment, the problem is managing one or more conferences and its attendees, which is the problem set that a framework must solve.

VENDOR LOCK-IN

When building an application, some type of technology must be used. Vendor lock-in occurs when an application is realized using a specific set of technologies that is provided only by one vendor. The larger the project, the larger the vendor lock-in. Vendor lock-in is a problem, because the corporation's business process is at the mercy of the vendor of the product.

But having said this, you will experience some form of vendor lock-in because you want to get things done. This situation doesn't just happen in building computer solutions. For example, if you own a Mercedes, you will not go to a BMW shop to get it repaired. The BMW dealership is not equipped to repair a Mercedes. So, you hope that you made a wise investment, and hope that the Mercedes vendor will continue to provide support. If not, you count the days until a better solution comes along. The point is that you should not have blind trust in a vendor; you should do your homework and determine which is the best option at the time and in the near future.

The Solution: Iterative Contextual Design

Currently, the best method for implementing the ADC is to use the Iterative Contextual Design pattern. This pattern is not described in the appendix, because the details are given here.

The Iterative Contextual Design pattern embodies two main concepts:

- **Iterative**: Solve problems in a step-by-step fashion. Great systems are built using evolutionary techniques.
- **Contextual**: Focus on serving the customer by listening and enhancing the communications between the various parties.

ITERATIVE DESIGN

An iterative approach is the process of building an application in an evolutionary manner. The advantage of evolution is that it does not attempt to solve all problems or achieve all goals at once. With iterative design, new systems can be designed from old systems by upgrading the old system.

In iterative design, solutions are repeatedly sought for the current problems. During the implementation of the solution, certain discoveries are made—some things may be optimal, whereas others are not. These inconsistencies are noted and dealt with in future versions of the software.

The best way to understand iterative design is to consider the application that you are developing as a series of islands that communicate with each other, as Figure 3–3 illustrates.

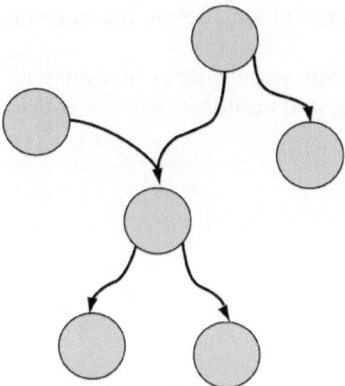

Figure 3–3: Islands of technology

Each island represents a piece of your application. An island is a grouping of functionality that is isolated from the other islands. Some islands are purely technological (for example, a database server or file server) and some islands are based on some logic (for example, a management system or manufacturing counter). Some of these islands may contain logic similar to that of other islands but use different technology, or vice versa.

When data is sent from one island to another, it does so using a protocol. The protocol is an agreed-upon communication between the two islands. This is like having two humans agree to speak to each other in the same language. Some examples of protocols include HTTP (Hypertext Transfer Protocol), DCOM (Distributed Component Object Model), and database access communications.

In an Iterative World

In an iterative approach, the islands are created step-by-step. Islands can be added, removed, or updated; they can be grouped to form "island chains" that could, for example, make up a management system. Various island chains can be grouped together to build an application.

Building the application is very similar to building your own world using islands. In the iterative approach, you begin with a few islands and then form the other islands as needed.

To organize the application, you can create a map on which you can plan out what your islands and island chains will do. The central islands should provide the core functionality.

Let's apply this design pattern by using a real-world example of a conference registration system that makes it possible for an attendee to register himself or herself for a conference.

The first step is to define the three main island chains (database, business logic, and Web pages). The database island chain is responsible for the database functionality. It contains the database, stored procedures, and database tables. The business logic tier contains the various business objects that have implemented the individual processes. The Web pages island chains define the various user interface pieces.

A closer look at the business-logic island chain shows three islands, as shown in Figure 3–4: registration, user maintenance, and conference-registration business logic.

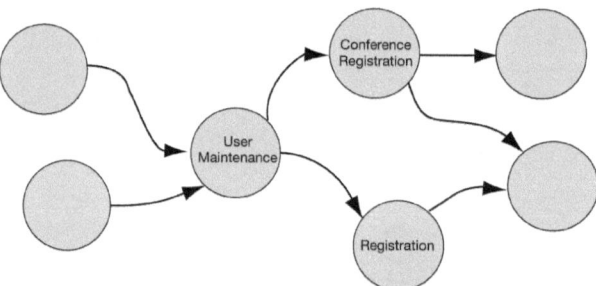

Figure 3–4: Map of islands and island chains

In an iterative approach, a few islands are sketched out first. The idea is to understand the concept of the application based on pieces of functionality. Then, based on those islands, the communications between the islands are defined. This establishes the dependencies of the various pieces of the applications. At this stage, a few islands are implemented so that the concept can be partially proven.

If some of the concepts prove to be incorrect, the islands can be redrawn and reorganized. This sets up a different set of dependencies; again, some of the islands are implemented to prove the new concepts and the concepts are assessed for their correctness. This process is repeated until the application is completed.

One criticism of this approach is that it is slow as well as trial-and-error in nature. The reason that this critique comes up is because people constantly want to improve and update; that is, create yet another iteration. This is like owning a house and constantly repairing it. The house is in a constant state of change. What you need to do is put your foot down and say, "this will be repaired later." There is always another version.

Now, consider the situation in which you have created a map and then you want to introduce new technology or business processes. The problem is that the new islands cannot be easily added—there is some legacy. And sometimes because of the time required to make the islands fit, hacks or shortcuts are introduced. (In fact, hacks and shortcuts are introduced regardless of the methodology used.) In the island-building approach, it is up to the designers to ensure a good design specification in the design phase. Experience shows that if the design specification is good, the interfaces can endure many design iterations and be more easily adapted to a legacy scenario.

One very large advantage of the island approach is that it is possible to build and test individual systems and then assemble them. The granularity of the system then depends on the various subsystems. Granularity is the amount of code in a specific island: if the code is large then the granularity is large, if the code is small then the granularity is small or fine. What you want to achieve is a medium granularity. Large granularity makes testing too difficult, because too many parameters need to be tested. Small granularity is easier to test, but keeping track of all of the various subsystems becomes too difficult. The exact definition of medium granularity is explained in following chapters.

In a Cathedral World

You could also build your systems using a cathedral approach. With a cathedral approach, a system is developed and then kept for a specific amount of time. The technology that is used is based on what is available at the time of development—this is called the *technology snapshot*. Any technology that is developed after this snapshot is taken is ignored, because it would disrupt the development cycle. The amount of time an application is kept depends on the amount of investment. Often designers and developers like to keep a life cycle of *n* years, and after that time is exceeded, an almost entirely new system is developed. Some legacy material may be kept, but that is only because it is too expensive in time and money to change it all.

The replacement of the technology is generally forced by outdated technologies. This means that the new system absolutely must work, which adds additional stress to the development team.

The problem with the cathedral approach is that it is not possible to develop a system based on one technology snapshot. A typical cathedral project has a technological requirement definition specifying the technology assumed for the system. However, the project will probably last about a year or so, and during that year, technology will change. At best, the changes will be minimal; at worst, the changes will involve major shifts, like the introduction of the Web. This means that the original technological definition will be obsolete before the project is completed. A new technological definition needs to be defined. This costs time and money.

Another downfall of the cathedral approach is that you cannot effectively future-proof the application. If the application has a life span of five years, a certain amount of brand new technology will need to be implemented to make this application last. However, the new technology will not have been fully investigated—there are no patterns that can be applied, because it is an entirely new domain. As a result, design mistakes, costing more time and money, occur.

Iterative versus Cathedral Design

The iterative approach is a constant-change approach, and constant change can be expensive. Bad management means that there is no real end to a project. The project is ongoing. This is why people tend to like the cathedral approach. In the cathedral approach, there is a set of goals that marks the beginning and end of a project. However, those goals are a trap, because the goals are constantly shifting.

Although I am saying that cathedral design is generally bad, sometimes you cannot avoid it. For example, there are old systems that exist in their own world, and these systems need constant tweaking. Bringing them into new-world development is simply not an option. Therefore, the simpler approach is to pour resources into the old system while developing a brand-new system that does the same thing. The solutions to the Y2K problem are examples of this. Not many companies integrated the old technology with the new. Instead, they took the two-route approach because it was simpler and less risky.

CONTEXTUAL DESIGN

The second part to iterative contextual design is defining the context. Often with iterative design projects, an initial map is laid out, but various teams do things their own way and build islands that are not defined. Sometimes the changes are valid, but more often these additions are the result of the initial design missing some details that should have been part of the overall application design. Those missing details create inconsistencies, which cause testing problems.

To feed those missing details into the island-building process, you need to create communication channels among your project teams. Communication is extremely important, because iterative design involves constant change. All of the teams need to be informed of the change, or subsystems will not function properly.

Contextual design involves project management, which is beyond the scope of this book. However, there is a good book called *Contextual Design* (referenced in the appendix) that explains the concepts in great detail.

PUTTING IT ALL TOGETHER

The advantage of iterative island-based development is that you can introduce new technology without rewriting the entire system. You can understand the ramifications of a newly developed island on the entire island chain. Based on those consequences, the island can be expanded or rejected.

Consequences are important because they indicate what your application is capable of doing. There are two types of consequences: those of technology and those of the interaction of technologies.

The consequences of technology are guessed at. Typically, this is because the technology is new and has never been used before. Or, perhaps the technology has never been used to solve that type of problem. Defining the consequences is difficult because there are no direct experiences that can be used as an example. However, very often there are indirect experiences that can be extrapolated.

Consequences are important to consider. A very useful technology that works well on its own may not integrate with the other components involved in the situation. In this case, the technology cannot be applied.

Consider defining the consequences of adopting HTML (Hypertext Markup Language) as a user interface. HTML is very different from any other type of user interface, so understanding the consequences would seem impossible. But HTML is not a new development; it is an evolution of SGML (Standard Generalized Markup Language). Therefore, to understand the consequences of HTML, consider the experiences with SGML. One consideration is that SGML is too complex; HTML has addressed this by being simpler. SGML is a standard that can be used across platforms, and HTML also has this benefit. However, SGML is document based, which means that rich functionality is not possible. In its pure form, HTML has the same limitations. Thus, the consequences of using HTML are that the user interface is cross-platform, but it is limited in functionality.

Consider the example of combining the HTML user interface with some data on the server side. There are many different ways to do this. One way is to generate all of the HTML pages using a batch process that is executed at some time. The consequence of this is that the freshness of the application data is dependent on when the batch process was last executed. Another way of doing this is to write some components to generate the page dynamically. However, this also introduces the consequence of choosing a technology to use. Should it be ASP (Active Server Pages) or ISAPI (Internet Server Application Programming Interface)?

The rest of this book focuses on how to apply technology and make it possible to intelligently guess the consequences.

Starting with a Project

Now, we define a project and build something, applying the concepts discussed thus far. The project that we use is one that was actually designed and implemented for Microsoft Germany. We refer to parts of this project throughout the entire book. However, because no one project can implement all features, we also look at other implementation scenarios.

To Build a Framework or Not?

When building an application, you must also decide whether or not to build a framework, which would make it easier to build other applications.

The answer is to build according to the application goals using iterative design. If the goal of the application is to build a framework, then do so in steps. Do not attempt cathedral building, because that will only create problems. If building a framework is not a goal, then do not build one—building frameworks is difficult and requires an in-depth knowledge of the domain and the technology that is being used.

Some Background Information

Combining the ADC, Iterative Contextual Design, and Context, the first step in taking on a project is to learn about its background—Why is the project being required in the first place? This is called building a project context.

In the case of our example, the answer is that Microsoft has become a large company and, as with all large companies, some processes move more quickly than others. Microsoft Germany needed a conference-registration system, and although Microsoft has a corporate conference-registration system, that system ignores the specific conditions of Germany. Microsoft corporate was investigating how to best address this issue for all of its subsidiaries, but this can't be done overnight. Hence, Microsoft Germany decided to develop an intermediate solution that would bridge the gap until the corporate system became available.

The key background assumptions for the project were these:

- **Short term**: This was a short-term project. There was absolutely no point to developing an evolutionary system because it would be discarded a year later.
- **Legacy data**: This application would create legacy data that would need to be inserted into the new corporate Microsoft system. It also needed to interact with the existing data and applications of other Microsoft suppliers.
- **Learning experience**: Appropriate technology needed to be used, but the implementation was also to test other Microsoft technologies so that experience could be gathered. To fully understand how to build the big corporate system, smaller experiences needed to be accumulated, and those experiences could then be used as patterns for the big system.

This background information gives you the context for the application—Microsoft wanted to invest little but experiment much.

BUILDING THE CONTEXT

Building the context for the conference registration system was not simple, because this solution was intended as a stopgap measure until the full system came into force. This situation makes developing an application especially interesting because you must consider both the time to market and the short life of the product.

Your context is developed from the information that was gathered in meetings and by talking to the people involved. You do not want to discuss project details, but project hopes and aspirations. At this stage, you will learn what things really are important and what is not important to people. For example, in the conference registration project, clean and reusable design was not important; time to market and robustness were the main priorities. This is important, because a clean design costs time and money. This does not mean the project does not need to be designed. It means that the design should focus on getting a running system using new technology.

By understanding what is important, you can focus on implementing the features that will make your client happy for the least amount of effort and money. The point of keeping your client happy for the least amount of effort is one that is misunderstood by most software engineers. Software folks often want to design for the sake of purity, but that purity costs time and money. You need to focus on what is important to the client.

Typically, you will want to talk to your end users. Do not solely rely on written documentation, because documentation does not express emotions or hopes; it expresses the corporate mentality. Emotions play an extremely important part of the application development process. If a client is unhappy about a small detail, selling the bigger detail may become impossible. If the client is happy about a small detail, selling the bigger detail is easier.

Talking to the end-users also ensures that what management wants is what end-users actually want. If there is a conflict, it must be dealt with immediately. Doing this at the stage of developing the context can make the difference between whether the application is accepted or not. In my experience, when the end user and management are at odds, the supplier of the application is typically the one who suffers. Often the application will not be deemed acceptable, and the contract will be deemed to have failed, meaning that the supplier may not be fully paid.

HOW MUCH BACKGROUND INFORMATION?

The problem of the information age is that you become swamped with information. What is too much information and what is too little information?

Successful projects follow this rule of thumb:

> *If you are responsible for an island of an application, then get the necessary information for that island. All other information is typically irrelevant.*

The one exception to this rule is that everyone needs to understand the big picture of what the application is doing, so that the common goal can be reached.

This is a bit of a blinder-type approach, but it is a successful one. If you don't follow this approach, you will often end up solving problems that do not exist or are not your responsibility, which costs extra time and money.

For example, one of the context items that we determined is that an island would be properly designed and implemented if doing so was of interest to clients of the conference registration system. Otherwise, the design and implementation needed only to be good enough. Again, this was a result of the project being a stopgap solution. The "good-enough" solution might be hard for some designers and developers to swallow, but the situation was that some parts of the system would soon be thrown away.

Application Requirements

After the context is determined, the first step of the ADC needs to be implemented. This is where we define the process. In this step, the general design of the islands and island chains on the maps are planned. Many books also refer to this as designing the baseline architecture. In this step, the dynamics of the application are described, and the intention of the application is defined. The combination of two aspects should give you an idea of what the tuning parameters are in your system. Tuning is when you change parts of a system and discover what the ramifications of the tuning are on the other parts of the system.

While you are defining the baseline architecture, the goals of the application are temporarily ignored. What you want to consider is how the various technologies and ideas could be used to solve your intentions. At this stage, you should try various ideas and concepts just for the sake of trying them. You want to ensure that the solution that you implement is optimal. Trying technologies at a later step will disrupt the development process.

In defining the process, the following things need to be created:

- A domain model that defines the application in understandable terms
- A defined technology platform that will be used to realize the application
- A list of use cases

The technology platform is not discussed because this book assumes that you are using Windows DNA. How the services of Windows DNA are applied is explained throughout the book.

DOMAIN MODEL

The domain model is used to describe the application in terms that can be understood by everyone. It is the foundation of your application.

Ideally, the domain model is a piece of written text. You want to be concise and interesting. The problem with a boring domain model text is that people's attention will wander, and as their attention diminishes, they might miss important points.

The domain model contains the terms that are fully described in the context in which they are being used. The word "title," for example, has several meanings—it could be the title of a person or of a book. The domain model explicitly defines what terms such as title mean.

A good domain model text has these characteristics:

- It is not simply a bulleted list because information cannot properly be communicated in a list; writing a good explanatory list is difficult. A poor list indicates either laziness or a lack of time.
- It does not have too many diagrams. Typically, diagrams are included to make the document look more impressive. Diagrams force a break in the reading stream, and if the diagram is not correctly placed, it distracts the reader from the subject or, worse, it may make the reader "read diagrams." The text will be ignored and important details may be missed, resulting in problems later in implementation.
- It is not long. It should explain the domain model of the application and no more. While it might seem more impressive to have 30 pages of explanation, this is not better. Conciseness is the key.

Writing a Domain-Model Text

How does one write a domain-model text? The answer is with practice and patience. Often in engineering and computer schools, report writing is not stressed. The schools (and perhaps you) assume that you learned how to write in high school. But there is a big difference between being able to write down your words and being able to write the best words in the right order so that you end up with a concise, organized presentation that people understand. Rightly or wrongly, people often consider the quality of a written presentation to be an indicator of the quality of the entire project. Being able to write well and explain yourself clearly is an incredibly valuable skill.

I know this lesson all too well, because English was my worst subject. In engineering school, one professor nearly failed me for the term because my report was not readable. However, he was kind enough to explain why my report was so bad. So, three rewrites later I was allowed to proceed to the next term.

This lesson, as you can imagine, has proved invaluable for my career as a technical author! The domain-model text should be written in a journalistic style, as a technical article rather than as a book. Writing a book and writing an article are two entirely different things.

In a book, you are telling a story that starts at the beginning of the book and ends at the end of the book. This book is a story about Windows DNA. In a book, you don't repeat the story, although you may refer to other parts of the story from time to time.

Book writing results in long detailed stories, which don't provide all the levels of summary that people want. For example, a manager who only wants a high-level synopsis of Windows DNA would not find it in this book. That manager would be better off going to another source.

In contrast, technical articles deal with a specific topic area and do not tell a story that begins in the first paragraph and ends in the last paragraph. Instead, technical articles provide a series of information loops, as shown in Figure 3-5:

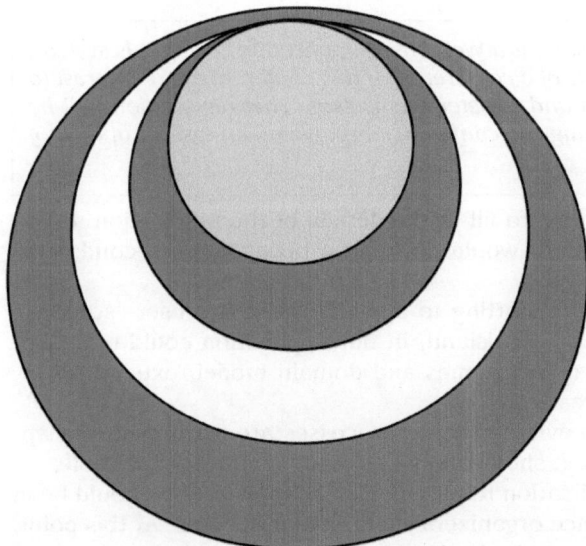

Figure 3–5: Ever increasing writing loops used in technical articles

In the diagram, there is a small circle. This represents the first paragraph of the article, which explains the focus of the article. The second circle is larger—the second paragraph, and maybe the third, expand on the first paragraph. They provide a detailed repetition of the first paragraph. And this process continues on and on.

Why is this better? It is easy to end the article at a specific point. If the original article was 5,000 words and contained three loops, then to create a shorter article for a higher level of management that wants the big picture but fewer details, you only need to cut the last loop. The article contains the same content with fewer details.

Using this approach, it is easy to present a single document to various levels of management, programmers, developers, and others on the team. Upper management will read only the initial summary, and programmers will read through all the details that apply to them. It is possible to skim certain areas and still understand the entire concept.

An Example Domain-Model Text

Now let's go through an example domain-model text used for the conference registration project:

> *It is required to build a conference registration application that is Web based.*

This is the first loop of explanation. It says what you want to achieve. In this case, it is a conference registration system on the Web. Let's expand the details a bit:

> *The conference registration system is a Web-based application. Using this system, the users can browse the details of a conference. If this conference is of interest to them, they can press a button and register themselves. This registration will be accomplished in real-time, giving the conference organizers an instant update of current activity.*

This second paragraph begins to fill in the details of the application. If you had not read the first paragraph, it would not matter because the second paragraph repeats it.

Certain system dynamics are starting to appear. There is a user—someone who attends conferences. An object (island) in our application could represent this user. It is important that object names and domain-model texts correlate. Doing otherwise will confuse readers.

Certain processes are also evident. These processes are features of our application. The domain-model text should define as many features as possible.

And finally, notice the application requirement. The registration should be in real-time because the conference organizers want instant updates. At this point, it would be interesting to dig into the background to find out why this was not done before. Gathering background information is an important aspect of working on projects. Very often, things have not been done because it was prohibitively expensive for one reason or another. But as time goes on, those reasons are forgotten, again it is attempted, and maybe again it will fail. If you find out why the real-time requirement was not implemented before, you can determine whether that reason is still valid. If it is, you can remove the requirement from the domain-model text.

Defining the Application

Now that the application has been investigated, described, and some of its features decided on, it is time to design the application. In terms of the ADC, this is the Designing the Model step. The best way to describe your design is to use Unified Modeling Language (UML). UML enables you to model the application without actually writing any code. It is an abstract modeling method that involves drawing figures and connecting them using arrows and lines.

WHAT ABOUT CASE?

Computer Aided Software Engineering (CASE) was a buzzword that brought a vision of greater productivity and simplicity to application development. The thinking was that a full application would be designed using some type of notation, an example being UML. The Generate button would be clicked, and a finished application would pop out of the CASE tool.

Yes, this is possible; but no, you shouldn't use it. The problems of CASE can be summed up as follows:

- **Code bloat**: It is easy to draw pretty pictures and then have the CASE tool generate the classes automatically. However, this type of action leads to laziness where the designer just draws and draws diagrams. I was called to help on one such project, and there were 350 business objects, which resulted in 15,000 Java class files.
- **Lowest Common Denominator**: Most notations only support a simple object-oriented framework. Simple concepts, such as inheritance and associations, are supported, but advanced programming concepts, such as C++ templates, are not. Therefore, when using CASE, you must write simple code. This is not bad in itself, but it can be bad if many constructs are added to make the simple code function like the more elegant complex code.

Does this mean it is not good to use CASE? No, it means that CASE should be used in the proper context. The reason why CASE was developed is because some programming projects are simply too big and complex to describe using a spoken language such as English. Using CASE makes it possible to simplify the concepts for some high-level constructs because you are using a notation invented to describe software design.

The key is to use CASE to help organize your thoughts. UML and application-modeling tools enable you to model some concepts and ideas. Those concepts and ideas enable you to understand the dynamics and possible problem areas of the application. Using a modeling tool is like building a miniature version of your application. It does not show all of the details, but it gives you an idea of what you are confronted with.

If the diagram writing exceeds its usefulness, then stop doing it. It will only waste your time. Some applications may not even need modeling tools, because they are so simple. Some applications may need huge amounts of modeling work, because they are so large or complex. It really depends on the application. The appendix has a list of recommended reading for further information on this topic.

FEATURE TRADE-OFF

When designing the model, you typically want all of the potential features to be designed into the model. However, some features are more useful and more important than other features.

There are usually absolute must-have features. These are not a problem, because they are the basis of the application. The problem is figuring out which of the large number of extra features can be implemented and which are to be delegated to the next version.

One way of figuring this out is to build an equation that considers these feature attributes:

- **Time**: How much time will this feature take to implement? This can be measured in units of time.
- **Benefit**: What is the direct benefit of adding this feature? The benefit can be measured in terms of extra usability, simpler code maintenance, or reduced testing. The more benefit, the higher the rating.
- **Impression**: Is this feature "eye candy"—something that will bring a smile to the user's face? The feature could be extremely trivial and not part of the entire application, but implementing it might make many people happy. Often the arguments in favor of this type of feature are irrational and are related to some kind of hype, such as Java, client/server, middleware, and so on. The better the impression they give, the higher the rating.
- **Consequences**: If this feature is added to the entire system, how much of the system will be affected? The consequences relate to how much testing will have to be done before a certain amount of stability can be achieved. The more the application is affected, the higher the rating.
- **Priority**: This is the priority that is assigned to the feature in the application. Some features must be implemented because they are part of the main functionality of the system. Those features will not need a trade-off evaluation. Other features are of varying priorities. The higher the priority, the higher the rating.

The ratings should be made on a common scale for all attributes. It could be 1 to 10, or it could be 1 to 100. Do not include 0 because that can result in a mathematical error. Calculate the time value by taking the time for implementation and dividing it by the total time remaining in the project.

Now apply the following formula:

(Benefit * Impression * Priority) / (Time * Consequences)

The resulting number represents nothing. It is simply used to compare with the results for other features. The highest results indicate the most important features.

One potential problem with this equation is that it assigns equal importance to the various feature attributes. However, there are times when time is a more important issue than impression or priority. In that case, you need to assign a weighting factor to each of the attributes. The best way to do this is to apply a fractional weight factor, making sure that all of the attribute weights, when added together, add to 1. If time is much more important than any other factor, you might use the following equation:

((0.1 * Benefit) * (0.1 * Impression) * (0.1 * Priority)) /
((0.6 * Time) * (0.1 * Consequences))

In your own development situation, you may well have different attributes. To accommodate them, you need only include the attribute value either above or below the divisor. When an attribute has a high value to indicate its desirability, it is placed above the divisor. When an attribute has a high value to indicate its undesirability, it is placed below the divisor.

Do not add together too many attributes, because this tends to dilute the answer. An example of dilution is the cost attribute. Cost would seem to be a valid attribute, but it is not because it is a consequence of another attribute. For example, higher cost is a result of more time, more consequences, or less benefit. Increasing the time for a feature naturally increases the cost, and if cost is also added to the equation and is not otherwise balanced, the equation will give misleading results. Math can give any result you want; it is how you interpret the answer that is important.

Using an equation to decide which features to implement means that features will be implemented based on their overall benefit to the application. Features are not implemented based on a single attribute.

USE CASES AND SEQUENCE DIAGRAMS

Based on the feature trade-off calculation, a set of features is decided on and needs to be designed. Features are implemented using a UML use case.

In UML terms, a use case is a description of the ways in which different users will use an application. The use case describes an interaction between the user and the application. The use cases give you an understanding of the various ways in which the application will be used.

The domain-model text gives a picture and an understanding of the entire application, and the use cases pinpoint various aspects of the application. After you have the full set of application use cases, you can determine which use cases can be reused, and you can establish the dependencies between the various use cases.

In UML, the use case is a very simple construct, but it is not very self-explanatory. Typically, you will want to combine a use case with a sequence diagram. A sequence diagram outlines a series of steps that accomplishes something. A sequence diagram typically shows an implementation of a use case. A use case may have multiple sequence diagrams associated with it.

A Simple Use Case

To begin, let's model the use case of the user browsing the conference Web site. The tool that I will use to diagram use cases is called Rational Rose and is developed by Rational Software Corp. This product is used here because I've often used that tool. You may be using a different tool. It doesn't matter right now, because we only want to be able to model the use cases—you can use Paint or PowerPoint if you want. Visual Modeler, included with Visual Studio Enterprise edition, is a subset of the Rational Rose tool that does not support use cases or sequence diagrams, although you could use it much as you could use Paint or PowerPoint.

The use-case diagram for a user browsing the conference site is as shown in Figure 3–6.

In this diagram, there are three pieces of information. There is a little stick person, an arrow, and an oval. The stick person is called an *actor*, which is an individual with a specific role. The oval is a use case. When there is a pointer from the actor to the use case, it is called an *interaction*.

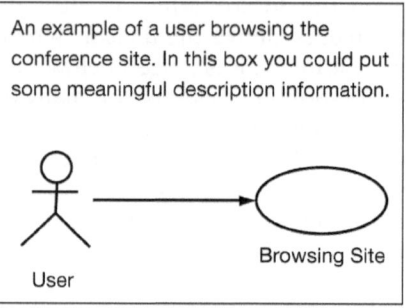

Figure 3–6: Simple use case for a user browsing a conference site

The Actor

The actor is an entity external to the application that interacts with the system in some way. Events are instantiated by an actor, and the actor can be described according to the role the actor plays.

In the example of the conference registration application, some of the actors were:

- **User**: An actor that browses the conference site and gathers information in order to decide whether he or she wishes to attend the conference or not. The identity of the user is not known.
- **Client**: A client is a user that has been promoted. The client is someone who has registered with the conference site and may or may not attend a conference. The identity of the client is known.
- **Conference manager**: The conference manager is responsible for the Web site's conference content. The conference manager periodically inspects the database to see the conference statistics.

All of the actors in the conference registration system are humans, but that does not need to be the case. An actor could be any entity external to the application, such as another application.

In the conference registration application, the following actor was added:

- **System manager**: Regularly checks the database to determine whether the data is consistent.

The system manager actor is a special actor. It is a task manager that regularly performs tasks such as cleaning up e-mail addresses.

Why is a system manager necessary? Often clients would register themselves but give an incorrect e-mail address (25 percent of the cases). The errors were minor (for example, substituting a hyphen with an underscore), but the errors caused e-mail failures. The system manager goes through the database to check for these errors.

In more complicated use cases, there might be multiple actors acting on a use case. The *initiating actor* starts the first event. The other actors are called *participating actors*.

The Use Case

The use case is represented as a simple oval. But to do anything useful, an interaction must happen. A good use case describes all of the interactions between the user and the application, but typically should not reference any specific technology.

In the conference registration application, one use case is the registration of the client for a conference. The process of filling out the client details is not a use case of its own—it is part of the registration use case. The granularity of our use cases is very important: it should describe all possible scenarios, but it should not be so specific as to bog us down in details.

Developing the various use cases is an iterative process and the number of use cases should increase with the number of iterations. In an iterative solution, the objective is to drill down to the specific solution.

A MORE COMPLEX USE CASE

The conference registration system has more use cases than just browsing the site. Other use cases include managing the conference information, registering for the site, and attending a conference. Figure 3–7 is a more complex use case diagram.

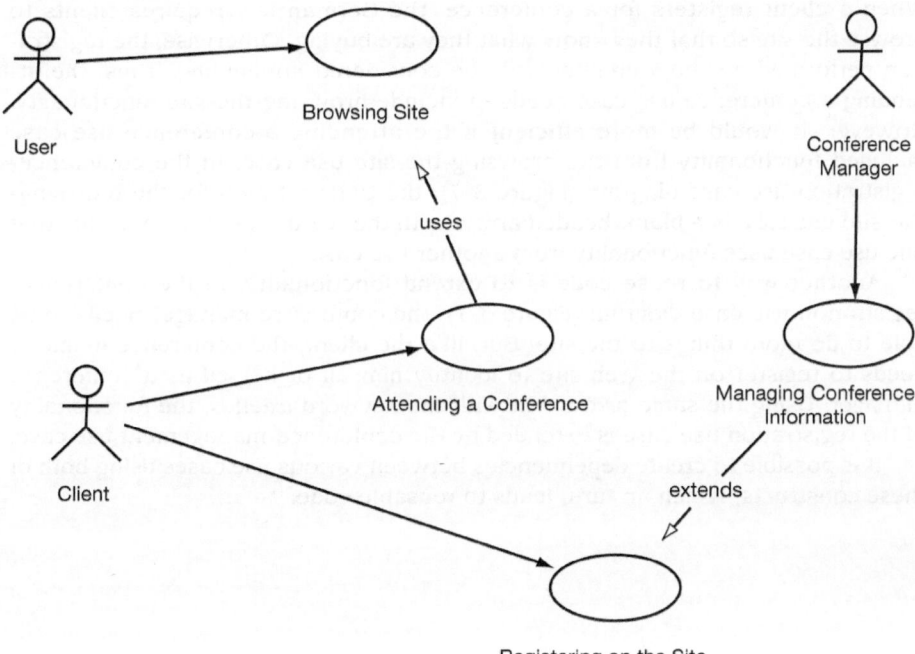

Figure 3–7: Conference registration use case diagram

There are four identified use cases in this figure: browsing the site, attending a conference, registering on the site, and managing conference information. In the original design and discussion, there was no difference in use cases between registering for a conference and for registering on the site. However, when the domain-model text was written, it was discovered that the two types of registration must be separated because registration for a conference involves a more sophisticated use case than site registration.

Interactions

In Figure 3–7, there are actor interactions and use case interactions. A simple arrow identifies the user interaction. But an interaction need not require human actors. The actors could be programs at the system level.

In the conference registration system, the databases will be merged on a batch basis by an Access database, which was designed part of the ADC process. How is that interaction modeled? The simplest way is to make the legacy system an actor. The legacy system actor is called a *system actor*.

Uses and Extends

When a client registers for a conference, the German law requires clients to browse the site so that they know what they are buying. Otherwise, the registration performed on the Web site could be considered nonbinding. Thus, the attending-a-conference use case needs to include browsing-the-site functionality. However, it would be more efficient if the attending-a-conference use case included functionality from the browsing-the-site use case. In the conference-registration use case diagram (Figure 3–7), the UML notation for the browsing-the-site use case is a blank-headed arrow with the word *uses*. This indicates that one use case uses functionality from another use case.

Another way to reuse code is to extend functionality. In the conference-registration use case diagram (Figure 3–7), the conference manager needs to be able to do more things to the site. But, like the client, the conference manager needs to register on the Web site to identify himself or herself as a conference manager. Using the same arrow, but with the keyword *extends*, the functionality of the registration use case is extended by the conference-management use case.

It is possible to create dependencies between various use cases using both of these constructs, which, in turn, leads to reusable code.

Defining the Model Details

After the context, domain-model text, and use cases are completed, you should have a good idea of what the application should be doing. However, up to this point the understanding of the application is very abstract.

Specifying the details depends on the previous operations. For example, if the use cases, domain model, or context is incorrect, then any details you base on them will be incorrect. This means that before you define model details, you need to make sure that the context, domain-model text, and use cases are correct to the best of your knowledge. Don't take any shortcuts.

There are four ways of refining the application design:

- **Sequence diagram**: The definition of a use case in the form of a series of steps.
- **Collaboration diagram**: A diagram similar to a sequence diagram, except that it has the capability of defining links between objects.
- **State diagram**: A diagram defining the different states that an object can exhibit across different use cases.
- **Class diagram:** A diagram that displays the classes of the applications and the relations between them.

With these diagrams, it is important to limit yourself to the ones you will use. Even though there are four different models, it is not necessary to implement a design model from each of them. Keep the number of models down to what is required. Creating too many makes the iterative process more complicated and code bloat will result.

A class diagram is needed, because it defines the overall object model of the architecture. This aspect of the design process will be discussed in Chapter 9, "Implementing COM Interfaces." The state diagram is not necessary for most systems. However, it becomes useful when transactions are used. Sequence diagrams or collaboration diagrams (described next) are also useful in the design process. It is not necessary to use both, because they do the same thing in different ways.

SEQUENCE DIAGRAMS

The sequence diagram defines a series of steps that completes a use case. One or more sequence diagrams can be associated with a use case. Figure 3–8 shows the sequence diagram for the attending-a-conference use case:

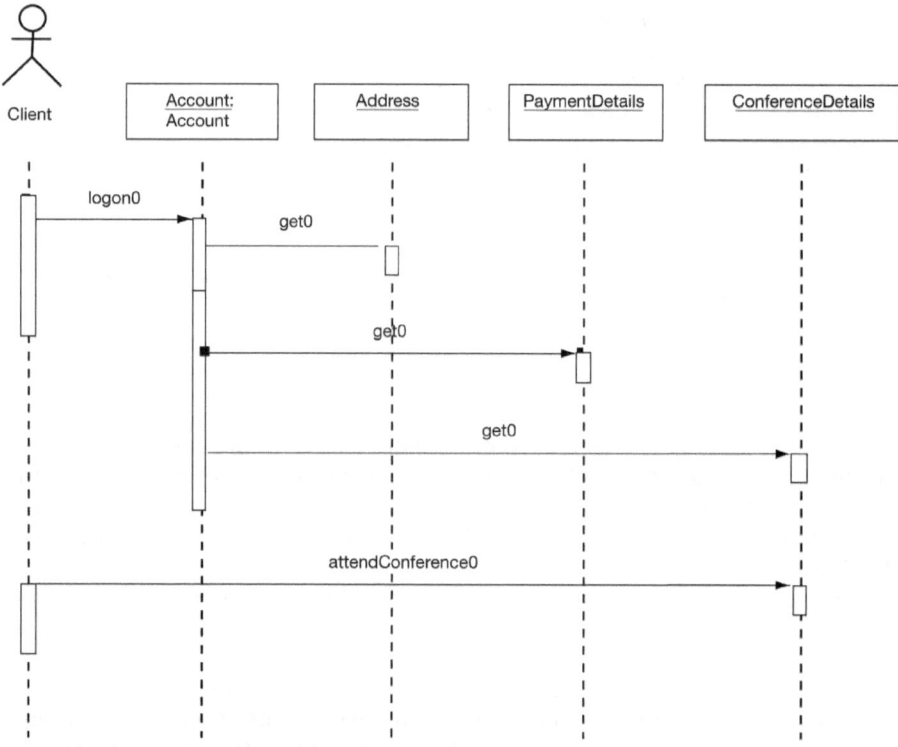

Figure 3–8: Sequence diagram for the attending-a-conference use case

In this figure, there is an actor and four boxes, which are the objects, along the top. Below each object is a series of vertical lines. Then, starting at the client actor there is a horizontal arrow that points to the second object from the left. This indicates the sending of a message from the client to the Account object. The message being sent is the logon.

Attached to the logon message are two narrow vertical boxes. These boxes define a focus of control. When a method call calls another method call, the focus of control switches from the first to the second method call. In a sequence diagram, the same thing occurs. Within each box in the diagram, the focus of control remains with the operation. However, when an arrow points to another box or to itself, the focus of control switches to whatever is being pointed at.

The logon message is attached on the right to a focus of control that includes three get messages. This indicates that the logon message has to wait until the three get messages have completed. In programming terms, this is like calling a function that calls other functions.

Messages in sequence diagrams are usually considered to be simple. Most UML tools make it possible to define other types of messages, such as asynchronous, blocking with timeout, or even periodic messages.

Once the logon message has completed, the message *attendConference( )* is sent. This registers the client with the *ConferenceDetails* object.

In this sequence diagram, the message flow is from left to right. It is also possible to define a message call from right to left, which would indicate a callback. It is also possible for an object to send an object to itself, as shown in Figure 3–9.

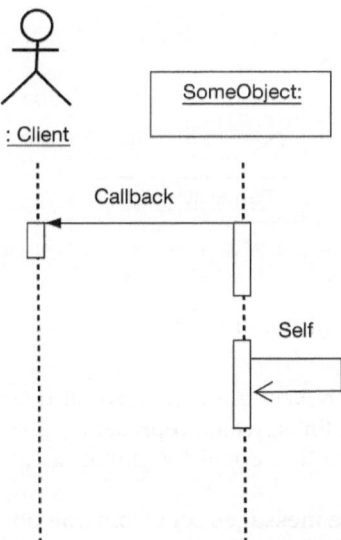

Figure 3–9: Sequence diagram showing callback and self-messages

When reading a sequence diagram, look at the focus of control to see which operations happen in one context. Also, note that the calling sequence starts at the top of the diagram and moves to the bottom.

COLLABORATION DIAGRAMS

The collaboration diagram is like a sequence diagram in that it represents a series of steps. It has the added capability to represent object interaction using object links. The attending-a-conference use case in a collaboration diagram looks like Figure 3–10.

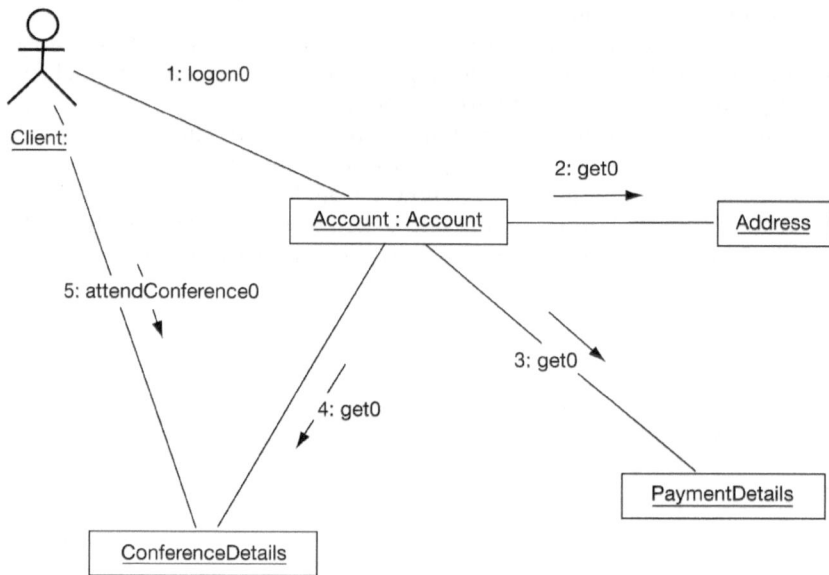

Figure 3–10: Collaboration diagram of attending-a-conference use case

In Figure 3–10, the various objects (actor and boxes) are scattered all over the diagram. The lines that connect the objects are links, which represent a programmatic way of associating the two objects. The link could be global, local, parameter, or a simple field.

Like the sequence diagrams, the arrows indicate messages sent from one object to the other. But to understand the order in which the steps are executed, a numeric identifier is associated with the message.

Sequence diagrams are very similar to collaboration diagrams. It is easier to see the steps of operation in a sequence diagram, because the steps are ordered visually. However, with a collaboration diagram it is possible to organize the objects to suit one's taste. In the end, though, which one you use is your choice.

Putting It in Perspective

This chapter gives you a firm understanding of how to define an application. Just creating some classes and putting them together in a haphazard fashion does not define an application. Instead, determining the context and writing a domain-model text starts defining an application. From there, use cases and sequence or collaboration diagrams can be created to give you a firm understanding of the application, enabling you to determine the ramifications when changes are required for whatever reason.

Why go through all these steps? It may seem as if I am suggesting that you do extra work or that this is just organizing for the sake of organizing. However, my experience has shown that projects that involve some type of logical planning ahead of time end up being better projects. If these planning stages are combined with an iterative development approach, the various factors can be tuned properly, and it is the tuning that makes the difference in the application.

Anyone can build an application. But to make the application robust, scalable, and useful for the future requires some consideration. In the end, software and technology change, and while planning is required, overplanning is not possible because you cannot see into the future.

Chapter 4

Building a Prototype

In the application-development cycle (ADC), after the design is complete, the initial prototype needs to be built, and building the prototype involves coding. To understand how to build a prototype, the concept of components must first be explained. Components are reusable modules that appear as black boxes to the programmer using them. The important point about components is that they separate the interface from the implementation.

Components

When discussing components, typically what comes to mind is COM (Component Object Model), CORBA (Common Object Request Broker Architecture), or even Java Beans. However, describing components in that manner is making a direct reference to a specific piece of technology. A more appropriate way of describing components is to say that it is a generic development strategy. This is more appropriate, because components are a way of encapsulating some logic and then exposing it using some type of protocol. This means that a component is like the islands that were mentioned in the last chapter.

A Bit of Component History

To understand components, a comparison can be made to object-oriented development. An object-oriented language, such as Java, C++, or Smalltalk, is a language that is based on classes. When you develop applications using one of these languages, you are creating an object to solve a specific problem.

The classic example is the shape class. It exposes generic operators to draw and describe the shape. From there, to create a specific class shape, such as a rectangle, you need to create a new class and then derive it from shape. The new rectangle class will have extra methods for the extra functionality. However, when the rectangle class is being operated on generically, only the shape class can be used.

Components are different because they work with interfaces and implementations. With components, the interfaces are generic and the implementation is specific. A more detailed explanation will follow, but some basic concepts of object-oriented development need to be defined.

ENCAPSULATION

The basic idea of encapsulation is that code that performs a particular function is hidden and is only accessible by a method call. This is a black-box approach in that the user does not need to know the implementation details. The user only needs to know how the method calls work.

The simplest example of object-oriented development is the foo class that says `Hello world`, as follows:

```
class foo {
public:
void sayHello() {
    printf("Hello world");
}
};
```

In this example, the class `foo` has the method `sayHello`, which calls a C library `printf` function. The function `printf` will send the text `Hello world` to the standard output.

The `sayHello` method is a public method that can be called by anyone who instantiates the class, as follows:

```
int main() {
foo ex;
ex.sayHello();
}
```

The consumer, which is called a client, does not need to know how the greeting is implemented. The programmer only needs to know that the `sayHello` method outputs a greeting. In this version of `sayHello`, the method outputs a static text.

Let's expand this and define the `setRepetition` method that defines the number of times `sayHello` will output its greeting. The extended `foo` class is as follows:

```
class foo {
private:
long m_repetition;
public:
foo() { m_repetition = 1L; }
void setRepetition( long value) {
    m_repetition = value;
}
void sayHello() {
    for( int c1 = 0; c1 < m_repetition; c1 ++) {
        printf("Hello world\n");
    }
}
};
```

The class `foo` was just revised from version 1 to version 2. However, because the users of version 1 do not want to set a repetition, that code still works—the constructor of foo initializes m_reptition to 1. This ensures that any users who call foo::sayHello will not be affected by the change. Users of foo version 2 have the added capability of setting the iteration count. Again, the user does not care how the repetition is handled. The user only knows the difference between the two method calls.

INHERITANCE AND POLYMORPHISM

Most object-oriented languages also have the capability to implement inheritance. With inheritance, you can create a new class based on another class. Inheritance provides the capability to add changes to the functionality of a class, while retaining existing base functionality. In the case of the foo class, we might want to have the option of saying hello in another language, such as French. The new class would be as follows:

```
class frenchFoo : public foo{
public:
void sayHello() {
    printf("Salut tout le monde");
}
};
```

The class frenchFoo is derived from foo using the C++ notation shown in the first line of code. Notice that frenchFoo has a sayHello method that has a method signature identical to foo::sayHello. This means that when any user instantiates a class of frenchFoo, all calls to sayHello will be diverted to frenchFoo::sayHello. Consider the following source code:

```
int main() {
foo ex;
frenchFoo fex;
fex.sayHello();
ex.sayHello();
}
```

In this example, the output would be as follows:

```
Salut tout le monde
Hello world
```

When the class foo is instantiated, the same sayHello outputs the greeting that we saw in the previous section.

Inheritance also has the capability of making classes appear like one another. For example, if the class frenchFoo is passed to an object that expects the type foo, the compiler will force a typecast. This means that users of the foo class think they have foo, but in fact they have frenchFoo. As a result, if the users of the foo class calls sayHello, they will be redirected to frenchFoo::sayHello.

Having a class appear like another class is called *polymorphism*. For example, if you want to have a generic greeting, then foo-class could be used as a basis. From there, any class that needed to issue a greeting would derive and implement the sayHello method. Various languages have techniques that force you to implement specific methods if they derive from a class. In C++, this technique is called a *pure virtual.*

THE PROBLEMS OF OBJECT-ORIENTED DEVELOPMENT

Object-oriented development is a benefit to the development process. However, there are problems associated with it, including these:

- **Must use a single language:** The previous code was written using C++, and that code cannot be mixed with Visual Basic code. The compiler can only understand a single language, and mixing two or more languages will make the compilation fail.
- **Must give full class descriptions**: When using a language such as C++, the foo class must be fully described to the compiler. Otherwise the compiler has no idea what the object does or how it does it. When inheritance and polymorphism need to be resolved, the compiler must know the definitions of all classes involved in order to define or determine the layout of the class. This is problematic, because when you want to share binary code, you must distribute extra information about a class. And because some compilers are different from others, full source code may have to be shared.
- **Not easy to design**: Designing good object-oriented applications is not easy. Because object-oriented design is more complex, and large applications written by several people often have differing programming styles, integration, testing and maintenance are more difficult.

Components–The Design Concept

When a computer is designed, a motherboard has a series of chips on it. The chips are wired together and electricity makes everything work. The designers of the motherboard do not care about the internals of the chips. They only need to know about the external connections and how they function. The chip is a black box to the designers of the motherboard.

Component development supports the same notion. The components are pieces of programmatic code that expose their functions using some type of signature. The interfaces, methods within the interfaces, and parameters within the method define a signature. Using the island concept described in the previous chapter, the islands are individual components.

I am trying not to use the terms *object-oriented programming* or *module programming* for an important reason. Programming has undergone incredible changes in the last 20 years. Twenty years ago, BASIC (Beginner's All-purpose Symbolic Instruction Code), COBOL (Common Business-Oriented Language), and FORTRAN (short for formula translation) were considered state of the art. Now there is CORBA, COM, C++, Java, and others. Limiting components to any technology is a bad idea, because it dates the concept.

Throughout the years, the one constant idea has been to develop software that can be reused. Sections of code with this functionality were first referred to as libraries, then modules, and now components. What all of these techniques attempted to do was package functionality in such a way that the details of the package were hidden in a black box. The user of the package only needed to understand the interfaces, which could be structures, methods, or objects.

With components, the goal is the same, but the concept of an interface and implementation is very explicit. A component requires an interface. To the consumer, the component is a static block. The implementation is not accessible directly nor can the consumer modify it. By using interfaces, the consumer builds in an abstraction that can later be used to define new functionality without changes to the consumer.

The best definition for summing up components is this:

> A software component is a unit of composition with contractually specified interfaces and explicit context dependencies only. A software component can be deployed independently and is subject to composition by third parties.

This definition was first formulated at the 1996 European Conference on Object-Oriented Programming.

MIDDLEWARE AND COMPONENTS

When a consumer and a server want to communicate, something has to bridge the technological differences between the two. This bridge is called *middleware*. It is like a translating service that makes it possible for people speaking two different languages to communicate. COM is an example of middleware; COM makes it possible for a Visual Basic object to communicate with a Visual C++ object. COM middleware is modeled as in Figure 4–1.

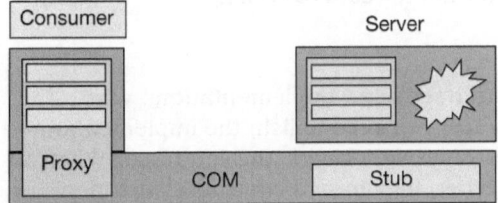

Figure 4–1: The architecture of COM middleware

In the architecture of middleware, the consumer and server are two separate entities, but at the abstract level they think they are connected directly. The middleware provides a ghost of the server to the consumer and a ghost of the user to the provider. This ghosting effect makes each party think it has a direct connection. In reality, when the consumer communicates to the server, it communicates to a proxy that is responsible for taking the information and packing it into a type of packet. COM manages the package and sends it to the stub. Then the package is unpackaged by the stub, and a call is made to the server.

The advantage of using middleware is that the consumer and server do not need to know about each other. The consumer only needs to know about the server's interface.

HOW STANDARDS AFFECT COMPONENTS

The reason for creating standards is to make it simpler for different parties to exchange information. Standards are a necessary part of our daily lives—without standards, there would be chaos. However, the software industry has repeatedly failed to use standards for one reason or another. Therefore, a couple of misperceptions need to be eradicated:

- *"The standards process is slow."* This is not correct anymore. ETSI (European Telecommunications Standards Institute) agrees that in the past, standards took years to define. But now, with the advent of the Web, it is possible to define a standard in less than a year.
- *"A standard forces products and features down to the lowest common denominator."* This is not true at all, and one example is the Internet. The protocols of the Internet are a standard, and they work for millions of people. Many innovative products have been developed that use these standards. The true innovation lies in making the standards do what you want.

Even though this is a Microsoft-oriented book using specific Microsoft technologies, there is no reason why you cannot use universal standards to build your applications. In this book, such standards are used whenever possible, because they give the option of using multiple tools, operating systems, and environments.

What about COM and standards? Microsoft developed COM, but with the passing of time, COM has become available on various platforms. There is even an effort now by the Mozilla group (open-source Netscape browser) to create an open-source cross-platform COM version called XPCOM. This means that COM component technology will be with us for many years to come.

Interfaces and Implementations

Let's look a bit more closely at how interfaces and implementations work. The interface defines the intent of what you want to accomplish; the implementation implements that intent. The consumer only works with the interface. When a consumer and a server are brought together, they form a contract that cannot be broken by either party.

The advantage of an interface-and-implementation approach is that it is a realization of the *bridge pattern*. A bridge pattern is a component-type pattern. By using the bridge pattern, the server can change its implementation without the consumer having to change or recompile its code.

The implementation also has the capability to support multiple interfaces. For example, when an interface needs to be changed, a new interface can be created. The new consumers will use this interface, but the old interface is still available to support the old consumers.

GRANULARITY

Components are meant to implement the island concept defined in the previous chapter. Granularity defines how much logic is implemented in a component. If a component is fine granular, then the amount of logic it contains is small. A coarse-grained component contains a large amount of logic.

Granularity is an important aspect of component development. Consider Figures 4-2 and 4-3.

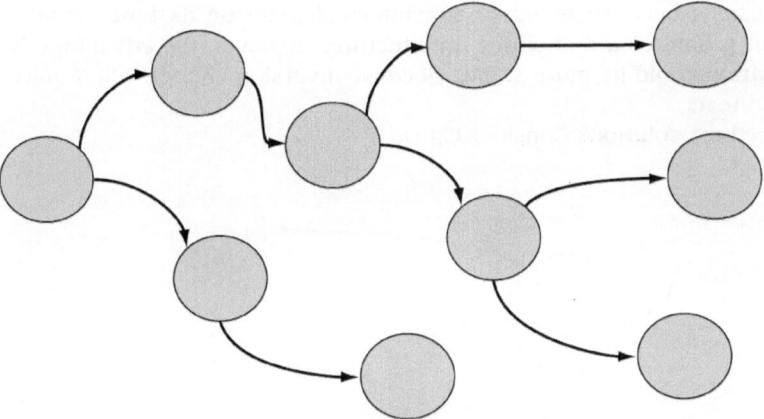

Figure 4–2: A more complex island diagram that includes many different contracts

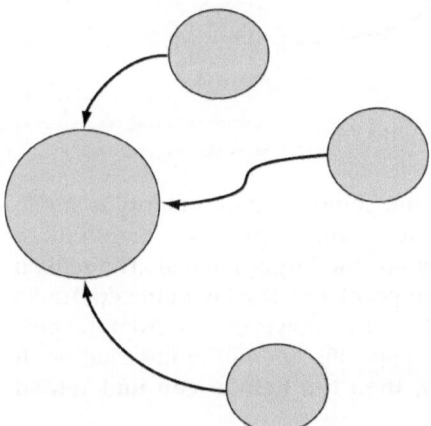

Figure 4–3: A simpler island diagram that has bigger islands but fewer contracts

The arrows in the figures are the contracts between consumer and server. From these diagrams, two relationships are identifiable. The larger the granularity, the fewer contracts there are. And, the larger the granularity, the more dependent we are on a specific component.

Figure 4–2 has many components but few contracts connect to any one specific component. In this small-granular system, a change in a single component will not have a great effect on the application. But because there are more contracts, managing them all may be very difficult. This problem will increase as the number of versions and interfaces increase. This, in turn, affects application stability.

Figure 4–3 has fewer overall contracts between the components, but they are more important. There is one component that is very large and all the other components have a contract with it. This means that this component cannot be changed very easily, because so many consumers depend on its functionality. This component promotes a monolithic architecture. However, the advantage is that the application could be more stable, because a version change will require a larger direct retest.

Which is the best solution? Consider Figure 4–4.

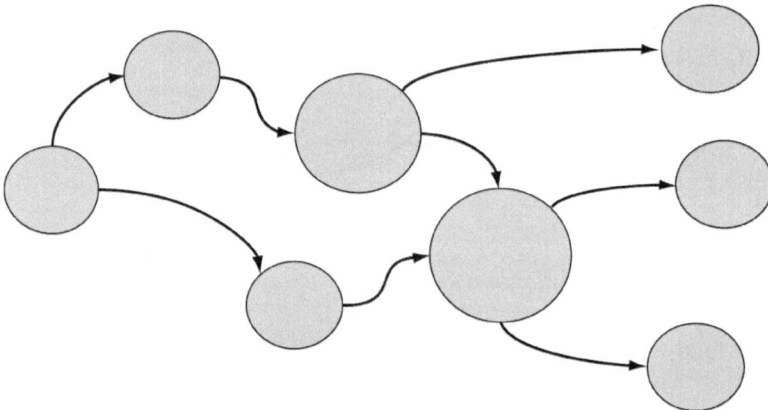

Figure 4–4: A hybrid-granularity component architecture

In the architecture shown in Figure 4-4, the component granularity is small, but there are a few key components. Those key components also contain more functionality than the rest (in the figure they are the larger circles). The reason for this approach is to reduce comprehension problems. Having many contracts is not bad from the perspective of the computer. It is, however, bad from the perspective of the human who can only take in a specific amount of information. If the contracts are organized in a hierarchy, then the human can understand everything in steps.

Another way to reduce complexity is to create specific components that act as intermediaries. These components hide a group of components that implement a specific functionality. This way the consumer only needs to understand the intermediaries and not the entire architecture. When the technology changes, the intermediaries can hide the alterations better than the individual components could.

LAYERED DEVELOPMENT

Typically, there are multiple components in an application and some components call other components. With an evolving system, the contracts increase and it becomes important to organize those contracts and the components. The way to do this is to use a layered architecture. A layered architecture is when the dependency direction of components points in one direction only.

For example, a one-direction dependency occurs when Component A depends on Component B, which in turns depends on Component C; there are no other dependencies between these components.

Cross-Dependencies in Components

What you want to avoid in a layered architecture are cross-dependencies, which are illustrated in Figure 4–5.

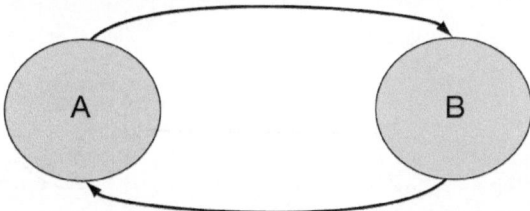

Figure 4–5: An example of cross-dependency in two components

The problem with cross-dependencies is that they cannot be easily compiled or tested because Component A requires Component B as part of its state. In a sequential compilation, Component B must first be defined. This makes compilation almost impossible. Many languages solve this problem by enabling forward definitions.

The problem with testing is more complicated. Consider testing both Components A and B and starting with Component A. Because the implementation relies on Component B, the results cannot be validated as correct, because Component B has not yet been tested and classified as correct.

Sometimes, though, it is not possible to avoid a cross-dependency. When that happens, there must be a way of testing the cross-dependency. When Component A is being tested, an artificial Component B implementation can be substituted. The artificial Component B implements the design constraints that are required. Regardless of how the implementation of Component A calls Component B, it will always get the correct result.

This approach may be unnecessary if the implementations of Components A and B are simple. It becomes very necessary when the implementations of Components A and B consume other components, which results in a more complex implementation.

Cross-dependencies do not need to be direct, as described here. They could be more than one component removed. The main issue is that a component depends on another component, which depends on the original component.

The Various Layering Techniques

When developing a layered architecture, what you want to strive for is a relatively strictly layered architecture. In the layered diagram in Figure 4–6, there is a core set of functionality as defined by the components to the right. These components implement the base functionality of the system. The next layer, to the left of the core components, defines another level of functionality. And to the left of those components is another layer of components. The consumer and server contracts flow from left to right, indicating a single direction. The components do not jump a layer when calling another layer. For example, components in the third column from the right do not call the core components directly. This is an example of strict component layering.

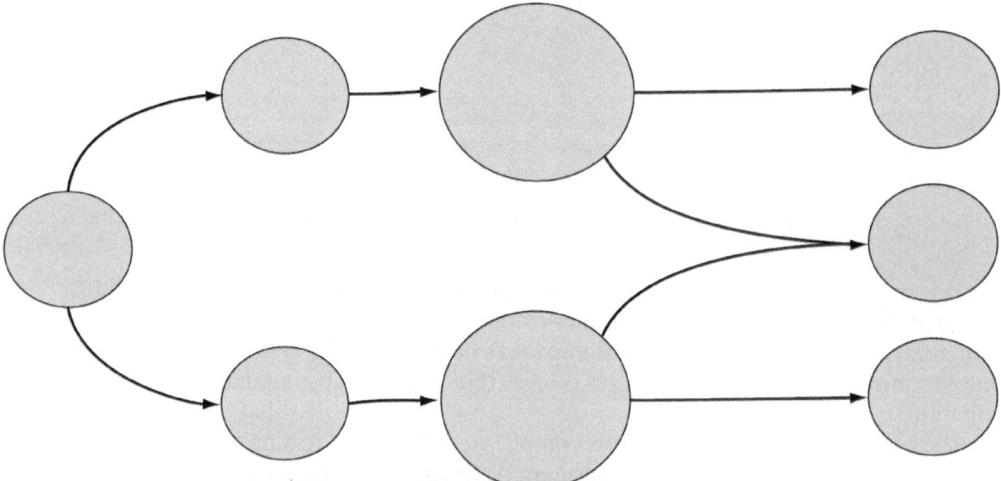

Figure 4–6: Example of a layered architecture

Figure 4–7 shows a nonstrict layering approach. In this example, the root calling component, the first component on the left side of the diagram, calls both the layer nearest to it and the layer below that. Also, a component in the nearest layer calls the core component layer.

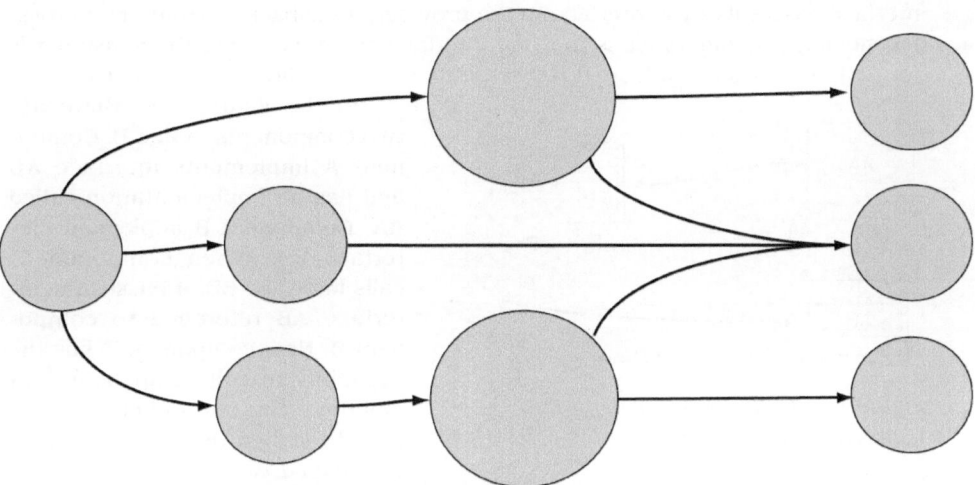

Figure 4–7: Example of a nonstrict layered architecture

The reason why you want a strict layered approach is so that you can assess the consequences of change within a layer. In a nonstrict layered approach, you cannot know which layers are affected by changes in a particular layer. Even if you did know which layers were affected by the change, managing this, with time, will become very complicated. The objective in a layered approach is to reduce the number of consequences resulting from a particular change.

So now let's talk about reality. I mentioned earlier that you should achieve a relatively strict layered architecture. The reason why I say "relatively strict" is because sometimes it is not possible to implement strict layering. Or if it is possible, then you end up with a monolithic application that consists of multiple components that depend on each other so much that replacing one may be impossible. The key is to layer and to design good interfaces. At times that may mean bypassing other layers to call a core set of functionality.

CALLBACKS AND EVENTS

The layered architecture assumes that a higher-level component will call a lower-level component—the calling sequence is sequential. However, there are situations in which you want to establish a callback situation, where a consumer of an interface passes its own interface to the provider. A callback is similar to a cross-dependency; the difference is that the interface being passed to the consumer is not part of the user interface. It is a separate entity, as shown in Figure 4–8.

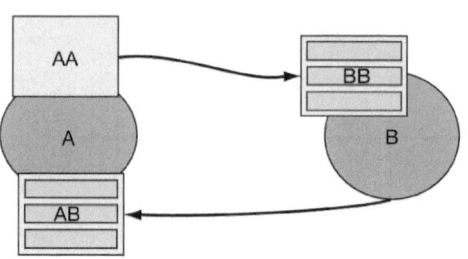

Figure 4–8: Callback implementation between two components

In the Figure 4–8, there are two components, A and B. Component A implements interface AB and has an implementation called AA. Component B implements interface BB. When component A calls interface BB, it passes the interface AB reference to component B. Now component B has the capability to call component A at any time. This sort of behavior can also be called *asynchronous calls* or *event based*.

Looking more closely at component A, it is apparent that the implementations of interfaces AA and AB share the same component, but are different areas of the component. This means a cross-dependency is not established because it is possible to continue testing. But this is a very fine line, because the internal structure of the component may share some code, which again creates a cross-dependency in that code. The point is that sometimes a cross-dependency must be implemented.

TESTING COMPONENTS

Testing is something that is often done, but it is often not done correctly. This is because it can become tedious, and when things become tedious, people either postpone it or do it quickly. In either situation, the testing is not done properly. Bad testing leads to bad software.

Testing components is different from testing an application because there is no user interface. A user interface makes testing components more difficult, because it can be difficult to determine what a correct or incorrect user interface is. With components, there is a definite interface that results in a measurable state.

Components can be tested by writing either a program or a script that calls the interface. However, testing components is not like testing a library module because, unlike a library, a component contains a state that is only partially defined by its parameters. To test a component, the parameters must be validated and so must the state within the component.

Some Component Examples

To understand the various types of contracts, the various component types need to be described. The component types are:

- **COM:** Component Object Model is a technology that is used to enable two separate pieces of application code to communicate. COM is based on a binary *vtable* concept. Vtables are discussed in Chapter 8 ("Designing COM Interfaces"), when COM is explained. In COM, the vtable represents an interface signature of methods that the piece of application code implements. COM has the capability to communicate with other COM components on the same machine or on a remote machine.

- **ADO/OLE DB:** Active Data Objects and Object Linking and Embedding Database are examples of COM interfaces that have specific vtable signatures. These interfaces are specific to database providers. Using these predefined interfaces, it is possible to let users choose various databases without requiring the users to rewrite code to match a specific database.

- **ODBC:** Open Database Connectivity is similar to ADO and OLE DB, except that ODBC is a DLL (Dynamic Link Library) specification. There are no objects, only function calls to a generic library. Again, like ADO and OLE DB, ODBC makes it possible to choose various databases without rewriting the client.

- **SQL Stored Procedures:** A Structured Query Language stored procedure is a way of interacting with the database without having to know any details about the database. A stored procedure is similar to a function call, and it resides on the database itself.

- **HTTP/CGI:** Hypertext Transfer Protocol is used to browse the Web. It defines a way of sending data between the consumer and provider. HTTP can be considered a type of standardized middleware that is universally accepted. While HTTP does not support components in the sense of COM, it does support Common Gateway Interface, which is a way of calling server-side functionality. HTTP is not typically classified as a component technology, but it should be, because it has middleware and a way of creating a consumer and provider.

- **XML:** Extensible Markup Language is the data aspect of a component technology. XML is an open standard of how data can be stored and exchanged between a consumer and provider. Combine that with HTTP/CGI, and it is a full, rich, component technology that is a standard. Throughout this book, this component technology is used to build applications.

Building Prototypes

In the application UML design discussed in the last chapter, the primary focus was to build a specification of functionality without considering what objects were involved. Now we build a prototype, which is the next step in the ADC.

The prototype is a preliminary realization of the components that will make up the full application. Building a good prototype is not as simple as it might seem, because people very often misconstrue what a prototype needs to accomplish.

What Is a Good Prototype?

As in the UML design, the prototype design will not contain any specific consideration of the object hierarchy. This is important, because rarely do you ever go into a project knowing all of the details. You may know some of the technology, but you do not fully know the application details, even if you think you do.

What you want to do with a prototype is experiment and try specific concepts. In the application-definition phase, you found some areas of concern regarding the implementation, perhaps relating to speed, availability, cost, reusability, or other factors. These factors might make you nervous, because they could affect the deadlines and the functionality of the application. In building the prototype, you want to lay those fears to rest and develop a firm understanding of what the application is doing. Using the prototype, you want to understand the consequences of applying a technology and a technique to certain application problems.

WHAT NOT TO DO

There are certain things that you do not want to do:

- **Don't think too much.** You will be tempted to think about the design and how to best design the objects. Resist the temptation. The objects will appear by themselves as your prototype is built.
- **Don't reuse the prototype.** You may be tempted to use the prototype as a basis for the application. While this may seem like a way of saving time, it generally does not. You can reuse specific code pieces, but not entire components. You should reuse the patterns from the prototype that work.
- **Don't build the complete user interface.** Many prototypes just build the user interface. The reason for this is that the user interface can easily be comprehended, and it makes for better demonstrations. However, the purpose of the prototype is not to be a demonstration, but to refine the application design. This is not to say that no user interfaces should be built.

What Features to Implement

Where do you start? The first step is to make a list of all the different technical parts that will make up the application. Do not worry if you do not understand the technical details—that is the whole point. Here is the list for the conference registration project discussed in Chapter 3:

- Web user interface
- Cross-platform user interface
- COM components that do not have any user interface attributes
- SQL Server database
- Stored procedures
- COM components in the middle tier
- Automatic import into legacy systems
- Fax generation

Some items in the list were not mentioned in the domain-model document. This was purposely done to keep the domain-model document simple. My intent was to show you how to approach the domain-model text. However, now that we are developing the prototype criteria, all aspects need to be defined.

With this list, go to your client and ask what technical aspects are very important. Now comes the difficulty of understanding your client. In our case, the client had studied business in college. He understood the business of conferences and supporting the developer community.

His knowledge of technical details was minimal. However, he did understand what features had to be included. I reworded the technical details in terms that he could understand, and he came up with the following list:

- Anyone with any Web browser should be able to access and administer the site, and it should contain all of the cool DHTML (Dynamic HTML) features.
- Some people do not have e-mail, so you need to be able to send faxes for conference-registration confirmation.
- The Web site will serve as the data center for all of our third-party suppliers.

This list now needed to be cross-referenced with the original technical list, which included the following concerns: One concern was the contradictory requirements of being able to use any browser to access all functionality and the requirement of using DHTML features. The fax confirmation was another problem area, because in previous versions of Windows NT, Microsoft did not provide a good network-based fax solution. And the last concern was that to be a data center, all of the third-party clients needed to have access to the Internet, which was not the case. Some third-party suppliers were still using DOS applications on Windows 3.1 stations.

Using this list, a prototype can be built.

Determining the First Line of Code

Based on the cross-referenced list, it would appear that the entire application would need to be written as a prototype, but this is not the case. From the UML use case model, we can look at the all the use cases and pick the minimum number of use cases that touch all areas in the cross-referenced list. This will result in a prototype that is incomplete and minimal, but one that explores the application maximally.

The use case that was decided on was the registration of a client for a conference. This use case implemented all of the core features that cause concern about the application. It also gave a representative picture of how complicated the entire application may become.

When building the prototype, do not use any UML tools; doing so will waste time. You want to get things done as quickly as possible. However, you do not want to take technical shortcuts either, because that is why you are building the prototype. You want to test some theories. This means that you should use your common sense and define components intelligently. If the components are badly thought out, they may mask certain component interactions that might cause problems in the application implementation.

Coding Standards

The prototype requires some coding, and the code is unlikely to be reused, although the lessons learned from building the prototype will be reused. To speed the development of the prototype, documentation should be avoided. However, with a lack of documentation, the requirement for easily readable code is very important. The code will be your documentation. When the team sits down and assesses the success or failure of the prototype, it is the code that will be inspected.

ADDING COMMENTS

Commenting is a skill and requires some thought. The key reason for a comment is to clarify the code's intent when the intent is not apparent from reading the code. Comments are not added when the function is clear and obvious. It is assumed that a certain amount of common sense is used. In the Microsoft Germany prototype, there was the following badly commented code.

```
Public Function updateUser()
Dim objUser As UserSite
Dim status As Long

Set objUser = CreateObject("VB_PDCRegistration.UserSite")
objUser.user.id = user.id
status = objUser.getStatus()

If status = 1 Then
    ' The user needs a full address so add an empty row
    Call addEmpty
End If

db.StoredProcedure "SQL_PDCRegistration", "clientUpdate200"
```

There is only one comment and it states The user needs a full address so add an empty row. What does that mean? By looking at the code, we can see that it happens when the status is equal to the value of 1. What does a status equal to 1 mean? Someone who has never seen the code must look at the implementation of objUser.getStatus to understand what is going on. This commenting is bad because the component call-tree must be followed in order to understand this code.

What needs to be commented? For starters, you must explain what you are trying to accomplish. The function name says that you are attempting to update a user, but the comment simply says that if the status is 1, then an empty row needs to be added. Because this functionality is not apparent, it needs to be commented. A better commenting of the code would be as follows.

```
Public Function updateUser()
Dim objUser As UserSite
Dim status As Long

Set objUser = CreateObject("VB_PDCRegistration.UserSite")
objUser.user.id = user.id
'Get the registration status of the user which
' could be empty, site registered, or conference registered
status = objUser.getStatus()
```

```
If status = 1 Then
    ' To save function calls, it is assumed that if the user
    ' status is empty, a valid but empty user record is added
    Call addEmpty
End If
```

Now, by reading the comments, the functionality is apparent. The first comment states that the status indicates how the user is registered in the database. The second comment says that, to save calls, an empty record is added if the user does not exist.

One more note regarding comments. The first comment is not necessary because the status flags could have been defined at the component method level in the method UserSite.getStatus. That would save time writing comments. It was added at this location because the status is used to decide whether to do something important—in this case, whether to add a record to the database. If the status were transferred to a variable for use at some later point in time, a comment would not be necessary. You want comments to explain a code sequence without requiring the reader to sift through pages, because this is confusing, unnecessary, and time-consuming.

NAMING CONVENTIONS

Comments explain the code, but naming conventions make it possible to read the code. Code with explicit naming often requires fewer comments.

What makes a good naming convention? That really depends on what you are used to. The first part of a good naming convention is to make sure your entire team understands the naming convention. Here are some rules of thumb:

- Use long names instead of short ones. The name .getStatus is better than .stat because the first name indicates that you are retrieving the status of the object. Stat just says stat, which may be understandable for a native English speaker, but not necessarily for someone who has learned English as a second or third language.
- Stay away from using acronyms, because they can be region- and language-dependent. This makes for code that can be misinterpreted. If you use acronyms, stick to a short, predefined list of acronyms that will be used by all the developers on the team. Be consistent in your use of acronyms—if you use "tbl" for "table," then use it everywhere in its short form.
- Use terms from the application domain-text model. Those terms are defined in the document, and anyone reading the document can comprehend what is going on by correlating the two.
- A variable or declaration must not be only one term. Several terms can be concatenated to form a single, more explanatory word.

If you are concatenating words, remember that this makes it more complicated to read. To make it easier to read, uppercase letters or underscores are used to indicate the start of new words. Consider the following four examples.

```
SoMevAriAble
SomeVariable
someVariable
some_variable
```

The first example shows how confusing case can make a word. The second example has a leading uppercase letter. You would typically use this style to indicate a data type, object type, or a function call. The third one is variable that can be an instance of an object. The last example is used in languages that are not case-sensitive, such as SQL.

The case of the first letter is not generally defined. In Java and Smalltalk, methods of objects are typically started with a lowercase letter. In Visual C++ and Visual Basic, the method name is started with an uppercase letter. Either choice is okay, so long as it is used consistently.

One very common rule of thumb is to use the Hungarian naming convention. For example, a string variable would be strVar. The data type is converted to an acronym and prefixed to the name of the variable. This makes it apparent what data type the variable is, without knowing the declaration. Some people find this notation helpful, and others say it makes the first set of letters very obtuse and difficult to understand. Again, if you do decide to use this notation, do so consistently.

SOME OTHER CODING TIPS

Whenever application code is written, don't take shortcuts, because shortcuts make the code more cryptic. For example, in C++ it is possible to use the ? : notation instead of an if statement. The problem is that this notation is not very self-explanatory. Sure, most C++ programmers know what it means, but why not use an if statement that even non-C++ programmers can follow? The if is easier to read and leads to clearer spacing of the various code pieces.

Putting It in Perspective

Components are the heart and soul of any modern multitier application system. A component is not specific to any technology—it is a way of thinking about an application design. Components force a separation of interface from implementation that is crucial to the success of an application. This makes it possible to update a component, without requiring an update to all of the clients that consume the component.

Before any application can be developed, the final step in the ADC design phase is to develop a prototype. Prototyping is an art. We constantly want to finish or implement most of the features, but that is the wrong approach. The idea is to implement the crucial pieces and then figure out whether the assumptions about the application proved correct. Businesspeople tend to call this "sending up a trial balloon."

With the next chapter, we begin coding. In this chapter the final design phase of the ADC has been completed and the implementation phase of the ADC starts in the next set of chapters.

Chapter 5

Creating the Thin Client

The simplest of client user interfaces is a thin client. A thin client is a client that is programmed using HTML 4.0—the simplest type of HTML (Hypertext Markup Language)—and it also has the least amount of client-side functionality. The server-side programming provides the interactivity. The thin client has the advantage in that it has the broadest reach on the widest possible number of devices.

This chapter outlines building a thin client application. HTML 4.0 is a relatively simple technology, so the focus is not on explaining every small detail of HTML 4.0, but on how to build HTML pages that can be read by other devices. As time progresses, the HTML versions supported by the various browsers will be the newest standards. However, because the type of devices reading those pages will become more diverse, the functionality will need to be simple and instructive; that is, the HTML page will need to indicate to the browser how to translate specific text pieces for optimum rendering. When an HTML page is generated from a database query or when an HTML form is processed, Active Server Pages (ASP) are used on the server side.

The Web Interface

What makes the Web interface unique? It is dynamic and simple. With the Web, it is possible to update content instantly and have those changes propagate through the entire network. The Web's architecture is shown in Figure 5–1.

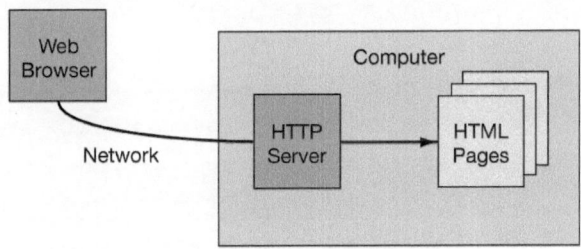

Figure 5–1: Plain-vanilla Web architecture

To use the Web, you need a browser, an HTTP (Hypertext Transfer Protocol) server, and a network that connects the two. A Web page contains a series of

tags that are translated into user-interface elements. The browser can display
the standard HTML tags any way it wants, but because HTML is a standard, the
user interface of the various browsers on various platforms will look similar.

The browser is responsible for sending a URL (Uniform Resource Locator)
command to the HTTP server. A URL command could be as follows:

```
http://www.infoworld.com/info.html
```

The URL is a string that defines where the resource is, using the DNS (Domain Name Service) Internet standard. DNS makes it possible to find the server
on the Internet. In this example, the resource type is HTTP. It also means that
HTTP is the protocol used when the client and server communicate. After the
double slashes (//), the server name is specified and then the content, which, in
this case, is /info.html. The content could be contained within virtual subdirectories. These are called virtual because the HTTP server maps the virtual directory to a directory on the hard disk or to some other application that can be
executed on the server side.

The content is sent to the browser with a tag that identifies the MIME (Multipurpose Internet Mail Extensions) type. The MIME type is used to identify the handler that will process the data. If the content is HTML, then the MIME type will be
text/html. If there is no handler, then the browser asks the user what to do next.

Navigation

A good Web site is like an English garden—the site is trim and clean, and interesting things are easy to find. A Web site that contains nothing interesting is like
a desert. And many Web sites are jungles that you must fight your way through to
find anything interesting.

Web documents are linked together with hyperlinks. A hyperlink is like a
pointer that, when activated, instructs the browser to retrieve some other content at the URL specified. A good navigation layout makes it easy to find information. The standard navigation layout is shown in Figure 5-2.

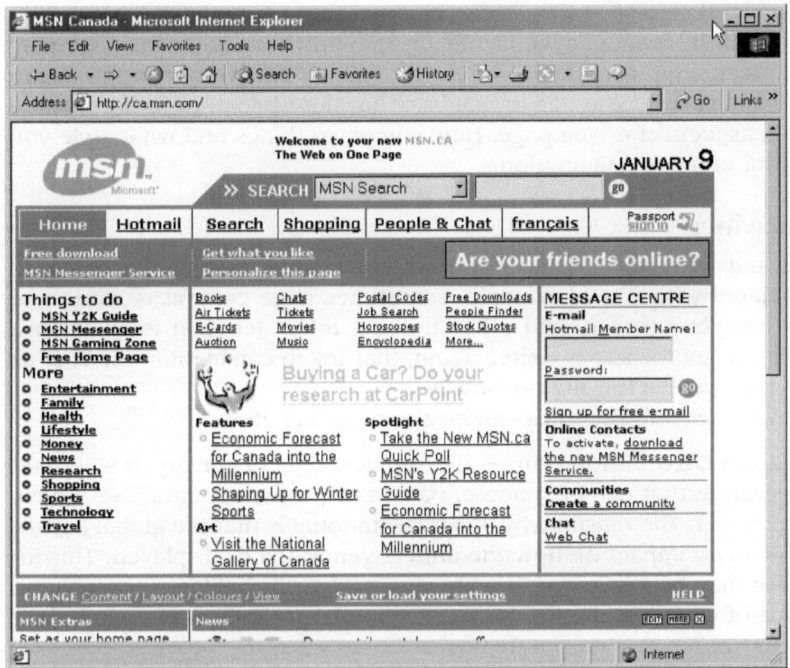

Figure 5–2: An example of a Web application

A Web page has three sections:

- **Banner**: This is the top of the Web page. The banner is a section that contains information that is nonessential to the task currently being pursued, but that may be useful. Banner bars may contain advertisements or informative references to other areas on the Web site.
- **Navigation section**: This section is usually at the left of the Web site. The navigation section provides a formal place for hyperlinks that will connect the viewer with different sections of the Web site. This section may use a hierarchical navigation scheme, images, or a search text box. A good navigation section will not contain too much information—if the navigation section is too complicated, then maybe the Web site contains too many different sections. In that case, breaking the site into multiple Web sites may be appropriate. An example is the breaking up of the Microsoft Web site into Microsoft and MSDN.
- **Body**: This section is the remainder of the Web site. It contains the main content and information that the user is actually interested in.

The individual Web page sections can be created using Web frames or a single page. They can be created dynamically or on a batch basis, or the page may be static. The technique used depends on the type of activity. Does this mean your Web page must resemble this format? No, but this style of page does define the three main aspects of a Web page. How you place things and what style you use is up to your creative imagination.

Web Site Activities

The purpose and features of a Web site will vary according to the business process associated with it. For example, sometimes page content is static and available for everyone to see, and other times a token (cookie) is given to a browser so that when the site is visited again, that token can identify the user as someone who has visited the site previously.

The different Web site activities can be classified as follows.

- **Information Distribution**: This is the simplest type of activity. It is a read-only operation that can be made of password-protected, database-driven, or static pages. The reason why it is informational is that the global key (or cookie) has no impact on how the data is generated or displayed. This information may be generated directly with ASP, or by calling a component. This type of task is a one-to-many distribution mechanism. An example is the display of news or corporate pages.
- **Interactive Information Distribution**: This is a read-only activity, like the information activity, but it is dependent on the global key. When the page content is generated, it is customized to the user's specifications. The global key then associates the user with the specific content and can be used to "recognize" the user if he or she returns. An example is displaying a paycheck, which is unique for each person.
- **Data Manipulation**: This is an input-output activity. It is dependent on the global key and it displays information that directly correlates to the global key. When data is input, the global key is required to correlate the data being saved with the user. A key characteristic of this task is that it uses server-side components for its input-output operations. An example is the buying and selling of your stock portfolio on the Internet.
- **Anonymous Data Manipulation**: This is an input-output activity, but it does not require a global key. The difference between this and the application task is that there is no global key. The input-output is a generic operation that can be performed by any user. An example is an attendee registering for a conference, where the details are filled out once and never seen again on the Web site.
- **Add-on Activities**: There are activities that do not fall into any of the preceding categories. They may require a global key or they may not. These tasks might not even be Web based. These tasks are designed to do certain things that are not part of the main business process. Code may need to be written, and some parts of other tasks may be reused, but they are still separate functions. Examples include data backups, database-filling operations, and system maintenance.

Partitioning a Web site is not simple. By defining the various activities it is possible to partition the Web application. When a Web site is partitioned, it is simpler to maintain and extend.

Another reason for partitioning a Web site is if the various activities use different Web site structures. Information-oriented sites can contain thousands of pages, whereas application-oriented Web sites may only contain a few pages. To manage thousands of pages, different tools are required than those used to build a data manipulation Web site. The types of Web sites that are focused on in this book are data manipulation and add-on activity Web sites.

The Thin Client User Interface

The conference registration application required both a thin client and a rich client user interface. This section focuses on the thin client user interface. When the project started, the thin client HTML standard was 3.2. Previously there was a difference between a rich client HTML standard and a thin client HTML standard—there was Dynamic HTML and HTML 3.2. Now there is HTML 4.0.

HTML 4.0 Defined

HTML 4.0 is different from other versions of HTML in that it does not describe a full working set. Instead, it defines a standard of subsets of HTML functionality. Using HTML 4.0, it is possible to reach any type of device. HTML 4.0 has these features:

- **Internationalization**: The Web is enormous, and English is an extremely popular language. However, there are other languages. To support these languages, HTML 4.0 has changed to support better indexing and international characters, text direction, and text-to-speech capabilities.
- **Accessibility**: The accessibility situation makes it possible to parse the document under various situations that do not include a general browser. For example a specialized browser intended for a car requires speech capabilities and has a smaller working area.
- **Tables**: Tables have been around for a long time, but with HTML 4.0 more control has been provided for defining the layout and look of the table and its columns. An example is incremental rendering.
- **Compound documents**: In the past, HTML pages included support for images. Then, support for Java applets was added with the introduction of the <APPLET> tag. The new <OBJECT> tag makes it possible to generically embed items within the HTML page.
- **Style sheets**: In early editions of browsers, it was not easy to control the look and layout of a document. Special tags were introduced, such as style sheets, that made it possible to separate structure from look and build better HTML pages.
- **Scripting**: With scripting it is possible to build client side-logic. This reduces the round trips to the server and makes for improved navigation and form processing.
- **Printing**: A large problem in the past has been how to print Web pages. This problem is specifically addressed in HTML 4.0.

Web Accessibility

With HTML 4.0, Web accessibility has become very important. Previously it was often ignored. The Web has become ubiquitous and accessible to almost everyone. However, the browser and operating system can only do so much. When you build your HTML content, you need to make sure your Web site is accessible to everyone. To be accessible, a Web site must address these points:

- A user may not be able to see, hear, move, or process certain types of information.
- A user may have difficulty reading or comprehending the text.
- The user may not be able to fluently speak and comprehend the language that the HTML page was written in.
- The user may be in a situation where his or her eyes, ears, or hands are busy (for example, driving a car, working on a machine).
- The device doing the browsing may not have a mouse or keyboard.
- The device doing the browsing may have a small screen, a text-only screen, a black-and-white screen, or a slow Internet connection.

The First HTML Page

Now the coding of the thin client begins. The coding focuses on building HTML pages that can be viewed on different browsers. A simple "Hello world" HTML page could be coded as follows.

```
<!DOCTYPE HTML PUBLIC "-//W3C//DTD HTML 4.0//EN" "http://www.w3.org/TR/
REC-html40/strict.dtd">
<HTML>
<HEAD>
<META NAME="GENERATOR" Content="Microsoft Visual Studio 6.0">
<TITLE></TITLE>
</HEAD>
<BODY>
Hello world
</BODY>
</HTML>
```

There are three sections to this document. The first is a DOCTYPE reference that indicates what kind of document this is. It is not necessary, but it should be added so that the parser can determine whether the document can be processed. The next tag, <HTML>, starts the document. Within it are two sections: <HEAD>, which defines some title and document-header definitions, and <BODY>, which contains the body of the document. In this body, the text "Hello world" appears.

SOME HEADER DEFINITION EXAMPLES

In the header area, the <META> tag should be used so that the client browser knows what to do with the document. For example, to help define keywords for the document to be searched on, the following could be used.

```
<meta http-equiv="Keywords" CONTENT="HTML, Reference">
```

The keywords are HTML and Reference.

If you want to specify when the document should be considered stale and be reloaded, the <META> tag would be as follows.

```
<META HTTP-EQUIV="Expires" CONTENT="Tue, 04 Dec 1996 21:29:02 GMT">
```

The Expires definition is always with respect to Greenwich Mean Time (GMT). The format of the date must be as defined in the example. The day and month are in a three-letter format.

If you are creating content that may potentially use a different character set, you could define the Content-Type as follows.

```
<META HTTP-EQUIV="Content-Type" CONTENT="text/html; CHARSET=EUC-JP">
```

In this example the CHARSET is defined as EUC-JP. It is not necessary to add the content type, but it does help the parser decide what to do.

Filling the Web Page with Content

The next step is to fill the page with some content. You should not add content by simply writing some HTML tags and then displaying them on the Web. If you do, your document may not be accessible to all. The better approach is to think about the structure first, and then add the content.

SEPARATING THE STRUCTURE FROM THE PRESENTATION

With HTML 4.0 it is possible to define your Web page presentation using style sheets. Style sheets make it possible to assign a location and style to various items on an HTML page. The advantage of using this approach is that it is possible to define various style sheets that will apply to different situations. For example, the style sheet for the visually impaired may require large fonts. Using style sheets also makes your site more extensible for future designs. Style sheets will be discussed in the next chapter.

USING IMAGES PROPERLY

One of the three sections on an HTML page is the banner. The banner is not as simple as it might seem. The problem with most banners on the Internet is that they are great for people who have the ability to read the page and the appropriate image. For those people who cannot, the banner is a waste of space.

The main element of a banner section is a series of images. However, images are a bit problematic. First, they are simply black boxes to many browsers, bots, indexers, and end users because the image itself cannot be deciphered like text. Images require some interpretation, which may or may not result in the correct presentation.

When using images, first consider whether the image is necessary. And what do I mean by a *necessary* image? In the past, some images have been used to overcome certain HTML layout shortcomings. For example, because there was a lack of style sheets, special fonts were created using images. Now that style sheets are not a problem, those old habits need to be broken. An image should only be used if it conveys information that cannot be represented using text.

If the image is required, then you need to provide some text to describe the image for users who cannot see the image for whatever reason. This is especially important when the image is used to convey some information that is not explicit elsewhere on the HTML page. The way that you do this is by providing some text for the alt attribute, as shown by the following example.

```
<img alt="Car driving tips" src="cardriving.jpg">
```

The tag <img> refers to an image and the alt attribute provides a description. The alt attribute can also be applied to the <applet> and <object> tags.

HTML 4.0 offers a way of providing a longer description, called the longdesc attribute. Using longdesc, it is possible to reference another Web page that describes in detail what the element is trying to indicate.

It is also possible to reference other documents using the <LINK> tag. This tag can be used in the <head> section to reference an alternative document that would be more appropriate for the end device. The following is an example link to a text-only document:

```
<HEAD>
<TITLE>Welcome to the Virtual Mall!</TITLE>
<LINK title="Text-only version"
rel="alternate" href="text_only"
media="aural, braille, tty">
</HEAD>
```

This example shows how to create an alternate Web site for users who do not have the capability to view the graphics.

MORE TEXT OPTIONS

When reading the Web-content accessibility guide, it is very apparent that developers should be more careful about how they write their text. Consider the following text:

In English we say car, in French we say voiture.

Typing that phrase in Microsoft Word produces a spelling error. This happens because Word assumes I am writing in American English. Word does not know that *voiture* is French. With the HTML 4.0 specification, the parser may be language-specific. Or, when pages are indexed, it may be useful to separate the indexes by language. You can indicate the language as follows:

```
In English we say car, in French we say <span lang="fr">voiture</span>
```

The <SPAN> tag is used to create a break area and the lang attribute is used to specify the language. If the main document was to be in French, then you should apply the lang attribute to the <BODY> tag.

Another language-related problem is acronyms. Unless you know the meaning of an acronym, it can be difficult to guess. In HTML it is possible to specify what an acronym means. The following example indicates that WWW stands for World Wide Web:

```
Welcome to the <ACRONYM title="World Wide Web">WWW</ACRONYM>
```

The acronym definition can then be used by the end device to indicate what the acronym means.

Using these tags to define sections of text is more complex. However, it is essential when they are being parsed by indexing devices or specialized browsers. For example, the acronym could be used to create a glossary for a Web site or a document.

Processing HTML Pages for the Thin Client

A standard HTML page does not invoke server-side processing. In a Windows DNA framework, to invoke server processing you use ASP. An ASP file is similar to an HTML page, except that the filename ending is .asp and it contains some scripting. The ASP framework combines a scripting engine and blocks of HTML code to generate an HTML page. ASP is extensible in that the scripting code can be extended with components that perform business operations and potentially generate more HTML content.

An Overview of ASP

When the HTTP server sends an HTML page to the client, it is sent in an HTTP packet, but this packet is sent in chunks over a period of time. These chunks can also be called an HTML stream. When an ASP page is processed, it also generates an HTML stream, but with an ASP page, the chunks are sent as quickly as the script is processed.

Figure 5–3 illustrates the architecture of ASP.

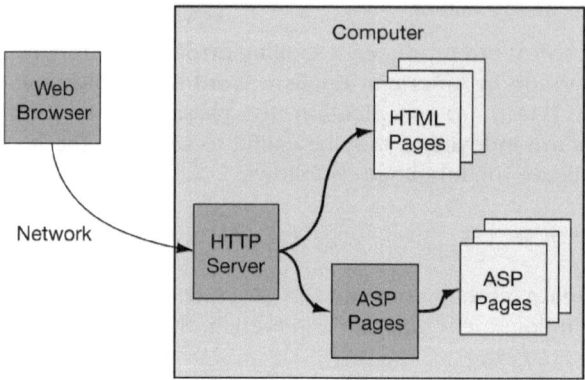

Figure 5–3: ASP architecture

ASP and IIS (Microsoft's Internet Information Server) are one architecture, and they work best together. (There is a company called ChiliSoft that does provide support for ASP on other Web servers and on other platforms.) When a browser requests the ASP file type, it is an ASP request. The ASP processing steps are:

1. The browser makes a request to the server, such as
   `http://server/something/default.asp`.
2. The request is converted to an ASP request. The ASP page is loaded in the processor and the page is parsed. The parsing starts at the top of the page and continues until the bottom of the page. At the start of this process, a return buffer stream is opened by default. The stream is defined by step 3.
   a. During the request processing, references can be made to the ASP built-in objects. These objects contain information about the client, server, and request. The built-in objects are Application, ASPError, ObjectContext, Request, Response, Server, and Session.
   b. During the request processing, COM+ application objects can be referenced. These objects perform some business process. Typically, these objects are custom designed.
3. Whatever stream content the script processing has generated is sent to the client. By default, the stream is sent as it is generated. It is possible to control the timing by using the Response built-in object.

It must be remembered that ASP works using a *stream* concept. For example, when a stream has a byte written, it is not possible to revoke that byte. The stream is serial and this means that information must be sent in a specific order.

For example, there are built-in object methods that send HTTP headers. These methods must be called before the HTML content is sent. If you attempt to use these methods after some HTML content has been sent, an error will result.

A Quick Script Example

In an ASP page, there are three types of script blocks. Two are server side and the other is client side. Because we are building a thin client, the client-side scripts do not interest us here. The server-side script execution happens on the HTTP server.

Consider the following ASP page script:

```
<%
var sum1;
obj = 1 + 1;
%>
<script language="jscript">
function clientFunc() {
var sum2;
sum2 = 1 + 1;
}
</script>
<script language="jscript" runat="server">
function serverFunc() {
var sum3;
sum3 = 1 + 1;
}
</script>
```

When the ASP framework parses this file, it searches for tags that cause a server-side script to execute. Those tags are called *escape sequences*. In this example, there are three blocks that cause an escape to scripting. The characters <% and %> bound the first block. This is code that is executed on the server side. The next block is bounded by <script> and </script> tags. This block is processed on the client side. The final block is again bounded by the <script> and </script> tags. The difference is that there is a runat="server" attribute that indicates the scripting code will be executed on the server side.

RETURNING AN ANSWER

You don't need to use the escape sequences to generate content for the HTML method. It is possible to use the intrinsic Response ASP object, as in the following example:

```
<%Response.Write("Hello world")%>
```

It is possible to embed the Response.Write method within a server-side <SCRIPT> or function block. But if you do this, the location of where the data is output depends on what has been written already to the stream.

In the following example, "Hello world" is written ten times to the HTTP stream using a loop:

```
<%for( c1=0; c1 < 10; c1++) {
Response.Write("Hello world");
}%>
```

Another way of writing content to the stream is to write to it directly, using the assignment operator; for example:

```
<%=value1%>
```

The only catch with this solution is that there can only be an assignment operator in the script block. Any other script operation will cause a script execution error. The following code is incorrect:

```
<%=value1;value1 ++%>
```

WHICH SCRIPTING LANGUAGE

Whenever an ASP page is called, it is possible to define the scripting language that is being used. In most of the examples in this book, either JScript or JavaScript is used. To indicate to the ASP framework which language is used, the following ASP command is added to the top of the page:

```
<%@ Language=JavaScript %>
```

This special command must be at the top of the page, and it specifies that JavaScript should be used as the default language. Other possible languages include VBScript, PerlScript, and Python, as well as many others. To use multiple scripting languages in the same page, the `<SCRIPT>` tag should have the `language` attribute to indicate which language is being used.

ASP Applications

An ASP application is not the same as a compiled executable. In ASP, each virtual directory is an application. When ASP pages are retrieved from the same virtual directory, they share the same ASP process space.

The HTTP server, which in this case is IIS, configures virtual directories. It is possible to define subdirectories on the hard disk, but these will not be recognized as separate ASP applications. The best way to create a virtual directory is to use Visual InterDev. This is because Visual InterDev performs the proper server-side modifications and uploads the correct initial ASP application state.

Traditional applications have the concept of global variables that can be shared in the application. ASP extends this concept to include global variables specific to a user or specific to the ASP application. You need to remember that the ASP application state is shared with other users, unlike traditional applications.

The HTTP protocol is stateless by default. This means that when a user requests one HTML page and then a second HTML page, the server will not recognize the requests as coming from the same user. With ASP it is possible to set the state, and it can extend to a page, a set of active objects, or a set of tasks. The following scopes are possible within ASP:

- **Function**: When a variable is declared at the function level, it only exists within that function. Once the function has been exited, the value of the variable is lost.
- **Page**: When an ASP page is being retrieved, the processing of the page starts from the top to the bottom. If a variable is declared during this processing, the variable exists for the life of the page.
- **User**: When a specific user accesses an ASP page, a token is associated with that user and a state is defined. It is possible to save data within that state. The state ceases to exist when a timeout or explicit state-ending method call is made.
- **Application**: When any user accesses an ASP application, a state is created. This state is shared by every user and may be accessed by any user whenever a page is retrieved.

PAGE SCOPE

Page scope can best be explained by comparing the ASP page to a serial stream. The processing starts at the top of the ASP page, and each escape sequence causes some processing. Let's say that the following code is the first piece of a JavaScript script:

```
<%
var value1;
value1 = 2;
%>
```

The variable value1 is being declared at the page level. It is then assigned a value of 2. The next section of scripting code is:

```
<script language=javascript runat=server>
var value2;

value2 = value1 + 3;
function getValue2() {
return value2;
}
function valueAdd() {
value2 = value2 + value1 + 3;
return value2;
}
```

```
function getValue1() {
return value1;
}
</script>
```

This time the <SCRIPT> tag causes the script escape. In this scripting code, there is a declaration of the variable value2. The variable value2 is then set to the value of value1 plus 3. Looking at this bit of code you would probably think that the value of value2 would be 5. However, that is not the case, because the code within the script block is not executed. It is ignored.

Now consider this ASP code fragment:

```
<p>Value1 <%=getValue1()%></p>
<p>Value2 <%=getValue2()%></p>
<p>ValueAdd <%=valueAdd()%></p>
<p>Value1 <%=getValue1()%></p>
<p>Value2 <%=getValue2()%></p>
```

Among the output, for the method call valueAdd the result is the error 1.#IND. This is because value2 has a nothing value. This is shown when the first get-Value2 is called. To solve this problem value2 needs to be set to 0. If this source code had been written in VBScript, there would be no error because VBScript does a data typecast, and a typecast of nothing is 0.

To declare page-level variables or process scripts, they need to be made within a server scripting block defined by the <% and %>tags.

To check whether the variable is actually declared, you can use the typeof function, as in this example:

```
typeof( value2)
```

This function will return one of the following strings: "number", "string", "boolean", "object", "function", or "undefined".

USER SCOPE

ASP has a series of predefined objects. One of them is the Session object, which is used to store information at the user-scope level. To use it, you assign variables as references, as in the following example:

```
Session("SomeData") = 3
```

Depending on the language, which typically will be either VBScript or JavaScript, there are no data types. Everything is a variant type. This means that when you are developing it is not possible to know what the data type is unless you check by using typeof.

Variables are stored in the Session object by assigning them as shown in the preceding example. But to identify a variable, a string identifier is associated with the assignment. In the preceding example, the string text is SomeData. To retrieve the value, the following code can be used:

```
=Session("SomeData");
```

To make user scope variables work, ASP uses cookies to identify the user with the data. Cookies are a nonintrusive technique used in HTTP to associate a user with an HTTP server.

APPLICATION SCOPE

The Application object is a built-in object that has application scope. Each client that establishes a unique Session will be able to see the same Application object. The purpose of the Application object is to enable data and information to be shared among the individual clients.

You can store a variable in the Application object just as you can in the Session object. A typical way of doing so is:

```
<%
Application.Lock();
Application("AValue") = "something";
Application.UnLock();
%>
```

In this example, the Application object's Lock and Unlock methods are called because there is concurrency for the same object. The concurrency occurs when multiple scripts attempt to modify the Application("AValue") value at the same time. The Lock method synchronizes access, preventing two clients from changing the contents of a variable simultaneously by enabling only one client to retrieve the lock. After the operations have been completed, Unlock must be called. If Unlock is not called, it will be called automatically after the ASP page has been processed. Be very careful about how the locking methods are called, because they are a bottleneck and can cause the Web application to be slower.

SETTING AND RESETTING STATE

When a Session-level and Application-level object are used, they need to be initialized. When an uninitialized value is read, nothing is returned, and depending on how that value is used, it may create problems. The global.asa file handles the initialization and destruction process. There are four events, which are defined as follows.

```
function Session_OnStart() {
}
function Session_OnEnd() {
}

function Application_OnStart() {
}
function Application_OnEnd() {
}
```

Consider an ASP application that is not running—no user has retrieved an ASP page. At this point, the ASP application is considered empty. When the first user retrieves an ASP page from the ASP application, then the user triggers a Session instantiation within the ASP framework. If the Session_OnStart event is implemented within the global.asa file, it is called. At this point, specific Session variables can be initialized. When the user is removed from the Web site as a user, the Session_OnEnd event is triggered. In this event, it is possible to release any objects that have been created, or to simply clean up operations.

If the user retrieving the ASP page is the first user retrieving any page, then the user triggers an Application instantiation. If the Application_OnStart event is implemented within the global.asa, then it is called. In this event, it is possible to set application-scope objects. It is not necessary to use the methods Application.Lock and Application.Unlock because the ASP framework ensures it is only called once. When the application shuts down because there are either no users, or the Web server is being shut down, then the Application_OnEnd event is triggered. Like its Session counterpart, it can be used to release object references or clean up operations.

TIMEOUT INTERACTION

Typically a user is removed from the application when the Session state has timed out. For example, if the time out is set to ten minutes, the user has a maximum of ten minutes to retrieve the next ASP page. If this time is exceeded, then the session times out and all values set are lost.

When writing code within the global.asa file, there can be a timeout conflict. For example, suppose the Session time out is ten minutes and a database query is stored within a Session object. However, the query has a timeout of five minutes. If the user waits for six minutes, the Session state is still available but the database query has expired. Any further database operations will cause a failure. The solution is to ensure that the Session timeout is the shortest timeout.

Processing HTML Forms

The most common HTML operation that will be programmed is the processing of forms. A forms process has two parts to it: the client side, which captures the data, and the server side, which processes the data.

THE CLIENT SIDE

Using the <FORM> tag within an HTML page specifies a form process. It creates a container that will be used to create a server process. To make a form work, the action and method attributes need to be specified as in the following example:

```
<FORM action="exampleform.asp" method=post>
...
</FORM>
```

The action attribute defines which URL will be called to process the form. A form action is a special kind of HTTP request. Unlike in the case of a regular HTML page, additional information is sent to the server. This information is used to generate a stream of HTML text that will be displayed by the end device. The stream most likely will not be a static page. In the example, an ASP page is called. The <FORM> tag does not need to be on an ASP page; it could be on an HTML page. But remember that if any server state is needed when the form page is requested, then the HTML page must have an .asp extension.

THE DIFFERENCE BETWEEN GET AND POST

There are two ways of sending information to the HTTP server. One way is to use a GET and the other is to use a POST. The GET or POST is specified in the method attribute of the <FORM> tag.

The difference between a GET and a POST is how HTTP handles it. When the client issues an HTTP GET command the various form fields are appended to the destination URL. The URL is sent within the HTTP header. In the POST variant, the form data is sent as an encoded piece of information after the HTTP header.

With respect to forms, GETs and POSTs call the same URL and pass the same information to it. The advantage with the POST is that different kinds and larger quantities of data can be sent. For example, a file could be sent using a POST, and it does not result in very long and cryptic URLs.

CREATING A SIMPLE FORM

To complete the form from the previous example, there are two more elements that need to be added. Both are of the type <INPUT>. Consider the following form implementation.

```
<FORM action="exampleform.asp" method=post>
<BR><INPUT type="text" name=text1>
<BR><INPUT type="submit" value="Submit" name=submit1>
</FORM>
```

The basic form element is the <INPUT> tag. It can represent many things, depending on the type attribute. In the first <INPUT> line in the example, the type attribute is text to denote a text field. In the second <INPUT> line, the type attribute is submit, which means that it is a button. The button is special because when it is clicked, it will call the action URL combined with the data-form variables. The value attribute associated with the submit button is the text that will be displayed on the face of the button.

It is important to identify each form element using the name attribute. When the data is combined with the URL and sent to the server, the data cannot be a large array. Instead the data is correlated with the name given in the <INPUT> tag. This information is then used on the server side.

ADDING MORE DETAILS TO THE FORM

Form elements need not be text boxes. They can include these elements:

- **Password**: This is a special field that is like a text box, but the individual characters are masked using a special character as they are typed. Example: <INPUT type="password" name=password1>
- **TextArea**: This is a multiline text field. The size of the text area is defined using the attributes rows (number of rows) and cols (number of columns). Example: <TEXTAREA rows=2 cols=20 name=textarea1></TEXTAREA>
- **Checkbox**: This is a checkbox that can be checked or unchecked. Example <INPUT type="checkbox" name=checkbox1>
- **Radio button**: This is a radio button and can be part of group of radio buttons. A group is defined by assigning multiple radio buttons the same name, but different values. Within the group only one button can be selected. Example: <INPUT type="radio" value="Value 1" name=radio1>
- **Reset button**: By pressing this button it is possible to clear the various form elements to their default value, allowing the user to start over. Example: <INPUT type="reset" value="Reset" name=reset1>

The combo box and list box form elements are a bit more complicated. When either is used, it is assumed that they have been prefilled with some data that can be selected; for example:

```
<SELECT size=1 name=select1>
<OPTION>Option 2</OPTION>
<OPTION selected="true">Option 1</OPTION>
</SELECT>
```

The <SELECT> tag can be used for either a combo box or a list box. If the size is 1, then the form element is a combo box. If it is greater than 1, it is a list box. To specify data within the combo box or list box, the <OPTION> tag is used. The text within the tag will be displayed. To select a default value, the <OPTION> has an attribute selected="true". If there are multiple selected="true" attributes, then the last one is the selected value. The exception is if the multiple attribute is set to true.

The CGI Call

When the submit button is clicked, the data is combined in a CGI (Common Gateway Interface) command and then sent to the server. CGI is a way of encoding the various parameters. Consider this simple page:

```
<FORM action="exampleform.asp" method=post>
<BR><INPUT type="text" name=text1>
<BR><INPUT type="text" name=text2>
<BR><INPUT type="submit" value="Submit" name=submit1>
</FORM>
```

If value for text1 was "Hello World" and for text2 was "folks", then the encoded CGI string would be:

```
text1=Hello+World&text2=folks%2C&submit1=Submit
```

When data is transferred between the browser and the server, many characters have a different meaning. Examples include carriage returns, spaces, and the special characters used in languages such as German and French. These special characters have to be converted into a neutral format by the browser, and then be decoded on the server side.

In the encoded string, the form elements are converted into a series of name pair values. The notation is [form field name]=[some value]. Individual form fields are separated using the ampersand (&) character. Spaces are replaced using the plus (+) character. Special characters are converted into an ASCII or short form prefixed with a percentage (%) character.

The reason for this explanation is not to make you write code to do the conversion—this is done automatically by ASP. However, there are times when raw HTML is sent. In those situations, it is your responsibility to encode the string. Chapter 7 has further discussion of this topic.

The Server Side

When a request is made and the ASP page starts processing, the Request object is instantiated. This object is responsible for parsing the CGI string into a series of variables. To access the form fields, the QueryString or Form method is used.

The following example page uses both methods and a third variant that is indifferent to how the information is passed from the client to the server.

```
<%@ Language=Javascript %>
<HTML>
<HEAD>
<META NAME="GENERATOR" Content="Microsoft Visual Studio 6.0">
</HEAD>
<BODY>

<p>Form collection
<br>Field 1: <%=Request.Form("txtField1")%>
<br>Field 2: <%=Request.Form("txtField2")%>
</p>

<p>Querystring collection
<br>Field 1: <%=Request.QueryString("txtField1")%>
```

```
<br>Field 2: <%=Request.QueryString("txtField2")%>
</p>

<p>Full collection
<br>Field 1: <%=Request("txtField1")%>
<br>Field 2: <%=Request("txtField2")%>
</p>

</BODY>
</HTML>
```

To access the value of a form field, you call the Form or QueryString method with the appropriate name attribute. This example form uses the POST method, so the Form method returns the appropriate values. The QueryString expects the individual values to be of the GET method, so those values are empty. The last way of retrieving the individual values is to call the Request object with no method specified. That action causes the form field to be searched in both the POST and GET sections.

The reason for the two method calls is to make it possible to build up custom CGI strings, which are beyond the scope of this book.

RETRIEVING UNKNOWN FIELDS

It is possible to retrieve the individual form fields by iterating through either the Form or QueryString collection, as shown in this VBScript:

```
<% For Each x In Request.QueryString %>
Request.QueryString( <%= x %> ) = <%= Request.QueryString(x) %> <BR>
<% Next %>
```

The looping technique used is specific to VBScript. The variable x is assigned an element of the QueryString collection. If the form method were a GET, the collection would contain the individual form elements. The variable x contains the name of the form field. This value is then used as an index to retrieve the value of the form field from the Request.QueryString collection.

Performing this operation within JavaScript requires a manual iteration to retrieve each element individually.

MULTIPLE FORM FIELDS WITH THE SAME NAME

There are times when two form fields have the same name. When the form is parsed, this element is a multivalued form element. This is an example of iterating through a multivalued form element in VBScript:

```
<%
For Each item In Request.Form("text1")
Response.Write item & "<BR>"
Next
%>
```

With ASP, a multivalued form element is converted into a collection. The iteration is identical to the previous collection example.

Data Validation

Form processing has the disadvantage that there is no client-side validation. This means the data is sent to the server to be validated. If there is an error, the user must fill out the form again. This costs time and bandwidth. A simpler approach, if scripting is supported on the client side, is to use client-side validation.

Data validation is not business-process validation. It is validating to make sure that the form-field values being sent to the server make some sense. There are different ways of doing this, but the simplest and most effective way is to do what was done in the conference registration Web site.

In the solution we used, some client scripting was implemented. This seemed acceptable because the browsers that supported HTML 3.2 were version 3.x browsers, and these browsers support a limited set of scripting. Based on that scripting, some client-side validation was implemented. This had the advantage of reducing the number of round trips required to submit a form. The <INPUT> tag of type attribute submit was changed to button so that the form submitting process could be controlled manually. The example source code is:

```
<INPUT type="button" value="Button" name=button1 LANGUAGE=javascript
onclick="return button1_onclick( this.form)">
```

To be able to catch the button-click event, an event handler is associated with the button by using the onclick attribute. (More details on this attribute are given in the next chapter.) When the button is clicked, the button1_onclick method is called. An example implementation of the event is:

```
<script language=javascript runat=server>
function button1_onclick( form) {
var dispString = "";
if( form.optSex.value == "") {
    dispString += "\nMale or Female";
}
if( form.txtFirstName.value == "") {
    dispString += "\nFirst name";
}
if( form.txtLastName.value == "") {
    dispString += "\nLast name";
}
if( form.txtPostCode.value == "") {
    dispString += "\nPostcode";
} else {
    var tempString = new String( form.txtPostCode.value);
    if( tempString.length > 5 || tempString.length < 4) {
        dispString += "\nPostcode is incorrect";
```

```
        }
    }
    if( form.txtCity.value == "") {
        dispString += "\nCity";
    }
    if( form.txtStreet.value == "") {
        dispString += "\nStreet";
    }
    if( form.txtTelephone.value == "") {
        dispString += "\nPhonenumber";
    }
    if( form.optCountry.value == "") {
        dispString += "\nCountry";
    }
    if( dispString != "") {
        window.alert( "The following fields have errors:" + dispString);
    } else {
        form.submit();
    }
}
</script>
```

The event handler passes the form that needs validating. The individual form fields are checked to see whether they are empty or contain an incorrect value. If there is an error, the variable dispString is appended with the error.

After all of the validation, if dispString is not empty, the various errors are displayed. If dispString is empty, then form.submit( ) is called. This method call has the same effect as clicking a submit button. The advantage of this method is that the errors are processed and displayed in one sweep. It also keeps all of the validation code in one function.

Putting It in Perspective

This was the first chapter in which we did some coding. We built a framework for creating Web applications.

The focus was on building a thin client, which means one that does not contain much functionality—a large amount of the processing of information occurs on the server side, using ASP. However, this means that the processing load on the server is that much greater, which, in turn, means that larger servers are needed to handle the load. This approach is sometimes necessary, particularly if the browser loading the content cannot handle a complex set of HTML elements. The techniques shown for building Web applications apply to both thin clients and rich clients. In either case, it is a form of distributed processing.

The questions that are still left unanswered include how to connect to a database, what other components are needed, and how to provide for a richer user interface. These are the focus of the next couple of chapters.

Chapter 6

Creating a Rich Client

A rich client is one that uses more of the functionality offered by the client browser than a thin client does. It assumes that the client browser is capable of this functionality, and a browser that does not have this functionality will display the extra information as garbled text.

We begin with a discussion of why you might want to use HTML (Hypertext Markup Language), followed by a look at some of the features offered by HTML 4.0. Many people develop for the Internet using HTML, but for an intranet using forms. There is a reason to use HTML for all types of applications, regardless of location and type. After our look at HTML's features, we look at how to format HTML using style sheets. Style sheets are a boon to Web developers because they make it possible to control the look and feel of HTML pages. Finally, the two types of browser applications—the browsing client and the workhorse client—are discussed. More advanced HTML topics, such as the DOM (Document Object Model) and scripting, are discussed within the discussions of these clients. And the discussion would not be complete without an explanation of XML (Extensible Markup Language) and XSL (Extensible Style Language): XML defines a data format, whereas XSL defines how the XML data is viewed.

As we look at these technologies, we also look at various situations in which the technologies should be applied.

Why an HTML Client?

Why use an HTML client? Why not use a language such as Java, Visual C++, or Visual Basic? The answer is that those languages solve other problems better. HTML in all of its flavors has two very powerful traits: simplicity and dynamism.

The Simplicity of HTML

HTML is simple because it is a text-based language. The tags are relatively simple, and putting together an HTML page can be accomplished with Notepad or with a development tool. HTML has a very low cost of entry, and in its simplicity is geared toward designers and user-interface people rather than programmers.

Creating a user interface using a tool like Visual C++ puts the designer at a disadvantage. The designer will see the user interface, but will not generally have the technical ability to tune it or tweak it without the intervention of a programmer. Other development languages, such as Java and Visual Basic, have the same problem in that they require a programmer. HTML enables designers to create and modify user interfaces without the help of programmers.

The Dynamism of HTML

When using a traditional language to create a user interface, the interface was designed and then the programmer wrote the code to implement the functionality. However, things change and so must user interfaces. Interface elements are added or removed, and although those elements can often just be dragged onto or off of a form, wiring them up can take quite a bit of work. Changes potentially require the programmer to rewrite some of the code, and there is a certain amount of lost programming effort.

HTML is different because elements can be added or removed dynamically. Defining templates and then applying the templates to specific situations can let you reuse code. While this is possible in other languages, it often requires a compile, distribute, and test cycle, which takes longer and is more complicated.

This brings us to HTML's strongest points. With HTML you have the option to distribute the HTML page without requiring the individual clients to manually reinstall them. The technologies used in this chapter are also cross-platform if you are using the newest major browsers (which, at the time of this writing, are Internet Explorer 5.0 and Mozilla (Netscape) 5.0).

Structuring Your Document

When developing HTML pages, you are not developing user interfaces; rather, you are developing dynamically generated documents. However, unlike in the previous chapter where the document was generated on the server, all of the content here is managed on the client side.

In a certain context, the rich client could be considered to be a fat client. In the pre-Web era, the fat client was a client application that took up many bytes and had a large installation footprint. However, in technical terms, the fat client contained the business logic on the client side.

With the introduction of the Web, a new era in server-based computing began and there is a move away from fat clients. However, the problem with a fat client is not that it is fat, but that it contains too much logic at one location. Some competing solutions have created a fat server, which in my eyes is just as bad. The key to a good solution is to properly distribute the tasks between the various machines—let each machine do what it can do best.

This section has the client process style sheets, XML, and XSL. Each of these is used to enhance the user interface of the rich client.

The Elements of a Page

A typical rich client HTML page has these elements:

- **DOM**: Document object model that represents the various elements on the Web page. The various elements can be controlled using a scripting language.
- **Style sheet**: A style sheet defines the look of a particular HTML element.
- **Component**: A component makes it possible to enhance the functionality of the HTML page by embedding logic that cannot be easily represented using scripting code.

- **XML**: HTML does not address the problem of managing data; it is just used for the user interface. XML is different in that it is used to manage data; there is no user interface with XML.
- **XSL**: XSL is like a style sheet—XML is represented on the HTML page using XSL. Conceptually it would be more accurate to define XSL as a series of HTML tags that select, filter, and illustrate XML data.

Designing a Look for Your Document

Every document has a look, regardless of what other functionality is included. So, the first thing that needs to be discussed is a style sheet. We begin with a very simple document, as shown by the following HTML code. Consider this initial HTML page:

```
<HTML>
<HEAD>
</HEAD>
<body>
<p>Hello world</p>
</body>
</HTML>
```

This page is not complicated. To enhance the page, all of the Hello World could be formatted using the <font> tag and color attributes. Instead, though, we want to separate the page content from its formatting using style sheets.

STYLE SHEETS

Style sheets enable you to separate the look of a Web page from its content. For example, a style sheet makes it possible to update the look of an HTML page without needing to update the body of that page.

Style sheets are very powerful because they are small and simple but create dramatic effects. Style sheets also promote the accessibility of an HTML page because they do not modify the content. Sometimes Web designers use images to create text effects; if these images are replaced with style sheet elements, then the page can still be processed.

How to Reference a Style Sheet

A style sheet can be referenced in various ways. The simplest way is to not have to reference it at all, but to integrate it in your Web page using the <STYLE> tag, as shown here:

```
<HTML>
<HEAD>
<STYLE>
BODY
{
COLOR: mediumblue;
```

```
FONT-FAMILY: Arial
}
</STYLE>
</HEAD>
<BODY>
```

This format is not recommended, because it is not possible to separate the style sheet from the document structure or to reuse the same style sheet in different documents. The better way is to use the `<LINK>` tag in your document, as follows:

```
<HTML>
<HEAD>
<LINK rel="stylesheet" type="text/css" href="SimpleStyleSheet.css">
</HEAD>
<BODY>
```

The attributes `rel` and `type` specify that the link is to a style sheet. When using this tag in your HTML pages, you use the same notation. The `href` attribute defines from where the style sheet is loaded. This attribute takes the form of a valid URL (Uniform Resource Locator).

How to Define a Style Sheet

When the HTML file is loaded, the various references to the style sheet are loaded and processed. Then the rendering process is started. The style sheet defines the rendering characteristic of an HTML tag. As the browser parses the HTML file, it encounters the individual HTML tags, and it will look in the style sheet for a definition. If there is a definition, the rendering characteristic from the style sheet is used. Otherwise, the browser's default is used.

When you define a style sheet, you create a set of "rules" for the rendering process. Consider the following rule:

```
BODY
{
COLOR: mediumblue;
FONT-FAMILY: Arial
}
```

The first item in the rule is called the selector. It is the HTML tag that will be rendered. The curly brackets then surround the declarations, which are listed in the form `attribute: value;`. The only exception is that the last declaration does not need a trailing semicolon. The rule in this example says that the HTML `<BODY>` tag should be rendered using the `mediumblue` color and the `Arial` font.

If you apply the style sheet to the Hello World HTML page we created in Chapter 5, the Hello world text would change color to blue, and the font would change to Arial.

Style sheets support inheritance. Consider adding the following HTML table fragment to the initial HTML page.

```
<table border=1>
<tr>
    <td>Hello</td>
</tr>
</table>
```

If the altered HTML page were viewed again, the content within the table would be blue also. Why? The style sheet tag defined previously applied only to the <BODY> tag. However, the <BODY> tag is the root of all tags in the rendering process. Because the <TABLE> tag does not have a specific rendering rule, it uses the parent rule, which is a blue color and Arial font.

Let's change the table to green with a different font and font size by using the following rule:

```
TABLE
{
COLOR: green;
FONT-FAMILY: 'Palatino Linotype';
FONT-SIZE: 20pt
}
```

Now, viewing the HTML page results in page content that is blue, but the table content is green and the font is larger.

Style sheets also have the ability to apply a rule to a specific context. Consider the following rule.

```
TABLE B
{
COLOR: blue;
FONT-FAMILY: 'Palatino Linotype';
FONT-SIZE: 10pt
}
```

In this example, the style listed will be applied to every <B> tag nested within a <TABLE> tag. Had the <B> and <TABLE> tags been separated by a comma, then the rule would be applied when one of the elements was encountered within the HTML page.

Style Sheet Classes

There are situations where you will not want to define a style sheet rule based on an HTML tag. You will want to define a generic style sheet rule that can be applied to an HTML element, when it is defined. In style sheet terms, this is called a class. The class can be defined in the HTML page or in the style sheet page. An example definition is as follows:

```
.exampleClass
{
COLOR: red;
FONT-FAMILY: 'Palatino Linotype';
FONT-SIZE: 10pt
}
```

To reference this style sheet rule, the HTML tag needs the appropriate attribute `class` set. You can apply the style sheet to a table cell as follows:

```
<TD class=exampleClass>Cost</TD></TR>
```

Now, when the `<TD>` tag is rendered, it will use the `exampleClass` rule.

It is also possible to define a context for when a specific style sheet rule is to be used. For example, suppose we want to define a style sheet class that can only be applied when a `<TABLE>` tag is encountered. The style sheet class definition would be as follows:

```
TABLE.exampleClass
{ ... }
```

MAKING STYLE SHEETS DO SOMETHING

The previous examples are very simple and show how to create some text effects. But the real goal is to do something interesting with a style sheet. The following discussions show how style sheets can be used to make an HTML page richer.

Working with Tables

Before Dynamic HTML and style sheets, tables were used to lay out information on an HTML page. But with style sheets, it is possible to manually define where things will be located and how. This is not to say that tables should not be used; rather, that they do not need to be used with the same frequency.

There are three elements to a table: declaration, row, and cell within the row, as shown in the following code:

```
<TABLE>
<TR>
    <TD>One row, one cell table</TD>
</TR>
</TABLE>
```

The `<TABLE>` tag begins a table, and each table should have at least one row `<TR>` and one cell `<TD>`. If it does not, then it is not a valid table, even though most browsers will still render the table. HTML tables are different from regular tables in that each row does not need to have the same number of columns. The data is written to the cell and not the table. An HTML table is dynamic, and the row and cell height and width will adjust to fit the data that is being rendered.

Designing a Banner

It is possible to explicitly define a style sheet attribute directly to an HTML tag. Consider the case of defining a banner on an HTML page. One way to define the banner is to create a table and have it extend the width of the page. But to make the banner stand out, its background color must be a different color. The way to do this is to alter the style sheet rule for the table cell. Consider the following HTML banner implementation:

```
<TABLE width="100%">
<TR>
    <TD style="BACKGROUND-COLOR: red>My Web Banner</div></TD></TR></TABLE>
</BODY>
```

The <TD> cell has the style attribute BACKGROUND-COLOR set to red, which changes the background color.

Working with Color

In the previous style sheet declaration, typing a text value (in contrast to defining it with a number) sets the color. This is because the browser understands the definition as being a specific color. Color is tricky because many browsers may not render color properly, and because many people are fully or partially color blind. In either case, you cannot count on viewers seeing the colors you use on the page. As a rule, color should be used to complement the page, but not to catch the attention of the user or convey information.

Color can also be problematic if the end user's system only supports 256 colors. When there is a 256-color palette and you have chosen your colors from a larger palette, you may have chosen colors that cannot be rendered as desired. To avoid this problem, use the safe color palette, which includes only colors that can be rendered properly. Visual InterDev has a color picker that offers only safe colors. If you are not using Visual InterDev, your safe colors are combinations of the following:

```
0x00, 0x33, 0x66, 0x99, 0xCC, 0xFF
```

Each of these values corresponds to one shade of a color of the RGB (red, green, blue) spectrum. To create a color, three of them are combined as in the following example:

```
0x003366
```

The "0x" notation is hexadecimal, and in HTML it is written as:

```
#003366
```

Playing with Text Alignment

On an HTML page, all text is bound by a boxed area. This is a result of the nested nature of HTML. When the first text is rendered, it starts in the upper-left corner because this is typical of Western languages. As items are rendered, it is possible to position text relative to the last rendered position. This is called managing a margin.

The following HTML creates a sample style sheet class containing a margin:

```
.quote { color: red;
font-size: 24px;
margin-top: -182px;
font-family: Impact }
```

In this case, the margin-top attribute says "please position the next element 182 pixels above the current position." Now, let's apply this apply this class to the following HTML fragment:

```
<table border="1">
<tr>
    <td ><div class="quote">Hello world</div></td>
</tr>
</table>
```

The <DIV> tag is discussed later; for now, consider it to be a space-holding token. Because the margin-top is negative, the text is rendered above the table cell. This means that the text disappears from the HTML page, because it is rendered in a nonexistent region. Positive values move the rendering position down the page. Positive and negative margins can be applied to any of the top, bottom, right, and left margins, as shown in Figure 6–1.

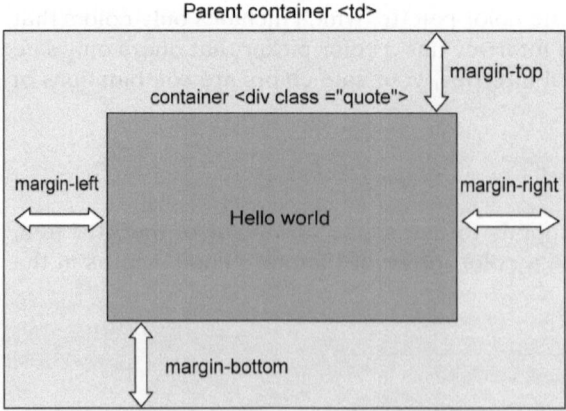

Figure 6–1: How margins are defined

Another way of providing a margin is to use the style attributes padding-left, padding-right, padding-top, and padding-bottom. They are identical in how they are calculated, except that the calculations are performed on the local HTML tag. In our example, this means the calculations are performed on the <DIV> tag. Figure 6–2 shows the page from Figure 6–1, extended to include padding definitions.

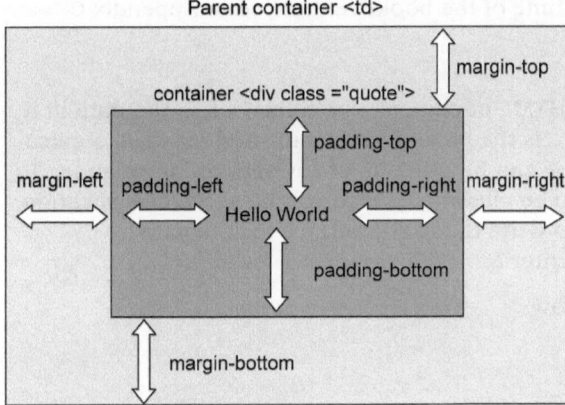

Figure 6–2: How paddings are defined

So which should you use use, and when should you use it? It depends on what positioning is required. Margins allow multiple HTML elements to be aligned relative to each other within a container. Padding is simpler; it provides a blank space for all elements within the container.

Another useful technique is to create floating text. When text is floated within an HTML page, other text wraps around it. This creates the effect of seamless text that fits into the HTML content. This might be used in an article where the first letter needs to bolded. An example class definition for floating text is:

```
.floatingText {
float:left;
width: 10px;
font-size: 80px;
background: #663366;
color: yellow;
text-align: left
}
```

Applying this to the previous HTML <DIV> fragment results in the following HTML:

```
<div id="something" style="background-color: lightblue; ">
<div class="float">H</div>ello world
</div>
```

The letter *H* appears to be in bold type and enlarged. A `float` attribute positions the HTML box within the container, and everything else floats around it in a seamless manner. The `float` attribute can be either `left` or `right`, and any surrounding text will flow to the right or left of the floating *H* element.

There are many other manipulation techniques that can be applied to text, such as indentation and line spacing, but they are beyond the scope of this book. If you need fine control, review some of the books referenced in Appendix C.

Understanding Your Data

HTML formatting is half of your HTML document; the other half is the data in it. Generating and working with data is the bulk of developing and using an application. The data can be simple or it can be millions of rowsets of information. To understand your data, it needs to be classified. Once you have the classification, it is possible to determine how to write the user interface for the data.

Data is classified using two criteria:

- The direction of the data flow
- The hardness of the data

DATA FLOW DIRECTION

The direction of data flow is connected to how the data is used. A data flow direction that is predominantly from server to client indicates a read-mostly client. A read-mostly client has the task of finding and presenting the various pieces of information easily. Because most of the time is spent moving data from one machine to the other, it is important that this is done efficiently.

DATA HARDNESS

Why the distinction between hard and soft data? Multitier computing involves moving data from the server to client and vice versa, which, in turn, requires network bandwidth. What you want to do is optimize that network traffic. One way to do this is to classify the data in terms of hardness, which makes it possible to manipulate data locally and only send it over the network when the data has become hard.

The difference between hard data and soft data is that hard data acts as a unit and is considered a packet of information. Consider the situation of entering an order. The order has an address, client, and items to be ordered, such as ten different types of widgets. When the order is being created the data is considered soft because when this order is for only five types of widgets, it is not valid—the client wanted ten types of widgets. After all ten types of widgets are ordered, the entire packet can be sent to the server for further processing. This packet is one piece of information and it reflects a business process.

You could argue that the information can be sent to the server in pieces, running within the context of a transaction. If the transaction is successful, the data is committed; otherwise, the data is rolled back. This form of manipulating data is identical to what was described previously, but without the complexity of data hardness. The problem with this solution is that it does not use the resources efficiently. When a piece of data is sent to the server, it is gone and cannot be returned. This means that the clients must know what they want. To delete that information, a delete operation would need to be sent to the server. This means that the network has been used to process information that will not exist in the database, and this is a wasteful use of network resources.

The Browsing Client

The browsing client is the first rich client to be discussed. It is a rich client and it is used for reading data and drilling down into specific pieces of data. The browsing client has these characteristics:

- Data flow is from the server to the client. The client wishes to browse and interpret large amounts of data.
- The data is neither hard nor soft, because browsing data is a read-only operation. As such there is no need to run transactions or keep database connections open on the server side.
- The most important consideration is to be capable of easily understanding the data and making it look attractive.
- Large amounts of data must be sent from the server to the client in the form of records.

The best way to write this type of client is to use server-side processing to generate XML data that can be formatted and processed using XSL. Please do not mistake this use of XML as being the only way of using it—it can be used in other situations. However, using XML and XSL is the optimal way of implementing the browsing client.

Introduction to XML

XML is a text-based technology used to define structured information. Traditionally, XML has only been used in documents, but this is not its only use. The power of XML is in its simplicity. Consider the following XML code:

```
<PERSON>
<NAME>Christian</NAME>
<LASTNAME>Gross</LASTNAME>
<SEX>Male</SEX>
</PERSON>
```

XML looks very similar to HTML. In HTML, the tags have a specific name and functionality, which XML does not require. XML is concerned with storing data, not displaying a user interface.

The above example can be either a full XML document or an XML fragment. In either case, you are defining an XML node. An XML node is created when there is both an opening and closing tag to bound the data. In the preceding example, the root XML node is <PERSON>. Another XML node is <NAME>, <LASTNAME>, and so on.

The opening tag set is defined with this notation:

```
<TAG>
```

The closing tag set is defined using this notation:

```
</TAG>
```

In this example, `<TAG>` could be replaced with a more meaningful tag name. For example, to define an address you could use `<ADDRESS>`. To represent a name, you could use `<NAME>`.

In the special situation where there is no information to be contained within the XML node, it is possible to use a simpler notation. For example, instead of using the following empty XML node:

```
<TAG></TAG>
```

the following simpler notation can replace it:

```
<TAG/>
```

XML is a nesting technology, in that the opening and closing tag sets must nest one within the other, like placing boxes in boxes. The sides may touch, but never can an inner box side extrude beyond an outer box. The following XML is considered invalid:

```
<PERSON><NAME>Christian<SEX>Male</NAME></SEX></PERSON>
```

The `<NAME>` closing tag set is presented before the `<SEX>` closing tag set. Because the `<NAME>` opening tag set is called before the `<SEX>` opening tag set, the correct notation would be the inverse, as shown here:

```
<PERSON><NAME>Christian<SEX>Male</SEX></NAME></PERSON>
```

A tag identifier must be a single word without any spaces. In XML, spaces are called white space.

XML ATTRIBUTES

Within each tag you can define an attribute. An attribute is like a property, in that it is specific to the entity in which it is defined. Consider the following example of an attribute:

```
<person age="31"><name>Christian Gross</name></person>
```

In this example, the `<person>` tag has an age attribute, which has a value of 31. The value of the attribute has a set of quotes (either single or double quotes) around it. This is a requirement.

The <person> tag and its nested values could also be represented as a series of attributes, as follows:

```
<person name="Christian Gross" sex="male"/>
```

In this situation, there are no nested values, just a single tag.

When is it best to use an attribute and when is it best to use explicit tags? There is no single answer, but there are a couple of rules of thumb:

- XML is supposed to be human readable and relatively easy to comprehend. Using too many attributes can make a tag difficult to read and use.
- Attributes can be used to define simple, short values, and using them otherwise produces unreasonably complex results. Long pieces of text or encoded data do not lend themselves to being defined as attributes.

HOW SPACES ARE HANDLED

Spaces in XML are not handled like spaces in HTML. In XML, all spaces are important. Consider the following XML.

```
<person>
<name>Christian Gross</name>
</person>
```

There is no significant spacing in this example, only formatted text. However, the XML parser sees things differently because there is some spacing. After the opening <person> tag set, there is a carriage return and a tab. The parser views this space as important—it says the <person> tag has a Return and Tab. What the parser does with this information depends on the parser and its settings. This book assumes that the Return and Tab are examples of white space, and if a text contains only white space, it is ignored. The Microsoft XML parser makes the same assumption.

Now let's look at an example in which the white space is important:

```
<person>
<name>Christian
    Gross</name>
</person>
```

In this example, the white space is important because there are other text characters.

IS XML CASE SENSITIVE?

Yes, XML is case sensitive, which means that the following are unique values:

```
<Person person="Christian" PERSON="another"/>
```

Even though all three person identities are spelled the same, the different cases make them unique in all situations. This is not like HTML, where case does not matter. In XML, no two attributes within a tag can have the same name and case.

Although the preceding notation might be valid XML, it is not recommended that you use the same word with a different case to represent different tags. Using the same word with a different case is likely to confuse readers.

CORRECT XML DATA

XML data is free flowing and can lack structure. But sometimes there is a need to define the data set as some type of structured information. This is done by building a DTD (document-type declaration). Using a DTD, the parser will validate the document data and ensure that the document data is what the DTD says it can be. If there are extra tags or missing attributes, the parser generates an error.

It is not necessary to define a DTD for all data. So when is a DTD necessary? The answer is that it depends on the context. If you are using a document editor such as Microsoft Word 2000, then a DTD is necessary to ensure that the data is fully correct before it is loaded in Microsoft Word. If it is not correct, Word generates an error. When building Web applications, however, a DTD may not be necessary because the browser only requires a correct XML form and parses the data as it arrives. Because the XML data is automatically generated in smaller pieces than what the DTD specifies, a DTD may complicate the entire scenario.

In general, using a DTD is a good idea because it documents what information is retrieved, stored, and sent on the network. In a large corporate scenario, this information might be important when debugging and testing applications and interoperability between those applications. The entire process of defining the DTD is beyond the scope of this book.

SPECIAL XML TAGS AND ATTRIBUTES

XML tags can be used to define a namespace. For example, a title for a person could be Mr., Mrs., or Ms. In the context of a book, a title is the title of the book. When the parser executes, it is good to know which title is being referenced. You can do this by defining a namespace.

An example namespace is:

```
<book xmlns:nsBooks="http://www.w3.org/books">
<nsBooks:title>Carpe Jugulum</nsBooks:title>
</book>
```

In this fragment, there is an XML attribute that has a special meaning. The xmlns attribute is used to define a namespace. This is a reserved attribute used by the XML parser to indicate that the namespace nsBooks is being defined. The value of the attribute specifies where the namespace is defined, typically using the form of a URL that references a file that contains the namespace specification.

The following special tags either exist or are under investigation and may become standards:

- xml:link: Enables an XML document designer to provide links to other XML documents. This is similar to HTML links.
- xmlns:[prefix]: Makes it possible to define a namespace to the given XML document. Namespaces are important because the <title> tag may refer to either the title of a book or the title of a person. The namespace provides the capability for distinguishing between the two.
- xml:lang: Specifies the language in which the XML fragment is encoded.
- xsl:[...]: A specific tag used in an XSL document that needs an XSL processor for proper parsing.

HOW DOES THE XML PARSER UNDERSTAND THE XML?

When text is being parsed, how does the parser know what to parse? The text may be in UNICODE or ASCII format. The answer is very simple. Each XML fragment needs to start with the following text:

```
<?xml ...>
```

The parser reads the first four bytes and, depending on what it finds and how it finds it, it invokes either the UNICODE or ASCII parser. Therefore, it is important that all XML fragments and documents include the reference.

XSL

On many Web sites promoting XML, users have expressed a difference of opinion on the merits of XSL. Some people think it is not good because it is too complex and could be avoided by using a different approach. However, I think XSL is interesting because of how it manages XML data.

When the receiving browser parses XML, which is raw data, the browser looks at the data but does not know what to do with it. Therefore, it is necessary to transform XML into some type of information that contains both the XML data and some HTML tags. This is done using a specification called Extensible Stylesheet Language (XSL). You could do the same thing with scripting and DOM, but doing it that way is not straightforward. That approach requires a series of functions and scripting techniques. XSL is a simple, one-step, optimized process that transforms data into user-interface information.

XSL transforms the XML data. A transformation requires a document in XML and the application of an XSL sheet. The first step is called a *tree transformation* because it takes raw XML and converts it to a filtered and sorted XML view. The second step is the formatter, which takes the newly generated XML and creates some type of view for a specific medium (for example, printer or screen). When we build the XSL pages, we are working with the tree transformation.

There are two ways of using an XSL sheet. The first is to reference it when viewing XML data. The more common way is to squirt the XSL-generated HTML tags into an existing HTML page.

STARTING WITH A SIMPLE XML DATA SET

Now we go through the process of displaying some XML data. The first step is to look at some XML data, as in the following example:

```
<?xml version="1.0" xml-stylesheet type="text/xsl"
href="exampleXSL1.xsl"?>
<population>
<person>
    <name>Isabelle Laurin</name>
    <age>31</age>
    <address>221 Avenue General De Gaulles</address>
</person>
<person>
    <name>Christian Gross</name>
    <age>31</age>
    <address>221 Avenue General De Gaulles</address>
</person>
<person>
    <name>Simon Gross</name>
    <age>19</age>
    <address>Napoul 21</address>
</person>
</population>
```

First, notice that this data is regular, which means that there are repeatable records. In this example, it is the <person> tag. The second item to notice is the <?xml-stylesheet ...> tag.

By default, when a browser reads XML, it attempts to parse it as HTML. If you have one of the latest browsers, such as Internet Explorer 5, it will create a raw XML view. When this document is loaded, however, the XSL sheet specified by the <?xml-stylesheet ...> tag is loaded and used to display the XML data.

In this case, the XSL sheet is defined as follows:

```
<?xml version='1.0' xsl:stylesheet xmlns:xsl="http://www.w3.org/TR/WD-xsl">
<xsl:template match="/">
<HTML>
<BODY>
<TABLE BORDER="2">
  <TR>
      <TD>Name</TD>
      <TD>Address</TD>
  </TR>
  <xsl:for-each select="population/person">
      <TR>
      <TD><xsl:value-of select="name"/></TD>
```

```
        <TD><xsl:value-of select="address"/></TD>
        </TR>
    </xsl:for-each>
</TABLE>
</BODY>
</HTML>
</xsl:template>
</xsl:stylesheet>
```

Notice that an XSL sheet is an XML application. This is because the first line contains the tag `<?xml ...>`. Because it is an XML application, care needs to be taken that all of the tags within the XSL document are XML complete. More details on this in a bit.

The next tag, `<xsl:stylesheet ...>`, indicates that this XML document is an XSL application. This `xsl:...` notation is similar to the XML special tags and attributes section. In XML, whenever there is a notation in the form *special:tag* the *special* refers to an XML namespace. In the preceding XSL document, the xsl namespace is defined.

Before any parsing of data can occur, the location of the data must be defined. This is defined in the XSL sheet with the tag `<template match = "/">`, which indicates a root location. The next step is to define a selection set of data that will be parsed.

The tag `<for-each>` starts a loop that will be iterated for each record that is found in the selection, and the loop ends at the closing `<for-each>` tag. The selection is defined by the `select` attribute that has a value of population/people. This selection says that in the XML population subdirectory, iterate through all of the people records. Whatever is within the loop will be output into the stream. Naturally, you would like to display the records, which is accomplished by using the `<value-of>` tag. The attribute `select="address"` defines the tag of the record that should be output, which is the `<address>` tag.

Formatting the HTML Tags Correctly

HTML tags need to be formatted correctly. While HTML is similar to XML, it does sometimes break some XML rules. Therefore, when you are including HTML within an XSL sheet, the HTML must be XML compliant. Otherwise, the parser generates document-parsing errors.

The following are some HTML syntax tricks to be careful with:

- `<P>` must have a closing `</P>`. Similarly, `<LI>` and table tags need to have closing tags. The lack of closing table tags is often the result of some HTML editing tools forgetting to add the closing tags.
- `<IMG src="somepic.jpg">` should be `<IMG src="somepic.jpg"/>`. The slash toward the end indicates a single tag.
- Watch your case. For example `<B>` and `</b>` are not matching tags and using them together will cause errors.

- The attributes need to be surrounded with quotes. Using `<img src= sompic.jpg/>` will cause problems, even though the HTML parser has no problem with it.

The last big thing to watch is the embedding of scripts. Consider the following.

```
<script>
function isLarger( value1, value2) {
if( value1 < value2)
    return false;
else
    return true;
}
</script>
```

The script looks harmless, but it will give the XML parser a fit. When the comparison is done, a less-than (<) character is used, and the XML parser will read this as an XML tag definition. Because it cannot find a greater-than (>) character to close the tag, a parsing error will result. The easiest way of fixing the problem is to change the script to the following:

```
<script><![CDATA[
function ...
]]></script>
```

The CDATA declaration specifies that whatever follows is data and should not be parsed by the XML parser.

SQUIRTING IN XSL-GENERATED HTML DATA

Another way of displaying XSL data is to combine both the XSL sheet and the XML data dynamically, and then inject the resulting HTML data in the document. The way to do this is to define the XSL sheet and XML data source as entities on the Web page. The XML data source is transformed using the transformNode method, with the transformation being the style sheet XMLDocument property. This results in a stream of HTML tags that then need to be injected somewhere in the document. Typically, this is done using a <DIV> tag and an appropriate script; for example:

```
<HTML>
<HEAD>
<TITLE></TITLE>
</HEAD>
<SCRIPT FOR="window" EVENT="onload">
injectSection.innerHTML = source.transformNode(style.XMLDocument);
</SCRIPT>
<BODY>
<XML id="source" src="example2.xml"></XML>
```

```
<XML id="style" src="examplexsl1.xsl"></XML>
<P>Here is some data</P>
<div id="injectSection"></div>
</BODY>
</HTML>
```

SORTING THE DATA

In the previous examples, the XML data was considered to be raw data, and records were displayed in the output. However, if the record set is large, viewing may be difficult because there may not be any order to the data. Fortunately, it is possible to sort the XML data before it is displayed. The following example sorts the XSL sheet by name:

```
<xsl:for-each select="population/person" order-by="name">
```

The order-by attribute identifies the XML tag that will be sorted on. It is possible to sort on multiple XML tags, as shown in the following example:

```
<xsl:for-each select="population/person" order-by="name;address">
```

Semicolons are used to separate the sorting keys.

Sorting Numeric Data

The sorting shown thus far sorts all of the data using alphabetic rules. But consider changing the sorting attribute to order-by="age". How will the information be sorted? XML by default does not understand the difference between a numeric, date, or alphabetic piece of information. To the XML parser, they are all bytes, which have some value. But when sorting dates or numbers those byte rules do not apply. In XSL, it is possible to sort using a numeric or date notation, and there are two ways to pass the information to the XSL processor. The first is to use the DTD that indicates the data type; for example:

```
<population xmlns:dt="urn:schemas-microsoft-com:datatypes">
<person>
    <name>Isabelle Laurin</name>
    <age dt:dt="number">31</age>
    <address>221 Avenue General De Gaulles</address>
</person>
</population>
```

In the declaration of the <population> tag, the data type (dt) namespace is referenced. This is then used as an attribute in the declaration of the <age> tag. The dt:dt type is number.

The other way of indicating that a specific value in the sort criteria is numeric or date based is to use the number or date function; for example:

```
order-by="name; number(age)"
```

Sorting Order

When sorting, it is possible to define whether the data is sorted in ascending or descending order. Ascending order is considered the default, but to explicitly define it, the following attribute setting is used:

```
order-by="+name"
```

The plus sign is for ascending sorts, and the minus sign is used for descending sorts, as shown in the following example:

```
order-by="-name"
```

FILTERING DATA

Filtering the data means that some records are displayed and some not, depending on the filtering criteria. A filter specifies a query for information that is of interest. A query could be similar to "select all of the people who have an age less than 20." To build a query, you need to understand XSL patterns, which haven't yet been discussed. Do not mistake an XSL pattern with the kind of pattern used to help you design applications. XSL patterns are used to create query strings for filtering XML data.

When filtering data, the context becomes important. XML has a hierarchy, which starts with the root node as defined by the tag <xsl:template match="/">. As we traversed the various nodes, the data nodes were enumerated. The base location of the enumeration is defined by the loop <xsl:for-each ...>, which referenced the location population/person. Because there is no leading backward slash (\) in this location definition, it is considered a relative location, that is, relative to the current absolute location, which was defined to be the root node, or /. (With respect to the loop, the absolute location is created by adding the relative location to the absolute location, which is /population/person.)

Why this explanation of absolute and relative locations? When you build XSL selection patterns, the location is used to filter the information. Different locations give different selection results. In this sense, creating XSL patterns is like navigating a directory tree.

A Simple Selection Pattern

Let's start with a simple selection based on the directory principle. What we want to do is select all of the people within a population. The XSL pattern is population/*, where the wildcard character (*) represents all of the XML nodes underneath the population XML node. The result is all of the nodes.

Let's now create a selection that returns all of ages within the population. The XSL pattern is population/*/age. This pattern says that all nodes containing an <age> tag should be displayed.

Now let's combine this with some actual XSL commands to display the data. The example that is illustrated will select all people who are 31 years old. The following XSL fragment accomplishes this:

```
<xsl:for-each select="population/person[age='31']" order-by="name">
```

The pattern population/person[age='31'] specifies that for every person, check whether the <age> tag has a value of 31. If age were an attribute of person, the query would change to population/person[@age='31']. The @ indicates that age is an attribute within the tag <person>. The selection could be used without comparison as follows: population/person[age]. This means that only <person> tags that have <age> tags should be selected.

Conditional Pattern Matching

When the XSL process is running, it is possible to apply conditional pattern matching. Consider the following:

```
<xsl:if age="qty[.$ge$10]">
...
</xsl:if>
```

This is an XSL if statement. It says that given the current context, check whether the <age> tag has a value greater than 10. The word qty refers to a <qty> tag and it then asks whether the value is greater than 10 using the ge operator. The ge operator is identical to the > character, which is a shortcut. (When using Microsoft XSL, the XML <age> tag is alphabetic, but the age is converted to a number automatically by the query.)

The following table defines all of the comparison possibilities.

OPERATOR	XSL SYNTAX
and	and
or	or
not()	not
=	eq
!=	ne
<	lt
<=	le
>	gt
>=	ge

This explains some of the basic and intermediate features of XSL.

The Workhorse Client

Data does not only flow from the server to the client. There is also a need to send data from the client to the server. With the workhorse client, data is sent to the server for further processing. Do not mistake sending a query for a specific piece of data as being a workhorse client operation—the query does not modify data on the server.

The workhorse client has these characteristics:

- Data flow is from the server to the client and client to the server. There is no need to navigate large amounts of data constantly. The key requirement is to interact with and manipulate the data.
- The data moves from soft to hard as was explained earlier in the chapter. Scripting objects or COM (Component Object Model) objects are used to gather the data on the client side.
- The workhorse client provides more functionality than browsing client.
- Bandwidth and processing power must be used intelligently, by involving both the client and the server.

The best way of writing this type of client is to use Dynamic HTML to position user-interface elements and dynamically interact with the user interface. Data can be transferred using XML and the XML DOM, and scripting can be used to glue all of the various elements together. If need be, custom COM objects can be used to implement functionality not possible using scripting.

Working with the DOM

The DOM is a very large object model that makes it possible to dynamically interact with the user interface. Elements can be added dynamically or statically, and the model is very flexible. It also requires some changes in thinking, because everything is dynamic. For example, when displaying a list of information, traditionally a list box was needed. However, with the DOM, that is not necessary. You can mimic a list using a table with the appropriate scripting handlers.

SCRIPTING

Scripting is the primary way of controlling the user interface. In the previous chapter, ASP (Active Server Pages) server-side scripting was introduced. Client-side scripting is similar, except that it is entirely event driven. Event-driven programming has events triggering pieces of code that react to the event. Let's start with the classic example, Hello world.

The Hello world display will result from clicking a button on an HTML page. The button triggers an onclick event, which is captured, and a message box appears. The full example is as follows.

```
<HTML><HEAD>
<SCRIPT LANGUAGE=javascript>
function button1_onclick() {
window.alert( "Hello world");
```

```
}
</SCRIPT>
</HEAD>
<BODY>
<P><INPUT type=button value="hello world" LANGUAGE=javascript
onclick="return button1_onclick()"></P>
</BODY></HTML>
```

Starting from the top of the HTML page, there is a <SCRIPT> tag. It contains a function called button1_onclick. This function will serve as a handler for the button click event. In this situation, the event handler has a significant naming convention (button name and then the event being handled). But the naming convention is just that—a naming convention. The function name could be someFunction. It does not matter, because the function is wired dynamically to the button.

To wire the function to the event, the <INPUT> tag needs two additional attributes. The LANGUAGE attribute specifies which language the event handler attribute is written in. Then the onclick attribute specifies which event is being handled. The onclick attribute value should contain scripting that calls the function in the scripting block, but this is not a requirement. The attribute could contain the scripting code itself, but that makes the <INPUT> tag much more difficult to comprehend. When the button is clicked, it calls up the function button1_onclick, which calls window.alert and says Hello world.

IDENTIFYING YOURSELF

Each element on an HTML page is an object. To be able to reference the element, it needs to have an ID. The ID is used within a script block for object-manipulation purposes. It is possible to write all of the code without using any IDs, but it is much more complicated. This time the Hello World example will not use a message box; instead, it will insert text in a table. Consider the following HTML page:

```
<HTML><HEAD>
<SCRIPT LANGUAGE=javascript>
function button1_onclick() {
insertionPoint.innerHTML = "<h1>Hello world</h1>";
}
</SCRIPT>
</HEAD>
<BODY>
<P><INPUT type=button value="hello world" LANGUAGE=javascript
onclick="return button1_onclick()"></P>
<table border=1>
<tr>
    <td id=insertionPoint> </td>
</tr>
</table>
</BODY></HTML>
```

The ID attribute is called `insertionPoint` and it has been associated with a `<TD>` tag, or table cell. In the script block, the code was changed to use the `insertionPoint` object. This object has all of the methods that a regular table cell object has. (For references on the DOM, please consult the Appendix C.) The most common properties that are used to add, remove, or manipulate text are `innerHTML` and `innerText`. These two properties contain the nested HTML tags, or text within the HTML tag. The difference between the two properties is that `insertionPoint.innerHTML` supports the parsing of HTML tags, whereas `innerText` does not. In the script block, `insertionPoint.innerHTML` is used to display the `Hello World` text. Be forewarned that if either `insertionPoint.innerText` or `insertionPoint.innerHTML` contains any information, that information will be erased.

Instead of replacing entire blocks of HTML content, it is possible to append HTML content to the element. This is accomplished using the `insertionPoint.insertAdjacentHTML` and `insertionPoint.insertAdjacentText` methods. These methods append the fragment to the end of the text or HTML tags that are within the object. By using the property `insertionPoint.outerHTML`, it is possible to replace both the inner fragment and the HTML element/object. Be forewarned that by removing content and replacing it with other content, you can invalidate references to elements that were part of the replaced content. Those references are thus made invalid, and attempting to use them will cause errors.

POSITIONING ELEMENTS

Style sheets make it possible to statically position HTML elements, but by combining scripting with positioning, it is possible to dynamically position HTML elements. When working with DHTML (Dynamic HTML), the most popular HTML tags used are `<DIV>` and `<SPAN>`. A `<DIV>` tag is a simple container that has some HTML rendering. The container is similar to a boxed region. The `<SPAN>` tag is different in that it is an inline region of text. The `<SPAN>` region integrates within the flow of the text.

The following example shows a box that can be moved from the left to the right, and vice versa, by clicking on a left or right button. The example illustrates wiring the button events, defining a `<DIV>` region and associating it with an ID, and defining the `<DIV>` region using style sheet classes that define the length, width, top, and left positions. This example is scripted with VBScript, but there was no particular reason to choose this language over another.

```
<HTML><HEAD>
<STYLE TYPE="text/css">
.Box {
position: absolute; left: 100px; top: 100px; width: 200px;
height: 80px; overflow: 'clip'; background: 00cc00;
}
</STYLE>

<SCRIPT LANGUAGE="VBScript">
```

```
Sub butMoveLeft_Click()
currBox.style.pixelleft = currBox.style. pixelleft - 10
end sub

Sub butMoveRight_Click()
currBox.style. pixelleft = currBox.style. pixelleft + 10
end sub
</SCRIPT>

</HEAD><BODY BGCOLOR=FFCCFF>
<DIV class=Box ID=currBox>
Hello from DHTML
</DIV>
<INPUT type="button" value="Move left" id=butLeft LANGUAGE=vbscript
onclick="butMoveLeft_Click">
<INPUT type="button" value="Move right" id=butRight LANGUAGE=vbscript
onclick="butMoveRight_Click">
</BODY></HTML>
```

The style sheet's Box class defines the dimensions and colors of the region. This is a good example of how to separate structure from the document, because the document's look can be changed without affecting its functionality. The <DIV> element has a class attribute that corresponds to the Box style sheet class. Following the <DIV> element are the two buttons that will cause the box to move left and right.

So, when this document is rendered, where are the buttons in relation to the box? The quick answer is that the button comes after the boxed region. However, this is not necessarily correct because of the way the <DIV> region and buttons are rendered. In the Box style sheet class rule, the declaration says that absolute coordinates are used (position: absolute), but the input buttons do not have any positioning mode associated with them, which means that relative positioning is used. Therefore, the correct answer is that the buttons are rendered before the box.

The Box class rule uses the declarations left, right, top, and height. However, in the scripting block, style.pixelLeft is used. This is important. In the Box class rule, the units are text-based and have a px appended to the end, which indicates that the units are pixels. When this property is referenced, the results are text. Therefore, to add values, you need to use the properties posLeft or pixelLeft—either one will be a numeric value. The same rule applies to top, posTop, pixelTop, right, posRight, pixelRight, height, posHeight, and pixelHeight.

Handling the Mouse
You've seen how to wire events to specific elements. With the DOM, the events can be wired to any element on the HTML page, but to make sure that the event is fired, the object must support the wired-in event. When an HTML object is

rendered, it occupies a specific region. Standard events can be raised on these specific regions, as defined by these groupings:

- **Mouse events**: These events all pertain to the mouse. They include events like clicking on or in a region. One set of powerful events indicates when the mouse has entered and left the region that the object occupies.
- **Keyboard events**: These are the standard keyboard events. They include events that trigger when a key is being pressed and is being released.
- **Cell events**: These events pertain to actions that occur to the cell as a result of some user interaction. They include cell activation, deactivation, and resizing. When a scrollbar is repositioned, a scroll event is fired.
- **Document events**: When the document, applet, control, or image is loaded or unloaded, specific events are being fired. These events are useful because they are global events that can be used to set global level variables. These events make it possible to build reliable DHTML scripts, because the state of applets and objects is predefined.

EVENT BUBBLING

Bubbling is the DHTML event model, and it has one major difference from other event models. Event bubbling causes events that are triggered to first call the event of the HTML element affected. Then, when the event handler has finished doing that processing, the HTML element that contains the triggering HTML element receives the event. The event is bubbled up until the top container object is reached. Let's look at a small example:

```
<HTML>
<HEAD>
<TITLE></TITLE>
<SCRIPT ID=clientEventHandlersJS LANGUAGE=javascript>
function baseCell_onclick() {
window.alert( "Clicked on the cell");
}

function bodyCell_onclick() {
window.alert( "Clicked on the body");
}
</SCRIPT>
</HEAD>
<BODY id=bodyCell LANGUAGE=javascript onclick="return bodyCell_onclick()">
<div id=baseCell LANGUAGE=javascript onclick="return
baseCell_onclick()">Here is a cell
</div>
</BODY>
</HTML>
```

There are two ID objects on this page: bodyCell and baseCell. The baseCell object is a <DIV> cell that has an associated onclick mouse handler. The bodyCell object is the <BODY> cell and it also has an associated onclick mouse handler. The region of the bodyCell is the entire client area that displays the HTML page.

If you click Here is a cell, there will be two messages. The first is Clicked on the cell and the second is Clicked on the body. The second message is an example of event bubbling from the <>DIV> to <BODY> HTML tag. If you click anywhere around there, there will be only one message—Clicked on the body—because the <DIV> HTML tag is not affected.

Why is event bubbling useful? With it you can create global handling routines. For example, you could create a routine that changes the font of the HTML element whenever anyone clicks on it. Instead of wiring each element to the global routine, it is only necessary to wire an onclick event to the <BODY> element.

Canceling an Event

It may be desirable to cancel an event so that the bubbling does not continue. To do this, the event object needs to be manipulated. Whenever an event is triggered, the browser instantiates the event object. This event object is a global object that contains the element that originally generated the event. From this object, it is also possible to cancel the event, as in this method:

```
function baseCell_onclick() {
window.alert( event.srcElement.tagName);
event.cancelBubble = true;
}
```

The event.cancelBubble = true property alteration will stop the bubbling process and not call any other event handlers after the current event handler ends.

The event bubbling process doesn't occur all the time. Some events do not event-bubble and only trigger on the specific element. An example of an event that does not bubble is onHelp. This is logical, because you would not want help on the parent objects of the element you click.

Which Element Is the Source of the Event Handler?

One problem of event bubbling is not knowing which element triggered the event. In the first example of event bubbling, the event Clicked on the body was called regardless of where you clicked. The difficulty is knowing which element called the event. The context of the event may be useful. Using the first event-bubbling source code as an example, change both window.alert methods to the following:

```
window.alert( event.srcElement.tagName);
```

Now when you click Here is the cell, which is the <DIV> element, two messages with the word DIV will appear. A click anywhere else on the page results in a message with the word BODY. This way it is possible to figure out the source of the event.

Using the tagName as identification may not be enough. There may be multiple HTML elements of the same type on the page. To be able to figure out the exact caller, it is necessary to use the srcElement property. From the original bubbling source code, change the bodyCell_onclick to the following:

```
function bodyCell_onclick() {
if( event.srcElement == baseCell)
    window.alert( "You clicked on the base cell");
else
    window.alert( "Clicked on the body");
}
```

It is possible to compare the property event.srcElement to the object baseCell directly. The property event.srcElement points to the object that triggered the event. One property of this object is the tagName, but there are more properties, such as innerHTML, innerText, and the methods insertAdjacentHTML and insertAdjacentText.

Writing Scripting Code

The usual way of integrating a script within the HTML page is to add the script directly. However, this means that structure is not separated from the document and makes reusability impossible. It is possible to link a scripting document to the HTML page using this syntax:

```
<script language="JavaScript"
src="/Webclient/workingclient/scripts.js"></script>
```

Again the script tag is used, but instead of writing the script directly into the page, the src attribute specifies where the script file is located.

DEFINING SCRIPTABLE OBJECTS

As in other programming languages, it is possible to define objects using JavaScript. However, unlike other languages, JavaScript objects need to be wired together. To show you what I mean by wiring JavaScript objects together, we look at a reusable JavaScript object that dynamically builds tables. The name of this object is TableBuilder, and it has the methods addTable, to add a table with the number of rows and columns, and setContents, to set the contents of the row and cell. The source code for the TableBuilder object is:

```
function TableBuilder() {
this.addTable = _TB_addTable;
this.setContents = _TB_setContents;

this.table = null;
this.rowCount = 0;
this.colCount = 0;
}
```

When declaring a JavaScript object, the first thing that is needed is a sort of super function. This function becomes the object constructor. In this case, it is the function TableBuilder. In this function, there are a series of this references. The this reference indicates that memory functions and variables are being built. The first two, this.addTable and this.setContents, are functions. They are being assigned _TB_addTable and _TB_setContents, which are also functions. The notation _TB_xxx is a naming convention to indicate a method used by the TableBuilder (TB) class. You can use any naming convention that you like, but be sure that there is a naming convention to keep things simple. The last three this items are variables that determine the state of the object.

The implementation of the _TB_addTable function is as follows:

```
function _TB_addTable( refObject, nameTable, rowCount, colCount) {
this.table = document.createElement( "table");

this.table.setAttribute( "id", nameTable, false);
this.table.setAttribute( "border", 1, false);

this.rowCount = rowCount;
this.colCount = colCount;
for( iRow = 0; iRow < rowCount; iRow ++) {
    this.table.insertRow( 0);
    for( iCol = 0; iCol < colCount; iCol++) {
        this.table.rows[ 0].insertCell( 0);
        this.table.rows[ 0].cells[ 0].innerHTML = "<B>Nothing</B>";
    }
}
refObject.appendChild( this.table);
}
```

In this function the parameters are:

- refObject: A DHTML object that will serve as an insertion point for the new table;
- nameTable: The ID-based name of the newly created table;
- rowCount and colCount: The number of rows and columns that the new table should contain.

The first step in this function is creating a new table object. In the DOM, it is not possible to create the Table object, because it does not exist. The way to create the table object is to instantiate it using the document.createElement method, where the parameter is a string to the HTML element. The return value of this method is the table. Because it is possible to navigate the table if the table object is referenced, the TableBuilder object has a reference to the table in this.table.

The table, when newly instantiated, is a raw table with no rows or cells. Using the method table.setAttribute, it is possible to set the ID attribute to the table name (nameTable). The other attribute, border, is set to show the table borders for illustration purposes. To make things easy, the row count and column count are assigned to the object state.

After that, it is necessary to create the individual rows and columns. The table object has a method called insertRow, which inserts a row at the point specified and returns the newly instantiated row. To keep referencing easy, this.rows[0].insertCell inserts an individual cell. The row and cell insertion operators are repeated until they reach the values of the variables rowCount and colCount. The last step in the function is to add the table to the insertion point using refObject.appendChild with the parameter being the table itself.

To instantiate and call the TableBuilder object, you could use the following HTML text:

```
<HTML><HEAD>
<script language="JavaScript"
src="/webclient/workingclient/tableBuilder.js"></script>
<SCRIPT ID=clientEventHandlersJS LANGUAGE=javascript>
function butAddTable_onclick() {
var tb = new TableBuilder();

tb.addTable( insertionPoint, "myTable", txtRowCount.value,
txtColCount.value);
}
</SCRIPT>
</HEAD>
<BODY>
<INPUT type="button" value="Add table" id=butAddTable LANGUAGE=javascript
onclick="return butAddTable_onclick()">
<BR>Row: <INPUT type="text" id=txtRowCount>
Columns: <INPUT type="text" id=txtColCount>
<DIV id=insertionPoint>
<table id=myTable></table>
</div>
</BODY>
</HTML>
```

At the top of the HTML, the script file is referenced using the `<SCRIPT>` tag. To keep things simple, add the references to the top of the page before any local scripting is done. This keeps the page clean and organized.

Then the script is wired to the `butAddTable_onclick` button event. In this event, the first step instantiates the `TableBuilder` object, and the second step calls the `TableBuilder.AddTable` method. The insertion point in this example is an empty `<DIV>` cell.

Putting It in Perspective

The Web has truly revolutionized the way we work with data. It has made some things simpler, and given us the capability to view information in ways we could not before. But with this new flexibility, the user interface has become more complex, because there are so many more options. This is not necessarily bad; we just need to determine when a feature is useful and when it is not.

In this chapter, the browser-based client was extended to include more functionality. However, the capability to classify becomes very important when using this type of client. For example, when viewing and reading data, the browsing client is useful. For working with data, the workhorse client is more useful. Of course, no solution is exclusively one thing. Most solutions are a combination of both situations, which is okay, so long as the data and code are kept granular. By keeping the data fairly granular, it becomes possible to define components that communicate using packets of hard data. And this, in turn, makes it possible to run through another iteration of the application's development cycle as business needs evolve and change.

The next step is to start generating some useful data. To do so, we'll connect ASP to a database using the ASP framework discussed in the previous chapter.

Chapter 7

Building a Web Application

Chapter 5 introduced the thin client and Chapter 6 introduced the rich client. Now, this chapter looks at the process of building a Web application. Understanding how to put the individual pieces of Chapter 5 and 6 together with some new techniques is very important in this chapter. Building Web applications is different from building traditional applications because with the Web there is a server side and a client side. The server side is not dependent on what the client browser is running—the server side can generate content for any type of HTTP-based browser.

Building Server-Side Logic

The simplest way to build a Web application is to assume that all critical work occurs on the server side. This means that the data kept on the server side is considered hard data. The client works with soft data. In the case of the thin client, keeping soft data on the client side is not possible. In that case, the state is built up in stages and stored temporarily in the ASP Session object.

To Use a Cookie or Not

Session variables are implemented using cookies, which are controversial. There are many end users who do not accept cookies and there are proxies that strip out cookies. The reason for using cookies is simple: When the original HTTP protocol was developed, it was considered stateless. While this may seem like a good thing for a transaction-processing system, it is not.

The real problem is that the statelessness is per request. For example, a request for a page is made, the page is served, and the connection is terminated. Therefore, unless the full transaction runs in one HTTP request, the process becomes very tedious—for every request, a context has to be created. To get around this limitation, ASP (Active Server Pages) uses cookies to identify the user and build a Session object. A cookie is a simple token used to identify the user. It is text based and does not execute any code. And because it is used to identify the current user and not the identity of the user there is no major invasion of privacy. If you do not like it, then flush the cookie buffer every day and nobody will be any wiser. Cookies are harmless!

Moving the Data

The next objective is to figure out how to move the data from the client to the server and from the server to the client. We have discussed several ways of doing this, for example, by using CGI (Common Gateway Interface) and XML (Extensible

Markup Language), which are the methods that we will continue to use. The advantage of using these methods is that both CGI and XML are open standards. This means that it would theoretically be possible to move the Web server from Windows 2000/NT to UNIX, or vice versa.

When moving the data, we assume that the data transfer will fail quite a bit. The programs will be written using a defensive programming style.

A Bit More about ASP

Chapter 5 explained the two built-in objects Application and Session. However, there are five other built-in ASP objects. These objects provide the mechanism that can be used to interact with ASP. For example, in a previous architecture diagram it was shown that there is a request stream and a response stream. Likewise, there are two built-in ASP objects called Request and Response. The formal definitions of these remaining five ASP objects are:

- **ASPError:** This is a new object introduced with Internet Information Server (IIS) 5.0. It makes it possible to retrieve an error that has been generated within the ASP execution context.
- **ObjectContext:** This object makes it possible to interact with the transaction context when the ASP page is executed.
- **Request:** This object represents the incoming stream and contains information about requests. It contains information about the incoming parameters, cookies, and client-side certificates.
- **Response:** This object represents the outgoing stream. It is possible to define Hypertext Transfer Protocol (HTTP) headers, create a buffer for delayed sending, and access other HTTP elements.
- **Server:** This is a simple utility object that is used to instantiate other Component Object Model (COM) objects. These COM objects can be used to enhance the functionality of ASP scripts.

USING COM OBJECTS

Within a Hypertext Markup Language (HTML) page or an ASP page, it is possible to consume, or use, COM components. COM components are binary units of execution that contain some logic and expose an interface to their functionality. The interface is what is consumed within the scripting environment.

A COM object is instantiated using either a PROG ID (program ID) or a CLSID (class ID). The difference between the two is that the first is human readable and the second is machine readable. An example of a PROG ID is:

```
COMSNAP.SnapinAboutImpl.1
```

There are typically three parts to the PROG ID. The first part represents the COM component in which the COM object is residing. The second part is the COM object reference, and the third part is the version number of the COM object. This style is a naming convention, however, and it may vary.

The PROG ID is resolved into a number that is called the CLSID, COM Co-Class. The computer uses the CLSID to reference a COM object. The CLSID has this form:

```
{52938292-1D8B-11d3-955F-0080C700807A}
```

This number need not be generated manually, but can be generated using the Microsoft Visual Studio tools.

Building the Web Application

Let's return to the original conference registration Web site project. The requirement that we are going to focus on is the presentation of a fancy Web site and of a simple Web site. Because of the requirements, the Web site needs to be split into a "cool and nifty" Web site and a functional Web site that can support the majority of end users. In the original domain-model text, there was a comment that if the user could not access either site via the Internet, the user could register by fax. This enabled us to enforce some rules and set some minimum browser requirements, because anyone who can't meet those requirements can still register by fax. For example, one rule was that the browser needed to accept cookies.

However, many other sites do not have these options. In that case, there is still the problem of figuring out how to build a Web site that is "cool and nifty" and functional at the same time. The way to do this is to figure out a way of sorting the various browsers by their capabilities. Using those capabilities, the server can then decide what kind of content to send.

Detecting Browser Capabilities

When a browser requests a Web page, the browser gives its identity to the server. This token is called the user-agent identifier, and it is present in the HTTP headers. To retrieve it on the server, write the following code:

```
Request.ServerVariables( "HTTP_USER_AGENT")
```

This returns the type of browser, for example:

```
Mozilla/4.0 (compatible; MSIE 4.01; Windows NT)
```

The text string starts off by defining what level of compatibility it supports. In this example, it states that it is compatible with Mozilla level 4.0 (Mozilla is the nickname given to the Netscape browser). But because the actual browser is Microsoft Internet Explorer (MSIE), an additional identification is necessary. In this case, the browser is MSIE 4.01 running on the Windows NT platform.

So, does this browser support scripting? Does it support frames? Looking at this descriptor you do not know. However, you can search for this information on the Internet and then create some scripting code for MSIE 4.01 or for other browsers. But what about MSIE 4.0, or MSIE 4.02, or MSIE 3.*x*, or MSIE running on a Windows CE device, or on Windows 95 or 98, or on a Macintosh? The number of possible browser and platform combinations for Internet Explorer is enormous, and writing an if statement to handle all of these cases would be very time-consuming. Fortunately, there is an easier method.

The original task was to determine which features the incoming browser supports or does not support. The browser type could be a key to a database of capabilities. The ASP framework has a COM object that retrieves the browser type and assesses its capabilities. This is called the *browser capabilities component*, and it does not expose what the browser is; instead, it exposes which feature set the browser supports. The browser does this by creating a series of variables that represents various browser functions. Consider the following ASP source code:

```
<%
var bc;
bc = Server.CreateObject("MSWC.BrowserType") %>
<table border=1>
<tr>
<td>Browser</td><td> <%=bc.browser%></td></tr>
<tr>
<td>Version</td><td><%=bc.version%></td></TR>
<tr>
<td>Frames</td><td><%=bc.Frames%></td></tr>
<tr>
<td>Tables</td><td><%=bc.Tables%></td></TR>
<tr>
<td>BackgroundSounds</td><td><%=bc.BackgroundSounds%></td></tr>
<tr>
<td>VBScript</td><td><%=bc.vbscript%></td></tr>
<tr>
<td>JScript</td><td><%=bc.javascript%></td></tr>
</tr></table>
```

What this code does is create an object that attempts to load a browser capability file. In the first section of ASP code, the object is instantiated with Server.CreateObject using the COM PROG ID MSWC.BrowserType.

When this object is instantiated, it attempts to load a file called browscap.ini. This file resides in the same directory as the browscap.dll, which is the browser capability component. In the initialization process, the object retrieves the browser type string and then attempts to cross-reference that string with a string in the browscap.ini file. The browscap.ini file is an .ini-type file that associates the browser-type string with a section in the file. An INI section is defined when a text is enclosed by a set of square brackets.

Let's search for the user agent as given in the beginning of this chapter.

```
[IE 4.0]
browser=IE
Version=4.0
majorver=4
minorver=0
frames=TRUE
tables=TRUE
cookies=TRUE
backgroundsounds=TRUE
vbscript=TRUE
javascript=TRUE
javaapplets=TRUE
ActiveXControls=TRUE
Win16=False
beta=False
AK=False
SK=False
AOL=False
crawler=False
cdf=True
[Mozilla/4.0 (compatible; MSIE 4.*)]
parent=IE 4.0
```

In this sample file, there are two INI sections, [IE 4.0] and [Mozilla/4.0 (compatible; MSIE 4.*)]. Neither one is an exact match for the original browser-type string. However, in the second section, the 4. is appended with an * character. This is a wild card character, and it means all version 4.*xx* browsers are included, which includes the browser type at the beginning of this section. Internet Explorer 4.0, 4.01, and 4.02 were basically identical in feature set. The difference between the various versions is some bug fixes.

When a section is matched, there are some associated INI values. In the case of the one we matched previously, there is a value of parent=IE 4.0. This is a reference to another section that contains all of the settings for the parent. And indeed, there is an IE 4.0 section heading, and under this heading is a series of values. Look at the values: Win16=False, cookies=TRUE. These values are exposed as COM properties on the created browser capabilities object. The value of these properties is false and true, respectively. This means that the browser is not Windows 16-bit and does accept cookies.

ADDING CUSTOM PROPERTIES

Installing ASP on an HTTP server also installs a basic feature set of capabilities for each browser. However, the browsercap.ini file is extensible, making the browser capabilities extensible, too. The extensibility is achieved by defining values under a section heading.

In the example of the conference registration application, we needed a flag to indicate whether a browser supports a minimum of rich features. Thus, the section value of supportsMinimumFeatures was added to the browsercap.ini file, as shown in the following example:

```
[Mozilla/4.0 (compatible; MSIE 4.*)]
supportsMinimumFeatures=true
```

The new section value can be set to any value. It does not need to be either true or false—it could hold a string or numeric value. To reference the supportsMinimumFeatures property in the ASP page, write the following code:

```
<%
var bc;
bc = Server.CreateObject("MSWC.BrowserType") %>
<p>My property</p><p><%=bc.supportsMinimumFeatures %></p>
```

The advantage of using a custom property is that retrieving it requires only one line of code. Other solutions require multiple lines of code, which could contain more errors and is more complex.

Returning the Correct Web Page

After the browser's capabilities are detected, it may be desirable to redirect the end user to the appropriate HTML page. In the conference registration application, users are required to have a security check for identity and level of access. If a user attempts to access a page without having undergone this security check, the user must be redirected to the correct page for the security check. There are several document redirection techniques.

AUTOMATIC CLIENT-SIDE REDIRECTION

The simplest redirection technique is called client-side redirection, which is an odd label, because the server initiates the redirection. When the client requests a document, the server sends back an HTTP command that indicates that the document has switched locations and that it should load that content. This was the technique used in the conference registration Web application. Consider the following source code:

```
<%@ Language=JavaScript %>
<%    if( Session("userId") == -1) {
    Response.Redirect( "../Logon/Default.asp");
}%>
<HTML>
```

In this example, the logon state is stored in the Session variable userId. If it is –1, that indicates that the user has not logged on. In that case,

the `Response.Redirect` method is called to send the user to the page
"../Logon/Default.asp", which is the security check HTML page.

Automatic Redirection within a Page

In the previously mentioned example, the redirection only works if no text was
sent to the ASP stream. Remember that text sent to the browser cannot be revoked, and text is anything that is not within the script code block. If it is necessary to do a redirection at the middle or end of a page, the ASP stream must be
buffered. When ASP is buffered, it is temporarily stored locally; then when indicated, the buffer can either be sent or deleted. The previous example could be
rewritten to use this technique, as follows:

```
<%@ Language=JavaScript %>
<%Response.Buffer = true%>
<HTML>
<HEAD>
</HEAD>
<BODY>
<%   if( Session( "userId") == -1) {
    Response.Redirect("../logon/default.asp");
    Response.Flush();
    Response.End();
}%>
</BODY>
</HTML>
<%Response.End()%>
```

Before any text is written to the stream, `Response.Buffer` must be set to `true`.
This prepares the buffer. If this is done later, an error will occur, because it is impossible to buffer content that has already been sent to the client. Once buffering
is enabled, `Response.Redirect` can be called anywhere within the HTML page. But
remember to add `Response.Flush` and `Response.End`—this avoids the "Object
Moved" message sent out by some proxies.

Sometimes it may be desirable to rebuild a buffered HTML page because the
content needs to change. To do this, use the method `Response.Clear`, which
clears the buffer and allows a restart.

If it is apparent that the amount of content to be sent to the client is large,
and the processing time required to send that content will take a long time, then
you can send the content in pieces. The method `Response.Flush` sends the ASP
stream content built up to that time. Once content has been sent, however, it is
no longer possible to use `Response.Redirect`.

The last step is to end the processing of the ASP page and send the content
that is in the buffer. The `Response.End` command does this. Be careful where you
place this method because calling it ends the processing of the current page.

AUTOMATIC REFRESH

Another way of automatically redirecting a Web page is to use the HTTP refresh command, as follows:

```
<head>
<meta http-equiv="Content-Type" content="text/html; charset=iso-8859-1">
<meta name="GENERATOR" content="Microsoft FrontPage (Visual InterDev
Edition) 2.0">
<META HTTP-EQUIV="REFRESH" CONTENT="5" URL="nextstep.asp">
<title>Document Title</title>
</head>
```

The <META> tag has an attribute HTTP-EQUIV, which specifies that this page will be refreshed after it is downloaded. In this case, the time is the CONTENT attribute and it is set to the value of five seconds. The URL (Uniform Resource Locator) attribute defines which page is loaded after the five seconds has expired.

The problem of using this method is where a user is not finished entering information in a form when the browser automatically redirects, which results in anything that the user typed up to that point being deleted. Also, with some browsers, reloading the page momentarily locks the browser up.

AUTOMATIC SERVER-SIDE REDIRECTION

With the introduction of Windows 2000, IIS-built objects are extended to include server-side redirection. Unlike client-side redirection, server-side redirection does not require a new client-side connection.

The Server.Transfer method makes the following possible:

- The Session and Application information is transferred between the multiple Web applications. This makes it possible to track a user through different Web applications.
- The redirection can occur in midstream of the script processing without needing to build a buffer.

The original conference registration example could be rewritten using the new method as follows:

```
<%@ Language=JavaScript %>
<HTML>
<HEAD>
</HEAD>
<BODY>
Logon process
<%    if( Session("userId") == -1) {
        Server.Transfer( "../logon/default.asp");
}%>
</BODY>
</HTML>
```

EMBEDDING AN ACTIVITY

The problem with redirection is that it is a permanent action. Without putting in some extra effort, it is not possible to return to the original calling page. Again, with the introduction of Windows 2000, the IIS Server object has a technique that enables a call to a separate Web page as if it were a function call. This way it is possible to build an HTML page in fragments, which is similar to using frames in a single page.

The method that permits this is called Server.Execute. An example is:

```
<%@ Language=JavaScript %>
<HTML>
<HEAD>
</HEAD>
<BODY>
Example site
<%         // Banner content
Server.Execute( "../banner/default.asp");%>

</BODY></HTML>
```

In this example, the Server.Execute method is used to add a banner to the current Web page. The Server.Execute method causes page processing to occur. Using the server side include directive to build a page in fragments does not involve any processing, and it can be faster. include is typically used when the content to be included is used as a reference in the Web page. Including works on both the client side and the server side.

WHEN TO USE WHICH REDIRECTION TECHNIQUE

The question is when to use which redirection technique. The answer is based on the limitations of each technique.

The Response.Redirect method is very powerful and easy to use, but many Web browsers and proxies do not interpret its message correctly. Instead of performing the client-side redirection automatically, a message appears. Another problem with using this technique is that the browser's Back button will not behave properly. The user is forced to click the button quickly and wait until the correct page appears.

The Server.Transfer and Server.Execute methods are the best techniques to use, if the redirection is on the same machine. These new methods could be used in the conference registration Web site. The problem with these methods is that they cannot call or transfer to another physical machine.

Language Support

On the Internet there is a multitude of languages and Web sites that have multiple languages. You may want to add text elements depending on the language displayed in the browser. As the popularity of the Web increases, the percentage of Web users who speak English will decrease. This means that the Web site must be localized so users can see pages in their own languages.

The traditional approach to multiple-language Web sites is to add national flags to indicate links to the various languages and then let the user choose. This is an okay solution, but it can be further enhanced.

An optimal solution is to have the server automatically choose the correct language depending on what the browser tells the server. The way to do this is as follows:

```
Request.ServerVariables("HTTP_ACCEPT_LANGUAGE");
```

The browser would return a setting such as en-us for American English or de for standard German. Both Microsoft's Internet Explorer and Netscape Navigator support this feature. The language setting is not dependent on which browser is installed, but on the settings for the computer. Therefore, if the Regional Settings, located in the Control Panel, are German, then the client sends de to the server whenever an HTTP request is made. The server can read the language setting and create the appropriate content or redirect the browser to a page that contains content in that language.

Building Web sites that support multiple languages, different browsers, or varying levels of technology is not easy. However, it is worth the effort because it gives the Web site that professional look and feel. Just remember that when you are developing a localized site, you'll need the assistance of someone who understands the language and the culture. Using a translation service to simply translate the English text will not help you avoid connotations, colors, or images that can have completely different implications in another culture.

Building the Body

As mentioned in Chapter 5, most of your development time is spent on the body of the Web application. All of the techniques learned thus far still apply. However, now the work is extended because you want to interact with the database, business objects, and data sent from the client.

When developing server-side content, you as a programmer are exposed to a new way of writing code, because ASP code is a mixture of HTML and scripting code. Most developers think it is a mess when they see it for the first time. After you become used to the notation, though, you will recognize that it is optimal for the Web application environment. This is because you do not want to embed HTML tags in the programming environment, as it makes reading the programming language more difficult. ASP is a kind of template approach.

I will explain the scripting code using both JavaScript and VBScript. Consider the following script:

```
<%@ Language=VBScript %>
<HTML><HEAD></HEAD>
<BODY>
<h2>Example Loop</h2>
```

```
<%
dim c1
for c1 = 0 to 10
Response.Write "<br> Count " & c1
%>
<br>Count <%=c1%>
<%next%>
</BODY></HTML>
```

In this code example, there is one loop (for...next) that counts from 0 to 10. Within the loop, there are two ways of dumping text to the stream. The first is to use Response.Write, which is a method call that sends a piece of data to the stream. In this example, the text is built dynamically. The second way of sending text to the stream does not use any methods explicitly. It uses the <%=c1%> notation to dump a specific variable. In this situation, it is not possible to add processing code within the dump block, because it would result in an error.

Either of these techniques will dump data to the stream, and there are many people who will say that one way is better than the other. However, they can both be right in different situations. When you are dumping text to the stream using the Response object, you need to ensure that none of the elements require any formatting. This is because it is very difficult to apply a style or formatting to those elements. If you do, you will need to code it by hand. This scenario is best suited to building scripting objects.

Using the second approach, the HTML and scripting code are more fragmented, but an editor can be used to modify the individual HTML tags. Where this method excels is in its capability to create special characters; displaying quotes using Response.Write, for example, is much more complicated than using the <%=c1%> notation. This second method makes HTML tag tuning much easier, but it is also better geared for direct editing of the ASP page.

When mixing HTML with scripting code, the formatting that I find works best is this:

```
<%@ Language=VBScript %>
<HTML><HEAD></HEAD>
<BODY>
<h2>Square of number</h2>
<table>
<tr>
    <td>Number</td><td>Square</td></tr>
<%
dim c1, c2

for c1 = 0 to 10
c2 = c1 * c1
%>
<tr>
```

```
        <td><%=c1%></td><td><%=c2%></td></tr>
<%next%>
</table>
</BODY></HTML>
```

The formatting is simple. The HTML tags and code both are indented using tabs. But the tabbing sequences in the code section and HTML tag sections are kept separate. The variable dump notations follow the tab notations of the HTML tag section, making the ASP page look like one continuous page.

The Visual InterDev Scripting Library

Chapter 6 introduced JavaScript objects. The Microsoft Visual InterDev product has a new library called the Scripting Object library. The Scripting Object library works with design-time controls to make it easier to develop Web applications using object-oriented techniques.

On the client side, there is an event model. The Scripting Object library also creates an event model on the server side and hides the complexities of the client and the server. This makes it easy to develop Web applications for basic browsers and for browsers that support the full DOM (Document Object Model). Using the Scripting Object library, it is possible to use data-binding techniques to navigate through the data. The scripting object library is written using JavaScript, but the ASP page-scripting code can be VBScript.

DESIGN-TIME CONTROLS

Design-time controls (DTC) have been around since Visual InterDev 1.0. A DTC is different from a regular COM control in that it only works at design time. The easiest way to understand these controls is to think of reusable wizards that generate code. The DTC has a series of parameters, set by the programmer, that generates the code. The code is generated when the HTML page is saved.

The DTC is the element in the center of Figure 7–1. The parameters are Connection (a data connection), Database object (a table, view, or stored procedure), and Object name, which depends on the Database object (Sports table). When the Web page is saved, it generates the following code.

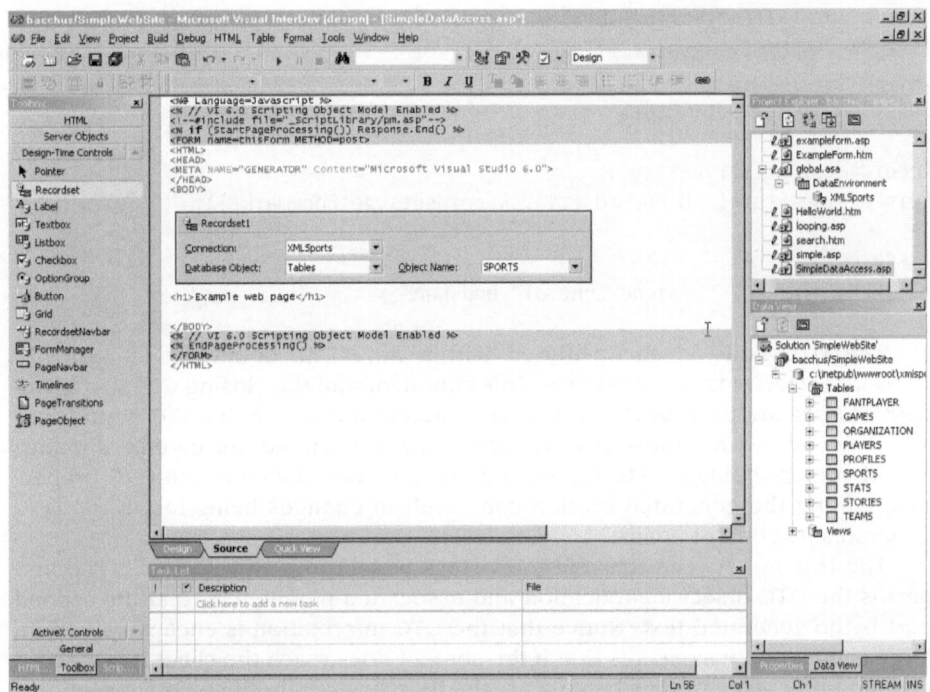

Figure 7–1: DTC diagram

```
<!—METADATA TYPE="DesignerControl" startspan
<OBJECT classid="clsid:9CF5D7C2-EC10-11D0-9862-0000F8027CA0" id=Recordset1
style="LEFT: 0px; TOP: 0px" VIEWASTEXT>
<PARAM NAME="ExtentX" VALUE="12197">
<PARAM NAME="ExtentY" VALUE="2090">
<PARAM NAME="State"
VALUE="(TCConn=\qXMLSports\q,TCDBObject=\qTables\q,TCDBObjectName=\qSPORTS\
q,TCControlID_Unmatched=\qRecordset1\q,TCPPConn=\qXMLSports\q,RCDBObject=\q
RCDBObject\q,TCPPDBObject=\qTables\q,TCPPDBObjectName=\qSPORTS\q,TCCursor
Type=\q3\s-\sStatic\q,TCCursorLocation=\q3\s-\sUse\sclient-side\scursors
\q,TCLockType=\q3\s-
\sOptimistic\q,TCCacheSize_Unmatched=\q10\q,TCCommTimeout_Unmatched=\q10
\q,CCPrepared=0,CCAllRecords=1,TCNRecords_Unmatched=\q10\q,TCODBCSyntax_Unmat
ched=\q\q,TCHTargetPlatform=\q\q,TCHTargetBrowser_Unmatched=\qServer\s(ASP)
\q,TCTargetPlatform=\qInherit\sfrom\spage\q,RCCache=\qRCBookPage\q,CCOpen=1,
GCParameters=(Rows=0))"></OBJECT>
—>
```

```
<—#INCLUDE FILE="_ScriptLibrary/Recordset.ASP"—>
<SCRIPT LANGUAGE="Javascript" RUNAT="server">
...
function _Recordset1_dtor()
{
Recordset1._preserveState();
thisPage.setState('pb_Recordset1', Recordset1.getBookmark());
}
</SCRIPT>
<!—METADATA TYPE="DesignerControl" endspan—>
```

The DTC code is encapsulated within an HTML comment `<!-METADATA TYPE="DesignerControl" startspan`. This comment and the closing `<METADATA>` tag with `endspan` are used by the DTC host to determine where the DTC boundaries are. Any code within these two boundary markers should not be edited manually. If you are going to edit the code manually, then only edit the DTC properties. Editing the generated section can result in changes being lost if the DTC generates its content again.

The text in between the `<METADATA>` tags is split into two sections. The first part is the DTC object identification and associated parameters, and the second part is the generated text. Notice that the DTC information is encapsulated in a large comment. This ensures that if the content does reach the client it is ignored and not processed. To save bandwidth, the IIS strips out these comment sections. The object identification section is defined using the `OBJECT` and `PARAM` tags. Here the generated text has been cut short because it is only shown as an example.

USING THE LIBRARY

Remember that ASP works from the top of the page to the bottom. With the Scripting Object library, there are page-enter and page-exit events. The page-enter event is called to indicate that page processing is about to start, and any necessary page-level initialization should be performed. The page-exit event is called to indicate that page processing is complete. This event makes it possible to write cleanup or persistence code.

The following example shows the implementation of the page-enter and page-exit events:

```
<%@ Language=JavaScript %>
<% // VI 6.0 Scripting Object Model Enabled %>
<!—#include file="../_ScriptLibrary/pm.asp"—>
<% if (StartPageProcessing()) Response.End() %>
<FORM name=thisForm METHOD=post>
<HTML>
<HEAD>
</HEAD>
<BODY>
<script runat=server language=javascript>
```

```
function thisPage_onenter() {
// Do something
Response.Write("<h1>Starting the page</h1>");
}
function thisPage_onexit() {
Response.Write("<h1>Ending the page</h1>");
}
</script>
<b>Some page content</b>
</BODY>
<% // VI 6.0 Scripting Object Model Enabled %>
<% EndPageProcessing() %>
</FORM>
</HTML>
```

The first step is to declare the programming language used. In this case, it is JavaScript. The following lines are crucial because they are responsible for initializing the Scripting Object library. If they were added using the Visual InterDev environment, these lines are grayed out and cannot be edited.

If you really want to edit the grayed out lines, simply add some content on the second line of the ASP page, as shown in this example:

```
<%@Language=JavaScript%>
<HTML>
<%//VI 6.0 Scripting Object Model Enabled%>
```

Save the page and then load it again. The grayed out zone disappeared. The downside is that you will not be able to use DTCs that require the Scripting Object library, because Visual InterDev thinks that the Scripting Object library is not enabled. Although this is not the case, all of the code must be typed in manually.

The <!— include statement includes the core Scripting Object library. The next line contains the function StartPageProcessing, which initializes the object library and creates a thisPage object. Right after that is a line that contains the <FORM> tag, which is explained later.

The thisPage Object

The Scripting Object library creates an event-driven architecture using the thisPage object. The thisPage object is an instantiation of the JavaScript _SOMObject. This object has multiple capabilities and it manages the events and the persistence of the server-side HTML page. The events onenter and onexit have no implementations, but they can be implemented on the ASP page by using the following naming convention:

```
[nameOfObject]_[eventName]
```

In the onenter case, this results in the thisPage_onenter and thisPage_onexit functions. When the StartPageProcessing function is executing, thisPage_onenter and thisPage_onexit are bound to the dispatch table and called. The dispatch table is part of the event mechanism in the thisPage object.

In the preceding example, the thisPage_onenter function writes some text to the stream using Response.Write as does thisPage_onexit. If the page were viewed, the generated source would look like the page shown in Figure 7–2.

Figure 7–2: Simple scripting output

The diagram appears to show the correct output. Each piece of text is where it is supposed to be. But consider the following HTML source that was generated by the thisPage_onenter function.

```
<h1>Starting the page</h1><SCRIPT LANGUAGE=JavaScript
SRC="/SimpleWebSite/_ScriptLibrary/pm.js"></SCRIPT>
<SCRIPT LANGUAGE=JavaScript>thisPage._location =
"/SimpleWebSite/scriptinglib/simple.asp";</SCRIPT>
<FORM name=thisForm METHOD=post>
<HTML>
<HEAD>
<META NAME="GENERATOR" Content="Microsoft Visual Studio 6.0">
</HEAD>
<BODY>
```

```
<b>Some page content</b>
</BODY>
<h1>Ending the page</h1>
<INPUT type=hidden name="_method">
<INPUT type=hidden name="_thisPage_state" value="">
</FORM>
</HTML>
```

This HTML source violates all HTML rules. Normally an HTML page is supposed to start with the <HTML> tag, but this starts with the <h1> tag. Why? Because this onenter event is called before any text has been written to the stream. The purpose of this event is to initialize data and objects on the page.

Another error on this page is that the <FORM> tag that precedes the <HTML> tag. Visual InterDev generates the HTML code in that way when the Scripting Object library is enabled on the ASP page. To move it to the correct place, disable the grayed out zone as explained earlier, and then move the <FORM> tag. To enable the grayed out zone again, remove the <HTML> element that disabled it.

Persistence of the Data

In the preceding HTML sources, there are FORM tags and a couple of INPUT tags that have the attribute type set to hidden. The Scripting Object library generates these fields. Although cookies aren't the problem that some people think they are, there are people who do not like to use cookies or who cannot use cookies. Hidden form variables enable you to create state like a Session variable, except that it travels from the server to the client and back again. All of this is accomplished without using cookies.

The way to create the hidden form variables is to use the _SOMObject. The _SOMObject saves or loads variables that are associated with the thisPage object. Consider the following code fragment:

```
thisPage.setState( "myObject", "somevalue");
```

When the EndPageProcessing function is called, it generates the following HTML text fragment:

```
<INPUT type=hidden name="_thisPage_state" value="myObject=somevalue">
```

When the form on the page is submitted to another ASP page, the StartPageProcessing method recreates the state. The following code retrieves the values:

```
thisPage.getState( "myObject");
```

JavaScript Objects

When creating JavaScript objects, the StartPageProcessing function calls all JavaScript object constructors and the EndPageProcessing function calls all JavaScript object destructors. A question that arises is this: Are there JavaScript constructors and destructors? There are JavaScript constructors when the new statement is called, but there is no instance-specific constructor that can be called generically. Similarly, there is no instance-specific destructor. The generic constructor and destructor are mimicked in the Scripting Object library by using a naming convention.

For the constructors, use the following:

```
[objectName]_ctor
```

For the destructors the naming convention should be as follows:

```
[objectName]_dtor
```

When the StartPageProcessing and EndPageProcessing functions execute, they search for functions that end with _ctor or _dtor, respectively, and if those functions exist, they call them.

ACCESSING THE DATABASE

There is enhanced database support within the Scripting Object library. It uses ADO (Active Data Objects) but extends them to include capabilities such as record-by-record navigation. We look now at how to access the database using the Scripting Object library.

Establishing the Data Environment

In the Scripting Object Library, there is an object called the Recordset object. Do not confuse this with the ADO Recordset. Even though both perform the same functions, this discussion is about the Scripting Object library Recordset object.

To use the Recordset object, you need to have an appropriate object and database definition in the global.asa file; for example:

```
    Application("XMLSports_ConnectionString") =
"DSN=xmlsports;DBQ=c:\inetpub\wwwroot\xmlsports\database\xml_sports.mdb;Dri-
verId=281;FIL=MS Access;MaxBufferSize=2048;PageTimeout=5;"
    Application("XMLSports_ConnectionTimeout") = 15
    Application("XMLSports_CommandTimeout") = 30
    Application("XMLSports_CursorLocation") = 3
    Application("XMLSports_RuntimeUserName") = ""
    Application("XMLSports_RuntimePassword") = ""
'— Project Data Environment
    Set DE = Server.CreateObject("DERuntime.DERuntime")
    Application("DE") = DE.Load(Server.MapPath("Global.ASA"),
"_private/DataEnvironment/DataEnvironment.asa")
```

The first set of Application definitions defines an OLE DB (Object Linking and Embedding Database) database connection. The DE object, though, is more complex. In Visual InterDev, you can build Data Connections and Data Commands by using the context-sensitive menus associated with the global.asa file. These operations create the Data Environment, which is saved to a file. In the preceding example, it is stored in the DataEnvironment.asa file. When the Web application is executed, the DERuntime.DERuntime COM object reads the Data Environment and, on demand, establishes the Data Commands and Data Connections.

When the data commands are read from the Data Environment file, they are associated with the global.asa file. This creates a centralized location for referencing the various Data Commands. When they are centralized, it is possible to reuse the same Data Commands in various HTML pages. This is part of component building.

Creating a Recordset

Typically, you want to display some data in an ASP page. To do this, you need to create the Recordset objects, and from those objects, the individual fields can be displayed. If there are multiple records, the Recordset will need to be navigated.

Creating the Recordset object or other objects in the Scripting Object library is not like creating a COM object. In the Scripting Object library, the constructor must be called first. For example, to create Recordset1, which is an instance of Recordset, the following constructor must be written:

```
function _Recordset1_ctor() {
CreateRecordset('Recordset1', _initRecordset1, null);
}
```

The _Recordset1_ctor name is based on a naming convention. The function could just as easily contain the construction of several objects. The function call to CreateRecordset instantiates the Recordset object. The first parameter is the name that is associated with the Recordset object, and the second parameter specifies the initialization function for the Recordset1 object. The last parameter is not currently used.

The initialization routine is responsible for associating the Data Command with the Recordset. The following is an example of the initialization routine:

```
function _initRecordset1() {
thisPage.createDE();
var rsTmp = DE.Recordsets('tabGames');
Recordset1.setRecordSource(rsTmp);
Recordset1.open();
if (thisPage.getState('pb_Recordset1') != null)
    Recordset1.setBookmark(thisPage.getState('pb_Recordset1'));
}
```

The initializer creates an instance of the DE Data Environment. The DE.Recordsets method call retrieves the Data Command tabGames. The returned object is an ADO recordset object that is then associated with the JavaScript Recordset object. If the user is navigating through the data set, the Recordset retrieves the current recordset location. This current Recordset location variable is stored as a hidden form element using the thisPage.getState mechanism. A variable without a null value indicates a bookmark, which is used to set the cursor.

The destructor saves the current cursor location to a hidden form variable. An example destructor is as follows:

```
function _Recordset1_dtor(){
Recordset1._preserveState();
thisPage.setState('pb_Recordset1', Recordset1.getBookmark());
}
```

Displaying Field Information

There are two ways to display fields from the database. The classic approach is to retrieve the field from the Recordset object, as follows:

```
Recordset1.fields.getValue("GAMEID")';
```

The Scripting Object library offers an additional way of encapsulating the various HTML elements as objects—the encapsulated objects can be bound to a Recordset. When the HTML element is generated, it can bind to a lowest common denominator HTML element or to a DHTML element. Like the Recordset object, the HTML elements have constructors and initializers. For display elements, there is no need to store data, so a destructor is not necessary.

The constructor format is similar to the Recordset format. For an HTML textbox, the initializer is as follows:

```
function _initTextbox1() {
Textbox1.setStyle(TXT_TEXTBOX);
Textbox1.setDataSource(Recordset1);
Textbox1.setDataField('GAMEID');
Textbox1.setMaxLength(20);
Textbox1.setColumnCount(20);
}
```

In HTML, it is possible to define a textbox as an area, password, or normal text field. In this example, the normal TXT_TEXTBOX is used. Then the data source and field are defined. The data source must be a Recordset object that has been instantiated on the page. In our example, it is Recordset1. The field that is of interest is GAMEID. Finally, a textbox length (setMaxLength) and column count (setColumnCount) are defined.

To display the textbox, the following method call is made:

```
<% Textbox1.display(); %>
```

Navigating Through the Data

To navigate the data, the `RecordsetNavbar` object is used. It creates a series of buttons that defines a navigation scheme. It is possible to create various combinations of navigation buttons, such as next only, next and previous, and so on. The buttons created are JavaScript `Button` objects; to navigate a data set, the navigation bar must be associated with a `Recordset` object. The style is defined in the `RecordsetNavbar` initializer. An example definition is as follows:

```
function _initRecordsetNavbar1() {
RecordsetNavbar1.setAlignment(RSNB_ALIGN_HORIZONTAL);
RecordsetNavbar1.setButtonStyles(RSNB_MASK_FIRSTCAPTION |
    RSNB_MASK_PREVCAPTION | RSNB_MASK_NEXTCAPTION
    RSNB_MASK_LASTCAPTION);

RecordsetNavbar1.updateOnMove = false;
RecordsetNavbar1.setDataSource(Recordset1);
RecordsetNavbar1.getButton(0).value = ' |< ';
RecordsetNavbar1.getButton(1).value = ' < ';
RecordsetNavbar1.getButton(2).value = ' > ';
RecordsetNavbar1.getButton(3).value = ' >| ';
}
```

The `setAlignment` method call defines whether the buttons are aligned horizontally (`RSNB_ALIGN_HORIZONTAL`) or vertically (`RSNB_ALIGN_VERTICAL`). The `setButtonStyles` method call defines which buttons are created and the style they use, which can either be an image or text. In this case, all of the buttons are caption based and are assembled using an `or` operation. The numeric values of the button styles are:

```
RSNB_MASK_FIRSTIMAGE = 1;
RSNB_MASK_FIRSTCAPTION = 2;
RSNB_MASK_PREVIMAGE = 4;
RSNB_MASK_PREVCAPTION = 8;
RSNB_MASK_NEXTIMAGE = 16;
RSNB_MASK_NEXTCAPTION = 32;
RSNB_MASK_LASTIMAGE = 64;
RSNB_MASK_LASTCAPTION = 128;
```

The Scripting Object Library Is Poorly Documented

At the time of this writing, the Scripting Object library was poorly documented. Many developers did not even know it existed. The question then is this: How does one learn to use the library without documentation? There are several tips that will help you code using the Scripting Object library.

- Look at the source code. The entire Scripting Object library source code is available, because it is written in JavaScript, though there are some situations where external objects are used, such as the DE database object. This does assume that you have a good working knowledge of JavaScript. The Scripting Object library is installed under the _ScriptLibrary folder of a Visual InterDev project.
- The library is very organized and easy to understand. The writers of the library did a good job.
- Each of the files in the library represents an individual object.
- The constructor or _Prototype function of the object contains the various events that are generated, methods that the object supports, and constants that are used in the various method calls.

Putting It All Together

Now it is time to build a piece of an application using the concepts learned in this and the previous two chapters.

Where to Start?

All Web applications should have these traits:

- The document is separated into various different pieces, such as the look and the functionality.
- The subsystem should be object oriented for reusability, using JavaScript objects.
- The application should support the lowest common browser and DOM-capable browsers.
- Scripting Objects should be used for common elements, such as buttons and text boxes.
- The application should be a self-contained unit that can be used in any situation.

Taking those goals into account, let's consider the domain-model text.

Conference Registration Web Site Security
The security subsystem needs logon and logoff capability. The security subsystem is needed because some pieces of information are sensitive and should not be made available to everyone. Examples include credit-card details and user addresses. This means that the subsystem needs to be applied to specific pages. It cannot be circumvented. Every page that is sensitive must have a security check. The information that is passed between the client and server should be time-limited and session-limited. This would stop the user from bookmarking the page and potentially have a colleague or other user access the Web site using their security descriptors. Not all users should see all information. Information display depends on their "need to know" status. The logon will occur using a standard form that is submitted and then validated.

What use cases and collaboration scenarios are available? The answer is simple. Consider a simple page for entering the user details. The entire input process may be spread over multiple HTML pages, and each HTML page will need a security descriptor. The collaboration scenario may be as follows:

1. Request address document.
2. Is user secure?
3. If not, retrieve logon page and return to user.
4. Make note of current process status.
5. When logon page is submitted, verify security status.
6. If unsuccessful, return to step 3.

Designing and Implementing the Pieces

To understand the process, let's consider a sensitive HTML page, such as the following:

```
<%@ Language=JavaScript %>
<HTML><HEAD></HEAD>
<BODY>
<% // VI 6.0 Scripting Object Model Enabled %>
<!—#include file="../_ScriptLibrary/pm.asp"—>
<% if (StartPageProcessing()) Response.End() %>
<FORM name=thisForm METHOD=post>
<!— Log on the user functionality here—>
<H1>Sensitive Content</h1>
If you can see this then you have been logged on
<% // VI 6.0 Scripting Object Model Enabled %>
<% EndPageProcessing() %>
</FORM>
</BODY></HTML>
```

The Scripting Object library framework was applied to this page. As well, there is a comment that states where the logon functionality should be inserted. It should be added before any sensitive content can be viewed.

As a user of languages such as C++ and Visual Basic, my first inclination was to write the following source:

```
<%if( user.isLoggedOn() == false) {
Response.Redirect("../logon.asp");
} else {%>
<H1>Sensitive Content</h1>
If you can see this then you have been logged on
<%}%>
```

There is a user object that checks whether the current user is logged on (isLoggedOn). If it returns false, then the current page is redirected to the logon page. Otherwise the sensitive content could be displayed.

This approach has many problems:

- Why is user an object? In ASP, each user has its own work area. It is not necessary to explicitly create a user object. Instead, creating a security object is more appropriate. The security is applied to the user.
- If the user is not logged on, then the page is redirected. This starts the logon process, but how will you return to the original page being requested? This method requires a logged-on user to perform an extra click. The Web application should "remember" where it was.
- The code written here is not reusable and requires quite a bit of typing. It would be simpler if the solution was a "one-liner." This would make for fewer maintenance issues.

The solution lies in thinking about how HTML and scripting objects work. When building a user interface, it is possible to build a JavaScript object that contains all of the user-interface code required. But this brings us back to the original problem of nondynamic user interfaces. The solution should separate the form's user interface from the functionality.

OUTLINING THE SOLUTION

In the solution, the Scripting Object library's state-management functions and ASP include statements are used to perform a security check. It is not necessary to redirect to another HTML page, which then requires the additional step of remembering which was the calling page.

Each and every sensitive page is built using two elements. The first element is the security element, and the second element is the content itself. When an ASP page is processed, it processes the security element first. If security indicates that it is necessary to perform a logon routine, those HTML elements are inserted in the page. The second element is aware of the results of the first element and reacts to them. If a logon routine was added, then the content is not generated.

This content is returned to the end user as a form. The end user fills out the form and submits it to the server. The URL is still the same, and the process of performing the security check is started again. However, the security check has a memory and realizes that it needs to process the information that was entered in the logon form.

If the processing of the form data is successful, the content element is aware of that and it inserts its HTML elements in the page. If the processing is unsuccessful, the security element generates the logon routine again for another logon attempt.

USER INTERFACE

Let's now consider how to implement a sensitive page. We'll create a piece of global information that can be reused. The global information could also be extended to include other information that would make it simple to realize workflow applications or to determine when data is stale. Consider this implementation:

```
<%@ Language=JavaScript %>
<HTML><HEAD></HEAD>
<BODY>
<% // VI 6.0 Scripting Object Model Enabled %>
<!—#include file="../_ScriptLibrary/pm.asp"—>
<% if (StartPageProcessing()) Response.End() %>
<FORM name=thisForm METHOD=post>
<%generateDocument = true;%>
<!— #include file="../logon/logon.asp"—>
<%if( generateDocument == true) {%>
<H1>Hello world</h1>
If you can see this then you have been logged on
<%}%>
<% // VI 6.0 Scripting Object Model Enabled %>
<% EndPageProcessing() %>
</FORM>
</BODY></HTML>
```

The document is a simple Hello World HTML page. However, it contains information considered sensitive and therefore needs some logon capabilities. The generateDocument variable is a global variable, and it can be changed by any subsystem to indicate whether or not the content should be shown. The logon functionality is contained within the logon.asp file. It is included using the <!–#include …> statement. This separates the functionality of the security subsystem from that of the sensitive page.

Normally the #include statement is used to include script, but in this case, it is used to include HTML tags and script. To make it possible to include content dynamically, the Scripting Object library constructor and destructor notation is used. It sets the state of the security subsystem, which, in turn, generates the content.

Consider this implementation:

```
<!—#INCLUDE FILE="../_ScriptLibrary/TextBox.ASP"—>
<!—#INCLUDE FILE="../logon/securitymgr.asp"—>
<script language="javascript" runat="server">
function _page_ctor() {
scrMgr.logon();
}
```

```
</script>
<SCRIPT LANGUAGE=JavaScript RUNAT= Server>
function _inittxtUsername() {
txtUsername.setStyle( TXT_TEXTBOX);
txtUsername.setMaxLength(20);
txtUsername.setColumnCount(20);
}
function _inittxtPassword() {
txtPassword.setStyle( TXT_PASSWORD);
txtPassword.setMaxLength(20);
txtPassword.setColumnCount(20);
}
function _creators_ctor() {
CreateTextbox( 'txtUsername', _inittxtUsername, null);
CreateTextbox( 'txtPassword', _inittxtPassword, null);
}
function thisPage_onshow() {
scrMgr.username = txtUsername.value;
scrMgr.password = txtPassword.value;
}
</script>
<%
if( scrMgr.isLoggedOn() == false) {
%>
<SCRIPT LANGUAGE=JavaScript>
function butSubmit_onclick( form) {
form.submit();
}
</script>
<table>
<tr>
    <td>Username</td><td><%txtUsername.display();%></td>
</tr>
    <td>Password</td><td><%txtPassword.display();%></td>
</tr>
<tr>
    <td><input type="button" value="Submit"
        name="cmdSubmit" onClick="butSubmit_onclick( this.form);">
    </td>
</tr>
</table>
<%
scrMgr.operationStep = STP_LOGGING_ON;
generateDocument = false;
}
%>
```

Let's dissect this code piece by piece. When this page is inserted into the previous ASP page, it either generates or does not generate the logon HTML elements. The page-constructor function page_ctor is called. Currently, it is empty, but it can be used to define any page-level state.

There is another constructor, _creators_ctor, on the page. This constructor is used to create two textboxes: txtUsername and txtPassword. Why create a Scripting Object Textbox when it might be simpler to use the <INPUT> tag? The answer is that yes, there is less typing in using an <INPUT> tag, but the form needs to be processed. By using a Scripting Object Textbox, the generation of the text, processing of the form, and retrieval of the value is one process. In a traditional form, this is not the case. The txtPassword textbox calls setStyle to define a password field. The txtUsername textbox calls setStyle to define a normal textbox. Both textboxes set their length and column count.

The Scripting Object library not only defines server-side Buttons and Textboxes. It is also possible to use client-side Buttons and Textboxes. A client-side Scripting Object Button was not used because it added more complexity than was needed. The button is a simple <INPUT type="button" …> tag with an associated event handler that submits the <FORM>.

In this page, a form.submit method is called, even though the page does not contain a <FORM> tag. The form is part of the Scripting Object library. The original sensitive page that included logon.asp has a line with the following <FORM> tag.

```
<FORM name=thisForm METHOD=post>
```

When the form is submitted, it references the above-mentioned form. It is not advisable to use your own forms because they will not submit the hidden text fields that are used by the Scripting Object library. This means that the state acquired in the Textbox, txtUsername, and txtPassword may not be carried forward. But the <FORM> attribute name references thisForm. What is thisForm? It is part of the client-side Scripting Object library, and it defines the current URL as thisForm. Therefore, when form.submit is called, it calls the current URL. This solves our problem of remembering which was the last page.

After the constructors are called, the event thisPage_onshow is called. It is an event that is generated to indicate that the page is about to be shown and that any values that need changing should be changed now. In this case, the scrMgr.username and scrMgr.password values are assigned. This assignment is not important when a logon is being generated. It becomes important when the logon form is being processed.

Finally, the method scrMgr.logon is called. But where did scrMgr come from? The answer is in the next section. For now, let's just say it is available. The scrMgr object manages the security attributes of the current end user. After that, scrMgr.isLoggedOn is called to see if the logon process was successful. If so, then the logon routine is generated and the flag generateDocument is set to false. This ensures that the included logon content is not generated.

IMPLEMENTING THE LOGIC

The logic is implemented in the included file `../logon/securitymgr.asp`. The securityManager is a global local object. Even though it sounds like a misnomer, it does exist. When the `securitymgr.asp` file is included, it contains a constructor and destructor. These functions create the scrMgr object. This object is global in the sense of the application, but local because only the current user sees it. This object is instantiated whenever a sensitive page is accessed. It is defined as follows:

```
<SCRIPT RUNAT=SERVER LANGUAGE="JavaScript">
function SecurityMgr() {
if (typeof(_SecurityMgr_Prototype_called) == 'undefined')
    _SecurityMgr_Prototype();
this.username = null;
this.password = null;
this.securityLevel = "";
this.operationStep = STP_NOTHING;
}
function _SecurityMgr_Prototype() {
SecurityMgr.prototype.logon = _SM_logon;
SecurityMgr.prototype.logoff = _SM_logoff;
SecurityMgr.prototype.isLoggedOn = _SM_isLoggedOn;
_SecurityMgr_Prototype_called = true;

STP_NOTHING = 0;
STP_LOGGING_ON = 1;
STP_LOGGED = 2;
}
function _SM_logon() {
// Do something to log on the user
if( this.operationStep == STP_LOGGING_ON) {
    this.operationStep = STP_LOGGED;
}
}
function _SM_logoff() {
// Do something to log off the user
}
function _SM_isLoggedOn() {
if( this.operationStep == STP_LOGGED) {
    return true;
} else {
    return false;
}
}
function _SM_ctor() {
```

```
if (typeof( scrMgr ) != 'object')
    scrMgr = new SecurityMgr;

scrMgr.operationStep = thisPage.getState( "operationStep");
}
function _SM_dtor() {
thisPage.setState( "operationStep", scrMgr.operationStep);
}
</script>
```

The function _SM_ctor allocates a new SecurityMgr. The scrMgr.operationStep is assigned the global state, which is an indicator of the security process step it is at. At the beginning, operationStep is STP_NOTHING. Then when the first sensitive page is called, and while the logon form is processed, operationStep is STP_LOGGING_ON. Finally, a successful logon indicates that the operationStep is STP_LOGGED_ON.

Notice that the state of operationStep is managed using thisPage.setState and thisPage.getState. These functions rely on there being only one <FORM> tag on the HTML page. The state could have been managed in the Session variable, but then the demo would not demonstrate an alternative state management. A Session variable does not send the data to the client, but it does require cookies. The catch with using thisPage is that it sends the data to the client, but it does work without cookies.

The last piece of interesting information is that there is a _SecurityMgr_ Prototype function, which is called in the constructor of SecurityManager. When building a method table in an object, it is possible to inherit default functionality. The way to do this is to use the Prototype keyword as shown by the _SecurityMgr_Prototype function.

Putting It in Perspective

This is the last chapter about HTML development, so I'll mention a few tips based on my experience building production Web sites:

- The number and variety of browsers are immense. There are simple browsers and there are fancy current-version browsers, and usually the problematic and vocal users are those who do not have a current-version browser. The Web site must support all of them.
  Solution: Use the Visual InterDev Scripting Object library to make it easier to write components that can work on any browser.
- People do not read what they type. In a past Web site, the number of users who entered the wrong e-mail address created a bounce rate of about 20 percent. Most often the error was very easy to trace to an incorrect hyphen or extra period.
  Solution: Chapter 5 showed how to write a form-checking routine. Always use one for validation. If necessary, add a dialog box that asks whether everything is okay, because incorrect input may waste many CPU cycles.

- When the Web site is too slow, people like to click the button again to make sure that they clicked the button previously.
Solution: There is none, other than teaching the end user about HTML.
- Proxies are nightmares, and they can cause many problems. A proxy also hides the internal user, making IP referencing useless.
Solution: Use form-based variables that pass state between the browser and server.
- Scripting, Java, and COM/ActiveX controls are often filtered out, making your page useless and dysfunctional.
Solution: Use as much server-side ASP code as possible.
- When people find something that they are interested in, they like to print out the details for reference.
Solution: Provide the option of a printing-oriented HTML page, or exploit browser-specific functionality.

Developing Web applications is not a simple task, especially if you have never done it before. It is a different world, and many people don't realize that. HTML offers many advantages that traditional user interfaces and traditional applications cannot offer. So when you develop your application, start small and learn from your projects.

Chapter 8
Designing COM Interfaces

This chapter begins our look at component development. As was mentioned in previous chapters, development should occur using interfaces and implementations; this chapter discusses what a Component Object Model (COM) interface is and what the ramifications of using one are. We begin with a discussion of COM and its interface concept, and delve into the technical details of COM and the COM IDL (Interface Definition Language) language. We also look at the practical issues of applying COM interfaces using Visual C++, Visual J++, Visual Basic, and scripting. This discussion focuses on the interaction between the various environments, and what can be expected.

Thinking with Interfaces

Designing applications with COM interfaces is a bit different from designing regular classes in Visual Basic, Visual J++, or Visual C++. When you design a class, you also design an implementation of the class. The classic object-oriented example is the implementation of shapes. In classic object-oriented programming (OOP), a base class called shape is defined to implement the functionality of all shapes, including circles, squares, and rectangles. The base shape class contains a function that would potentially be implemented in the square or circle class. Using this technique, a consumer of shape does not need to know about the individual workings of square or circle.

Developing an Architecture

Object-oriented programming techniques apply to interfaces, but in a different context. When you are building a system, it is vital to consider the architecture first. The separation of the interface from the implementation enables the architecture team to consider the big picture without having to consider the various implementation details. Sherlock Holmes once said, "Watson I do not listen to news because my brain is like an attic of a limited size. The more clutter there is, the more likely something important will be discarded or hidden." And the same is true when developing large applications. It is only possible to focus on a limited range of goals at once. Beyond that, things get forgotten.

The architecture team is responsible for designing the core interfaces that represent the various use cases and collaboration diagrams in the application. If you followed the book chapter by chapter, you should have created a domain-model text and a prototype that explores the various technical difficulties. We are now at the stage where certain objects and program behaviors can be extracted.

Now you want to be concise. For example, if a use case leads to the impression that one COM interface can be applied, then do that. Do not attempt to design interfaces that are secondary to the use case. While you may think they are important, you will run into problems at the implementation stage, because this will present yet another interface to be implemented. However, do not be extreme and dictate that all interfaces must be associated with a use case. What you want is a compromise where the main COM interfaces are directly related to the different use cases and collaboration diagrams, including some secondary COM interfaces.

The development process could be converted into the diagram shown in Figure 8–1.

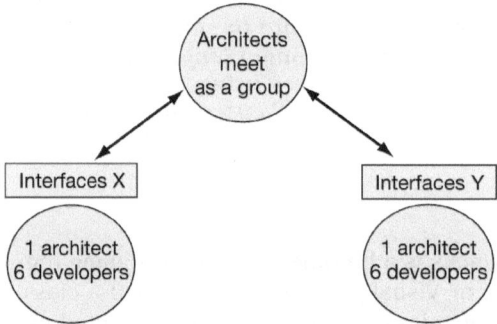

Figure 8–1: Team structure showing architecture team at core

In Figure 8–1, there is an architectural team that meets as a group, and they develop the interfaces for the entire application. These interfaces are documented and then handed off to the two teams. The individual teams implement their interfaces, and if the architecture team did their job correctly, the individual pieces fit together.

COMPONENTS AND TESTING

When developing interfaces and components, it is absolutely vital that a testing scenario be developed. This is further explored in Chapter 19. However, proper testing is not the only factor affecting application stability.

In Figure 8–2, there is an architectural team that has defined two interfaces, IAccount and IUser. Two different development teams then implement these interfaces. Because all of the teams are part of one larger team, they know about each other and sometimes meet as a group. During one of these meetings, one member of the team that implemented interface IAccount talked to a member of the team that implemented interface IUser. They discovered that both teams had partially implemented some common functionality. To reduce development efforts, both teams decide to pool efforts and build a component, My-CommonObject, that solves both problems.

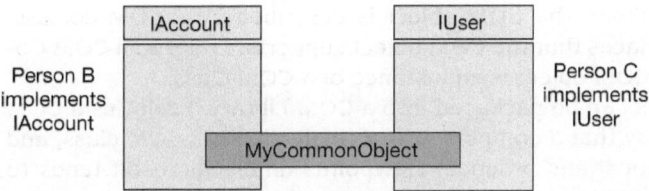

Figure 8–2: Development diagram showing implementation of interfaces

While this may seem like a noble effort, it is actually a problem because reuse is being applied without understanding the ramifications. First, only the team members know about this reuse—the architects and testers are not aware of its existence. When this application is tested, interface IAccount is tested independently of IUser. Let's now say that interface IAccount is okay, but interface IUser needs work. To solve those bugs, the common component is changed. The testers only retest interface IUser, but for proper testing, interface IAccount needs to be retested also. The noble effort may cause a disaster, which will require a patch.

The solution is not to reuse components, but to cut and paste the code so that two source codes are developed. When there is some time available, the architects can inspect the component and consider the ramifications of the component. Then, maybe, the components can be reused. Writing good components is not easy, and stability is the result of a good testing process that recognizes the boundaries of the components.

Building a COM Component

The COM component is a series of interfaces that are grouped into classes and a library. The question for the architecture team is how to design the interfaces. There is no simple answer. Ideally, a UML (Unified Modeling Language) tool is used, but because the current batch of UML tools supports COM interface design extremely poorly, the use of UML is saved for a later section. Some projects have used Microsoft Word to document and create interfaces for both CORBA (Common Object Request Broker Architecture, a competing component technology) and COM.

How COM Works

COM is a binary technology, which makes it possible to define components. COM components are reusable black boxes that expose a specific functionality. It is a good component architecture because a COM component is language-independent. COM makes it possible to focus on interfaces and using those interfaces.

The COM technology is built up in levels. At the lowest level is a COM interface. The COM interface is a vtable (virtual table) that groups a series of function pointers, which point to an implementation of the interface. This part of COM follows the *bridge pattern (appendix patterns)*, because the interface and implementation are independently definable.

In the COM environment, the COM object is described by a COM coclass, which identifies the interfaces that the COM object supports. I refer to a COM Co-Class as a COM class; a COM object is an instance of a COM class.

Multiple COM classes can be packaged into a COM Library. I call this a COM component. You might say that a component is a single physical COM class, and this is where the theoretical and practical viewpoints differ. Microsoft tends to refer to a single DLL as a COM component, which is a COM Library.

Every COM interface, class, and library needs to be uniquely identified. This is done using a *GUID* (Globally Unique Identifier). It is a 128-bit value that consists of a group of 8 hexadecimal digits, followed by 3 groups of 4 hexadecimal digits, followed by 1 group of 12 hexadecimal digits. An example GUID is as follows:

```
6B29FC40-CA47-1067-B31D-00DD010662DA
```

This identifier is used when the consumer wants to call a COM class, interface, or library.

IDL and What It Does

The interface is a central part of the COM technology. Interfaces are defined with a language called IDL. In the past, Microsoft has had two separate ways of defining interfaces: ODL (Object Definition Language) and IDL (Interface Definition Language). The first was for OLE Automation and the latter for RPC (Remote Procedure Call). A more detailed description of OLE Automation is given later. But with time ODL became superfluous. The decision was made to use IDL for both RPC and COM descriptions. ODL is still supported, but IDL is the recommended way of describing interfaces.

IDL has one basic concept to understand. Every labeled keyword can have associated attributes and contain other keywords. An example of the notation is:

```
[attributes] keyword  label
{
keyword member descriptions
};
```

or

```
typedef [ type_attributes] type_keyword label
{
keyword member descriptions
};
```

The keyword is a single command such as interface, coclass, or library. In the square brackets are the attributes that are associated with the keyword. Examples include object, uuid, and helpstring. The keyword contains child elements within curly brackets.

A SIMPLE EXAMPLE

When developing larger applications with many COM classes, it is really easy to become confused. The confusion is caused not by the complexity of the COM classes, but by too much information. You are mixing COM implementation code with COM interface descriptions; we want to separate the COM interfaces from the implementations. The way to do this is to create an IDL file.

There are different ways of using an IDL file, and which you choose depends on the environment that you are programming in. Visual C++ has the capability to use IDL files natively and integrate them in your project, whereas Visual Basic and Visual J++ require a type library for integration. To create a type library, you would use the MIDL program to compile the COM library into a COM-type library. A COM-type library is a compiled binary representation of the IDL file.

Consider the following IDL file:

```
import "oaidl.idl";
import "ocidl.idl";

[
    object,
    uuid(8895EECD-0915-11D2-9C50-00A0247D759A),
    dual,
    helpstring("ISimpleInterface Interface"),
    pointer_default(unique)
]
interface ISimpleInterface : IDispatch
{
    [id(1), helpstring("method method1")] HRESULT method1( long param1);
};

[
uuid(8895EEC1-0915-11D2-9C50-00A0247D759A),
version(1.0),
helpstring("ServerPackage 1.0 Type Library")
]
library SERVERPACKAGELib
{
importlib("stdole32.tlb");
importlib("stdole2.tlb");

[
    uuid(8895EECE-0915-11D2-9C50-00A0247D759A),
    helpstring("SimpleUser Class")
]
```

```
coclass SimpleComponent
{
    [default] interface ISimpleInterface;
};
};
```

With Visual Studio Enterprise Edition you do not need to manually use MIDL to compile the file into a COM type library. The Visual Studio C++ shell lets you create a utility project and add the IDL file to that project. When the utility project is compiled it automatically calls MIDL and compiles the IDL file.

For this example, after having created the utility project, create a new file and call it InterfaceComponent.idl. Add the preceding source code, and execute the Build menu item. Once the build is complete, you'll have the InterfaceComponent.tlb file, which is the type library.

IDL may seem ugly to read and hard to write, but it is not. You only need to remember the organization presented previously. A COM component is a package that is defined by the keyword library, and it has the label SERVERPACKAGELib. Contained within the package can be multiple COM classes, which are defined using the keyword coclass, and they have the label SimpleComponent. With a COM class you have the ability to define multiple interfaces using the keyword interface, and they have the label ISimpleInterface. All of the keywords presented have an associated GUID using the uuid attribute.

HOW A COM INTERFACE IS INSTANTIATED

When the previous IDL is compiled, a *type library* results. In the previous example, when clients want to use an implementation of the ISimpleInterface, they do not instantiate the interface itself. Instead, the consumer instantiates a COM class (coclass) that has implemented the interface. After the coclass is instantiated, COM uses a QueryInterface to search for the ISimpleInterface. If the QueryInterface fails, COM returns an error indicating that the interface does not exist. If the ISimpleInterface interface does exist, it is returned to the consumer, which can then call the various methods.

WHY THE NEED FOR THIS COMPLICATION?

It may seem silly to use IDL. Why not save data to a structure, and then pass that piece of data between operating systems and programming languages? The answer is that regardless of how an operating system or programming language is written, there is a need to speak a common language. Every language, every operating system, and every piece of hardware differs in the way it communicates. For example, on a 16-bit platform, an integer is 16 bits in size. On a 32-bit platform, the integer is 32 bits in size. If a structure is compiled and a piece of data is exchanged between the two platforms, they may not read the value in the same way. COM uses IDL to create a neutral format that specifies the size and alignment of data. Using a technique called *marshaling* and *unmarshaling*, the COM layer converts the data from one operating system or programming language to COM, and back to the other operating system and other programming language.

A COM Package

When building COM applications, an in-depth understanding of IDL is not required, but you'll need to know how IDL behaves. Understanding IDL makes it possible to diagnose problems related to component management.

THE COM COMPONENT

The COM component is defined by a library keyword, as presented in the simple example section. It contains all of the classes that are exposed by the COM component. The common attributes are:

- uuid: The ID used to define this library. This is a required parameter.
- version: Supplies the version number of the library.
- helpstring: A text describing the library. This is useful for object browsers.
- lcid: An ID that indicates which language this library applies to.
- hidden: Hides the object from an object browser.

THE COM CLASS

The coclass keyword is used to define an implementation in a COM component. When defining an IDL file that is to be compiled into a type library, you must define a coclass. If you do not, MIDL, by default, will not include the interface in the compilation phase. The coclass in the interface-definition phase does not need to be special, because it will not be used to reference any implementation. The typical syntax for a coclass is as follows:

```
[attributes]
coclass classname {
[interface attributes] [interface | dispinterface] interfacename;
};
```

In the implementation phase, the coclass is important. The coclass has these attributes:

- uuid: This identifies the CLSID (Class ID) that will be used to identify this object.
- version: Supplies the version number of the library.
- helpstring: A text describing the class. This is useful for object browsers.
- licensed: Tells the class that the object is licensed and that it should be checked. In this case, the interface IClassFactory2 should be used as the class factory.
- hidden: Hides the object from a COM object browser.

Within the coclass definition, the various interfaces can have these attributes:

- source: This specifies that the interface is a source of events and is used in conjunction with the IConnectionPoint container.

- default: Used by macro programmers (VBScript) to define the default interface called when none is specified.
- restricted: Prevents the interface from being used by macro programmers.

The COM Interface

The bulk of your time will be spent designing good interfaces. The interface in COM terms is defined as follows:

```
[attributes]
interface interfacename [:baseinterface] {
functionlist
};
```

Valid attributes are these:

- dual: Specifies that the interface defined supports both custom and IDispatch interfaces.
- object: A special tag that tells the MIDL compiler to generate COM-compatible code. If this tag is specified, it must have an associated uuid. Without this tag, the interface is compiled as a DCE (Distributed Computing Environment) RPC call.
- uuid: This identifies the CLSID that identifies this object.
- helpstring: A text describing the interface. This is useful for object browsers.
- pointer_default: This is used whenever an interface uses pointers within their interfaces as parameters. This does not include top-level pointers, only things such as double pointers.
- oleautomation: This specifies that the interface will only support parameters that are considered standard automation types.

In the method parameter list, there are other attributes that specify how the parameter memory is allocated and how the information is sent. They are combined in the attribute list using commas.

THE QUERYINTERFACE PROCESS

What sets COM apart from all other component technologies is its capability to deal with the unknown. Consider the situation of a consumer instantiating a COM class. How does the COM layer know that the COM class has implemented the COM interface? It asks the COM class whether it has implemented the interface using the QueryInterface process. What we are going to do is look at which interfaces and methods must be implemented.

Every COM class must implement IUnknown, and every COM interface must inherit from IUnknown. The interface definition of IUnknown is as follows:

```
[
local,
object,
uuid(00000000-0000-0000-C000-000000000046),
pointer_default(unique)
]
interface IUnknown {
HRESULT QueryInterface( [in] REFIID riid, [out, iid_is(riid)] void
**ppvObject);
ULONG AddRef();
ULONG Release();
}
```

There are three methods in the IUnknown definition: QueryInterface, AddRef, and Release. COM calls the first method, QueryInterface, when the COM class is instantiated. The first parameter, riid, is the GUID of the interface that is being requested. In the implementation, this parameter is checked against the list of implemented interfaces. If there is a match, the implementation returns, via the ppvObject pointer, a vtable pointer that represents the interface.

At this point, COM trusts that the interface implementation vtable signature matches the IDL interface vtable signature. Using the programming languages Visual Basic, Visual C++, and Visual J++, this is not an issue, because a vtable signature mismatch would result in a compilation failure. With other languages, it will most likely be the same, but you should check the COM implementation details of the language.

IDL supports a concept called interface inheritance, and an interface that inherits from IUnknown has the following IDL:

```
[
object,
uuid(E05034D2-8EB8-11d2-86CB-0000B45FCBCB),
helpstring("ISimpleInterface2 Interface"),
pointer_default(unique)
]
interface ISimpleInterface2: IUnknown {
[helpstring("method1")] HRESULT method1();
};
```

The vtable signature for ISimpleInterface2 has four function pointers in this order: QueryInterface, AddRef, Release, and method1. The first three function pointers are the result of interface inheritance.

IMPLEMENTATION REFERENCE COUNTING

The other two methods of the `IUnknown` interface are `AddRef` and `Release`. These two methods manage reference counting.

In Figure 8–3, consumer A instantiates COM class `SimpleComponent`. Then consumer B instantiates the COM class `SimpleComponent`. But the instance of `SimpleComponent` is a singleton and returns a reference to itself. A singleton is a special kind of object in which only one instance of the class can exist in memory. Consumer A terminates, and in keeping with good programming practices, it deletes the `SimpleComponent` instance. However, consumer B still requires the instance of `SimpleComponent` to be executing. So, does consumer A actually delete `SimpleComponent`? The answer involves reference counting. Whenever a consumer instantiates or references a COM class, the reference count is incremented using `AddRef`. When the consumer does not need the reference anymore, the reference count is decremented using `Release`. Once the reference count hits zero, the COM class instance deletes itself.

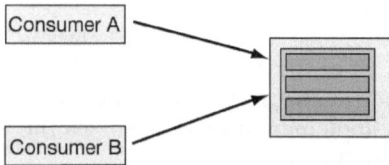

Figure 8–3: Two consumers referencing a single COM object

This scheme may sound good, but one might think it could be prone to miscounts. However, miscounts do not happen in a multitasking 32-bit or 64-bit environment such as Windows 2000. The operating system accounts for processes that die mysteriously and that present other nasty problems. Of course, if the program that performs reference counting is not properly written, the reference count will be incorrect, but when you are using languages like Visual Basic or Visual J++, the language manages the counting. Reference counting in Visual C++ is managed by helper classes.

CUSTOM INTERFACES AND EARLY BINDING

When an interface inherits directly from `IUnknown`, it is called a custom interface, and custom interfaces use *early binding*. Early binding means that the interface's vtable signature is known when the consumer is compiled. Early binding means that there is a contract between the consumer and the implementation, which is defined by the type library.

The run-time speed is higher with early binding, because the consumer knows where to find the implementation functionality. However, early binding also has problems if the implementation alters the contract without informing the consumer application—such vtable signature changes can cause the application to fail.

LATE BINDING

Sometimes you create a COM class that determines its methods dynamically. Consider the situation of creating a COM interface to a database. You want the capability to dynamically generate methods that represent database functions. There is no way of creating a type library, because it would be out of date once it is created. In this situation of not being able to create a type library, or in the case where you do not wish to expose a type library, *late binding* applies.

Late binding is also called OLE Automation. Late binding is interesting because the consumer can call the method or property of the method using a general function as a negotiator. The negotiator accepts the structure and parameters, and then attempts to decipher which method in the application is being called. The negotiator then calls the method and returns the data in form of another structure populated with information. This negotiator is called the IDispatch interface, which is part of the implementation. ASP uses this method of binding when it calls COM classes.

DUAL INTERFACES

When an object is created, it must support either early binding or late binding. Early binding is a faster access technique, but it is not as flexible. If there is another version of a server and certain methods have changed or disappeared, the application will crash because the vtable is not correct.

If the object should remain flexible and provide a soft crash or a recoverable crash, then using late binding is the answer. The price of using late binding is speed. In late binding, the consumer of a COM class asks it whether there is a method that has a specific signature. The COM class then searches its function table and returns an ID. The consumer then creates a structure that contains all of the parameters and passes it to the COM class, which translates the structure into a function call. Also, because the methods are general and the parameters and methods are stored in arrays, the implementation must decipher what the structures are. Because of the question and answer process and the interpretation involved, everything does slow down.

Both methods have their advantages and disadvantages. If you want the object to support both methods, you can implement both early binding and late binding. This is called a dual interface. It is a bit more work to implement, but it makes sure that all clients can make use of the object. With most languages, the dual technique is hidden within the programming environment.

WHICH BINDING IS BETTER?

Many people believe that custom interfaces are much better, because they promote faster applications and better versioning. Generally, early binding is preferable, but there are specific instances where late binding is better.

For example, in the previous chapter, the Visual InterDev Scripting Object Library used the Data Environment COM component. This object translates stored procedure calls directly to COM method calls. The Data Environment does this trick by using late binding and exposing functions dynamically that represent stored procedure calls. This technique would seem to be slower, but let's take a closer look.

If the Data Environment were implemented using custom interfaces, then methods for setting the various parameters and for calling the stored procedure need to be written. This means that the implementation must translate the parameters and stored procedure call to a specific stored procedure. In other words, the implementation must do quite a bit of work before the actual stored procedure can be called.

The Data Environment object, on the other hand, is an example of a technology-bridging object. It does nothing but translate a method call from one technology to another (COM to SQL (Structured Query Language)). Using the Data Environment promotes a simpler programming syntax at virtually no cost in performance.

The rule of thumb in choosing binding methods is to always use a dual interface, but if the situation warrants it, use late binding.

Some COM Interface Design Techniques

Now that you have a basic understanding of COM and interfaces, some COM interface design techniques need to be discussed.

Interfaces Are Immutable

When an interface has been published and released to the public, it is considered immutable and cannot be changed. Making an interface public does not necessarily mean making it public to the general consumer; it simply means making it public to the development team.

MAKING AN INTERFACE IMMUTABLE

Making an interface immutable should not be a simple process. It is like the decision to get a puppy. Once the puppy is there, it needs attention and can't be put aside. Similarly, once you make an interface immutable, you are stuck with it, and even if you'd like to make changes, you can't. The general philosophy behind developing applications in this book is to use iterative development techniques. However, when interfaces are made immutable, they can't be developed incrementally.

In our design process, we want to have multiple COM interfaces to promote fine granularity. However, there can be too much of a good thing. Fine granularity can make things more complex than necessary. The solution is to apply the *façade* pattern to simplify something complex. This can be done by using an iterative *layered* pattern approach or by using a fully flowing approach.

Now let's apply this to what was said in the previous section about an architectural team splitting off the work. And let's consider the situation of developing the application using iterations. Again, the architectural team develops a series of COM interfaces that solves the application. But instead of implementing all of them, a few of them are implemented. The criteria used to determine which interfaces to implement depend on the team and the priority. Consider the case of implementing the entire application with some COM interfaces, as shown in Figure 8-4.

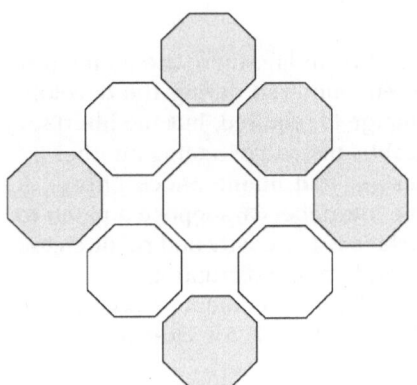

The solid blocks represent implemented COM interfaces; the empty blocks are COM interface definitions only. In this approach, the core COM interfaces are developed and implemented. Then, as the implementation continues, the testing team starts to test the implementations. Testing is done incrementally.

Now that the architectural team has tentatively finished the interface design, it is free to process the tests results. Some results may indicate problems; the architectural team is immediately aware of them and can make the appropriate changes. These changes may require new COM interfaces or changes to the testing specifications. These incremental changes do not affect the entire application, but yet the entire application adapts.

Figure 8-4: Entire application

Where to Start Implementations

The iterative approach sounds good until you have to start implementing and testing objects. The reason is because you do not know which COM interfaces to implement. The COM interface implementation process is like digging a tunnel, with the business tier being the tunnel that binds the presentation tier and the data tier. So, do you start the tunnel at the presentation end and dig to the data end, or do you start at the data end and dig toward the presentation end, or do you start at both ends and hope to meet in the middle?

Which technique is better depends on the nature of the team. If you use the start-from-one-end approach, you will build a core set building the various layers in sequence. This is a sequential and iterative approach because plan changes are made in mid-step. The problem is that the layers cannot be changed significantly after they are made immutable—making changes requires complete retesting and a new evaluation, which can cost time and money. However, this approach is easier to quantify than building from both ends.

The start-from-both-ends approach is a much more flexible technique, because interfaces are made immutable when they have been used in various scenarios and proven their effectiveness. A badly designed interface is changed, and anyone using that interface must also change his or her use of it. This approach also means that more changes can potentially occur, and if some teams make changes to the interfaces without informing the others, errors will occur. It is up to the architectural team to control these changes and inform all parties of the changes.

This approach will not work if the team does not have the discipline, experience in gauging implementation changes, or effective communication channels. It will cause budget and time delays, resulting in application development failure.

Experience has shown that the second approach works better. It is a more responsive approach, and it leads to an application that is more to the end users' liking.

When an Interface Must Be Extended

The term *immutable* means "never changing." But as in life, there are many gray areas. These gray areas are most likely to be encountered during the development phase. For example, suppose a design change is required, but the interface has already been tested and made semi-immutable. Instead of adding another interface, which would add documentation, design, and maintenance efforts, it would be simpler to modify the semi-immutable interface. Or suppose a patch to fix a small bug is required. Adding another interface is too costly and requires too much time, when the goal is to minimize costs and system disruption.

Making such changes is not condoned as a design technique. Good design and planning can often prevent situations that would call for changes to immutable interfaces.

EXTENDING THE INTERFACE

The first method of modifying the interface is to simply add the extra method to the end of the vtable, while keeping the original vtable intact. This technique is called extending.

Consider the following immutable interface:

```
[
uuid(BE1FFD3B-E489-11D1-B44D-00A0247D759A),
version(1.0),
helpstring("Math 1.0 Type Library")
]
interface IMath : IUnknown
{
[id(1)] HRESULT add(long param1, long param2, long *retvalue);
};
```

This is a proposed math interface that has the capability to add two numbers (param1 and param2) and return the result in the variable retvalue.

The following example adds an extra subtract method to the end of the original vtable.

```
[
object, dual,
uuid(BE1FFD3B-E489-11D1-B44D-00A0247D759A),
version(2.0),
helpstring("Math 2.0 Type Library")
]
interface IMath : IDispatch
{
[id(1)] HRESULT add(long param1, long param2, long *retvalue);
```

```
[id(2)] HRESULT subtract(long param1, long param2, long *retvalue);
};
```

In this new extended interface definition, the `subtract` method has a totally different functionality. In comparison to creating a new interface with the associated overhead, this technique is the least painful and simplest. When releasing this interface, make sure to change the version number of the interface attributes. This way the client can distinguish between the different versions.

ADDING COMPLEMENTARY FUNCTIONALITY

In the previous example, the `subtract` method was added. But both methods are only capable of adding integer-type numbers. Suppose you need to change the functionality so that real numbers can be added. The extending technique is used, but the method is called add2 to reflect similar functionality. The solution is as follows.

```
interface IMath : IDispatch
{
[id(1)] HRESULT add(long param1, long param2, long *retvalue);
[id(2)] HRESULT add2(double param1, double param2, double *retvalue);
};
```

The number at the end of the add2 method indicates a different version, which typically means different parameters are required. This technique is applied if there are only a few similar methods. Under no circumstance should there be an add100, because that would mean that your interface has been changed one hundred times.

ADDING COMPLEMENTARY INTERFACES

Consider the case in which your application needs to be radically changed. For example, suppose we learn that the cost difference between using longs and doubles for addition are nonexistent, and that in some situations the double is faster. If this radical change happens, the interface needs to be updated.

A radical change requires a new interface definition. Consider the following interface definition:

```
interface IMath2 : IDispatch
{
[id(1)] HRESULT add(double param1, double param2, double *retvalue);
[id(2)] HRESULT subtract(double param1, double param2, double *retvalue);
};
```

In this solution, instead of adding an incremental value to the method, it is added to the interface (IMath2). The interface could also be called IMathDoubleVersion, but consider the situation in which the interface implements long doubles. The interface would now be called IMathLongDoubleVersion. Extend this to potentially 100 interfaces, and very quickly the names of the interfaces become extremely long and lose their meaning. This is a question of semantics, but there is a benefit in the large scale. The advantage of using an incremental approach is that any developer who uses the interface knows that the interfaces are complementary and if they understand one, they should be able to guess at what the other does.

Using a Programming Language to Develop COM Interfaces

Now, we want to define COM interfaces. We have learned that IDL is the basis of COM, so it makes sense to use IDL. However, because a COM-compatible language generates COM-type libraries, that language could be used to define the interfaces. This is called creating an empty implementation. Let's try this technique and see what kind of COM IDL is generated.

SIMPLECOMPONENT IN THE VARIOUS LANGUAGES

To compare the IDL we generate, we will use the COM interface definition shown earlier in the "A Simple Example" section of this chapter. Specifically, we will attempt to define SimpleComponent.

Defining SimpleComponent Using Visual C++

To build a COM component that will be used as an empty implementation, it needs to be an ATL (Active Template Library) component. It is possible to use MFC (Microsoft Foundation Classes), but ATL is better geared for COM interfaces (both ATL and MFC are libraries that simplify the process of building Windows applications). When creating the ATL component, ensure that it is a dynamic link library. The interface is designed by using the ATL Wizard to add a new Simple Object type. There are two dialog boxes, shown in Figure 8–5 and Figure 8–6, that should be filled out carefully.

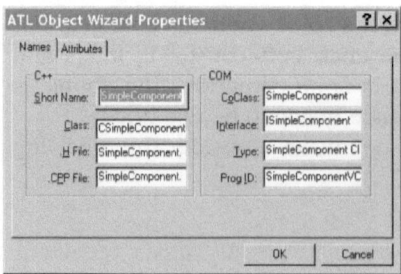

Figure 8–5: SimpleComponent Wizard Properties Names tab

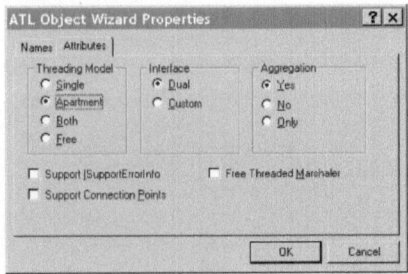

Figure 8–6: SimpleComponent Wizard Properties Attributes tab

The short name defines the name of the component, and the COM coclass has the same name as the short name. The wizard does not create a COM co-class independently of the COM interface—it creates the two items in one step. The interface has the letter "I" prefixed to it, indicating that it is a COM interface. The prog ID is SimpleComponentVC.SimpleComponent, which is a concatenation of the COM library name and the COM coclass.

Figure 8–6 defines the attributes of the interface being added. The only at-tribute that is of interest to us is the Interface attribute, which can be Custom or Dual. If it is Custom, then ISimpleComponent derives from IUnknown. Dual means that the interface is based on IDispatch. In this case, the Custom interface at-tribute was selected.

To complete the development, it is necessary to use a small wizard to add method1 as part of the interface. This is all that is required to create a type library that contains a series of interfaces that can be implemented in other develop-ment environments.

What does the wizard generate in the type library? This does not need to be shown because it is nearly identical to what was displayed in the original IDL file, earlier in this chapter. The important point Visual C++ provides the capability to tune the IDL and create the interface that you desire.

Defining SimpleComponent Using Visual Basic

In Visual Basic, like Visual C++, it is possible to define a type library by defining empty Visual Basic classes. To do this, create a Visual Basic Active X DLL (Dy-namic Link Library) project. Name the project SimpleComponentVB; it will contain a single VB class called SimpleComponent. The definition of the class is:

```
Public Sub method1(ByVal param1 As Long)
End Sub
```

When this is compiled, this type library is generated:

```
[
uuid(FC81A421-2A94-11D3-957D-0080C700807A),
version(4.0)
```

```
]
library SimpleComponentVB
{
importlib("STDOLE2.TLB");

// Forward declare all types defined in this typelib
interface _SimpleComponent;

[
    odl,
    uuid(78C21322-2A95-11D3-957D-0080C700807A),
    version(1.0),
    hidden,
    dual,
    nonextensible,
    oleautomation
]
interface _SimpleComponent : IDispatch {
    [id(0x60030000)] HRESULT method1([in] long param1);
};
[
    uuid(FC81A423-2A94-11D3-957D-0080C700807A),
    version(1.0),
    appobject
]
coclass SimpleComponent {
    [default] interface _SimpleComponent;
};
};
```

Some of this type library generation is not correct, because the type library was viewed using the OLE Viewer. The OLE Viewer will translate some of the IDL keywords into its own representation, which will not always match the original IDL. What we will focus on is the naming convention and the types of interfaces. Unlike Visual C++, Visual Basic does not prefix the interface name with the letter "I"; instead, it uses an underscore. Like Visual C++, Visual Basic associates the COM coclass with the COM interface. But unlike Visual C++, Visual Basic can only generate one interface from a specific class—the interface that is created by Visual Basic is dual. With Visual Basic, it is not possible to define a custom-only interface. There is also a limitation on the parameters and parameter types.

Defining SimpleComponent Using Visual J++

To create a COM interface with Visual J++, create a Visual J++ project that represents a COM DLL. Then rename the added Java class file to SimpleComponent and define the sources as follows:

```
/**
 * This class is designed to be packaged with a COM DLL output format.
 * The class has no standard entry points, other than the constructor.
 * Public methods will be exposed as methods on the default COM interface.
 * @com.register ( clsid=4D559511-2A97-11D3-957D-0080C700807A,
typelib=4D559512-2A97-11D3-957D-0080C700807A )
 */
public class SimpleComponent
{
public void method1( long param1) {
    return
}
}
```

When this class is compiled, this type library is generated:

```
[
uuid(4D559512-2A97-11D3-957D-0080C700807A),
version(1.0),
helpstring("SimpleComponentVJ")
]
library SimpleComponentVJ
{
// TLib     // TLib : OLE Automation : {00020430-0000-0000-C000-
000000000046}
importlib("STDOLE2.TLB");

// Forward declare all types defined in this typelib
dispinterface SimpleComponent_Dispatch;

[
    uuid(72AA2BB7-2A97-11D3-957D-0080C700807A)
]
dispinterface SimpleComponent_Dispatch {
    properties:
    methods:
        [id(0x00000064)]
        VARIANT wait(
            [in, out] VARIANT* Parameter0,
            [in, out] VARIANT* Parameter1);
        [id(0x00000065), helpstring("hashCode")]
        long hashCode();
        [id(0x00000066), helpstring("toString")]
        BSTR toString();
        [id(0x00000067), helpstring("equals")]
        VARIANT_BOOL equals([in] IDispatch* Parameter0);
```

```
        [id(0x00000068), helpstring("method1")]
        void method1([in] long Parameter0);
        [id(0x00000069), helpstring("notify")]
        void notify();
        [id(0x0000006a), helpstring("getClass")]
        IDispatch* getClass();
        [id(0x0000006b), helpstring("notifyAll")]
        void notifyAll();
};

[
    uuid(4D559511-2A97-11D3-957D-0080C700807A),
    helpstring("SimpleComponent")
]
coclass SimpleComponent {
    [default] dispinterface SimpleComponent_Dispatch;
};
};
```

What is generated is something that is not desired in an interface. Visual J++ adds various methods that are part of the Java object class, and considers the interface to be a dispinterface. This is a COM specification that says that the methods of the interface can be invoked only using late binding. This means our COM calls will be slower, which is not what we want. Another small problem is the naming of the COM interface, which is SimpleComponent_Dispatch. When this client is used in the context of a Visual C++ or Visual Basic client, different naming conventions will arise.

And the Best Solution Is?

The simplest way to develop an interface is to use either Visual C++ or write a utility project and compile the IDL file using MIDL. When manually editing the IDL file, you have ultimate control over how interfaces and methods are defined and can fine-tune them. In the future, the IDL file may change and require a new writing. However, the concept of interfaces and implementations will not change.

PARAMETERS WITHIN METHODS

COM provides the capability to define parameter data types. You can choose either general data types or strict data types. A general data type is a VARIANT, which can accept any type of data. A strict data type, such as a long or double, can only contain a specific type of value.

Strict parameters offer these advantages:

• The specific data type makes it easy to identify what type of data to pass.
• No data is lost in conversion from one data type to another.
• Strict data types are faster than variants.

General parameters also offer a few advantages, including:

- It is easy to update implementations without requiring an interface change because the parameters can accept any kind of data.
- The parameters can handle multiple data types without requiring the client to call different methods or interfaces specific to different data types.
- It is easier to decouple interfaces. With general parameters a specific interface is not dependent on another interface or functionality.
- They do not require a scripting language data conversion function call. Many scripting languages will default to the string data type, which is often an incorrect assumption.

Choosing whether to use a general or specific data type is not a simple decision, because each option has strengths and weaknesses. There is no rule of thumb for when to use a specific technique.

For example, ADO (Active Data Objects), which is used in Visual Basic and scripting, is written using general data types. General data types make it possible to create generic methods to retrieve data. ADO works with Recordsets from databases. When retrieving a value, it is silly to write methods such as getDouble, getLong, getString, and so on. The interface would be too long and complex. It is simpler to return a VARIANT using a method called getValue. And because the typical data provider has many different data types, using a VARIANT is appropriate.

OLE Automation Data Types

There is a difference in the types of parameters that can be used in custom interfaces and dual interfaces. This is because a dual interface can be implemented in any programming language, but not all consumers support all data types.

There is a category of data types called OLE Automation compatible. The core OLE Automation data type is the VARIANT, which is a structure that contains a value of reference to the data type that it represents.

The data types that you will use most often are these:

- long, BYTE, short, float, double, BOOL, DATE, char: These are the core data types used to represent numbers.
- BSTR: This is the COM string data type.
- IDispatch: This is a data type that contains a reference to another COM interface.
- SafeArray: This is a data type that contains an array of elements that can be of one of the above types or a VARIANT. The array is safe because it contains the element count, starting point, and ending point.

Outside of the OLE Automation data types are all the other data types. Although they are useful in their context, they cannot be used in many programming environment. In the context of Windows DNA and application development, any data type that cannot be used everywhere should be ignored unless there is a good reason to use it.

Using the Variant Data Type

Let's step back and consider how the VARIANT data type is represented in the various languages. Consider the following IDL method declaration:

```
[ id(1)] HRESULT method2([in] VARIANT newVal);
```

This VARIANT is represented in Visual C++ as,

```
STDMETHOD( method2)(/*[in]*/ VARIANT newVal);
```

The VARIANT data type is a raw structure that contains the information about the data contained within it.

In Visual J++, the VARIANT is represented as,

```
public void method2 (Variant newVal);
```

The Variant data type is a Java class that encapsulates the VARIANT data structure. Visual J++ does not use the COM VARIANT data type directly because COM at its basic level is low level. To make COM programming easier, it is possible to create libraries or create helpers. Visual J++ has created the helper object Variant that manages the details of that data type.

In Visual Basic, the VARIANT is represented as,

```
Public Sub method1(ByVal newVal As Variant)
```

In Visual Basic the Variant data type is a native data type. It can be manipulated using a series of functions, but because it is a data type, it can be used directly like an integer, long or double.

Regardless of which language is using the VARIANT data type, it requires some extra work, and depending on how it is being used can make it slower. This is because the VARIANT data structure needs to have some flags set for it to be considered correct.

So, why is there a VARIANT data type? The VARIANT creates a pseudostructure and enables flexible parameters. In the ADO example, the VARIANT data type solved the problem perfectly. When interfaces are going to be used mostly in scripting environments, then using the VARIANT data type is the simpler option.

Using the Object Data Type

Consider the following method declaration that contains a reference to an object:

```
[ id(1)] HRESULT method3([in] IDispatch* newVal);
```

The object is a reference to the IDispatch interface. It might seem more logical to reference IUnknown as an object, but the problem with this is that if the interface is an IUnknown, the consumer of the interface must know which interface it is using, and in many scripting languages this is not possible. Visual Basic has problems understanding the IUnknown interface and expects all object references to be based on IDispatch. The IDispatch reference makes it possible for the scripting language to query for various methods.

In Visual C++ the method is declared as:

```
STDMETHOD(method3)(/*[in]*/ IDispatch* newVal);
```

This is a pointer to the interface itself.

In Visual J++ the method is declared as:

```
public void method3(Object newVal);
```

The Object data type is a root Java object. To use it you need to typecast it to the desired interface.

In Visual Basic the method is declared as::

```
Public Sub method3(ByVal newVal As Object)
```

As in Visual J++, the Object data type is a root Visual Basic object. However, unlike Visual J++ you do not need to typecast the object to use it. Visual Basic uses the IDispatch interface when you make method calls on an Object data type.

When building interfaces, it might seem more intelligent to use strict interface data types, as shown here:

```
[ id(1)] HRESULT method3([in] ISimpleComponent* newVal);
```

Either way is acceptable. The only catch with using a strict interface is that ISimpleComponent must at some point be derived from IDispatch. And while it may seem quicker to use interface pointers directly, that is only true when the server and the consumer are Visual C++. @T:Visual C++ has the capability to use interface pointers directly. In other languages there may be a QueryInterface, and in some environments, such as scripting, it is only possible to use IDispatch.

Using the String Data Type

Strings in a C programming language context are buffers of characters terminated by a NULL character. The characters could be single-byte or double-byte characters. The number of bytes before the NULL character defines the length of the string. With COM and OLE Automation, a string uses the BSTR data type. A BSTR is different from a regular string in that it is UNICODE data and stores the length of the string. Consider this method declaration:

```
[helpstring("method method3")] HRESULT method3(BSTR param1);
```

In Visual C++, the declaration is:

```
STDMETHOD(method3)(BSTR param1);
```

In Visual J++, the declaration is:

```
public void method3(String param1);
```

In Java, the `String` object is a Java base class.
In Visual Basic the declaration is:

```
Public Sub method3( ByVal param1 as String)
```

As in Visual J++, in Visual Basic the `String` object is a part of the language.

The string object is not a problem in either Visual J++ or Visual Basic because there is a direct mapping. In Visual C++, however, it is a bit more complicated—there is quite a bit of legacy, with the result that there are many string wrapper classes. Chapter 9 outlines a way of dealing with strings in Visual C++.

Defining Return Values

When declaring functions, you typically want to declare return values to the caller. In all of the past IDL examples, the return value was an HRESULT. In COM IDL, it is customary to return an HRESULT, which is an error-handling mechanism.

COM handles exceptions based on the return value of the method being called. This is because exceptions cannot be thrown across COM interfaces. This was an early design decision in COM. At that time, there was no consistent exception mechanism, and not all languages supported exceptions. Therefore, all methods of COM interfaces must return an error code that indicates whether the method call was successful. Even though most languages now support the concept of exceptions, it is still not possible to throw an exception in COM.

To define a return value in COM, the function needs to be declared using this IDL:

```
[id(1)] HRESULT method2(long param1, [out,retval]long *retval);
```

In Visual Basic and Visual J++, you won't need to do return an HRESULT to indicate whether a method worked because the run-times mask the details of the HRESULT. They correlate their internal error-handling mechanism to an HRESULT and then, depending on the HRESULT, throw either an internal error or the HRESULT.

The implementation of the preceding IDL method in Visual Basic is as follows:

```
public function method2( ByVal param1 as long) as long
```

And in Visual J++ the method is:

```
public int method2(int param1);
```

Because Visual C++ is working at the raw level, the method declaration is identical to the IDL declaration and has two parameters.

Directional Parameters

When a COM consumer calls an implementation, it passes data from the consumer to the implementation, and the data needs to be marshaled and then unmarshaled. The problem that we have is that data from one compiled programming environment needs to be sent to another compiled programming environment. The environments may be on the same machine or they may be on two totally different networks on different parts of the planet, so the data may need to travel on the machine or across the network. COM resolves this situation, because COM is location independent, but the price is that the interface must declare the direction of the parameter.

Consider this function declaration:

```
HRESULT someMethod( long value);
```

This method declaration says that the parameter will be sent from the consumer to the implementation. The COM marshaling routines will create a buffer to hold the long value. But consider a string that is 40,000 characters—such a buffer is not insignificant. Moving it from the consumer to the implementation and back again uses bandwidth. In the preceding method call, the buffer is only required when sending the data from the consumer to the implementation. It is not necessary for the return trip. An optimization would be to only send the buffer to the server and to ignore it on the return trip.

In fact, you can optimize this by applying the directional attribute to the parameter indicating the direction of the parameter. The default is in, which means that the data flows from the consumer to the implementation only. The attribute out means that the data flows from the implementation to the consumer. Combining in and out indicates that the data flows from the consumer to the implementation, it is deleted and reallocated, and it then again flows from the implementation to the consumer. This entire process may seem long-winded, but it is necessary, because COM is not location dependent.

An example interface that implements all three variations is as follows:

```
interface ITest : IDispatch
{
    [id(1)] HRESULT onlyInput(long param1);
    [id(2)] HRESULT onlyOutput([out]long *output);
    [id(3)] HRESULT inputOutput([in, out]long *value);
};
```

The directional attributes are very important when it comes to implementing an interface, because the languages treat the interface differently if the interface is consumed. In this chapter, only the implementing aspect is discussed.

If Visual C++ were used to implement the interface, the method declarations would be identical to the IDL, except that it would be based on the C++ syntax.

Where the implementation does differ is when the Visual Basic language is used. Visual Basic has no problem with the methods `onlyInput` and `inputOutput`, but it cannot do anything with `onlyOutput`. If you attempt to implement the `ITest` interface as it stands, Visual Basic will generate a compilation error. This is because it cannot do `output` parameters. The method `inputOutput` has this signature in VB:

```
public sub inputOutput( value as long)
```

This Visual Basic method declaration has no `ByValue` in the parameter list. This is because with an in,out COM parameter, the Visual Basic run-time will handle the COM parameter memory management.

Visual J++ can implement any of the methods defined in the interface. However, it does not make a distinction between `out` and `in, out`. @T:The method definitions are:

```
public void onlyOutput( int[] output);
public void inputOutput( int[] output);
```

The parameter is considered as an array. This creates a reference, which is almost like a pointer.

A SPECIAL METHOD CALLED A PROPERTY

Up to this point, all of the discussion has revolved around the implementation of methods, but COM also can define properties. Properties are different from methods in that properties can be assigned values like variables. However, properties, while being very effective, cannot be implemented in some languages (such as Visual C++ and Visual J++) because there is no equivalent concept. But Visual Basic and scripting can understand properties in the correct sense.

To understand properties, consider this JavaScript:

```
var temp = myObject.simpleProperty1;
```

This is known as a *property get* because it retrieves the value of the property from the object. The converse is called a *property put*, which is as follows:

```
myObject.simpleProperty1 = temp;
```

MIDL treats properties like functions with the attributes propput and propget as shown by the following:

```
[propget] HRESULT simpleProperty1([out, retval] VARIANT *pVal);
[propput] HRESULT simpleProperty1([in] VARIANT newVal);
```

In Visual C++, the method declarations are:

```
STDMETHOD(get_simpleProperty1)(/*[out, retval]*/ VARIANT *pVal);
STDMETHOD(put_simpleProperty1)(/*[in]*/ VARIANT newVal);
```

The method declarations are prefixed with get_ and put_. This is purely notational and is generated by the MIDL compiler. COM translates the properties to these methods.

In Visual Basic, the function declarations are:

```
Public Property Let simpleProperty1(ByVal RHS As Variant)
Public Property Get simpleProperty1() As Variant
```

Visual Basic supports the notion of properties by adding the Property attribute to the front of the method declaration. The Let property keyword is equivalent to an IDL put. The Get property keyword is equivalent to an IDL get. Visual Basic has one more property keyword, Set, which is similar to Let, except that the parameter of the function does not have a ByVal.

In Visual J++, the function declarations are:

```
public Variant getSimpleProperty1();
public void setSimpleProperty1(Variant pVal);
```

The key to making properties work in Visual J++ is to add the *get* and *set* prefixes to the IDL method names. Incidentally, this is also part of the Java Beans specification. However, if the resulting IDL is inspected, something very interesting occurs:

```
[id(0x0000006c)]void setSimpleProperty1([in, out] VARIANT* Parameter0);
[id(0x0000006d)] VARIANT getSimpleProperty1();
[id(0x0000006e), propget] VARIANT simpleProperty1();
[id(0x0000006e), propput] void simpleProperty1([in] VARIANT rhs);
```

The Visual J++ compiler creates two IDL declarations. The first (IDs 6C and 6D) treats each of the functions, which are properties, as functions. The second (ID 6E) treats the functions as properties by adding the propget and propput attributes.

Putting It in Perspective

This chapter introduced COM interfaces. You've seen how they are designed and programmed in various languages. Throughout the entire process, you've seen IDL equivalents. It should be apparent that the simplest way of writing interfaces is to write them in IDL—using any other language is not as good, because each language adds extra pieces of information. Visual C++ adds the least amount of extra information, Visual Basic some, and Visual J++ adds so much extra information that using Visual J++ as a COM interface-definition tool is not a good idea. We look next at implementing the various interfaces using the different languages.

Chapter 9

Implementing COM Interfaces

In this chapter, the interfaces designed by the architectural team are implemented, and those implementations are then consumed in other implementations. Combining an implementation with an interface results in a component. We first look at an example set of interfaces that represents the typical work of a Windows DNA application and consider why the interfaces are designed the way they are.

Then we look at how to best implement the interfaces using Unified Modeling Language (UML). UML was not used in the Component Object Model (COM) development phase, but it is partially used in the implementation phase. The components are implemented using the three different programming languages (Visual Basic, Visual C++, and Visual J++). The focus is on how to implement them most efficiently.

The last aspect of the implementation is to consider how to consume the interfaces. This is important because the application architecture has layers. Again, the consumption is illustrated using the three programming languages. While scripting is not specifically discussed, scripting notes are included throughout the chapter.

Understanding the Dynamics of Implementing Components

When developing a Windows DNA application, there are two basic operations: gathering data and then operating on the gathered data. This may seem like a simple approach, but sometimes the data is not gathered properly, and sometimes the operations are complicated. If things are not done properly, then errors or bugs result.

To minimize the number of bugs, you can test the application. However, use debugging to ensure that the component is stable, not to excuse sloppy code-writing practices, as even good testing can never catch all the bugs introduced by sloppy programming. Debugging is a secondary process, and it can be time-consuming, but if the program is properly designed and implemented, that secondary process can be minimized.

One programming technique that can be used to improve code quality is a data-set verification operation. This is implemented at the object level in property-setting operations, as follows:

```
Private mvarexampleProperty As Long 'local copy
Public Property Let exampleProperty(ByVal vData As Long)
If vData < 0 Then
    mvarexampleProperty = vData
```

```
End If
End Property
```

The first step in this property-setting function is to make sure that the data member contains a valid value by using the if statement. If the value is valid, the vData parameter value is copied to the local data member.

The purpose of having functions that mask property assignments is to check their value. This is a good programming practice. Even in object-oriented programming textbooks, it is recommended that value checking be used, both to ensure that the data structure is valid and to give the developer the flexibility to change the underlying data structure.

However, practice shows that this does not work. In reality, changing the data structure within the object requires changes in the manipulation of the functions that interact with the objects, because components do not live in isolation—they use each other's data. Only if the component is very large and contains a lot of functionality might the good object-oriented programming technique be the appropriate choice.

Separating Data Gathering, Data Operations, and Data Checking

A better way of managing the implementation is to consider the three basic operations—data gathering, data operations, and data checking—as three separate objects. The objects can then be dynamically bound together to perform the operation. An advantage of this approach is that it increases the granularity, which means that it is possible to gradually shift the architecture to reflect new resource technologies or operations. As previous chapters taught, we want fine granularity so that the pieces of the architecture can shift individually.

The data abstraction pattern complements this approach. This pattern solves the problem of the changing data access and data resources. For example, data is stored in a database, which may be an object-oriented database or a relational database. Regardless of the database technology used, you want to store the same data, such as an address. However, the problem is that when embedding the data access in a set of objects, you can never know how the access works. ODBC (Open Database Connectivity), ADO (Active Data Objects), and OLE DB (Object Linking and Embedding Database) all work differently. Typically, library developers attempt to write abstraction layers that provide a neutral format, which is a good idea, but it requires constant tuning. The data abstraction pattern addresses this problem by dividing the problem into two pieces, only one of which is tweaked. The data abstraction pattern uses data processing objects and neutral data format structures.

This pattern has been extended to include data verification, because data consistency often depends on the context. A related problem arose in the conference registration system—when the data abstraction objects were filled out, they were sometimes required to have an address and sometimes not. If the address verification routines were bound directly to the data abstraction, a special context selection was needed, and this added complexity.

When the three operations are separated into their individual objects, a typical consumer scenario is this:

1. The three objects are created.
2. The data abstraction structures are filled out.
3. An operation routine is executed.
4. The operation routine creates a verification object.
5. The verification object is applied to the data set.
6. If the verification is okay, then the operation is executed.
7. (Optional; done for more effective debugging) After the operation finishes executing, another verification object may be applied to ensure that the state that was modified is correct.

The advantages of this separation are:

- The testing team can use external data-verification objects to test the correctness of the individual operations.
- The data abstraction makes it possible to move data from operation to operation without needing to reassign or copy data.
- The data abstractions make it possible to save state to a stream, which can then be used in a distributed processing scenario.
- The operation objects can be designed individually and only concern themselves with processing data.

An Example Set of Interfaces

Returning to the conference registration example, the next step is to define the objects needed to manipulate a user. I am not going to show the database code, because that is left to the database chapters (Chapters 15 to 17). The focus here is on implementing the various interfaces in the different languages. There are three sets of interfaces that will be defined in an Interface Definition Language (IDL) base-type library:

- ISimpleData represents a simple data set.
- ISimpleOperations represents the operations on the ISimpleData COM class.
- IVerification represents the state verification of ISimpleData COM class.

For ISimpleData, the COM interface is defined using this IDL:

```
interface ISimpleData : IDispatch
{
[propget, id(1)] HRESULT username([out, retval] BSTR *pVal);
[propput, id(1)] HRESULT username([in] BSTR newVal);
[propget, id(2)] HRESULT password([out, retval] BSTR *pVal);
[propput, id(2)] HRESULT password([in] BSTR newVal);
[propget, id(3)] HRESULT userId([out, retval] long *pVal);
[propput, id(3)] HRESULT userId([in] long newVal);
};
```

This interface is a data object, and there should be no methods in this object. The ISimpleOperations interface is defined as:

```
interface ISimpleOperations : IDispatch
{
[id(1)] HRESULT addUser([out,retval]long *userId);
[id(2)] HRESULT deleteUser();
[id(3)] HRESULT findUser([in]long userId, [out, retval]BOOL *didFind);
[propget, id(4)] HRESULT simpleData([out, retval] IDispatch* *pVal);
[propput, id(4)] HRESULT simpleData([in] IDispatch* newVal);
};
```

This interface has three methods (addUser, deleteUser, findUser) and a property (simpleData). The methods operate on the ISimpleData COM class, which is the simpleData property. As shown by the IDL, the simpleData property is read and write (propput and propget). This is necessary because the dataset could be used in another operations class. Passing the ISimpleData interface pointer to the various classes is more efficient than moving the parameters.

The addUser method adds a user based on the data in the simpleData property. If everything is okay, the userId is returned as the return value. Why return the userId? For the sake of simplicity; extracting the userId from the structure is easy to do, but it involves an extra programming step.

The findUser method is different from addUser in that the search criterion (userId) is passed as a parameter and not as part of the simpleData property. Again, this is done for the sake of simplicity and ease of use. If something is found, a BOOL TRUE is returned; otherwise, a BOOL FALSE is returned.

The last method, deleteUser, deletes the user as specified by the simpleData property. It is important to understand that the deleteUser method not only deletes the ISimpleData interface pointer, but also removes the user from the database. You may notice that this method does not have userId as a parameter. This is because it is assumed that the user you are about to delete is already found. If, however, you want both options, then make the deleteUser method have an optional parameter. If you want to know how to define this optional parameter, review the IDL attributes for parameters in Chapter 8.

The IVerification interface is as follows:

```
interface IVerification : IDispatch
{
[id(1)] HRESULT doVerification(IDispatch *pDisp);
[propget, id(2)] HRESULT isOk([out, retval] BOOL *pVal);
[propget, id(3)] HRESULT context([out, retval] long *pVal);
[propput, id(3)] HRESULT context([in] long newVal);
};
```

The interface has one method, doVerification. This method expects as a parameter the object on which the verification will be performed. In this case, that object is an implementation of ISimpleData. The property isOk is used to check on how the verification performed. If the return value is TRUE, then all is okay. The context property is an additional property that defines the context of the verification. It indicates which verification routines should be activated. This property is optional and is added for demonstration purposes. What you might want to add are properties and methods that extract the various errors when isOk returns FALSE.

Extending the Interfaces with Multiple Data and Operation Classes

The interfaces here are really simple. In your scenarios, you are likely to have multiple data, operations, and verification objects. What I want to show here is what a simple scenario looks like so as to give you a general rule of thumb.

Data objects can have references to other data objects and a parent-child relationship with multiple COM objects. A data object never contains code, reference verification, or operations objects. Data objects should be simple and represent the data of your system.

An operations object can reference different data objects. However, in the context of a method call, only one verification object should be referenced when the method is called. The verification object is created dynamically and all of the required information should be passed to it. A typical verification object implementation does not reference an operations object or internally store a data object.

Registering the Type Library

The IDL that we defined can be compiled into a type library. However, if we were to use the interfaces in a production COM setting, they would not work because the interfaces defined in the IDL are not yet registered with the registry. To do that, you need to register the type library.

Registering a type library is not like registering an executable or DLL (Dynamic Link Library) because the registration routines are embedded in the executable or the DLL. The way to register a type library is to use the Win32 API (application programming interface) function LoadTypeLibEx. There is a little utility that can be used on the command line to register a type library with the LoadTypeLibEx function. You can find this utility in the book's source code in the directory RegInterface.

Implementing the Interfaces Using Visual Basic

Our next step is to implement the previously defined interfaces. We will use Visual Basic as our first programming language. To do this, start Visual Basic, create an ActiveX DLL project, and then reference the type library.

You can reference a type library by selecting the Project -> References menu item. Then search the list for COMPONENTLib 1.0 Type Library. This library name is given to the type library in the IDL file. Select it and click OK. After the type library is referenced, it is possible to view it in the object browser, as shown in Figure 9–1.

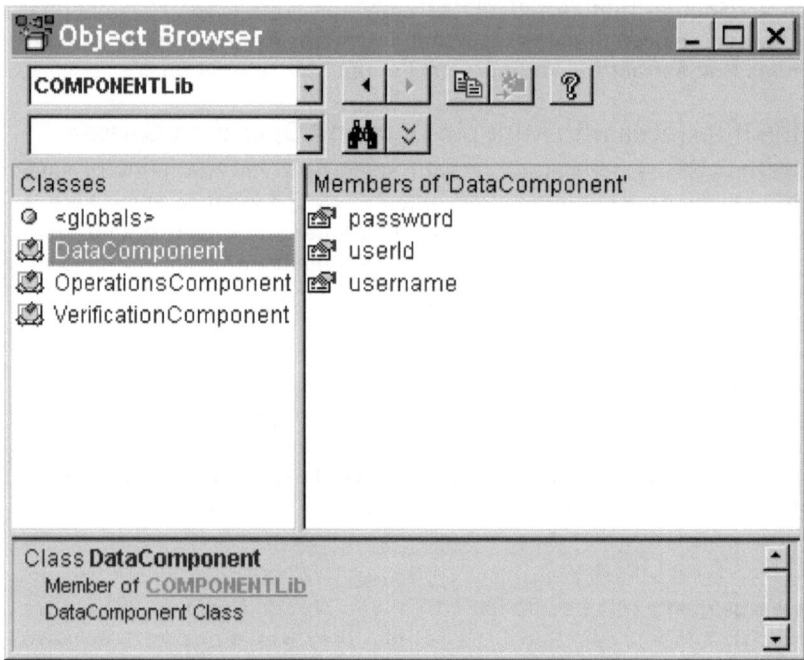

Figure 9–1: Object Browser showing the component definition

Next, create a new class object and give it a name, such as clsImplData. We are going to implement the ISimpleData data COM interface.

To implement a COM interface, use the Visual Basic keyword implements. The implements keyword works in conjunction with any COM-type library that is referenced in the project. In the Visual Basic class, add the following line to the top of class file:

```
Implements DataComponent
```

This line instructs the Visual Basic compiler to implement the DataComponent or ISimpleData interface. The name DataComponent is the coclass defined in the IDL file. If you attempt to compile right now, errors will occur because the ISimpleData properties are not implemented. The implementation is as follows:

```
Private myPassword As String
Private myUserId As Long
Private myUsername As String
Private Property Let DataComponent_password(ByVal RHS As String)
myPassword = RHS
End Property
Private Property Get DataComponent_password() As String
DataComponent_password = RHS
End Property
Private Property Let DataComponent_userId(ByVal RHS As Long)
myUserId = RHS
End Property
Private Property Get DataComponent_userId() As Long
DataComponent_userId = myUserId
End Property
Private Property Let DataComponent_username(ByVal RHS As String)
myUsername = RHS
End Property
Private Property Get DataComponent_username() As String
DataComponent_username = myUsername
End Property
```

There are three private variables, myPassword, myUsername, and myUserId. They will store the values of the properties. The property implementations do nothing but transfer the parameters to the private variables and vice versa.

THE CATCH

It seems that the implementation should work properly, but compile it and look at what it generates in the IDL:

```
coclass clsImplData {
[default] interface _clsImplData;
interface ISimpleData;
};
```

The IDL says that the default IDispatch interface is _clsImplData. This is not good, because that interface does not contain any of the properties of ISimpleData, which means that any client that uses automation (late binding) cannot access the properties and methods.

One technique to solve this problem is to add a member function that does an interface casting. The example method is as follows:

```
Public Function getOther() As DataComponent
Set getOther = Me
End Function
```

What this does is force a QueryInterface call to retrieve the DataComponent interface. This interface can then be used to call the various properties and methods using the IDispatch method. This technique only works in some programming languages. At the time of this writing, it does not work with the Windows Scripting host, but it does work with Visual Basic for Applications.

If, however, you need to access the properties regardless of the programming language, then you need to add Visual Basic properties that do the same as the ISimpleData environment. This also applies for methods. For example, consider the following ISimpleData properties:

```
Private Property Let DataComponent_userId(ByVal RHS As Long)
myUserId = RHS
End Property
Private Property Get DataComponent_userId() As Long
DataComponent_userId = myUserId
End Property
```

To expose these methods as properties, the following code needs to be added to the clsImplData file:

```
Public Property Let userId(ByVal RHS As Long)
myUserId = RHS
End Property
Public Property Get userId() As Long
DataComponent_userId = myUserId
End Property
```

This solves the problem because the methods are exposed as part of the _clsImplData interface, and this is the interface that IDispatch will be routed on. This is extra work, and you might question the need for writing an IDL file. However, when it comes to larger-scale applications, doing everything with VB is asking for problems. If the COM libraries are not managed correctly just once, everyone will have to recompile everything. IDL files are more foolproof.

Implementing the Interfaces Using Visual J++

To implement the interfaces using Visual J++, you need to create an ActiveX DLL project. This creates a project with a class that needs to be renamed to SimpleImplementation.java. As in Visual Basic, the COMPONENTLib type library needs to be referenced. The difference in Visual J++ is that a series of stubs and wrappers is generated. To do this, select Project —< Add COM Wrapper from the menus. From the list, select COMPONENTLib 1.0 Type Lib. The stubs are generated and added to your project as a subfolder with the name of the COM component given to the folder, as shown in Figure 9–2.

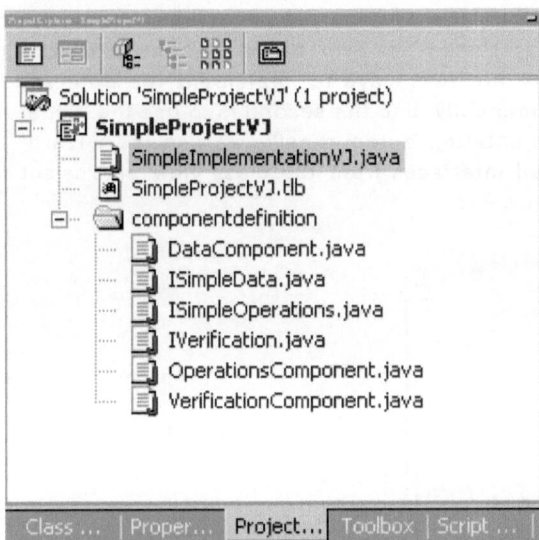

Figure 9–2: Visual J++ project showing added generated stubs

In the componentdefinition stubs directory, there are six Java class files. When Visual J++ creates the COM stubs, it creates both the coclass stub and the COM interface stubs. There is DataComponent, the coclass-based class, and ISimpleData, the interface-based interface. Which one you use depends on the scenario. If you are implementing a COM interface, then the Java class file will inherit from the ISimpleData Java interface. If you are writing a Java class that will be consuming a COM object, then you declare a Java class and instantiate it. It is possible to typecast the instantiated class to a specific interface.

Because we are writing an implementation, the SimpleImplementationVJ class should be implemented as follows:

```
import com.ms.com.*;
import componentdefinition.ISimpleData;
public class SimpleImplementationVJ implements IUnknown,
componentdefinition.ISimpleData
{
...
}
```

When implementing COM interfaces, the base COM classes need to be imported from the Java based packages com.ms.*. They provide the COM framework that you will use in the implementation. The other interface that needs to be imported is componentdefinition.ISimpleData. This is the interface that we want to implement.

From looking at the declaration of the SimpleImplementationVJ class, the IUnknown and ISimpleData COM interfaces need to be implemented by the SimpleImplementationVJ class. There are two ways to implement the different methods. The first is to write them manually, and the second is to use the Visual J++ wizard that creates the implementation automatically. To use the wizard, right-click the selected implemented interfaces from the class view and select Add Method Stubs, as shown in Figure 9–3.

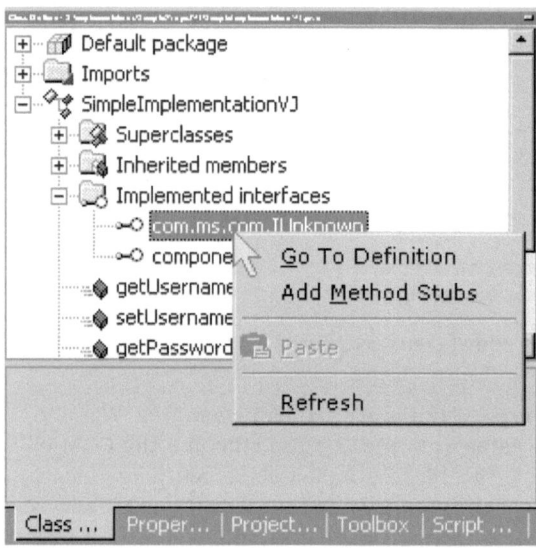

Figure 9–3: Visual J++ context menu for adding empty methods

After the methods are added, the class is ready to be compiled. The methods for IUnknown are not added to the implementation of the Java class because when the Java class file is compiled, the Java run-time provides a default IUnknown implementation. The Java run-time provides default implementations of IUnknown and IDispatch.

HOW SCRIPTING HOSTS ARE SUPPORTED

The class SimpleImplementationVJ supports both scripting and custom-interface consumers. To understand how, let's look at the generated IDL:

```
dispinterface SimpleImplementationVJ_Dispatch {
methods:
[id(0x00000066), helpstring("setUserId")]
void setUserId([in] long Parameter0);
[id(0x00000067), helpstring("getPassword")]
BSTR getPassword();
```

Visual J++ generates a series of IDL method and property declarations that implements the interface for IDispatch-based consumers. But let's consider the case of a Visual C++ type consumer—it is possible using Visual C++ to QueryInterface for the ISimpleData interface. It might seem that Visual J++ solves the problem of supporting both scripting consumers and custom-interface consumers, but if two implemented interfaces have the same method, then a conflict in the IDL occurs.

Implementing the Interfaces Using Visual C++

To implement the interfaces in Visual C++, create an ATL (Active Template Library) DLL project called SimpleProjectVC. Then add an ATL object of the type Simple Object to the project. Name the object ImplData. In the attributes, accept all of the default settings by clicking OK.

The next step is to compile the project. This is necessary, because for the next step to work, the type library needs to be generated.

Then select the CImplData class and right-click. A context menu appears, as shown in Figure 9–4.

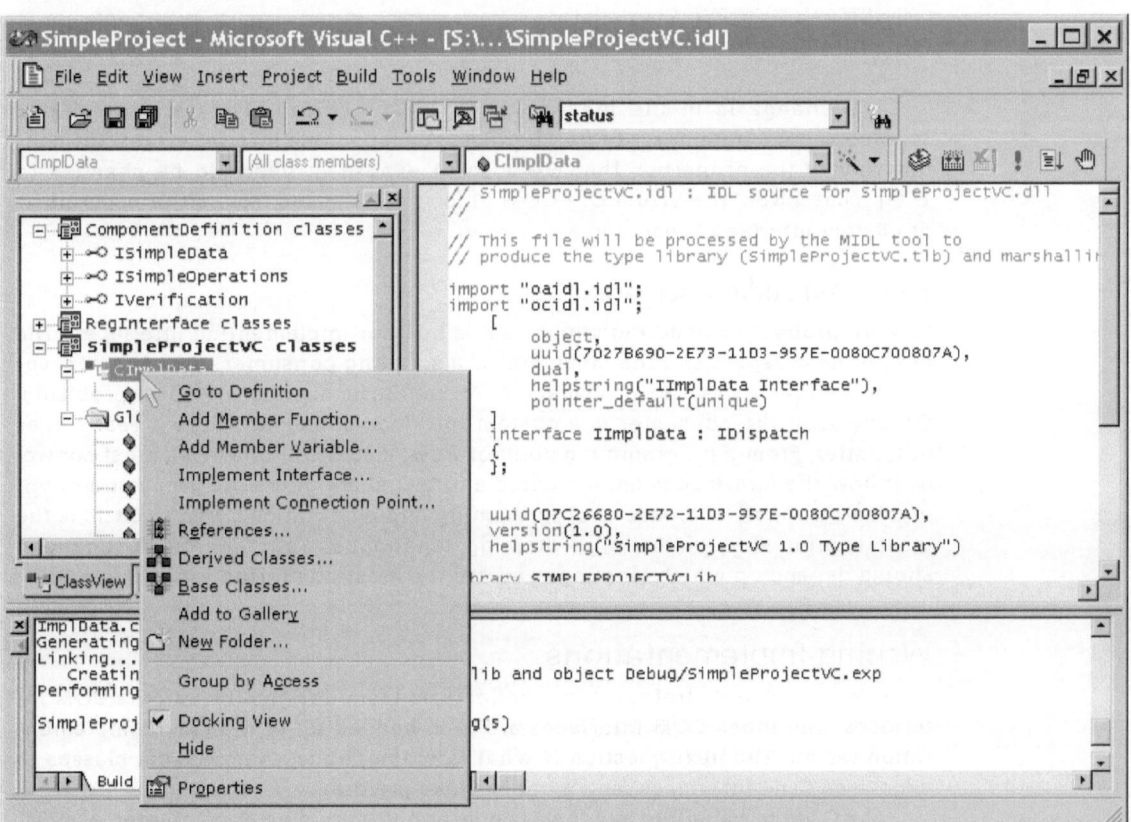

Figure 9–4: Context menu used to implement the ISimpleData interface

Select Implement Interface from the menu. A dialog box appears and states that there are no interfaces to implement. Click the Add TypeLib button. Another dialog box appears that contains a list box of all registered components. Search for COMPONENTLib 1.0 Type Library. Select it and click OK. Now the original dialog box has three interfaces available: ISimpleData, ISimpleOperations, and IVerification.

Select ISimpleData and click OK. What this does is activate a code generator that modifies the CImplData class that implements ISimpleData. Visual C++ uses a tool called the COM compiler to help implement the interface. The COM Compiler is a utility that generates a COM stub that is easier to use in the Visual C++ environment than raw COM is to use. The other step is the generation of the methods that need to be implemented from the ISimpleData interface. The one change that needs to be made is the changing of the IDispatch mapping to the following:

```
BEGIN_COM_MAP(CImplData)
COM_INTERFACE_ENTRY(IImplData)
//DEL    COM_INTERFACE_ENTRY(IDispatch)
COM_INTERFACE_ENTRY2(IDispatch, ISimpleData)
COM_INTERFACE_ENTRY(ISimpleData)
END_COM_MAP()
```

The change is in the macro COM_INTERFACE_ENTRY2. The code generator sets the second parameter to be IImplData. Because this interface does not contain any of the properties that we wish to expose, it needs to be changed to ISimpleData. Now the Visual C++ COM object can be used from either a scripting or custom interface consumer.

Some Concluding Remarks

You are probably wondering which tool is best for implementing interfaces. The answer is, it depends. If the consumer is a scripting consumer, then the best solution is either Visual C++ or Visual J++—Visual Basic has the IDispatch problems. Otherwise, if the consumer is a custom-interface consumer, then it really does not matter. From a programming point of view, Visual C++ offers the most control over how the interface is implemented and Visual J++ offers the greatest amount of wizard support and ease of programming implementations. Visual Basic is the least complicated of the programming languages. Your choice of language should depend on which language you are the most comfortable with.

Writing Implementations

In our development strategy, the architectural team designs the various COM interfaces, and those COM interfaces are then handed off to individual implementation teams. The next question is what to make public, that is, what classes to expose as COM interfaces, and what to make private.

The COM purist might say that all operations should be implemented as COM interfaces and that there is no reason to use anything other than COM interfaces. However, consider the situation of writing a COM component with Visual C++. In

C++, templates can be used to solve some programming problems very elegantly. Unfortunately, COM does not understand the concept of a template, so when writing a pure COM component, it is not possible to use templates. This means that you are making your C++ programming life more complicated if you only use pure COM interfaces.

Because the architectural team decides which interfaces are used publicly, it does not matter whether the implementation uses pure COM interfaces or some language-specific extensions for the private classes. The private interfaces are not exposed, and if the private interfaces change there are no ramifications to the other COM interfaces.

But in the future, you might want to expose some of the private functionality as a public interface. If this is likely, then implementing the classes as COM interfaces initially would give you the experience necessary to determine the efficiency and feasibility of these COM interfaces.

When deciding where to use COM interfaces, make sure that you do not go "COM crazy" and make everything a COM interface. Remember that invoking the overhead of COM is still slower than using native programming code.

Using UML

There is quite a bit of programming code involved when writing the implementations of COM interfaces, and you need to manage this code and do some code planning and organizing. While Visual Studio does an okay job of this, it can be improved on. One alternative is to use a UML tool to build the class diagram.

In previous chapters, we used UML to define our use cases and sequence and collaboration diagrams. Now we use the UML tool to create a set of class diagrams. Be forewarned though. At this stage, people often use UML to develop the entire application, which is easy to do because UML tools generate code automatically. And some people like to draw lots of diagrams, which is really easy to do with UML. Converting these UML class diagrams directly into programming code leads to a bloated application.

UML should be used to make your implementation comprehensible. Using UML lets you capture the essence of the design in a diagram. UML is used to lay out the architecture of the individual components.

There are several UML tools that are usable in conjunction with Visual Studio. If you intend on programming with Visual Basic, then the Visual Studio application Visual Modeler may be okay. Visual Modeler does not support use cases, collaboration, or sequence diagrams. If you intend on writing components using Visual C++, then Visual Case from Rogue Wave or Rational Rose may be the best solution. For good well-rounded multitool capabilities, Rational Rose or MicroGold may be the best solution. Look for these attributes in a UML tool:

- UML 1.2 (including things like use cases, collaboration, and sequence diagrams)
- Roundtrip engineering, which means that when the programmer creates classes in the UML tool or the development tool, the changes are reflected in the UML tool and the development tool

- Version control integration, which makes it easier to control changes
- Team development, which makes it possible to work in multiuser teams
- Documentation generation, which makes it possible to automatically generate documentation based on the description given. Integration with the Web or with a word processor is a good bonus.

Writing Components Using UML

When writing the implementation of the application, you need to implement the COM interfaces defined by the architectural team, and you should not use the UML tool to do this. The COM support currently provided with UML tools is poor, at best. The COM interfaces are easily implemented without using the UML tool, which will also give you a good footing in your component implementation.

To create the base implementations for all COM interfaces, use the wizards provided by the programming tools.

As an aside, the naming convention that I like to use when implementing COM interfaces is to drop the leading I and add Impl to the end of the interface name. The Impl at the end indicates that it is an implementation of the interface. For example, if the COM interface is called ISimpleData, then I call the COM implementation component SimpleDataImpl.

After the base COM implementations are defined, the project is converted to a UML project using the reverse engineering wizard available with most UML tools. A cleaned up example is shown in Figure 9–5.

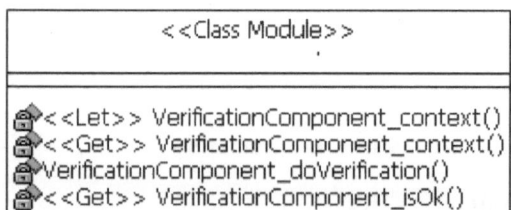

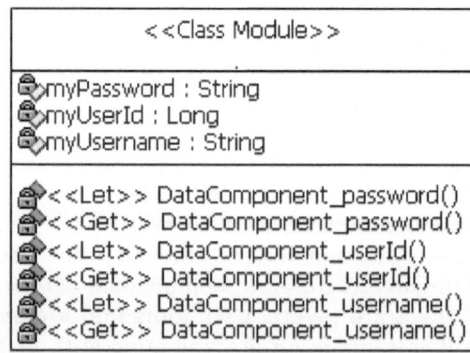

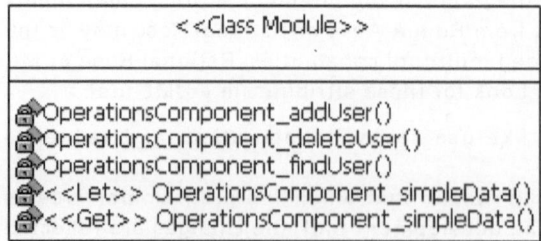

Figure 9–5: Initial class structure after reverse engineering was run

There are three classes that represent the individual implementation classes. In UML, a box represents a class, but the term class is very generic. You can identify different types of classes in UML with stereotypes. A stereotype is a meta-classification of an element. All UML tools provide some default stereotypes, and it is possible to define your own. In Figure 9–5, the << text >> tag at the top of the class identifies the stereotype.

The diagram is incomplete because the various classes implement interfaces. With UML it is possible to define an interface as a different stereotype of the class, but the UML tools cannot actually create the COM interfaces. You need to add them manually. An example of adding the DataComponent/ISimpleData interface is shown in Figure 9–6.

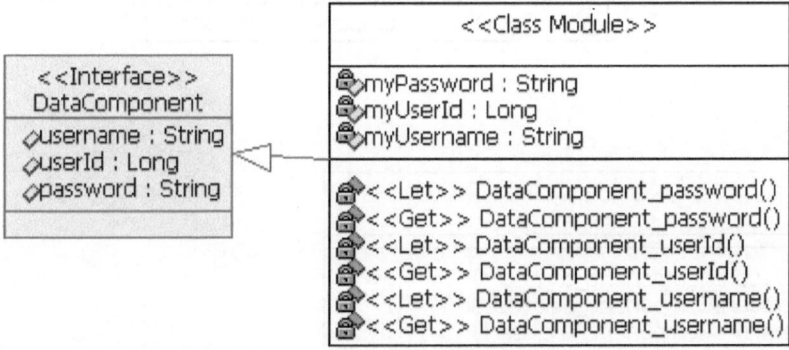

Figure 9–6: Interface definition and generalization of it in clsDataImpl

In Figure 9–6, the DataComponent interface and the clsDataImpl class have an arrow connecting them. The arrow is called a generalization. A generalization can indicate an inheritance or an implementation. Because the one class is an interface and the other is an implementation, the generalization is called an implementation generalization. The implementation generalization is the only type of generalization understood by Visual Basic and COM. Visual C++ and Visual J++ understand inheritance generalizations, too.

The operations implementation reference various data implementations. However, when the project was reverse engineered, it did not pick up those connections because the various implementations are empty and do not contain any significant information. The first association that we need to create is the association between clsDataImpl and clsOperateImpl. The clsOperationImpl implementation exposes the simpleData property, which is from the OperationsComponent/ISimpleOperations::simpleData interface. We need to reference the DataComponent/ISimpleData interface because that is what the property simpleData is referencing.

The UML diagram of these relationships looks like Figure 9–7.

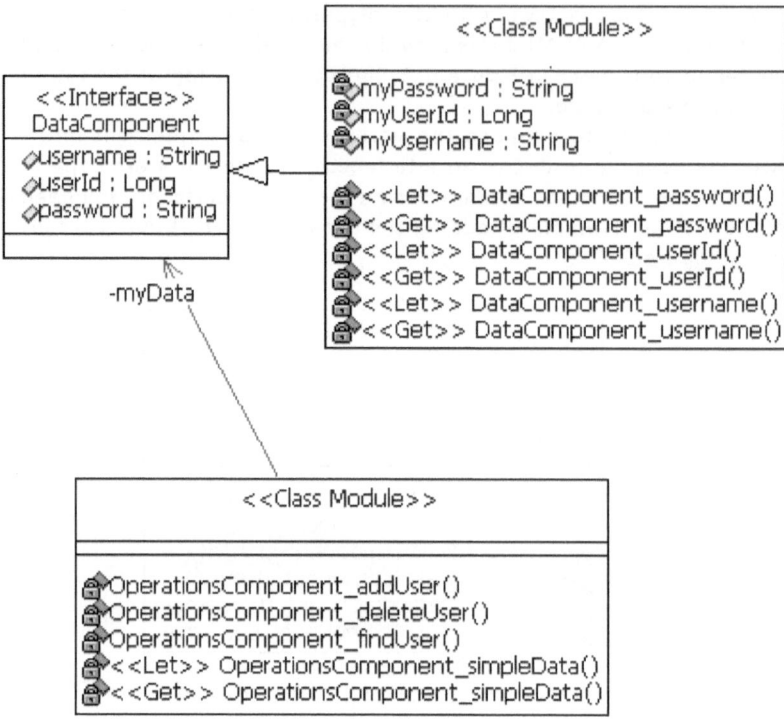

Figure 9–7: UML association between the implementation and interface

The association is between the clsOperateImpl and DataComponent, and it is
called a unidirectional association because navigation is in one direction only;
navigation is the process of being able to move between object references. In
this association, it is possible to move from clsOperateImpl to DataComponent, but
not from DataComponent to clsOperateImpl. A bidirectional association enables
navigation between the two components. In comparison to linked lists, unidirectional associations are like single-linked lists and bidirectional associations are
like double-linked lists. In the example association, there is a private reference
to the interface within the clsOperateImpl class called myData. You can tell that it
is a private association from the minus sign in front of the myData variable. If
there were a plus sign, it would be public. A hash mark indicates that the variable is protected, and no mark indicates implementation. Associations are class-
level declarations and are supported by all Visual Studio programming
languages.

   In the implementation of the clsOperateImpl class, the verification object is
instantiated. It is a good practice to create a reference between the interface and
the clsOperateImpl class. In UML-speak, this is called a dependency and is indicated by a dashed arrow, as shown in Figure 9–8.

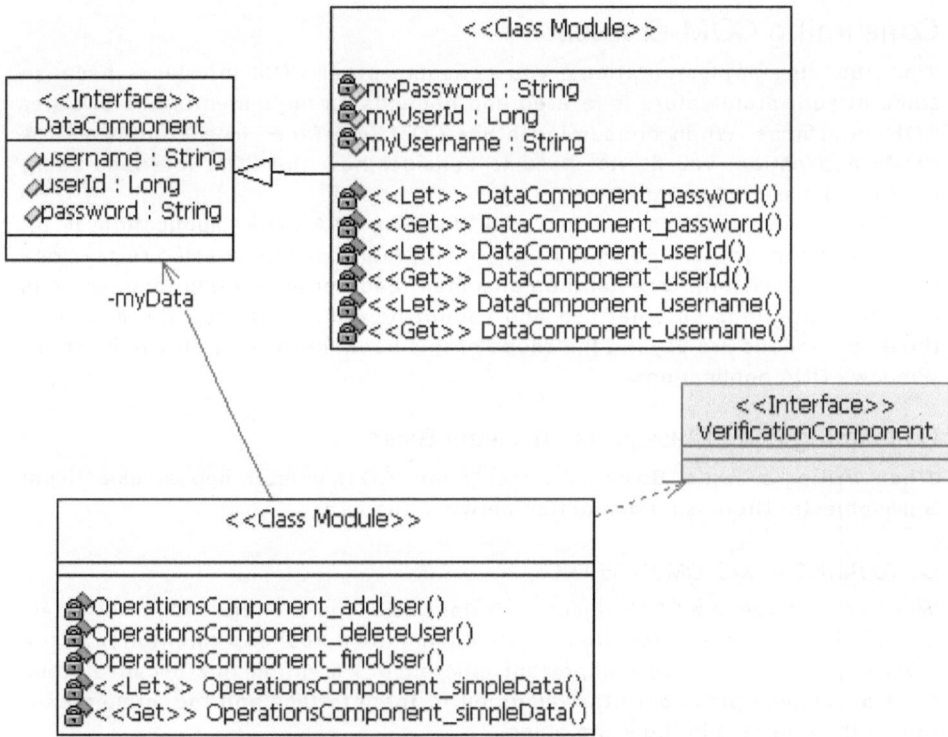

Figure 9–8: UML dependency between the Verification Component and
clsImpl Operate

   The dependency is necessary because when code is generated it will cause
the appropriate COM interface references or include statements to be inserted.
From this point on, the UML diagram can be code-generated, and you can implement your COM component.

   This is the basic UML required to be productive. Each UML tool has its own
capabilities. For example, Rational Rose has the capability to create properties
from associations. This is a good feature, but remember that the purpose of
UML is to provide an overall architectural layout of the COM component, so you
want good support for basic features. You also want extremely good code-gen-
eration and reverse-engineering capabilities. Otherwise your code may become
an unsightly mess.

When doing development work as a team, it may be desirable to package the various UML diagrams into one bigger UML team diagram. UML tools enable you to do this by defining components. Components make it possible to reference implementations that contain the details of how they are implemented.

Consuming COM Classes

When building implementations, you consume other COM interfaces because some of your architecture is layered and depends on implementations of other COM interfaces. When consuming other COM interfaces in a Windows DNA COM+ application, you do not need to consider how the COM interface being consumed was implemented.

This is only true in the context of a Windows DNA COM+ application. If, on the other hand, you are doing multithreading, there may be specific restrictions on how the COM interface can be consumed. Each programming language has its own restrictions on what can and cannot be done. However, the details of those restrictions are beyond the scope of this book, because it only talks about Windows DNA applications.

Consuming COM Classes Using Visual Basic

When writing a Visual Basic implementation, COM objects appear like Visual Basic objects. There is no distinction between the two.

CONSUMING A CUSTOM INTERFACE

When you reference a COM object in Visual Basic, you are referencing the interface of the COM object. You are not referencing the actual implementation of the COM object. This is a very important difference. I mention this because many COM developers place both the definition of the interface and the implementation of the interface in the same object.

To better understand this distinction, let's consider the example of using the verification object. Whenever an operation method is called, the verification object needs to be instantiated and called. The verification object ensures that all of the parameters are correct. The example source code of the operation method is as follows:

```
Private Function OperationsComponent_addUser() As Long
Dim tempVerification As VerificationComponent

Set tempVerification = New clsVerifyImpl
tempVerification.context = 1
tempVerification.doVerification (myData)

If tempVerification.isOk = False Then
    'Error cannot proceed
Else
    ' Do the operations that need to be done
```

```
End If
Set tempVerification = Nothing
End Function
```

The object tempVerification is declared as a VerificationComponent object using the Dim statement. This is an example of declaring an interface that is not defined with any object implementation. Because we want to associate a specific implementation with the variable, there cannot be a new keyword in the variable declaration.

To assign a specific COM implementation to the interface, the next statement, New clsVerifyImpl, instantiates the object and does a QueryInterface for the VerificationComponent interface. If clsVerifyImpl did not implement the VerificationComponent interface, clsVerifyImpl would still be instantiated, but it would be destroyed when the QueryInterface fails. As a result, the variable tempVerification needs to be set to nothing.

After the tempVerification object is instantiated, the methods of VerificationComponent can be called. The first step in the verification process is to set the context, which is the value 1. Then the doVerification method is called. At this point the implementation of VerificationComponent inspects the state of the object and ensures that everything is okay. To determine if everything went well, the property isOk is checked. If this is false, an error occurred and the operation cannot continue. A value of true allows the operation to continue.

CONSUMING IDISPATCH INTERFACES

The other way of instantiating the object is to use CreateObject. An example of using it instead of the New function is this:

```
Set tempVerification = CreateObject( "SimpleImplementationVB.clsImplVerify")
```

CreateObject does the exact same thing as New, except that it explicitly uses COM. In the past, this technique was recommended because using New bypassed specific COM routines. Because tempVerification is still a specific interface, a QueryInterface for the interface is still performed.

To use the IDispatch interface, the declaration of the tempVerification object needs to be as follows:

```
Dim tempVerification as Object
```

In this case, the object is of the type Object, which is an IDispatch object. Now, if the same method calls are executed, they are routed using the IDispatch interface.

WORKING WITH CUSTOM AND IDISPATCH INTERFACES

If the tempVerification object were left as an Object data type, all calls would result in an error. This is because of the problem we discussed earlier—Visual Basic objects derive their IDispatch interface from the class methods and properties that are declared public. However, there is a technique in Visual Basic for using the IDispatch interface of the interface you want. Consider the following example:

```
Dim genericObject As Object
Dim typeVerification As VerificationComponent
Dim usableObject As Object

Set genericObject = CreateObject("SimpleImplementationVB.clsVerifyImpl")
Set typeVerification = genericObject
Set usableObject = typeVerification
usableObject.context = 1
```

Look at the line where genericObject is assigned after the object is instantiated using CreateObject. Because genericObject is of the type Object, the IDispatch interface it contains is from clsVerifyImpl. The next step is to do a QI for the VerificationComponent interface using the typeVerification assignment. Now typeVerification contains a reference to the VerificationComponent interface. When the usableObject is assigned, the IDispatch interface is QI'd for. But this time, because the last custom interface is VerificationComponent, the IDispatch interface is from that interface. Now when the usableObject.context property is assigned, it will work.

It may seem that all of this typecasting, which is being converted to a Query-Interface by Visual Basic, is a bit too complicated. But when dealing with COM classes that implement multiple interfaces, you need to extract specific interfaces. This technique makes it possible to implement polymorphism.

Consuming COM Classes Using Visual J++

The simplest and least complicated language to use for consuming COM interfaces is Visual J++. To consume a COM interface, it is only necessary to generate the various COM wrappers of the components COMPONENTLib, and in our case, the Visual Basic library SIMPLEIMPLEMENTATIONVB. The following source code is a Visual J++ version of the same verification code that was presented in the Visual Basic section:

```
import componentdefinition.*;
import simpleimplementationvb.*;

...

IVerification tVerification;

tVerification = new clsImplVerify();
tVerification.doVerification( objData);
tVerification.setContext( 1);
if( tVerification.getIsOk() != 0) {
    // Do nothing
} else {
    // Do some error handling
}
}
```

The first step is to declare the IVerification interface object (tVerification). To assign a COM object instance, the clsImplVerify object is instantiated. But because it is being assigned to tVerification, a typecast is performed. This is standard Java, but the added twist is that the Microsoft Java VM (Virtual Machine) realizes that this is a COM interface and does a QI for IVerification. From this point on, it is possible to use the tVerification interface instance.

CONSUMING IDISPATCH INTERFACES

One thing that the Visual J++ environment does assume is that all interfaces have type libraries associated with them. When the COM wrapper executes, it searches for the type library, so that it can generate the correct stub. If there is no type library and the calls must be made using IDispatch, then things become a bit ugly. In the Visual J++ packages, there is a class named com.ms.com.Dispatch. This is a class that has many different methods, and by using those methods, it is possible to call an IDispatch-based implementation. It is not necessary to fill out a structure, but it is necessary to call various methods with varying numbers of parameters. This works, but it leads to very messy code. If it does become necessary to use the Dispatch class, create a stub class that encapsulates the functionality. This makes it much more maintainable.

That is all you need to know to consume COM implementations. It is by far the least complicated and least stressful approach.

Consuming COM Classes Using Visual C++

The last programming language that needs to be discussed is Visual C++. Previously, consuming COM implementations with Visual C++ was very ugly and not much fun. It tended to lead to interesting debugging sessions. But with the release of Visual C++ 5.0, matters are simplified by something called the COM compiler.

Using the COM Compiler, it is possible to reference and use a COM class by using a simple notation. The COM compiler support is like a preprocessor that is executed when C++ code is compiled. By specifying a specific type library, the COM classes within it are read. Then a series of C++ classes is generated on the type library information. This is very similar to what Visual J++ does, except it is for Visual C++. The advantage of using the COM compiler is that it blends in fully with C++ and does not resemble raw COM programming code.

An example of using the COM compiler is as follows:

```
#import "file" attributes
#import <file> attributes
```

The use of the import with quotes or brackets follows the same rules as for including a file in C or C++. The file specified must contain some type library information. An example implementation of the verification routines is as follows:

```
COMPONENTLib::IVerificationPtr ptr( "SimpleImplementationVB.clsImplVerify");
ptr->doVerification( ptrData);
if( ptr->GetisOk() == FALSE) {
// Do error handling
```

```
} else {
// Do something
}
```

   In this code example, the COMPONENTLib is a C++ namespace that contains the three interfaces defined previously. The one that is of interest to us is IVerification. However, it is not possible to use the IVerification interface directly; instead, the class definition with a Ptr appended must be used. (More about this later.) Then the ptr object is declared. As part of the constructor, the PROG ID of the implementation that implements IVerification is specified. This one line instantiates the COM object and then QIs for the IVerification interface. The next line, ptr->doVerification, passes in the COM data instance to the routine. The check of the verification is the method call GetisOk(), which is the IDL COM property isOk.

HOW THE COM COMPILER WORKS

The COM compiler is an interesting tool because it does several things. The COM compiler:

   - Automatically manages the reference count of the COM interface
   - Converts COM properties and return values as function return values, as is the case already in Visual Basic and Visual J++
   - Automatically retrieves the correct interface

   The COM compiler does all of these things by using smart pointers and operator overloading in some custom-generated stubs. When a file that contains a #import is compiled, the COM compiler generates two files: a TLH (typelib header) and TLI (typelib implementation). An example source is as follows:

```
#include <comdef.h>
namespace COMPONENTLib {
// Forward references and typedefs
struct /* coclass */ DataComponent;
struct __declspec(uuid("88950010-0915-11d2-9c50-00a0247d759a"))
/* dual interface */ ISimpleData;
struct /* coclass */ OperationsComponent;
struct __declspec(uuid("88950011-0915-11d2-9c50-00a0247d759a"))
/* dual interface */ ISimpleOperations;
struct /* coclass */ VerificationComponent;
struct __declspec(uuid("88950012-0915-11d2-9c50-00a0247d759a"))
/* dual interface */ IVerification;

// Smart pointer typedef declarations
_COM_SMARTPTR_TYPEDEF(ISimpleData, __uuidof(ISimpleData));
_COM_SMARTPTR_TYPEDEF(ISimpleOperations, __uuidof(ISimpleOperations));
_COM_SMARTPTR_TYPEDEF(IVerification, __uuidof(IVerification));

// Type library items
```

```
struct __declspec(uuid("88950003-0915-11d2-9c50-00a0247d759a"))
VerificationComponent;// [ default ] interface IVerification

struct __declspec(uuid("88950012-0915-11d2-9c50-00a0247d759a"))
IVerification : IDispatch
{
__declspec(property(get=GetisOk))
long isOk;
__declspec(property(get=Getcontext,put=Putcontext))
long context;

HRESULT doVerification ( IDispatch * pDisp );
long GetisOk ( );
long Getcontext ( );
void Putcontext ( long pVal );

virtual HRESULT __stdcall raw_doVerification ( IDispatch * pDisp ) = 0;
virtual HRESULT __stdcall get_isOk ( long * pVal ) = 0;
virtual HRESULT __stdcall get_context ( long * pVal ) = 0;
virtual HRESULT __stdcall put_context ( long pVal ) = 0;
};
} // namespace COMPONENTLib
```

There is quite a bit of source code generated, but the COM compiler does things in a specific manner. The first step is a declaration of a C++ namespace. This is identical to the COM IDL library name. Then, within the library name, the various coclass and interface UUIDs are defined. These are required by the COM library calls. Then the various interfaces are declared. All of the interface declarations, except IVerification have been removed for clarity. Within the interface declaration there are two method declarations for doVerification. The first is doVerification and the second is raw_doVerification. When the class declaration is used, the doVerification method is used. When the compiler attempts to map the vtables to the COM interface, raw_doVerification is used. There are two methods so as to generate a user-friendly version of the method. User-friendly means being able to use return values, such as the property GetisOk, instead of passing in a pointer.

Smart pointers are a technique of mimicking garbage collecting using reference counting. The idea is not to have access to the interface pointer, but to have a class that manages the interface pointer on behalf of the user. Consider the following code:

```
template < class managed>
class smrtPtr {
public:
smrtPtr() { }
~smrtPtr() {
```

```
ptr->Release();
}
managed *operator->() {
return ptr;
}
managed *ptr;
};
```

This is an annotated version of a smart pointer to show the important bits. The manager, which is the smrtPtr template, contains a typed interface member. When the object is destructed, the manager does a reference decrement by calling IUnknown::Release. To access the managed ptr without having to use the notation smrtPtr::ptr::method, the -> operator is overloaded. This makes it possible to use the notation smrtPtr->method to get access to the method managed by the smart pointer. Access to the managed method makes it impossible to use methods within the smrtPointer class using the -> operator, but that is okay, because a smart pointer is never allocated using a memory allocation.

When the smart pointer and the stub that the COM compiler generates is combined, it results in an easy-to-use COM object-consumption technique. One thing that the smart pointer class adds is the automatic capability of converting from one interface to another. For example, the following code is legal:

```
SimpleImplementationVB::_clsImplDataPtr
ptrData( "SimpleImplementationVB.clsImplData");
COMPONENTLib::ISimpleDataPtr ptrInterface;

ptrInterface = ptrData;
```

The initial object that is allocated, ptrData, is the interface _clsImplData. What is desired is the ISimpleData interface. It is known that _clsImplData implemented ISimpleData. To retrieve it, ptrInterface is assigned ptrData. The QI for the ISimpleData interface occurs automatically. The QI is embedded in the smart pointer class.

It was mentioned earlier that it is necessary to append the interface name with Ptr. This is because of the following macro:

```
#define _COM_SMARTPTR_TYPEDEF(Interface, IID) \
typedef _COM_SMARTPTR<Interface, &IID> Interface ## Ptr
```

To save time and effort, all generated interfaces in the stub have a typedef interface that embeds the smart pointer.

A Catch with Smart Pointers

When working with smart pointers, there is one instance where they do not work. In the implementation of the property ISimpleOperations::simpleData, an interface pointer must be passed back. When a COM compiler-generated class is assigned to the double pointer, it does not increment the reference count. This needs to be done manually, as in the following source code:

```
STDMETHOD(get_simpleData)(IDispatch * * pVal) {
if (pVal == NULL)
    return E_POINTER;
*pVal = ptrData;
(*pVal)->AddRef();
return S_OK;
}
```

The pVal is assigned to the COM compiler class ptrData. After the assignment is complete, pVal->AddRef needs to be called.

TAKING ADVANTAGE OF THE COM COMPILER SUPPORT CLASSES

The other thing that the COM compiler support gives you is extra classes that manage interface pointers and the non-C++ based types. Although in ATL there are counterparts to these classes, the counterparts are specific to ATL. The classes defined by the COM compiler are not specific to any library and can be reused in straight COM components, if need be. While ATL and MFC are good libraries, they are specific libraries and are not as simple to use as the COM compiler support.

Defining Your Own Smart Pointer—Based Classes

There are interfaces in which the smart pointer is not defined. To define your own smart pointer class using the COM compiler notation, do the following:

```
_COM_SMARTPTR_TYPEDEF(IMyInterface, __uuidof(IMyInterface));
```

This creates a smart pointer class called IMyInterfacePtr, which is managed. But be forewarned: because the COM compiler could not generate a stub, the methods are raw COM methods.

Working with Any Data: _variant_t

Using the COM compiler VARIANT class _variant_t makes development very easy. Because of its simplicity, there is not really much to explain except to show some source code that demonstrates how the variant data type could be used:

```
_variant_t var;
_variant_t var2((long)12);

var = (short)12;
var = "Hello";
```

This may seem very simple, but there is quite a bit of work that occurs in the background. When var is assigned a value of 12, a type has to be declared. The reason for this is that 12 could be an int, a long, or a short. Encapsulated in the class is all of the functionality to ensure that the variant is properly declared and assigned. If however, you are passed a VARIANT and want to convert it to a _variant_t type, then assign it, as in the following example:

```
VARIANT vtText;

VariantInit( &vtText);
V_VT( &vtText) = VT_BSTR;
V_BSTR( &vtText) = SysAllocString( L"12");
testCopy = vtText;
```

Another necessary operation is changing the variant from one type to another. For example, in the preceding source code, the variant type was VT_BSTR. We want to convert the string to a number, because referencing a number is more efficient than referencing a number as a string. To do this, we need only change the types using this method:

```
void ChangeType( VARTYPE vartype, const _variant_t* pSrc = NULL );
```

The first parameter, vartype, is the destination variant type. This is directly analogous to the types introduced with OLE Automation, and examples are VT_BSTR, VT_I4, and so on. The second parameter defines a source used for conversion. This means that if pSrc is not NULL, the contents of pSrc are converted to the type vartype and then copied to the referenced _variant_t object. Anything that is being referenced in the current object is lost. The default is NULL, which means the reference object is converted to the type desired. Finally, you may need to clear the variant using the Clear method.

Working with COM Strings: _bstr_t

The final class that is outlined is one of the most needed classes. This class makes it easy to convert strings from bstr to a wide char or to a normal char. Like the variant, the _bstr_t class wraps most of its conversions within a set of overloaded operators. Typical scenarios are:

```
_bstr_t bstrVar( "Hello");
char *tempHello;

tempHello = bstrVar;
```

This example does nothing but convert a string to a _bstr_t in the constructor, and with the overloaded assignment operator, it is converted back to normal char string.

There is a catch to using this class. Consider this example:

```
void func( BSTR input) {
_bstr_t var( input, true);
char *result;

result = var;
return;
}
```

The reason that the BSTR input parameter is used as the _bstr_t constructor parameter, is because it is easier to convert, as the next few lines show. However, the problem is that the raw bytes are manipulated and the caller of the class creates the BSTR that is passed in. Therefore, the input BSTR has to be copied into another buffer. If this did not occur, then when the _bstr_t variable destructs itself, it will attempt to free the BSTR, and because it was not created by the function, an error will occur.

Handling Errors

In Visual Basic, COM errors are called run-time errors. In Visual J++, COM errors are called exceptions, and you must use them. In Visual C++, COM errors are called exceptions, but using them is optional. In general, programmers do not use exceptions. Java programmers do use exceptions, though, because Java itself enforces the use of them. From this point on, all code samples in this book use exception handling in all languages. Exception handling is useful when properly applied.

COM Errors

Before we look at error handling, though, we must look at COM errors. If you remember the IDL method and property declarations, they all returned HRESULT because COM currently does not support exception handling. Errors are returned using a method return value called the HRESULT.

DECIPHERING THE HRESULT

The HRESULT is defined as a 32-bit integer, and it is laid out as follows:

```
3 3 2 2 2 2 2 2 2 2 2 2 1 1 1 1 1 1 1 1 1 1
1 0 9 8 7 6 5 4 3 2 1 0 9 8 7 6 5 4 3 2 1 0 9 8 7 6 5 4 3 2 1 0
+-+-+-+-+-+-+————————+————————-+
|S|R|C|N|r|    Facility      |          Code      |
+-+-+-+-+-+-+————————+————————-+
```

The most important parts of the HRESULT that concern the developer are the severity, facility, and the code itself. Severity is the S, and it is a single bit that determines the type of message. The message could be either a Success (0) or Failure (1). The facility determines where the message originated. Is it a Windows error message, COM system error message, or a message that is specific to the interface itself? And then, finally, the code is stored in the rest of the bits. By building an HRESULT on these three parts it is possible to define almost any message. When an HRESULT is received, it is important to separate it into its individual parts. This is done in the following example:

```
HRESULT hr;
hr = ptrData->callMethod();
if( SUCCEEDED( hr)) {
printf( "This is not an error, but Facilty %ld, Code %ld\n",
HRESULT_FACILITY( obj.Error()), HRESULT_CODE( obj.Error()));
} else if( FAILED( obj.Error())) {
printf( "This is an error, but Facilty %ld, Code %ld\n",
HRESULT_FACILITY( obj.Error()), HRESULT_CODE( obj.Error()));
}
```

The facility is determined by using the macro HRESULT_FACILITY. It can be one of the following:

```
#define FACILITY_WINDOWS          8
#define FACILITY_STORAGE          3
#define FACILITY_RPC              1
#define FACILITY_SSPI             9
#define FACILITY_WIN32            7
#define FACILITY_CONTROL          10
#define FACILITY_NULL             0
#define FACILITY_INTERNET         12
#define FACILITY_ITF              4
#define FACILITY_DISPATCH         2
#define FACILITY_CERT             11
```

The list is from the header file winerror.h. When a custom facility error message is given, it is of the type FACILITY_ITF. This means that the error is specific to the interface. If this error is given, then it is important for the error receiver to understand that the code is specific to the interface. So, error code 100 from custom interface IInterface1 and error code 100 from custom interface IIInterface2 do not mean the same thing. This is a potential problem, because if a FACILITY_ITF error is propagated up the method tree, the error could be mistaken for another error. Hence an error must be handled locally. To retrieve the error from the HRESULT, the macro HRESULT_CODE is used. An error specific to the facility is returned. Using the macros SUCCEEDED and FAILURE, it is possible to determine whether the error code refers to a success or failure.

The macros FAILURE and SUCCEEDED are used to determine what has occurred.

How to Generate Errors

Generating errors is a tricky process. On the one hand, the simplest way is to generate custom HRESULTs for your framework. This works, but all it does is cause an application to exit, a general protection fault, or, worse, display a dialog box. For simple end-user applications, handling an error is not so complex, but it becomes very complex for distributed applications running thousands of instances. In these scenarios, it is not easy to do any debugging because it is not often possible to reestablish the problem.

The solution that works is to create an error object that works in conjunction with the COM error-handling facility. While it may seem silly to create yet another error object, this approach has proven to be very effective in actual distributed applications. Within a custom error object, it is possible to develop custom tracing facilities and state management. And once the error object is created, it can be reused in various projects.

The interface definition of the custom error-handler COM class is as follows:

```
interface IErrorHandler : IDispatch
{
[id(1)] HRESULT setError(long code, BSTR module, long lineNumber);
[propget, id(2)] HRESULT errorLevel([out, retval] long *pVal);
};
```

The first method is called setError, which generates an error. In a typical implementation, this method writes to the event log or to the trace log. The second and third parameters of the method are file location indicators. Within C++, this can be compiled into the code. In other languages, it needs to be set manually. It is absolutely critical that this information be included—when the code is running, it is possible to pinpoint the error exactly.

THROWING THE OBJECT

Many languages support the notation of throwing objects as errors, so it would make sense to throw the implementation of IErrorHandler. However, because COM does not function in that way, it is not possible. The error object can only be used as an object to record the error.

WRITING TO THE EVENT LOG

Windows 2000 has the capability to log events in something called the event log. Writing to the event log is not very complicated. Writing to the Windows 2000 event log can be better than writing to a file. Consider the situation of an internal network. A server is not performing properly and errors are occurring. Using

Windows 2000, it is possible to retrieve the event log from a central machine. In an Internet scenario, a file might be better.

An example implementation of writing to the event log is as follows:

```
public void setError(int code, String strModule, int lineNumber)
{
EventLog log;

log = new EventLog( "bacchus", null);
log.reportEvent( EventLog.ERROR, lineNumber, 100, strModule);
}
```

Visual J++ has a class that encapsulates the event log functions. In Visual Basic or Visual C++, there are three equivalent Windows API functions (RegisterEventSource, ReportEvent, and DeregisterEventSource).

The basic process of event logging is to first register a source. This is identical to the EventLog constructor, which takes two strings: the name of the server where the event will be logged and the source that is doing the event logging. A source can either be null or it can be a subkey under the HKEY_LOCAL_MACHINE\System\CurrentControlSet\Services\EventLog **Registry key.**

The next step is to report an event. When reporting an event, it is possible to indicate an event with a string, or an event with a string and binary piece of information. An analysis tool for figuring out what went wrong could use the binary information. This is where the state could be stored.

There are four parameters in the reportEvent method. The first parameter indicates what kind of event is being logged. It could be a warning, informational, or, in this case, an error. The second parameter defines the event category. This number is specific to the component generating the event. Using this number, an analysis tool could categorize the various events according to subsystem location. The third parameter defines the event ID, which depends on the source. This could be an internal error code sequence. The fourth parameter is a string, and its content depends on whether there is binary information about the error to store.

Using Error Handling in Visual Basic

An error-handling framework in Visual Basic is set up using On Error Goto. To show how to use error handling, I created a COM object called BadCOM, which always throws an error. To integrate this COM object, the following Visual Basic code was written:

```
Private Sub method2()
On Error GoTo ErrorHandler:

Dim tmpObj As BadCOM

Set tmpObj = New BadCOM
tmpObj.alwaysAnError
```

```
Exit Sub
ErrorHandler:
Dim errObj As New ErrorComponent.implErrorHandler
Call errObj.setError(Err.Number, Err.Description, 1)
Err.Raise 2 + vbObjectError + 512
End Sub
```

The first thing that the method has to do is declare a local error handler using On Error Goto. The error handler only applies to the local context of the method. If during a method an error is generated, then Visual Basic finds the last handler created in the calling stack. After the Goto, it is necessary to specify where to jump to. In this case, the jump is to ErrorHandler.

The next step is to create the BadCOM object, and then call the method alwaysAnError. It is very important to add the exit sub (exit function) statement before the error-handling routine. Otherwise, if no errors occur, the error handler is still called. In the error handler, the first step is to create the Error COM object. If this fails, then an exception is thrown, which then is caught by the next available handler or by the application itself. The method setError is called to indicate the error.

Notice the parameters of setError. When Visual Basic generates an error, it creates the Err object. The Err object is an object that contains all of the error information. What is of interest to us is the number (err.number) and the description (err.description).

After an error is handled, it is possible to continue processing. But before that is done, the error needs to be cleared using the method called err.Clear. Then the resume statement can be called to resume processing of the current method. Another option is to exit from the method and let the calling method continue.

Let's now step back and consider Visual Basic error handling in a larger context. If an error occurs because of a bad COM call or some incorrect value, how do you exit the function? Do you exit the function without returning an indication of failure? The answer is no—that could cause another error to occur, because the object state is not consistent. What you want to do is inform the caller of the method that something has gone wrong. This is done in Visual Basic by creating an application-specific error code using the following formula:

[error number] + vbObjectError + 512

The error is then raised using Err.Raise as explained previously.

In this framework, when an error occurs, the error-handling mechanism catches the error. The error is then recorded and it generates an application-specific error. The caller will most likely do the same thing and also generate an error. This process continues until the application can no longer continue. This makes it possible to build a calling stack trace. Inspecting a log file enables you to see what path led to the error.

You might think that this will cause any error to lead to an automatic shutdown of the task, and that this may be too drastic a solution. There might be a way to resolve the problem. However, this is generally not the case. In most cases, when an error does occur, it is a drastic error and recovery is not possible.

The other thing to remember is when to apply exceptions and when not to. Exceptions are only applied when exceptional situations occur. For example, if you are opening a file, an exception is generated when the file that you are reading is corrupt. You should not generate an exception if you cannot open the file because that is an error that you can recover from by asking for another filename. However, if the file can be opened but it is corrupt, that problem cannot be fixed by asking for a new file, and an exception must be generated.

Using Error Handling in Visual J++

COM error handling in Visual J++ is similar to catching a Java exception. The difference is that the object to be captured is called ComFailException, which is part of the package com.ms.com. This class contains the error that has occurred. There is a counterpart class called ComSuccessException, which indicates that the COM method call went okay. Typically, you do not want to capture this error, because it indicates that everything went ok. The following implementation functions just as the previous Visual Basic example does.

```
try {
BadCOM tmpObj = new BadCOM();

tmpObj.alwaysAnError();
} catch( ComFailException e) {
implErrorHandler errObj = new implErrorHandler();

errObj.setError( e.getHResult(), e.getMessage(), 1);
throw new ComFailException();
}
```

The try and catch block defines a region where exceptions will be caught, but the only exception that is of interest to us is of the type ComFailException. To retrieve the error code, the method e.getHResult is called. The error message is retrieved using e.getMessage. To generate an exception, the throw statement is used. In this example, the ComFailException object is instantiated without defining the error value. This is okay, because the class ComFailException uses a default error value of E_FAIL.

Using Error Handling in Visual C++

It is possible to capture errors using exceptions within C++. With C++, however, some methods generate exceptions and some methods do not. This complicates things, because it is necessary to capture exceptions. For those methods that do not generate exceptions, the exceptions must be wrapped in methods that do generate exceptions. When the COM compiler generates the stubs, exception handling is included within the stubs. Those same routines will be used in the Visual C++ exception-handling mechanism. Converting the Visual Basic code to its Visual C++ counterpart, you get the following:

```
try {
ERRORTHROWERLib::IBadCOMPtr ptr( "ErrorThrower.BadCom.1");
ptr->alwaysAnError();
} catch( _com_error err) {
COMPONENTLib::IErrorHandlerPtr ptrError(
"ErrorComponent.implErrorHandler");
ptrError->setError( err.Error(), err.ErrorMessage(), 1);
_com_raise_error( E_FAIL);
}
```

An exception block is set up using a try and catch block. Like Visual J++, the exception that we are interested in is _com_error. This is a COM compiler class defined in the header <comdef.h>. To access the error code, the method err.Error is called. To access the error message, the method err.ErrorMessage is called. It returns a _bstr_t. To raise your own error you do not use throw; instead, you use the function _com_raise_error with the COM error code as a parameter.

BUILDING YOUR OWN HRESULT

In Visual C++, building your own COM error is a bit more complicated. However, there is a macro to make it easier. Consider the following source code:
```
HRESULT retCode = MAKE_HRESULT( SEVERITY_ERROR, FACILITY_ITF, 600);
```
The macro MAKE_RESULT masks all of the bit operators. The first parameter determines whether the error is an error (SEVERITY_ERROR) or a success code (SEVERITY_SUCCESS). The second parameter determines the facility, and because this is a custom error message, it must be FACILITY_ITF. The last number is the error code. The error code cannot be in the range of 0 to 0x1FF, because this range is reserved for COM facility errors.

CAPTURING EXCEPTIONS WHERE THERE ARE NONE

It is important that all COM methods generate exceptions that work with the COM compiler classes. To do this, the helper function CheckError is available. It accepts as a parameter an HRESULT. Typically, most raw COM interfaces return an HRESULT, which can then be passed to the helper function. An example implementation is as follows:

```
_com_util::CheckError( intf->noExceptionThrown());
```

If the HRESULT is an error, then a COM error object _com_error is thrown. If the HRESULT is a warning, however, an exception will not be thrown.

Putting It in Perspective

Previous chapters explained how to design the application using sequence diagrams, collaboration diagrams, and use cases. This chapter introduced the technologies that you use to implement your COM objects. This chapter is important because there are some very important technical details to implementing COM objects.

For example, generating errors is an underdeveloped skill. I know from personal experience that having a good error-handling framework makes the difference between a stable run-time product and an unstable run-time product. This is because run-time errors are very difficult to trace, and being able to determine where the error is occurring is important.

We also looked at implementing COM objects in the three different languages. You now have some understanding of what the differences are so that you can judge how these factors impact your project.

The rest of the book focuses on the various technical details of implementing the business objects that we have designed thus far.

Chapter 10

Developing Transactional Components

Writing COM (Component Object Model) components and objects is not complicated. Writing COM components and objects that are stable, robust, and scalable is complex. The difficulty in writing these components is that the programmer must typically write server-side code that manages things such as threading and concurrency. Debugging this type of code is very complex, because a run-time error may not be reproducible in a debugging session.

This chapter looks at how to write COM objects that take advantage of the COM+ services of Windows 2000. The basic COM+ service enables a COM object to be registered in a COM+ application. At that point, the COM object becomes a COM+ object, and it can then take advantage of the COM+ transaction service. This chapter begins with what it means to use the COM+ transactional service. Parts of the chapter are theoretical, because using the COM+ framework does involve the use of a different programming model. After the theory is discussed, we look at the practical issues of writing COM+ objects.

Introducing Transactions

A transaction in software is the act of performing some process that involves two parties or components. In more general use, a transaction is often a business process.

Consider a bank. You go to the nearest ATM machine and decide to get some money by following these steps:

1. Put your card in the ATM.
2. Enter your PIN number.
3. Select the amount of money to withdraw.
4. Press the validate option to process the transaction.
5. Wait while your account is debited by the amount asked for.
6. Remove your card from the machine.
7. Remove the money from the machine.

All of these steps are involved in one transaction. Imagine the ATM delaying the debiting of your account, with the debiting ultimately failing. The ATM has given you your money, and it cannot run after you and ask for it back. This is a very important fact about transactions. After they are done, they cannot be rolled back. After the money is given, it is gone, and can't be recalled. While you may think that the worst part of this failure is that the bank loses money, there is a bigger problem—money is produced. The money that ATM gives you must be accounted for. If your account is not debited, then the money given by the ATM is added to the system. In other words, due to an error in the process, money is created. This is illegal and should never happen.

ACID: The Four Commandments of Transaction Processing

ACID is an acronym assembled from the first letter of each of the four commandments that all parts of a transaction system must follow: atomicity, consistency, isolation, and durability. Unlike other systems in which certain parts of the system are exempt from some of the rules, in a transaction-based system everything must follow the rules. This includes the transaction system, server components, and client components. It must be stressed that shortcuts and hacks should never be used and could cause problems in the long run. A transaction system is like a chain that is only as strong as its weakest link.

ATOMICITY

A transaction will either commit or abort. If a transaction commits, all of its changes remain in effect; if it aborts, all of its changes are undone.

In the example of withdrawing money from an ATM, the requirement was for the account to be successfully debited a certain amount of money. If that transaction was interrupted or a crash occurred, the transaction must fail. And, if the transaction fails, the person making the withdrawal expects the account to remain at the same level. Atomicity requires that either the entire transaction commits or aborts, and with that success or failure situation it is absolutely imperative that the correct state be maintained. It is an all or nothing situation.

CONSISTENCY

A transaction is a correct state; it preserves the state invariants. Correct state is when data is defined to be a correct value. When a state is transformed, there are an initial set of values and a final set of values. For the state to be correct, either the initial set of values or the final set of values must be in place. Any other set of values is incorrect, creating a wrong state. The state can be corrupted because the transformation of the state cannot occur instantly. It takes time, and during that time, a problem can occur.

Consistency does not mean a program without bugs. Consistency is the application of a consistent methodology. For example, when interest is calculated, half cents cannot be paid or collected. The amount must be rounded off to the nearest cent. Rounding off is not a simple issue because there are multiple ways of doing it. One approach is the regular mathematical approach of rounding up or down to the nearest value. This is what banks generally do—it is a simple and consistent approach. It would be incorrect for the bank to round down when paying interest and round up when collecting interest because that does not apply the rules consistently and makes the application inconsistent.

Consistency is a much-desired aspect of transaction code. When an account is credited a sum of money, the way of crediting the account should always be the same. An example of inconsistency is to credit an account using two amounts at one point in time and using one amount at another point in time. The result is the same, but the way of doing the calculation is not the same, and this difference can cause problems. When interest is calculated, it should always be calculated the same way. Consistency ensures that a finalized transaction always results in the same end result. Consistency cannot be enforced by the transaction system—only good testing and good programming techniques can enforce consistency. A good way of enforcing consistency is to document your rules and business processes.

ISOLATION

Concurrent transactions should be isolated from the results of other transactions, which may be incomplete.

During a running transaction, data is altered and can be considered to be in a state of limbo. Consider the situation of the bank transferring money from one account to another. When money is debited from one account and credited to another, there is the period when the original account has been debited and the other account is not yet credited. This limbo period lasts a certain amount of time, and if at this time another transaction wants to credit the account, what account balance does it see? Does it see the old balance or the new balance? Transaction systems take the point of view that the data has not been altered. This means that if the other transaction wants to see the data, then it sees the old data.

The job of the transaction system is not yet complete. If the other transaction system wants to modify the data, the two transactions must be kept isolated. Otherwise a potential update could occur on data that could still be rolled back.

The other problem that may occur is stale data. Transaction A reads some data. Transaction B reads and updates the same data. Transaction A updates the data. The data held by transaction A is considered stale. Some databases solve this problem by locking the data, but this creates another problem: you get long transactions (this is not good and is discussed later). A better solution is to write relative or version-checking code. Relative code is code in which the value in the record does not matter, because the other value increments or decrements the original value, rather than providing a new value based on the original value. Version checking is when the version of the data is checked before it is updated.

DURABILITY

Once a transaction commits, its effects persist even if there are system failures.

The concept of durability requires that if anything goes wrong, the transacted data will still be there. This concept is very important, because the scope extends beyond software. Returning to the ATM example, if the transaction went through and the money is given out, then a crash in the system must not influence the outcome of that transaction. When the system reboots from the crash, the state that results from the transaction is still there. If the system crash results from hard disk corruption and a new hard disk is required, the transaction is lost if it were only stored on the one hard disk. Therefore, it is imperative that a certain amount of redundancy exist. The concept of durability requires that whatever the cause or whatever the problem, a completed transaction must remain completed. There is no way of undoing, changing, or deleting it.

Durability within a transaction is not simply a software issue—it is both a hardware and software issue. COM+ only supports the software aspect of durability. Once the transaction is written to hard disk, it is assumed to be durable. To get durability beyond this, a cluster server with RAID (redundant array of independent disks) needs to be implemented.

Types of Transactions

A transaction is a series of business process steps that are completed together to achieve some result. To make a transaction system complete, transaction coordinators are required. These coordinators make it possible to roll back or commit the transactions.

There are several types of transactions, but COM+ services only supports the simplest transaction type, which is a flat transaction.

FLAT TRANSACTIONS

A flat transaction is when the series of business processes occurs in a sequential order. There is a starting point and an ending point, and if anything goes wrong in between, then all of the work is rolled back and removed from the various resources.

In the previous transaction example, the first transaction occurs when the money is removed from the account and the database containing the account is updated. In this case, the database is our resource. To remove the money, the following transactional business logic is executed:

1. A BEGIN transaction command is issued to the resource by the transaction monitor. It tells the resource that some work will commence and a transaction context needs to be associated with the system user. If there are any other currently running transactions, they are not associated with the new transaction. A brand new context is created.

2. The client ID is retrieved from the resource and stored within the logic. The transaction context manages any references to the resource. The client ID is used to modify the client's account.

3. The last step is for the logic to issue the COMMIT WORK transaction command. Any work that has been done will be made durable if the two-phase commit is successful. The two phase commit will be discussed shortly, but for now consider it to be a way of stating that the data will be made durable. If anything fails, then a ROLLBACK WORK command is issued, which causes all work in the context since issuing the BEGIN transaction command to be removed from the resource.

A flat transaction is flat because it can only contain one BEGIN transaction command and a COMMIT transaction command to make the data durable. Once one BEGIN starts, another BEGIN starts another independent transaction.

Flat transactions need to be timed properly because depending on the amount of time between a BEGIN and COMMIT or ROLLBACK the system is either scalable or slow. A scalable system can process a large number of requests, whereas a slow system forces the client to wait a lot. A transaction requiring a long time to process locks resources, and any ROLLBACK would require many steps to be performed. A group of transactions individually requiring a short time to process would cause complicated resource states.

I have referred to long and short processing times, and there is no way to define these times absolutely. They are dependent on the business process and what seems like a long or short time to the user. Of course, something like two hours is definitely a long time and should always be avoided. The "Activities" section, later in this chapter, provides a better idea of what long and short processing times are.

Two-Phase Commit

When a transaction needs to make the data durable, it calls a two-phase commit. A two-phase commit solves the time-delay problem of coordinating numerous resources and the entities that are manipulating those resources.

A two-phase commit is like a traditional marriage ceremony. In a traditional marriage ceremony, the two people come together and hold hands. The priest will ask the groom whether he wants to marry the bride. The groom replies yes. Then the priest asks the bride whether she wants to marry the groom. The bride says yes. Then the priest declares them to be married. In a two-phase commit, the bride and groom are the resources, and the priest is the transaction monitor.

Applying the above example to a computer scenario gives us these steps for a two-phase commit:

1. **Local prepare:** Each local resource prepares for the commit.
2. **Distributed prepare:** Send a prepare request to each transaction's outgoing session.
3. **Decide:** If all the resources voted to commit the transaction, then a commit is issued.
4. **Commit:** Invoke each resource, inform each of the voting commit outcome, and send the message on the outgoing transaction session.
5. **Complete:** When all resources have acknowledged the commit message, write a complete commit log record. When the message is durable, free the resources needed for the transaction.

It is important to understand that the transactions are placed in the middle tier. It is not possible to have the transaction context stored on the presentation tier. The exception is when the client desktop being used is Windows 2000. In that situation, the transaction service is installed by default and is usable in a distributed transaction.

COM+ Applications

In Windows 2000, MTS and COM+ have been integrated and they are one and the same. This integration goes beyond a simple transaction context and extends into an infrastructure concept. A graphical user interface (GUI)-less COM object can exist as is. However, when it is grouped into something called a COM+ application, it becomes a COM+ object. A COM+ object has the capability to interact with the various services offered by COM+.

Why use a COM+ application? A COM+ application builds an application based on components. Within a COM+ application, there are specific things going on, such as transactions and database connections. When the COM+ objects are grouped, the COM+ application manager has the capability to optimize the cache and make the application more scalable and robust.

HOW A COM+ APPLICATION WORKS

Building COM+ applications requires a bit of a change in thinking. In a classical application, there is a main function that is executed, and it is responsible for performing some actions, such as displaying a user interface and executing database logic. COM+ is different in that there is no main loop. There are only COM interfaces that are executing within a COM+ context. The COM interfaces are like services that are used to perform specific tasks. Everything is exposed as a series of COM+ objects.

Figure 10–1 has a box that represents a COM+ application. Contained in it is a box that is the Activator and Interception. This box is very simplistic, but from the perspective of the COM+ object developer, it is sufficient to illustrate the architecture of a COM+ application. Within that box are three items: Context, Attributes, and the COM object.

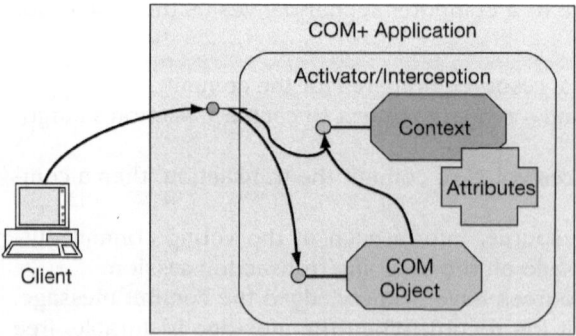

Figure 10–1: Activator and Interception architecture

The COM+ application is what was earlier called an MTS package. It is a surrogate process that contains the various COM objects. When the client wants to instantiate the COM object, it does not instantiate the COM object directly. Instead, something called the activator instantiates it. The activator is responsible for instantiating a COM object at the right moment with the right context. Essentially, this is an automatic feature and it just happens.

What is more important is the creation of an interception model. When you use plain COM, the consumer has direct access to the COM object and its various interfaces. The problem with this is that any problems or errors will have a direct effect on the consumer. COM+ interception, on the other hand, provides a certain amount of shielding from errors. The interception model also makes it possible to dynamically query the context for information.

The context of the COM object contains information about the environment that the COM object is executing within. Information such as security, IIS availability, and transaction capabilities are all stored in the context. If the COM object needs some run-time information, it asks the context for the appropriate COM interface. If the context has that information, the COM interface will be returned.

This is a better solution than using application programming interfaces (APIs) or regular COM because it is possible for the context to anticipate certain actions and prepare for them. Consider the case of connecting to a database. Using an interception model, it is possible for the context to cache information about the database connection. When the client asks for that connection, the COM interface exposure will be extremely quick. In a regular API scenario, the connection would require a long time because there is very little caching.

Using the attributes defined by the COM object, it is possible for the context to figure out what services the context should load. For example, if the COM object said, "I want transactions," then at activation the context would preload the transaction context information and manage it. If this information is cached, the information is loaded extremely quickly.

In the end, the interception model makes everything quicker because it gives the infrastructure a chance to create a cache of recently used data. The cache is generally stored in RAM and is more readily accessible than the original data source. This, in turn, makes the application faster and more scalable. However, the COM object that uses COM+ services must abide by the COM+ programming model and use the context.

THE DISTRIBUTED TRANSACTION COORDINATOR

The context is not responsible for managing the transaction, nor is it responsible for managing the two-phase commit. This is the responsibility of the Distributed Transaction Coordinator (DTC).

Figure 10–2 shows two computers and two COM+ applications. When the context is loaded, the requirement is that a transaction is added to the context. The context communicates with the DTC, and then a transaction is started. When other COM+ objects are referenced, the DTC on the two machines communicate and the transaction is extended to the other machine. Any resources that are used are associated with the transaction shared by the two COM+ objects.

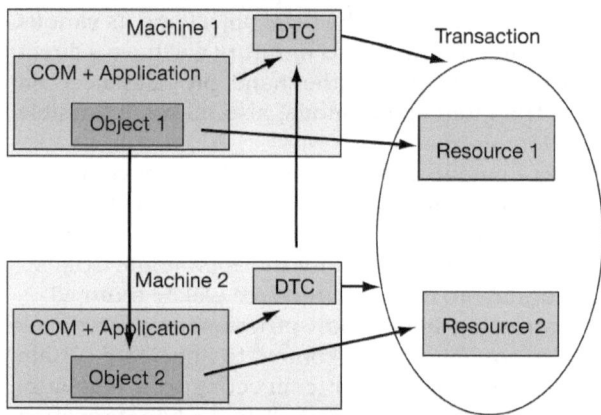

Figure 10–2: Architecture of DTC and COM+ objects

The context does not manage the transaction; the context is connected to the DTC. The DTC provides the "wiring" between the various COM objects and the resources. For example, if the new COM object were to access another resource or modify an existing resource, the DTC would attempt to communicate with the new entity and make itself available for transaction management. The DTC remains passive, because resource dispensers and resource managers must initiate communication.

Resource Dispensers

As a comparison, consider the situation of sitting in a restaurant and ordering a meal. A waiter typically takes your order and relays it to the kitchen. The kitchen makes the meal, and the waiter brings you the meal from the kitchen once it's ready. In effect, the waiter is providing a way of accessing the kitchen resource.

So, the waiter is a resource dispenser, and the person being waited on is a COM object. The COM object, when it connects to the resource, has no idea of where the resource comes from. It simply receives the information just as the restaurant customer receives the food. Essentially, the food could have been shipped from several time zones away.

Once it receives the data, the COM object can do what it wants with that data, just as the waiter does not care whether you eat the food, take it outside to your dog, and so on. The resource dispenser simply manages the various connections and tries to optimize access to the resources. Examples are the Shared Memory and Open Database Connectivity (ODBC) resource dispensers.

Resource Managers

Consider the situation in which the waiter dispenses all of the meals. When the client is finished with the meal, the client must pay for it. At this point, the waiter returns with a tab listing all the things the client was served. This is the state information. Where was that state information kept when the original order was submitted? In the restaurant, it was kept on a piece of paper or a computer, but generally not in the waiter's mind, because the waiter has other things to think about. In the COM scenario, it is the resource manager that manages the state of the data. The resource manager is not involved in dispensing its own resources, because the resource dispenser does that. A typical resource manager is Structured Query Language (SQL) Server.

Writing a resource manager is much more complicated than writing a resource dispenser because of the state issue. Managing state efficiently is not simple.

The Shared Memory Manager is a resource dispenser even though it may seem to take on the job of a resource manager. It isn't a resource manager, though, because the Shared Memory Manager, when it crashes, does not retain state, whereas a resource manager does retain memory. Returning to the restaurant example, a waiter may remember things such as how many people are at the table and the number of soup spoons needed. The waiter will not remember how many potatoes were consumed from the storage area. The resource manager does that.

A Good Transactional COM+ Object

A good transactional COM+ object is an object that uses a context and does not hold on to resources. It manages resources as needed and releases them when they are no longer needed.

COM+ objects are state managed, which means that they are neither stateless nor persistent. Experience shows that this is the best approach for building scaleable robust applications. To understand why we are creating state-managed objects, let's look at what was done in the past.

A Bit of History

Imagine that there are no COM+ services. The tools we use are traditional tools and some parts are from other vendors. Figure 10–3 has an object called client. User represents some data used when the client logs on to the Web site. In its simplest form, User only contains things such as name, e-mail, and password. However, client can be more complicated and contain other data, such as address, conferences attendees, and so on. The question is how the user object is instantiated when the client is instantiated.

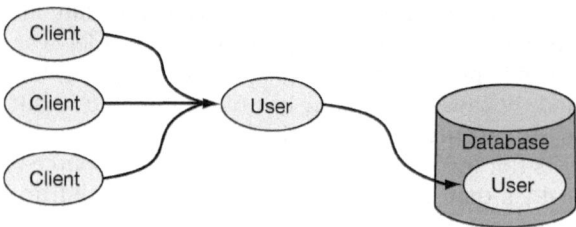

Figure 10–3: Example of Web architecture

In a pure object-oriented context, the answer is that the data is retrieved from an object-oriented database and then moved to memory. During the various operations performed by the different clients, the User is kept in memory.

This seems correct, because using a SQL approach, the data has to be converted from SQL database to a native format. With an object-oriented database, this is not necessary and it makes our lives simpler.

In either approach, the data is moved to memory and kept there. This is a flaw in program design. When data is kept in memory there are two copies of that memory. This creates cache and concurrency problems.

For example, what happens in a situation of concurrency? When the first Client object is instantiated, the User data is loaded in memory. When a second Client object is instantiated and references the same User data, what does the second Client get? Is it given a handle to the User instance in memory, or is a new User object instantiation created? Let's walk through both cases.

In the case of getting a handle to the existing object in memory, there are concurrency issues that the programmer of the Client and User object must handle. What happens if Client 1 modifies the address and Client 2 modifies the address again? Who writes the correct address?

In the case of creating a new copy of the User data there are no concurrency problems, because each client has a copy of the data. However, the extra copy of data requires extra resources—instantiating the object requires extra processing cycles. And if either client changes the object, the other client does not see the changes, because each client instantiates the object for the lifetime of the application.

In both of these two scenarios, the object is kept in memory. Now imagine that the object has been changed and the machine crashes. The current data may or may not have been written to the resource, and a crash will erase all of the data in memory. If it was not saved, all of the steps must be redone.

Code could be written to solve all of these problems, but this type of code is not simple, nor is it easy to debug. This kind of extra programming is not good, because it requires the developer to write system code that has nothing to do with the solution, but simply provides a framework for the application code. Also, system code is better written by companies that are focused on those types of products. In a Windows DNA scenario, we are concerned with writing application code to solve a given business process.

State-Managed Objects

In a COM+ environment, we write state-managed objects. The context manages a cache, which knows the resources that are required by the COM+ object. A state-managed object performs a specific set of operations and then removes itself entirely. In other words, we are constantly instantiating and destroying COM+ objects. This is fine because COM+ caches everything, which means that instantiation time is largely dependent on the time of initialization of the COM+ object. If that time is small, then the system is fast. There is a certain amount of overhead for COM+, but it is very small when compared to the amount of time required to perform the business operations.

In a state-managed application, the client COM object is responsible for passing some state information to the COM+ object. This small amount of information is used to build a new state for the new business process.

There is a catch to using the COM+ context. If the resource that is being manipulated is not capable of using the COM+ context or COM+ transactions and does not cache its information, then the COM+ application will not be faster. It may even be slower.

JUST-IN-TIME (JIT) ACTIVATION

When a consumer communicates with a COM object, there is some COM runtime that needs to be created between the two. For example, you need a proxy and stub and some communications information to create a COM communications infrastructure, as shown in Figure 10–4.

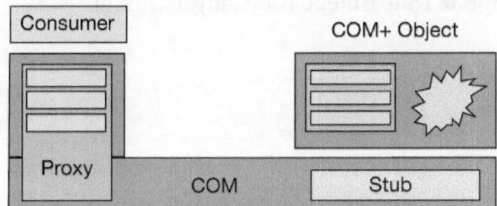

Figure 10–4: COM communications infrastructure

In COM+, the proxy and stub information is still used, but cached, which makes the references to COM+ objects quicker. This caching of COM+ communications infrastructure is called just-in-time (JIT) activation. When a transaction is started, the COM+ infrastructure creates a proxy and stub and the COM+ object implementation itself. When the transaction is done, the COM+ object is destroyed, but the proxy and stub are not destroyed; they are cached instead. The consumer thinks that it still has a reference to the COM+ object. When that reference is used, it causes a new transaction to start, and it instantiates a new COM+ object. The consumer does not realize what has happened behind the scenes.

This means that the COM+ object is instantiated and it is used when it is needed. The length of the transaction defines the life of a COM+ object. Because the same communication infrastructure is reused, the COM+ object instantiation is that much quicker.

THE TRUTH ABOUT OBJECT RECYCLING

The COM+ infrastructure, by default, does not recycle COM+ objects. For each transaction there is a new object instantiated, and when the transaction ends, that object is destroyed. In the past, Microsoft did say that in future versions of MTS, object recycling will be implemented, and it has been implemented, but perhaps not in the form that you expected.

The purpose of COM+ object recycling was to make applications quicker. But consider the model where COM+ object recycling is implemented. In that model, there is a language constructor or object initialization, and then there is a COM+ initialization. This makes for a tedious programming model because there are two initialization routines. Which initialization routine you should use is a complex question. The same problem applies to the destruction phase because there are two destruction routines, as well.

The question that must be asked in this recycling model is this: Is there a speed advantage to object recycling? The answer is yes, because there is no COM communication infrastructure that needs to be created. The initialization step is still there because in object recycling the object does need to be initialized.

Now let's contrast this with a JIT activation solution. When the object is referenced, the COM+ infrastructure has already cached the necessary information, such as class factory and database connections. The only step necessary is to recreate the object. Thus, it would appear that object recycling is faster. However, the truth is that with object recycling the object must reset its state, and in most cases the object resetting step takes the same amount of time as it takes to recreate the object. So, object recycling works, but an intelligent infrastructure also works and it is simpler to program.

The only case in which there is an advantage is with slow resources. In those situations, the initialization of the COM+ object takes a long time, and using object recycling is the faster solution. COM+ supports object recycling, but it requires that the COM+ object manage the transaction and the transaction-to-resource association. This is not difficult, but it does involve an extra step.

In short, object recycling does not provide performance gains for most situations, and the simpler programming model is to just instantiate and destroy the individual objects.

ACTIVITIES

Because objects are instantiated at the beginning of the transaction and destroyed at the end of the transaction, the programming model cannot assume an ongoing state. The object must be state managed, and the simplest way to manage state is to define activities.

An activity follows the same rule as the writing of a paragraph. A paragraph is a grouping of sentences that covers a single concept. Starting a new concept means that you must start a new paragraph. The new paragraph is not randomly chosen, but builds on the thoughts created in the previous paragraph.

The same is true of activities. An activity is an execution of a business process, and activities are pieced together to create an application. Between the various activities, a small amount of global state is used to create the context for each activity. Most activities should be short and last only minutes or seconds. They should never be hours long, because that creates unnecessary resource locks.

Designing for Activities

Building an activity-based object is very different from designing a pure object-oriented application. With activities, specific tasks are accomplished, which means that nouns representing objects are not the center of the design. Instead, verbs describing tasks are the core of the object design.

Let's go through the conference registration project and see how it is activity based. First, let's look at the Unified Modeling Language (UML) class model, shown in Figure 10–5, because I use it to discuss the activities concept.

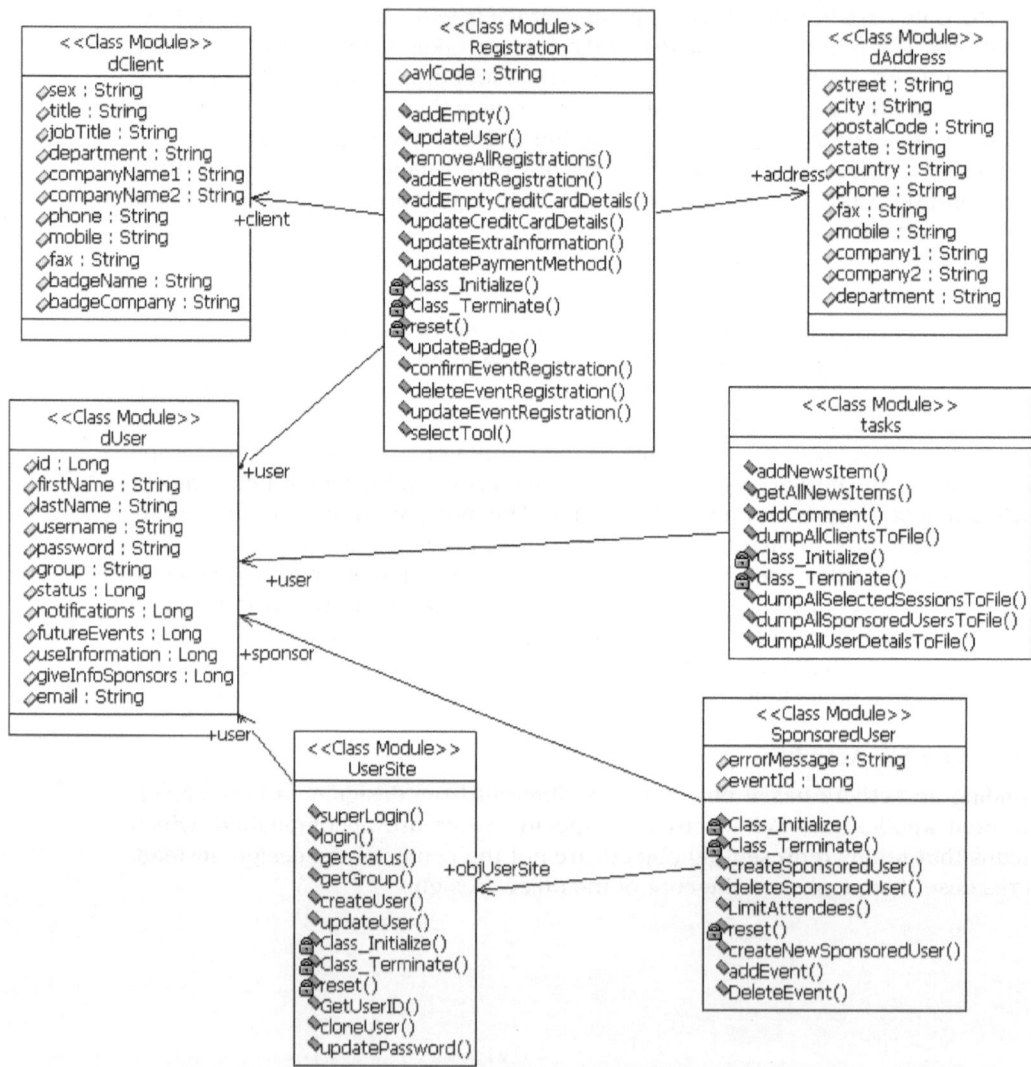

Figure 10–5: Conference registration Web application object model

The object model comes from Chapter 9, where we were creating a set of data and operations classes, and the only class missing was the verification class, which was omitted for the sake of simplicity.

There are three data classes: dClient, dUser, and dAddress. These classes contain all of the data that will be used in the application. They were designed using classical noun-based object-oriented design.

To realize the activities, operations classes needed to be designed. In this model, there are four operations classes: Registration, tasks, SponseredUser, and UserSite. These classes are based on the four major activities in the conference registration application: registration, sponsored user management, user management, and miscellaneous. The class names, while still being nouns, are based on actions. To make the activities more obvious, they could have been called Register, AccomplishTasks, ManageSponsoredUser, ManageUser, respectively. In any case, this is an activity-based design.

Now look inside the Registration class. This class contains a series of methods that perform operations such as adding, updating, and deleting. These methods are operations that can be combined into transactions.

When you are designing your activities-based class model, follow these steps:

1. Define all of your noun data objects in the design. This information could typically be taken from the domain model and use cases.
2. Attempt to group multiple sequence or collaborations diagrams into groups and look for similarities. What you want to do is create a series of operations classes that realizes the various operations of the application.
3. Combine the various data objects and operations objects, and convert them into a series of transactions. These will typically realize your sequence or collaboration diagram. Based on those transactions, you will have a set of required states that represent your verification objects.

When you are going through this process, do not attempt to take shortcuts by assigning one operation object per sequence or collaboration diagram. This creates code bloat and bad applications. Use common sense and judgment. Each application is unique and needs its own design.

If the preceding steps do not seem to apply to your project, then do not use them. However, in my experience, these steps for designing objects have proven useful.

Writing Transactional Components

The COM+ objects that we write here will not access any data. That is left to Chapter 16, which discusses how to access a data resource. The COM+ objects will just manipulate data. This raises the question of whether we need to use transaction services if we are not using a resource. The answer is probably not. The transaction service that is included in Windows 2000 does more than just provide transaction capabilities; it provides stability and COM-object management. But this is not a big deal if the COM objects are written properly (if they have an error-handling mechanism, do data verification, and so on). In that situation, it is okay to not use the COM+ transaction service.

Based on the previous explanations some rules about writing transactional COM+ objects can be developed:

- All COM+ objects must be state managed. This means that when they are activated, they always appear as fresh objects.
- All COM+ objects are initialized by the COM+ framework or application. Only use the constructor or object initialization to reset private object variables.
- All COM+ objects get resources late and release them early to promote scalability. Because of the COM+ caching and optimization, it is okay to retrieve a database connection at the method call level.
- All COM+ objects use activities to do their work. The activities are directly related to business operations.

How to Declare a COM+ Transactional Object

When a COM+ object is written, it is important to declare it as being transactional. This can be done at the Interface Definition Language (IDL) level. In the attributes section of an interface, the transaction type is defined; for example:

```
[
object,
uuid(E0B99A70-324D-11D3-868C-0080C700807A),
dual,
helpstring("IExTransactionVC Interface"),
pointer_default(unique),
TRANSACTION_REQUIRED
]
interface IExTransactionVC : IDispatch
{
[id(1), helpstring("method method1")] HRESULT method1();
};
```

In this example interface, the attribute is set to transaction_required. This is the way that a transaction attribute is specified in the Visual C++ programming environment.

In the Visual J++ programming environment, the transaction attribute is specified at the class level. In the class view, right-click the class and then select Class Properties. A dialog box, similar to that shown in Figure 10–6, appears, and you can choose the required transaction attribute.

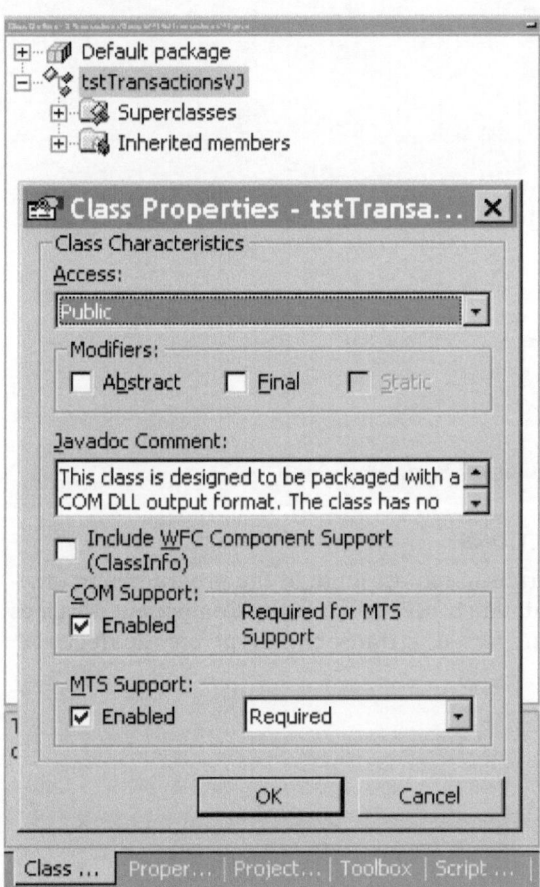

Figure 10–6: Transaction attribute in Visual J++

In the Visual Basic and Visual J++ programming languages, it is possible to set the transaction attribute at the class level. If, in your dialog box, the transaction attribute is not enabled, it is because COM must first be enabled.

In the Visual Basic programming environment, the transaction attribute is specified at the class level. The transaction attribute is located in the Class Properties list box, as shown in Figure 10–7.

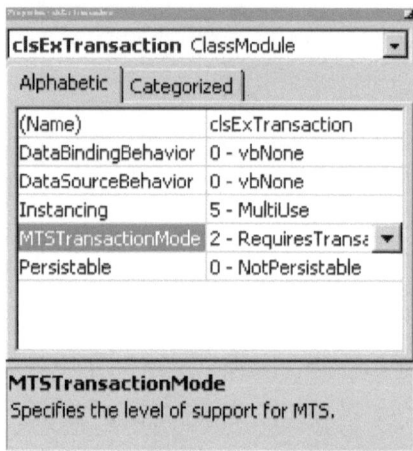

Figure 10–7: Transaction attribute in Visual Basic

THE DIFFERENT TYPES OF TRANSACTIONS

It is not necessary to declare the transaction attribute in the programming environment; this can be done at the administrative level. In the Component Services Explorer, when a COM+ object is imported, a transaction type can be declared, as shown in Figure 10–8.

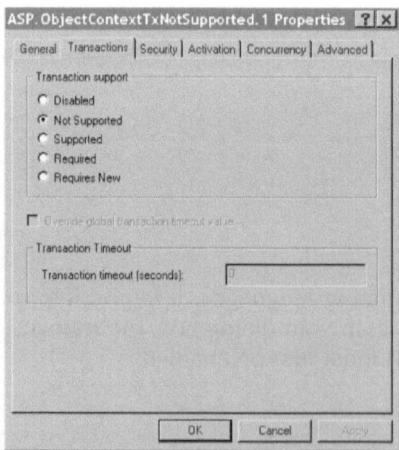

Figure 10–8: Transaction attribute in Component Services Explorer

Previous figures show that there are different types of transaction attributes. Consider the situation of a COM+ object being referenced by a consumer—there is a relationship established between the consumer and the COM+ object. Does the relationship mean that the same transaction will be shared? What happens if the consumer does not have a currently running transaction? The actual nature of this relationship is what the transactional attributes determine. There are these possibilities:

- **Disabled:** This is a big on/off switch that is off, and it says that you cannot use the COM+ transaction support at all. There may be a transaction being used, but COM+ should not influence it and should not automatically enlist a transaction. The transaction ID still flows and is part of the entire transaction stream.
- **Not Supported:** The COM+ object does not want a transaction context.
- **Required:** A transaction context is required. If the consumer has a transaction context, then the COM+ object that has just been instantiated will share it. Otherwise a new transaction context is started.
- **Requires New:** A new transaction is started regardless of whether one already exists or not. Do not confuse this with nesting, because the new transaction outcome does not affect any other currently running transaction.
- **Supported:** If the consumer has a transaction context, then the COM+ object that has just been instantiated will share it. Otherwise no transaction context is shared.

It might seem that Disabled and Not Supported are similar—in both cases the COM+ object does not share any transaction context. What is different is that Disabled enables hand-tuning of the transaction. There are a few situations in which it may be desirable to modify the DTC transaction manually, such as when optimizing resource access. By setting the transaction attribute to Disabled, it is possible to not use transactions, but still use the benefits of COM+ applications, such as JIT.

SYNCHRONIZATION

Consider the situation of writing a COM+ object that is part of a transaction. Suppose this COM+ object instantiates two other COM+ objects, but each of these objects executes in a different transaction. This means that there are three different transactions running concurrently. In our application, we execute multiple threads in order to promote scalability, but what does this mean in the situation of these three COM+ objects calling each other?

The answer depends on the COM-threading model. COM threading is beyond the scope of this book, but it defines how COM objects interact with multithreaded applications. If the COM+ objects are running in a free-threaded apartment model, they call each other directly without any restraint. This is not good, because the called COM+ object could be in the process of doing something, and should not be interrupted. The solution to this problem is to write synchronization code.

If you do not want to write synchronization code, another solution is to make the COM+ object execute in the apartment model, which is a COM-threading model that synchronizes the calls. In this situation, the calls are queued to the COM+ object. This is okay, but still not ideal—it is expensive in terms of processing time, because the COM+ object needs to execute a thread-context switch.

One solution to this switch of context is to introduce the Neutral Apartment (NA), which is another COM-threading model concept. When a COM+ object executes within a NA, it does not execute within any specific thread. The thread that it executes in is determined at call time.

Going back to our three different COM+ objects, note that they are running in three different transaction contexts. If one object attempts to manipulate another COM+ object, it influences that transaction. One COM+ object could be telling the object to commit the transaction, and the other could be telling the object to abort the transaction. This means that concurrency code needs to be written yet again, but COM+ offers a simpler solution.

The COM+ solution is to introduce synchronization. With synchronization, a COM+ object is locked in an apartment, but it extends beyond the apartment to include the activity, which in our case is the transaction, and the transaction can extend to other computers. This makes it possible to lock out callers and actions that could cause the transaction to corrupt itself.

Figure 10–9 shows the dialog box in the COM+Explorer that lets you adjust the various synchronization settings. COM+ has five synchronization settings:

- **Disabled:** When the COM+ object is instantiated, the synchronization attributes are ignored. This means that the COM+ object executes in its own context. It is important that these types of objects not use any resources.
- **Not supported:** The instantiated COM+ object never participates in the synchronization.
- **Supported:** If there is an existing synchronization, it is used; otherwise, it is not.
- **Required:** Synchronization is required; if it does not exist, it is created. When used in a transaction context with JIT, this setting is the default value.
- **Requires new:** A new synchronization context is created when the COM+ object is instantiated.

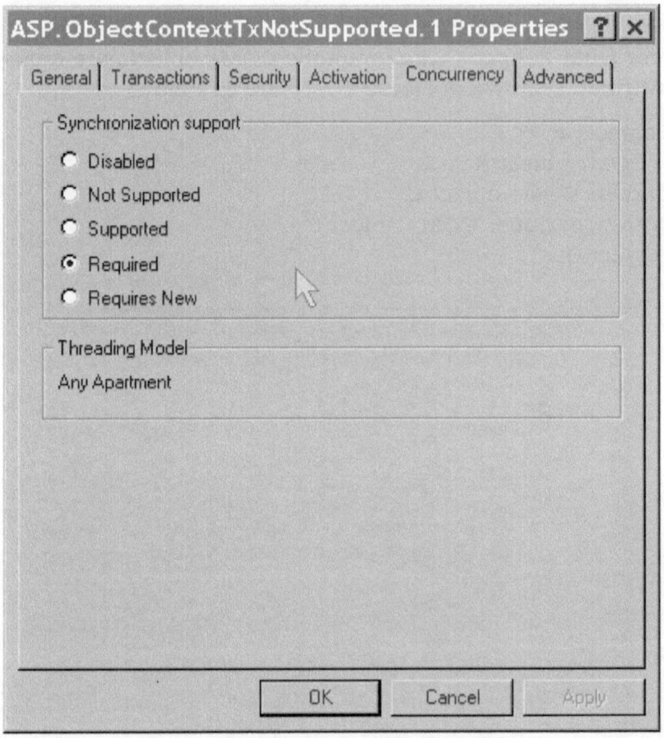

Figure 10–9: COM+ synchronization attributes

The synchronization setting is dependent on the transaction attribute. For example, when the transaction attribute is Supported, Required, then the synchronization can only be Required. When the transaction attribute is Requires New, then the synchronization can be Required or Reqes New. This means that when building transactional COM+ objects, there are no options on the synchronization.

Synchronization can only be tweaked when there is no transaction context. Synchronization is useful because it makes it possible to write COM objects without needing to write Win32 synchronization code. It is simpler.

Multiple COM+ Object Transaction Scenarios

It is important to consider what happens when multiple COM+ objects are combined. The transaction attributes shown in Figure 10–10 are as follows:

- **Required:** COM+ objects A, D, F
- **New transaction:** COM+ object B
- **Supports transactions:** COM+ object C
- **Does not support transactions:** COM+ object E
- **Disabled:** COM+ object G

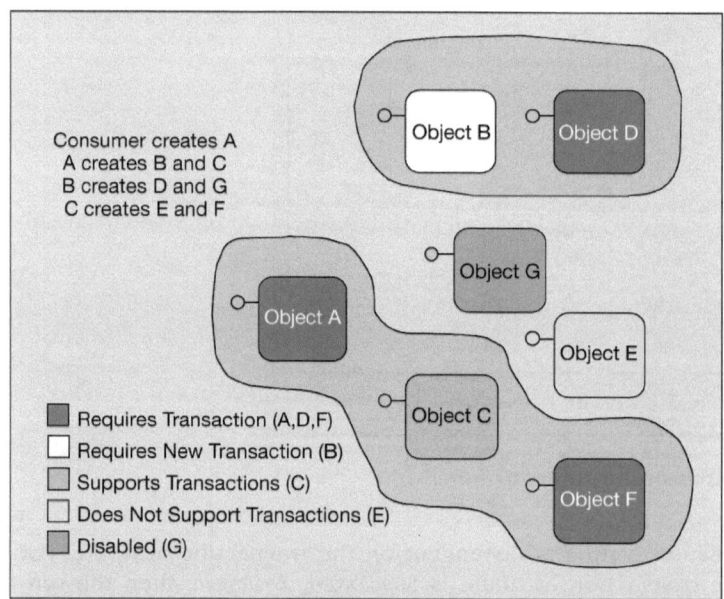

Figure 10–10: Example scenario of multiple COM+ transactions

The consumer creates COM+ object A. As a result, a new transaction stream is started. COM+ object A requires a transaction context, and because the consumer does not have any transaction contexts, a new one is started. COM+ object A is special, because it is the root of the transaction stream.

Next COM+ object A instantiates COM+ objects B and C. COM+ object B has the transaction attribute New Transaction. This means a new transaction context is started, and it becomes the root of the new transaction stream. COM+ object C has the transaction attribute Supports transactions. Because COM+ object A has a transaction context, COM+ object C shares the context and is added to the transaction stream of COM+ object A.

COM+ object B instantiates objects D and G. COM+ object D has an attribute of Required, which means it is added to the transaction stream of COM+ object B. COM+ object G has a Disabled attribute, meaning that it is not part of any transaction stream. It could be, but that is a decision that object G makes, and

COM+ does not decide how it should manage the context and transaction stream.

COM+ object C instantiates objects E and F. COM+ object E has the transaction attribute Does not support transactions, and therefore is not be part of any transaction stream. And finally, COM+ object F has the transaction attribute Requires Transactions, and because COM+ object C has a context, object F shares that context and is part of the transaction stream created by COM+ object A.

ROOT OF THE TRANSACTION STREAM

Both COM+ objects A and B are the roots of their transaction streams. Being a root is important because roots are responsible for the validity of the stream and the objects contained in them.

Consider the situation in which the consumer holds COM+ object F as a reference. The consumer at some point in time decides to let go of the reference to COM+ object A. Because it is the root of the transaction stream, all COM+ objects in the stream are deactivated as well. This means that if the consumer attempts to reference COM+ object F, it will cause an execution error.

WORKING WITH MULTIPLE TRANSACTION STREAMS

When working with multiple transaction streams, problems can occur. Consider the following situation. There are two transaction streams, and each stream is modifying some data. The first stream is modifying dataset A, and the second stream is modifying dataset B. If the activity has each stream updating the other's data, a deadlock will occur.

A deadlock is when two entities are holding locks on resources that each wants. Because neither is willing to give up its lock, they wait indefinitely. They are deadlocked. This usually doesn't happen in COM+.

To understand why it doesn't happen in COM+, let's consider how a deadlock can be unlocked. A deadlock can be unlocked in two ways. The first is a simple timeout. Each transaction waits for a period of time for access to the locked information. If that time is exceeded, a timeout occurs and the transaction is aborted. This means that one transaction is applied, while the other is aborted.

The second solution is called deadlock detection. A resource knows which transaction is accessing which information, and if it detects a deadlock situation, it can instantaneously take steps to stop it, by resolving or aborting the transaction, depending on the resource.

Deadlocks can also be avoided even if you are writing code that does lock data that will be used in other transactions. The main factor is the scope of the data. For example, a username or a client's address has a narrow scope. The chance of two applications changing the same data at the same time is remote. This means that a transaction that modifies and queries narrow-scoped data can keep a transaction running longer. A data object that has a large scope, or that is used by many different applications, must not be locked for long periods of time, because this will slow down an application. Following these guidelines reduces the chance of deadlocks occurring, but it does not give you the right to execute long transactions.

But even with the best activity design, sometimes there are problems with resource sharing. For example, Microsoft SQL Server 6.5 uses page locking. This means that two separate transactions could deadlock if they shared data from the same page. Microsoft SQL Server 7.0 uses record locking and does not have this problem.

Getting the Transaction Interface

When a COM+ object is activated, it has the capability to manage the transaction context. It does not access the transaction context directly, but it accesses the transaction context interface called IObjectContext. Using this interface, it is possible to influence the outcome of the transaction, create other transaction COM+ objects, or check specific run-time characteristics.

The transaction context is a shadow object and is retrieved using the method call GetObjectContext. In Visual J++, it is done as follows:

```
import com.ms.mtx.*;
import com.ms.com.*;
IObjectContext objContext = MTx.GetObjectContext();
```

The transaction interfaces are stored in the package com.ms.mtx.

In Visual Basic, the transaction context is retrieved as follows:

```
Dim objContext As ObjectContext
Set objContext = GetObjectContext()
```

Because Visual Basic does not support the notion of using interfaces, it uses the coclass ObjectContext as the IObjectContext interface. All of the transaction interfaces are defined within the references type library COM+ Services Type Library.

And finally, in the Visual C++ environment, the transaction context is retrieved as follows:

```
#include <autosvcs.h>
_COM_SMARTPTR_TYPEDEF(IObjectContext, __uuidof( IObjectContext))
IObjectContextPtr objContext;
_com_util::CheckError( GetObjectContext( &objContext));
```

The transaction interfaces are defined in the COM+ services header <autosvcs.h>. To simplify the use of the IObjectContext interface, a smart pointer is defined using the _COM_SMARTPTR_TYPEDEF. Then, to retrieve the interface pointer, GetObjectContext is used, but it is wrapped in the error checker _com_util::CheckError. It is possible to use the & operator because the COM compiler classes overloaded the operator to get the correct interface pointer.

Changing the Outcome of the Transaction

There are four different methods for influencing the outcome of a transaction. They are presented here in IDL, which is usable by all COM-capable languages.

```
HRESULT SetComplete();
HRESULT SetAbort();
HRESULT EnableCommit();
HRESULT DisableCommit();
```

These four functions can be grouped into two types: transaction termination and transaction delaying.

TRANSACTION-TERMINATION METHODS

In a transaction, it is possible to indicate that the transaction was completed and how everything went. The two options are to say all went okay or all didn't go okay. The following indicates all okay:

```
objContext.SetComplete();
```

This says that the transaction is to be considered done and the results are fine. This starts the two-phase commit, and if all transactions have said okay, as well, the data written to the resource is made durable.

The other option is to say that something went wrong and that the transaction should be aborted. Writing the following code does this:

```
objContext.SetAbort();
```

A two-phase commit is not started, and all data written to the resource is removed.

In either case, the transaction stream is released. All of the COM+ objects currently active in the stream and all resources and locks held in the transaction stream are released. It is important that all COM references to the transaction stream are set to NULL, because now the references are considered invalid.

TRANSACTION-DELAYING METHODS

When a method on a COM+ object is called, the COM+ object is activated. When the method is finished, the COM+ object is deactivated if any of the transaction-termination methods are called. Business processes tend to use multiple COM+ object method calls, and it can be useful to delay the termination of the transaction, because doing so makes undoing data changes much simpler. Data that has been updated is much harder to restore to its initial state.

To delay determination of transaction outcome, it is necessary to call other methods of the IObjectContext interface.

To delay the outcome of a transaction and abort it if a two-phase commit starts, use the following code:

```
objContext.DisableCommit();
```

To delay the outcome of a transaction and enable a commit if a two-phase commit starts, use the following code:

```
objContext.EnableCommit();
```

To integrate these methods into the conference registration application, the operations classes are extended. There are two ways to extend the methods. The way chosen in the conference registration application was to delay the transaction outcome on every method. To abort or commit a transaction, explicit methods are called. In the conference registration application, the transaction was aborted by calling the Registration.reset method.

Having these explicit methods to abort or commit a transaction is not required. It is a design decision, and it depends on the business process that you are carrying out. Having these explicit methods sometimes leads to long transactions, because the activity that is associated with the transaction takes too long to complete.

HOW THE TRANSACTION OUTCOME IS MANIPULATED

The SetComplete, SetAbort, EnableCommit, and DisableCommit methods are what I call bit-toggling methods. In the context of a method call, these methods can be called in any order. However, the method that is applied is the last method called in the context of a method.

The way to understand this is by remembering that these methods toggle the Done and Consistent switches. If the Done switch is ON, it means that any resources held by a transaction can be released. If the Consistent switch is ON, it means that the data is correct—when combined with an ON Done switch, it will start a two-phase commit. The following table visually explains the relationship among these methods.

METHOD	SWITCH: DONE	SWITCH: CONSISTENT
DisableCommit	OFF	OFF
EnableCommit	OFF	ON
SetAbort	ON	OFF
SetComplete	ON	ON

During the method call, the switches are flipped. At the end of the method, the state of the switches is then used to determine what to do to the transaction stream.

Sometimes you need to know whether the COM+ object is running within a transaction context. Or, it may be desirable to know which user is currently executing the COM+ object. These methods fall into the category of transaction-context querying.

The whole discussion of transactions is not much use if you don't know whether the object is participating in a transaction or not. The `IsInTransaction` method checks whether an object is in a transaction.

```
BOOL IObjectContext::IsInTransaction ( );
```

If the method returns a TRUE, then the object is executing in a transaction. A FALSE indicates that the object is not executing in a transaction. This method can also be partially used to check whether the object is configured properly in the COM+ services catalog. For example, if a check proves that the object is not in a transaction but the object is registered in a package, then the transaction property is set to Does not support transactions. If this is unacceptable, the object can stop executing the current method and send an error back to the caller.

COM+ Object Instantiation Method

In previous editions of MTS, it was necessary to use special methods when you wanted to instantiate a new COM+ object: `IObjectControl::CreateInstance`. And you had to call the `SafeRef` method when passing COM+ object references between various COM+ objects. None of this is necessary now. The methods are still supported, but their use is not required. In COM+, you just need to call the regular COM instantiation calls and pass the object references.

Converting a COM Object to COM+

When a COM object is instantiated and it uses COM+ services, it must be part of a COM+ application. If it isn't, there will be an application failure, because there is no context. The COM+ object must be added to the COM+ catalog by registering it with a COM+ application.

There are two ways to manipulate the COM+ catalog. The first and simpler way is to use the Component Services Explorer and create a COM+ application by just pointing and clicking. When creating a COM+ application, the default settings are good enough to get things working. After the COM+ application is created, you can then point and click to add a COM object to the application. After the COM+ objects are installed, you can manipulate their properties, such as transaction support and synchronization support.

The second way is to write scripting code that manipulates the COM+ administrative objects. This is more complex to do, but it provides the capability to manage every aspect of the COM+ application and objects. It is also useful for creating installation routines if you are doing larger-scale tests.

Putting It in Perspective

Writing transaction code is not just a matter of using some interfaces and then committing or aborting a transaction. To write transaction code, you need to understand transaction processing. The best way to understand transaction code is to compare it to business processes. You carry out a number of steps and then you decide whether to commit it or abort it. With transaction processing, state becomes very important.

To manage state effectively, your activities must be well designed, and this can only be accomplished if your sequence and collaboration diagrams are well thought out. They influence the design of the operations classes. A good activity-based design makes it possible to carry out transactions in packet form. This is the point at which it becomes obvious how closely linked the design and implementation really are.

Most of your time is spent writing transaction code. For example, you may use messaging in your application, but the messages are not meant to solve business problems. They are used to solve infrastructure and timing problems. When a message is processed, it carries out a business process, which means carrying out a transaction.

The next step is to build infrastructure to support the construction of distributed applications.

Chapter 11

Developing Messaging COM+ Objects

This chapter introduces the messaging services offered by Microsoft Message Queue (MSMQ). We begin with a description of why you would want to use messaging, or MSMQ, followed by a look at how MSMQ functions by using the MSMQ application programming interface (API) tester. Finally, we go over the details of writing distributed applications that use transactions and messaging.

Introduction to MSMQ

What is Microsoft Message Queue (MSMQ) and why use it? What purpose does it serve? Consider the situation of a company based in Germany, that works on a global basis creating widgets, and that buys the copper for the widgets is from a Chilean company. Communications with Chile are expensive and can be unreliable (because of the long distances involved), so the company orders copper from the Chilean company, communicating with a synchronous call using Distributed Component Object Model (DCOM). The object in Germany instantiates the object in Chile.

One limitation of this system, aside from the time taken to instantiate the objects and communicate between them, is that all orders in Germany must be entered while the company in Chile is doing business, or nobody will be at the other end to confirm the order. Now imagine that the line breaks down somewhere in the process. With COM+ transaction services, everything will be rolled back and the order will have to be reentered. If this happens often, it will be expensive and annoying. What can we do to create a better system?

Microsoft Message Queue is Microsoft's response to the need for reliable asynchronous communication between applications. It is the only software that provides a guarantee that a message will travel from one point to another point. Using MSMQ, applications can communicate with each other without actually establishing a direct connection. This means that even if one application is not online, the other application can send its message without having to worry that it will not reach the other application.

MSMQ is a network of queues and messages. A *queue* is a place where messages are stored. Queues are like mail addresses—to send a message you simply need to send it to the correct address, or queue. *Messages* can be any sort of data: text, binary, objects, and so on. MSMQ doesn't place any limits on the contents. It is only responsible for sending the message, not for what is inside.

An application interacts with a queue using a series of APIs. These APIs are simple: Open, Close, Send, and Receive. They provide an access layer to the underlying MSMQ service, which is the Queue Manager. Using the Queue Manager, it is possible to put messages in a specific queue. It does not matter whether the queue is on a local machine or a remote machine because the Queue Manager manages the routing of the message.

MSMQ API and the MSMQ ActiveX Component

MSMQ offers two programming interfaces. There is the basic MSMQ API and then there is the MSMQ Component Object Model (COM) component. I prefer using the MSMQ COM component because it fits in the component architecture and is simpler to use than the API. The only time that you would ever need to use the API is if the MSMQ COM component cannot do what you want it to.

Comparison of DCOM and MSMQ

You may think that MSMQ is a technology that could be replaced by DCOM, but each technology has its own uses. DCOM is a connection-oriented technology, whereas MSMQ is a messaging technology. To fully understand the role of each technology, let's look at what each offers and requires.

First, DCOM requires a connection. Consider the case of a base client calling a component on another machine. When the call is made, the component on the other machine must exist and be capable of running. Thus, the connection between the component and base client must exist. With MSMQ, a connection is not required. When the message is sent from the base client to the component, the base client does not care whether the component exists.

Similarly, DCOM requires a working source network and computer, and the receiver must be working, as well. If anything is not working, then the method call will not succeed. With MSMQ, the only thing that needs to work is the local machine that receives the message. Once the message has been accepted by the queue, it is part of the system. At this point, the action is considered completed.

When a DCOM system makes a method call or a stack of method calls, they are executed in a first-in, first-out model. This is because it is a serial process—the first call must be processed first. Otherwise, it is not possible to determine the outcome of the method calls. In a MSMQ system, the order of the messages is based on a prioritization model. This means that the first message in may not be the first message to be processed. Although this may seem to be a problem, it is not, as you'll see when we look at developing applications later in the chapter.

In a DCOM system, resources tend to be locked. Consider the calling of a component located in Frankfurt, which then calls New York, which then calls Tokyo, which finally calls Santiago. Because of the long distances involved, the call will not be immediate. There will be a small delay. Therefore, calling Quito can become a longer proposition. During this call the components are locked, waiting for the component method call to return. In an MSMQ-based system, the calling mechanism is local. If the same message were to travel to Quito, then at each location there would be a lock, but the next and previous locations would be free to call or accept calls from other locations.

The DCOM system also has a data model that is *immediate*. Again, consider the calling sequence to Quito. When a change is made at one location, that change is immediate. When the original caller at Frankfurt is free to process something else, the data across all of the locations is up to date and in a known state. With MSMQ that is not possible, because it is not known when the receiver will get and process the message. However, with messaging it is guaranteed that eventually the message will get to the receiver and be processed. Therefore, the data integrity is considered to be *eventual*.

Finally, when something does go wrong, the DCOM system fails. While it is possible to retry the connection, that must be done manually. With MSMQ, retry is done automatically.

CHOOSING BETWEEN DCOM OR MSMQ

So, given the preceding arguments, should you exclusively use MSMQ components? The answer is that you should use the two technologies in different situations.

Use MSMQ in these circumstances:

- When the sender and receiver communicate with each other at different times. For example, a sales-processing system that communicates across continents. In that case, there is very little overlap of sales people, and a series of messages is better.
- When the cost of sending a message and then having it fail is high. MSMQ reduces the cost because of the automatic retry, which does not disrupt the entire process. It only delays the eventual result.
- When the sender wants to send off a message and do some other processing. MSMQ allows the sender to do a certain amount of parallel processing.
- When the messages must be logged for possible auditing or potential recovery purposes.
- When creating a physical connection between the sender and receiver is impractical. This could involve batch-processing applications. Notebook users who are on the road would also be ideal candidates for messaging because they could do their work and then later send it off to be processed.

Use DCOM in these situations:

- When the sender and receiver have a reliable high-bandwidth connection. The DCOM protocol requires a higher bandwidth to be reliable and responsive.
- When the sender cannot wait for an answer from the receiver. If the communications must be synchronous, or if making the communications asynchronous would offer no benefit, then it is simpler to use DCOM.

Experimenting with MSMQ Using the API Testing Sample

In the Platform Software Developer's Kit (SDK) (samples directory *COM\MessageQueueingdirectory*), there is an application called the MSMQ API tester. This application shows how to interact with MSMQ using the MSMQ APIs. This sample is structured so that it exposes the MSMQ API as methods. If the MSMQ method requires any parameters, the dialog box that is displayed defines them. I will demonstrate how messages can be sent and received using the MSMQ API testing sample.

So that you do not have to build the application, look in the book's source code for the util directory, start the MqAPITst.exe application, and then start another instance of the same application. Arrange them one above the other, as in Figure 11–1.

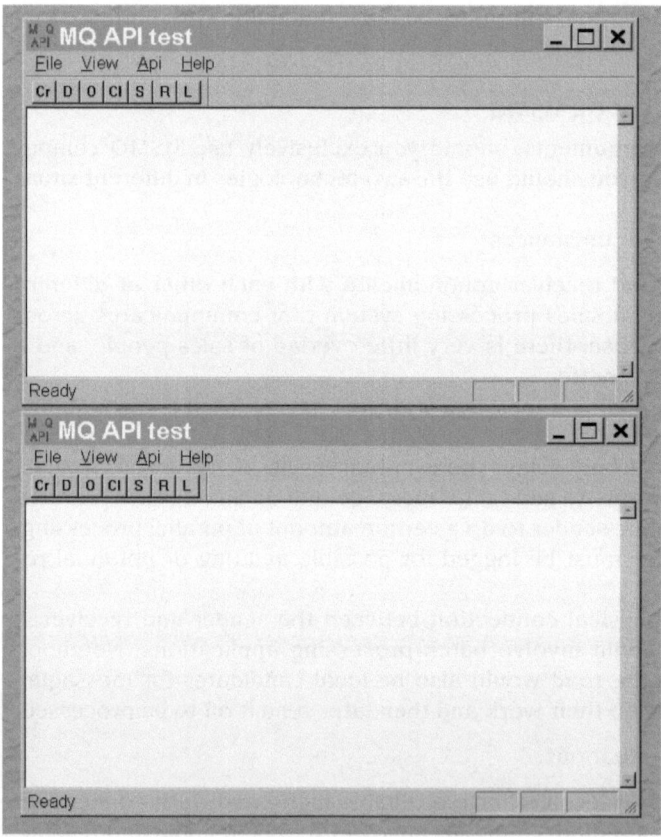

Figure 11–1: Arrangement of two MSMQ windows

The top window is the receiver, which means that it will receive the message. The bottom window is the sender and will send the message. The aim is to send a message from the bottom window to the top window. In this demo, both the sender and receiver are started. However, the receiver could just as easily have been started after the message had been sent.

STARTING A RECEIVER

When a message is to be received, there must be a listener. When MSMQ delivers messages to a queue, it does not trigger an application—the receiver must perform that task. Hence, in our demo, the receiver must be started so that it can listen for messages arriving in the queue.

Because this is the first time you will be running the application, you first need to create the queue so that you can listen to it. Create the queue by selecting API -> MQCreateQueue from the menu. The dialog box shown in Figure 11–2 displays.

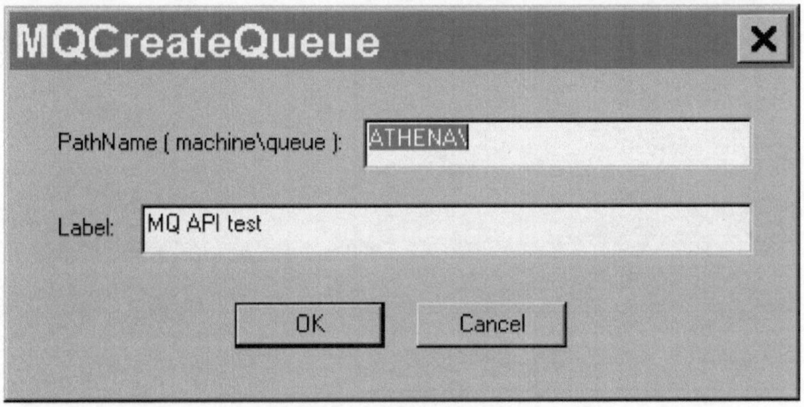

Figure 11–2: The MQCreateQueue dialog box

The top text box defines the message queue name and the machine where the queue will be found. The name of the machine is defined by entering a name, or a period (.) to specify the local machine. You can specify any name for the queue. For example, you could type in the name MACHINE\SampleQueue, where MACHINE is the name of the machine on your local network.

The lower text box specifies the label that is assigned to the queue. A label is like a description, except that it can be used to reference a specific queue. The label is easy to read and makes it easy to figure out what the queue does. To better explain the queue name, remove what was entered by default and type in MQ API test. Then click OK. If the queue did not already exist, you should see a message in the window stating that the queue was created successfully.

Now that the queue is created, the new queue needs to be opened. From the top window select API –> MQOpenQueue from the menu, and the dialog box in Figure 11–3 displays.

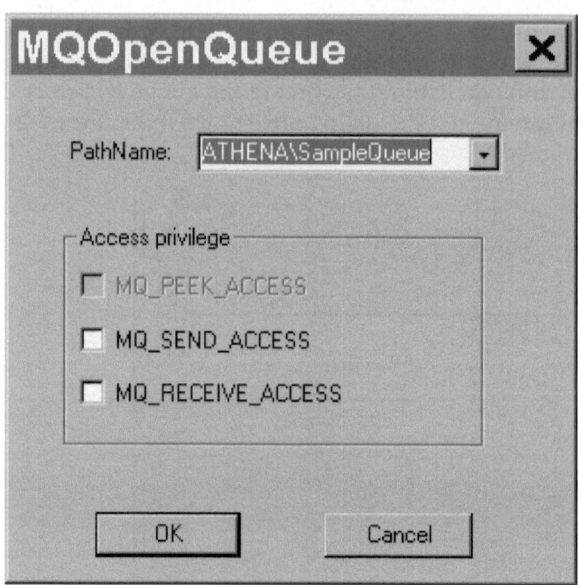

Figure 11–3: Opening a queue

If a queue was created successfully, then a queue path resembling the one in the previous dialog box is automatically displayed in the combo box.

When a program opens a queue, it can perform three types of message operations: sending, receiving, and peeking (retrieving a message without removing it from the queue). For each reference to a queue, the program can only perform one operation at a time. From the program's point of view, the queue is a one-way operation. To send and receive from a queue at the same time, the program has to open two references to the queue, each of which is a one-way operation.

Because we are manipulating the receiver, check the MQ_RECEIVE_ACCESS checkbox. The MQ_PEEK_ACCESS option, which applies to a receiver, is grayed out. Click OK when you are done, and a message should appear in the client area stating that the queue handle was successfully opened.

The last step in setting up the receiving application is to start listening for messages to arrive on the queue. The application can listen for messages in either a synchronous or asynchronous manner. Synchronous listening is like issuing a method call and then waiting for an answer, except that a timeout can be issued so as not to lock the process. Asynchronous listening acts like a callback in Windows.

Writing messaging applications using MSMQ is a form of asynchronous programming, but in the previous paragraph, I stated that it is possible to retrieve messages either synchronously or asynchronously. Many people assume that be-cause MSMQ is asynchronous, messages are retrieved asynchronously, but that is not necessarily the case. MSMQ gives you the capability to process messages whenever you want.

This means that you can either retrieve the message by asking for it or you can wait for a message to arrive, which is called polling the queue. Polling the queue is a synchronous operation in which you call a method periodically. When a COM+ transaction-capable object interacts with MSMQ, it has to use this method.

An asynchronous MSMQ operation works differently. When a COM object is instantiated, it connects to MSMQ using a MSMQ API. The COM object then in-forms MSMQ that it wants to receive messages asynchronously. MSMQ will send the messages asynchronously using COM connection points. However, COM connection points require that both the sender and receiver of COM connection point events be alive at the same time—this cannot always be ensured with COM+ components because COM+ transaction services will deactivate the COM+ component when the transaction is done, killing the COM connection point. To get around this problem, you can still use COM+, but you should not use COM+ transaction services. This will keep an active reference to the COM+ object re-ceiving the MSMQ COM connection point events.

The MSMQ API testing sample uses a synchronous method call to receive MSMQ messages. To begin listening, select API –> MQReceiveMessage from the menu. The dialog box in Figure 11–4 appears, giving you three options to enter.

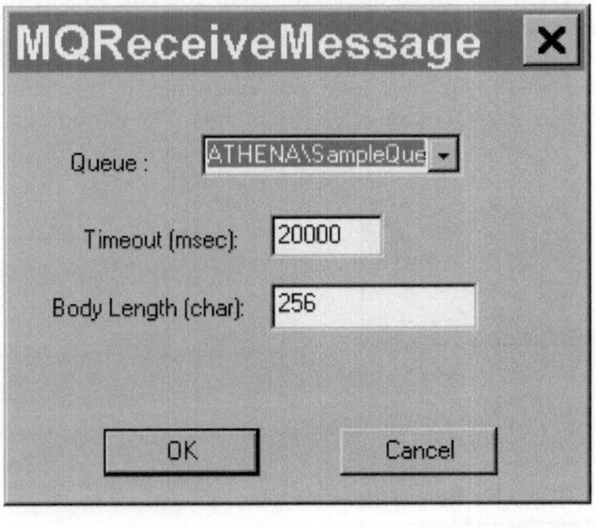

Figure 11–4: Receiving a message

The Queue combo box defines which queue we will be receiving messages from. If you have followed the preceding steps, the queue name will contain the name of the queue you created.

The Timeout text box specifies the time in milliseconds that the listening MSMQ method will wait before returning. Type in 20000.

The Body Length text box specifies the length of buffer that will be sent from the receiver to the sender. It is important to understand that there is a contract between the sender and receiver. Whenever the sender sends a certain number of bytes of data, the receiver must read the same number of bytes of data. If this contract is violated, problems can arise. The default value of 256 is fine, so click OK.

A dialog box will now be displayed, explaining that the receiver is waiting for a message. If a message is sent, the method will return and display the message in the client area of the receiver process. If the time exceeds 20000, the method will timeout and return without displaying anything. If you know that there is a message, call the MSMQ Receive Message dialog again.

STARTING AND TESTING A SENDER

The sender is responsible for sending a message to a queue, and to do this the sender needs to be capable of opening the queue. Although it is possible to open a queue directly, doing so does not always make sense because of how MSMQ manages queues. There may be many machines on an MSMQ network, with each holding some queues, and some queues on the different machines may have the same names. So, you need to determine which queue to open. You can specify a path containing a machine name and a queue name, but this locks the application to a specific machine and queue. To make the application generic, you, instead, need to locate the queue, possibly from a collection of queues.

To locate the queue, select API –> MQLocate from the menus. The dialog box in Figure 11–5 appears.

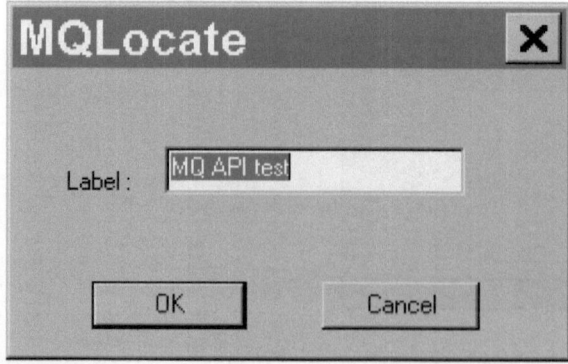

Figure 11–5: Locating a queue

This dialog box contains only a *Label* text box. Do not confuse the Label with the Windows element label. The Label of a queue is an identifier that is used by the MSMQ API testing sample to locate a queue. Type in MQ API test, which is the label we used earlier in the chapter when creating the queue. Then click OK. The receiver should find the queue that was just created and return a "locate queue operation completed successfully" message.

This is not the only way to locate a queue. The most common way is to use a Universal Unique Identifier (UUID), which can be like COM Globally Unique Identifier (GUID). The UUID approach was not used in the MSMQ API testing sample because typing in a UUID is very complicated and error prone.

After you have found the queue or queues, they can be opened for use. Opening a queue for the sender is exactly the same as opening a queue for the receiver, except that you need to choose MQ_SEND_ACCESS from the checkbox options instead of MQ_RECEIVE_ACCESS in the dialog box. A "queue was successfully opened" message should be visible in the client area. You can now send a message to the queue. Select API –> MQSend from the menus, and the dialog box shown in Figure 11–6 displays.

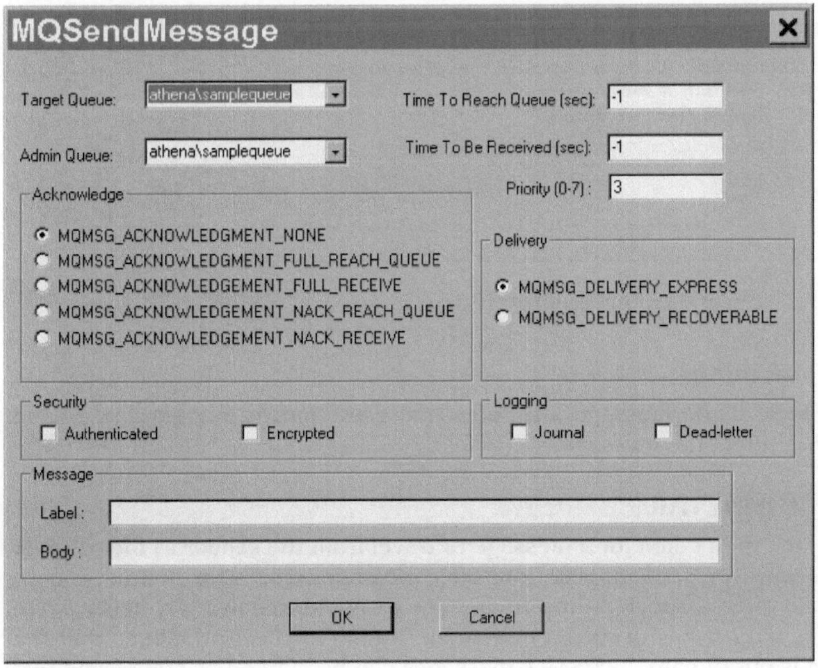

Figure 11–6: Message sending properties

This dialog box is much more complex than the others we have seen in this chapter. In the simplest case, you will need to fill in the Label and Body text boxes and click OK. The Label specifies a message header or description, and the Body contains the main content of the message.

We will go through the various options in the next section, so for now just enter some Label and Body text, and click OK to send the message to the receiver. The receiver should show results similar to those shown in Figure 11-7.

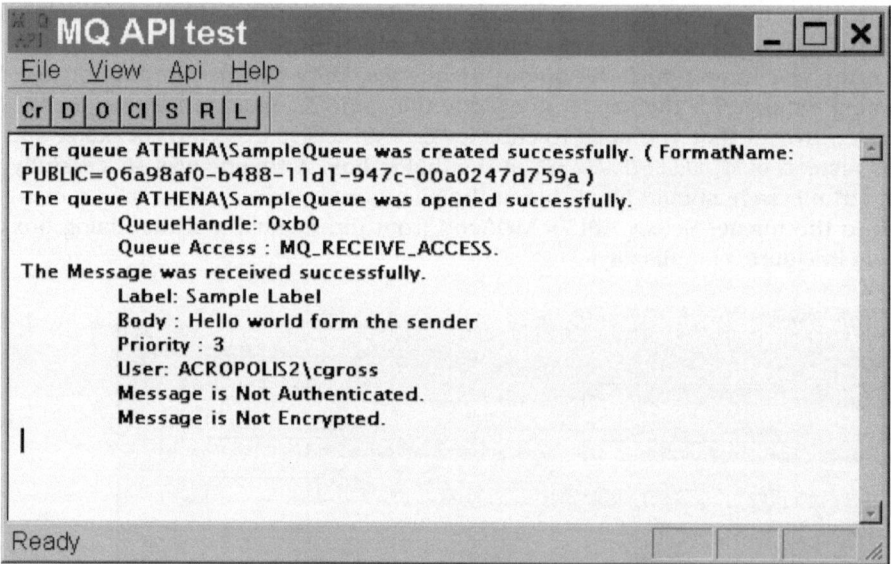

Figure 11–7: Receiver showing received message

Message Attributes

Let's now look at the message attributes that were shown in Figure 11–6, and see how they affect the message.

MESSAGE DELIVERY TIME

By default, the time taken for a message to travel from the sender to the receiver is ignored. However, some applications have messages where the content is considered stale after a specific time frame. For example, receiving a ticker value three weeks after it has occurred in a stock trading application means that the calculation is out of date. In MSMQ, messages can be marked as stale using two measurements: time to reach queue and/or time to be received. When a message is stale, the MSMQ network processes the file according to the queue and message properties.

When a sender sends a message, it is only considered sent at a programmatic level. In reality, the message is added to the MSMQ network and is in the process of being sent to the queue. The queue may be located on another machine in another country, and this traveling may take time. The time taken to reach the queue is called the *time to reach queue*. When the message is retrieved from the queue, the total time it has taken, from sending to retrieval, is called the *time to be received*.

The time taken to reach the queue is always less than the time to be received. If timeouts for both events are defined, then the time-to-be-received timeout takes precedence. This means that if the time to be received exceeds the timeout limit, and the time to reach queue is still within the limit, the message is still considered stale.

When you send a message, it is possible to specify the priority of a message. When sending two or more messages with MSMQ, you cannot specify the order in which the messages are received. They could arrive in any order, depending on factors such as traffic and processing capabilities. However, you can *influence* the order in which messages are received by setting the priority of the messages. In high traffic situations, this ensures that some messages are sent before others. MSMQ has a message Priority property, and the priorities can range from 0 to 7. The higher the priority, the higher the precedence of the message in the MSMQ network.

HOW A MESSAGE IS DELIVERED

There are two ways of delivering a message: express and recoverable. There is a large difference between the two. In *express* mode, the message is delivered at high speed. To maximize the speed, the message is not written to the hard disk—it stays in RAM and nothing is logged. The disadvantage of this method is that if the computer crashes, all traces of the message are lost.

In *recoverable* mode, the message is stored on the hard disk. When the MSMQ message travels through the network, at every node a backup copy of the message is made. This ensures that if the machine crashes, the message will still be sent. There is a trace of the message. The downside of this approach is that it requires extra processing time to write the data to the hard disk.

THE BODY OF A MESSAGE

In MSMQ, a message body is a series of bytes. The MSMQ ActiveX component has an extra capability. If the body is a COM object, MSMQ is capable of serializing the object using the IPersistStream COM interface. This simplifies writing and reading the message because the MSMQ ActiveX COM object takes on extra responsibilities.

FINDING OUT WHAT HAPPENED TO A MESSAGE

Sending a message is a one-way communication mechanism, in that there is a sender and a receiver, but it is helpful to know what happened to the message by receiving an acknowledgment. There are various types of acknowledgments, both positive and negative. When either type of acknowledgment is sent, it is sent to an administrative queue. The user specifies the administrative queue. In MSMQ 1.0, there were only basic acknowledgments.

In MSMQ 1.0, the acknowledgment was sent using the MSMQMessage.Ack property. With the release of MSMQ 2.0, though, the MSMQMessage.Ack property still exists, but it has lost significance. In MSMQ 2.0, message types are associated with a class of message (MSMQMessage.Class).

The different MSMQMessage.Ack property values are as follows:

- **MQMSG_ACKNOWLEDGMENT_FULL_REACH_QUEUE:** Posts a positive or negative acknowledgment depending on whether or not the message reaches the queue. A negative acknowledgment is posted when the *time-to-reach-queue* timer of the message expires, or when the message cannot be authenticated.
- **MQMSG_ACKNOWLEDGMENT_NACK_REACH_QUEUE:** Posts a negative acknowledgment when the message cannot reach the queue. A negative acknowledgment is posted when the *time-to-reach-queue* timer of the message expires, or when the message cannot be authenticated.
- **MQMSG_ACKNOWLEDGMENT_FULL_RECEIVE:** Posts a positive or negative acknowledgment, depending on whether or not the message is retrieved from the queue before its *time-to-be-received* timer expires.
- **MQMSG_ACKNOWLEDGMENT_NACK_RECEIVE:** Posts a negative acknowledgment when an error occurs and the message cannot be retrieved from the queue before its *time-to-be-received* timer expires.
- **MQMSG_ACKNOWLEDGMENT_NONE:** This is the default. No acknowledgment messages (positive or negative) are posted.

There are many details for using the various MSMQ message class values, and the different acknowledgments can be grouped into *arrival acknowledgments* or *read acknowledgments*. In the Microsoft Platform SDK Documentation the terms *arrival acknowledgments* and *read acknowledgments* are used to define the events associated with the arrival of the message in the queue and the reading of the message from the queue. (I have been referring to these events as sending the message to the queue and retrieving the message from the queue.) There are acknowledgments for encryption, for being able to write the message to the queue, for exceeding the quota, for the success of transaction, and so on. All acknowledgments are sent to an administrative queue.

TRANSACTIONS AND MSMQ

There are four different types of MSMQ transactions:

- **MSMQ transactions:** These transactions are internal to MSMQ. They only affect MSMQ messages and will not propagate to external resources.
- **DTC transactions:** These transactions explicitly combine MSMQ with the DTC (Distributed Transaction Coordinator). If resources are involved with the DTC, then they will be affected by the MSMQ transaction.

- **COM+ transactions:** These transactions are like the MSMQ with DTC transactions, except that the transaction association is done automatically. There is no need to write additional programming code.
- **XA-compliant transactions:** It is possible to send a message using transactions based on a transaction monitor using the XA protocol. In this scenario, you must still interact with the DTC, because it will be the resource monitor for the MSMQ resource provider.

Combining transactions and messaging changes how messaging works. First, to make transactions work on MSMQ messages, the queue to which the message is being sent must be transaction capable. This is accomplished by setting the queue transactional flag to true. After that is done, the message must use transactions and determine which transactions will be used from the four different models defined above. By default, you use the COM+ transaction capability, because it integrates with the Windows DNA architecture.

Now comes the tricky part. When an application sends a message in the context of a running COM+ transaction, the message is not sent immediately—it is only sent if the transaction commits successfully. If the transaction aborts, the messages are purged and not sent. While this may seem odd, there is a very important reason for doing this. Consider the problem of a transaction sending a message and then having the transaction abort. The MSMQ network would have to retract the message. If the message had been retrieved and processed, MSMQ would also have to retract the transactions executed by the processing of the message. The simpler approach is to not send out messages until the transaction is complete. However, this does mean that you can't send a message and wait for a response—this would cause an automatic deadlock because the transaction must first complete before a message response could be generated.

Now let's consider the situation of creating a Windows DNA application and running transactions on the sender and the receiver. It is possible to start a transaction context at the sender and have it extend to the receiver, but doing so is not recommended because it could create a long transaction. A long transaction is undesirable because it tends to lock resources and reduce scalability as explained in Chapter 10. What you want is to create a transaction context on the sender side and a separate transaction on the receiver side.

Sending and Receiving Transactional Messages

When a transaction is used, the message may or may not be transactional and the queue may or may not be transactional. This means that you could have a situation in which a message is transactional and the queue is not. This is further complicated in that the queue could be either local or remote. So, what combinations of transactions and queues are allowed? The following table shows which senders are permitted to send messages to a queue.

	LOCAL QUEUE		REMOTE QUEUE	
	Transactional	Non-transactional	Transactional	Non-transactional
Transactional Send	Yes	No	Yes	No
Nontransactional Send	No	Yes	No	Yes

When sending messages, the message must be transactional if the queue is transactional. The location of the queue is not a factor in whether a transactional message can be or cannot be sent.

The following table considers the situation of a receiver retrieving a message from queue.

	LOCAL QUEUE		REMOTE QUEUE	
	Transactional	Non-transactional	Transactional	Non-transactional
Transactional Received	Yes	No	No	No
Nontransactional Received	Yes	Yes	Yes	Yes

In this scenario, a transactional message can only be retrieved within the context of a transaction if the queue is local. But if you really want to retrieve a message, it is possible in all different situations. The question is whether there is an associated transaction context with the retrieved message. MSMQ assumes a transactionless retrieval model because MSMQ cannot assume that the receiver has a transaction content.

The advantage of using transactional queues is that messages arrive only once and in the proper order. The order of the messages' arrival reflects the order in which they were sent during the execution of the transaction. However, when messages that were created in different transaction contexts are being retrieved, they are not in order.

THE DIFFERENT QUEUES

In MSMQ, there are different types of queues: message queues, administration queues, response queues, journal queues, dead letter queues, and report queues.

Message Queues

The most commonly used queues are the message queues. Message queues are created by applications and are responsible for the sending of the data from a sender to a receiver. When a message queue is created, there are two variants: public and private. There can be any number of either. The *public* queue is stored within the MSMQ framework. This means it can be searched for and found. They are also persistent and can be backed up. The public queue provides basic functionality so that it can be used in an enterprise situation. The *Private* queue is stored on the local machine and cannot be searched for. A private queue has none of the overhead of the public queue and therefore is much faster.

Administration Queues

When a message queue is created, messages can be tracked. This may be important if the message contains sensitive information or if the information needs to be sent in a timely manner. In those instances, it can be important to know whether the message was sent and if it was sent in a timely manner. Or it may be important to know whether something went wrong with sending the message. Whenever these properties of the message are required, the data is returned in the form of a message. So as not to confuse these messages with actual application messages, there is an administration queue that contains all of these status messages.

Response Queue

When a sender sends a message to the receiver, often the sender can request a response. This type of response message is similar to the previous message type, but there is a very big distinction. The typical administrative message gives limited details, and it is sent if things went wrong. A response message contains application data, and it works only if the message did get through. If the message did not get through, the sender waits for the message to return and does not know what happened if there is no response.

Journal Queues

The journal queue is created whenever a machine is added to an MSMQ enterprise. The purpose of the journal is to track messages. The messages are only journaled when it is specified at the queue. Messages need to be journaled so that they can be sent again if anything happens to the sent messages. A journal is kept on the local machine, because after a message is journaled, the message is considered part of the system.

There are two types of journals. The *machine journal,* which tracks all messages from the machine, and the *queue journal,* which is a queue that is created at the location of the message queue. The queue journal tracks the messages removed from the main queue.

Dead Letter Queues

The dead letter queue is a queue like the journal queue that is created on a per machine basis. It stores the messages that could not be delivered. There are two types of dead letter queues: one for nontransaction-based messages and the other for transaction-based messages. Each case treats messages differently.

A dead message sent in nontransaction mode is stored in the dead letter queue of the machine that could not deliver the message. This nondelivery could be caused by the network not functioning or simply result from the message expiring. This means that if a message is being journaled, and it was entered into the journal queue on the previous machine, the message will stay there. A dead message does not change anything on the machines that it has already visited.

If a message is sent in transaction mode, and subsequently is considered dead, then the sending computer moves the message to the dead letter journal. Whatever happened on the network is erased, and no presence of the message is left.

Report Queues

Report queues are queues that track the progress of messages moving toward their destinations. Report queues are useful for the administrator who needs to track messages.

Writing a Messaging Application

Writing messaging applications is not as easy as it might seem. The process of sending data from one location to another is relatively simple. The complexity arises from the variety of options and the lack of specification on how the data is encoded.

To write effective messaging applications, two problems need to be overcome. The first is recreating a data structure. A typical messaging solution involves saving a structure of data as a message. The message is then sent somewhere where it is read and converted to a structure again. Thus, the solution has two pieces, a sender and a receiver, which may be written in the same language or not. The sender and receiver each require maintenance and explicit routines must be created that write and read the data.

The second problem is setting up an effective communication scheme. When a message receiver picks up a message, it does so from a specific queue. Ideally, the receiver returns a response, but it cannot use the same queue that it received the message from, because once the message is put in the queue, the receiver could then read its own message. Therefore, the sender and receiver must read messages from their own queues.

A Solution to Messaging

The solution to the problem of creating and maintaining separate senders and receivers is to implement the Command pattern. The command pattern simplifies the development process because it encapsulates the sender and receiver in one object. The sending process only sees the message as an object to be manipulated as part of a business process; the receiving process sees the message as a generic object that exposes an interface that is instantiated.

The object is sent from one location to another using the process of serialization. The sender process serializes the object into an MSMQ message. The receiver process unserializes the message, instantiating and executing the object. The execution is a method of a defined interface that the object implemented. This method then performs some business operations based on what the sender has saved to the object.

Using the command pattern, the sender and receiver processes do not need to know the details of the implementation. They only need to search for the IPatternCommand interface and invoke the appropriate method. The official Command pattern is defined to only have a single method, but a reply method can be tagged onto the IPatternCommand interface. The reply method makes it possible to send a message, do some processing, and then send a return answer.

In COM Interface Definition Language (IDL), the IPatternCommand interface is defined as follows:

```
interface IPatternCommand : IDispatch
{
[id(1)] HRESULT execute();
[id(2)] HRESULT reply();
[propput, id(3)] HRESULT service([in] IDispatch* newVal);
};
```

The property service is used to set the context of the current execution environment. When a COM object is to be defined as an MSMQ COM object, it must implement the IPatternCommand interface and the IPersistStream interface. The IPersistStream interface is a standard COM interface that is used to implement serialization.

When the sending process is sending a message and when the receiving process is receiving a message, they need to define the name of the queue, machine, and path. It is best to abstract these pieces of information. Do not hard code the queue name or machine name, because hard coding is generally a bad idea. The abstraction could be added to a Visual C++ header file or a Visual Basic global module file, but that means that a scripting client could not send a message. The solution is to define a COM interface that defines methods that will retrieve the correct machine or queue name. As an example, consider the following IDL interface:

```
interface IMsgProp : IUnknown
{
[propget] HRESULT machine([out, retval] BSTR *pVal);
[propget] HRESULT serviceType([out, retval] IID *pVal);
[propget] HRESULT queueName([out, retval] BSTR *pVal);
[propget] HRESULT description([out, retval] BSTR *pVal);
[propget] HRESULT fullPath([out, retval] BSTR *pVal);
};
```

The properties are read-only because they will depend on the implementation. The sender and receiver process instantiate the COM object that implements this interface, and they send the message or receive the message using the machine name or queue name properties defined by the implementation of the IMsgProp COM interface. The advantage of this approach is that the names of the queues and their locations can be updated without requiring a recompile of the sender or receiver processes or of the COM object that implements the IPatternCommand interface.

Writing an Implementation

The concept of implementing the IPatternCommand interface has been discussed, but what has not been discussed is the implementation of the IPersistStream interface. It is possible to implement this COM interface like any other COM interface. However, doing so makes extra work for ourselves if we are using Visual Basic or Visual J++. These tools offer built-in support for implementing this interface.

IMPLEMENTING IPERSISTSTREAM USING VISUAL BASIC

Look at the Visual Basic class file properties shown in Figure 11–8.

(Name)	clsLine
DataBindingBehavic	0 - vbNone
DataSourceBehavic	0 - vbNone
Instancing	5 - MultiUse
MTSTransactionMo(	0 - NotAnMTSObji
Persistable	1 - Persistable

Figure 11–8: Visual Basic class properties

The clsLine class has a property called Persistable. It can either have the value Not Persistable or, as shown in the figure, Persistable. What this does is implement IPersistStream, IPersistStreamInit, and IPersistStorage in the resulting COM object. The IPersistStreamInit and IPersistStorage interfaces have not been discussed; for now, consider them to work like IPersistStream does, except that they store the data differently. After the class is set to Persistable, then the Visual Basic class needs to implement the Class_ReadProperties and Class_WriteProperties methods, which are persistence events. Within the persistence events the object property values have to be written using the PropertyBag.

In Visual Basic, the data is streamed to something called a *property bag*. A property bag can be considered a piece of memory that contains the state of a COM object, and in this case, it is the Visual Basic class. The property bag is used for controls, for Active Documents (an advanced COM document concept that is beyond the scope of this book), and for MSMQ persistence.

The property bag contains a snapshot of the COM objects' state. Initializing an object and loading it with the state contained in a property bag, wipes out the existing state of the object. Because of this, if the state of the object changes because of operations performed on the object, it is good practice within Visual Basic to inform the property bag that changes occurred. Otherwise, some property bag implementations will not realize that the state has changed and so will not save the COM object. (It isn't necessary to inform the property bag about changes when the property bag represents an MSMQ message.)

Now let's consider implementing a COM object in Visual Basic to support persistence. This Visual Basic COM object has a state. Some private data members typically define the state. Performing some business operation on the COM object modifies these private data members. The simplest way to modify the private data members is to expose them as a series of COM properties. Consider the following example of defining a COM property in Visual Basic.

```
Public Property Let x1(ByVal vData As Long)
mvarx1 = vData
PropertyChanged "x1"
End Property
```

The COM property is assigned to the private value mvarx1, and then calling PropertyChanged with the name of the property indicates a change of state in the property bag. The name x1 is a key that is used to associate the property with a specific value. A property bag property name and a COM interface property name do not need to be the same. They can be named anything you want and represent anything you want. A property bag property is a key value pair identifier.

Data variables are read from the property bag in the Class_readProperties event. An example implementation is as follows:

```
Private Sub Class_ReadProperties(PropBag As PropertyBag)
mvarx1 = PropBag.ReadProperty("x1", 0)
…
End Sub
```

The variable mvarx1 is assigned by retrieving it from the PropertyBag using the key x1. The last parameter of ReadProperty is a default value if the key does not exist in the PropertyBag.

To write the property value, the following code is used:

```
Private Sub Class_WriteProperties(PropBag As PropertyBag)
PropBag.WriteProperty "x1", mvarx1, 0
…
End Sub
```

The method WriteProperty writes a key value pair in the PropertyBag. The last parameter is used to define a default value.

When reading or writing data to and from the property bag, the data is stored as a VARIANT. Hence, the data can be almost anything that Visual Basic can handle. For example, when passing in an object, the object is serialized. What is not supported is the serialization of collections; collections must be serialized using manual techniques. Nonbyte arrays are not supported at all.

Building a Serializable Collection Class

Because collection classes are not automatically serialized, we need to create a custom implementation of a collection class that can be serialized. This can be coded by hand, or it can be generated using the Visual Basic class builder. When the class builder window is active, it is possible to add a new collection. The class that will be built will be a collection that contains a number of line objects and it will be called clsLines. (At the time of this writing, the Visual Basic add-in that allowed automatic collection class generation was not functioning, so the collection class is coded manually here.)

A collection class is nothing more than a class with a number of specific method calls. The methods that we need are these:

- **Add:** Adds a line to the collection of lines. The add method parameter list is based on the data needed to define a valid line. In the implementation of this method, a clsLine object is instantiated and is assigned the parameters passed in. The newly instantiated object is then returned as a return value. An optional parameter is a key value that provides the capability to index the newly instantiated object in the collection using a meaningful identifier.
- **Item:** Retrieves the element based on the index passed in. The index can be a numeric or alphanumeric value.
- **Count:** Retrieves the number of elements contained within the collection.
- **Remove:** Removes the element pointed to at the current index.

To make it possible to iterate through the collection class using a Visual Basic FOR EACH loop, an extra method needs to be added. This method is responsible for creating a copy of the collection. This copied collection does not copy the contents of the local collection (mCol). The following is an example implementation:

```
Public Property Get NewEnum() As IUnknown
'this property allows you to enumerate
'this collection with the For...Each syntax
Set NewEnum = mCol.[_NewEnum]
End Property
```

The property mCol.[_NewEnum] is a special property that returns an IEnumVARIANT from the Visual Basic collection. To make everything work, the last step exposes this method with a special ID. To do this from the Visual Basic menu, select Tools -> Procedure Attributes. In the resulting dialog box, click Advanced to expand the dialog box. Then, from the Name combo box select the NewEnum method name. In the Procedure ID combo box, type -4. In the Attributes group box check Hide this member. The dialog box should look similar to the one shown in Figure 11–9.

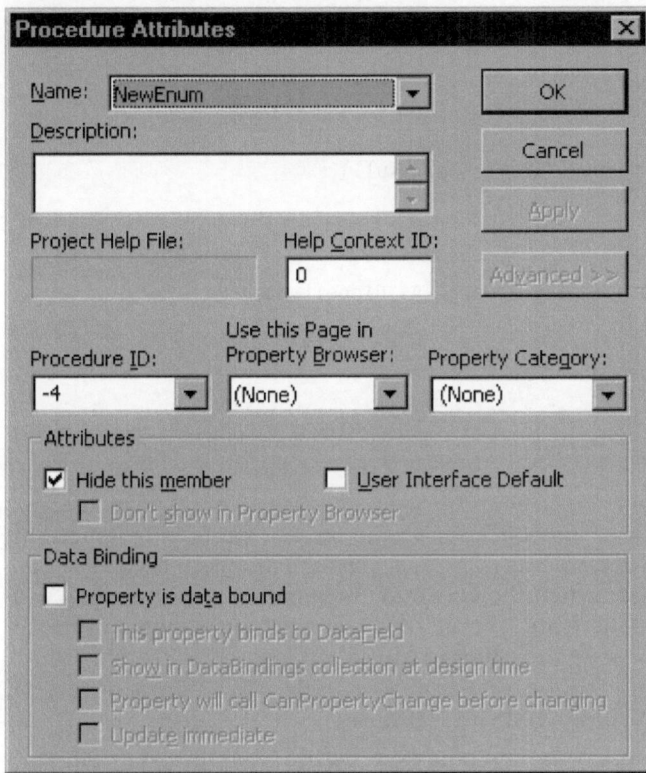

Figure 11–9: Procedure Attributes dialog box

The reason that the NewEnum method needs a special tag is because of how the Visual Basic FOR EACH loop operates. When a Visual Basic FOR EACH loop is started, it searches the collection object for a COM method with a dispID of –4. If that exists, then it calls that method and attempts to instantiate and return a IEnumVARIANT COM interface. Based on the IEnumVARIANT interface, the various elements are retrieved and assigned to a Visual Basic object.

This newly created collection class does not persist the individual elements. The next step is to make it persistable by setting its persistable property to persistable. **This adds the** InitProperties, ReadProperties, **and** WriteProperties **methods to the Visual Basic class.**

The implementations for reading and writing to the PropertyBag **are as follows:**

```
Private Sub Class_ReadProperties(PropBag As PropertyBag)
Dim tmp As Object
Dim count As Long
Dim c1 As Long
count = PropBag.ReadProperty("CollectionCount", 1)
For c1 = 1 To count
    tmp = PropBag.ReadProperty("Item" & c1, Null)
    mCol.Add tmp
Next
End Sub
Private Sub Class_WriteProperties(PropBag As PropertyBag)
Dim c1 As Long
PropBag.WriteProperty "CollectionCount", mCol.count
For c1 = 1 To mCol.count
    PropBag.WriteProperty "Item" & c1, mCol.Item(c1), Null
Next
End Sub
```

When the serialization of the collection to the stream starts, it is important to write the total number of elements (mCol.Count) as the first item to the stream. You have to do this because when the collection is being read in, the class will not know how many items there are. Therefore, to specify how many items are to be read, the class needs to save the count to the collection.

IMPLEMENTING IPERSISTSTREAM USING VISUAL J++

The IPersistStream interface is implemented within the Java Virtual Machine (VM). However, the Java COM object does not need to implement the IPersistStream. Instead, the Java COM object implements the standard Java serialization interface (java.io.Serializable). Implementing this interface implements IPersistStream, IPersistStreamInit, **and** IPersistStorage, as follows:

```
import java.io.Serializable;
public class cLine implements Serializable {
private long x1, x2, y1, y2;
...
}
```

When the Serializable interface is implemented in Java, it makes the Java VM inspect the class declaration and look for data members that can be written to a buffer. If the data types are the Java data types or other objects that have implemented the Serializable interface, then the serialization works. If the data declaration is either transient or static, then the data member is not serialized. An example of each is as follows:

```
transient long var1;
static long var2;
```

In the situation where the programmer has either declared all of the variables as transient or as object declarations, you need to implement the methods ReadProperties and WriteProperties to serialize those elements. An example of converting the individual values of the Java cLine class to transient and then implementing the persistence methods is as follows:

```
transient private long x1, x2, y1, y2;
private void writeObject(ObjectOutputStream s)
    throws IOException
{
    s.writeLong( x1);
    s.writeLong( x2);
    s.writeLong( y1);
    s.writeLong( y2);
}
private void readObject(ObjectInputStream s)
    throws IOException, ClassNotFoundException
{
    x1 = s.readLong();
    x2 = s.readLong();
    y1 = s.readLong();
    y2 = s.readLong();
}
```

The PropertyBag in Java is called an ObjectInputStream. They are both the same conceptually, but unlike in Visual Basic, Java requires that the type of data being written be specified. In the preceding code the readLong and writeLong methods were used. It is also possible to write objects (writeObject), floats (writeFloat), and so on.

IMPLEMENTING IPERSISTSTREAM USING VISUAL C++

If you are using Visual C++ to make the object persist, one of the COM interfaces (IPersistStream, IPersistStreamInit, and so on) must be implemented. By default, there are no helper classes.

The source code for this book has a sample class that handles the default implementation. This class is a template called MsgIPersistStreamImpl, which functions much like the Java Serializable interface. It needs to be added to an ATL (Active Template Library) COM object inheritance list. Then the COM MAP needs to be extended to indicate that the IPersistStream is available. The data members that are serialized are stored in the structure. In this implementation of the serialization an entire structure is written and then read from the stream.

An abbreviated ATL COM object with the added pieces is as follows:

```
class ATL_NO_VTABLE CLine :
public MsgIPersistStreamImpl< CLine >,
{
public:
CLine () {
    clearMemory();
    resetParameters();
}
BEGIN_COM_MAP(CLine)
COM_INTERFACE_ENTRY_IMPL_IID(IID_IPersistStream, MsgIPersistStreamImpl)
END_COM_MAP()
private:
typedef struct {
    long x1;
    long x2;
    long y1;
    long y2;
} structCLine;
public:
structCLine m_value;
DWORD m_size;
BOOL m_bRequiresSave;
};
```

The template `MsgIPersistStreamImpl` relies on public exposure of the data member `m_value`. This is a structure that contains all of the data members that will be serialized. The data member `m_size` is the size of the structure to be saved. This is used by `MsgIPersistStreamImpl` to determine how much data to write or read. The flag `m_bRequiresSave` is a dirty flag. If any properties are changed, it should be set to `TRUE`.

Saving COM Objects

This technique of serialization works correctly so long as the data types in the structure are simple. If the contained data type is complex, such as an object, it requires additional serialization. The template `MsgIPersistStreamImpl` has two virtual functions that make it possible to perform custom serialization. The `LocalLoad` method provides additional object-reading capabilities, and the `LocalSave` method provides additional object-writing capabilities. In either case, the method passes a `PropertyBag` equivalent that represents an `IStream` interface implementation. The reading and writing methods assume that the `IStream` interface pointer is reading and writing to a stream of bytes. This stream of bytes can only be read once.

The following is an example of implementing LocalLoad or LocalSave:

```
private:
PRJBATCHEXLib::UserDataPtr ptrUser;
public:
void LocalLoad( LPSTREAM pIStream) {
    ptrUser.CreateInstance( "PrjBatchEx.UserData.1");
    IPersistStreamPtr ptrStream = ptrUser;

    ptrStream->Load( pIStream);
}
void LocalSave( LPSTREAM pIStream, BOOL fClearDirty) {
    IPersistStreamPtr ptrStream = ptrUser;
    ptrStream->Save( pIStream, TRUE);
}
```

The object ptrUser is a private variable that has implemented IPersist-Stream. It is a nested COM object. When the implementations of LocalSave save the data, the ptrUser interface is converted using IUnknown::QueryInterface to an IPersistStream interface. Then the Save method is called and the passed-in IStream is passed to that object.

The loading of the nested object is similar (LocalLoad), but to make it work, the parent must instantiate it first. Then, like the saving of the nested object, the IPersistStream is QueryInteface'd for. This time Load is called with the passed in IStream interface pointer.

SERIALIZATION, DATA TYPES, AND VERSIONING

Serialization does have a downside. When the data is persisting, there are no version numbers included. This means that if the serialized COM object is updated, it may not work, because additional data fields may have been added or removed. This situation can arise in a messaging situation, because with MSMQ it is possible to keep a backlog of messages that have been sent. The solution to this versioning problem is to add a version field in the class definition. If the version numbers do not correspond, the object being serialized must take some action.

Consider the situation of Visual Basic creating the serialized buffer. Can this buffer then be read using Visual Basic or Visual J++? The answer is, probably not. This is because IPersistStream does not define the format of the data being stored. This problem is made worse if the data was created on one platform and will be read on another platform. The solution to this problem is to read the stream using the same tool that created the stream.

An Example of Distributed Application

If you are writing a good distributed application, messaging will be involved. So far in this book, we have considered everything that is necessary to fill in the details of the presentation and business logic tier.

The Web client will call a Web server, which is Internet Information Server (IIS). IIS, in turn, will call an Active Server Page (ASP) page, which will call a COM+ object. This COM+ object will run within the context of a transaction. The COM+ object may do some processing in the context of the transaction, and during this processing one step will be the creation of a message, which is sent to the queue when the transaction commits successfully. A receiver picks the message up, starts another transaction context, and carries out the rest of the work.

In Chapter 9, I explained that the COM objects in our business logic are separated into three types of objects: data, operations, and verification. Sending messages is not accounted for in this architecture. To send messages, the previously mentioned command pattern will be used. In this case, the data objects are assigned to the command pattern object.

When the IPatternCommand object is serialized to a messaging message, it also serializes the data objects. This means that the data objects have to be changed to implement IPersistStream so that they can be serialized to the MSMQ message. When the receiver picks the message up from the queue, the IPatternCommand object is also responsible for unserializing the data objects and instantiating them.

This is an optimum way of writing distributed applications. The implementation of the data objects is the only modification necessary for sending the state to another location. The operations and verification objects do not travel and are not affected by data objects traveling from another location. The operation and verification objects are only interested in the state of the data object. This makes the solution very granular.

A granular solution such as this makes it possible to focus on specific characteristics. For example, the operations object only operates on a state. The data object is only responsible for managing state, and that state can be serialized to a message. The command object is responsible for moving messages from one location to another and then starting a batch job to process that message. In the big picture, there has been a minimal amount of data copying.

DESCRIBING THE ARCHITECTURE IN UML

Now let's consider what a full implementation would look like in the form of a Unified Modeling Language (UML) diagram. The implementation we will look at is the process of a user registering and then passing on that registration to another location. The UML and the programming source code are available in the app-Conference directory of the source code for the book.

We first look at a UML diagram that shows the high level objects. Then we consider the activity excluding messaging. And then we split the activity into two operations: sending the activity to a message and reading the activity from a message.

So let's start with the UML class diagram. The registration process in a UML class diagram looks similar to Figure 11–10.

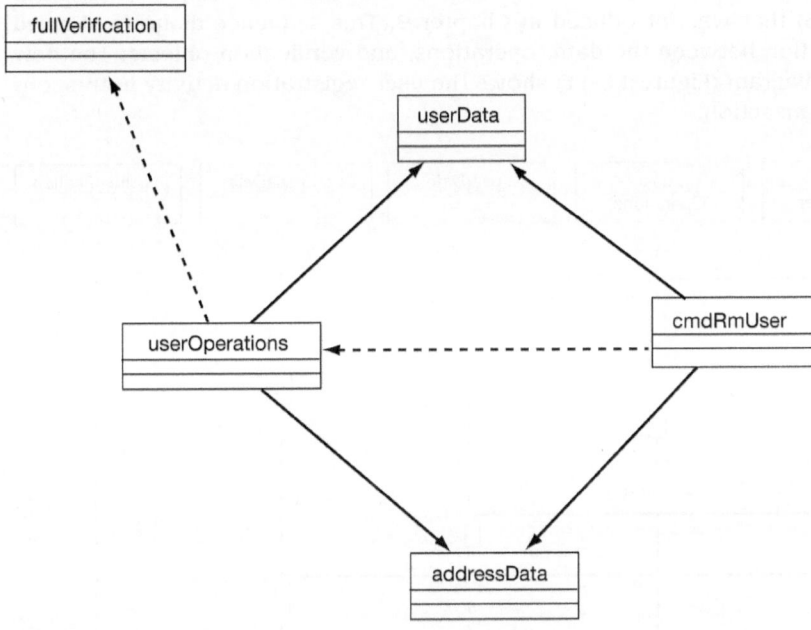

Figure 11–10: Architecture in terms of a UML class

There are two data objects: userData and addressData. These data objects contain data about a user and the user's address. The data objects are associated with the userOperations object. This object has methods such as Find (to find a specific user), Add, and Delete. There is a dependency between the userOperations object and the fullVerification object. This is a result of the operations object's method calls. The cmdRmUser object is a command object. It has an association with the userData and addressData objects. The dependency is established in the Execute method of the command object.

An Activity in a Distributed Application

What the class diagram does not show is the sequence in which the objects are manipulated and altered. Our activity diagram will extend the sequence diagram (Figure 9–5) that was introduced in Chapter 9. This sequence diagram showed the interaction between the data, operations, and verification objects. The new sequence diagram (Figure 11–11) shows the user registration activity in the context of a transaction.

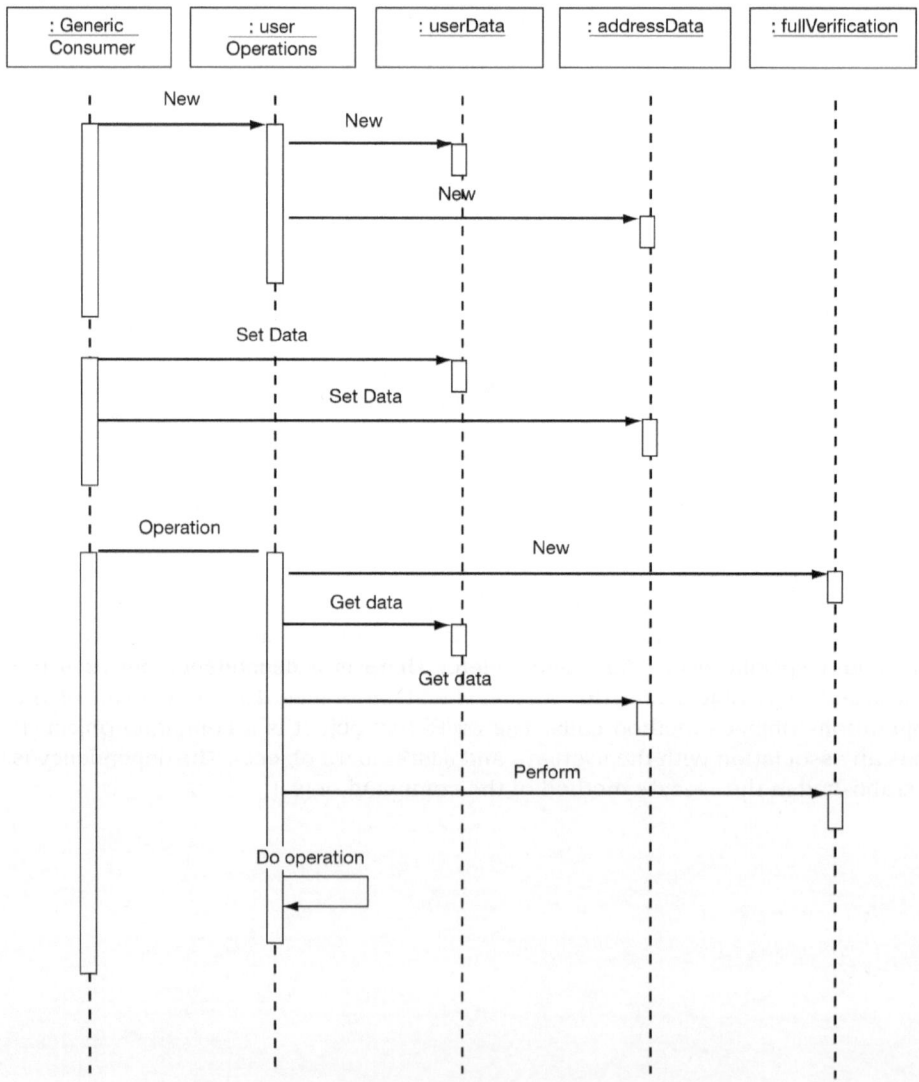

Figure 11–11: Sequence diagram showing details of an activity

The basis of an activity is a genericConsumer object that instantiates the userOperations object. In turn, this instantiates the userData and addressData objects. You could choose to have either the genericConsumer or the userOperations object create the data objects. I prefer to reduce the amount of method calls required by the consumer and let the operations object create the data objects that it needs.

You can also introduce an optimization at this point. Some data objects can be very large and they may not be used by certain operations. If you delay the object's creation to the point at which the data object is first referenced, you can avoid using unnecessary resources. This works well with transactions because it upholds the ideal of getting resources late and letting them go early.

After the different objects are instantiated, the generic consumer needs to set data to the data objects. And the next step in the sequence diagram is to call up the individual operation on the userOperations object. This then instantiates the verification object fullVerification. The data is retrieved in the form of object references and verification is performed. The last step is to do the operation on the object.

In Chapter 10, I stated that when a transaction is finished, all of the objects involved in the transaction are deactivated and deleted. The sequence diagram in Figure 11-11 shows see that there is a problem—the userOperations object is responsible for creating the data objects, and this means that the data objects could be part of the transaction stream and be deleted when the transaction is completed. We obviously do not want this because it would mean we would lose the state stored in the data objects. You might point out that in a state-managed environment, this is okay, but you need to remember that we do need some state for this sequence of operations. Therefore, when adding data objects to a COM+ application, make sure that they do not use transactions and that you have the transaction attribute set to *transaction not supported*.

Writing a Message in a Distributed Application

The previously defined user registration activity now needs to be converted to a messaging application, which means that the application will send messages when it wants some task accomplished. The sequence diagram in Figure 11–12 goes through the process of writing a message.

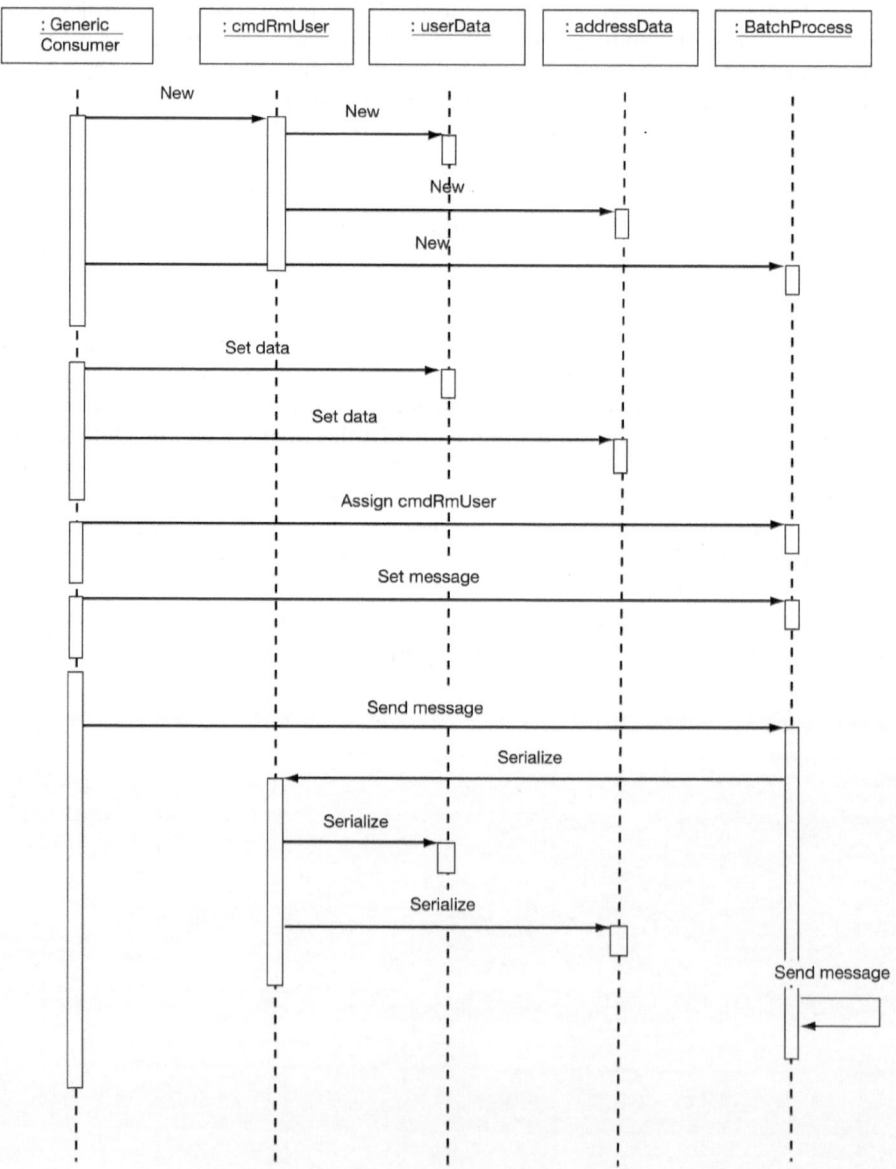

Figure 11–12: Sequence diagram of writing a message

In writing a message, there are two general objects: genericConsumer and BatchProcess. The BatchProcess object is a generic process that manages the messages. (The batch process is described in the last chapter of this book.) The genericConsumer instantiates the command object cmdRmUser using the new operation. This, in turn, instantiates the two data objects userData and addressData. The genericComponent is also responsible for instantiating the BatchProcess object by creating a reference to the actively running BatchProcess.

When the various objects are instantiated, the genericConsumer assigns the data objects userData and addressData. This operation need not involve a data transfer—it could be an assignment of already active userData or addressData objects.

The object hierarchy is now complete. In our messaging application, the operation is carried out on the receiver end. The cmdRmUser object represents the object that implements the IPatternCommand COM interface. The BatchProcess object is responsible for sending the message to the queue. Therefore, the object cmdRmUser needs to be assigned to the BatchProcess object. The genericConsumer will indicate to the BatchProcess object that the message should be sent.

When this happens, the BatchProcess object takes control and serializes the object hierarchy pointed to by cmdRmUser. According to our serialization outlined in a previous section of this chapter, the cmdRmUser causes the serialization of the userData and addressData object. The serialized stream of information is saved to a buffer that the BatchProcess object uses as contents for an MSMQ message. Once the serialization process ends, the BatchProcess object calls itself and causes the message to be sent to the MSMQ queue.

Reading and Executing a Message

The second part of the messaging activity involves reading and processing the message. In the processing the message, the business logic is executed. Messages do not cause an event on the receiver side, so there must be an active process using either polling or MSMQ COM connection points to wait for a message.

In the receiving message sequence diagram, the active process is called BatchProcess, which is identical to the BatchProcess in the message sending sequence diagram. These can be the same applications or two different applications. The term BatchProcess is used to indicate that it is an external process used to send or receive messages from MSMQ.

In the sequence diagram of reading the message (Figure 11–13), the process of waiting for the message is not shown. The sequence diagram assumes that the BatchProcess has received the message and is about to start processing the MSMQ message.

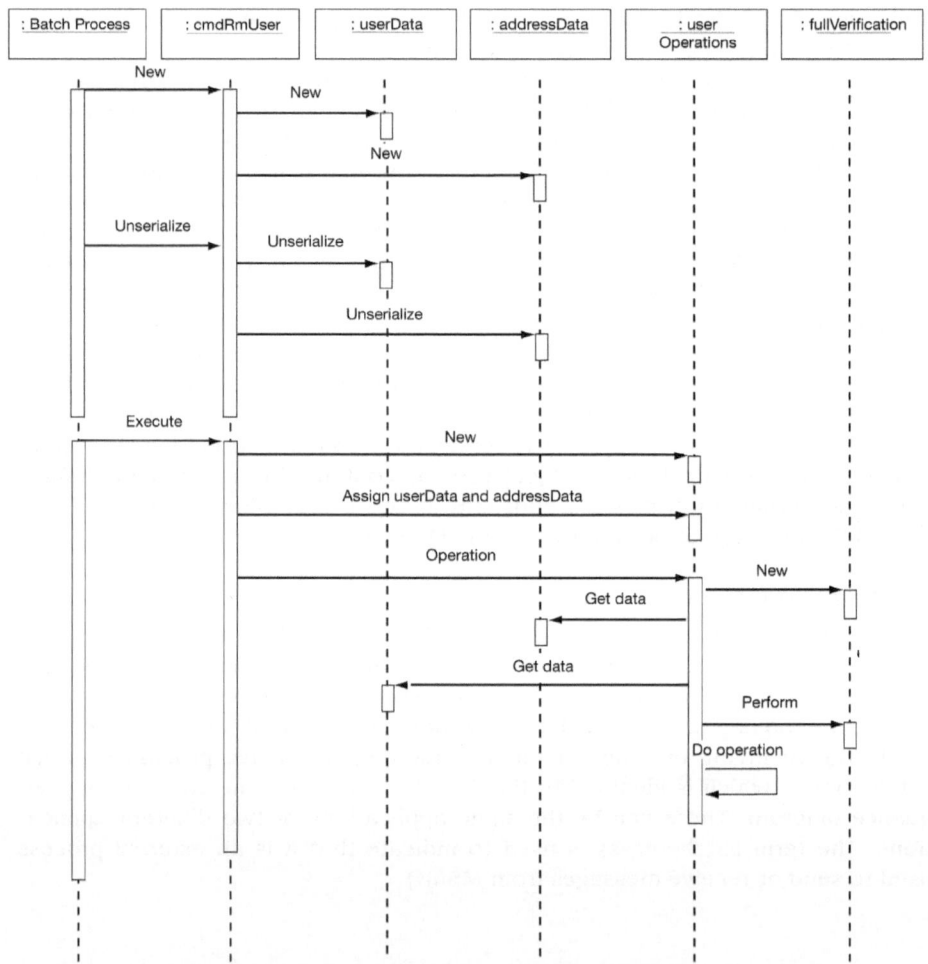

Figure 11–13: Sequence diagram of reading a message

When a message has arrived, BatchProcess has a buffer containing a serialized stream of objects. Therefore, the BatchProcess object needs to instantiate the cmdRmUser object. This, in turn, causes the instantiation of the userData and addressData objects.

After the serialization process recreates the object state, the BatchProcess object does a QueryInterface for the IPatternCommand interface from the cmdRmUser object. Then, as previously described, the IPatternCommand::Execute method is called by the `BatchProcess` object. This carries out the registration activity that was described at the beginning of this section.

ABOUT THE BATCH PROCESS

The `BatchProcess` object is a generic batch process that makes it possible to carry out a task on any remote location. However, because of the batch process, the transaction is split into two parts. There is a transaction executing on the sender side and a transaction executing on the receiver side. The sending process assumes that if its transaction is successful, the receiver transaction must be successful, as well.

But what happens if the receiver process transaction aborts? This can become very complicated. If any processing work was made durable on the sender side, it has to be undone.

Undoing a Transaction Theoretically

Undoing a transaction is not something that is supported at the theoretical level. When a transaction is completed, then any state resulting from it is considered correct. However, in reality there are times when state changes must be undone. The trick to undoing a transaction is not to undo it, but to perform an opposite transaction in addition to the first one. Consider how CAD (Computer-Aided Design) software handles undoing elements of a design.

In the CAD software world, undoing is extremely important. But the undo must be intelligent, in that it must undo some things and not others. For example, if you are designing a house, undoing the design of the door should not affect the windows or walls surrounding the door. When the door is removed from the drawing, all that should be left is a wall with no door. The CAD solution to this problem is to use Euler operators. In a CAD designing process, every operation should have an equal opposite that undoes whatever was done. In the case of the door, there are operators for adding a door and for removing a door.

In another context, let's consider the process of adding and subtracting numbers.

$$1+2+3+4=10$$

The opposite of the first step is -1. Adding this to the mathematical equation changes it to

$$1+2+3+4-1=9$$

This is the same answer as if the first step didn't occur:

$$2+3+4=9$$

In a business process, every object must have equal and opposite methods. For example, if you have a method to add a user, you must have a method to delete the user.

The important question is how do you know what to delete and what the original parameters were? To provide this information, you can add a logging facility that tracks the operations that have occurred. The undo method will retrieve the parameters used in the original method call from the log file.

Undoing a Transaction Practically

Now let's consider how all of this can be implemented in reality. Part of the solution is already available in a technology called Queued Components. Queued Components are discussed in detail in Chapter 12. For now, you just need to know that Queued Components have a built-in undo mechanism. The undo is provided by a COM interface called IPlayControl, which is defined as follows:

```
interface IPlaybackControl : IUnknown {
HRESULT FinalClientRetry( void);
HRESULT FinalServerRetry( void);
};
```

When a Queued Component method fails, it calls FinalServerRetry on the receiver side to indicate a failure. Then the Queued Component calls the sender-side FinalClientRetry method to undo the effects of the message.

To implement this in our application, the operations objects would implement the IPlaybackControl COM interface. When either method of the IPlaybackControl COM interface is called, the operations object knows to do the opposite (undo) of what it normally would have done. According to our previous sequence diagrams, the cmdRmUser and userOperations objects would implement IPlayBackControl.

What the BatchProcess would then do is call the IPlayBackControl interface to indicate that an error has occurred. Then the BatchProcess would go through the same calling sequence, and each method call in the calling sequence would undo the operations previously applied. The playback control uses the same approach as the CAD Euler operators. The difference is that there is a specific COM interface that is responsible for setting the negative operations flag.

This technique of undoing a transaction sounds easy from a technical point of view, but it is not simple from a business point of view. For example, if an ATM (Automated Teller Machine) gives out US$100 and then finds that there was an error, the ATM cannot run after the individual and ask for the US$100 back. Another path of action must be taken to retrieve the money, and that other path is not a simple solution.

Putting It in Perspective

Messaging changed the tone of our application. Messaging provides the capability to send state from one location to another. The most important part of this entire exercise is to understand that by separating the data objects from the operations objects, moving state is simplified.

So, why are we changing to messaging? Because it provides scalability and robustness. In many of my projects, messaging has proven itself to be the most robust way of writing applications that work. The only problem is that you need to change your programming model. This is why the Command pattern was introduced. By using this pattern, it is possible to distribute a task over different locations without it affecting our programming model.

There is also a technology called Distributed COM (DCOM), which makes it possible for one COM object to call another COM object on a different machine. I personally have found this to be a rather poor technology—it tends to be very "chatty" on the network and is complicated to configure. I consider it a kludge that does work in some situations. Messaging is better because an administrator can control all aspects of the messaging application, such as which server handles the request, and resending of messaging when things go wrong. The challenge lies in converting the programmer to write event-driven server-side applications.

Chapter 12

COM+ Asynchronous Services

This chapter introduces two new Component Object Model (COM)+ services: queued components and event services. COM+ queued components are Distributed Component Object Model (DCOM) components using Microsoft Message Queue (MSMQ). The advantage of COM+ queued components is that they can cope with failure. COM+ queued components are an easy way of distributing processing power on an as-needed basis.

COM+ events make it possible to publish information and to subscribe to that information. If you have some experience using COM, youíll find COM+ events to be similar to connection points, except that COM+ events are more robust and scalable. When you are using COM+ events, you do not need to know who wants to subscribe to the information.

COM+ Queued Components

COM+ queued components are designed to provide reliable communications between a client and a server. At the end of Chapter 11, I mentioned that I was not impressed with DCOM. This is not because of the DCOM concept but because of the implementation. DCOM is a very chatty protocol and its security can be complicated to set up correctly. Over a long distance connection, DCOM can be unreliable.

What we would like to have is a stable and robust DCOM, and with the release of Windows 2000 there is a stable and robust DCOM-like technology called COM+ queued components. With COM+ queued components, the method of communication between two COM objects is similar to using DCOM, except that MSMQ is used as a transport mechanism.

How Queued Components Work

COM+ queued components are a layer that was programmed on top of MSMQ. The problem that we had with MSMQ in Chapter 11 was that sending raw structures and messages made programming much more difficult. The solution that we used in that chapter was to use the Command pattern to distribute the task from the sender to receiver. This did make things simpler, but this chapter considers another solution that solves a problem that was not solved by the Command pattern.

COM+ queued components work by intercepting property assignments and method calls for a COM+ object that was defined as queueable. These operations are recorded in a buffer by the COM+ infrastructure, and the buffer is then converted to an MSMQ message, which is sent to an MSMQ queue. On the listener side, the COM+ infrastructure plays back the operations that were recorded. This is like a COM-based macro recorder.

Figure 12-1 shows how COM+ queued components work. The COM+ queued component infrastructure includes devices called recorder and player. When a client instantiates a queueable COM+ object, the COM+ queued component infrastructure instantiates a ghost interface. The ghost COM interface is identical to the queueable COM+ object's COM interface and is directly tied to the recorder. Hence, whenever the client makes a method call or a property assignment, it is automatically recorded. When recording has stopped, the recording information is sent as a message to the listener. The listener opens the message and then plays back the different method calls and property assignments.

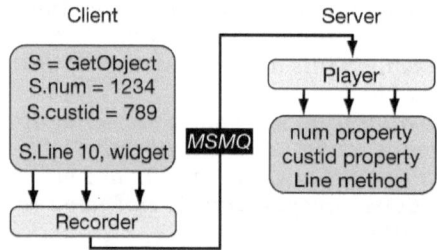

Figure 12–1: Queued component infrastructure

Implementing a Queueable COM+ Component

A queueable COM+ component does have some restrictions imposed on its interface. The restrictions are identical to the restrictions imposed by ordinary COM+ objects using MSMQ. This means that the communication is asynchronous, so we cannot expect a response to our method calls. When the restrictions are applied, they are not applied to the COM+ object but to a specific COM interface that the COM+ object has implemented.

The following points sum up the COM interface restrictions:

- The queued component message must contain parameters by value. It is not possible to send parameters by reference. This means that queueable COM interface method parameters and properties must be tagged with the Interface Definition Language (IDL) attribute [in] only.
- If the parameter is an object that supports the IPersistStream interface, it is serialized.
- The communication is one way and no response can be sent.
- The recorder finishes recording everything before any messages are played on the server side.

Apart from these restrictions, consuming a queueable COM+ object is just like making a COM call.

A SAMPLE QUEUEABLE COM+ INTERFACE

We will implement the messaging activity defined at the end of the last chapter. As you may recall, there were two core objects in the distributed messaging application: BatchProcess and cmdRmUser. In the last chapter, the BatchProcess object was defined as single or multiple processes that would handle the sending and receiving of MSMQ messages. The cmdRmUser object implemented the IPatternCommand interface. The main responsibility of the cmdRmUser object was to carry out the remote task when the IPatternCommand::Execute method was called.

We begin with the implementation of BatchProcess. This COM+ object has a single interface with a single method and a single parameter. If this COM interface is defined using either Visual J++ or Visual C++, it is possible to add the queueable attribute to the IDL interface. With Visual Basic, the interface is either manually or programmatically registered as queueable. An example of defining the queueable attribute in IDL is as follows:

```
[
helpstring("IBatchProcess "), uuid(CB34A1A4-28C2-11D2-B5B6-00C04FC340EE),
object, dual, nonextensible, hidden, pointer_default(unique),
QUEUEABLE
]
interface IBatchProcess: IDispatch {
[id(1)] HRESULT execute([in] IDispatch *obj);
}
```

The IBatchProcess serves as a service that can be called by any client. It contains one method, execute, which has one parameter. The parameter represents the remote operations object to be executed. In our example, this is the cmdRmUser object. An example Visual Basic implementation of the IBatchProcess::execute method is as follows:

```
Public Sub execute(ByVal obj As Object)
Dim tmp As PatternCommand

Set tmp = obj
tmp.execute
End Sub
```

The obj object is converted to the variable tmp, which is the IPatternCommand (PatternCommand) COM interface. Then the IPatternCommand::Execute method is called. That is the entire implementation of BatchProcess.

You may look at this and ask where the rest of the code is. The answer is that it is in the COM+ queued components framework. So, why not expose the cmdRmUser object as a queueable component? The answer is that COM interface restrictions make development a bit tricky, and doing so means that each COM interface needs to be exposed as queueable. By using a neutral object such as BatchProcess, it is only necessary to create one queueable COM+ object per machine. This architecture also fits very elegantly into our previously defined architecture. The restriction on sending objects as messages means that they must implement the IPersistStream interface. However, doing that is trivial, because it was already done in the last chapter.

REGISTERING A QUEUEABLE COM+ COMPONENT

A queueable COM+ object must be added to a COM+ application that accepts COM+ queued component messages. Remember that a COM object is a COM+ object once it has been added to a COM+ application. In the context of a COM+ application, it is possible to set up the COM+ queued component listener. To do this, create a new COM+ application. Then, right-click the node of the newly created COM+ application and open the Properties dialog box for a COM+ application. Select the Queuing tab, which should look similar to the one shown in Figure 12–2.

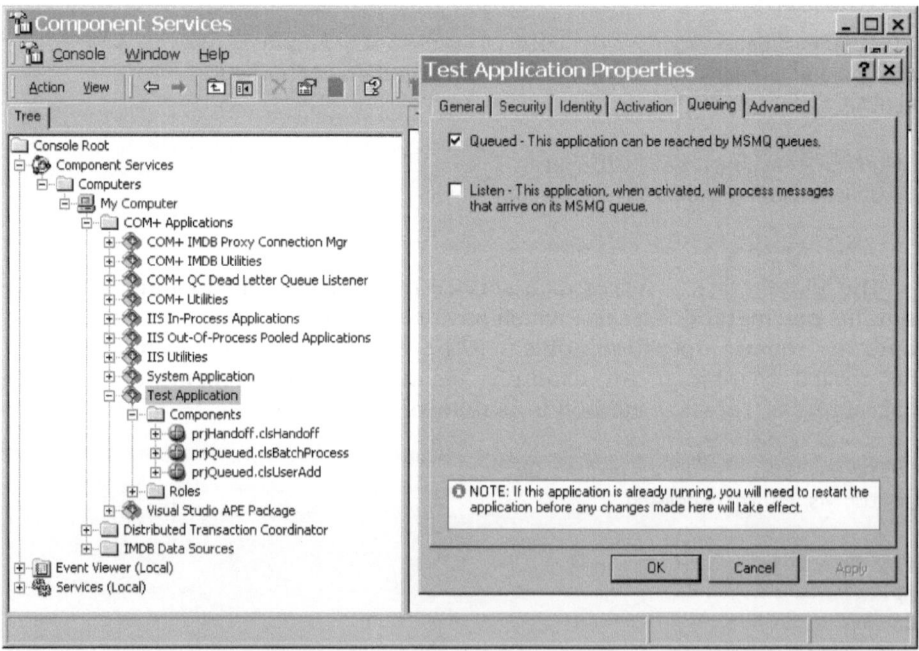

Figure 12–2: COM+ queuing properties

In this sample, the COM+ application is called Test Application. The Queued checkbox in the dialog box is checked, which enables the application to receive COM+ queued component messages. The Listen checkbox has not been checked, which means that COM+ queued component messages will be stored in the queue but not retrieved. If the Listen checkbox were checked, the messages would be picked up automatically and processed.

As it stands, the COM+ application needs to be started manually. This can be done using either the COM+ Explorer or the COM+ catalog manager.

Looking at the MSMQ Queue

Let's consider how a COM+ queued component application works with a MSMQ queue. This is important because it determines where the queue must be located and what messages can be sent to it.

The COM+ queued component framework creates a queue that has the same name as the COM+ application. This means that when you are writing MSMQ applications as outlined in Chapter 11, you cannot send or receive messages to a queue with the same name. This can and will cause conflicts with the COM+ queued component infrastructure.

Figure 12–3 shows that the queue is transactional. This is necessary because the COM+ application works with transactions. As we saw in the previous chapter, if the MSMQ queue is not transactional, any failures will result in lost messages. And this is something that we need to avoid at all costs.

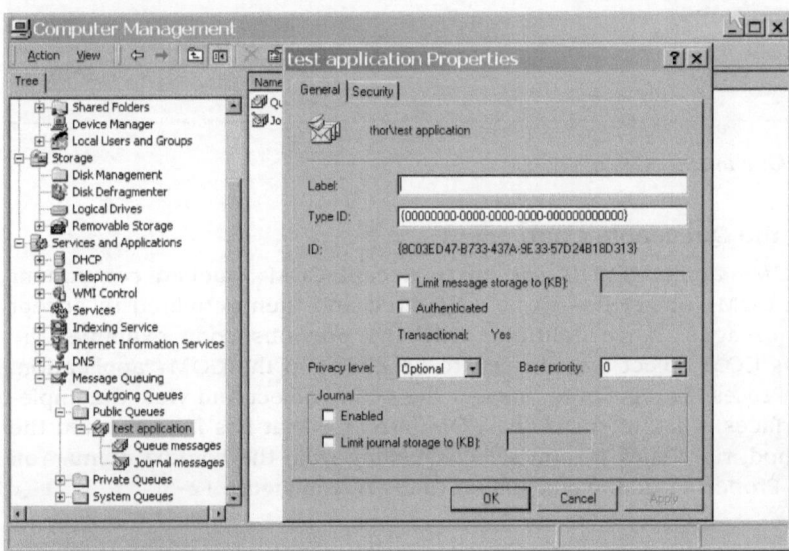

Figure 12–3: MSMQ queue properties

Now I am going to jump ahead because I want to show some messages in the queue. Figure 12–4 shows some simple messages. If you were to open one up and inspect its contents, you would see that they are messages with binary content. The structure of the binary content is not defined. Hence, it is not possible to manipulate the MSMQ messages manually using MSMQ COM object calls. Doing so could confuse the COM+ application and possibly introduce errors.

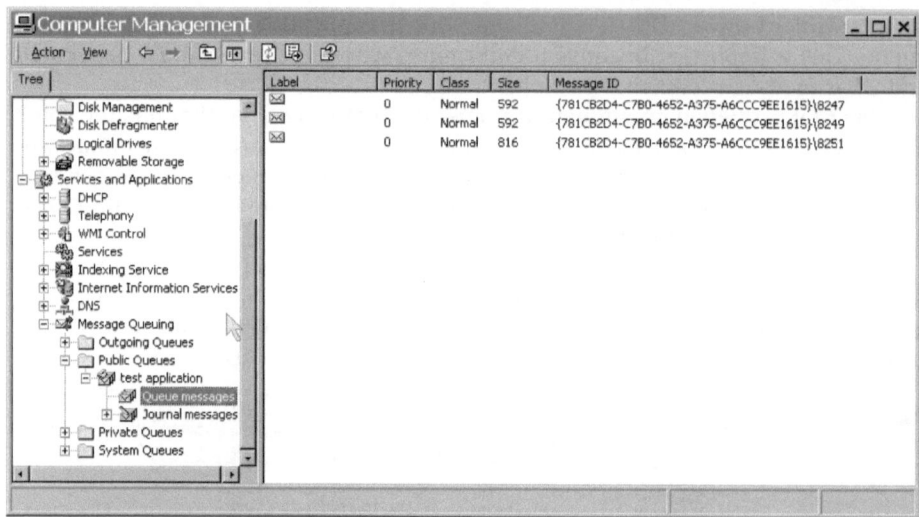

Figure 12–4: Queue with messages

Registering the Queueable Component

After the COM+ application is set up to accept COM+ queued component messages, a COM+ object has to be registered and then activated to accept individual messages. If we continue with the previous code example, the IBatchProcess COM object would need to be added to the COM+ application. When IBatchProcess is registered, inspect the COM+ object and view the implemented interfaces. Click to select the COM interface that has implemented the execute method, right-click it, and select Queuing from the context menu. You should see a Properties dialog box similar to the one in Figure 12–5.

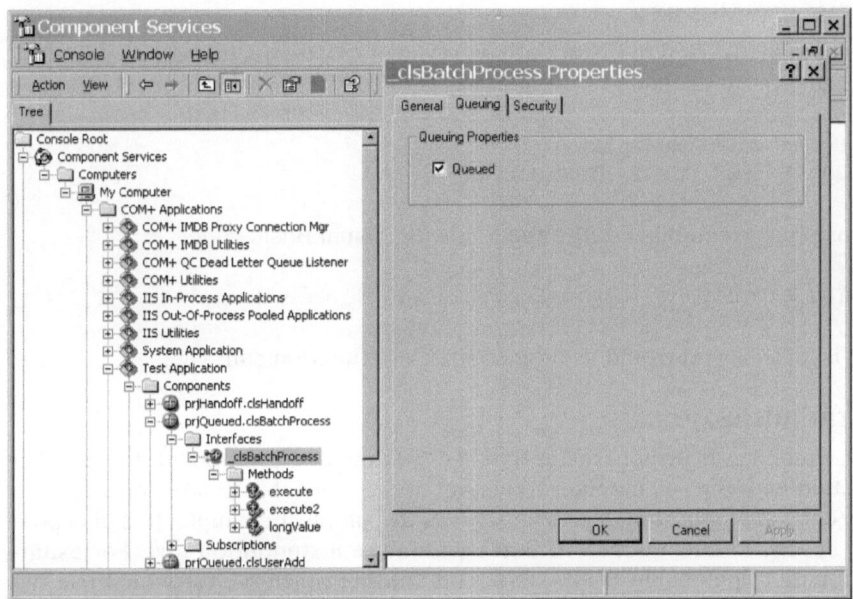

Figure 12–5: BatchProcess COM interface activated as queueable

In this figure, the Queued checkbox is checked and indicates that this interface will accept COM+ queued component messages. If this COM interface were defined in IDL and had the QUEUEABLE attribute, then it would be automatically set. If this COM interface violated one of the COM+ queued component restrictions, the Queued checkbox would be grayed out.

Click OK to accept the properties, and the application will be set to receive COM+ queued component messages.

Instantiating a Queueable COM+ Component

Instantiating a queueable COM+ component is slightly different from instantiating a regular COM+ object. The difference lies in the instantiation string. With regular COM+ objects, you would call CreateObject and pass in the CLSID (Class ID) or the PROG ID of the desired object. With COM+ queued components, the string uses a different object creator. Consider the following example, which instantiates a queueable COM+ object:

```
Set userOp = GetObject("queue:/new:prjQueued.clsBatchProcess")
```

The GetObject function retrieves an existing object from a stream. This code is written using Visual Basic, but the same type of function is used in other programming languages. Historically, GetObject was used to instantiate a COM object from a file because it uses COM monikers. With Windows 2000 there are two new COM monikers: new and queue.

USING THE NEW MONIKER

The new moniker is used to instantiate any type of COM object based on its PROG ID or its CLSID. An example of using either is as follows:

```
new:prjQueued.clsBatchProcess
new:{812DF40E-BD88-11D0-8A6D-00C04FC340EE}
```

To use the new moniker, write the following Visual Basic code:

```
set userOp = GetObject( "new:prjQueued.clsBatchProcess")
```

In Visual C++, you would use the CoGetObject function call.

USING THE QUEUE MONIKER

The queue moniker is used to instantiate a COM+ queued component. It is used in conjunction with the new moniker to instantiate a queueable COM+ object.

The code example shown previously was the simplest example. It is also possible to specify MSMQ queue attributes within the instantiation text. For example, to create a queueable COM+ object on another machine, we would use the following string:

```
queue: ComputerName=cronos/new:prjQueued.clsBatchProcess
```

In this example, the COM+ queued component message is routed to the queue located on the *cronos* machine. This then makes it a DCOM type call, in that the call spans multiple machines.

There are other options that can be specified. In all of the preceding examples, it was assumed that the queue name was identical to the name of the COM+ application. However, let's consider the situation of the remote client. The COM+ queued component infrastructure will not know what the name of the remote COM+ application is, so the queue's name must be defined as the attribute QueueName.

It is also possible to specify attributes that indicate how the message is to be sent. Examples include the encryption, label, MaxTimeToReachQueue. The attributes would be added to the COM+ object instantiation string. As you will notice, they map directly to MSMQ message and queue properties. This is the point, because COM+ queued components are built on top of MSMQ.

And If Something Goes Wrong

To this point, we have assumed that everything has gone well. But what happens if something goes wrong? For example, suppose the network is interrupted. With COM+ queued components, problems are handled and messages are always accounted for in one way or another. COM+ queued components do not lose messages. This is the advantage of queued components over a standard DCOM call.

Let's consider the scenario of a client and a server on two different machines. If you are using COM+ queued components, the message is sent to the server, and then the COM+ application processes the message. To make this scenario work on the server machine, a COM+ application proxy must be created. To do so, select the COM+ application and then export it as an Application Proxy. Then install this proxy on the client machine, and a COM+ application identical to the server COM+ application is created. However, when the components within the COM+ application are instantiated on the client machine, the requests are sent to originating server.

In this client server type of situation, many different errors can occur, but they always end up being two basic types of errors. The first is that the message cannot reach the destination queue and the other is that server-side processing failed.

CANNOT REACH THE QUEUE

The simplest type of error is when the message cannot reach the destination queue. This could happen if the network is not available or if the destination queue is not accepting messages. When the message cannot be sent, it is moved to the Transactional Dead Letter queue. This queue can be found under the System Queue heading in the Message Queue explorer.

COM+ queued components have an associated queue scanner that scans the Transactional Dead Letter queue for messages. If the scanner finds a message and finds a queued COM+ object message, it attempts to instantiate the exception class associated with the queueable COM+ object. The exception class is a COM+ object that is instantiated when a COM+ queued component message fails.

The purpose of the exception class is to undo a transaction that has occurred as a result of the original message. We saw this type of functionality at the end of the last chapter, where we built an undo framework.

To specify an exception class, select the COM+ object in the COM+ application, right-click it, and select Properties to retrieve the properties of the COM+ object. The Advanced tab of the dialog box is shown in Figure 12–6.

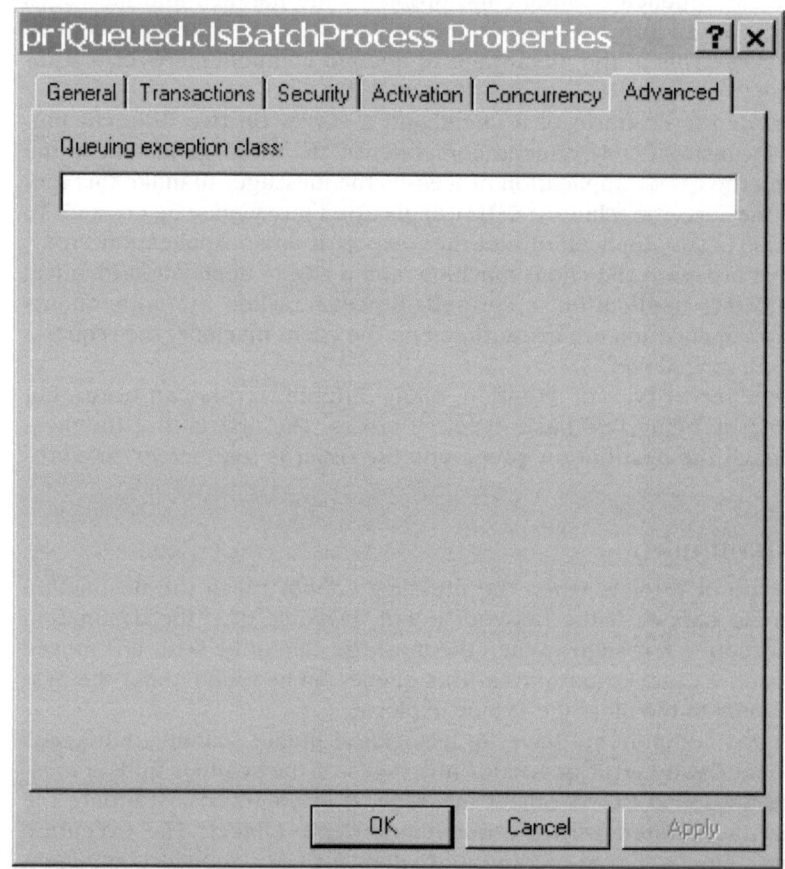

Figure 12–6: Queuing Exception class definition

The Queuing Exception class is a class that implements the same interface as the queueable COM+ object that has failed, and it implements one additional COM interface called IPlaybackControl. This COM interface was discussed in the last chapter. Its purpose is to indicate that an error has occurred by calling the IPlayBackControl::FinalClientRetry method. Then the final playback of the failed message is executed, and the exception class attempts to undo the transactions that have been done. If the undoing works, the failed message is removed from the Transactional Dead Letter queue. Otherwise, the message remains in the Transactional Dead Letter queue. Once the message is in the Transactional Dead Letter queue, it must be removed manually using either an administrative tool or a program.

CANNOT BE PROCESSED ON THE SERVER SIDE

The other error scenario is when a message reaches the server side and the COM+ queued components' playback control cannot successfully carry out the COM+ queued component message. This is considered a failure. At this point, a very long series of attempts is carried out. I will not get into the details, but essentially it works like this:

1. The message is retried.
2. If the message fails, the message is put back in the queue.
3. If the failed message count exceeds the maximum, the message is put in a different queue. The name of the queue is *Application_X* where *X* is the retry level. The retry level is incremented with each failed retry.
4. If the retry level exceeds five, the message is moved into the queue with the name *Application_DeadQueue*. The message stays here until an administrator using the MSMQ Explorer or some other tool moves it.

On the last retry before the message is moved to the `Application_DeadQueue` queue, the associated exception class is retrieved with the failed queueable COM+ object. If this exception class exists, then the `IPlaybackControl` interface is retrieved, and the `IPlaybackControll::FinalServerRetry` method is called. Then the methods and property assignments are played back. It is up to the exception class to undo the effects of the message. If this operation does not fail, the message is deleted instead of being moved to *Application_DeadQueue*.

You might expect an indicator to be kept to point out that something failed. However, this isn't needed because the exception class undoes any operations that have been done. If you do want a message, an event can be logged in the exception class.

Getting an Answer Back

So, how does the calling application get an answer back? The solution is to implement the Command pattern in reverse. One way of doing this is to add the name of the sender in the implementation of the Command pattern. This way, when the caller requires an answer, it has the location of the sender. The sender can then create a message that will be sent to the caller.

The point is that this is not a difficult solution, and it requires only a small amount of development effort. The best way of looking at this problem is not to consider the individual computers as client and server, but as peers. You are really just sending messages from one peer to another.

COM+ Event Services

COM+ events are another type of asynchronous communication. COM+ events implement a subscription type of asynchronous communication. Consider this problem: a user has a mortgage with a flexible interest rate and may want to convert it to a fixed interest rate when the rate goes above a certain level. The classic way of providing this functionality is to create a periodic application that queries the interest rate. The problem with this approach is that it requires a certain amount of processing even if no change has occurred. A simpler solution is to subscribe to interest changes and then react if there is a need. This solution requires less bandwidth, but only works if there is an infrastructure to support it.

COM+ events are an implementation of the publisher/subscriber event model. In this model, there is an event described by some COM interface. The subscriber indicates to the COM+ events subscription database its interest in receiving information described by the event. A publisher is responsible for generating an event by instantiating the event COM interface. At this point, the COM+ events service intercepts the interface call and delegates any method invocations to the individual subscribers.

COM+ events permit multiple subscribers to the same event. Neither the publisher nor the subscriber needs direct knowledge of the other. This is called an LCE (Loosely Coupled Event). The only connection between the publisher and subscriber is the COM+ event interface. Figure 12–7 shows an implementation of COM+ events.

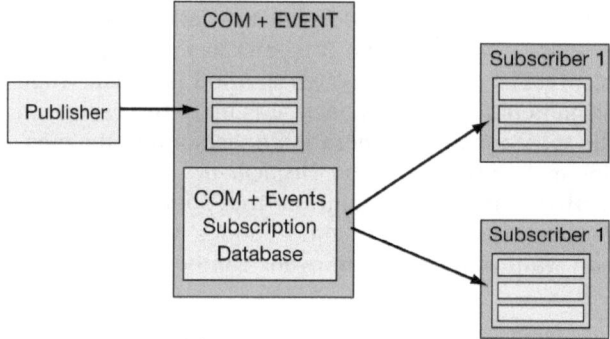

Figure 12–7: COM+ events architecture

It is possible to build a COM+ event type of service using COM connection points. However, COM connection points are TCE (Tightly Coupled Events)—the subscriber and publisher know about each other and depend on each other. COM connection points are not reliable and cannot perform any type of filtering.

Building a Publisher/Subscriber Application

Let's build a simple COM+ event application. There are three pieces of code that need to be implemented. They are the event class, a subscriber, and a publisher.

The COM+ event application that we will write is based on the conference registration application that we have worked on in previous chapters. Currently in the conference registration application, when a user registers for a conference, that information is only written to the database. The administrator of the conference registration application has no way of knowing which users have registered. To improve this situation, we will create a COM+ event that is triggered each time a user registers.

DEFINING THE EVENT INTERFACE

The event class that is being defined is a COM interface only. The COM+ event service uses this COM interface as a reference when building its ghost COM interface. This means that any functionality implemented by the COM interface is ignored.

The simplest way of implementing this interface is to use Visual C++ and then define the COM interface using the ATL object wizard. However, you could use either Visual Basic or Visual J++. Keep in mind, though, that with either Visual Basic or Visual J++ you may not end up with a correctly named interface, as was explained in Chapter 8.

For our sample application, the event interface is defined using the following IDL:

```
interface IVCEventRegistration : IDispatch {
[id(1), helpstring("method newUser")] HRESULT newUser(long id);
[id(2), helpstring("method updateUser")] HRESULT updateUser(long id);
};
```

After the event library is defined, it is necessary to compile the COM component.

ADDING THE EVENT CLASS TO THE COM+ CATALOG

The next step is to register the COM object as an event class by following these steps:

1. Start the Component Services Manager.
2. Either use or create a new COM+ application.
3. Right-click the folders node within the context of a COM+ application, and select New Component from the pop-up menu.
4. The Welcome to the COM Component Install Wizard dialog box will appear. Click Next, and you will see the dialog box shown in Figure 12–8.

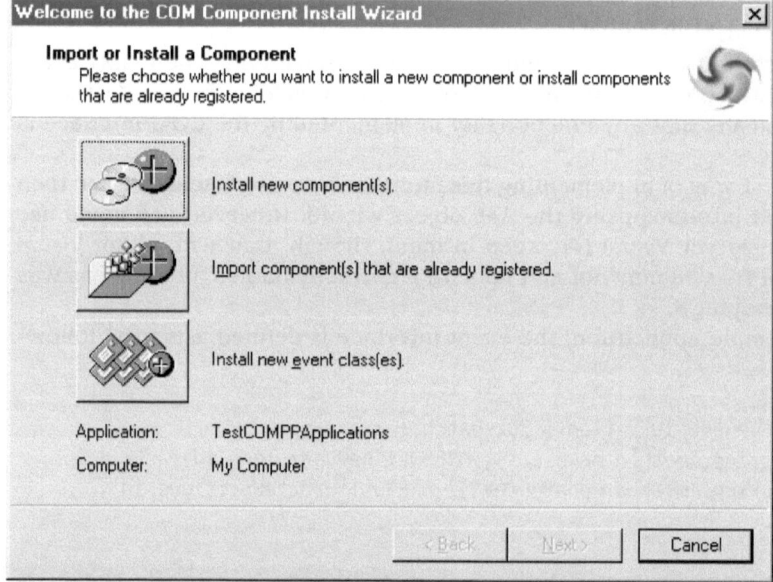

Figure 12–8: Event class registration

5. Click Install new event class(es) and an Open dialog box will appear.

6. Select the Dynamic Link Library (DLL) that contains the implementation of the event class (IVCEventRegistration). Click OK and you should see the dialog box shown in Figure 12–9, displaying the information found in the COM component.

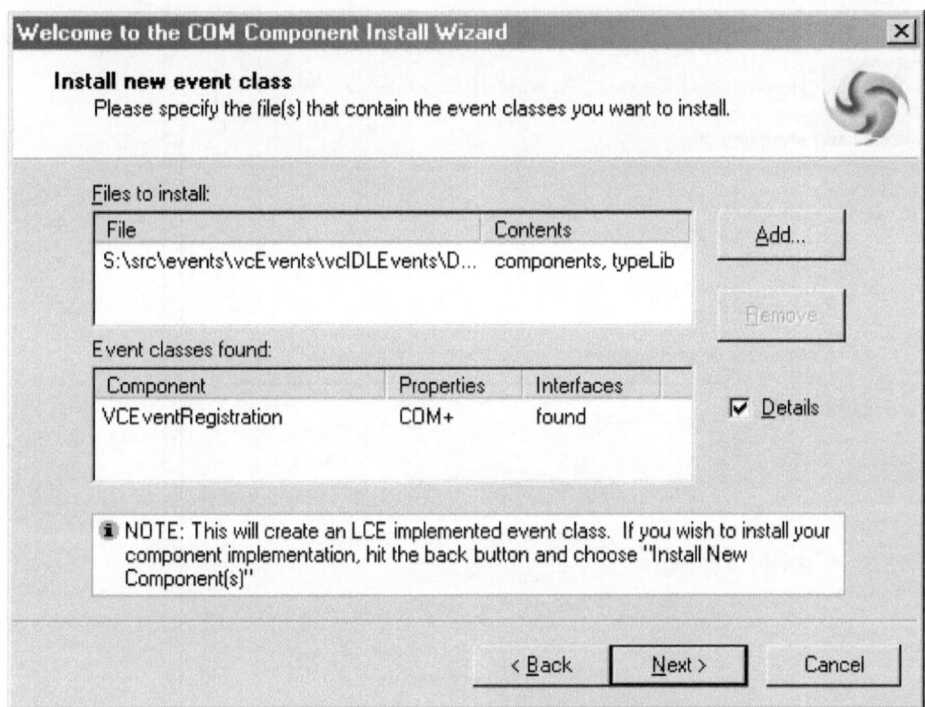

Figure 12–9: Event class description display

7. Click Next, and then click Finish in the final dialog box.

The COM object that has just been added to the COM+ catalog looks just like any other COM+ object. The difference is that it is defined as Event class. To verify this, right-click the COM object, select Properties, and click the Advanced tab. The dialog box should look like the one shown in Figure 12–10.

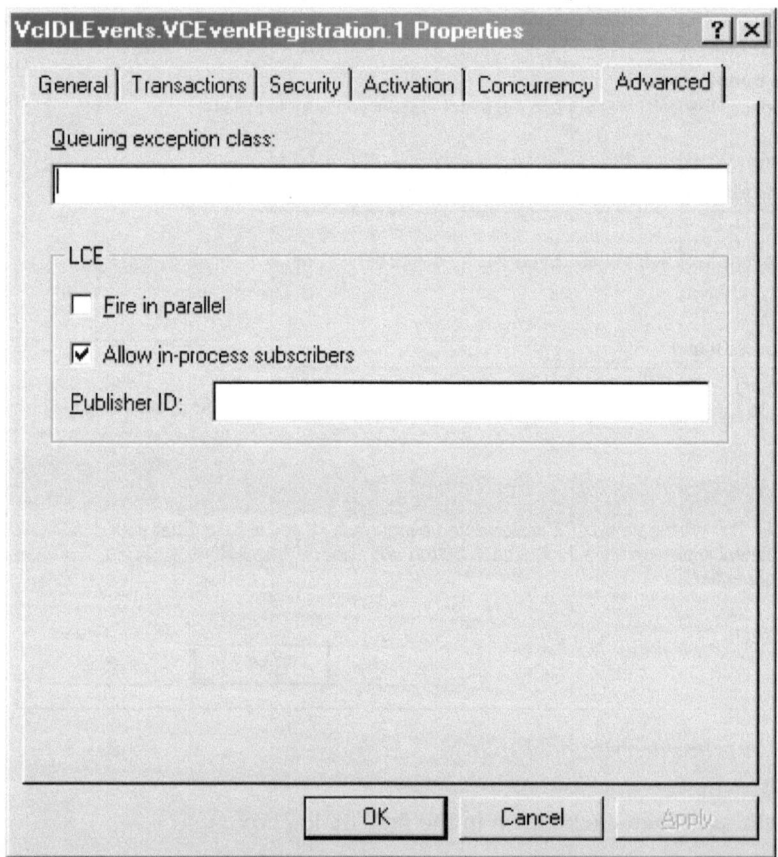

Figure 12–10: Properties of a class, showing its event status

The LCE group box only appears on COM+ objects that are defined as Event class. The Allow In-Process Subscribers checkbox should be checked, because COM+ applications are in-process COM objects.

IMPLEMENTING A SUBSCRIBER

At this point, a publisher could start generating events. But because there are no subscribers, those events would go nowhere. A subscriber needs to be implemented. The subscriber is another COM+ object that implements either a method of the event class or the entire interface of a COM+ event interface.

In our example, the event interface is called IVCEventRegistration. Because we have already gone through the steps of implementing an interface, we will assume that the COM interface was implemented and that the implementation was registered in a COM+ application.

To associate a subscription with the COM+ object that we implemented from the Component Services Manager, open the COM+ application that contains the IVCEventRegistration event class. Then open the IVCEventRegistration event class that was implemented. This should show the various COM interfaces that were implemented, as is shown in Figure 12–11.

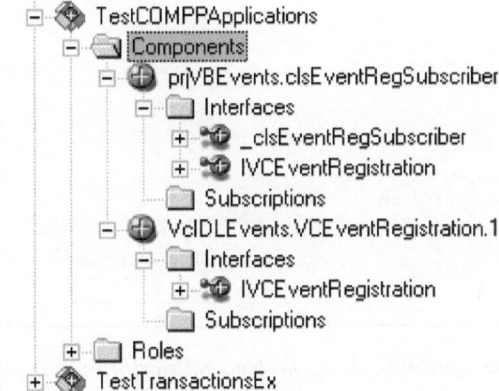

Figure 12–11: COM+ object showing the Subscriptions folder

The prjVBEvents.clsEventRegSubscriber COM object has implemented two COM interfaces: _clsEventRegSubscriber and IVCEventRegistration. The subscription is based on the registered event class, which happens to be IVCEventRegistration.

To create a new subscription, follow these steps:

1. Right-click the Subscriptions folder and select New -> Subscription. Then click Next.

2. The COM New Subscription Wizard displays all of the interfaces. Select the interface that will accept a subscription, as shown in Figure 12–12.

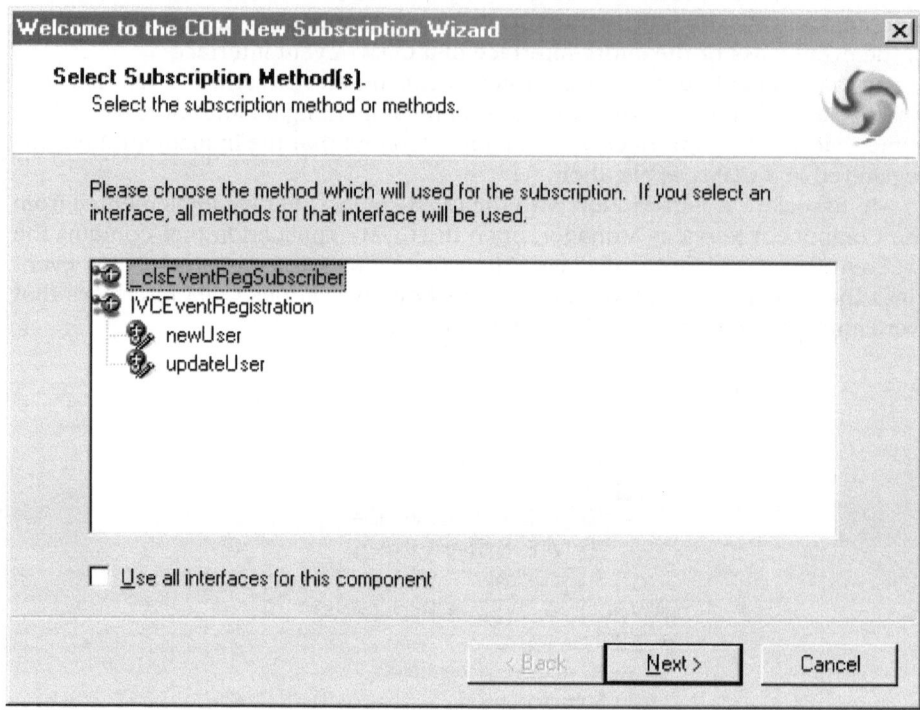

Figure 12–12: Selecting a subscription in the COM New Subscription Wizard

3. You can select either an entire interface or a specific method on an interface. Select the IVCEventRegistration name so that the subscription will apply to the entire interface. Then click Next.

4. The selected interface is now cross-referenced with an available Event class, and this may take a moment. When it is complete, you should see the wizard screen shown in Figure 12–13.

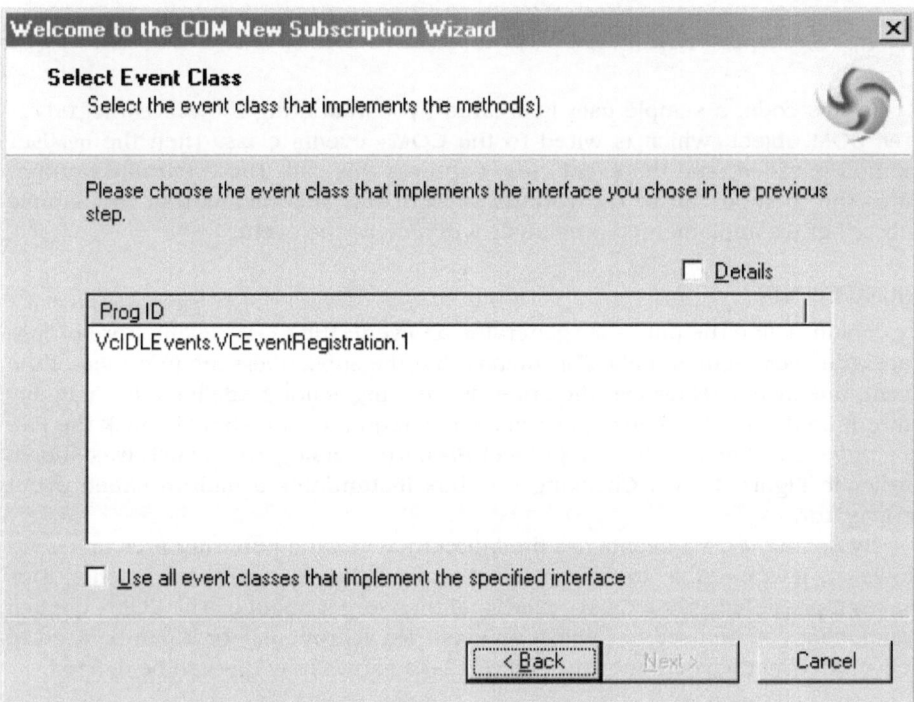

Figure 12–13: Selecting an event class in the COM New Subscription Wizard

5. Select the only option, and then click Next.
6. The last wizard screen asks for a name for the subscription. Type First subscription, and check the Enable This Subscription Immediately checkbox. Click Next, and then click Finish.

The subscription is added to the Subscriptions folder, and the subscriber is ready to accept events. This is an example of a persistent subscription. More details about this are provided later in the chapter, in the "Defining a Transient Subscriber" section.

PUBLISHING INFORMATION

Now we need to create a publisher. In this case, we will use a test program to generate a new user registration event. The publisher only needs to instantiate the COM+ events class (IVCEventRegistration) and then call the registration method (IVCEventRegistration::newUser).

A sample Visual Basic implementation of this is as follows:

```
Private Sub tstRegisterUser()
Dim obj As New VCEventRegistration
obj.newUser 13
End Sub
```

In this code, a sample user is created by instantiating the VCEventRegistra-tion COM object, which is wired to the COM+ events class. Then the newUser method is called, and the event class captures this call. The event class propa-gates the method call to the various subscribers. This means that the sample subscriber we implemented previously will receive the event.

FIRING EVENTS

By default, when the publisher generates an event, the COM+ event store propa-gates the event sequentially. This means that the subscribers are informed of the event, one by one. However, the order of the firing is not predefined, nor can any pattern be deduced. If better performance is required, you should check the *Fire in parallel* checkbox in the COM object Properties dialog box, which was shown earlier in Figure 12–10. Checking this box instantiates a multithreaded event propagator.

By default, COM+ events are fired directly when the publisher fires an event. However, it is possible to fire an event using COM+ queued components. This makes it possible to fire a COM+ event and then forget about it. The COM+ queued component can be used to publish an event asynchronously or it can be used to deliver an event asynchronously. Figure 12–14 shows how this can be defined.

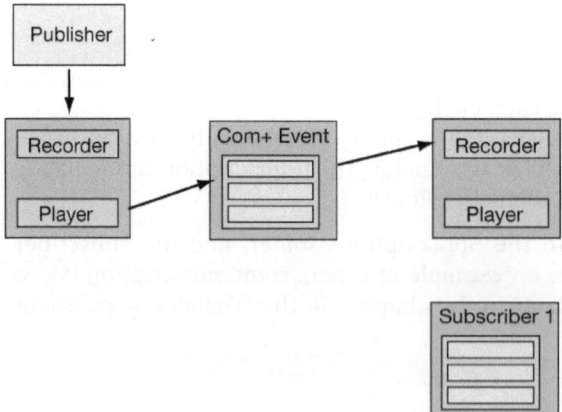

Figure 12–14: COM+ events using COM+ queued components

When publishing events, the recorder and player are between the publisher and the COM+ events service. In practical terms, this is implemented by defining the event class as queueable. In the example that we went through, the publisher refers to the COM interface `IVCEventRegistration` that is part of the component `VcIDLEvents.VCEventRegistration.1`.

The second way of adding COM+ queued component functionality is to define the subscriber event interface as queueable by modifying the subscription properties. From the COM+ explorer, select the subscription that we created in the previous example, right-click, and select Properties. In the Properties dialog box, select the Options tab, which is shown in Figure 12–15.

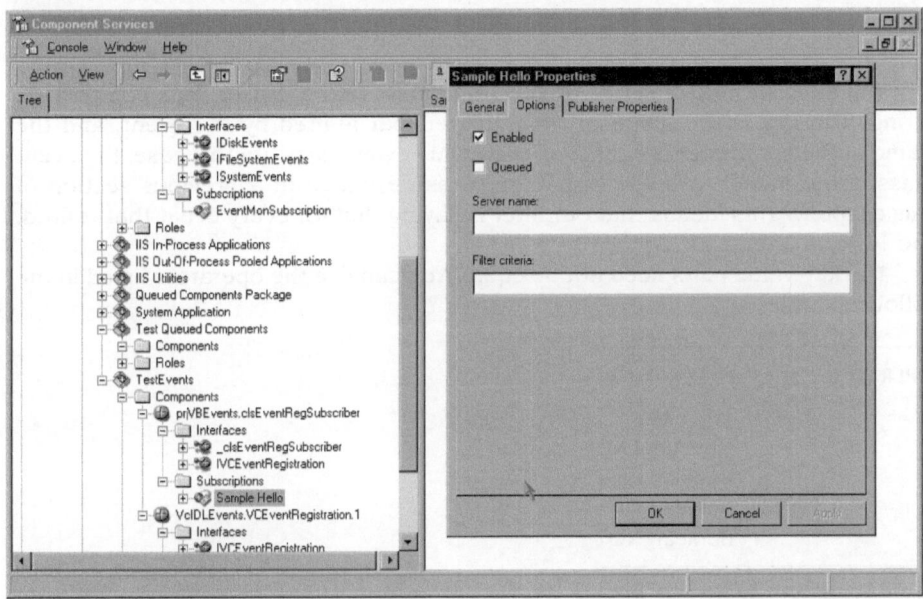

Figure 12–15: Subscription properties

To make this subscription a COM+ queued component message, check the Queued checkbox. This makes it possible to remote COM+ events and store messages for roaming users.

It is possible to remote a COM+ event by setting the *Server name* in the Properties dialog box shown in Figure 12–15. Doing so calls up the subscriber residing on the other machine. While this approach may work, it is not intended to be used for thousands of users.

Filtering Events

With COM+ events, it is possible to filter events so that subscribers only get the information that they are interested in. There are two types of filtering. The simplest is subscriber-side filtering. In that scenario, the subscriber defines a filter string that specifies the parameter values. The more complicated filtering option, in terms of programming, is called publisher-side filtering. In that scenario, a COM object implements a specific interface that is called whenever an event occurs. The publisher-side filter can then determine which subscribers will see the event.

SUBSCRIBER-SIDE FILTERING

Defining a subscriber-side filter is the simpler of the two options because it can be defined within the COM+ explorer. If you look again at Figure 12–15, you will see a text box labeled Filter Criteria. The filter string can be defined in this text box. A filter string for the IVCEventRegistration interface might be the following:

id=10

The filter string is a series of key value pairs that are used as a comparison string. The key is the name of a parameter that is fired by the event, and the name of the parameter is defined in the COM+ event class. (In this case, the event class is the interface IEventRegistration as described in a previous section of this chapter.) This means that our filter is saying that for every event that is fired, the id parameter must equal 10.

The key value pairs need not be equal. You can use the operators listed in the following table.

OPERATOR	DESCRIPTION
=, ==	Equal to
!=, ~=, <>	Not equal to
&	Boolean AND
|	Boolean OR
!,~	Boolean NOT

To combine multiple key value pairs, use brackets. For example, having the id equal either 10 or 20 is represented as follows:

(id=10) | (id=20)

You can nest brackets and use many different combinations of operators. The only requirement is that the key must be a simple data type (numeric, string, and so on). It is not possible, for example, to validate object data types.

PUBLISHER-SIDE FILTERING

Publisher-side filtering occurs when the event is preprocessed by a publisher-side COM object that implements the IMultiInterfacePublisherFilter COM interface. At the time of this writing, it was not possible to implement this interface with Visual Basic because Visual Basic Object Linking and Embedding (OLE) Automation does not support one of the methods of this interface. As a result, the implementation details are done with Visual C++. It is difficult to know whether Visual Basic will have this capability in the future.

Figure 12–16 outlines the big picture of what we are trying to accomplish with publisher-side filtering.

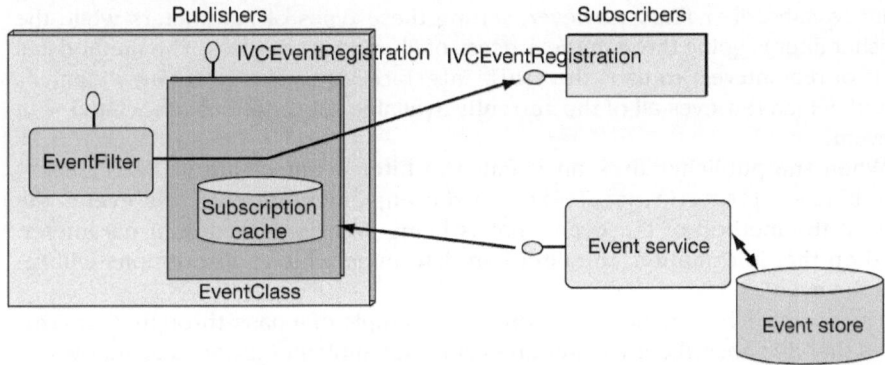

Figure 12–16: Architecture of COM+ publisher filter

In this figure, the publisher interacts with the IVCEventRegistration **COM in-**terface. But instead of the COM+ event service propagating the event directly to the subscribers, it sends the event to the EventFilter. The EventFilter **has the** capability to inspect the subscription cache and determine which subscribers will receive the event.

Implementing a General Filter

There are several ways that a publisher-side filter can implement its functionality. It really depends on how you want your filter to operate.

Let's start with the general implementation. With this technique, your publisher-side filter will only implement IMultiInterfacePublisherFilter. In this situation, when the publisher calls the event, the COM+ event service calls the method IMultiInterfacePublisherFilter::Initialize. The publisher filter will use this method to initialize the COM+ object and to store the IMultiInterfaceEventControl **COM interface.**

A simple implementation of this filter is as follows:

```
STDMETHODIMP CVCEventRegFiltImpl::Initialize(IMultiInterfaceEventControl *
pEIC) {
try {
    m_ptrEIC = pEIC;
} catch( _com_error err) {
    return err.Error();
}
return S_OK;
}
```

Let's look more closely at the IMultiInterfaceEventControl interface. This interface provides the capability to control the filter characteristics of the event class. For example, you can use IMultiInterfaceEventControl::SetPublisherFilter to programmatically set the publisher filter class. Or, if there is no publisher filter set, you can use IMultiInterfaceEventControl::SetDefaultQuery to set a string similar to subscriber filter. However, setting these types of parameters while the publisher filter is going through the process of filtering is pointless. The method call that is of real interest to us is the IMultiInterfaceEventControl::GetSubscriptions method, which retrieves all of the currently available subscriptions associated with the event.

When the publisher fires an event, the filter event called is IMultiInterfacePublisherFilter::PrepareToFire. In the implementation of this event, the name of the method of the event that is being fired is passed as a parameter. Based on that information, the filter can determine which subscriptions will receive the event.

The sample event implementation is an example of a pass-through filter. This means that all subscribers will get an event. The implementation is as follows:

```
STDMETHODIMP CVCEventRegFiltImpl::PrepareToFire(REFIID iid,
BSTR MethodName, IFiringControl * firingControl) {
try {
    int error;
    IEventObjectCollectionPtr ptrEventCol;

    _com_util::CheckError( m_ptrEIC->GetSubscriptions(
iid, MethodName, NULL, &error, &ptrEventCol));

    IEnumEventObjectPtr ptrObjEvent;
    _com_util::CheckError( ptrEventCol->get_NewEnum( &ptrObjEvent));

    m_ptrObjEvent = ptrObjEvent;
    m_ptrFireCtrl = firingControl;

    ULONG count;
    IEventSubscriptionPtr pes;

    while( ptrObjEvent->Next( 1, (IUnknown **)&pes, &count) == S_OK) {
        firingControl->FireSubscription( pes);
    }
} catch( _com_error err) {
    return err.Error();
}
return S_OK;
}
```

In this implementation, the various subscriptions associated with the event are retrieved using the m_ptrEIC->GetSubscriptions method. This method returns a collection of objects, and what we want to do is iterate through this collection and retrieve the individual subscriptions.

The way to do this is to create a new collection and iterate through it using the IEnumEventObject interface (ptrEventCol->get_NewEnum). The individual elements of the collection are COM interfaces of the type IEventSubscription, and these COM interfaces contain all of the details regarding an individual subscription, such as the subscription name, event class ID, method name, and machine name identifying where the event class is located. With this information, it is possible to determine whether the subscriber should receive the event. It is also possible to use this information in conjunction with an external database to formulate the answer.

If the subscriber is to receive the event, then the IFiringControl::FireSubscription method is called. The subscription that is to be fired is passed in as a parameter.

Implementing a Method-Based Filter

The general filter does not take the parameters of the individual method into account. If that is required to make the decision as to which subscriptions receive the event, then the publisher event class must also implement the COM interface of the event class. In our example, this means that the event class must implement the IVCEventRegistration COM interface. In the filtering process, the event class is queried for after the IMultiInterfacePublisherFilter::PrepareToFire method has completed.

As in the general filter example, we will use a simple pass-through, such as the following:

```
STDMETHODIMP CVCEventRegFiltImpl::newUser(LONG id) {
try {
    ULONG count;
    IEventSubscriptionPtr pes;

    m_ptrObjEvent->Reset();
    while( m_ptrObjEvent->Next( 1, (IUnknown **)&pes, &count) == S_OK) {
        m_ptrFireCtrl->FireSubscription( pes);
    }
} catch( _com_error err) {
    return err.Error();
}
return S_OK;
}
```

Without going into too much detail, you can see that the implementation of this method is very similar to the implementation of IMultiInterfacePublisher-Filter::PrepareToFire. However, in that method, the collection of subscription objects and firing control were stored for later reference in the m_ptrObjEvent and m_ptrFireCtrl variables. In this example, the publisher filter can inspect the value of the id parameter and make the decision about which subscriptions get the event.

You may have noticed that the publisher filter as it is implemented here calls the FireSubscription method twice for each subscription, which means that the event is called twice. It is called twice because the subscriptions were fired in the two phases of the filter—the general filter and the method filter. Doing this in technical terms is valid, but it may violate a business rule if the filter is called twice.

Registering the Filter

After implementing the publisher-side filter, you need to register it. However, there is nothing in the COM+ explorer that lets you define a publisher-side filter. The way to register a publisher filter is to bypass the COM+ explorer and program the COM+ administrative objects directly. Using the COM+ administrative objects, it is possible to manipulate all aspects of COM+ applications.

The COM+ administrative objects are arranged in a hierarchy, which means that we start at the root, then find the COM+ application, and then find the event class. From that class, the publisher filter is defined.

The COM+ administrative objects are instantiated by creating the COM object defined by the COMAdmin.COMAdminCatalog PROG ID. An example implementation is as follows:

```
Dim catalog As COMAdminCatalog
Set catalog = CreateObject("COMAdmin.COMAdminCatalog")
```

The instantiated object that is returned represents a root node for all COM+ services and COM+ applications. To find the specific COM+ application that contains the event class, we need the COM+ application collection. You can retrieve it as follows:

```
Set appcoll = catalog.GetCollection("Applications")
appcoll.Populate
```

Notice the call to appcoll.Populate in this implementation. This method reads in all of the COM+ application data from the COM+ catalog. After we have this information, we need to find the COM+ application that contains our event class. An example implementation is as follows:

```
For i = 0 To appcoll.Count - 1
If appcoll.Item(i).Name = "Test Application" Then
    Set compcoll = appcoll.GetCollection("Components",
```

```
appcoll.Item(i).Key)
    compcoll.Populate
End If
Next
```

After the COM+ application is found, which in this example is Test Application, the collection of components can be retrieved using the appcoll.GetCollection method and populated using the compcoll.Populate method. The components collection identifies the individual objects using the PROG ID.

Because this collection of components could be any number greater than zero, we need to iterate through the collection to find the event class, which in this case has a PROG ID of VcIDLEvents.VCEventRegistration.1. Code such as the following can be used to do this:

```
For i = 0 To compcoll.Count - 1
If compcoll.Item(i).Name = "VcIDLEvents.VCEventRegistration.1" Then
    Set comp = compcoll.Item(i)
    comp.Value("MultiInterfacePublisherFilterCLSID") = _
"VCEventFilter.VCEventRegFiltImpl.1"
    compcoll.SaveChanges
End If
Next
```

After the event class is found, the identifier of the event class is assigned to the PROG ID of our publisher filter, which is the comp.Value property. It is important to save the changes that were made by using the compcoll.SaveChanges method. After all this is done, the publisher filter is completed and will be called whenever a publisher calls the IVCEventRegistration event.

Defining a Transient Subscriber

There are two types of COM+ subscriptions: persistent and transient. A persistent subscription is where the subscriber is an inactive COM+ object, and this is what we have been dealing with to this point. In the case of a persistent subscription, a publisher publishes some information, and when the COM+ event is propagated, the COM+ event object is instantiated.

In contrast, a transient subscription is when a subscriber is currently executing in the context of an application. Any event that is propagated is sent to the active subscriber, but the subscription lasts only for as long as the subscriber is alive, or for the life of the computer session. Rebooting the computer ends the subscription. To make sure that the subscriber remains active, the COM+ events services adds a reference count to the COM object.

A transient subscriber in our conference registration example would still need to implement the IVCEventRegistration interface. However, unlike a persistent subscription, a transient subscription needs to be added using the COM+ administrative objects. We will add a transient subscription and then remove it.

ADDING A TRANSIENT SUBSCRIPTION

To add a transient subscription, the COM+ administrative catalog object needs to be instantiated, and then the transient subscriptions need to be retrieved. An implementation of this is as follows:

```
Dim catalog As COMAdminCatalog
Dim subColl As COMAdminCatalogCollection

Set catalog = CreateObject("COMAdmin.COMAdminCatalog")
Set subColl = catalog.GetCollection("TransientSubscriptions")
```

There is no need to populate the subColl object, because a subscription will be added to the collection. After a subscription object is added to the collection, it is necessary to define the various attributes of the subscription. An example implementation is as follows:

```
Set comp = subColl.Add
comp.Value("EventCLSID") = "{BF72A012-3312-4C17-AA41-B8F98A243EBF}"
comp.Value("Name") = "Sample Transient Subscription"
comp.Value("SubscriberInterface") = objEvent
comp.SaveChanges
transId = com.Value("ID")
```

There are three attributes that need to be defined. The first is a definition of which event class is being subscribed to. In this example, the event class is defined by the EventCLSID property, which in our case is the CLSID of the VCEventRegistration COM class. The Name property describes the name of the subscription, which can be any type of string. The last property, SubscriberInterface, is defined to contain the currently active object that will be the subscriber. After these properties are set, they must be saved using the SaveChanges method.

To help find and remove the transient subscription, the ID property can be retrieved and stored. This property defines the ID of the transient subscription, and it uniquely describes the transient subscription that was added to the collection.

REMOVING A TRANSIENT SUBSCRIPTION

You can remove a transient subscription from the collection of transient subscriptions by iterating through the collection and finding the subscription that is to be deleted. In our case, we stored the subscription ID and we will use it as the key to determine which subscription to delete.

To delete the subscription, the COM+ catalog object needs to be instantiated and the transient subscriptions collection retrieved. Because we will be iterating through the different elements, the Populate method must be called to populate the collection. The following source code could be used:

```
Set catalog = CreateObject("COMAdmin.COMAdminCatalog")
Set subColl = catalog.GetCollection("TransientSubscriptions")
subColl.Populate
```

Now it is possible to iterate through the different subscription elements and delete the subscription that has the ID that was generated when the transient subscription was added. The implementation of this is as follows:

```
For i = 0 To subColl.Count - 1
If subColl.Item(i).Value("ID") = transId Then
    subColl.Remove (i)
    subColl.SaveChanges
End If
Next
```

To remove the subscription, the `Remove` method is called with the index location as a parameter. To make the changes permanent, the `SaveChanges` method is called.

Transactions and COM+ Events

When writing COM+ events, transactions are automatically integrated. It is possible to set the transaction attributes on the event class or on individual subscribers. That is your choice. But remember that if you set the transaction attribute on the event class, all of your subscribers may be involved in the same transaction.

Putting It in Perspective

This chapter introduced the concept of asynchronous communications. However, I tend to think of this not as asynchronous communications but as a sort of push technology. To push data means that the consumer of the data expects to see some data at some period in time. In the other models, you have to be active and call objects to move data.

The difference between the two models described in this chapter is that with COM+ queued components you get the pushed data automatically. With COM+ events you get the pushed data if you subscribed to it.

Writing applications for a push model is different from writing a normal application because you are a passive participant in the programming model. That is okay, though, because the Windows programming model is based on events, and requires the application to be passive, as well. The difference in the server-side push model is that we are not used to seeing an event-type architecture when there are no graphical user interfaces (GUIs).

After having read this chapter and the last chapter, you should have a pretty good idea of how to write robust messaging applications. If you are not very familiar with writing messaging applications, start by writing a small application to get a feel for how things happen, and then write bigger and better messaging applications.

Chapter 13

More COM+ Services Programming

This chapter focuses on controlling specific aspects of Component Object Model (COM)+ objects. These features are not needed in all COM+ objects, but sometimes you may want some extra control. The first part of the chapter is concerned with tuning COM+ transactions. The second part of the chapter focuses on integrating a COM+ object within an Active Server Page (ASP).

Scalability and COM+ Lifetime Management

When developing COM+ applications for large environments where there are potentially thousands of concurrent users, scalability is an important issue. Scalability was addressed in Windows 2000 by adding various services, such as better caching and dynamic load balancing. So, when a COM+ application is too slow, you will want to hand-tune it so that it goes faster.

Implementing Object Pooling

Object pooling is used to solve slow object instantiation or the dispensing of legacy resources. Slow object instantiation can occur when the COM+ object requires a long time to connect to a particular resource. This could be the case with a legacy resource that is not optimized to use COM+ transaction services. Or, it could happen when the COM+ object has many different steps to accomplish before it can be used to carry out some business logic. In any of these cases, you will want to use COM+ object pooling.

What is object pooling? In the Microsoft Transaction Server (MTS) era, object pooling was the soon-to-be-released feature that allowed an instance of an object to be recycled for later use. This would substantially increase performance because the object would not need to be instantiated again.

Object pooling has been implemented in COM+, but its purpose has changed. Now the purpose is not to enhance general performance, but to enhance performance of slow instantiating components. In Chapter 10, we learned that the COM+ object is not recycled—the information is cached in some location and is managed by the resource and the COM+ run-time. This does not slow the system or decrease scalability. However, if the caching is poor, due to environmental conditions or because the resource is poorly written, it becomes necessary to implement object pooling.

The easiest way of knowing when to use object pooling is to consider the amount of time spent doing system-level work as opposed to application work. System-level work is work such as connecting to a resource, building a network connection, and so on. Application-level work includes the business processes. An object that should be pooled is one in which the time spent doing system-level work is greater than the time spent on application-level work. A pooled object can reduce the instantiation time by caching it or doing the work ahead of time.

POOLED OBJECT REQUIREMENTS

Using object-pooling code is a bit more complicated than using COM+ objects because you need to write system-level-type code. It can be written in either Visual C++ or Visual J++; it cannot be written in Visual Basic because of the way that Visual Basic implements COM objects. Depending on the resource, writing this code can be either complex or simple.

Pooled objects have these requirements:

- **Stateless**: Pooled objects must be stateless. They cannot carry forward state determined by another transaction.
- **No thread affinity**: Pooled objects cannot be bound to a specific thread. This means that thread-local storage cannot be used. A pooled object should not manage the thread that is executing it, but this does not mean that it cannot manage other pooled threads.
- **Aggregatable**: The pooled object must be COM aggregatable. If you are using ATL (Active Template Library), then the Aggregation checkbox must be checked.
- **Transactional**: The pooled object must support transactions. It has the option of whether or not it will participate in the transaction. A pooled object must associate a transaction context with a resource.
- **Implement IObjectControl**: Pooled objects should implement this COM interface, which makes controlling the pooled object much simpler.

DEFINING THE OBJECT-POOLING INTERFACE

Implementing the object-pooling interface is simple. The ATL wizard will do it, if requested, when an MTS COM object is created. The IObjectControl interface is defined as follows:

```
interface IObjectControl : IUnknown {
HRESULT Activate( void);
HRESULT Deactivate( void);
HRESULT CanBePooled( void);
};
```

There are three methods in this interface. The first two methods, Activate and Deactivate, work together to form the life cycle of the pooled object. Consider the pooled object lifetime diagram in Figure 13–1. There is a physical lifetime and a transaction lifetime, and a pooled object often switches from physical to transactional and back to physical.

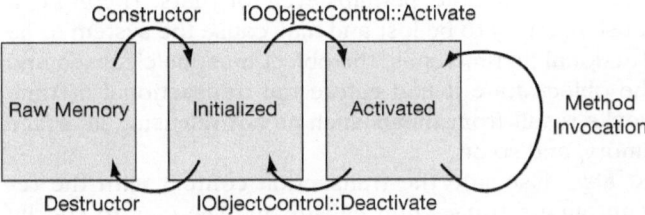

Figure 13–1: Pooled object lifetime

A physical lifetime begins when the COM+ object is physically instantiated—when the constructor of the C++ object is called. When an object is in a physical state, it is not in the context of a transaction or even of a COM+ application. It is in memory and doing nothing in particular. When the COM object is destroyed and removed from memory, the physical lifetime ends.

When a consumer wants to use a COM+ object of the type that is currently in a physical state, COM+ switches the lifetime to transactional, which means it is in an active state. To do this, the IObjectControl::Activate method is called. This indicates to the COM+ object that it is about to be consumed and that the COM+ object should get itself prepared. After that method has been called, the COM+ object performs some type of business logic. The transactional lifetime ends when the consumer finishes the transaction. Then the COM+ object's active state is ended by the call to IObjectControl::Deactivate, and that it should clean up after itself. Now the COM+ object is in a physical state again. It is called a pooled object because the object is constantly moving from a physical state to an active state and back again.

The method CanBePooled indicates to the COM+ run-time whether or not the object can be pooled. Because we want the object to be pooled, it should return TRUE. Had it returned FALSE, the object would not be pooled, but the IObjectControl::Activate and IObjectControl::Deactivate methods would still be called.

How Object Pooling Works

The object pool is a pool of active COM+ objects. There is a minimum and maximum number of objects in the pool. The minimum specifies the number of active COM+ objects that must exist in the pool, and the maximum specifies the maximum number of active COM+ objects that can be in the pool.

Suppose a consumer wants to instantiate a COM+ object that is being pooled. The interception framework inspects the pool to determine whether an available object exists. If one does not exist, and the maximum number of pool objects has not been reached, then an object is instantiated. If the maximum has been reached, then a queue of waiting objects is created. This queue is a FIFO (first in, first out) buffer. If a request exceeds the timeout value as specified by the COM+ application, an error is returned.

Some Techniques of Object Pooling

There are some important considerations when using pooled objects. First, your pooled object may be active for a long time, perhaps even for years. Therefore, a small memory leak can cause memory to be lost and may cause the system to be rebooted. When the transactional lifetime ends, the object must be cleansed and it must be returned to the object state it had before the transactional lifetime started. Object memory leaks result from things such as not releasing interface pointers, not deleting memory, and so on.

A pooled object must also associate the transaction context with the resource, so it cannot use automatic transaction enlistment. The way to specify this is to set the COM+ transactional attribute to disabled. This means that the pooled object is still part of the transaction stream, but the method decides whether the resource is enlisted or not.

A SIMPLE IMPLEMENTATION

Let's consider a simple situation. We have an open database connectivity (ODBC) driver that supports Distributed Transaction Coordinator (DTC) transactions, but it does not support connection pooling, and connecting to it takes a long time. Therefore, if we created a pooled object, the pooled object would have to manage the connection and management of the resource.

When writing system-level-type code, or when writing code that tends to repeat itself, it is advantageous to convert that code into a helper object. Helper objects abstract complex or repetitive tasks into objects that only require a few lines to use.

I mention helper objects in the context of pooled objects. The task of the pooled object is to make something slow be quicker by using pooled objects. However, if we step back and look at what we are doing, you will notice that we are talking about system-level code. System-level code has nothing to do with the overall application, except to increase the efficiency in programming terms or execution time. Helper objects should always be used in this context. They are objects that reduce the amount of programming code or increase the efficiency of the application.

It is important to make helper objects separate objects because they may be replaced in later versions of the application. For example, consider using a pooled object to increase the efficiency of the application. In a new version of the resource, there may be a COM+ optimized resource dispenser, which means that a pooled object is no longer necessary. If the pooled object code were scattered throughout the application code, making changes to the application would be difficult. But because the code is centralized in a helper object, the change is relatively painless.

Building a Physical State

When implementing a pooled object, the main task is to optimize the acquisition of a resource. Because we are using Visual C++ to implement the COM+ object, there are three constructors that are executed.

When a COM+ object is instantiated, the first constructor called is the C++ class constructor. This constructor instantiates only private class members that have nothing to do with COM. This is done because the COM and COM+ services are not yet available.

Because we are using Visual C++ and ATL, there is a COM-type constructor called FinalConstruct. If the COM object implements this method, the ATL library will call it, and at that point it is okay to call COM. For example, you could use this method to instantiate other COM objects. After that method is called, the COM+ object is considered to be physically active.

In our pooled object implementation, the FinalConstruct method is used to initialize the database connections. An example implementation is as follows:

```
HRESULT FinalConstruct() {
RETCODE rc;
HRESULT hr= S_OK;

rc = SQLAllocEnv(phenv);
ASSERT_SQL_SUCCESS(rc);
if (bUseObjectPool) {
    rc = SQLSetEnvAttr(*phenv, SQL_ATTR_CONNECTION_POOLING,
(void*)SQL_CP_OFF, 0);
    ASSERT_SQL_SUCCESS(rc);
}
rc = SQLAllocConnect(*phenv, phdbc);
...
}
```

The database that we will be connecting to has an ODBC driver. Therefore, in this step, the ODBC environment and handle are allocated. In this initialization phase, it is recommended that none of the variables be stored as static or global variables. Depending on the situation, doing so could require the writing of synchronization code, which is a bottleneck that will slow the pooled object.

In the process of destroying an object, the method FinalRelease is called when the object shifts from an active state to a physical state. In our sample pooled object, this method deletes the ODBC environment and ODBC connections created in the FinalConstruct method. A sample implementation is as follows:

```
void FinalRelease() {
if (m_hstmt)
    SQLFreeStmt(m_hstmt, SQL_DROP);
if (m_hdbc) {
    SQLDisconnect(m_hdbc);2:
    SQLFreeConnect(m_hdbc);
}
...
}
```

Enlisting the Transaction

When a pooled object is used in the context of a transaction, it moves from a physical state to an active state. At this point, the pooled object needs to indicate to the resource that a transaction is being started and that it should participate. This means that the pooled object has to manually enlist itself in the transaction.

In the pooled object implementation, the resource is being connected to using ODBC. ODBC has the capability to associate a COM+ transaction with the underlying resource because ODBC is an official COM+ resource dispenser. However, this transaction enlistment is only useful if the underlying resource supports ODBC transactions.

By default, ODBC uses automatic transaction enlistment, and in our example, it needs to be turned off, and a transaction needs to be manually associated with the DTC transaction. The automatic transaction association option can be turned off by using the SQLSetEnvAttr method.

When the pooled object moves from a physical state to an active state, the IObjectControl::Activate method is called. The COM+ context being passed in does have a valid transaction context. It is up to the pooled object to enlist the transaction to the resource. The only case in which the transaction context is not valid is when the COM+ object attribute is set to *not supported*.

An example implementation of enlisting a transaction is as follows:

```
IObjectContextInfo    * pObjTx = NULL;
hr = CoGetObjectContext(IID_IObjectContextInfo, (void**)& pObjTx);

if (pObjTx) {
ITransaction * pTx = NULL;
pObjTx -> GetTransaction ((IUnknown **)&pTx);
RETCODE rc ;
if (pTx) {
    rc = SQLSetConnectOption(m_hdbc,
SQL_ATTR_ENLIST_IN_DTC, (UDWORD)pTx);

}

}
```

In a traditional MTS COM object (Microsoft Transaction Server, predecessor to COM+ transaction services) the transaction context is retrieved using the GetObjectContext method call. However, with COM+ it is possible to call the CoGetObjectContext function. This function call can retrieve these interfaces: IObjectContext, IObjectContextInfo, IObjectContextActivity, and IContextState. We will talk about these interfaces later, so do not worry yet about what these interfaces do.

If the pObjTx interface pointer is not NULL, then the DTC transaction interface ITransaction (pTx) is retrieved. If pTx is not NULL, then it is passed as a parameter to the SQLSetConnectOption ODBC function. The ODBC function then enlists the resource being manipulated with the transaction given to it.

When the transaction ends, the `IObjectControl::Deactivate` method is called. The pooled object now switches from an active state to a physical state. It is up to the pooled object to reset the database connection. Because we are using ODBC with transaction support, we don't need to do anything in particular. The ODBC resource manager manages all of the details automatically.

However, we do need to be consistent with our COM interface pointers and memory. For example, if memory was allocated in the `FinalConstruct` method, then it needs to be freed in the `FinalRelease` method. If a COM interface pointer was instantiated in the `IObjectControl::Activate` method and stored as a class-level variable, it needs to be de-referenced in the `IObjectControl::Deactivate` method.

Dynamic Load Balancing

Another way of achieving scalability is by using load balancing. Load balancing makes it possible to consider a group of computers as one communication point. This is not clustering, because clustering ensures fail-over. (Fail-over is when servers, memory, and other things are replicated on different machines.) Clustering is beyond the scope of this book.

With load balancing, if a machine fails, all running transactions are lost. However, it is possible to start over immediately because another machine automatically takes on the extra load. With fail-over, when a machine fails, the transactions are not lost because another machine has a mirror of the state of the failed machine and automatically continues the transaction. Neither system is better than the other—the choice really depends on what you want to achieve.

Implementing load balancing is an administrative issue, because it does not involve any specific programming techniques. However, when you are writing applications, it is important to understand the ramifications of load balancing.

Consider the situation of two servers that a client considers to be one machine. This means the operating system will load balance between the two machines. Now suppose a client is accessing an invoicing application on the server using a Web browser. When the client makes one request, the load balancer directs that request to one server, and the client establishes some state on that server. Meanwhile, other clients make their own requests. Now the client makes another request, and the load balancer determines that the request should be directed to the other server. This creates a problem. The original state that is required to carry out the task is held on the other server. The application assumes that there is a state, and because there is none, the server-side application crashes.

Nothing was done incorrectly, but the computer program was not equipped to deal with that problem. So what should a program do? The answer is that the program should keep the state in a database or force the load balancer to balance users rather than objects. Load balancing was removed as a service from the Windows 2000 operating system and added to a new application called Application Server. At the time of this writing, too few details were known about Application Server to be able to write about it.

More Transaction Management Interfaces

The new COM interfaces, IObjectContextInfo and IContextState, enhance the capability to interact with the COM+ transactional services.

IContextState

When IObjectContext::SetComplete, IObjectContext::SetAbort, IObjectContext::DisableCommit, or IObjectContext::EnableCommit is called, it flips the consistency and doneness bits. (These two bits were explained in Chapter 10.) Using the IContextState interface, it is possible to manually control each bit. The interface is defined as follows:

```
interface IContextState : IUnknown {
HRESULT _stdcall SetDeactivateOnReturn(VARIANT_BOOL bDeactivate);
HRESULT _stdcall GetDeactivateOnReturn([out] VARIANT_BOOL* pbDeactivate);
HRESULT _stdcall SetMyTransactionVote(tagTransactionVote txVote);
HRESULT _stdcall GetMyTransactionVote([out] tagTransactionVote* ptxVote);
};
```

The deactivate methods define the doneness, and the transaction methods define the consistency of the transaction.

Why use these methods? Wouldn't it be simpler to just use the methods from IObjectContext? The answer is generally yes, but the IObjectContext methods set both the consistency and doneness bits at the same time—it is not possible to set bits individually. Nor is it possible to figure out what bits are set. When you are manipulating the transaction manually, this interface helps you tune the transaction outcome.

IObjectContextInfo

As we saw in the pooled objects example, it is sometimes necessary to manipulate the underlying DTC transaction. The IObjectContextInfo COM interface retrieves information regarding the context that is associated with the COM+ object. You can get the transaction, but more importantly, you can find out whether you are in a transaction and what IDs are associated with the transaction, activity, and context. This interface is purely informational. In Interface Definition Language (IDL), the interface is defined as follows:

```
interface IObjectContextInfo : IUnknown {
long IsInTransaction();
HRESULT GetTransaction(IUnknown** pptrans);
HRESULT GetTransactionId([out] GUID* pGUID);
HRESULT GetActivityId([out] GUID* pGUID);
HRESULT GetContextId([out] GUID* pGUID);
};
```

RETRIEVING IOBJECTCONTEXTINFO

In the pooled object example, you saw how to retrieve the IObjectContextInfo COM interface using CoGetObjectContext. This time, let's use the GetObjectContext function to demonstrate the other technique. Calling this function returns the IObjectContext COM interface. To retrieve IObjectContextInfo, a QueryInterface for IObjectContext is performed. An example implementation is as follows:

```
IObjectContextPtr pObjectContext;
_com_util::CheckError( GetObjectContext(&pObjectContext));
IObjectContextInfoPtr pObjTx;
pObjTx = pObjectContext
//pObjectContext.QueryInterface(IID_IObjectContextInfo, (void **)&pObjTx);
```

This example uses COM compiler support and smart pointers, which means that the hard work is done for you. I added a commented out line at the bottom of the code example to show you what the smart pointer assignment (pObjTx = pObjectContext) does.

Coding this in Visual Basic is similar to how we coded it for a COM+ transaction-capable object. First, you must retrieve the ObjectContext COM object. Then, from the ObjectContext COM object the IObjectContextInfo COM interface is retrieved via the ContextInfo property. An example implementation is as follows:

```
Dim ctxt As ObjectContext
Dim ctxtInfo As ContextInfo

Set ctxt = GetObjectContext()
Set ctxtInfo = ctxt.ContextInfo
```

WORKING WITH THE RAW TRANSACTION

In the pooled object example, the ODBC function needed to directly communicate with the DTC raw transaction. The IObjectContextInfo::GetTransaction method returns an interface pointer of the type ITransaction. This interface is also used in the OLE DB provider framework. The main feature of this interface is that it is possible to manipulate the transaction directly by calling Commit or Abort. The interface is defined as follows:

```
interface ITransaction : IUnknown {
HRESULT Commit(
            [in] long fRetaining,
            [in] unsigned long grfTC,
            [in] unsigned long grfRM);
HRESULT Abort(
            [in] BOID* pboidReason,
            [in] long fRetaining,
            [in] long fAsync);
HRESULT GetTransactionInfo([out] XACTTRANSINFO* pinfo);
};
```

Our other COM interfaces that commit or abort the transaction are much simpler—they do not expect a parameter. The ITransaction interface is much more complex than IObjectContext::SetComplete and IObjectContext::SetAbort. This is because when you are working with the raw transaction, it is possible to commit the data in different ways.

So why work with the raw transaction using this complex interface? The answer is that it provides the capability to work with the transaction without having the COM+ framework in your way. Remember the pooled object example. Passing a COM+ transaction is meaningless for the ODBC resource, because it does not know what to do with it. However, the resource knows what to do with a DTC transaction.

The last method, GetTransactionInfo, retrieves the properties of the currently running context, such as the isolation level of the transaction. This is part of the currently running resource-locking level.

Specifying Construction Parameters

We have learned about three different C++ constructors or methods that can be used to initialize a C++ COM object when it is instantiated. Let's now put this in the context of a generic COM object written using any type of language. The problem with initializing a COM+ object is determining when to do it. In the pooled object example, the solution was to wait until IObjectControl::Activate was called. However, this only applies if the object is a pooled object. In COM+, there is another constructor implemented by the IObjectConstruct COM interface. This COM interface makes it possible to initialize a COM object that was implemented in any programming language.

Before you become confused about what code to place where, let's look at the various initialization routines based in a pseudo-programming-language context and the order in which they are called:

- Language constructor: This is a language-supplied constructor or class initialize method. Memory is initialized.
- IObjectConstruct::Construct constructor: This is the new constructor that is called when the object is instantiated. This is passed in a configuration string defined in the COM+ catalog.
- IObjectControl:Activate constructor: This is the transactional lifetime constructor that indicates that a transaction has started. This is typically only used for pooled objects.

The IObjectConstruct COM interface is defined as follows:

```
interface IObjectConstruct : IUnknown {
HRESULT Construct([in] IDispatch* pCtorObj);
};
```

The object that is passed in as a parameter to the Construct method (the pCtorObj parameter) has the following IDL definition:

```
interface IObjectConstructString : IDispatch {
[id(0x00000001), propget]
HRESULT ConstructString([out, retval] BSTR* pVal);
};
```

Now let's consider where this COM interface might be implemented. The ConstTest COM+ object implements the IObjectConstruct COM interface, so ConstTest needs to be added to a COM+ application. Then selecting the Activation tab of the COM+ object's Properties dialog box activates the IObjectConstruct interface. The Properties dialog box would look much like the one shown in Figure 13–2.

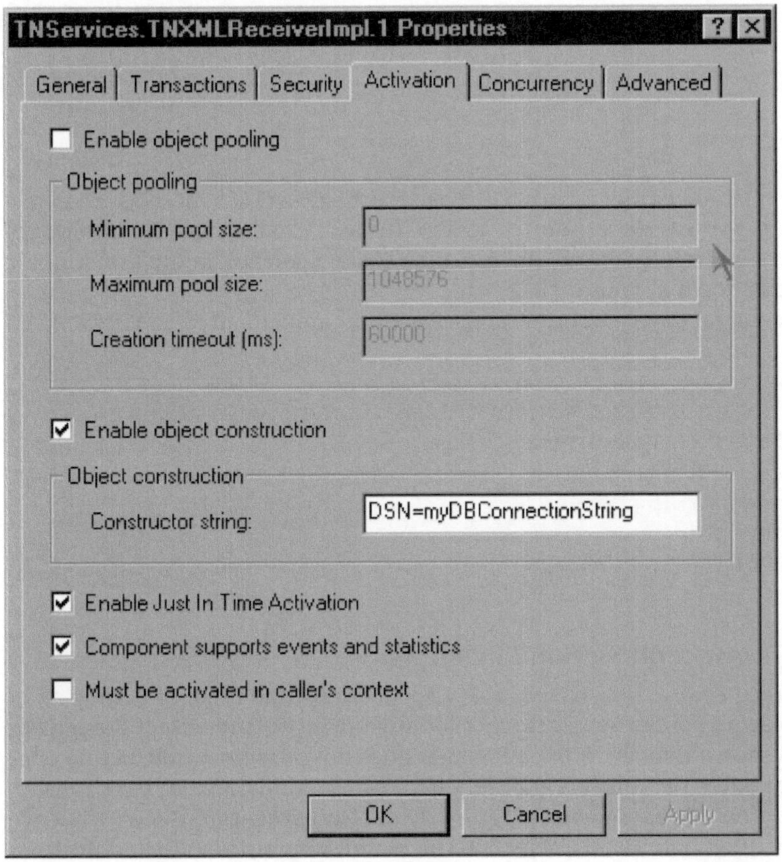

Figure 13–2: COM+ object activation specification

To make COM+ call the IObjectConstruct interface, check the Enable Object Construction checkbox on the Activation tab. When the ConstTest object is instantiated, the COM+ infrastructure calls the IObjectConstruct::Construct method. A sample implementation of the method in Visual C++ is as follows:

```
STDMETHODIMP CConstTest::Construct(IDispatch * pDisp) {
try {
    IObjectConstructStringPtr pString = pUnk;
    if( pString != NULL) {
        BSTR szConstruct;
        pString->get_ConstructString(&szConstruct);

        // do some work

        SysFreeString(szConstruct);
    }
} catch( _com_error err) {
    ;
}
return S_OK;
}
```

As was explained earlier, the IObjectConstruct::Construct method pDisp parameter is a COM interface pointer to the IObjectConstructString interface, which contains a property that is the run-time string specified in the Constructor String text box shown in Figure 13-2.

The same IObjectConstruct::Construct method implemented in Visual Basic is as follows:

```
Private Sub IObjectConstruct_Construct(ByVal pCtorObj As Object)
Dim obj As IObjectConstructString
Dim strRuntime As String

Set obj = pCtorObj
strRuntimw = obj.ConstructString
End Sub
```

Creating a Transaction Stream of Objects

When developing transaction-based COM+ applications, the issue of getting all of the COM+ objects in the same transaction context must be addressed. From all of the examples shown thus far, if the consumer does not possess a transaction context and instantiates two objects that require a transaction context, two transactions will be created, as shown in Figure 13-3. However, this is not what we wanted. We wanted both COM+ objects to be in the same transaction context.

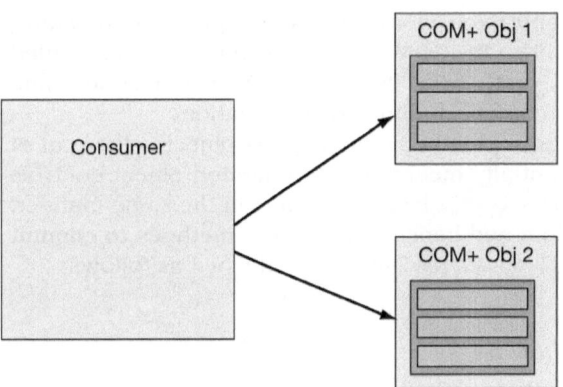

Figure 13–3: Example of consumer instantiating two COM+ objects

In Figure 13–3, both COM+ objects 1 and 2 have the transaction attributes *Require a transaction*. When the consumer instantiates COM+ object 1, a transaction context is started because the creator of the COM+ object does not have a transaction context. When the consumer instantiates COM+ object 2, the same thing happens. This means that there are two COM+ objects in two different transaction contexts.

One solution to getting both COM+ objects to execute in the context of one transaction is to create a handoff COM+ object. The handoff COM+ object would be responsible for creating COM+ objects 1 and 2. The references from these COM+ objects would then be given back to the consumer. This scenario is shown in Figure 13–4.

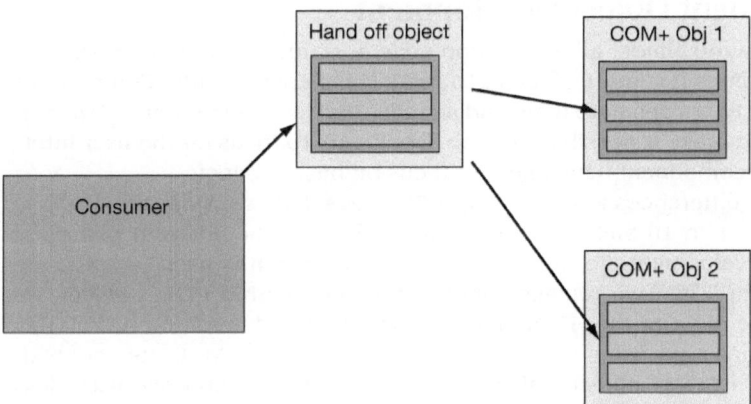

Figure 13–4: Diagram of a COM+ object that instantiates other objects

The handoff COM+ object approach works and is simple to implement, but it creates unnecessary work. In COM+ there is an interface called ITransactionContextEx that does exactly what the handoff COM+ object does and it has the additional capability to commit or abort the transaction.

In the handoff COM+ object example, the handoff COM+ object is the root of the transaction stream. This essentially means that the handoff object controls the transaction. The ITransactionContextEx interface works in the same manner. It is responsible for the transaction, and hence, it needs the methods to commit or abort the transaction. In IDL, ITransactionContextEx is defined as follows:

```
interface ITransactionContextEx : IUnknown {
HRESULT CreateInstance( [in] GUID* rclsid, [in] GUID* riid,
              [out, retval] void** pObject);
HRESULT Commit();
HRESULT Abort();
};
```

This interface is similar in Visual Basic, except that the CreateInstance method uses PROGIDs.

Despite the apparent usefulness of this interface, you are unlikely to use it. This interface is only useful when you are using a DCOM-based client. Because we are using the Web to provide our presentation, IIS and ASP already have integrated transaction-management capabilities.

If you need to use this interface, consider your business process again. In my experience, I have found that this interface can usually be avoided by implementing the façade pattern. The façade pattern is similar to a handoff object except that it contains some business logic.

ASP Component Object Development

It is possible to write almost all application code in script or using JavaScript objects. But sometimes it is more efficient to write using components. Components make it possible to encapsulate logic and simplify the development of ASP pages. Components also make it possible for Web developers to focus on the user interface and for the component developers to focus on business logic.

To show the differences in developing ASP pages, let's consider the problem of counting from 1 to 10 and take this example through the different phases of COM+ object development. To begin, a pure ASP approach is used to solve the counting problem. Then we replace some of the code with a COM+ object. Finally, we replace most of the HTML and ASP scripting code with an ASP COM+ object. Notice that I am using the term COM+ more than COM. In this context, when I refer to a COM+ object I also mean graphical user interface (GUI)-less COM objects.

A Simple ASP Page

An implementation that solves the counting problem in a pure ASP page looks like the following:

```
<%@ Language=Javascript %>
<HTML>
<HEAD></HEAD>
<BODY>
<table border=1>
<%
var counter;
var c1;
counter = 0;
for( c1 = 0; c1 < 10; c1 ++) {
counter = (counter * 2) + 2;
%>
<tr><td><%=c1%></td><td><%=counter%></td></tr>
<%
}
%>
</table>
</BODY></HTML>
```

In this example, JavaScript is used to count from 0 to 9, and some output is generated in the form of a table. There is an additional calculation performed, and the output is put in the generated table.

Integrating a COM+ Object

When building Web applications, business logic and complex calculations are not to be written in JavaScript on an ASP page because JavaScript does not have the sophistication that a programming language does. The solution is to create a COM+ object that contains the business logic or complex calculation. Building a COM+ object also means that the programming code must be distributed between an ASP page and a COM+ object. It is possible to integrate a COM+ object into an ASP page by having the ASP page call the COM+ object.

We will not go through the details of creating this COM+ object. Let's just say that the COM object IDL is the following:

```
interface IASPComponent : IDispatch {
HRESULT reset();
HRESULT getValue( [out,retval]long *value);
};
```

In this interface, there are two methods: reset, which resets the count and value, and getValue, which retrieves the calculated value and increments the count for the next getValue call. We could then integrate the COM+ object in the ASP to incrementally generate the same table as in the pure ASP approach.

The changed ASP page looks like this:

```
<%@ Language=Javascript %>
<HTML>
<HEAD></HEAD>
<BODY>
<OBJECT RUNAT=server PROGID=ASPComponent.Counter.1 id=objCounter> </OBJECT>
<table border=1>
<%
// Following commented-out code is used if the OBJECT tag does not exist
// var objCounter;
// objCounter = Server.CreateObject("ASPComponent.Counter.1");
objCounter.reset();
var c1;

for( c1 = 0; c1 < 10; c1 ++) {
%>
<tr><td><%=c1%></td><td><%=objCounter.getValue()%></td></tr>
<%
}
%>
</table>
</BODY></HTML>
```

In this piece of code, the difference is that the COM object is instantiated on the ASP page. There are two ways to do this. The first is to use the OBJECT tag, and the other is to use the Server.CreateObject method.

To use the OBJECT tag, you need to supply three parameters:

- RUNAT=server: This is necessary because it tells the ASP parser that the object will be instantiated on the server side. If this is not added, the object is instantiated on the client side.
- PROGID: This is the COM PROGID used to instantiate the object. It is possible to use the CLSID, but that is more abstract and harder to understand.
- ID: This defines the object identifier used by the scripts to reference the instantiated objects.

The Server.CreateObject method requires as a parameter the PROGID of the COM object. If the COM object instantiation is successful, the object is returned. In the preceding code, this technique was commented out but is included for reference.

After the object is instantiated with either technique, it can be called like the built-in ASP objects. In this example, objCounter.reset is called, and in the loop, the objCounter.getValue method is used to access the value.

An ASP COM+ Object

The last bit of optimization that can be done is embedding both HTML and script-ing in the COM+ object. This is called *building an ASP COM+ object*. An ASP COM+ object can be referenced on an ASP page like the COM+ object that was inte-grated in the previous example. However, the ASP COM+ object goes beyond the capabilities of that COM+ object in that it is able to access the ASP object model in the COM+ object. The advantage of this approach is that scripting code does not need to be written to input or output HTML or scripting content. It creates a compact COM+ object that only needs a few parameters to be set for it to gener-ate some very meaningful content.

IIS can pass the ASP object model from a scripting environment to a COM object because of the COM+ context. When a COM+ object is instantiated within the context of an ASP page, there is already an ASP context. In a normal COM+ object, the ASP context is not referenced, but with an ASP COM+ object it is, which is why it is called an ASP COM+ object. But don't think that the ASP COM+ object must use COM+ transactional services for it to work properly. Remember that the context-programming model enables the COM+ object to choose the functionality that it needs.

RETRIEVING THE ASP OBJECTS

As was mentioned previously, the ASP object model is referenced within the COM+ context. To access the object model, the GetObjectContext function is called. This retrieves an IObjectContext COM interface pointer. Based on this COM interface pointer, it is possible to do a QueryInterface and retrieve the IGetContextProperties COM interface pointer. From this COM interface, we can retrieve the various ASP objects (Session, Application, Response, and so on) as properties. The ASP COM objects are defined in the Microsoft Active Server Pages Object library (ASP.TLB).

Let's start with a simple ASP object manipulation. An example of retrieving the ASP Response object in Visual Basic is as follows:

```
Dim objResponse As Response
Dim objContext As ObjectContext

Set objContext = GetObjectContext()
Set objResponse = objContext("Response")
```

Judging from this Visual Basic code, it seems that retrieving the Response ob-ject is not very difficult. However, that's because Visual Basic hides much of the complexity from the developer.

Let's look at how the ASP Response object is retrieved using Visual C++ code.

```
IRequestPtr ptrRequest;
IObjectContextPtr ptrCtxt;
IGetContextPropertiesPtr pProps;
```

```
GetObjectContext( &ptrCtxt);
pProps = pObjContext;

_variant_t vt;
pProps->GetProperty( _bstr_t( "Response"), &vt);
if( V_VT( &vt) == VT_DISPATCH) {
IDispatch* pDispatch = V_DISPATCH(&vt);
ptrRequest = pDispatch;
}
```

This code is more complex. But again, I am using COM+ smart pointers. This builds the reference counting and the QueryInterface process into the programming code. The only difference between this code and the preceding Visual Basic code is that you have to explicitly call the IGetContextProperties::GetProperty method. This method returns a VARIANT data type that contains the IDispatch based Response COM object.

Optimizing Visual C++ ASP Object Referencing

In the preceding Visual C++ example, repeatedly writing the same ASP COM object reference code becomes very tedious. A better solution is to abstract this functionality to another class that contains this logic.

In the common directory of the source code associated with this book, there is a set of header files, and in the *implementation.h* header file is a class called ASPObjReference. This class encapsulates all of the steps defined above. You would typically use this class within another class as a class-scoped data member.

USING THE ASP OBJECT MODEL

Now that we have retrieved the ASP object model, it is time to actually do something with it. The simplest approach is to write a COM+ object that does the work and manipulates the ASP object model. However, there is a problem with this kind of development.

Throughout the book, we have been striving to make our components more granular. By combining the ASP object model with the business logic, we are reducing granularity. While ASP may be the "in" thing in this version of your application, things may have changed by the time you create the next version. If that happens, you may need a larger rewrite to extract the business logic from the ASP object model manipulation code.

The solution that we will use here is to write an ASP COM+ object that manipulates the IASPComponent COM+ object. This approach may seem redundant because there is a piece of script that manipulates an ASP COM+ object, which then manipulates a COM+ object. However, this is not excessive because the ASP COM+ object is an encapsulation of ASP functionality. Writing script code to manipulate the ASP COM+ object is always simpler than writing script to do the work of the ASP COM+ object. Because the ASP COM+ object is compiled, there is no chance that a scriptwriter will write the wrong script generation. The one exception to this rule is that JavaScript objects could be implemented instead of the ASP COM+ objects, but the ASP COM+ object still offers the advantage of speed and programming richness.

The ASP COM+ object encapsulates the iteration within the CASPWrapper::generate method. Hence, the ASP script only needs to call one method. The method requires a parameter that defines the number of iterations that will be executed. This method is called generate, and it is implemented as follows:

```
STDMETHODIMP CASPWrapper::generate(long iterations){
try {
    m_refASP.Init( ASPObjReference::get_Response);

    ASPCOMPONENTLib::ICounterPtr ptr( "ASPComponent.Counter.1");
    long c1;
    char buffer[ 512];
    ptr->reset();
    m_refASP.Response()->Write( _variant_t( "<table>"));
    for( c1 = 0; c1 < iterations; c1 ++) {
        sprintf( buffer, "<tr><td>Iteration %ld</td><td>%ld</td></tr>", c1,
ptr->getValue());
        m_refASP.Response()->Write( _variant_t( buffer));
    }
    m_refASP.Response()->Write( _variant_t( "</table>"));
} catch( _com_error err) {
    return err.Error();
}
return S_OK;
}
```

In this example, the generate method has as a parameter the number of iterations that will be generated. This code also uses the ASPObjReference object. The way to use this helper class is to call the ASPObjReference::Init method and pass in the ASP objects that should be retrieved. In this code, only the Response object (get_Response) should be retrieved.

After the Response object is retrieved, the COM object that performs the actual business logic is instantiated (ptr). Then, as in the previous ASP source example, the ptr->reset() method is called to reset the internal counter.

Next a TABLE is generated. But let's look more closely at this. Content is sent back to the client by calling the Response->Write method. This is something that we did in ASP, but it does have an important ramification—the ASP COM+ object does not know where the content will be placed on the HTML page. From the point of view of the ASP COM+ object, it is just adding more HTML content to the stream. As a result, where you place the ASP COM+ object on the ASP page is very important. For example, you would not place the CASPWrapper object between the <HEADER> and </HEADER> HTML tags. Instead, the CASPWrapper object is placed in between the <BODY> and </BODY> HTML tags.

Also notice that the VARIANT tag is used in this code example. This is something that you will have to get used to as a Visual C++ or Visual J++ developer. In Visual Basic, it is an inherent part of the programming language.

Now, let's see how this ASP COM+ object is integrated into the ASP page.

```
<%@ Language=Javascript %>
<HTML>
<HEAD></HEAD>
<BODY>
<OBJECT RUNAT=server PROGID=ASPComponent.ASPWrapper.1 id=objASPCounter>
</OBJECT>
<%objASPCounter.generate(10);%>
</BODY>
</HTML>
```

Notice the simplicity of this ASP page. There is only one method call and the table is automatically generated. As a designer, you can then focus on building the application and the user interface. The downside is that whatever the COM object generates cannot be easily modified. If the table is not to your liking, you may need to modify and recompile the COM object. However, because the ASP COM object is a wrapper for the underlying object, it is possible to use the underlying object directly, bypassing the ASP object.

Transacted ASP Pages

A Web application does not use DCOM when the client wants to manipulate COM objects on the server side. Instead, what a Web application is most likely to use is IIS and an ASP page. This, however, leaves open the question of how to manage transactions on an ASP page.

With IIS 5.0, it is possible to manage transaction-based Web pages. Here is an example of using a transaction within an ASP page:

```
<%@Language=JavaScript transaction=supported%>
```

The transaction keyword must be added to the first line of the ASP script. The transaction attribute is used to define which types of transactions are supported. In this example, the Web page has the transaction attribute supported. Other transaction attributes include required new, required, and not supported. Their meanings are equivalent to the COM+ transaction attributes, except that they apply in the context of an ASP page.

ASP works with transactions at the page level. This means that at the end of a page script, the transaction is committed or aborted. A transaction instantiated by ASP can only last for the duration of the page. If this is adequate, then it is good to use this type of transaction, because multiple components can be used within the same transaction context. This way, whatever action is taken by any of the components can be committed or aborted.

Consider the following source code:

```
<%@ Language=JavaScript transaction=required%>
<HTML>
<HEAD></HEAD>
<BODY>
<h1>The transaction example</h1>
<%
try {
var tempObject;
tempObject = Server.CreateObject("Registration4.UserImpl4.1");
tempObject.firstname = "Christian";
tempObject.lastname = "Gross";
tempObject.email = "cgross@eusoft.com";
tempObject.password = "cc";
tempObject.writeObject();
Session("tempObject") = tempObject;
} catch( e ) {
%>
<h2>Error is <%=e%></h2>
<%}%>

<%
function OnTransactionCommit(){
Response.Write( "Transaction Complete");
}
function OnTransactionAbort(){
Response.Write( "Transaction Abort");
}
%>
</BODY>
</HTML>
```

In this example, a transaction is started when the page is loaded, and then the ASP script is executed. However, the OnTransactionCommit and OnTransactionAbort functions are not executed. They are events called by the ASP transaction support to indicate the success or failure of the transaction on the page. When a page has finished executing, a two-phase commit is started. If the two-phase commit is successful, the OnTransactionCommit event is called. Anything else is an error, and the OnTransactionAbort function is called.

The other item to notice on this ASP page is the use of JavaScript exception blocks. By using these blocks, it is possible to give presentable feedback to the user on what went wrong instead of having an error page with some cryptic error code on it.

INTEGRATION OF ASP TRANSACTIONS AND COM+ TRANSACTIONS

It is possible to combine the CASPWrapper ASP COM+ object with a transacted ASP page. The COM+ object manipulated by the CASPWrapper ASP COM+ object could be using COM+ transactions. However, the COM+ object transaction ID and the ASP transaction ID are not the same because COM+ transactions are known as flat transactions, as described in Chapter 10. This means that there are two distinctly separate transactions.

This makes our transaction management more difficult, because we need to determine which transaction is running when and how. There are several simple rules to determining this:

- If a COM+ object is instantiated in the context of a transaction-supported ASP page, then the transaction ID of the COM+ object and the ASP page is the same. A call to abort the transaction from either the ASP page or the COM+ object will result in the failure of the transaction.
- If the COM+ object is instantiated on an ASP page that does not support transactions, a separate transaction is started. If a transacted ASP page manipulates that object, the changes made by any script on the ASP page will not be part of the ASP transaction.
- If the COM+ object is assigned to a Session variable, then when the transaction of the COM+ object ends, the object reference becomes invalid and should not be used. Instead, the value should be set to NULL.

Putting It in Perspective

This chapter ends our discussion of the middle-tier business object. This chapter introduced some advanced topics on using COM+ transactions. They are specialized scenarios, but they can occur.

For example, while it is interesting to build brand-new applications using brand-new data, the reality is that you are likely to need to integrate some type of legacy data. Converting the legacy data is not possible, but the data needs to be integrated into your COM+ application. Pooled objects are your solution. It is possible to write resource dispensers, but doing that is much more complicated.

The other part of this chapter focused on building ASP-enabled COM+ objects. This is a specialized scenario, but you need it for development purposes. Server-side business objects need to be optimized—ASP developers and HTML designers do not want to spend their time developing large pieces of ASP code to display a table of users. An ASP COM+ object optimizes this. It does not remove any flexibility in formatting because style sheets can be applied to the overall HTML page, which affects the HTML content generated by the ASP COM+ object.

Chapter 14

Building the Hybrid Client

So far we have discussed Hypertext Markup Language (HTML) and Component Object Model (COM). In this chapter, we combine them to build the hybrid client, which mixes Internet technology with desktop windowing technology. The combination of the two technologies makes it easier to write maintainable distributed applications.

In this chapter, we look at the various pieces of a hybrid client and at how they are combined to build a hybrid application. The core technology used is Microsoft Internet Explorer, because Internet Explorer is not just a Web browser—it is a component-based document and Internet browser.

Defining the Hybrid Client

We talked about using the thin client as a way of easily solving the problem of wide distribution. However, the thin client doesn't solve the data management problem. A thin client assumes that all of the data remains on the server, but often this is simply not possible. Many applications require intensive client-side interaction, because having a richer interface can sometimes help in carrying out the task. Sometimes, an HTML user interface is not enough.

The problem that we will face in the future is the problem of not having enough processor speed to be capable of managing large volumes of data. I, for example, have an Apple Newton and multiple Windows CE devices that I use to distribute my tasks. My bottleneck becomes moving and manipulating data. I regularly work with about 300 MB of data and need access to many megabytes more of archived data from older projects.

In general, the volume of electronic data easily outstrips available network capacity, and this problem will not decrease in the future, because technologies such as XML (Extensible Markup Language) will increase those requirements dramatically. What we need is a computer software solution that optimizes this network traffic. And the only solution that has resulted to date is a device that has a CPU, RAM, and a hard disk (a PC) running a hybrid client.

So, what is a hybrid client? Suppose you are using a word processor to edit a document. Is it better to have the word processor installed locally, rather than to retrieve the word processor executable from a remote server? If it is installed locally, when the word processor application is started, it is faster and does not require a network connection.

You could argue that networks in the future will be faster, and that is true. What is likely to happen is that you will buy and install software locally for tasks that you do everyday, and for occasional tasks, you may put up with the slower network connection and rent the use of a remote application.

Now let's apply the concept of the hybrid client to the task of editing a document. An intelligent word processor is a hybrid client. In the future, features that are required every day would be installed locally, and specialized features would be installed on demand. This process of installing on demand would be embedded within the word processor. Interestingly, Microsoft Office 2000 has this functionality built in. The only behavior that has not been implemented is the capability to charge a fee for one-time use of specific features.

The next question is where to keep the documents we are editing with the word processor—they, too, can be local or remote. The user doesn't need to define this location—they just need to see a domain of documents that they can work with.

When you look at the functionality required, it is apparent that we need a hybrid client. The role of the hybrid client is to abstract the difference between network and local storage to a single domain of documents and features. When those documents are modified, the hybrid client manages the details of whether to save them locally or remotely based on the name of the domain. When features are installed and deleted, the hybrid client manages it automatically. The point is that the user is never aware of what is a local manipulation and what is a remote manipulation.

The Architecture of the Hybrid Client

The hybrid client that we discuss is based on Microsoft Internet Explorer. It is possible to use another browser, like Mozilla, but that is beyond the scope of this book. Microsoft Internet Explorer, itself, is a hybrid client application, albeit a simple one. On your Windows 2000 desktop, the Microsoft Internet Explorer icon is only a reference to an executable that instantiates an application that hosts the Web Browser COM control. The Web Browser COM contains the functionality of being capable of browsing any type of document, including HTML. Figure 14–1 shows the architecture of Microsoft Internet Explorer.

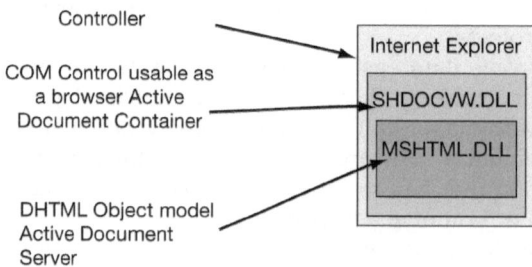

Figure 14–1: Microsoft Internet Explorer architecture

So, the Microsoft Internet Explorer application is a COM control controller because it hosts the Web Browser COM control. This control is located in the SHDOCVW.DLL library. It is a COM control, but it is also an Active Document

Container. An Active Document Container has the capability to host and contain an Active Document Server.

An Active Document Server is something like OLE (Object Linking and Embedding). The basis of OLE is the capability to cut and paste information from one type of document to another type of document. Implementing that type of functionality has been very complex. An Active Document Server is a simplified version of OLE, because you cannot cut and paste, but you can create a generic document framework that is controlled by the content of the documents.

The Web Browser COM control is a generic document framework in that it enables you to browse any type of document that has an Active Document Server. Granted, for the most part you will be navigating HTML and XML documents. However, to create a more complex hybrid client application, you could integrate Microsoft Word or Microsoft Excel as a remote document.

When an HTML page is loaded into the Web Browser COM control, the HTML Active Document Server, MSHTML.DLL, is loaded. This dynamic link library (DLL) contains all of the Dynamic HTML COM objects and it is our HTML COM component. The JavaScript that manipulates Dynamic HTML object model on the client side manipulates the HTML COM object model.

Business Logic on the Client

Many people consider fat clients to be bad because they are too large both in byte size and programming logic. However, the bad reputation of the fat client is not entirely deserved. Sometimes a client needs to be fat because of the things that it must accomplish. I am not going to try and point out the advantages of a fat client. I will just say that a hybrid client can be fat, and a fat client is only bad when it tries to do too many things and does not attempt to distribute the logic. A hybrid client will never attempt to do all things.

Some tasks need to be carried out on the client side, such as word processing. A word processing application focuses on the word processing task. Sometimes the word processing needs to be augmented by managing forms and word processing content. This is typical of a workflow application. In this case, the word processor acts as a shell application that manipulates the content. In contrast, a server-side process would process the content on the server side.

Now we come to the question of where the logic should be put. In Chapters 6 and 7, we discussed some techniques for generating and manipulating data. Specifically, we looked at the concept of hard and soft data. With the introduction of the hybrid client, the difference between hard and soft data becomes very blurred, because some data is saved on the client side. We need to focus on solving tasks and determine where to store the hard and soft data.

In the case of the workflow application, the content at the beginning is considered soft, but once the content is processed on the server side, it becomes hard and is sent back to the client. At this point, the client stores the hard data on the local hard disk. However, because it is hard data, the server will take a copy of the data and store it for reference purposes. In effect, the client has cached the hard data on its local hard disk to optimize access time. The client will consider the hard data to be read-only data, and the moment the data is manipulated, it is once again considered soft data that must be sent to the server to be made hard again. This is called optimizing the resources. The hybrid client is an exercise in figuring out how to store data on the network; the challenge lies in making the data hard and ensuring that, after it is hard, anyone who has a copy of the hard data has the correct information.

For the purposes of this book, I assume that the concept of COM+ transactions and COM+ activities does not extend to the client side. Even though we will be using Windows 2000 on the client side, which does include COM+ transaction services, we will disregard that. The reason for doing this is that the resource managers have not yet become diverse enough to add COM+ capabilities to the client side. For example, there is no way yet to relate client-side transactions to the server securely using hypertext transfer protocol (HTTP) or XML. This particular example is important, because it affects the location of where data is made hard.

DEFINING THE SHELL

In the hybrid client, there is the concept of the shell, and the shell that we will be working with encapsulates the Web Browser COM control. The main function of the shell is to seamlessly integrate the functionality of the network. This means that the user of the hybrid client does not notice the difference between using network resources and using local resources.

The `Remote Control` pattern defines the type of functionality in the shell. With the remote control pattern, you can provide seamless integration of the network and still make it updateable. Let's put this in the context of the traditional application. In that scenario, an application is written using the classic Windows Application Programming Interfaces (APIs) with some controls. To distribute that client, a setup program is written that is executed on the machines needing the functionality. This process of distribution and installation costs money and time.

With the remote control pattern, the solution is to provide a data navigation application, but the content for the data manipulation is provided by a resource that is simpler to distribute. In our example, the data manipulations are performed using the techniques described in Chapters 6 and 7. The data navigation application is a simpler application that does not need constant updating to fix bugs. The data manipulations, on the other hand, need regular patches and updates to reflect changes in the business process. You still have to distribute the data navigation application, but less often than you would have to update traditional applications.

Building a Corporate Desktop

In every corporation, there is a corporate computer desktop. The desktop is grouping of company applications that are used to carry out daily operations. In a banking situation, it might be applications relating to the processing of mortgages, savings, and portfolio management. In a manufacturing situation, it might be applications related to production output, invoicing, and client account management.

We will go through a simple example of building a computer desktop application for a custom software company. A quick domain-model text for the project would be similar to this:

> The custom software desktop is used to control all aspects of the custom software development process. The desktop contains applications for managing project files, project time card management, software bugs, version control, and administrative tools.

Building the Shell

We begin by building the shell, which is modeled after the remote control pattern that will provide our data navigation of the custom software applications. We want to navigate the project time card management, software bug management, and message board applications.

To represent and navigate the various applications in the shell application interface, three different push buttons on a toolbar could be used. The problem is that toolbar buttons are not dynamic. A data navigation shell needs to be able to self-adjust when new data manipulation applications become available. We don't want the user to have to manually install the various data manipulation applications. This is an incorrect way of navigating the various applications, but it is the technique most people use for navigation.

A computer user's work is organized according to a series of tasks, and the desktop software needs to be organized similarly. The data navigation and data manipulation applications need to represent the tasks that the user wants to accomplish. The tasks, themselves, can be organized in individual portfolios, which can be applied to both the server side and client side to organize the user's work.

Another function that the data navigation framework needs to offer is the capability to keep notes. Notes are useful for storing spur of the moment thoughts. This notepad data should not be stored on the server, because it is soft data that changes daily.

Let's now consider the options for building a data navigation shell. The first option is to move the data navigation core to a server and let the client-side application reference the information on the server. Such an implementation could use HTML frames, with a navigation frame, banner frame, and so on. However, the problem with this solution is that it requires a constant connection to the server, and HTML frames are restrictive in their functionality. For example, having multiple different views of the same data is not easily done.

The second option for building a data navigation shell is to create an MDI (Multiple Document Interface) application, and then let the data navigation shell monitor the various navigation steps. With an MDI shell application, it is possible to open the same document data twice, but each view of the data is different. To realize this solution, create a Windows MDI application that hosts the Web Browser COM control in multiple child windows.

BUILDING THE APPLICATION MENU

Regardless of how the portfolio or data manipulation applications are represented, we need to define an application menu. Do not confuse the application menu with a Windows application menu. The `application menu` is an HTML page that contains links to the various data manipulation applications.

The simplest way of building this application is to have it download and parse an XML file that contains a link to an HTML file. The XML file is a data repository that contains references other than the HTML file. For the time being, though, we are only interested in the HTML file.

The HTML file references one or more data-manipulation application references. This HTML file is downloaded and stored on the local hard disk for faster access, and it is loaded into the Web Browser COM control for display purposes. When one of the links on the reference HTML file is clicked, it opens another MDI child window and displays the content in it.

The most important component within the data navigation shell application is the Web Browser COM control itself. It is a central piece of your hybrid client application. I do not go into the details of how to reference the Web Browser COM control in your programming environment—the DLL SHDOCVW.DLL contains all of the COM-type library information required. In the COM-type library references, this library is called *Microsoft Internet Controls*.

Integrating the Web Browser COM Control

Even though the Web Browser COM control is a document browser, it is a COM control, and every COM control has methods and properties. In the case of the Web Browser COM control, there are methods, such as `GoBack`, `GoForward`, `Search`, and `Refresh2`, which are identical to their browser counterparts. Some of the methods provide for the interaction between the Web Browser COM control hosting application and the Web Browser COM control. There are also other properties. An example could be `WebBrowser.busy`, that tell you that the Web Browser COM control is busy doing other things and should not be disturbed.

The Web Browser COM control is a COM control, where everything can be queried, and all of the statuses can be retrieved. Or the Web Browser COM control can inform the hosting application when some status has changed. This is important, because loading a specific document takes an undetermined amount of time. There is an event that indicates that the Web Browser control is about to change documents (`WebBrowser.BeforeNavigate`). There is also an event that indicates that the document was downloaded (`WebBrowser.NavigateComplete`). All of these events can be redirected to individual HTML frames or generic content files such as ASCII text.

The Microsoft Internet Controls type library has two versions of the Web Browser COM control: `WebBrowser` and `WebBrowser_V1`. The difference between them is that `WebBrowser_V1` is an older implementation that has fewer events and methods. The `WebBrowser` object is the current version as described by the Microsoft Internet Explorer documentation.

In the hybrid client navigation architecture, the XML needs to be downloaded. The Web Browser control is placed on the Visual Basic form and then the

XML file is retrieved from a Web server, which can be done using the following programming code:

```
Private Sub Form_Load()
WebBrowser1.Navigate2 "http://bacchus/desktop/applications.asp"
End Sub
```

When the Web Browser COM control is placed on a Visual Basic form, the first control of its type is named Webbrowser1. Navigating to a specific document on a local hard disk or remote network is accomplished by using the Navigate2 method. In this case, the simplest form is used, which only specifies the Uniform Resource Locator (URL). Notice the use of http:// in the URL. This is very important. Internet Explorer does not require an explicit http:// (it assumes the HTTP protocol when none is specified), but it is good programming practice to add it to the URL. Notice also that the URL specifies an Active Server Page (ASP) page. Typically, an ASP page contains HTML commands, but it can contain any text, and in this case, the text is XML.

In Visual C++, the Navigate2 method has five parameters instead of one. The other four parameters can be ignored in Visual Basic because they are considered optional. The full definition of the Webbrowser.Navigate2 method is as follows:

```
Webbrowser.Navigate2(URL, [Flags], [TargetFrameName], [PostData], [Headers])
```

The additional parameters are defined as follows:

- Flags defines how the new content is to be downloaded. In Internet Explorer 5.0, content can be cached on the local hard disk or it can be downloaded every time it is requested. An example flag setting is navNoWriteToCache, which means download the content but do not write the results to the cache.
- TargetFrameName is used to specify in which frame the content is to be displayed. If there are no frames, or the identified frame cannot be found, a new window is opened.
- PostData is used to provide additional information regarding the request. This information can be in any form. It can be a stream of binary bytes or form-encoded variables. What is important is that the Multipurpose Internet Mail Extensions (MIME) type is set correctly and that the server is expecting that type of content during the request that is being made. If this parameter is used, the HTTP request is automatically converted from a GET to a POST.
- Headers makes it possible to provide additional HTTP headers to an HTTP request. The last two parameters of the Navigate2 method assume that the request is made using the HTTP protocol. If the request isn't made using the HTTP protocol, then the parameters are ignored. For example, if the request is ftp://ftp.myserver.com, then the last two parameters are ignored because the URL represents an FTP request.

So why the detail on this single method? The answer is that the `Navigate2` method is the most important method that you use in the hybrid client.

Avoid Hard Coding

Going back to the previous source code sample, the `Navigate2` method used a hard-coded URL, but this is not a typical programming practice. Or at least it should not be. The URL should either be a constant defined in the program or it should be dynamically read into the application.

You may be thinking that the better approach is to read in the URL dynamically, but I recommend defining the URL as a constant in the program. The URL is not likely to change. For example, how often has the www.microsoft.com URL changed? Not since it was first introduced. The servers that represent the URL may have changed, but not the URL. This is the point of the Web.

As a result, the best way of creating a dynamic data-navigation architecture is to create a corporation-wide central URL that is resolved using Internet technologies. Then the server is responsible for dynamic content that specifies where the various resources are stored. The advantage of this approach is that the hybrid client application can be installed anywhere, and it will automatically configure itself based on the network server settings and local environment.

NAVIGATION

Now let's apply some of the techniques we have discussed to our shell application. Our basic task is to display the HTML data applications navigation page. That page will have a series of links, and when someone clicks a link, another MDI child window will open. By default, HTML does not do this. The way to implement this functionality in our shell application is to implement the `WebBrowser.BeforeNavigate2` event. An example implementation is as follows:

```
Private Sub WebBrowser1_BeforeNavigate2(ByVal pDisp As Object, URL As
Variant, Flags As Variant, TargetFrameName As Variant, PostData As Variant,
Headers As Variant, Cancel As Boolean)
If redirect = True Then
    Dim tmpFrm As Object

    Set tmpFrm = New frmBrowser
    tmpFrm.Visible = True
    tmpFrm.brwWebBrowser.Navigate URL
    Cancel = True
End If
End Sub
```

Before we delve into the details of this implementation, let's look at the various parameters of this event.

- pDisp represents the Web Browser COM control that is currently being affected. When a document is loaded that contains multiple frames, the BeforeNavigate2 event is called for each frame. The pDisp parameter represents the local frame, which is a Web Browser COM control.
- URL defines the URL of the resource that is about to be loaded.
- Flags has not yet been defined and should be ignored.
- TargetFrameName represents the string name of the frame that is being currently loaded. This is only filled in if the document loaded in the Web Browser COM control contains HTML frames.
- PostData represents the content that is sent with a POST request. An example of this is the filling out of the HTML form elements.
- Headers represents the individual headers sent with the HTTP request.
- Cancel is a flag that determines whether or not the URL is retrieved. This is the only parameter that is sent as a reference and is actually used by the Web Browser COM control. If the Cancel flag is set to TRUE, the document is not retrieved. A FALSE setting downloads the document.

Now let's consider the implementation of the BeforeNavigate2 event. The redirect flag is required because otherwise all documents, including the data applications navigation HTML page, will be redirected. This is the problem: Suppose you have a form, and on it you implemented the BeforeNavigate2 event. Every time the event is called, the content is redirected to another document. In this instance, the event implementation creates a child window, which means that the browser window doing the redirecting is never loaded with an HTML document. The purpose of the redirect flag is to enable the initial loading of the data applications navigation HTML page.

If redirect is True, then a new MDI child window is created. This new MDI child window contains an instance of the Web Browser COM control, and then the URL to be navigated to is assigned to the new browser window instance (tmpFrm.brwWebBrowser.Navigate). Finally, setting the Cancel parameter to True stops the navigation in the current window.

If you are developing your application in Visual Basic, and in the main window the frmBrowser and frmNavigation are started using [form].visible = True, then the BeforeNavigate2 event is shared between the forms. This is not desirable. All forms should be instantiated using the new keyword to avoid this problem.

CREATING A PORTFOLIO

Now that we have made it possible to navigate and work with the individual data manipulation applications, we want to make sure users can keep track of their work. This means keeping a locally stored portfolio of applications that are currently being used.

The challenge in creating the portfolio is not in managing the individual pieces of data and writing them to a file. The challenge is writing a file format that can be shared by any tool and any environment. I won't get into the details of how to write the buttons to create the portfolio—you can look at the accompanying source code for that information. Instead, I want to focus on the mechanism of storing the portfolio information.

Defining the XML Persistence

The task is to be able to persist the contents of the portfolio to an XML file. The first step is to build the object model that represents the portfolio. The Unified Modeling Language (UML) class diagram is shown in Figure 14–2. The root object is the portfolio object. It is responsible for managing the entire portfolio.

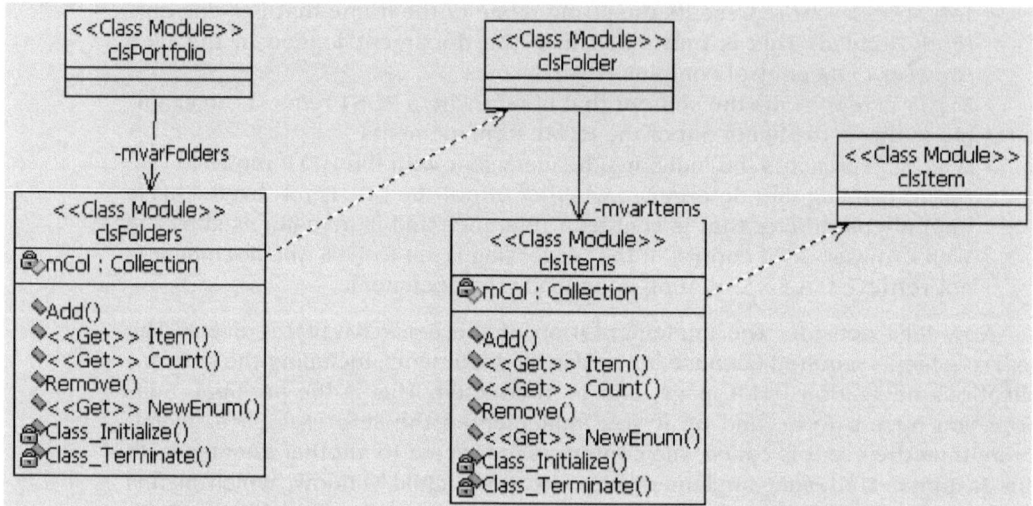

Figure 14–2: Portfolio class

Within a portfolio, you can define folders, which make up a desktop that contains various URLs. The folder is the object clsFolder. Because there are multiple clsFolder objects within a portfolio, a clsFolders collection is created to contain them. The clsFolder contains multiple URLs that are to be loaded when the folder is loaded. A URL represents a browser window, and there are various attributes, such as window dimensions, that need to be considered. This information is grouped in a class called clsItem. The clsItems collection contains clsItem objects.

An example XML output is as follows:

```
<portfolio>
<folders count="1">
    <folder>
        <items count="1">
            <item>
            </item>
        </items>
    </folder>
</folders>
</portfolio>
```

As you can see, there is a root-level node called portfolio. Contained in it is an XML node called folders with an attribute named count, which indicates the number of folder XML subnodes that exist. In the folder XML node is an items XML node. This serves the same purpose as the folders node, and it also has a count attribute. Finally, there is the item node. This object model is a direct copy of the UML object model, and at first glance it seems like a good approach, because typically in a file format you do not know how many items will be stored.

In XML, it is not necessary to define boundaries that explicitly define where one node ends and another starts. This is because XML can be an ad hoc collection of different items. The XML tags define the boundaries of the collection. Therefore, it is not necessary to add the folders and items nodes. The attribute count will be lost, and it will not be possible to know how many folder or item nodes there are, which means that the loading routine must dynamically allocate the objects. But that is not a problem, because good programming routines allocate objects dynamically. Setting limits is not a good idea and can cause bugs.

If we remove the folders and items XML tags from the previous XML document, we get the following:

```
<portfolio>
<folder>
    <item>
    </item>
</folder>
</portfolio>
```

Working with the XML DOM

The best way to write the portfolio is to use XML. Using XML ensures that our data can be shared in different environments. We discussed using XML to view data in Chapters 6 and 7. However, XML can also be used as a file format to store data for an application.

For manipulating the XML document, there is a something called an XML DOM (Document Object Model). The XML DOM is based on the concept of nodes. The root of the XML document is the XML document object. Within the XML document object, there are XML nodes. These XML nodes can contain other collections of XML nodes, which, in turn, can contain other XML nodes.

The XML data hierarchy resembles a directory tree structure. To reach a specific piece of information, you move up and down the XML data hierarchy. The problem with this approach is that navigating the XML data hierarchy requires explicitly referencing various nodes. In other words, you must search each node individually. This makes finding a specific piece of information very tedious. And trying to relate the individual XML nodes to a specific COM object is also very tedious and difficult.

Serializing COM Objects to XML Data

The challenge in persisting the portfolio to an XML file is mapping a set of COM objects to XML data. The best way to do this is to build helper objects that handle this functionality automatically.

Why is the XML DOM not sufficient? When you are extracting information from the XML DOM tree, you need to constantly go up and down the XML DOM tree to find something. The helper objects can define anchor points in the XML DOM tree where a COM object would parse the local XML nodes for its state. This means that in most cases, a maximum of one level of XML DOM tree navigation is required, which then makes everything much simpler.

How is this all implemented? The answer is that our helper objects are COM objects that define COM interfaces that the persisted objects must implement. The helper objects do the automatic COM to XML serialization, then call these COM interfaces. It is important, though, that these helper objects use the XML DOM, because it is a standard. Building the solution any other way would introduce a proprietary solution that does not fit in the bigger picture.

One alternative method is to develop a wizard that takes an XML description and automatically generates the source code to manipulate the XML DOM. While this is a noble goal, the problem is that for an XML document of significant size, the generated code will be large and hard to read and use, which means that fixing bugs and making changes would require more effort than necessary. Again, the better approach is to develop a set of helper objects that abstracts the XML DOM standard.

Chapter 11 described the persistence of COM objects using `IPersistStream`. However, these objects were saved to a proprietary format that is not XML compliant. When persisting the COM objects to XML, the same persistence technique that was described in Chapter 11 is used. This technique involves defining an XML Persistence COM interface that each COM object must implement.

The XML COM persistence framework will then query for the XML Persistence COM interface from each COM object that wants to save its state to the XML stream. The XML Persistence COM interface needs two methods: `save` and `load`. In the implementation of the XML Persistence COM interface, the process of saving data and child objects is identical to the process presented in Chapter 11.

However, there is a problem with the loading of the various COM objects that have implemented the XML Persistence COM interface. The save process does not save the PROG ID or the CLSID of the COM object, as the save process does in Chapter 11, and we do not know which objects to load at what time. The XML tags have no indicator to say which object is associated with the tag. The solution is to register XML tag handlers with the helper objects. The handler associates itself with a specific tag, and in the process of loading the document, the helper objects constantly check their lists of handlers to see if there is a match. If there is a match, then the handler redirects the XML node-parsing process to the XML tag handler.

The XML serialization interface is a custom COM interface only, which is declared as follows:

```
interface XMLSerialize : IUnknown {
HRESULT save([in] XMLService* service);
HRESULT load([in] XMLService* service);
};
```

The save method is used to save the current state of the COM object to the XML stream. The converse is the load method, which is used to load the state of the COM object from the XML stream. In both of these methods, an interface pointer of the type XMLService is passed in. This is a custom interface used to manage the serialization process.

Creating XML Documents, Nodes, and Attributes

The COM objects clsPortfolio, clsFolder, and clsItem need to implement the XMLSerialize COM interface. Let's take the example of saving the clsPortfolio COM object. When the XMLSerialize::save method is called, it would serialize the collection of clsFolder COM objects, which in turn would serialize the collection of clsItem COM objects. The serialization is recursive, because serializing clsPortfolio serializes the various child objects. In this way, an XML hierarchy is built that reflects the hierarchy of COM objects. This recursion is handled by the XMLService interface.

The XMLService COM interface is responsible for managing the serialization process. Its interface is defined as follows:

```
interface IPXMLService : IDispatch {
[id(0)] HRESULT addHandler( BSTR handler, IDispatch *item);
[id(1)] HRESULT removeHandler( BSTR handler);
[id(2)] HRESULT load( BSTR url);
[id(3)] HRESULT save( BSTR url, IDispatch *ptrVal);
[propget, id(4)] HRESULT currNode([out, retval] IDispatch **pVal);
[propput, id(4)] HRESULT currNode([in] IDispatch *newVal);
[propget, id(5)] HRESULT XMLDocument([out, retval] IDispatch **pVal);
[propput, id(5)] HRESULT XMLDocument([in] IDispatch *newVal);
};
```

To explain this COM interface, let's look at what functionality it contains. We will assume that IPXMLService was implemented as COM object XMLService. The XMLService COM object is used to load and save the XML document—it is responsible for managing the COM to XML persistence process. Contained in the implementation is the list of handlers. The XMLService COM object is responsible for setting the local XML anchor node, which is the IPXMLService::currNode property.

When an application wants to save a set of COM objects to XML, the applications needs to instantiate XMLService. An example of doing this is as follows:

```
Dim objXMLService As New XMLService

objXMLService.save mvarfilename, rootObject
```

To add content to the XML hierarchy, the objXMLService.save method is called. The first parameter represents the name of the XML file where the objects will be persisted. The second parameter is the COM object that represents the root COM object, which, in turn, will be the root XML node.

In the implementation of XMLService.save, the DOMDocument COM object is instantiated. This object is part of the Microsoft XML library and when instantiated, it creates an empty XML document. Because this is a save serialization process, it is up to the rootObject to add XML nodes to the XML document. The XMLServer.XMLDocument property represents the DOMDocument that was instantiated in the XMLService.save method. Then the rootObject.save method is called to persist its state.

Here is an example implementation of a COM object IPXMLSerialize.save method:

```
Private Sub PXMLSerializeClass_save(ByVal service As Object)
Dim pService As XMLService
Dim pHelper As XMLHelper
Dim pNode As IXMLDOMNode

Set pService = service
Set pHelper = pService.XMLHelper
Set pNode = pHelper.setRootElement("folder ")
Set pService.currNode = pNode
Dim c1 As Long

pHelper.addNodeTextCombo "CollectionCount",CStr( mCol.count)
For c1 = 1 To mCol.count
    mCol.Item( c1).save service
Next
End Sub
```

In this implementation, the code starts out converting the service parameter to an XMLService data type. It is possible to not convert the parameter, but then you would be relying on the IDispatch COM interface, which would make the entire persistence process slower. The pHelper variable represents an XML helper object that encapsulates specific operations, such as adding child XML nodes.

When an empty XML document is created, there is no root element. Therefore, when the first COM object is being serialized, it is necessary to create a root XML element. It is up to the COM object being serialized to create the root XML node. The XML helper object has the setRootElement method to create a root node with the XML tag as defined by the folder parameter.

The mCol collection needs to be serialized to the XML stream. It is identical to the collection introduced in Chapter 11, and serializing the collection to an XML stream is identical to serializing the collection to an Microsoft Message Queue (MSMQ) message stream. The only difference is that instead of using the property bag to write to the MSMQ message, the XMLSerialize.Save method is called.

The instantiation of the XML nodes is encapsulated in the XML helper class. In the XML DOM, it is not possible to create XML elements by instantiating the XML node COM object. The DOMDocument has methods that create the XML nodes, such as comments, attributes, and elements. We are interested in creating nodes. This is done using the DOMDocument::createNode method, as shown in the following example:

```
Dim obj As IXMLDOMNode
Set obj = mvarXMLDocument.createNode(NODE_ELEMENT, tagName, "")
```

The first parameter specifies the type of node being created. In this case, it is a NODE_ELEMENT, which in XML terms could be:

```
<ELEMENT />
```

However, the node could be NODE_TEXT, which in XML terms could be:

```
<TAG>some text</TAG>
```

Or the node could be any other valid XML node type, such as entity declarations, comments, a CDATA section, and so forth.

The second parameter defines the identifier of the tag, which is the same as the nodeName property. In the previous example, if the value of tagName were *folder*, then the following would be generated:

```
<folder/>
```

The last parameter is a text string that specifies the namespace that the identifier of the tag is defined in. This parameter is optional. If it is not used, the parser assumes that the identifier is defined in the local document-type declaration (DTD), if it exists. After a successful creation, the new node, which is a COM interface of IXMLDOMNode, is returned.

The returned variable obj is an IXMLDOMNode COM interface pointer. It is not part of the XML document and needs to be added to the document.

Now let's consider the following XML fragment:

```
<ELEMENT attribute="value">some text</ELEMENT>
```

To create this fragment, you have to create two XML nodes. The first is the XML node that represents the XML tag *ELEMENT*. I'll call this the parent XML node. The attribute = value attribute is part of the XMLDOMNode.attributes collection. This XML tag is of the type NODE_ELEMENT.

To create the *some text* XML content, another XML node needs to be created, but this time it is of the type NODE_TEXT. This XML node is added to the child XML nodes collection of the parent XML node that was created in the previous paragraph using the XMLDOMNode.appendChild method.

It is also possible to insert a child node in a specific location using the insertBefore method. This method inserts a node before a specified node in the children collection.

Adding attributes to an XML node can be done in two ways. The more complicated way is to call DOMDocument::createAttribute and then set the various values of the attribute. This object is then added to the attribute collection of the node. A simpler way is to do a QueryInterface for the IXMLDOMElement interface, and then use the setAttribute method as shown in the following example:

```
Dim obj As IXMLDOMNode
Dim obj2 As IXMLDOMElement
...
Set obj2 = obj
obj.setAttribute "attribute", "value"
```

Once the serialization has finished, the XMLService.Save method will save the contents to a file using the DOMDocument.save method.

Building the Content

The data manipulation HTML pages are downloaded dynamically on request from a Web server. To this point, the data manipulations have occurred on the server side, although we did use some client-side techniques, such as JavaScript and XSL (Extensible Style Language). Now, though, what we really want is to have very rich functionality that enables us to save state to a locally stored portfolio. The way to do this is to create a custom COM control, more commonly known as ActiveX control.

ENHANCING THE DATA MANIPULATIONS

ActiveX controls work with Microsoft Internet Explorer and can be inserted into an HTML page. The ActiveX Control is distributed on demand, like the HTML page. If the user does not have the ActiveX Control, then it is automatically downloaded and installed. Installing an ActiveX Control in the context of an HTML page is a simpler and smaller installation process than a full Windows application installation.

Now, because some logic can be built into the ActiveX control, we must decide on the criteria used to determine which logic is added. The way to do this is to use the Separating format from logic pattern. This pattern addresses the question of how to structure the content on the client side. We need to create very granular COM objects that can be dynamically wired together using client-side HTML scripting. The various COM objects will know about each other's COM interfaces, and the HTML scripting will dynamically associate and introduce the various COM implementations to each other.

Let's focus on the physical characteristics of ActiveX controls. They are similar to COM objects, except that they have a graphical user interface (GUI) or user interface. They also support the notion of COM interfaces and COM implementations.

When you are working with ActiveX controls and developing them using Visual Basic or Visual C++, be sure that they are executed on the correct processor. Visual J++ is different, because it only requires that the Microsoft Java virtual machine (VM) exist on the client side. There are also implementations of the Microsoft VM on UNIX and Macintosh platforms. Compiled ActiveX controls have the capability to do serious damage to your computer, such as reformatting a hard disk.

You might think that because of the lack of restrictions and lack of cross-platform capabilities, ActiveX controls should be avoided. And many people would agree. However, ActiveX controls do have proper uses, such as these:

- When some desired functionality cannot be accomplished using DHTML, XML, and XSL, such as graphing, mathematical calculations, and some types of business logic
- When the performance of scripting is too slow
- When you need special effects using ActiveX controls to enhance the end user experience
- When network bandwidth is to be used more efficiently by offloading some of the server-side processing to the client side
- When a different client protocol is to be integrated into the Web application

On the desktop application, there is a need to keep control of how much time is spent on the various projects. An ActiveX control on the client is useful because it makes it possible to gather the data, and then send it to the server for persistence at a later time. To display the various pieces of data on the client side, a recordset is created. This control introduces two new concepts: Dynamic HTML data binding, and interacting with the Dynamic HTML object model.

USING DYNAMIC HTML DATA BINDING

With the introduction of Internet Explorer 5.0, it is possible to define XML as a data source, and then bind it dynamically to the HTML page. This is called Dynamic HTML data binding. DHTML data binding makes it possible to store a set of data on the client side and then to iterate through it like a recordset.

DHTML data binding works as follows. An HTML page is downloaded. On this page is a data source object (DSO) reference to a recordset. This reference could be a URL or data on the page. When the DSO is loaded, it binds the data to itself. Then, on the HTML page, references are made to the DSO using scripting. These references move through the recordset or display the data. The point is that it interacts with the DSO recordset.

Using a DSO is very powerful technique because it abstracts the concept of data to a generic recordset. Because it is very simple to write a custom DSO, there is no learning curve for HTML designers—they only need to understand the concept of the recordset.

The example application that we will build is a time-card application. The time-card application will allow us to punch in and out of a task, which could be a project or a vacation. The reason for choosing a time-card application is that there is some server-side and client-side processing. Also, the most effective way to display the various time cards is to use a DSO and manipulate the time cards as if they were recordsets.

An Example Using the XML DSO

To understand how a DSO works, let's consider a simple time-card application that only displays and navigates through the data. The source code to do this is as follows:

```
<HTML>
<HEAD>
<META NAME="GENERATOR" Content="Microsoft Visual Studio 6.0">
</HEAD>
<BODY>
<XML ID=xmlSample>
<Projects>
<Project><id>Root Project</id></Project>
<Project><id>Other Project</id></Project>
<Project><id>Another Project</id></Project>
<Project><id>Some more Projects</id></Project>
</Projects>
</XML>
<P>Project name: <INPUT TYPE=TEXT DATASRC=#xmlSample DATAFLD=id id=txtId
name=txtId>
<BR><BR>
<INPUT ID="first" TYPE=button VALUE="<<"
onClick="xmlSample.recordset.moveFirst()">
<INPUT ID="prev" TYPE=button VALUE="<" onClick="if
(xmlSample.recordset.absoluteposition > 1)
xmlSample.recordset.movePrevious()">
<INPUT ID="next" TYPE=button VALUE=">" onClick="if
(xmlSample.recordset.absoluteposition < xmlSample.recordset.recordcount)
xmlSample.recordset.moveNext()">
<INPUT ID="last" TYPE=button VALUE=">>"
onClick="xmlSample.recordset.moveLast()">
<BR><BR>
</BODY>
</HTML>
```

In the above HTML source code, there is an XML island, which represents some data. In this example, the data is embedded directly into the Web page, which is bounded by the XML tag <XML>. Internet Explorer 5.0 recognizes this as an XML data fragment. The data fragment is a repeating set of project names (<ID>). When Internet Explorer 5.0 loads the XML data fragment, it loads the XML DSO, and the XML DSO then loads the XML data fragments and converts them to a recordset. To access the recordset, special HTML attributes need to be used. They are DSO attributes that bind the various HTML elements to the recordset. In the preceding source code, the `<INPUT>` HTML tag binds its value to the recordset `xmlSample` and the field ID.

The following are the DHTML data-binding attributes:

- `DATASRC`: Reference to the DSO providing the data
- `DATAFLD`: The column or field in the DSO recordset that is to be retrieved
- `DATAFORMATAS`: The format of how the DATAFLD is to be expressed, when it is used
- `DATAPAGESIZE`: The number of records that should be shown on the Web page in a table display

The elements that can be bound like this are all the form elements, the object elements, and `IMG`, `FRAME`, `IFRAME`, `DIV`, `SPAN`, and `LABEL`.

To navigate the recordset, scripting moves the cursor forward or backward (for example, `xmlSample.recordset.movePrevious`). The object model exposed by the DSO is the Active Data Objects (ADO) object model. (The DSO is an example of using the OLE DB simple provider interface.) When the XML DSO consumes the data, it is a fixed size, so it is possible to use the `RecordCount` property to identify the last record. When moving forward and backward, the `AbsolutePosition` property indicates which record is currently displayed.

Generating the Data

It is possible to reference the DSO data using a URL. The notation is as follows:

```
<XML ID=xmlid src = "projects.xml"></XML>
```

References to XML URLs in a data island have the same retrieval rules as if the references were to HTML pages. In the preceding example, this means that the `projects.xml` file must exist in the directory or virtual directory from which the HTML page is retrieved.

It is also possible to generate the XML content dynamically using ASP by substituting `projects.asp` for `projects.xml`. If you create a `projects.asp` file, then it must generate a text stream similar to the following format:

```
<ROOT>
<RECORD>
    <FIELD1>...</FIELD1>
    <FIELDn>...</FIELDn>
</RECORD>
</ROOT>
```

It is possible to create more complex XML documents with more hierarchies, but that is beyond the scope of this book. In the Microsoft Platform Software Developer's Kit (SDK), in the XML source code directories, there are some examples of this.

In the XML document fragment, the XML tag names `ROOT` and `RECORD` need not be used, but can be changed to something more meaningful. Instead of the

RECORD tag name, the tag name PROJECT could be used, but the hierarchy that is created must be maintained. The <ROOT> tag defines a beginning recordset.

Within the recordset is a series of records, and within the record is a series of fields. The name of the field is very important, because this is the name that will be used when it is referenced in the HTML tag attribute. An example implementation of projects.asp with a database query is as follows:

```
<%@ Language=JavaScript %>
<%
var registration;
projects = Server.CreateObject("ADODB.Connection");
projects.Open( "DSN=Projects", "sa", "");
cmdTemp = Server.CreateObject("ADODB.Command");
DataCommand1 = Server.CreateObject("ADODB.Recordset");
cmdTemp.CommandText = "select * from projects";
cmdTemp.CommandType = 1;
cmdTemp.ActiveConnection = projects;
DataCommand1.CursorType = 0
DataCommand1.LockType = 1
DataCommand1.Open(cmdTemp);
%>
<?xml version="1.0" encoding="windows-1252" ?>
<ROOT>
<%
while( DataCommand1.EOF != true) {
%>
<project>
    <id>
        <%=DataCommand1.Fields("id")%>
    </id>
</project>
<%
DataCommand1.MoveNext();
}
%>
</ROOT>
```

This page generates the same XML format as in the XML data fragment. Be forewarned, however, that if you are going to use the Visual InterDev Scripting Object library, there may be some extra tags generated. If this does happen, you will need to tweak the Scripting Object Library source code. Typically, this means that you will not be able to use design-time controls (DTC).

The preceding examples show that ASP does not need to generate HTML text. ASP can generate XML text or any other text formatted to the developer's liking.

Showing a Page of Data

It is possible to navigate through the data as a group. The group can be the entire recordset, or it can be pages of data that have a specific size. Referencing the DSO using the <TABLE> HTML tag navigates the data as a group. The table is like a loop that generates rows according to the definition. The following example shows two things: a paged table size and record sorting capability.

```
<html>
<head><title>Paged example</title>
<script language="JavaScript">
function forward() {
tbl.nextPage();
}
function reverse() {
tbl.previousPage();
}
function description_onclick() {
xmlSample.Sort = "description";
xmlSample.Reset();
}
function id_onclick() {
xmlSample.Sort = "id";
xmlSample.Reset();
}
</script>
</head>
<XML id=xmlSample src="portfolio.asp"></XML>
<table id="tbl" datasrc="#xmlSample" border=1 datapagesize=5>
<THEAD>
<tr>
<td style="cursor:hand">
    <b><u><DIV id=id onClick="id_onclick();">Id</DIV></u></b>
</td>
<td style="cursor:hand">
    <b><u><DIV id=description
onClick="description_onclick();">Description</DIV></u></b>
    </td>
</THEAD>
<TBODY>
<tr>
<td align=center>
    <DIV datafld="id"></DIV>
</td>
<td align=center>
    <DIV datafld="description"> </DIV>
</td>
```

```
</tr>
</TBODY>
</Table>
<input type=button value="Prev Page" onClick="reverse();">
<input type=button value="Next Page" onClick="forward();">
</body>
</html>
```

The page of data is built using a table. The <TABLE> tag needs to have the DATASRC attribute assigned to it. This lets Internet Explorer know it needs to generate multiple rows. To specify the number of records, the DATAPAGESIZE attribute in the <TABLE> tag is also assigned. If it does not exist, then all records are shown. Within the body of the table, a prototype row template with the desired fields is defined. This template is filled with data from the DSO, and for each DSO record, it is repeated. This template is inserted in the table as many times as is specified by the DATAPAGESIZE attribute. Therefore, do not be misled into believing that it represents the number of rows in a table. In this case, there are two <DIV> tags with DATAFLD attributes within a row (<TR>). This is not the only valid scenario. There could be two or three or *n* rows.

To move between the various pages of records in the table, extra methods are exposed—tbl.nextPage and tbl.previousPage—that enable navigation. The rebuilding of the table is handled automatically by Internet Explorer. For the DSOs that support it, it is possible to sort the records using xmlSample.Sort.

This brings up another point about DSOs. The XML DSO only has the ability to manipulate read-only data. Another DSO called Remote Data Service (RDS) makes it possible to update data. The DSO we will be developing has the ability to update data using transactions.

BUILDING CLIENT-SIDE LOGIC

The time-card application has some client-side logic. It gathers the various time-card information pieces, displays them, and sends some to the server for durability when necessary. This client-side business logic uses two pieces of COM technology: DHTML data binding and DHTML integration, which I discuss later. Building client-side logic is very similar to building server-side logic. Interfaces that represent the business logic must be defined, and then some COM objects implementing those COM interfaces must be defined. The source code presented is in Visual C++, but the same thing can be done in Visual Basic or Visual J++. In the Microsoft Platform SDK in the directory \Samples\Web\Author\DataSrc\arraycontrol is a Visual Basic DSO example.

Defining the Interfaces

What is the business process in this project? The managing of the time and costs associated with each individual project. What operations are required? The use cases indicate that it is the capability to punch in and punch out of a specific project; the time card should also have the capability to punch in and punch out of vacation time and sick time.

There is a controller that exposes COM interfaces that enable a user to punch in and out of the time card. HTML scripting associates the various business operations objects with the controller and the objects all implement a COM interface that the controller uses to process data. Therefore, when a user punches in or out, the controller notes the current conditions, such as the time, and then passes that information to the business operations object. The business operations object then processes the conditions and returns to the controller a set of data that is added to the controller recordset, which is the time-card recordset. The controller is a DSO, so the designer only needs to associate the various HTML elements with the controller DSO.

The COM interface that the business operations objects must implement is defined by the following interface definition language (IDL):

```
interface ITimeCard : IUnknown {
HRESULT PunchIn( BSTR time);
HRESULT PunchOut( BSTR time);
HRESULT SetService(IUnknown *serviceProvider);
}
```

The controller calls the PunchIn and PunchOut methods when the user wants to punch in or out of the time card. In this implementation, the only condition is the current time, which is managed by the controller. A good distributed application requires that the controller retrieve the time from some central network timekeeper. The method SetService is a housekeeping method used by the controller to expose an operational interface used by the business operations object implementation.

Building the Controller

The controller implementation has very little to do with business processes. The controller implementation is a system-level COM object. It does three things: manages the various business operations objects, manages the time-card recordset, and exposes a COM interface that is called by the HTML scripting environment.

The controller is the CExDataProv COM object and it implements two core interfaces: OLEDBSimpleProvider and IExDataProv. The IExDataProv interface exposes generic punch-in and punch-out methods and is defined as follows:

```
interface IExDataProv : IDispatch {
[id(1)] HRESULT punchIn();
[id(2)] HRESULT punchOut();
[id(3)] HRESULT activeInterface(IUnknown *currInterface);
[id(4)] HRESULT resetActiveInterface();
[restricted, id(-3900)] HRESULT msDataSourceObject(BSTR qualifier, IUnknown
**ppUnk);
[restricted, id(-3901)] HRESULT addDataSourceListener(IUnknown *pEvent);
};
```

The IExDataProv interface contains the PunchIn and PunchOut operations. The ActiveInterface method defines which ITimeCard implementation is active when IExDataProv::PunchIn or IExDataProv::PunchOut is called. To reset the current ITimeCard reference in the IExDataProv implementation, the IExDataProv::ResetActiveInterface method is called. None of the methods discussed thus far modify the user interface, but they are wired to the user interface by the script.

Because we defined the controller as DSO, it must implement the standard defined OLEDBSimpleProvider COM interface. When Microsoft Internet Explorer attempts to bind data to an ActiveX control, it does a QueryInterface for the OLEDBSimpleProvider COM interface. This COM interface is used to build a recordset. To make DHTML data binding work, the DSO COM interface (IExDataProv) must add two methods with specific IDs (msDataSourceObject and addDataSourceListener). These methods reset and bind the DSO to Internet Explorer.

Storing the Recordset Data

When data is moved from the browser to the DSO, the COM VARIANT data type is used. Although it is possible to convert the data type internally, ideally it should be left as a VARIANT. This wastes less processing time converting the data from one type to another. Internally, the controller must store the time card data, and this is managed by the CRow class. CRow stores the data as an array of VARIANTs.

The definition of the CRow class is as follows:

```
class CRow {
public:
_variant_t getData( long iCol);
void setData( long iCol, _variant_t var);
CRow();
virtual ~CRow();
private:
_variant_t m_arrData[ 5];
};
```

The setData and getData methods set and retrieve individual values of the array.

Binding the Interfaces

When the Web page is loaded, the DSO HTML tag will cause Internet Explorer to check whether the control has the msDataSourceObject method implemented. If it does, the controller needs to return a reference to the COM object that implemented the OLEDBSimpleProvider interface. It is possible for the OLEDBSimpleProvider interface to have multiple data sets, but Internet Explorer can only retrieve one.

The implementation of Microsoft Internet Explorer calls the msDataSourceObject method to retrieve the COM object that has implemented the OLEDBSimpleProvider COM interface.

```
STDMETHODIMP CExDataProv::msDataSourceObject(BSTR qualifier, IUnknown
**ppUnk){
if( ppUnk == NULL) {
    return E_FAIL;
}
*ppUnk = GetUnknown();
return S_OK;
}
```

The first parameter, qualifier, is always NULL and should be ignored. The OLEDBSimpleProvider COM interface is returned in the parameter ppUnk. This is an IUnknown COM interface pointer. We want to return the current object in the ppUnk parameter in the form of an IUnknown. This is done by calling the COM object's local GetUnknown() method.

If this method call is successful, then the addDataSourceListener method is called. This method passes in a DataSourceListener COM interface. The controller uses this COM interface pointer when data has changed within the controller's recordset. This forces Microsoft Internet Explorer to update the content displayed on the HTML page. The following is an example implementation of the addDataSourceListener:

```
STDMETHODIMP CExDataProv::addDataSourceListener(IUnknown *pEvent) {
DataSourceListener *temp = m_pListener.Detach();

if( temp != NULL) {
    temp->Release();
}
m_pListener = pEvent;
return S_OK;
}
```

This DataSourceListener COM interface has the capability to inform Internet Explorer of changes in these column definitions, record size, and sort order recordset elements by calling DataSourceListener::dataMemberChanged(NULL). There are other methods that indicate multiple data set changes, but because Internet Explorer does not support multiple records, they are ignored.

Binding between the Data and the Interface

In the HTML, the DHTML data-binding attributes bind a field name to a field in the recordset. The problem is that the OLEDBSimpleProvider interface does not provide any methods or properties to cross-reference a numeric field ID to a field name. The OLEDBSimpleProvider interface binds everything based on a row and column.

The solution that the OLEDBSimpleProvider COM interface uses is to bind the column header information to the recordset row index of zero. When the contents of row zero are requested, they should be the field names. By iterating through all columns, Internet Explorer has the capability to cross-reference a field name (DATAFLD) to a field ID. If the fields referenced in the HTML do not exist in row zero of the recordset, then those fields are not bound.

Another special value is when either the row or column of the recordset has an index ID of –1. This means that all elements in the row or column are selected. For example, iRow = –1 and iCol = 2 means the entire column 2. The capability to select all elements using the special row and column index is optional and does not need to be supported.

Some Data Characteristics

In the example of the XML DSO, the data came from a different source and was retrieved from a specific URL or from within the HTML page. When custom DSOs are used, they can do anything they want. A custom DSO can bind itself to a stream of information that is being presented to the client, or it can bind itself to a database on the local machine. This is an implementation detail of the DSO.

After the DSO is retrieved and the HTML page is ready to display the recordset, it needs to follow a number of steps. The first step that Microsoft Internet Explorer does after it loads the DSO, is retrieve the row and column count using the OLEDBSimpleProvider::getRowCount, OLEDBSimpleProvider::getColumnCount methods of the recordset. For an empty data set, the values for the row and column should be zero and zero, respectively. If the data set isn't empty, any value greater than zero is okay.

The next step depends on whether there is any data in the recordset. If there is, then the status of each individual data item is retrieved. The status defines the update capability of the individual data items. Two valid status flags are read-only and read-write.

The following is an example controller implementation in which the data is read-only. An implementation of the status retrieval is as follows:

```
STDMETHODIMP CExDataProv::getRWStatus(LONG iRow, LONG iCol, OSPRW
*prwStatus) {
*prwStatus = OSPRW_READONLY;
return S_OK;
}
```

In this example, all of the items are updateable. However, remember that the row and column index could be 0 or –1. Taking the CExDataProv::getRWStatus method implementation into account, this means that the recordset headers or an entire column or row could be updateable.

When the data set changes as the result of a row being inserted, or deleted, or of elements being updated, the Internet Explorer consumer must be notified. It does this by calling the OLEDBSimpleProvider::addOLEDBSimpleProviderListener method. An OLEDBSimpleProviderListener interface is passed to this method as a parameter. This interface is similar to the `DataSourceListener`, except that it deals with individual rows and cells of the data set.

When Internet Explorer is not interested in receiving data set events, it calls `OLEDBSimpleProvider::removeOLEDBSimpleProviderListener` and passes the interface that should be removed from the list as a parameter.

Working with Rows

When working with the individual rows, it is useful to be able to add and delete records. The `OLEDBSimpleProvider` interface provides these two methods:

```
OLEDBSimpleProvider:: deleteRows(LONG iRow, LONG cRows, LONG *pcRowsDeleted)
OLEDBSimpleProvider:: insertRows(LONG iRow, LONG cRows, LONG *pcRowsInserted)
```

When a row is to be inserted or deleted, the first parameter, `iRow`, specifies the row number. The second parameter, `cRows`, specifies the number of rows that will be deleted or inserted. The last parameter, `pcRowsxxx` is the number of rows that were inserted or deleted. When either of these operations is executed, the operation is on the row number. For example, if you insert a record on the tenth row, it moves the current tenth row record to the eleventh row.

When implementing these methods, it is important that boundary checks be done. Be sure the row to be deleted is an actual row.

Working with the Data

Working with the data is a bit more complicated. There are two possible operations: setting the data and getting the data. The definition of the method for getting the data is as follows:

```
OLEDBSimpleProvider::getVariant(LONG iRow, LONG iCol,
OSPFORMAT format, VARIANT *pVar)
```

The first two parameters specify the row, `iRow`, and column, `iCol`, of the cell of the data that is to be retrieved. The values must be within the boundaries of the underlying data set, with one exception. That exception is when Internet Explorer cross-references the `DATAFLD` values with the column ID. In this case, the row is zero.

The third parameter defines the format of the data when it is retrieved. There are three possible values:

- `OSPFORMAT_RAW`: The raw data format of the internal data set can be kept. No conversion is necessary.
- `OSPFORMAT_FORMATTED`: The internal data set value, regardless of type, must be converted to a BSTR within the VARIANT.
- `OSPFORMAT_HTML`: The internal data set value, regardless of type, must be converted to a BSTR within the VARIANT that can contain HTML tags.

The last parameter is the outgoing `VARIANT` data type. When passing `VARIANT`s from the internal data set to Internet Explorer, the data must be copied using

VariantCopy. **Visual Basic programmers do not need to worry about this, because it is done automatically.**

To save data, the status of the row, column, or cell must have a read-write status. The status of the row, column, or cell was set when Microsoft Internet Explorer called the OLEDBSimpleProvider::getRWStatus method. It is defined OSPRW_READWRITE, which means updating is enabled. An example implementation of setting the data is as follows:

```
STDMETHODIMP CExDataProv::setVariant(LONG iRow, LONG iCol,
OSPFORMAT format, VARIANT var)
{
if( iRow > m_rows.GetCount() || iCol > 5) {
    return E_FAIL;
}
try {
    _com_util::CheckError( Notify(CHANGECELL_ABOUTTODO, iRow, iCol, 1));

    CRow *element = m_rows.GetAt( m_rows.FindIndex( iRow - 1));

    element->setData( iCol, var);

    _com_util::CheckError( Notify(CHANGECELL_DIDEVENT, iRow, iCol, 1));
} catch( _com_error err) {
    return err.Error();
}
return S_OK;
}
```

Like the getVariant method, the data is set using a row, iRow, and column, iCol. The format in this case is not as important, because it can be converted to the internal data set. The last parameter defines the data to be stored.

In the implementation of this method, it is important to indicate to Internet Explorer what is happening by calling the methods of the OLEDBSimpleProviderListener interface. For example, when the value is about to be set, the method aboutToChangeCell is called. When the cell has changed, the method cellChanged is called. These methods need to be called because Internet Explorer uses the methods to update the visual interface.

Building the Implementation

The controller interacts with the various business operations implementations of ITimeCard. The controller does not bind the user interface to the business operations implementations—the business operations are self-contained and must do this themselves.

Let's look at a sample business operations implementation of punching in and out of a project. There are two pieces of user interface: the project being selected and the description of the task being accomplished. The implementation will be a COM object that implements the IWorking interface. The values could be assigned to two properties using scripting, but that requires extra coding. Another approach is for the business operations implementation to access the HTML page and retrieve the values from two HTML elements. This uses the DHTML integration technology, which is available in the MSHTML.DLL.

Consider the following HTML fragment:

```
<table>
<tr>
    <td>Project:</td>
    <td>
        <select id="optProjects" size="1">
            <option value="ProjectX">Project X</option>
            <option value="ProjectY">Project Y</option>
            <option value="SinkManufacture">Sink Manufacture</option>
            <option value="CarWindshield">Car Windshield</option>
            <option value="Motor">5 Liter Motor</option>
        </select>
    </td>
</tr>
<tr>
    <td>Comment:</td>
    <td><input id="txtWorkComment" type="text" name="txtComment"
size="20"></td>
</tr>
</table>
```

The business operations implementation needs to search the HTML page for the optProjects and txtWorkComment HTML elements. There are two ways to do this. One is by passing in the HTML elements when the implementation is instantiated on the HTML page. The other is to let the business operations implementation find the elements on the page. Either way is acceptable. The approach used here is the passing in of the HTML elements. With this approach, it is only necessary to do a QueryInterface for the interface IHTMLInputTextElement. COM compiler support is useful because it hides all of the complexities of the various interfaces.

Consider the following implementation for setting the comment text box:

```
#import "mshtml.dll"
STDMETHODIMP CWorking::SetCommentElement(IUnknown * inpElement) {
try {
    MSHTML::IHTMLInputTextElement *temp = m_comment.Detach();
    if( temp != NULL) {
        temp->Release();
    }
    m_comment = inpElement;
} catch ( _com_error err) {
    return err.Error();
```

```
};
return S_OK;
}
```

The variable m_comment is a direct reference to the HTML element on the HTML page. Any events or properties associated with this variable are available to the implementation. The business operations implementation now has the capability to manipulate the HTML element without requiring the intervention of HTML scripting. But there is a price. In this implementation, there is a reference to an HTML tag. Suppose this tag was within a frame, and the frame was loaded with a different page. The <INPUT> tag does not exist anymore, but the reference within the implementation still exists. If this interface pointer is used, the results are unpredictable and could result in the program crashing. The dynamic nature of the Web is something that must be accounted for, which is different from traditional applications.

Adding to the DSO Recordset

When the controller calls the punchIn method, the values are retrieved from the HTML page. The following source code does this:

```
_variant_t strComment = m_comment->Getvalue();
_variant_t strProject = m_project->Getvalue();
```

Again, the values are VARIANT-based. When working with the client-side DHTML model, VARIANTs are used often.

After the values are retrieved, the implementation sets the values in the DSO. The controller doesn't set the DSO values itself, because the DSO does not know how the data is processed. The DSO exposes a generic data set. The implementation receives generic information, performs some business operations, and then sets the new values in the generic data set.

An example of setting the data is as follows:

```
_com_util::CheckError( m_service->getRowCount( &m_currRow));
m_currRow ++;
long actualInserted;
_com_util::CheckError( m_service->insertRows( m_currRow, 1,
&actualInserted));

_variant_t value( _bstr_t( "work"));
m_service->setVariant( m_currRow, 1, OSPFORMAT_RAW, value);
```

The data that is being added in the example source code is a new record. To add a row with the OLEDBSimpleProvider interface, a location must be given. Typically, you want to add the row at the end, so you need to retrieve the record count using getRowCount. This value is then used to add a row using insertRows. And then, finally, the row values are set using setVariant.

SOME ISSUES WITH CLIENT-SIDE LOGIC

The source code shown is specific to Visual C++, but both Visual Basic and Visual J++ can make use of this technology. Visual J++ was not discussed because it does not use the exact same object model—it uses a library called Windows Foundation Classes (WFC). The models are almost identical, and they have the exact same output.

When building client-side business logic, Visual Basic is better to use because it hides the complexity of capturing events from the HTML page. For example, when a button is clicked on the HTML page, some scripting captures it. With Visual Basic, it is only necessary to use the keyword withEvents. DHTML events are possible with Visual C++, but the coding is very complex because there are no default event sink implementations for the MSHTML.DLL.

However, writing implementations using Visual Basic means that the Visual Basic run-time must exist on the client side, and this could be a large download. In an Intranet scenario, the download size may not be an issue.

Putting It in Perspective

This chapter introduced the concepts of writing a hybrid client, which is a more sophisticated version of the original Windows 3.1 client. The hybrid client is special, because it makes use of the Internet and integrates it seamlessly using HTML and XML. By using a hybrid client, the processing power can be distributed between the client and server sides. Doing some business logic on the client side is not a bad thing—it all depends on the business process being accomplished.

A word about using Visual J++. Visual J++ is a great environment, but at the time of this writing, there were simply too many unanswered political questions that made the question of whether to use Visual J++ to write client-side components and desktop shells a difficult one. I used Visual J++ on the server side because there is no GUI, which means that the code could be partially ported to Sun Microsystem's Java without too much effort.

The hybrid client will significantly change how we build user interfaces. While some parts of it are currently not cross-platform, that will change. At the time of this writing I do not know much about Transmeta (www.transmeta.com) other than it is developing a flexible CPU, which just might make the cross-platform issue go away.

Chapter 15

Building Your Resource

We have discussed the presentation tier and the middle services tier. Now, we turn our attention to the data services tier. The data services tier is where your data is persisted. In the data services tier, we consider how data can be persisted reliably, consistently, and with scalability in mind. Saving data for later manipulation is very simple in theory, but the implementation of it is very complex. A data service can be a database or a product such as Microsoft Exchange. Both of these examples persist data for later manipulation, although one product is based on relational data and the other on workflow data.

Most books that are based on a database focus on the administrative aspect of the database. In contrast, this book focuses on how to write code for the database. This chapter focuses on the Structured Query Language (SQL) Server data service and on how SQL is used to manipulate data in a relational database. Specifically, you learn how to write a stored procedure. A stored procedure is a function in a programming language, but the stored procedure only executes on a database.

SQL and Portability

Structured query language is a standard that is designed to be portable. It is not a comprehensive standard, and it only includes the basic operations that can be performed on a relational database. At the time of this writing the current standard is SQL 2 (SQL 92), but SQL 3 (SQL 99) was almost totally defined. SQL 3 has many more options and possibilities—it is described as an object-oriented language that can go beyond the stored procedure architecture.

However, because we are working with current technologies, there are still some problems. For example, the stored procedures that we will look at are specific to Microsoft SQL Server—the same procedures will not work on Oracle. Fortunately, this isn't really a problem because moving data from one database to another is a very complicated and tedious process. Transferring stored procedures in that situation is likely to be one of the less complex issues.

Why Not Use an OODBMS?

An OODBMS is an object-oriented database-management system. Although many people say that using an object-oriented database is better because it is a more object-oriented solution, the reality is that OODBMSs have not lived up to their expectations in the Windows DNA market. Where OODBMSs do excel is in specialized fields, such as science and mathematics, because in those fields the database only needs to fulfill one or two major requirements. Contrast that to a

Windows DNA market, where security, performance, scalability, and extensibility are all equally important. So, although SQL is not object oriented, it continues to be used because it is a well-defined and robust query language that offers these advantages:

- Supports high-volume transactions
- Stores huge amounts of data
- Supports parallel processing, load balancing, and indexing tools
- Provides data backup for huge volumes of data
- Offers security implementations for large volumes of users and data
- Provides for disaster recovery
- Includes concurrent user support

It all boils down to being able to keep, maintain, and use data on a 24x7 basis. As OODBMSs mature and SQL 3 becomes more popular, databases will become a hybrid between the object-oriented and relational types.

Which Version of Microsoft SQL Server?

At the time of this writing, SQL Server 7.0 was the current implementation of SQL Server. Normally, it is not recommended to jump to a new database, but in this case, there is a good reason to do so. Microsoft SQL Server 7.0 is the first version that implements row locking—the other versions use page locking. The page-lock mechanism can cause massive scalability problems when using database access layers that rely on dynamic querying of the database.

A good rule of thumb is that if the database has at least two transactions per second, you should use SQL Server 7.0. SQL Server is a true enterprise-based database and it is very fast.

SQL Basics

If you have never used a SQL database, then the first thing to learn is how to write a command in a language called SQL that selects all of the records from a table. To understand relational databases, it is important that you understand how a table works and how data is associated between the various tables.

Tables

The table is the basis of the relational database—tables are where the database data is stored—and tables are, therefore, the first thing that we will work with. A table is rectangular, its dimensions defined by a number of rows and columns. Each row in a table has the same number of columns as every other row in the table. If a row is added to the table, then it will have a certain number of columns to represent each of the fields in the table. The added row can have column values that are empty or contain a NULL value. The row in a database is called a record.

When SQL is executed on a specific table, some records may be returned in a result set. However, SQL will not define the location of any particular record in the table. This is something that only the database needs to know. SQL does not care about the location of data because SQL works with data on a result set basis.

WORKING WITH DATA TYPES

A table consists of a series of columns that have specific data types. The data types are native to the SQL environment. Some data types are part of the SQL standard, whereas others are defined specifically for the database.

String Data Types

By far the most common data type is the string. There are two types of strings: char and varchar. char is a character string of fixed length; varchar is a character string of variable length. Be careful which string format you use. A char field of size x bytes takes up x bytes in the database, regardless of the data contained, whereas a varchar field of size x takes up a maximum size of x bytes, but may take up less space, depending on the size of the data stored in that field. This difference becomes very important when a specific programming language manipulates the string. For example in C and C++, a string is NULL-terminated. A char field does not have a null termination until it reaches the end of the buffer. This means that the C and C++ string manipulations must find the last significant character and then insert a null character. Visual Basic has this facility built in, but it is a function that must be called. Typically, it is better to use varchar.

It's better to use the char string when the string that you are working with is a fixed string, such as an international three-letter currency symbol (e.g., USD, CAD, DEM). However, there is a catch to doing this. Remember that the Y2K problem was caused by using a two-digit year to save space and write efficient code. If you are going to use a fixed length, think carefully about what the length should be before you implement.

In SQL Server 7.0, both the char and varchar data types have a maximum data length of 8,000 characters. This is an increase from the 256-character limit that existed in SQL Server 6.5x. That change in limit is very significant, because the varchar or char often has to be converted to a text data type. The text data type extends the upper length limit to 231 characters. In other words, very large. Of course, the downside of this type of field is that it slows things because of its sheer size.

Large Data Types

Handling large data is not simple, and there are several ways of doing it. The first is to use the text field. To handle pure binary data there is the image field. This field is meant for binaries, and it handles up to a length of 231 bytes.

Numeric Data Types

The most misused data type is the integer. The integer data type is defined by two attributes: signed and length. The signed bit reduces the number range, but negative numbers can be defined. The length can be 16, 32, or 64 bits, although 64 bits is not yet commonly available. Adding to the confusion of the integer is the fact that it is often defined and redefined as other data types, such as a a HANDLE and/or resource HANDLEr. The following table identifies what is 16-bit and what is 32-bit.

| 16-bit | short, WORD |
| 32-bit | int, long, DWORD, UINT, ULONG |

In Microsoft SQL Server, there are integer data types also, but they are named differently than in the programming language. A 16-bit integer is mapped to a SQL smallint, which is 16 bits. The smallint is a signed integer, meaning that both positive and negative numbers can be stored in the data type. The highest and lowest values are 32,767 and –32,768, respectively. If the program exceeds these values, then a wrap around occurs, which will yield an incorrect answer. Or, if a positive number that exceeds 32,768 is written to the variable, the number will be automatically converted to a negative. The value has not been corrupted, but the signed bit will be incorrectly interpreted as a negative value in a signed context.

In those instances when the 16-bit integer is not large enough, the integer size needs to be increased to 32 bits. For 32-bit integers, the database type is int. Don't get this int confused with the C++ int. This value is signed and therefore has an upper limit of 2,147,483,647 and a lower limit of –2,147,483,648. If a value larger than this is written, it will either wrap around or be converted into a negative.

The other type of numeric value is a real value. The difference between a real and integer is that a real has decimal points. There are two types of floating point numbers: the 4-byte float and 8-byte double. Mapping these types to appropriate SQL data types is simple, except that a naming conflict arises. An SQL float is 8 bytes, whereas a C++ float is 4 bytes. The correct mapping is from a C++ float to an SQL real, which is 8 bytes, and from a C++ double to an SQL float.

Unicode String Data Types

The newest data-type addition to SQL Server is the capability to handle UNICODE using nchar, nvarchar, and ntext data types. They are similar to their respective character counterparts except that they are double-byte characters. Because the UNICODE character uses 2 bytes per character, the maximum ntext field size is 2^{30} characters. For nchar and nvarchar, the maximum number of characters is still 8,000.

SQL Numeric Data Types

The SQL numeric data type is a special data type that is similar to a number, but which is defined as a string. The data types are called decimal and numeric. Consider the number 123.456. This number has a precision of six digits and a scale of three. The terms *precision* and *scale* are SQL terms that define the accuracy of the number and the number of positions to the right of the decimal point, respectively. To store the number 123.456, the declaration would be decimal(6,3) or numeric(6,3). The scale cannot exceed the precision, and the precision is defined as a maximum value of 38.

Time Data Types

Another data type is the time field. It can contain a time and date. There are the datetime and smalldatetime time fields, and the difference is the amount of accuracy. The smalldatetime data type is accurate to the minute, whereas the datetime data type is accurate to 3.33 milliseconds.

Cursor Data Type

The cursor data type is useful in the context of stored procedures (which are discussed shortly). The cursor data type makes it possible to iterate through a query and inspect each record.

BUILDING A TABLE

Adding a series of column data types to the basic table definition creates a table. This is accomplished using the SQL command CREATE TABLE. An example of the SQL code is as follows:

```
Create table myTable (field1 datatype, field2 datatype, ...)
```

In the conference registration Web site, the basis table is the user table. It defines each user of the registration systems and contains the first name, last name, password, and e-mail address of each user. The SQL command that defines the table is as follows:

```
CREATE TABLE users (
first_name varchar (255) ,
last_name varchar (255) ,
password varchar (255),
email varchar (255)
)
```

Vagueness and Redundancy of Data

When designing an SQL table, a couple of things must be kept in mind:

- The order of columns need not be specified. This means that if you refer to a column by a numeric index, you may introduce errors. Instead, all of the references should be done on an abstract level, such as by referencing the column name.
- Each record in the table needs to be unique in some form. The unique aspect of record can be a single column value or a combination of column values. Working with duplicate records in a database is potentially hazardous to your data. Duplicate records could cause a consistency problem in the database, resulting in incorrect updates and queries.

Thus, a table cannot be entirely defined by the function it serves, because it is partially defined by the information that it will contain. As a result, it is important to understand the data that will be stored in the database.

Another important thing to understand about tables is the difference between data duplication and data redundancy. *Data duplication* is when data appears twice in a table, but with different attributes. A simple example is shown in the following table:

PART	PART DESCRIPTION
123	Processor
124	RAM
125	Hard Disk
126	Processor

It might seem that all records in this table are unique, but this isn't actually true. Consider how this table would be used in an application. A user could do a text search on the part description and type in *processor*. The result would be two records with two different part numbers (123 and 126). The question then becomes this: Which processor is correct? There is no correct answer because both products have the same product description—the two records are duplicates. To solve this problem, the two processors must be distinguished from each other. A couple of solutions are:

- Create a better description such as *Big Processor* and *Small Processor*.
- Upgrade the field containing the processor description to be a type field and create an identifier field.

Now, let's consider a table where there is redundant information:

SUPPLIER	PART	PART DESCRIPTION
1	123	Processor
2	124	RAM
3	125	Hard Disk
4	123	Processor

In this example, there is redundant information for part 123. Suppliers 1 and 4 both supply this part, which is a processor.

Consider what would happen if the table was updated and the first row's part description was changed to *Fast Processor*. There would be an inconsistency, because part 123 would have two different descriptions from the two suppliers. The data would be inconsistent. To prevent inconsistencies, the data needs to be normalized—the process of normalization is discussed shortly.

Using Indices

Table indexes make it quicker to search for data. An index orders the records in a table or a view, but it does not order the records itself. What it does is create an ordered set of record indices that is kept internal to the database engine. When the SQL engine can use an index to find the desired information, the search is extremely fast. If there is no index for the information, the SQL engine must inspect each record, which costs quite a bit of processing time.

When records are added to the database, the database decides where they are placed. The database places the record in a lowest-cost place, as determined at run-time. An index is then used to access the data as if it were sorted according to specific criteria. In the conference registration project, for example, the user could be searched for by name or e-mail address.

Consider the following sample reference data:

FIRST NAME	LAST NAME	E-MAIL ADDRESS	PASSWORD
Joe,	Smith	jsmith@company.com	cc
John,	Hank	jhank@another.com	d
Mary,	Handle	mary@mail.com	ff
Joe,	Smith	jsmith@someother.com	gg

Depending on how the index of the table is defined, the *Joe Smith* record could be a duplicate record. If a unique index consisted of first name and last name, the two Joe Smith records with different passwords and e-mail addresses could not have been added without an error occurring.

However, there are multiple Joe Smiths, so the index must either allow duplicates or the index must be based on something other than just first and last name. When defining an index, you must consider how the data will be searched. In the previous table, the unique attribute is the e-mail address. An e-mail address is unique, so we can use it for our main index.

But a search for a person is typically not based on the e-mail address—people generally search for a first name and last name. As a result, it would also be useful to create an index that allows duplicates on the first and last name.

Normalization

Normalization reduces redundancy and inconsistency in database data by placing table data in multiple tables. For example, in the conference registration application, the user had an associated address. So, where is this information stored? Is a new table created or is the Users table extended? Let's consider what would happen if the Users table were extended. The new table definition is as follows:

```
CREATE TABLE users (
first_name varchar( 255), last_name varchar( 255),
password varchar(255), email varchar(255),
street varchar(255), postcode varchar(32),
city varchar(64), country varchar(64)
)
```

The table is now a bit larger. It associates an address with the user. This is okay—because the unique index is based on the e-mail column, all records will be unique and there will be no duplication or redundancy.

However, there is a problem. Some users may have billing addresses that are different from their mailing addresses. At present, there is no space to represent this other piece of data, and the table must be extended again, as follows:

```
CREATE TABLE users (
first_name varchar( 255), last_name varchar( 255),
password varchar(255), email varchar(255),
street varchar(255), postcode varchar(32),
city varchar(64), country varchar(64)
bill_street varchar(255), bill_postcode varchar(32),
bill_city varchar(64), bill_country varchar(64)
)
```

When you are extending tables, there are two things to consider. First, you are making changes, which may or may not be an indication of good planning. There is a planning problem if changes are constantly being made. Second, you should generally avoid extending tables because it might mean that old data will need to be adjusted, which can be quite a bit of work. Instead, you can add tables that reference the old tables. The old tables can continue to exist without changes, which results in a more stable system.

Normalization is the process of removing the fields from one table and using them to create a new table, adding reference fields to the new table that link its data to records in the original table. We could normalize the Users data to create the following table design:

```
CREATE TABLE users (
id int,
first_name varchar( 255),
last_name varchar( 255),
password varchar(255),
email varchar(255),
)
```

```
CREATE TABLE address (
user_id int,
address_type int,
street varchar(255),
postcode varchar(32),
city varchar(64),
country varchar(64)
)
```

These two tables will contain all the data from the Users table we extended earlier. However, to make it work, one change had to be made to the original Users table. When two tables are referenced, each table must have a unique identifier that can be indexed without duplication; typically, this identifier is an autoincrementing numeric value. The identifier can be indexed to improve speed when creating relations between two tables.

In a real database scenario, the identifier is typically the main index. In this example, the identifier is users.id and address.user_id fields. The users.id field was added because using the users.email field as an identifier would require more space and be less efficient when relations between tables are processed. In the address table, the main identifier cannot be the address.user_id, because a single user could have multiple addresses (different mailing and billing addresses, for example). So, in the address table the main index is the combination of the address.user_id and address.address_type fields. The address.address_type field indicates the type of address, which includes mailing, or billing address.

Another choice for the main index is to create an address.id field to uniquely identify the address. This would work, but because of the way the address table is being used, this information would not be useful. An address will never be retrieved for the address information alone. The address will always be retrieved because it is being manipulated in the context of a user. Hence, the address index needs to have a user id reference.

To understand SQL associations, you have to think about them in reverse. For example, you would think that a user is associated with an address, but the referencing of the address table is from the address table to the User table. This means that it is not possible to figure out which addresses are associated with a specific user based on the User table. However, it is possible to figure out the users based on the address table alone. It might seem that a logical next step would be to add references to the various addresses in the User table. But while this may work in object-oriented programming in the form of a double-linked list, it does not prove very efficient in an SQL context. In an SQL context, the explanation that is provided in this paragraph makes more sense, because when you want to associate new data with a specific user, you do not need to change the User table. In an object-oriented database scenario, you would have to.

In the process of normalization, multiple tables are created where there previously was only one. With normalization, there is no data redundancy because the relevant data is moved into a table of its own. The association between the tables is called an SQL relation. By splitting a large table into multiple tables, the overall table complexity is reduced, making it simpler to understand each table and causing each table to use fewer resources.

But there is such a thing as too much normalization. The first sign of this is when too many relations are required to retrieve any meaningful information from the database. Using too many relations slows the performance of the database.

Generally speaking, programmers will not be very involved in database design, and this type of planning can generally be left to the database administrator. However, if a programmer understands the dynamics as explained here, working with the database administrator will be much easier.

Why Use Stored Procedures?

Stored procedures in a database are like functions in a programming language. Using stored procedures makes it possible to pass information, such as a function call, to a database. When you do not use stored procedures, the information is added to the database in the form of a larger SQL command—it is larger because it contains more SQL logic than does a similar stored procedure. The difference with a stored procedure is that the commands are already resident on the database server.

In the proposed database access architecture, the Component Object Model (COM)+ objects on the business tier will interact with the data services tier by issuing SQL stored procedures. The reason for using stored procedures is that they encapsulate the database functionality. A stored procedure is an SQL component, and the stored procedure function call definition is the interface.

There are four major advantages to using stored procedures: simplicity, abstraction, security, and performance.

REASON #1: SIMPLICITY

A COM+ business object contains business logic, but part of that business logic involves accessing data in the data services tier. Typically, business logic data services code contains multiple lines of SQL commands, and SQL is not like code in a programming language such as C++, or Visual Basic, or J++. This means that you will be mixing two different programming styles. This is not bad in itself, but what is bad is that the two programming styles will make the COM+ business objects very large and complex.

A stored procedure lets the two programming styles be separated and self-contained. The COM+ code will still need to run some SQL code, but less than in the previous approach. Much of the SQL code is moved to the stored procedure.

REASON #2: ABSTRACTION

The stored procedure architecture creates a number of interfaces that are defined by functions. Using a view or stored procedure architecture, the underlying data structure can change. It is possible to make changes when needed.

For example, standard normalization works on medium-sized databases, but when databases approach the terabyte size, normalization must be handled differently because of the costs that normalization incurs. For example, in a terabyte database, doing a query that involves two tables may be less efficient than performing the same query using a single table. The table designs cannot be easily changed if the COM+ objects make use of the tables directly. A stored procedure, however, can change its implementation without changing the interface. The COM+ object will not know the difference.

This means that by using stored procedures and views, you can create versions to update the database and still keep backward compatibility. Or you might want to create different databases, and if you need to access the old data, you could merge it with the new. This becomes important when doing data warehousing and data mining.

REASON #3: SECURITY

In an SQL database, security is based on the tables and it is implemented on a per-user basis. In the conference registration application, consider the case where the user is assigned a Windows 2000 security token. When the user wants to modify the database, the COM+ business object will be executing with the user's security token, which means that for users to be able to update their data in the database, they must have the rights to the entire table. Thus, users could view the contents of other registration applications, creating a security leak.

One way of plugging this leak is to make every user use a COM+ object to communicate with the database. While this might work most of the time, it provides a false sense of security. If the user can communicate with the server using a COM+ object, then the user could communicate with the database using the same username and password via a database-querying tool. Again, the user would have the ability to view all of the records for which the user has security privileges.

What you need is a database that has the capability to apply security tokens on a record level. Sadly, only a few databases implement this functionality, and they do so in a very database-specific way. Microsoft SQL Server 7.0 does not have this functionality.

Fortunately, the problem can be solved using stored procedures. The way to do this is to assign all tables an administrative privilege to view and manipulate the data. However, the stored procedures used to manipulate the data can be assigned a user privilege, and within the stored procedure, the security level is changed to administrative level, enabling the tables to be viewed and manipulated. This solution makes it possible for all users to access the stored procedure, but not the table. As a result, they will not be able to corrupt the database or view information that they should not be viewing.

REASON #4: PERFORMANCE

Under the previous simplicity point, the code was separated into two parts for reasons of simplicity. However, another reason for doing this is performance.

When compiled SQL is executed, it is much faster than fresh SQL code that needs to be compiled before it can be executed. SQL Server compiles things such as parameter and value validations. It also assesses what is the fastest way to call the statement. Those steps are cached when stored procedures are used. Every time a fresh SQL command is sent to the server, a recompile is forced, which takes more time.

SOME OTHER CONSIDERATIONS

The stored procedure architecture does not preclude the use of transactions. Note, however, that if the stored procedure adds transaction code, it is then in charge of the transaction. For certain operations, this may be desirable. For example, an invoice number is incremental, and once it is retrieved, it cannot be given back because it would represent a missing number when being audited—special reasons have to be assigned to invalid invoice numbers.

The use of stored procedures does result in a certain amount of nonportability. However, this is usually outweighed by the business advantages.

Creating Simple Stored Procedures

To this point, we have only written SQL code to create a table. We will now write a stored procedure. To create a stored procedure, you must execute a SQL command. The following is the simplest stored procedure that can be created:

```
Create Procedure simpleProcedure
As
return (0)
```

This stored procedure has no parameters and does nothing when called except return a 0 value. In SQL talk, a stored procedure generally does not return parameters, but it returns a result set. In our simple stored procedure, the result set is a table of zero columns and zero rows. A result set can also contain one or more tables of a number of columns and number of rows. In a programming language context, this is like having the capability to return a number of two-dimensional arrays.

When you are writing multiple stored procedures, remembering what each does becomes difficult. With Microsoft SQL Server, it is not possible to group them. However, you need to group them so that it is possible to quickly search and understand a specific stored procedure. One way of grouping stored procedures is to define a naming convention. The naming convention that I use is this:

```
[area][function]
```

This is an example:

```
userGetSimple
```

The term *area* refers to the working area. For example, in the conference registration application there is a working area that is used to manipulate the user details. An appropriate area title is user. The term *function* defines what operation is attempted, such as retrieving a specific user, and in the conference registration application, there is a difference between a simple user and a full user. Thus, the name of a stored procedure to retrieve a simple user is userGetSimple.

The advantage of using this naming convention is that the stored procedures are grouped according to area in the stored procedure list box.

VERSIONING STORED PROCEDURES

If you have released a stored procedure publicly, it is legacy code that needs to be maintained. If you create a new version of the stored procedure that has some fundamental differences, the changes cannot be applied to the original stored procedure. Some consumers of the original stored procedure may rely on specific functionality, or on a set of existing parameters.

In this situation, the stored procedure needs to be renamed. For example, you could name the new version of userGetSimple to be userGetSimple2. The old version could still exist and function. Over time, the old version would be deprecated and then removed from the database.

PARAMETERS

Stored procedures use parameters, specified by a name that starts with an @ symbol followed by the data type. The @ is important, because that is what the SQL Server uses to indicate a local variable. It is declared in the Create Procedure command and added after the name of the procedure.

The following is a simple example:

```
Create Procedure clientAdd @firstname varchar(255), @lastname varchar(255),
@email varchar(255), @password varchar(64)
as
return @0
```

When this stored procedure is called, all of the parameters must have explicit values specified by the caller. Otherwise, a function calling error will result.

To specify an optional parameter, which is a parameter that does not need to be specified by the caller, you can assign a default value to the parameter. The assignment is placed on the same line as the stored procedure declaration, as shown here:

```
Create Procedure clientAdd @firstname varchar(255), @lastname varchar(255),
@email varchar(255), @password varchar(64) = 'nothing'
as
return @0
```

In this example, the @password parameter was assigned a default value. Here the data type was a string, but it is also possible to use a numeric data type.

All of the parameters that have been shown are input parameters. In Chapter 8 we discussed directional parameters in COM IDL; that same concept of directional parameters also applies to SQL parameters. An input SQL parameter is a value that is sent from the consumer to the server only. If the value of an input parameter is altered within the stored procedure, the alteration is not returned to the consumer.

To return the value of a parameter to the caller, a directional attribute needs to be added. In SQL, there is an output attribute that indicates that the parameter will only return a value to the caller. There is also an input output attribute that indicates that the parameter will travel from the caller to the database and back again.

An example of using the output parameter declaration is as follows:

```
Create Procedure addTwoNumbers @param1 int, @param2 int, @result int output
as
SELECT @result = @param1 + @param2
```

In this example, the parameter @result is assigned the result of adding @param1 and @param2. Assignments must use the keyword SELECT. We will get to the explanation of the SQL SELECT command a bit later.

RETURN VALUES

A stored procedure can return a value that can indicate the success of the stored procedure. The caller uses this value to indicate the success or failure of the stored procedure call. Return values are not like parameters that return a value to a caller. Return values are used by the middleware to define a return code.

Here is a simple example of returning an error value when a specific client search fails:

```
Create Procedure clientDoesExist
@usr_name varchar(255)
as
declare @var int

select @var = count(*) from clients where usr_name = @usr_name
if @var <> 0
    return 0
else
    return -100
```

This time the SELECT statement is used to count the number of records (count(*)) that are available in the table with a user_name (@user_name) input parameter. If the record count is 0, then we know that there is no client and so a value of –100 is returned. If there are one or more records, then 0 is returned to indicate no failure.

While it is possible to return the actual record count, doing so is incorrect. SQL Server reserves the return values 0 to –99. A return value of 0 indicates that the stored procedure was successful. A return value of –100 is used to indicate a search failure. Do not use the return value to return anything but an error, because doing otherwise will confuse SQL Server, and the associated database access layer.

Simple Table Manipulation with SQL

Typically, there are four things that you will do in your stored procedures: selecting, inserting, updating, and deleting data. Four commands to do this are available: INSERT, SELECT, DELETE, and UPDATE. With these four commands, most of your stored procedures can be written.

SELECTING DATA

To understand the process of selection, you must understand the relational model. A table is nothing more than a selection of data that has a number of columns and rows. When you perform a SELECT on this data, you are creating a temporary table that is a subset of the original table.

Let's assume that there is data in a Clients table. To retrieve the all contents of the table, you would issue this command:

```
SELECT * FROM clients
```

This is the simplest form of the SELECT command. The asterisk (*) tells the SQL command interpreter to select all columns and place them in the result set. The word clients states which table the data should be selected from. Because there are no constraints, all of the records of the table are selected.

To search for a specific client, you might use something similar to the following SQL:

```
select * from clients where id=123
```

The addition of the WHERE statement indicates that the command interpreter should search for rows that have an ID column value of 123.

The following example is a bit more complex:

```
select * from clients where firstname='george' or firstname='mary'
```

This is a search that looks for rows that have a firstname of george or mary. The OR operator says the row must fulfill either criterion; an AND operator specifies that both criteria must be fulfilled.

In each of these examples, it is the equality operator that works on the column. You can also search based on ranges, using the comparison operators (=, <, >, <=, >=, and <>). It is also possible to select based on a string range by using the BETWEEN operator, as in this example:

```
select * from clients where firstname between 'c' and 'r'
```

This will select all clients with a firstname that starts with c or r or anything in between. The comparison operators could have been used instead, but that would have required more coding. If a NOT BETWEEN operator were used, then everything that falls outside the range would be selected, but nothing within the range.

To select only records within a specific list, use this syntax:

```
select * from clients where first_name in ('c', 'r')
```

This example selects all records that have a firstname of c or r. To get something more useful (such as names that start with c or r), the search needs to be converted to a wildcard search. This is explained in the "Searching with Wildcards" section, below.

In the preceding SELECT examples, the data in the result set included all columns. It is possible to slice the data so that only the columns you need for data processing are returned. The following example returns a data set of three columns and an undefined number of rows:

```
select id, firstname, lastname from clients
```

In the previous examples, the asterisk (*) was used to indicate that all columns should be returned in the result set. However, there is a catch to using an asterisk and its use should be monitored.

Consider the situation in which the table definition changes. If you are using an asterisk-based SELECT, the result set will be based on the new number of columns in the modified table. This means that some COM+ business objects could fail because they are not finding the expected information. Alternatively, if you reference specific fields in a SELECT, the SELECT automatically breaks, giving you a database error message if you attempt to change the table and save the changes.

INSERTING DATA

Selecting data is a large part of SQL development. Another important task is the adding of data to a database. This process is simpler and has fewer possible options. Consider this example:

```
insert into clients ( id, username, password) values (123, 'cgross', 'cgross')
```

This example creates a new record and stores the values 123, cgross, cgross, respectively, in the columns id, username, and password. Because not all columns were specified when the record was created, the other columns will contain NULL values, unless the columns have default values specified.

If the three columns in the preceding INSERT statement were constrained to not being NULL values, this would be the minimum INSERT statement that could be used to create a valid record (although the values could change).

It is also possible to insert rows depending on the outcome of a SELECT, as the following data shows:

```
insert into oldclients (id, username, password)
select id, username, password
from clients where username between 'c' and 'r'
```

In this example, a backup table oldclients, which is an almost identical copy of the original clients table, is copied from the clients tables.

DELETING DATA

To remove or delete records from a database, use the DELETE command. The DELETE command is similar to the SELECT command, because they both search for specific rows to act upon. The difference is that the DELETE command does not return any result sets—it deletes rows from the table. An example of the DELETE command is as follows:

```
delete from clients where username='cgross'
```

Once you specify a table, everything after the WHERE is identical to the SELECT command.

UPDATING DATA

The last major operation is altering existing records. This is done with the UPDATE command, as shown in the following example:

```
update clients set password='newpassword' where userid=1234
```

The UPDATE command is like the DELETE and SELECT commands, in which a record is updated based on the selection outcome. You can update either a single row or collection of rows. The UPDATE command can operate on a single column or on multiple columns. In the example shown above, there is only one column being updated (password).

More SQL Techniques

We've now covered the fundamentals of using SQL and working with its result sets. The next step is to define additional operations that can be done within a stored procedure.

Working with Variables

When you write stored procedures using Microsoft SQL Server, you write code in T-SQL (Transact SQL). In fact, we have been using T-SQL without even knowing it. T-SQL is an extension of the SQL 92 standard.

In T-SQL, all variables are declared using a leading @ symbol. They can be defined using the standard SQL Server data types. To declare them within the context of a procedure, use this format:

```
Declare @myVar int
```

Because SQL works is a group-set language, assigning a value to a variable is not like assigning a value to a variable in a normal programming environment. Therefore, assignments must be done using a SELECT statement. The basic assignment format is as follows:

```
select @var = 123
```

In SQL Server 7.0, a new extension provides the capability to assign local variables using the SET statement, as follows:

```
set @var = 123
```

As mentioned earlier, SELECT statements return a result set of zero or more records. You work with a result set rather than with an individual record. However, there are times when you would like to work with the individual records in a result set. Using a cursor can do this.

When a result set is generated, the caller has a general reference to the data, but not to specific records. A cursor refers to the individual record that is being manipulated by the caller. Cursors enable you to iterate through the various values in the result set. Cursors are good for doing some things, but their general use is not recommended because cursors are slow as compared to programming code. Cursors are discussed in more detail later in the chapter.

In the case in which you know that there is only one record in the result set, it is not necessary to open a cursor. Instead, the variables can be directly assigned within the SELECT statement, as follows:

```
Select @var = username from clients where id=123
```

This SELECT must only return one record. If it does not, the variable @var returns the last record in the result set. Because of the way indexes work, the last record may not be the record that you are searching for.

Searching with Dates

Working with dates is a tedious and painful operation, because different countries have their own date formats, and many computer systems have their own date formats. What some developers do is create yet another date format in a string data field. However, although this may seem easier for the programmer, it is not useful in other applications—you have simply created another proprietary date format.

The simplest way to search with dates is not to search for a specific date, but to search in a range. Searching for a specific date sometimes fails because the search is not specified carefully enough. For example, if you search for a record that occurred two days ago, Microsoft SQL Server only returns records that occurred exactly two days, zero minutes, and zero seconds ago. Searching with a range, as shown in the following example, returns the correct result:

```
select * from sampleDate where date >= convert( datetime, '1997-03-09') and
date < convert( datetime, '1997-03-10')
```

This method of date searching is very robust, and it works regardless of whether the date is in a datetime or a smalldatetime column type.

Searching with Wildcards

Using wildcards is a powerful way to search a database. Wildcards are only useful when the SELECT command is combined with a LIKE. The LIKE search criterion searches for everything that is similar to the criteria. A LIKE is a more nebulous type of search when compared to an equality—it can be useful when searching a string-based column. A LIKE is only effective when the criterion includes a number of wildcards—the three wildcards are explained in the following table.

WILDCARD	DESCRIPTION
%	Matches any characters in the string
_	Matches a single character within the string
[ ]	Specifies a range of valid characters within the string

Wildcards can look very cryptic, but they can also return very powerful results. The following is a series of SELECT commands and its results:

```
Select * from clients where first_name like 'c%'
```

Returns all first names that start with c.

```
Select * from clients where first_name like 'c%n'
```

Returns all first names that start with c and end with n.

```
Select * from clients where first_name like 'c__'
```

Returns all first names that start with c and have two trailing letters.

```
Select * from clients where first_name like '[Cc]%'
```

Returns all first names that start with c, regardless of case.

```
Select * from clients where first_name like '[CD]%'
```

Returns all first names that start with a capital C or D.

```
Select * from clients where first_name like '[c-f]%'
```

Returns a range of first names that start with c, d, e, or f.

```
Select * from clients where first_name like '[^c]%'
```

Returns all first names that do not start with c.

Advanced Data Manipulation

Sometimes you will need to perform some extra data-manipulation operations. For example, you may need to define a unique identifier field or specify simultaneous updates.

INSERTING WITH AUTOINCREMENTING FIELDS

In the Building a Table section, we discussed defining the main index of the Users table using a unique numeric identifier. When you are adding data to the database, it is fairly simple to create a unique identifier by looking up the number of records in the table and then setting the newly added record's unique identifier to one more than the record count. But what happens when some records are deleted? The formula for figuring out the unique identifier will not work, resulting in duplicates.

Microsoft SQL Server comes to rescue with the autoincrementing data field. The autoincrementing data field guarantees that each record contains a unique value. When adding a new record to a table that contains an autoincrementing field you do not specify a value for the field in the SQL INSERT statement. This is because it is not possible to manually set the value of an autoincrementing data field.

So how do you know what the value of the data field is? There is a global variable named @@IDENTITY that you can use to retrieve the next autoincrementing value. You must retrieve the value directly after a record insertion—otherwise, it may change.

An example of using @@IDENTITY is as follows:

```
insert into clients ( id, username, password) values (123, 'cgross', 'cgross')
select @@IDENTITY  as 'Identity'
```

@@IDENTITY is not returned as an output parameter, but as a record set of one row and one column.

There is a problem with using an autoincrementing field in a multiple database scenario. Consider the situation in which there are two Users tables in two different databases and the ID in the two tables is autoincrementing. If a user is added to the Users table in the first database, that user will have an ID of 1. If, in the other database, a different user is added, that other user also will have an ID of 1. If either of those user records were to be replicated to the other database, they would get an ID different than the ID they had in their original databases. This means that any JOINS performed on those users will not be correct.

ADDING TEXT AND LONG BINARY DATA

SQL Server supports the manipulation of text and images, but some thought must be given to how one works with these large items. Simply creating a variable and then storing 2 GB of data in it is not something to be treated lightly because of the large sizes involved. All of these large items are called either a binary data object (image) or text data object (text).

When you read and write those types of data fields, the data is not directly written or read like it is for other types of data fields. Instead, data is read and written using a series of functions (writeText, readText, updateText) that read or write the data as a number of data chunks.

A large data field actually stores a reference rather than the actual data. The reference, in turn, points to the location in the database where the actual data is stored. This is unlike the other data types, whose data is stored within the record.

This is relevant in your development because when you read a record that contains a large data field, you will not be reading the data field content, itself. You will need to use the writeText, readText, and updateText methods to gain access to the data.

The writeText command is used as follows:

```
declare @ptrField varbinary(16)
select @ ptrField = textptr( textField) from testText where id=3
writetext testText.textField, @ptrField, 'Hey dude, how's it going!'
```

The pointer is a 16-byte reference variable. When the record is selected using a single record SELECT statement, the pointer is retrieved using the function textptr. The next line has the writeText function, which uses the pointer to write the text to the record.

PREVENTING SIMULTANEOUS UPDATES

Often in a transaction-processing environment, there are problems with two or more people modifying the same data. While COM+ transaction services will stop both people from altering the data at the same time, it will not stop both from retrieving the old data and then sequentially altering the data without seeing the other's changes.

To prevent this problem, a timestamp column can be added to the table. A timestamp is like a version stamp—whenever a row is added or updated, the timestamp column updates. So let's say that user 1 adds a record and it has a timestamp of A, where A is some date and time. Now along comes user 2, who executes a SELECT and wants to update the newly added record. At the same time, user 1 also decides to update the record. At this point in time, both users have a record with a timestamp of A. User 2 calls a stored procedure to update the record, and passes in the timestamp of A. The stored procedure sees that the record's timestamp and the passed-in timestamp match, so the record is updated and given a new timestamp of B. One millisecond after user 2 updates the record, user 1 attempts to update the record. But because user 1 called the stored procedure just after user 2, the database puts user 1 on hold because everything is executing within the context of a transaction. Once user 2's transaction completes, the stored procedure matches timestamps and notices that the original user has a timestamp of A, whereas the record's timestamp is now B. The stored procedure realizes that there is a problem and returns an error. It is now up to the original user to either get a fresh data set and try again, or to just forget about the update.

In reality, it could be implemented by extending the Client table with a field called verStamp. When a selection is made, it would look like the following:

```
select id, username, password verStamp from clients where  id = @id
```

The verStamp field is then used in the update as follows:

```
update clients set ... where id = @id and tsequal( verStamp, @inpVerStamp)
```

As a result, if anyone updates the record while another person is working with it, the second update will fail. At that point, the business object can perform some alternative action.

I have also seen some clients add two fields called mod_when and mod_by. These fields define not only when the change was made, but also who modified the data. This is done to implement auditing and security features to record who edited which records when. This approach also makes it possible to implement row-level security features.

BULK INSERT

Often you may want to batch-add a large amount of data that does not come from a relational source. An example is data from the stock exchange or from some type of reading device. In such cases, the source data is often in the form of a file.

The file could be added to the database by using some type of COM component, or you could use the BULK INSERT command. Consider this statement:

```
BULK INSERT Northwind.dbo [Order details]
FROM 'f:\orders\lineitem.tbl'
with (
FIELDTERMINATOR = '|',
ROWTERMINATOR = '|\n'
)
```

In this example, the bulk insert is into the SQL database Northwind. The table that is being specified is Order details. The table name is enclosed in square brackets—this is because the table name contains a space, which would confuse the command. The FROM specification indicates the file that is to be loaded.

Loading files is not simple, because files can be of various data types and formats. For example, the different data types could include char, native, wide char, and wide native. The char is a text file as is the wide char, the difference being that the latter uses the double-byte string notation. The native and wide native data types are files in the native data format. For example, a long would be stored as 4 bytes. The only catch with this file type is that it can only be created using the BCP (bulk copy) utility supplied with SQL Server 7.0.

For the files of the text variant, the next important consideration is to define the delimiters. When BULK INSERT reads files, it needs to know what values are fields and what values are rows. Using delimiters—defined characters that indicate field and row breaks—it is possible to specify fields and rows.

Each text row in a file is separated by the newline character, which, by default, specifies a new database row. The default delimiter for fields in the row is the tab character. Either of these default delimiters, however, can be changed. In the previous example, the pipe (|) character is specified as separating the fields, and the | and newline characters together specify the next record.

Programming in Transact SQL

The SQL Server commands presented thus far are statement-based. However, T-SQL also has more advanced concepts. For the programming tasks, such as control-of-flow, the language is similar to BASIC.

CONTROL-OF-FLOW

One very important mechanism for writing stored procedures is to be capable of controlling the program flow. Control-of-flow is the capability to decide, based on program results, which statement to execute. It also involves the capability to loop through program steps a variable number of times.

The simplest control-of-flow statement is the if statement. With if it is possible to do something based on a decision. Consider this example:

```
declare @var int
set @var = 21
if @var < 10
print 'The value is less than 10'
else if @var <= 20
print 'The value is more than 10'
else
print 'The value is more than 20'
```

This example shows a multi-branch if statement. The first statement declares the variable @var, and then a value is assigned to using a SELECT. Then the if comparison begins. In the example, the last branch of the if is executed because the value is 21 and the first two comparisons fail.

To complicate the first example, suppose you wanted to do two things if one branch of the if is executed. The problem with this is that each T-SQL statement only executes one statement based on some condition.

To create a block of multiple statements, the commands BEGIN and END are used. This example uses BEGIN and END to perform two statements in the last branch of the if:

```
declare @var int
select @var = 21
if @var < 10
print 'The value is less than 10'
```

```
else if @var <= 20
print 'The value is more than 10'
else
begin
select @var = @var + 20
print 'The value is more than 20'
end
```

If there are multiple if statements that only perform an assignment, the case statement is more efficient. Consider the following code example:

```
declare @var int
set @var = @anotherValue
set @var =
    case
        when @var = 1 then 3
        else @var
    end
if @var > 10
break
set @var = @var + 1
print @var
```

The purpose of the case statement is to enable an assignment based on a specific value. In the example shown, if @var is equal to 1, it will be set to 3. Otherwise @var will be set equal to @var. It is important to understand that the case statement only allows simple Boolean comparisons and setting operations. It is not possible to add complex logic.

The other flow control operation is looping and executing specific tasks repeatedly. The command to be used is the while statement, as shown here:

```
declare @var int
set @var = 0
while @var < 20
begin
if @var < 10
    print 'The value is less than 10'
else if @var <= 20
    print 'The value is more than 10'
else
    begin
        set @var = @var + 20
        print 'The value is more than 20'
    end
set @var = @var + 1
end
```

   The while loop contains either a statement or, more commonly, a BEGIN and END block. The loop is repeated until the test is false, at which point the while ends, and processing continues with the statement following the while loop. To break a loop prematurely, you can use the break statement. Consider the following code:

```
declare @var int
set @var = 0
while @var = @var
begin
set @var = @var + 1
print @var
if @var = 10
    break
end
```

   In this example, there is an endless loop created with the while statement. The condition @var = @var will always be true. This type of notation is used because T-SQL is a simple language, and it is not possible to write while @var as you could write it with a programming language such as Visual Basic, J++, or C++. T-SQL also cannot have multiple statements embedded on one line.
   In a full programming language, you can have the while depend on the outcome of a function call. This is not possible in T-SQL. Instead, you need to store the output of the function call in a variable, and then use the variable in the while statement. In the preceding example, the break command is used to break out of the infinite loop.
   Sometimes you want to restart a loop at the top without processing the remaining code for that loop; to do this, use the continue command. Consider the following code:

```
declare @var int
set @var = 0
while @var = @var
begin
set @var = @var + 1
if @var = 5
    continue
print @var
if @var = 10
    break
end
```

In this example, the first `if` statement restarts the loop when @var is equal to 5. In this case, the `print` statement and second `if` would not be executed.

The last statement will help you call up other stored procedures within your stored procedure. The command is EXECUTE and can be used as follows:

```
declare @var int
EXECUTE SimpleAdd 1, 2, @var OUTPUT
print @var
```

In this example, the stored procedure's name is SimpleAdd, and it takes three parameters. The first two parameters are input parameters and represent the numbers to be added. The last parameter is the returned value that is to be stored in the variable @var. To indicate that the value is to be returned, the OUTPUT keyword is added.

The interesting thing about the EXECUTE command is that it is not limited to executing stored procedures. It can be used to dynamically execute any SQL command. Consider the following example:

```
EXECUTE( 'SELECT * from authors')
```

This EXECUTE will perform a standard SQL SELECT and then return a result set to the caller. However, there is a side effect. In the first EXECUTE example, a stored procedure was called and parameters were passed in. When EXECUTE is called with a SQL command, it is not possible to pass in parameters. For example, the following would *not* be legal:

```
EXECUTE( 'SELECT * from authors where id=?')
```

The question mark in the above code example requires that a parameter be substituted.

For those stored procedures that allow default values as the stored procedure, it is possible to replace the parameter with the keyword DEFAULT. This automatically uses the default value.

Finally, it is possible to execute remote stored procedures that exist in other databases. Consider the following example:

```
declare @var int
declare @retstat int
execute @retstat = NEPTUNE.pubs.dbo.SimpleAdd 1, 2, @var output
```

In this example, the stored procedure name was prefaced with a reference to another computer with a specific database. The notation is *server.database.user.storedProcedure*. The variable @retStat is the return parameter.

TRANSACT SQL FUNCTIONS

Within T-SQL, there are series of functions that are part of the system and that make it simpler to do certain operations. The functions include string, mathematical, date, metadata, security, system statistical, and system programming functions. Discussion of these functions is beyond the scope of the book, but you can find more information in the Microsoft SQL Server books online, which is installed when either SQL Server 7.0 or SQL Server 7.0 utilities are installed.

Temporary Information and Cursors

When working with databases and executing stored procedures you will need to work with groups of data. However, groups of data cannot be easily stored in single variables, because each variable is a single instance of data. In this situation, cursors or temporary tables solve the problem.

CURSOR MANAGEMENT

When a command, such as a SELECT, is executed, it returns a result set. Based on the stored procedure functionality, you may want to go through the data record by record and do some other sort of processing. What we need is an SQL cursor that makes it possible to iterate through the various records in the result set.

What I am about to show you should not be used on a general basis. Performance tests show that it is faster to have a COM+ object iterate through the data. Of course, this assumes that the COM+ object and the database are on the same computer. This technique works well if the result set is a small subset that needs individual attention.

Consider this example:

```
declare @myCursor cursor
declare @autName varchar(255)
declare @autLastName varchar(255)

set @myCursor = cursor scroll for
select au_fname, au_lname FROM authors for read only

open @myCursor
fetch next from @myCursor into @autName, @autLastName
while( @@fetch_status = 0)
begin
print @autName
print @autLastName
print '————————————————'
fetch @myCursor into @autName, @autLastName
end
```

In this example, a cursor is declared using the declare statement and the data type is cursor. Cursors are not simple types, because they represent data sets. Before the cursor is used, it must be associated with a SELECT statement. In this example, this is done with the set@myCursor = line.

The SELECT statement is carefully put together, because the cursor opens a recordset. The first cursor option is the scroll keyword. It enables the cursor to move to the first, last, previous, or next location. The other cursor option is for read only. It makes the recordset a snapshot of the database data, and therefore does not allow for updating. To make a recordset updateable, the keywords for update are used, instead. This set statement could also be used in the declaration of the cursor.

After the cursor has been defined, it needs to be bound by calling the open function and passing in the cursor as a parameter. The function executes the SQL statement associated with it.

Then, the only step is to retrieve the data associated with the cursor by using the fetch statement and passing in the cursor name and variables that will be used to store the fields. Notice the keywords next from; they specify that the next record should be retrieved. This works in combination with the scroll for specified in the cursor assignment. The fetch variables are only bound once; a subsequent call to fetch must again specify where the variables will be stored. The next line is a loop that breaks when the global variable @@fetch_status = 0. When the status is 0, there are no more records to retrieve.

TEMPORARY TABLES

Instead of moving through the result set block of data dynamically with cursors, it is possible to copy the data to a temporary table that can be accessed with regular SQL commands. There are two types of temporary tables: local and global.

A local temporary table is one that is visible only to the user who created it. This makes it possible to write a generic stored procedure that manipulates a table, without having to worry about data conflicts. Consider the scenario in which a new table called tempLocation is created, and there are two users who are adding data to the table. You want to know who added what data and to hold it separately. A temporary table solves this problem. The local temporary table is created as follows:

```
CREATE TABLE #MyTempTable (cola INT PRIMARY KEY)
INSERT INTO #MyTempTable VALUES (1)
```

The table name is preceded with a hash (#) mark. The advantage of a temporary table is that when the user disconnects, SQL Server automatically drops it.

Global temporary tables only differ in that their names are preceded with a double hash (##) mark. Global temporary tables are visible to all users. A global temporary table is dropped when the last user who has a reference to the table disconnects.

Accessing System Information

When building stored procedures, it is often useful to access some system information. The system information available extends from global variables that are defined by SQL Server to a series of stored procedures that help work with SQL Server.

Our first global variable was defined in the cursor example, but there are other global variables. Global variables are identified by the double @@at the beginning of their names, and the different global variables are defined in the SQL Server 7.0 Books Online help file that is installed with SQL Server 7.0.

In addition to global variables, there are some stored procedures that are global and generic. They are typically called system-stored procedures. These stored procedures are preceded with sp_. The main purpose of generic global stored procedures is to make it simpler to administer the database. While it is possible to do all of the operations using standard SQL, doing so is more complicated. The system-stored procedures leave the data permissions intact.

Creating and Using Views

We looked at how stored procedures can be used to abstract database tables. SQL views also let you abstract a table. A view is like a table, but it is not a table.

A view is based on a SELECT statement, which creates a result set that is mapped as a permanent fixture in the database. A view can be queried like any other table, but updating is not always possible. If an update is permitted, it will not generate an error when it is attempted.

In this book, we use views to read data but not to update. Stored procedures are efficient, but if you are doing a simple SELECT, using a stored procedure may seem like overkill. The SELECT could be executed on a view. Because the SELECT is a simple view selection, the view offers the advantage of abstraction, performance, simplicity, and security.

When we discussed normalization earlier in this chapter, we split the Users table into two tables. While this is a good idea, it makes navigating through the data a bit more difficult. If you want to view a client and the client's address at the same time, you would need to create a SELECT statement and join the two tables. Instead of creating this SELECT statement each time you want to view the combined data, you could create a view that joins the two tables and then just look at the view as if it were a combined table.

Such a view is created as follows:

```
create view userView as
SELECT users.first_name, users.last_name, address.street, address.city
FROM users INNER JOIN address ON users.id = address.user_id
```

Whenever the userView view is referenced in a SELECT statement, it retrieves the preceding SELECT and combines it into a new result set. What this operation does is create from multiple SELECT statements another result set that is based on a specific number of columns and undefined number of rows.

The SELECT used to create the view is an extension of the original SELECT, in that it combines two tables using an INNER JOIN. An INNER JOIN means that whenever a record is selected from the first table (the Clients table, in this case) there must exist in the second table (the Address table) a corresponding record, using the clients.id and address.client_id to match the records.

It is possible to control what you can see in a view by hiding specific records or columns. To do either is simple, because the underlying SELECT statement determines what is seen in the view. You might think that because you have access to the view, that it includes access to the tables. Microsoft SQL Server has the added capability to encrypt the underlying mechanisms of views or stored procedures. Being capable of encrypting the code is good if the product is to be distributed commercially, or if you want to prevent people from being able to alter the contents.

An example of creating an encrypted view is as follows:

```
create view clientView with encryption as
SELECT      clients.first_name, clients.last_name, address.street,
address.city
FROM        clients INNER JOIN address ON clients.id = address.client_id
```

Working with Joins

When developing views, you frequently use the keyword JOIN. Joins are very powerful, flexible, and potentially confusing to a programmer. We will create a simple example with two tables that will demonstrate the various types of joins. One table will have a series of conferences, and the other will have a series of planning stages. The views will combine the two tables in different configurations. The Planned_schedule table is shown in Figure 15–1 and the Conferences table is shown in Figure 15–2.

id	conference_id	country_id	planning_phase
1	1	1	Just started
2	1	2	Finished
3	1	3	Cancelled
4	2	1	Started
5	2	2	Conference finishe
6	6	6	A fake record
*			

Figure 15–1: Planned_schedule data

id	description
1	SQL Server Confer
2	Windows 2000 Con
3	Exchange Conferer
4	Devdays Conferen
*	

Figure 15–2: Conferences data

SIMPLE JOINS

Let's start with the simplest of all joins—the JOIN. A JOIN has the following notation:

```
FROM [table1] JOIN [table2] ON (criteria)
```

The first table is the base table. The second table will be joined to the first table based on the criteria in the parentheses following the ON keyword. The criteria can use comparison operators, such as =, <>, and so on.

Suppose, for example, we wanted to look at all conferences being planned, and see what stage they are at. The SQL command for that is as follows:

```
SELECT Planned_Schedule.id, Planned_Schedule.planning_phase,
Planned_Schedule.conference_id,
Conferences.description
FROM Planned_Schedule JOIN
Conferences ON
Planned_Schedule.conference_id = Conferences.id
```

This SQL command selects from the Planned_Schedule table and joins an appropriate value from the Conferences table. What the SQL database does underneath is up to the database. It will attempt to optimize its actions so that it will have the lowest I/O (input/output) cost.

Another way of writing the same statement is as follows:

```
SELECT Planned_Schedule.id, Planned_Schedule.planning_phase,
Planned_Schedule.conference_id,
Conferences.description
FROM Planned_Schedule, Conferences WHERE
Planned_Schedule.conference_id = Conferences.id
```

In this example, there is no join. This is because the join will be created automatically when Planned_Schedule.conference_id = Conference.id is evaluated. If there are records in either table that do not have a counterpart that meets the joining criteria in the other table, then those records are not displayed.

Many tools, such as the ones in Visual Studio, automatically prepend JOIN with the INNER statement. This results in the INNER JOIN statement, which is the same thing.

Joining multiple tables together gives duplicates in the result set. The duplicates result because one record value in a table may be joined to multiple values in another table, which results in a record being displayed multiple times in a result set. To remove the duplicates from the result set, use the keyword DISTINCT. An example of using it is:

```
SELECT DISTINCT Planned_Schedule.id, Planned_Schedule.conference_id, ...
```

CROSS JOINS

The opposite of a simple join is a CROSS JOIN. It is a SELECT that is a Cartesian product of the tables involved. A cross join maps each row of one table to a row of the other table without restriction.

An example of a CROSS JOIN is as follows:

```
SELECT Planned_Schedule.id , Planned_Schedule.conference_id,
Planned_Schedule.planning_phase, Conferences.description
FROM Planned_Schedule CROSS JOIN
Conferences
```

If a WHERE statement is added to the cross join then it will behave like a simple join. A CROSS JOIN is like combining each record of one table with a record in another table. It is a permutation and combination type of operation and is rarely used.

OUTER JOINS

The OUTER JOIN is often called a right join. In the case of a simple join, the Planned_schedule records with the ID 6 and the Conferences records with the IDs 3 and 4 are not displayed. This is because these records have no equal counterparts in the opposite table. An outer join makes it possible to display records that do not have counterparts.

Why is an outer join useful? Consider the situation of a conference application. You want to plan the conferences for the full year, so to check the return status you perform an INNER JOIN query. However, as a result, some conferences do not appear because there are no status records. The other solution is to use OUTER JOIN queries. Depending on the type of outer join used, the records that are not displayed are tagged to the result set.

Let's start with the FULL OUTER JOIN, as shown in the following example:

```
SELECT Planned_Schedule.id, Planned_Schedule.planning_phase,
Planned_Schedule.conference_id,
Conferences.description
FROM Planned_Schedule FULL OUTER JOIN
Conferences ON
Planned_Schedule.conference_id = Conferences.id
```

In this case, the first set of records displayed are those that match the criteria after the ON keyword. Then, whatever has not been displayed in either table will be tagged onto the end. The output based on the data in Figures 15-1 and 15-2 is shown in Figure 15-3.

	id	planning_phase	conference_id	description
▶	1	Just started	1	SQL Server Confer
	2	Finished	1	SQL Server Confer
	3	Cancelled	1	SQL Server Confer
	4	Started	2	Windows 2000 Con
	5	Conference finishe	2	Windows 2000 Con
	<NULL>	<NULL>	<NULL>	Exchange Conferer
	<NULL>	<NULL>	<NULL>	Devdays Conferen
	6	A fake record	6	<NULL>
✳				

Figure 15–3: FULL OUTER JOIN output

To display all of the conferences in the output, a RIGHT OUTER JOIN could be used. A RIGHT OUTER JOIN displays all the rows from the right table, which in this case is all of the conferences. The SELECT statement in this case would be as follows:

```
SELECT ...
FROM Planned_Schedule RIGHT OUTER JOIN
Conferences ON
Planned_Schedule.conference_id = Conferences.id
```

The output is shown in Figure 15–4.

	id	planning_phase	conference_id	description
▶	1	Just started	1	SQL Server Confer
	2	Finished	1	SQL Server Confer
	3	Cancelled	1	SQL Server Confer
	4	Started	2	Windows 2000 Con
	5	Conference finishe	2	Windows 2000 Con
	<NULL>	<NULL>	<NULL>	Exchange Conferer
	<NULL>	<NULL>	<NULL>	Devdays Conferen
✳				

Figure 15–4: RIGHT OUTER JOIN output

The last outer join is a LEFT OUTER JOIN. It works identically to a right outer join, except that all of the records of the left table are displayed. The left outer join is written as follows.

```
SELECT ...
FROM Planned_Schedule LEFT OUTER JOIN
Conferences ON
Planned_Schedule.conference_id = Conferences.id
```

The output of this join is shown in Figure 15–5.

	id	planning_phase	conference_id	description
▶	1	Just started	1	SQL Server Confer<
	2	Finished	1	SQL Server Confer<
	3	Cancelled	1	SQL Server Confer<
	4	Started	2	Windows 2000 Con
	5	Conference finishe<	2	Windows 2000 Con
	6	A fake record	6	<NULL>
✱				

Figure 15–5: LEFT OUTER JOIN output

NULLS AND JOINS

When two data fields are joined, there is a relation between the two. Consider the example of a relation that says that two data fields must be equal. If both data fields have a value of 7, the relation is fulfilled. However, if both data fields are SQL NULLs, is the relation fulfilled? The answer is no and they will not be joined because NULL means undefined. To retrieve all of the NULL records, an outer join must be used. This works so long as the JOIN criteria does not exclude NULL values.

SUBQUERIES IN A SELECT

The last type of multitable join is a multiple SELECT. Using this technique, it is possible to select specific records based on another SELECT statement. For example, let's imitate a simple join, but do it using multiple selects. The SQL command is:

```
SELECT DISTINCT
Planned_Schedule.conference_id,
Planned_Schedule.planning_phase
FROM Planned_Schedule
WHERE (Planned_Schedule.conference_id IN
    (SELECT id
FROM country))
```

The second SELECT is part of the criterion used to search for the data in the original table. If the record is in the second SELECT then the IN keyword specifies that it should be displayed. The DISTINCT keyword is important. It removes the duplicate records that are generated.

GROUP BY

In a SELECT statement, it is possible to organize records into specific groupings. This is accomplished using the GROUP BY statement in conjunction with a SELECT. A common use of GROUP BY is to compute the total number of items sold for a specific product. It is implemented as follows:

```
SELECT prodID, SUM( Quantity) as AmountSold FROM orders GROUP BY prodID
```

The GROUP BY keyword works in conjunction with an aggregate function. An aggregate function is an SQL function that does something with a group of fields in a result set. In the preceding example, the grouping is based on the prodID field.

COUNTING THE NUMBER OF RECORDS

A common task is counting the number of records in a result set. The SQL command COUNT(*) is used to do this, as follows:

```
SELECT COUNT(*) FROM users WHERE first_name='s*'
```

In the SELECT statement, the only field that can be selected is the COUNT(*). It generates a one-column, one-row result set that contains the record count.

Putting It in Perspective

Many books ignore the topic of this chapter—building a database resource using SQL. They discuss business objects and leave the SQL issue to another book. Unfortunately, you cannot ignore the issue. A business object is tied to its resource, and the database is your biggest speed bottleneck. This means that no matter how good your COM+ object design is, the application will still be slow if the database is slow. One of my friends was responsible for a *PCWeek* shoot out that involved building a Web application. He said that designing good objects is important, but understanding how to write SQL code and stored procedures is also very important.

You will not become a database administrator by reading this chapter, but at least you will understand what the database administrator must consider. If a programmer understands what the database administrator is doing, building applications should be that much simpler and the resulting applications that much faster.

Chapter 16

Accessing the Data

The concept is simple enough: access the data and perform some operations. However, data can come in various shapes, sizes, and forms. This chapter explains how to access data using Microsoft's Universal Data Access (UDA) model.

I begin with a discussion of what UDA is, and then I discuss how to access the data and how to write data access code. The database access layer that we will look at is Active Data Objects (ADO), which is a Component Object Model (COM)-based technology.

Universal Data Access

When files contained only text data, life was simple. Now, though, data is contained in spreadsheets, databases, e-mail, and other interesting formats. Microsoft's Universal Data Access framework was created to be a general solution for data access. Using the UDA framework, we can access information on the data services tier. Remember how hypertext transfer protocol (HTTP) bound the presentation tier to the business object tier—the UDA does the same thing between the business object tier and the data services tier.

The reason for creating the UDA framework is a simple one; people want access to all types of data. People want the ability to combine multiple types of data sources without problems. For example, a spreadsheet has information that is cross-referenced with an e-mail, which is cross-referenced with a database. Combining these data sources enables the developer to create data warehousing applications that can retrieve information from any data type. In the past, the developer had to convert all of the data to a uniform format, which took quite a bit of development time.

The makeup of the UDA framework is shown in Figure 16–1. It is important to understand that all of the objects shown in the diagram are based on COM. At the bottom of the figure, there is a series of boxes labeled SQL Data, Non-SQL Data, and Mainframe. These boxes are your data services tier.

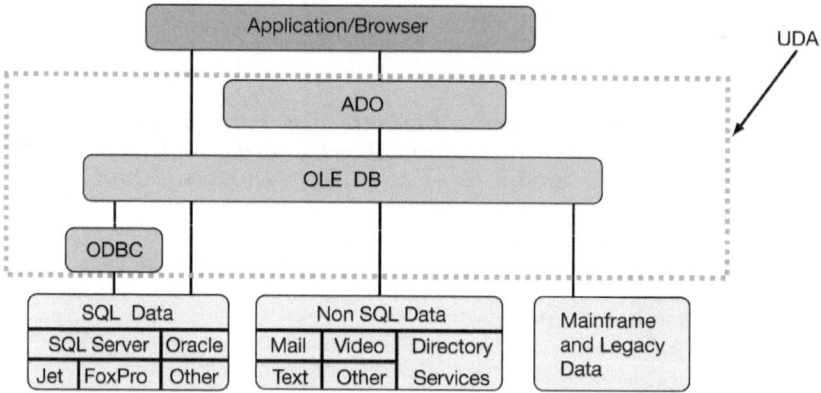

Figure 16–1: UDA architecture

Above those boxes is OLE DB (object linking and embedding database), which is a data-neutral layer used to directly access the data. OLE DB does not require the intervention of any kind of OLE DB manager. When a data source is connected to the consumer, the consumer uses the interfaces provided by the OLE DB provider directly. There is no COM object sitting between the consumer and the interfaces. OLE DB is a specification that contains a series of required and optional COM interfaces, which ensures that all OLE DB providers provide the correct COM interface. This type of standard makes everything faster and more stable.

Sitting on top of the OLE DB box is ADO. ADO was invented because only Visual C++ can use OLE DB directly—ADO is an abstraction that is COM friendly. ADO is a very powerful interface because any language can use it. It uses the VARIANT as a basis data-type and keeps things very generic.

Off to the side of both object layers is ODBC (Open Database Connectivity), which can be used to access Structured Query Language (SQL) data. Although UDA takes over much of the role of ODBC, ODBC is maintained because a lot of software makes use of it and because it remains the best interface for SQL. ODBC is a dynamic link library (DLL) based technology. When a consumer connects to the database, it first connects to an ODBC manager, which then redirects the call to the database itself. A discussion of ODBC is beyond the scope of this book and you are not likely to be using it for development anymore.

Finally, above the ADO and OLE DB box is the application or browser, which is what I call the consumer.

Why Use UDA?

So, why use UDA if SQL is the killer database application? Why not store every-thing in our SQL database? The answer is that although the SQL database is very important, it cannot accommodate all data.

In a typical office scenario, the office workers will get to the office and boot their computers, which could be networked computers, PCs, or terminals. Then they retrieve their e-mail and reply to some. They might even open some of the attached documents and view them. These attached documents may require using a word processor or a spreadsheet. Then they may browse the Internet and retrieve some current news documents. After all of this is done, they will start to open the corporate applications and begin entering or changing information.

There are two ways that an office worker interacts with data. The first is in creating the content. This could take the form of e-mail, word-processing docu-ments, spreadsheet documents, and hypertext markup language (HTML) docu-ments. After this content is created, it needs to be stored somewhere. Storage could be on an e-mail server, a database, or a Web server. An e-mail message could be stored in either a database or on an e-mail server. Thus, there are dif-ferent types of data and different places to store the data. The problem with this scenario is not in creating the data, but in knowing how to store and manipulate it. Some vendors use a single database server to store the documents, but the problem with this is that database data and e-mail data cannot be stored or ma-nipulated in the same ways.

What is needed is to develop a consistent and all-encompassing data ser-vices strategy. To realize this, a standard is needed that is flexible enough to cover everything. The UDA does this quite well, because the UDA has a set of re-quired COM interfaces that can be extended. This gives you the best of both worlds. And because everything is COM-based, it automatically integrates with your business objects or hybrid applications.

Extensible markup language (XML) might also be suggested for this role, but the tools are not yet rich enough. There are also many people who believe that XML will excel as a communication interchange and not as a data store.

How to Access the Data

The biggest problem with writing data-access code is making it efficient. When data is moved from a server to a client, the movement of the data requires a cer-tain amount of processing time and network bandwidth. What you want to do is minimize the amount of processing time and network bandwidth required. This process of transferring data from the server to client and back again is expen-sive. This is why we design the data objects at the business object tier.

While I do believe in good object-oriented design rules when it comes to the data services tier, we need to think first about efficiency and then about good ob-ject-oriented design. Toward this end, we will look at the two types of data ma-nipulation: read-only operations and data-modifying operations. It is important to separate the two types of data manipulation because there are different ways of optimizing each.

Read-Only Operations

Data is being read when the flow of data is from the server to the client. This flow is large, so to transfer the data quickly, the data should take the shortest route from the server to the client. It is best not to create an abstraction between the server and client using an object layer. The various approaches to moving data were demonstrated throughout this book at the various tiers.

In Chapter 7, we looked at how to access SQL data directly. Many developers may not accept this approach because it means bypassing the business services tier and directly accessing the database. But let's step back and look at how the data services tier was designed. The data services tier uses stored procedures and SQL views to encapsulate the database data. So, while it may seem that the business services tier is being bypassed, we are not sacrificing any componentization. The stored procedures and SQL views already take care of this.

There were four reasons why we used stored procedures and SQL views: simplicity, abstraction, security, and performance. These were explained in the previous chapter. Creating a tier of business objects to read the data is creating an unnecessary object abstraction. In this instance, it is simpler to read the data using the stored procedures or views. However, this approach only works because data is being read and not manipulated.

In Chapters 5, 6, and 7, the Web application chapters, XML was used to transfer data from the server to the client, and even though UDA makes it possible to use ADO recordsets, I still recommend XML. The problem with ADO recordsets is that they are very specific to an implementation of a technology—if you use an ADO recordset to transfer data, the versioning of the client and server are bound. For example, if the recordset is version 1.1, then both the server and client must be capable of consuming that version. If an upgrade is done, then both client and server must be upgraded. In contrast, consider the XML approach. If the server is upgraded to generate XML more efficiently, the client will not need to be upgraded because XML is implementation-neutral. The same is true if the client is upgraded.

Data-Modifying Operations

The other way of interacting with the data is to process it. The operation could involve reading, modifying or deleting data, or a combination of those. The point is that the data needs to be processed before it can be stored or displayed, and these operations require the business object tier. In previous chapters, we learned that a business object operates in the context of a transaction. This enables operations to be called in any order without any need to worry about undoing the operations. The undo is handled automatically by aborting the transaction and letting the resource manage the removal of the details of the transaction.

In Chapter 9, there were three different types of objects: operations, data, and verification. The data-access technology should not be written into the data object, although it might seem logical from a design point of view that the data object should contain the data-access routines. The problem with this approach is that it does not take into account the operation that is being performed.

Consider the conference registration application. There are completely different requirements for resetting the password and for displaying a user's address. If the data access routines are embedded in the data object, each instantiation of the object will require all of the data to be retrieved, and when you only want to change the password this is an unnecessarily expensive operation. One solution is to develop a context in which only specific pieces of data are loaded. However, although this solution works, you are creating work for yourself. A cleaner design is to separate operations and data, so that the operations object loads only the data required. This is another example of bending the object-oriented design rules to minimize the amount of data being copied.

A SPECIAL SITUATION REGARDING DATA OPERATIONS AND DATA ACCESS

This doesn't mean that no data objects should contain data-access routines. There are some very specific situations in which data-access routines are required in the data object. Consider the situation of a merchant selling widgets worldwide. To be friendlier worldwide, the merchant wants the price and shipping conditions to be displayed on a Web page in local currencies.

The best implementation in this situation is to use a data object that loads a table of information regarding the exchange rates and shipping costs. When the data object is instantiated, it loads the information from a database. And to make the data object be fast, it is converted to a COM+ pooled object so the information does not need to be repeatedly read from the database. This object would do everything automatically and would not require an explicit operations object. It breaks our design methodology, but it makes everything more efficient, which is what we want.

An Introduction to ADO

The database access technology that you will use in about 60 percent of your COM+ business objects is ADO. You do not use it for all of your objects if you are developing using Visual C++, or if you need components that do special things, such as read large binary images, or if you need high performance. For those environments, you use the Visual C++ OLE DB Consumer Templates, which are described in the next chapter. The ADO object model is a very simple COM-based architecture. This means that it can be used in any environment where COM can be consumed.

The Architecture of ADO

The architecture of ADO 2.5*x* is shown in Figure 16–2. The COM objects in the diagram are the core ADO COM objects. There are others that are not shown, but they are used to perform special functions. We will get to those special functions a bit later.

The release of ADO 2.5 made some fundamental changes. There is now both a static object model and a dynamic object model. A static object model is like the one in Figure 16–2. When one object is instantiated, it begets another object as defined by the object model. The dynamic model is when ADO exposes methods and objects depending on how the resource is being used by the business object.

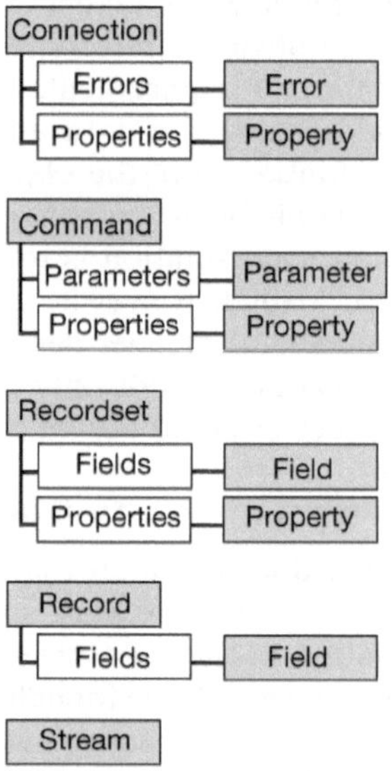

In the context model, the ADO object model exposes things such as stored procedures depending on the database connection. The stored procedures are exposed as COM object methods, with the parameters representing the parameters of the stored procedure. This is much simpler than the previous technique of filling out parameters and then calling a method that bundles the created parameters in a stored procedure call. Of course, the previous technique remains available for legacy applications.

ADO is also dynamic when it uses optional parameters. The optional parameters can be used to create other ADO objects explicitly or implicitly. For

Figure 16–2: ADO architecture

example, if you use the ADO Recordset object, you have the option to use it without creating a Connection ADO object. The Recordset object creates a Connection object internally, but does not expose it to the developer.

This approach may seem like a waste of processing cycles, but it works just fine. You need to count your cycles where they really matter, and they really matter in the transfer of data between the various network connections and within the database itself. Creating an object implicitly or explicitly does not matter with most business objects. This implicit creation is an even smaller factor with COM+, because much of that information is cached. The only place where it may matter is if the business object calculates something that involves the iteration of the data—that is a reason to use OLE DB Consumer Templates.

CONSUMING ADO

ADO is based on a series of COM interfaces. Hence, to use ADO in the various development environments, it is only necessary to reference the ADO type library.

In Visual Basic, the ADO library is referenced by using the Visual Basic Reference dialog box. The COM library that you will want to find is Microsoft ActiveX Data Objects (Library 2.5).

In Visual C++, the ADO library is referenced using COM compiler support and a header that enhances the ADO binding functionality. The ADO header that will interest you is called *icrsint.h*.

And finally, Visual J++ has embedded ADO using the Visual J++ ADO for Windows Foundation Classes (WFC) library classes.

Performing Processing Data Operations

The database access layer accesses the resources using exposed stored procedures and SQL views. And when you use either a stored procedure or view, you will have a resultset. Hence, the first step in understanding the database access layer is to learn how to manipulate a resultset using ADO.

The stored procedure that is called is used to add two numbers together and then return that result to the user. So let's look at the stored procedure to acquaint ourselves with it:

```
Create Procedure addTwoNumbers @param1 int, @param2 int, @result int output
as
Select @result = @param1 + @param2
```

There are three parameters, the first two being input and the last one being an output. What we want to do is write some ADO code that will call this stored procedure and then return the answer to us.

CALLING A STORED PROCEDURE THE HARD WAY

Let's first consider the hard way of calling this stored procedure. The hard way is to create each parameter in an ADO collection and then call the stored procedure using an ADO method. If you understand this hard method, then the easy one will seem simple because it is an encapsulation of the hard method.

Connecting to the Resource

The first step in using any ADO objects or recordsets is to create a Connection object. The Connection object represents a connection to the OLE DB resource being consumed. The following code sample does this:

```
Dim objConnection As New Connection
strCon = "Provider=sqloledb;Data Source=bacchus;" & _
"Initial Catalog=TestDatabase;User Id=sa;Password=; "
objConnection.Open strCon
```

The connection string (strCon) specifies the connection to the resource. Typically, a wizard generates this code, but it is important to know what each piece means. The connection string is a series of token and value pairs, separated by a semicolon. In every connection string, it is necessary to specify what the consumer will connect to. This is referred to as specifying a provider. By default, all providers are native OLE DB providers. It is possible to use ODBC because there is a bridge that binds an ODBC resource to a native OLE DB provider.

In the connection string example, the `Provider` is very important because it defines which OLE DB provider is used. In the above example, the provider used is for SQL Server. The consumer can also define a provider that connects to a file that represents a persistence of an OLE DB data source. This time, you do not specify a `Provider` in the connection string but a `File Name`. If the provider is a File Name, then the value of the `File Name` must be a valid Uniform Resource Locator (URL), similar to the following:

```
File Name=http://www.myserver.com/samplefile.conn
```

After the `Provider` or `File Name` has been specified, the other connection string items are specific to the `Provider` or `File Name`. Their specification is dependent on the OLE DB provider. As a result, the following description only applies to Microsoft SQL Server. If you use a different data source, check the OLE DB documentation for that data source. From this point on, all OLE DB settings will be SQL Server specific.

The `Data Source` keyword specifies the server where the SQL Server database is hosted. The keyword `Initial Catalog` is the database that will be connected to. And the `User Id` and `Password` are the username and password that will be used to connect to the database.

If the OLE DB for ODBC provider is used, then the OLE DB connection string changes slightly. In that case, OLE DB will use the OLE DB to ODBC bridge, which will connect to the database. The following connection string would work:

```
strCon = "DSN=TestDatabase;UID=sa;PWD=; "
```

Notice that there is no `Provider` or `File Name` setting. This is okay because when the `DSN` keyword is used, it is automatically recognized as the OLE DB for ODBC provider. If you wanted to be OLE DB pure, you could specify the `Provider` to be ODBC and then pass in the information specified by the previous code example. The `DSN` is the name of the data source as defined in the ODBC settings. In the previous code example, the `DSN` specifies that all of the database connection settings are stored in the ODBC `TestDatabase` configuration.

Calling the Stored Procedure

There are many different ways of executing a stored procedure using ADO. I will show two different ways and leave the others to you as an exercise in coding.

A stored procedure in the OLE DB sense is considered a command. In ADO, there is a `Command` object that is used to issue commands. The stored procedure is therefore assigned to the `Command` object. The code that does that is as follows:

```
Dim objCommand As New Command
objCommand.CommandText = "addTwoNumbers"
objCommand.CommandType = adCmdStoredProc
objCommand.ActiveConnection = objConnection
```

The CommandText property is the assigned the name of the stored procedure that is to be called. The CommandType property is assigned the type of data that is being stored in CommandText. In this case, it is a stored procedure text, so the type of data is adCmdStoredProc. When the Command object is executed, it needs to know which connection to use. This is stored in the ActiveConnection property.

The stored procedure being called has three parameters. Parameters are represented in ADO using the Parameter object. Here is an example of assigning the first parameter:

```
Dim param As New Parameter

param.Type = adInteger
param.Size = 4
param.Direction = adParamInput
param.Value = 2
objCommand.Parameters.Append param
```

When assigning the Parameter object, you must indicate what the parameter is and which direction the information is traveling. The first parameter of the stored procedure is an Int, which is of the Type adInteger and has a Size of 4 bytes. The parameter is an input, so the Direction is adParamInput. Finally, the Value is assigned, which will be consumed by the stored procedure. The parameter is then appended to the Command object. Because the parameter is added as an append operation the order in which the parameters are appended must reflect the order of the parameters in the stored procedure. The second parameter is added to the parameter list using the same steps as the first parameter.

The third parameter is an output, so the third Parameter object has the following outputDirection specification:

```
output.Direction = adParamOutput
```

And the last piece of code calls the stored procedure. It is implemented as follows:

```
objCommand.Execute
```

When this method returns, the output parameter contains the value obtained by adding the two numbers in the input parameters.

CALLING A STORED PROCEDURE THE EASY WAY

In Chapter 7, we discussed using the Visual InterDev Data Environment to call a stored procedure. In that situation, the stored procedure could be called like a method call based on the Data Environment object. The ADO Connection object has similar functionality in that it exposes all stored procedures as methods, so you can call the stored procedure like this:

```
objConnection.addTwoNumbers 1, 2, result
```

The names of the methods are identical to the stored procedure names. The Connection object attempts to decipher the parameter types and how they map to the stored procedure. Usually this works out, but it won't in this case. The result parameter is an output parameter that stores the result of the addition, but the Connection object does not understand this. This is a general problem with output parameters. Calling the method this way will not produce the correct result in result.

In any case, there is a very simple workaround to get the output parameters to work. You need to revise the stored procedure to create a resultset. Consider this rewritten stored procedure:

```
Alter Procedure addTwoNumbers
@param1 int,
@param2 int
as
declare @retVal as int
set @retval = @param1 + @param2
select @retval
```

The stored procedure now has only two parameters, and both are inputs. They are added together and the result is stored temporarily in the variable @retVal. Then, using the SELECT command, a resultset of one row and one column is created. This resultset can be picked up by the stored procedure by modifying the ADO call as follows:

```
Dim resultSet As New Recordset
objConnection.addTwoNumbers 1, 2, resultSet
```

The stored procedure is still called using three parameters, but the last parameter is a special one. It is an optional parameter that is used when the stored procedure returns a Recordset. The resultSet variable contains the one row-one column result, which can be read.

CALLING A STORED PROCEDURE ANOTHER WAY

The previous solution does not always work with multiple resultsets, parameters, and database providers that do not have dynamic querying capability. There is, however, another solution that uses the Connection and Command objects to set up a custom command that can be called using the Connection method technique.

The Command object is set up using the following code:

```
objCommand.Name = "sp_addTwoNumbers"
objCommand.CommandText = "addTwoNumbers"
```

```
objCommand.CommandType = adCmdStoredProc
objCommand.ActiveConnection = objConnection
objCommand.Parameters.Refresh
```

This is very similar to the hard method shown earlier. The `Name` property that is assigned represents the custom method so that it can be called. I like to append a `sp_` to the method so that I do not confuse it with the real stored-procedure mappings of the database.

The other difference is that the last statement calls the `Parameters.Refresh` method. This method is key to making output parameters work. This method causes the ADO layer to tell the OLE DB provider to retrieve all of the information regarding the parameters of the stored procedure. This step requires that ADO call the resource and ask it about this information. If you are trying to save bandwidth, then this is not an optimal solution—you would be better off doing it the "hard way" and specifying each parameter.

The final step is to call the method as in the following code:

```
objConnection.sp_addTwoNumbers 1, 2, result
```

Now the `result` variable contains the result of the addition.

When the `Parameters.Refresh` method is called, the `Parameters` collection is filled with a number of `Parameter` objects. Therefore, it is not necessary to add `Parameter` objects. If you do, they will cause a `Command.Execute` error. If you do need to change a parameter, it is possible to replace the Parameter objects directly using the `Parameters.Item(index)` method. The only situation where that might be useful is if you are using prefilled objects.

For example, suppose you are working with a specific user id. To store the value of the user id, a `Parameter` object is created and the correct properties are assigned. Now, instead of storing an `integer`, the `Parameter` object is stored and then assigned to the various ADO commands when needed.

When you use the `Parameters.Refresh` method, you are making a round trip to the database server, because ADO attempts to read the various parameters required to make a proper stored-procedure call. When the method `Parameters.Refresh` is called, it assumes that the database server supports dynamic querying of its properties. If it does not, then the `Parameters.Refresh` method will not work. Because we are using SQL Server, this is not a concern. However, Microsoft Access is an example of a database in which this will not work.

Performing Read-Only Operations

Read-only operations are a two-step process. First, you execute a stored procedure or a `SELECT` on an SQL table or view, which generates a resultset. Then, you iterate through the resultset using a database cursor and display the individual records to the user for further processing. This process constitutes most of your application.

THE PROBLEM OF DISPLAYING DATA

Previously we learned how to call a stored procedure to manipulate data and possibly return a specific value depending on what occurred in the stored procedure. However, let's look at managing result sets in more detail.

One data display technique that has been used extensively in the Visual Basic developer community is to use data-bound COM controls located on a Visual Basic form. Data-bound controls take a database connection and a command string to generate a resultset. This resultset is then displayed within the COM controls. The technology is very easy to use.

But there is a big problem with data-bound controls—they bind directly to the data. There is no way for a developer to interject code to perform any business logic, which means that incorrect data could be stored on the database. Nor does this scenario permit you to control the business process. In other words, this is a solution to avoid. I mention it here because many people like to use data-bound grid COM controls. I suggest that you avoid them.

DISPLAYING RESULTS USING STORED PROCEDURES

Now let's generate some read-only resultsets using stored procedures. Let's consider a stored procedure in the conference registration application that is used to retrieve the conferences that correspond to a specific conference ID. The stored procedure implementation could be as follows:

```
Create Procedure conferenceGet
@confId int
as
select id, description from conferences where id = @confId
```

This stored procedure will return a resultset that contains two columns with an unknown number of rows. To call this procedure, use the following ADO code:

```
objConnection.conferenceGet 2, resultSet
```

The resultSet parameter is an ADO Recordset object that contains the results from a command or from opening a table. The Recordset object contains a collection called Fields, which represents the columns of the resultset. As you can see from the stored procedure and the resultset it generates, there should be two Fields: id and description.

Accessing the Data

It is possible to retrieve the data from the Recordset using either an index or a field name. Based on the preceding example, the following code samples reference the resultset columns using a numeric index:

```
resultSet.Fields(0)
resultSet.Fields(1)
```

And the following code references the result columns using field names:

```
resultSet.Fields("id")
resultSet.Fields("description")
```

In both examples, the data is displayed in the same order. However, there are some very big differences in how each is retrieved. When using an index to reference a resultset column, the data is retrieved from the Fields collection using a simple index. You must make sure that your index value is within the valid limits for the collection. If you attempted to reference the resultset column with an index of 2, an error would have occurred, because there are only two columns in the Fields collection. By referencing a resultset column using a numeric index, you also do not know which column is being retrieved. If the stored procedure switched the order of the id and description columns, the data would be different and your application could have problems.

When referencing a column with a field name, the Recordset object searches the column names for a match. By default, because most SELECT statements are the result of searching in a table or view, column names correspond to the name of the column of the table or view. However, if there are column aliases in the SELECT statement, they are used as the column names. In this scenario, switching the order of id and description would not make any difference in the data output. The only disadvantage to this solution is that it takes slightly longer to retrieve the data, because a string comparison is made between the column name that is passed in and the column name in the resultset.

Using an Alias

It is often necessary to define a column name alias in a SELECT statement when doing a JOIN between multiple tables, because columns frequently have the same names. The Recordset must have a unique column name when it attempts to retrieve a column value based on the field name, or an ambiguous result occurs.

Let's consider the stored procedure from earlier in the chapter that added two numbers and returned the result as a resultset. Attempting to use a Recordset field name reference would have yielded nothing, because the resultset had no column name. An alias can be used to give a column name, as shown in the following example:

```
Alter Procedure addTwoNumbers
@param1 int,
@param2 int
as
declare @retVal as int
set @retval = @param1 + @param2
select @retval as out_value
```

The last SQL statement in this example creates a one row one column result-set with a column name of out_value. You could reference this value using a Recordset object, as follows:

```
resultSet.Fields("out_value")
```

Navigating Through the Data

In most cases, multiple records are returned to the client, which means that you need the capability to navigate through them. When navigating through a result-set, it is necessary to know whether there are any records. You may be tempted to read the value of the RecordCount property, but you should not because of the problems it creates.

The reason why you should not attempt to read the RecordCount is because of database optimization. Consider an SQL statement that retrieves one million records from a two-million-record table. To get an accurate record count, you could call Recordset.MoveLast and then call Recordset.RecordCount. This means that you have navigated through 1,101,123 records to get the record count. Also, the resultset is so large that the record count takes time. This is not effi-cient. Let's look at how to navigate and count records properly.

A Recordset looks something like the representation in Figure 16–3. A Recordset is a collection of records, which can also be called a resultset, that can be navigated using cursors. A cursor holds the location of the current record and reads the values of that record into the Recordset. The Fields collection contains that data.

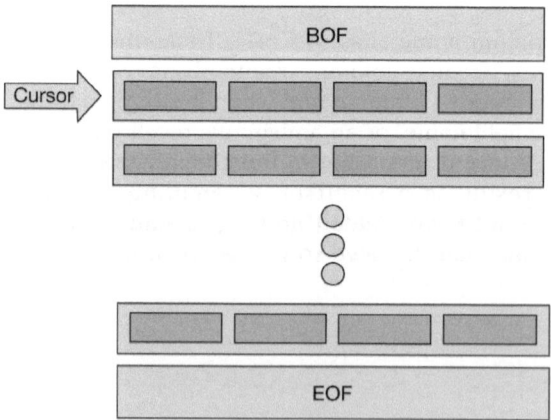

Figure 16–3: Conceptual diagram of Recordset

Before the first record in the resultset is a record that has the BOF (beginning of file) identifier. The BOF record is not an actual record—it is a position that the Recordset cursor can reach. The same goes for the last record, which is called EOF (end of file). Both of these locations were created so that there is a final end point when the cursor is moved forward or backward.

To determine whether your `Recordset` cursor has actually landed in one of the special locations, there are two properties, called `BOF` and `EOF`, which are `FALSE` if the cursor is in the resultset. If the cursor lands in the `BOF` location, then the `BOF` property is `TRUE`. If the cursor lands in the `EOF` location, then the `EOF` property is `TRUE`.

When the cursor moves through the records, it is possible to define a bookmark at any location other than `EOF` or `BOF`. The bookmark uniquely identifies the location of the record in the recordset. If at a later time you need to return to the bookmarked record, you simply move your cursor to the bookmark.

Your main task in navigating through a collection of records is to move the cursor. The following `Recordset` methods will help move the cursor:

- `Recordset.MoveFirst`: This moves the cursor to the first record of the recordset.
- `Recordset.MoveLast`: This moves the cursor to the last record of the recordset.
- `Recordset.MoveNext`: This increments the cursor to the next record or forward location. If the current cursor location is the last record, then it moves it to a location after the last record and the `EOF` property is set to `TRUE`. Moving forward when `EOF` is `TRUE` results in an error.
- `Recordset.MovePrevious`: This decrements the current cursor position to the previous record location or backward direction. If the current cursor location is the first record, then it moves to a location before the first record and the `BOF` property is set to `TRUE`. Moving backward when `BOF` is `TRUE` results in an error.
- `Recordset.Move`: This moves the cursor a number of records forward or backward with respect to the current cursor location. The number is passed in as an argument to this method and it is a signed number. A positive number means moving the cursor forward and a negative number means moving the cursor backward. If the number results in a location beyond `EOF` or `BOF`, then the cursor is moved to that location and the appropriate property is set to `TRUE`. It is possible to specify a starting position as a parameter, from where the cursor should start moving. This location must be a bookmark that has been previously defined.

Using Bookmarks

Bookmarks are easy to define. When a cursor is at a location, that location is stored in the `Recordset.Bookmark` property. This can be retrieved and assigned to a variable. When you want to move to the bookmark, you pass the bookmark variable to the `Recordset.Move` method.

The bookmark is a value that has no relation to anything. I mention this because some resources define the bookmark to be the row location in the resultset. This might lead you to think that you could define your own bookmark without retrieving it first. This isn't possible, because the value of the bookmark only has relevance to the database and should not be generated in your code.

When Is the Resultset Empty?

It is also necessary to find out when a resultset is empty. The value provided by `Recordset.RecordCount` is incorrect, so it can't be used. However, when the `EOF` and `BOF` properties are both `TRUE`, the resultset is empty.

USING THE COMMAND OBJECT WITH SQL

The other way of creating a read-only resultset is to call an ADO `Command` object and pass in an SQL command. While you might think that the ADO `Command` object requires SQL commands, it is possible to use a `SELECT` command. Issuing an SQL statement is like issuing a stored-procedure statement. For example, when you use `addTwoNumbers` as the text for a `Command` object, as we did earlier in the chapter, it is similar to using the following SQL command text:

```
{ ? = call addTwoNumbers( ?, ?, ?) }
```

The question marks represent parameters that are inserted at run-time using the `Parameter` object. It is possible to do the same thing using ordinary SQL. To make this work, the `Command.CommandText` property needs to be an SQL statement, and the `Command.CommandType` property needs to be set to `adCmdText`. An example of a parameterized `SELECT` statement is as follows:

```
SELECT id, description FROM conferences where id = ?
```

Here the parameter is the search criterion on the `id` column. The advantage of using the `Parameter` object is that the same command can be issued multiple times with different parameter values. When SQL Server sees this command, it uses the parsed and compiled version, which increases performance. If, however, the SQL command will only be used once, then there is no advantage gained in using the `Parameter` objects.

There are two ways of creating the `Command.Parameters` collection. The first is manually, by instantiating a `Parameter` object and then appending it to the collection. The second is by calling `Command.Parameters.Refresh` after the `Command.CommandText` property is set. In this case, calling the `Refresh` method call will not force a server round trip, because the command is client-based. After the parameters are defined, it is possible to call `Command.Execute` to retrieve the resultset.

USING CURSORS

One thing we have not discussed is how resultsets are transferred from the server to the consumer and how this affects the cursor. Consider the following code, which opens a `Recordset` and then moves the cursor forward and backward:

```
objConnection.conferenceGet 2, resultSet
resultSet.MoveNext
resultSet.MovePrevious
```

When the MovePrevious command is called, an Operation not allowed in this context error occurs. This happens because the Recordset is by default opened as read-only and forward-only. The Recordset object assumes that you will move through the data once and then be done with it, which in our display context would be correct. Why does it assume this? Knowing that the cursor cannot move backward means that any record visited can be discarded—the OLE DB provider uses this as an optimization when managing the resultset cache.

If the resultset is no more than a few records, an inability to move the cursor backward isn't likely to be a problem. The entire data set could be loaded into the client browser without many problems. But let's consider the situation in which there are several thousand records. Then moving the cursor backward may be important.

To do so, the cursor must be declared as having the capability to move backward. The way to do this is to modify the Recordset.CursorType property to the value adOpenStatic, adOpenDynamic, or adOpenKeyset. The default property type is adOpenForwardOnly. A modified version of the preceding example is as follows:

```
resultSet.CursorType = adOpenDynamic
objConnection.getAllItems 2, resultSet
resultSet.MoveNext
resultSet.MovePrevious
```

The Different Types of Cursors

Let's consider the situation of multiple users, each opening a resultset that has the same data, and based on that resultset some data is read and modified. The question is this: How does ADO handle the conflict when two users are working with one record? For example, suppose one user selects a resultset and another user modifies one of the records in the resultset. Does the user who performs the selection see the changes? It depends on the type of cursor. By default, the forward-only cursor creates a snapshot of the data. This means that any changes, additions, or deletions are not visible because only the original resultset is shown.

The adOpenStatic cursor type opens a snapshot resultset, except that the cursor can move forward and backward. If the OLE DB provider supports bookmarks, then using them is allowed.

The adDynamic cursor type opens a resultset where the cursor can move forward and backward. However, bookmarks are not supported. When there are additions, changes, and deletions by other users, they become visible in the current resultset.

The adOpenKeyset cursor type opens a resultset where the cursor can move forward and backward with full support of bookmarks. Any data additions are not visible in the resultset. Deleted records become inaccessible to the resultset.

Client-Side and Server-Side Cursors

The cursor location is determined by the `Recordset.CursorType` property, which can be either `adUseServer` (server-side cursor) or `adUseClient` (client-side cursor). The default is a server-side cursor. When a cursor is declared in Transact-SQL, it is a server-side cursor.

When a consumer iterates through a data set, the cursor used depends on where the resultset is kept. If it is kept on the server side, it is a server-side cursor and if it is on the client side it is a client-side cursor.

When a cursor is declared as a client-side cursor, all of the resultset is downloaded to the client. The SQL Server driver considers this data to be a snapshot. Hence, the cursor type can be only `adStatic` or `adForwardOnly`. The client-side cursor is fast, so long as the record count of the resultset is small, typically less than 50. A client-side cursor typically requires less bandwidth when iterating through the data, but it requires more time to initially load the data.

Using a server-side cursor stores all of the data in the resultset on the server. When moving through the records, the data is moved from the client to the server. The OLE DB provider can optimize and cache old records, so that they need not to be accessed.

By default, the cache size is set to one record. To increase the cache size, the `Recordset.CacheSize` property can be set to any number larger than one. However, changing this value can affect performance, depending on the cursor type. For example, if the cursor type is `adDynamic`, then the cache must make sure it includes any changes that occur. If the cache size is large, this may add extra network processing.

When we use COM+ business objects in the context of ADO cursor locations, caches, and cursor styles, things could very quickly become messy, but they don't. This is because our stored procedure and SQL view architecture make some assumptions for us. When we use a `Recordset` to retrieve data, it is for read-only purposes and we only need a snapshot of the data. This snapshot contains a timestamp for the record, which means that when we do our data update, the stored procedure architecture will ensure that we are working with a current data set. As a result, things are relatively simple.

Navigating Multiple Resultsets

The last situation that needs to be discussed is navigating through multiple resultsets. Consider the following stored procedure:

```
Create Procedure conferenceGet
@confId int
as
select description from conferences where id = @confId
select id from conferences where id = @confId
```

In this example, there are two SELECT statements generating two resultsets that have one column each. The way to access the second resultset is by using the following code:

```
dim resultSet2 as new Recordset
set resultSet2 = resultSet.NextRecordset
```

Record and Stream Objects

The release of ADO 2.5 added two new objects: Record and Stream. These are useful in several different situations.

In the case of a relational database, a record is a flat entity—a group of columns that contain data. Now consider querying a resource that is an e-mail system. A record may be a single e-mail message, which is not a flat structure. The e-mail may contain attachments, which are variable and which may contain yet other attachments. The point is that some data is not predictable, as it is in a relational database. The Record object makes it possible to navigate hierarchical data.

It is also often useful to store the contents of a resultset for purposes other than manipulation. XML has proven itself to be a neutral data-exchange format and it is sometimes desirable to convert an ADO Recordset to an XML document. Another situation is the asynchronous processing of a data set. A snapshot of the data could be persisted to a stream, which is represented by a message. The message could then be sent somewhere for further processing.

Records

To test the Record object's functionality, we can apply it to an OLE DB provider that treats most of its data as Record objects. Windows 2000 includes an OLE DB provider for Internet publishing. Using this provider it is possible to access Web resources and to upload, download, manipulate, move, or copy resources on an Internet Information Server (IIS) or Front Page-capable server.

OPENING A RECORD OR RECORDSET

When working with a Record and Recordset, there is a sort of symbiotic relationship. A Recordset can be a Record and vice versa. When a resultset is created, the top-level node is a Record object. It contains a series of child objects in a collection that can be iterated through using the Recordset object. One of the fields of the Recordset object may be another Record object, which, like the top-level Record object, can contain children that may be iterated through using a Recordset.

The example that we will look at is connecting to a Web server and then iterating through the various documents contained on the server. The connection can be direct, using the Record object, or it can use an existing connection and then assign that to the Record.ActiveConnection object. If a Connection object is used, then the data provider must be defined. Here is an example:

```
Dim grec As Record
strCon = "provider=MSDAIPP.DSO;data source=http://bacchus/XMLProject/"
objConnection.Open strCon
grec.ActiveConnection = objConnection
```

The provider that is used is MSDAIPP.DSO. The data source keyword defines the URL that will be used as a connection. The Connection is made and then assigned to the Record object. The direct way of doing this is to use the Record.Open method, as follows:

```
grec.Open "", "URL=http://bacchus/XMLProject/", , adOpenIfExists Or
adCreateCollection
```

When a Record is opened using the Open method, there are two things that can happen. The first is that the URL references a collection of items. In that case, the Open method will return a Recordset. If a Recordset is to be created, then you need to specify the adCreateCollection flag. The second possibility is that the URL references an individual object. In that case, the Open method will return a Record object, and you will need to specify the Record object for the first parameter of the Open method.

In our example, this parameter has not been specified. Later in this chapter, we will see a Stream example where a Record object will be passed in as a first parameter.

NAVIGATING THE RECORDS

When iterating through a Recordset and retrieving individual Record objects, those Record objects could represent single items or collections of subitems. The individual Record objects may contain child objects that are part of a Recordset collection. To retrieve these collections, the GetChildren method can be called, which returns a Recordset object.

The following code example, based on Active Server Pages (ASP) server-side scripting code, illustrates this:

```
Dim grs As Recordset
Set grs = grec.GetChildren
While Not grs.EOF
value = grs.Fields.Item( 0).Value
grs.MoveNext
Wend
```

The grec variable represents a record that contains a collection of items. To get at those child objects and iterate through them, the grec.GetChildren method is called. This returns a Recordset object, which is assigned to grs. From there, it is possible to iterate through the records of the resultset.

In the preceding code example, we are not iterating through the objects themselves. Instead, we are iterating through objects that have properties that represent the individual elements. This means that in our code example, we are not iterating through the files and subdirectories, but through objects that have properties describing those files and subdirectories. The OLE DB provider is responsible for creating those objects and filling them with the appropriate property values.

A complete list of the properties and their names is given in the following table.

RESOURCE_PARSENAME	The name of the item being parsed. If the document name is sample.doc, then the parsed name will be sample.doc.
RESOURCE_PARENTNAME	The name of the parent of the file or directory. If the item were a document named sample.doc, then the parent would be the URL at which the document can be located.
RESOURCE_ABSOLUTEPARSENAME	The full name of the document. This is a complete URL. If you combine the RESOURCE_PARENTNAME with the RESOURCE_PARSENAME you will get this value.
RESOURCE_ISHIDDEN	Is the document hidden from the selection? To make hidden documents visible they need to be specifically selected.
RESOURCE_ISREADONLY	Is the item read-only? It is not possible to write to a read-only item.
RESOURCE_CONTENTTYPE	The type of content of this document. Usually this is the MIME type (e.g., text/html).
RESOURCE_CONTENTCLASS	Defines the most likely use for this document.
RESOURCE_CONTENTLANGUAGE	Defines the language of the document.
RESOURCE_CREATIONTIME	Defines when the item was created.
RESOURCE_LASTACCESSTIME	Defines when the item was last accessed.
RESOURCE_LASTWRITETIME	Defines when the item was last modified.
RESOURCE_STREAMSIZE	The size of the file or stream that this item represents.
RESOURCE_ISCOLLECTION	Indicates whether the item is a collection that contains children. An example is a directory.
RESOURCE_ISSTRUCTUREDDOCUMENT	Indicates whether the document is structured. A structured document is one that uses OLE to save the contents of the document to a stream. Office documents are an example.
DEFAULT_DOCUMENT	Indicates what the default document in this collection is.
RESOURCE_DISPLAYNAME	The user-friendly name of the item.
RESOURCE_ISROOT	Indicates whether the item is the root of the collection or a structured document.
RESOURCE_ISMARKEDFOROFFLINE	Indicates whether the item is marked to be read offline.

When iterating through a row of a Recordset, you need to retrieve the Record object to manipulate the data associated with the record. To do this, you must instantiate a Record object, and in the Record.Open method, the first parameter is the Recordset object. This automatically binds the current recordset cursor to the Record object. An example of binding the grs Recordset to a Record is as follows:

```
Dim rec As New Record
rec.Open grs
```

To determine whether a `Record` is a collection, you need to check the `RecordType` property. There are three types:

- `adSimpleRecord`: A simple record that does not contain any child nodes
- `adCollectionRecord`: A record that contains child nodes
- `adStructDoc`: A document that represents an OLE-structured document

These flags are used before opening the `Record` object to make sure that there is indeed a subcollection of objects.

Streams

Records can be moved, deleted, or copied directly from the `Record` object. To be able to read or to write to a document, you need to use a stream. A stream is a series of bytes that moves in a specific direction. The ADO `Stream` object is like any other COM `Stream` object and is manipulated like a file.

READING A STREAM

Suppose you are building a Web browsing and administration application and want the capability to download or upload files. The way to download a file is to create a `Stream` object and then associate it with the current `Record` object. When the `Stream` is opened, the direction and mode of the stream must be specified. An example follows:

```
Dim s As Stream
Dim str as string
s.Open grec, adModeRead, adOpenStreamFromRecord
str = s.ReadText(1)
```

The grec object represents the current `Record`, and the last line of the code reads one byte of text into the string variable `str`. Reading data from the stream is not as simple as it appears. Sometimes binary text can be encoded as text, or vice versa. (Encoding specifies how escape sequences are handled. Binary does not handle escape sequences, whereas text does.) To read text using the method `Stream.ReadText`, the property `Stream.Type` needs to be `adTextType`. Otherwise, the `Stream.Read` method should be used to read the data—it can also be used to read text streams. A stream assumes that any text to be read is Unicode.

It is possible to force the data to be read in a specific manner. For example, most HTML files are not Unicode-based; they are ASCII-based. Therefore, before a stream can be read, the `Stream.Charset` property needs to be set to "ascii". This is an example of reading an HTML file:

```
s.Charset = "ascii"
s.Type = adTypeText
str = s.ReadText(adReadAll)
```

When reading data, it is possible to read a block of a specified size, the entire stream (adReadAll), or a line (adReadLine). This is specified as the first parameter to Stream.ReadText.

WRITING A STREAM

It is also possible to upload a file. To do this, a Record must be created, which represents a new file. To add content, a stream needs to be associated with the Record, and then the contents of the file can be written.

```
Dim rec as New Record
Dim s as New Stream
rec.Open "http://bacchus/XMLProject/newfile.txt", , adModeWrite,
adOpenIfExists Or adCreateNonCollection
s.Open rec, adModeWrite, adOpenStreamFromRecord
s.WriteText "<HTML><BODY>Hello2last:world</BODY></HTML>"
```

When the Record is opened, it does not require an explicit creation of a Connection object. This is created implicitly. The resource that is created is passed in as the first parameter. The second parameter is ignored, because the operation is specific to a single entity.

The next parameter, adModeWrite, indicates what the item is to be written to. There are also other usable modes—the concept to keep in mind is that manipulating a stream is like manipulating a file. It is possible to open a Record in read-write mode, or in exclusive-access mode.

The last parameter specifies how the Record is to be opened. For example, when creating a document it may be desirable to open it if it already exists (adOpenIfExists) and to create it as a flat document (adCreateNonCollection).

After the record is opened, it is created on the server. The server creates an empty document. To write data to the document, a Stream object has to be opened. This is done using the method Stream.Open and passing in as the first parameter the opened Record. When the Stream object is opened, the correct direction (adModeWrite) is indicated. The last parameter (adOpenStreamFromRecord) indicates that the first parameter is a Record object.

Finally, data can be written to the stream using Stream.WriteText. The rules regarding binary and text data also apply to writing a file.

PERSISTING AS XML

It is possible to persist a Recordset as an XML file. This can be very useful for interacting with other systems that may not be Windows 2000-based or OLE DB-based. On the Recordset object, there is a method called Save that will persist the contents of the resultset to a file or a stream. For example, to write a resultset to an XML file, the following code is executed:

```
objConnection.conferenceGet 2, resultSet
resultset.Save "c:\example.xml", adPersistXML
```

In the `resultset.Save` method, where the `resultset` is of the data type `Recordset`, the last parameter `adPersistXML` indicates that the contents should be saved as XML. It is possible to save the resultset as a Microsoft data format (adPersistADTG). To edit the file, the *destination* URL is specified in `Recordset.Open`.

Data Shaping with ADO

When you are working with relational data, you may be required to drill down to a specific piece of data. Drilling into the data means opening a recordset and reading some values. Based on those values, you may open another recordset and retrieve some more data, and this process could go on for several iterations. What you are doing is creating a parent-child relationship between various data sets. All of this can be optimized using the OLE DB data-shaping provider.

Using the Data-Shaping Provider

Consider the following situation. Every conference has attendees, and to represent this in database terms there would be a `Conference` and an `Attendee` table. To determine which attendees are attending which conference, a `JOIN` could be created. The `SELECT` statement could be as follows:

```
SELECT Conferences.id, Conferences.description, attendees.name
FROM Conferences INNER JOIN
attendees ON Conferences.id = attendees.conference_attend
ORDER BY Conferences.id
```

This statement is correct, but it is not optimal. Let's say that there are 20 attendees of a particular conference. That means the `Conference.id` and `Conferences.description` are repeated 20 times.

A better approach is to create a hierarchy, where the details of the conference are displayed and then the details of each attendee would follow. This, in effect, means that there would be two recordsets, and the standard OLE DB providers do not offer this functionality.

The previous `SELECT` statement could be converted into a generic-shaped statement, as follows:

```
SHAPE  {select * from conferences} As conferences
APPEND ({select * from attendees} RELATE id TO conference_attend) AS con-
fAttend
```

Every `SHAPE` command starts with the `SHAPE` keyword, followed by a set of curly braces. Inside the curly braces is the parent command. This command is dependent on the database being used. In this example, we are using Microsoft SQL Server, and therefore the command is a `SELECT` statement. The parent command initializes a recordset.

A resultset can be appended to the parent that is based on a value of a field in the parent command. To do this, the APPEND command is used in the context of the SHAPE command.

The APPEND command contains a subcommand between curly braces. To relate the subcommand to the parent command, a JOIN must be created using the RELATE command. In this case, the relation is from the attendees.conference_attend field to the conferences.id field. The first field identifier after the RELATE command is the field that is used to establish a child relationship. The field is from the resultset of the parent, and in this case, it is exposed as the confAttend data field.

Many of the things that the SHAPE command can do can be replicated with a more complicated SQL JOIN. However, the SHAPE command uses resources more effectively, because it queries and retrieves information on an as-needed basis.

Coding a Shaped Command

Now let's put the preceding explanation into practice. To code a shaped command, we will use two different OLE DB providers. The primary one is the Shaped OLE DB Provider. The secondary one will accept the commands to create resultsets. In our example, the secondary OLE DB provider is Microsoft SQL Server.

The two different OLE DB providers are realized by defining the correct OLE DB connection string. For our example, the implementation is as follows:

```
strCon = "Provider=MSDataShape;Data Provider=sqloledb;Data Source=bacchus;" & _
"Initial Catalog=TestDatabase;User Id=sa;Password=; "
objConnection.Open strCon
```

In the connection string, the primary OLE DB provider is MSDataShape and it is associated with the Provider keyword. The secondary OLE DB provider is sqloledb, which is defined by the key Data Provider.

Navigating the Data

After the data connection is established, we need to execute the SHAPE command that we just created. To do this, we'll create a Recordset object and then pass the SHAPE command in to the Open method. The Recordset that is created will be based on the primary SHAPE command.

To retrieve the results of the subcommand, the confAttend data field is retrieved, and this field contains another Recordset that can be navigated. This establishes our drill-down pattern.

The sample implementation code is as follows:

```
rsConference.StayInSync = False
rsConference.Open "SHAPE  {select * from conferences} " & _
"APPEND ({select * from attendees} " & _
"RELATE id TO conference_attend) AS confAttend", objConnection
While Not rsConference.EOF
```

```
Debug.Print rsConference.Fields("id"), rsConference.Fields("description")
Set rsAttendee = rsConference.Fields("confAttend").Value
While Not rsAttendee.EOF
    Debug.Print rsAttendee.Fields("name")
    rsAttendee.MoveNext
Wend
set rsAttendee = nothing
rsConference.MoveNext
Wend
```

The root Recordset is rsConference, and it opens the main Recordset. The Recordset.StayInSync property is set to FALSE. In default mode (TRUE), when a recordset is opened using a parent-child relationship, the child recordset changes whenever the parent changes. Navigation is therefore more complicated because the subcommand is automatically executed.

The child rsAttendee recordset is assigned from the field rsConference.Fields("confAttend").value. From there the Recordset is navigated until there are no records available. After the Recordset subcommand is exhausted, the parent command moves to the next record and the Recordset subcommand is retrieved and navigated.

Performing Computations

When using data shaping, it is possible to apply aggregate functions. An aggregate function is one in which a calculation is performed over a number of records but only the end result of the calculation is of interest. For example, instead of retrieving all of the attendees of the conference, you might want to count how may attendees there are per conference. The SHAPE command would be used as follows:

```
SHAPE {select * from attendees} AS rs
COMPUTE Count( rs.id) as conference_count, rs BY conference_attend
```

Here, a new form of the shape is to use the command COMPUTE. This command makes it possible to select a series of rows, perform a computation, and then display the details of that computation. In the previous example, the main command that selects all of the attendees is a child command. The main command is what follows the COMPUTE statement. The statement says that for all of the attendees, Count the number of records grouped by conference (conference_attend). This is the main query. Then, as a subquery, select all of the attendees that correlate to the individual conferences, as per the result set rs. The implementation of this code is as follows:

```
rsConference.StayInSync = False
rsConference.Open "SHAPE {select * from attendees} AS rs " & _
"COMPUTE Count( rs.id) as conference_count, rs BY conference_attend",
objConnection
```

```
While Not rsConference.EOF
Debug.Print rsConference.Fields("conference_count")
Set rsAttendee = rsConference.Fields("rs").Value
While Not rsAttendee.EOF
    Debug.Print rsAttendee.Fields("name")
    rsAttendee.MoveNext
Wend
rsConference.MoveNext
Wend
```

The COUNT(rs.id) column has the alias conference_count. This is needed so that it can be specified in the Recordset. Notice that the main recordset iteration is the COMPUTE statement and that rs is a field that contains the child recordset. You could also use other commands, such as SUM, AVG, or STDEV (standard deviation).

Embedding Multiple SHAPE Statements

It is possible to have multiple SHAPE statements. This could be coded manually, but that would be too complicated and too error prone. A better way of building a multiple-level SHAPE statement is to use the Visual Basic Data Environment designer and then embed commands. Consider the following multiple-level command structure.

Figure 16–4 shows a multiple-level command structure. There is a top-level shape command called shpCountry, and this shape command could be a table, a stored procedure, a view, or a complicated SELECT. Whatever the command is, it will have a resultset. In this case, the resultset is the fields id and country. You can add a child command by right-clicking and using the context menu. Again, like the parent, it could be a table, a stored procedure, or something else. The only catch is that a relationship must be established.

Figure 16–4: Example of multiple commands

To edit one of the relationships, right-click the relationship and select Properties to display a dialog box similar to the one shown in Figure 16–5. In that dialog box, the child command has set up a relationship to the parent object shpCountry, and the relationship is that the parent field id is joined to the child field country_id.

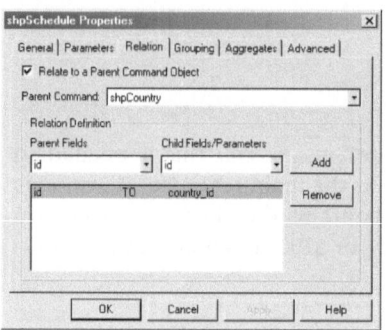

Figure 16–5: Example of relation to parent

Finally, as was shown in Figure 16–4, there is yet another child object called shpAttendee, which has a relationship with shpSchedule. As a result, the following SHAPE command is generated from the Visual Basic Data Environment:

```
rsCountry.Open " SHAPE {SELECT * FROM Country} " & _
"APPEND (( SHAPE {SELECT * FROM Planned_Schedule} " & _
"APPEND ({SELECT * FROM attendees}  " & _
"RELATE 'conference_id' TO 'conference_attend') AS shpAttendee) AS
shpSchedule " & _
"RELATE 'id' TO 'country_id') AS shpSchedule", objConnection
```

The result is that the two SHAPE commands are nested like an XML command. You can access them as you would access a nested Recordset.

Writing More Complex SHAPE Commands

Instead of reading about all of the details of the SHAPE command, it is much simpler to simply use the Data Environment Shape Editor. It has support for not only the nested SHAPE, but for COMPUTE and grouping functionality. By using this environment, you do not need to manually edit the SHAPE command. I tend to design the SHAPE in the editor, and then copy it to the appropriate programming code.

Putting It in Perspective

This chapter introduced the UDA data-access technology. The ADO and OLE DB providers are a large part of that technology. ADO can be used in various languages because it is COM based. However, the true power of the ADO and OLE DB data-access technology shows up in its capability to access and work with any kind of data.

ADO and OLE DB provide a very clear line between COM+ business object functionality and data-access technology, which makes for applications that are much more robust. You should keep this clear distinction in mind when you develop your applications. For example, if you have written business objects that manage persistence, perhaps you should think about writing an OLE DB provider. If you are using Visual Basic, you could write an OLE DB Simple Provider (this was discussed in Chapter 14).

So, how does XML fit in this picture? It is likely to become yet another OLE DB provider. However, the exact details won't be apparent until the release of Visual Studio 7.0. The only thing that we can be certain of now is that XML will be used to exchange data between different platforms.

Chapter 17

Optimizing the Data Access Tier

This chapter introduces you to optimizing the data access tier. Adding data to the database is not complicated, and the code to do it can be written relatively quickly. But, Active Data Objects (ADO) is slower when used in iterative programming scenarios, and there are instances when you want to optimize the data-access layer.

The technology that this chapter discusses is Object Linking and Embedding Database (OLE DB) consumer templates. These templates are a thin wrapper for the OLE DB consumer interfaces. They make it easier to write Visual C++ code without sacrificing speed. We'll look at the various OLE DB consumer templates and how they relate to our database access architecture. Then, toward the end of this chapter, we'll look at various specialized topics, such as reading larger amounts of data and tuning data access using multiple accessors.

OLE DB Consumer Template Classes

The OLE DB consumer template classes are intended to be used by Visual C++ programmers, because Visual C++ programmers need speed and native data access. When using ADO, the native data type is a VARIANT, and while this is okay for Visual Basic or scripting, it is more cumbersome than using a native data type. The OLE DB consumer templates solve this problem by converting the native SQL data types to their C++ counterparts.

To understand the OLE DB consumer templates, you only need to think of connecting to a data source and then viewing the data as two separate steps. In an ADO data connection, you execute an SQL command that returns a resultset. The consumer of the resultset has a view of the data as defined by the SQL command. OLE DB consumer templates go one step further, because they enable you to define how you want to view that resultset.

Let's look at a really simple example of viewing some data based on a resultset. Suppose you are building an Internet-based music Web site that will sell MP3 audio files. The client should be capable of building a query based on the genre of music and current hits. When the query returns a resultset, it will contain description information and the MP3 files represented by data fields in the resultset. Because the client is searching, the client will not want to listen to every MP3 data field. Hence, creating a query that returns every MP3 file would be inefficient. In ADO, you could optimize this by returning a Uniform Resource Locator

(URL) data field that defines where the actual MP3 file is stored instead of returning the MP3 files. With OLE DB consumer templates, you can define your resultset view such that it only loads the contents of the fields that you want. This means you can have MP3 data fields and only load them on demand. This optimizes data access when you are working with large data fields.

Here are some points that should be kept in mind when developing consumers of OLE DB consumer templates:

- All data items should be kept in structures. Other database middleware layers use disparate variables, but by keeping the data within a structure, it becomes more object-oriented and manageable. However, this does require centralized structures and access. Doing this will keep in tune with our database access strategy which is an implementation of the *data abstraction* pattern.
- Use the right class for the right task. Each OLE DB consumer template class provides for specific functionality, and each should be used for that specific purpose.
- Treat stored-procedure resultset interfaces like COM interfaces. It is okay to add features, but bad to remove them. When interfaces change, a numeric identifier should be appended to the stored procedure or view. Changes have ramifications for the structures used to retrieve the resultsets.
- If you do not like the functionality being offered by the OLE DB consumer templates, create your own classes that use the base functionality contained within the OLE DB consumer templates. Do not worry that your classes may be incompatible—the OLE DB consumer templates are designed with this capability.

There are three pieces in the OLE DB consumer template architecture: Connection classes, Execution classes, and Viewing classes. These classes are implemented as shown in Figure 17–1.

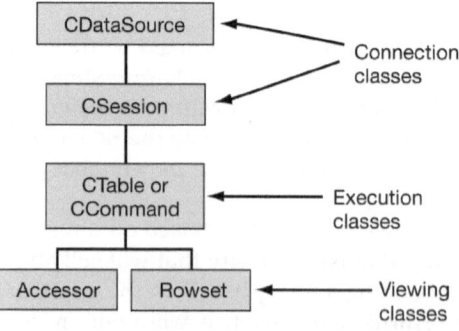

Figure 17–1: Architectural layout of OLE DB templates

Connection Classes

Three classes are used to connect to the resource: CDataSource, CEnumerator, and CSession. With these classes, it is possible to iterate through the OLE DB Connection attribute objects and connect to the resource.

OLE DB providers are Component Object Model (COM) objects written to a specific set of interfaces. This is unlike ODBC, in which the provider dynamic link library (DLL) implements a series of functions, and there is an open database connectivity (ODBC) manager that redirects each ODBC call to the appropriate DLL. With OLE DB, everything is a COM interface and there is no thinly layered OLE DB manager.

Execution Classes

The next group of classes—CTable, CCommand, and CMultipleResultsCommand—let you retrieve a resultset. These classes bind a resource command (in our case it is a Structured Query Language (SQL) command) and the resultset to a view. The three classes can be grouped into two separate groups: CTable accesses a database table directly, and CCommand and CMultipleResultsCommand execute some command and get a resultset. It is possible to write your own execution class, but you will need to derive your functionality from the CAccessorRowset or CCommandBase class.

The Viewing Classes

Once a resultset is returned, it needs to be bound to a view. In the lingo of OLE DB consumer templates, this is called an *accessor*. There are multiple accessors: CAccessor, CDynamicAccessor, CDynamicParameterAccessor, and CManualAccessor.

Each accessor is different and solves a different problem. Here is a short explanation of what each is best suited for:

- CAccessor is a static accessor and is generated by the ATL (Active Template Library) OLE DB consumer wizard. It maps SQL data types to C++ data types, creating a C++ structure that is based on the resultset created by the Execution classes.
- CDynamicAccessor and CDynamicParameterAccessor are dynamic accessors that dynamically generate all of the information needed. The dynamic accessor does this by querying the database for resultset and command-type information. That information is then used to instantiate a series of COM objects that represents the SQL command parameters and resultset data fields. The downside to using this class is that it requires a round trip for the type information. Using this class is not as efficient as using CAcessor.
- CManualAccessor is an accessor for which the developer must specify all the characteristics of the resultset view. This is a low-level accessor, and it enables you to tune the resultset view to fit any condition. It is the most complex and tedious accessor to use.

An OLE DB Consumer Template Example

When writing an OLE DB consumer template client, you will often use the same programming code. The accessor that you generally use is CAccessor. It offers the best performance and the fewest problems in terms of coding. It also fits into our stored procedure architecture very well.

Building the Template Class

Our simple example is based on the process of manipulating a user in the conference registration Web site. The user will be manipulated using a direct table connection, and later by using stored procedures.

Let's look at the SQL table definition again, because it will be used to generate our resultset.

```
CREATE TABLE users (
id int,
firstName varchar (255) ,
lastName varchar (255) ,
password varchar (64),
email varchar (255) ,
group int,
status int
)
```

The resultset that is created is a direct mapping of the Users table. The CAccessor template is used to map this information to something that Visual C++ can manipulate. The CAccessor based class can be automatically generated using the OLE DB consumer template wizard. Running the OLE DB consumer template wizard against the Users table generates the following C++ data class:

```
class CdbousersAccessor
{
public:
LONG m_id;
TCHAR m_firstName[256];
TCHAR m_lastName[256];
TCHAR m_email[256];
TCHAR m_password[65];
LONG m_groupId;
LONG m_status;

BEGIN_COLUMN_MAP(CdbousersAccessor)
COLUMN_ENTRY(1, m_id)
COLUMN_ENTRY(2, m_firstName)
COLUMN_ENTRY(3, m_lastName)
COLUMN_ENTRY(4, m_email)
COLUMN_ENTRY(5, m_password)
```

```
COLUMN_ENTRY(6, m_groupId)
COLUMN_ENTRY(7, m_status)
END_COLUMN_MAP()
};
```

There are two sections to this C++ data class. The first part of the class contains the various data types that correlate to the Users table. The data types are of fixed length. This is a very important characteristic of accessors and the OLE DB architecture.

When an OLE DB consumer and provider communicate, they need to exchange resultset data. In previous technologies, the way in which this data was exchanged was not specified. With OLE DB, though, it is specified. In OLE DB, a record in a resultset has to be a contiguous piece of data in memory, which means that no pointers are allowed within the context of an accessor. This is enforced because it is more efficient when transferring data in memory. However, it also has a downside. Suppose you decided to change the position of m_lastName and m_groupId in the C++ data class declaration. There is no error when the data in memory is copied, but because the definition of the resultset does not match the C++ class, the data will be corrupted.

The second part of the C++ data class defines a series of macros that are required by OLE DB because they define the boundaries and types of the individual data fields represented within the memory block. If we were to change the positions of m_lastName and m_groupId, we would also need to change the positions of the m_lastName and m_groupId COLUMN_ENTRY macros, and then the data would be copied properly again.

Opening the Table

The CdbousersAccessor class is used to view the resultset, but there needs to be a class that generates the resultset. This is an execution class, and it is responsible for opening the database and performing the execution. In this case, the execution is performed directly on the Users table. When the OLE DB consumer template wizard is used to generate the viewing class, it also generates the execution class. In this case, the execution class is based on CTable and is defined as follows:

```
class Cdbousers :
public CTable<CAccessor<CdbousersAccessor> >
{
public:
HRESULT Open() {
    HRESULT       hr;
    hr = OpenDataSource();
    if (FAILED(hr))
        return hr;
    return OpenRowset();
}
```

```
HRESULT OpenDataSource() {
    HRESULT        hr;
    CDataSource db;
    CDBPropSet    dbinit(DBPROPSET_DBINIT);

    dbinit.AddProperty(DBPROP_AUTH_USERID, OLESTR("sa"));
    dbinit.AddProperty(DBPROP_INIT_DATASOURCE, OLESTR("SQLRegistration"));
    dbinit.AddProperty(DBPROP_INIT_PROMPT, (short)4);
    dbinit.AddProperty(DBPROP_INIT_LCID, (long)1033);
    hr = db.Open(_T("MSDASQL"), &dbinit);
    if (FAILED(hr))
        return hr;
    return m_session.Open(db);
}
HRESULT OpenRowset() {
    // Set properties for open
    CDBPropSet    propset(DBPROPSET_ROWSET);
    propset.AddProperty(DBPROP_IRowsetChange, true);
    propset.AddProperty(DBPROP_UPDATABILITY, DBPROPVAL_UP_CHANGE |
DBPROPVAL_UP_INSERT | DBPROPVAL_UP_DELETE);

    return CTable<CAccessor<CdbousersAccessor> >::Open(m_session,
_T("dbo.users"), &propset);
}
CSession    m_session;
};
```

This class declaration shows how the execution classes bind a resultset accessor together with rowset functionality. Rowset functionality refers to how data in the view of the resultset is retrieved and stored.

All of the execution classes have default parameters, but to make them do something useful you need to specify the accessor that will be used. In this example, the resultset will be mapped to the CAccessor class, and the CAccessor template requires a data structure to hold the record of the resultset, which in this case is CdbousersAcessor. This results in the CAccessor template being expanded in the CTable template. While this is a more complex version of a template, the different parameters of the data-access layer are bound at compile time and this results in a more efficient application. The other option is to bind all of the elements at run-time, which is slower.

There are three methods in this class providing two basic functions. The first function is to open a database connection to the resource (this is the OpenDataSource method). The second function is to open a resultset based on the open data connection (this is the OpenRowset method). The Open method combines the two functions in one method.

OPENING THE DATA SOURCE

The `OpenDataSource` method is used to build a connection to the data source that contains the data. Within the `OpenDataSource` method are a series of calls to `dbinit.AddProperty`. These calls are wrappers that create structures used by the OLE DB interfaces.

OLE DB does not use explicit methods to set the properties of the data resource because there is no single set of properties. Each data provider can have its own properties. The simpler way of setting properties is to use a method that sets the data provider properties using a key value technique.

After the properties are set, use the `db.Open` method to open a connection to the resource. In our example, the resource is `MSDASQL`, which is the OLE DB-to-ODBC bridge. For our testing purposes, this is okay, but in production, you should use a native OLE DB provider, because it is faster.

After the connection is open to the resource, a session for the user is opened using `m_session.pen(db)`.

OPENING THE ROWSET

The `OpenRowset` method uses `m_session` to open a particular table. And when you build a database connection, the properties specifying how the table is to be opened are defined by calling the method `propset.AddProperty`.

When the table is being operated on, you can specify a database cursor location and operations to be performed on the table. For example, the `DBPROP_UPDATEABILITY` property enables resultsets to be updated. Multiple operations can be `OR`'d together. After the properties are set, the table is opened using the following template expansion:

```
CTable< CAccessor< CdbousersAccessor>>::Open
```

Now, let's consider how we can use the different open methods. If you are going to instantiate the `Cdbousers` class once and use the resultset once, then you only need to call the `Cdbousers.Open` method.

However, if you intend to open the resultset and then open it again at a later point in time, you need to change your calling sequence. The first time that you open the resultset, you need to call the `Cdbousers.Open` method, and when you are done using the resultset you need to close it by calling `Cdbousers.Close`. Then, when you are ready to open another resultset, you need to call the method `Cdbousers.OpenRowset` because the connection is already open. Calling `Cdbousers.Open` results in an open database connection error.

Testing the Classes

To fully understand the calling sequence for using the OLE DB consumer templates, consider the following client implementation code:

```
int main(int argc, char* argv[])
{
```

```
CoInitialize( NULL);
try {
    Cdbousers users;

    _com_util::CheckError( users.Open());
    if( strcmp( argv[ 1], "-add") == 0) {
        // We want to add a record to the database
        strcpy( users.m_email, "cgross@eusoft.com");
        strcpy( users.m_firstName, "Christian");
        strcpy( users.m_lastName, "Gross");
        strcpy( users.m_password, "something");
        users.m_groupId = 0;
        users.m_status = 1;
        users.m_id = 1;
        users.Insert( 0);
    }
    users.Close();
} catch( _com_error err) {
    printf(" Oooops an error happened.... %s\n", err.ErrorMessage());
}
CoUninitialize();
return 0;
}
```

This program first calls user.Open to open the resource and connect to it. At this point, the resultset is open, but it is not bound to the CdbousersAccessor class. What we want to do is insert a record, so binding to the first record in the resultset is not necessary. To add a record, the data needs to be set by assigning values to the CdbousersAccessor data members (m_email, m_firstName, and so on). After the values are set, the data is inserted into the database using users.Insert. The 0 parameter in the users.Insert method specifies the accessor that is being used. We discuss this parameter in the "Using Multiple Accessors" section of this chapter.

Suppose that instead of inserting data in the database that we want to read the resultset and display it. After the users.Open method is called, we need to bind the data to the CdboUsersAccessor. This is done automatically when the users.MoveNext method is called. After that method is called, the data members of CdboUsersAccessor will contain a valid record from the resultset. Here is an example implementation of this scenario, added as a second if statement to the previous code example:

```
...
} else if( strcmp( argv[ 1], "-read") == 0) {
        while( users.MoveNext() == S_OK) {
            printf( "Record is %s %s email: %s password: %s\n",
                users.m_firstName, users.m_lastName,
```

```
users.m_email, users.m_password);
        }
    }
...
```

Calling Stored Procedures

Now let's consider how to write OLE DB consumer template code using stored procedures or SQL commands. We will use the CCommand execution class instead of the CTable class because it fits better in our architecture. The stored procedure that we will call in this example adds two numbers and then returns the value. In contrast to ADO, which provided a one-column, one-row resultset for the return value, this return value will use an SQL out parameter.

The definition of the addAndReturn stored procedure is as follows:

```
Create Procedure addAndReturn
    @var1 int,
    @var2 int,
    @value int OUTPUT
As
    Select @value = @var1 + @var2
    return 0
```

The stored procedure adds two numbers (@var1@var2@value). The return value of 0 is used to indicate that everything went correctly.

You can use the OLE DB consumer template wizard to generate the OLE DB consumer template for the addAndReturn stored procedure. The OLE DB consumer template wizard will generate a CCommand template as the execution class. For the viewing class, the following source code for the CAccessor structure class will be generated:

```
class CdboaddAndReturn1Accessor {
public:
LONG m_RETURNVALUE;
LONG m_var1;
LONG m_var2;
LONG m_value;

BEGIN_PARAM_MAP(CdboaddAndReturn1Accessor)
SET_PARAM_TYPE(DBPARAMIO_OUTPUT)
COLUMN_ENTRY(1, m_RETURNVALUE)
SET_PARAM_TYPE(DBPARAMIO_INPUT)
COLUMN_ENTRY(2, m_var1)
COLUMN_ENTRY(3, m_var2)
SET_PARAM_TYPE(DBPARAMIO_INPUT | DBPARAMIO_OUTPUT)
```

```
COLUMN_ENTRY(4, m_value)
END_PARAM_MAP()

DEFINE_COMMAND(CdboaddAndReturn1Accessor, _T("{ CALL dbo.addAndReturn;1
(?,?,?,?) }"))
};
```

The first part of CdboaddAndReturn1Accessor is a C++ mapping of the SQL data types. In this case, they represent the stored-procedure parameters. There are no resultset data members because when the OLE DB consumer template wizard generated the code, it queried Microsoft SQL Server for resultset information. This only works if the data provider supports dynamic querying, which Microsoft SQL Server does. Otherwise, the OLE DB template wizard will not generate a proper accessor mapping and you will have to tweak it so that it matches what the stored procedure generates.

The middle part of the CdboaddAndReturn1Accessor class defines the stored procedure parameter mapping. Notice that this mapping is very similar to the previous C++ CdbousersAccessor data class mapping of the resultset columns, which are defined by the BEGIN_COLUMN_MAP macro. Both mappings are similar because OLE DB passes the stored procedure data as a contiguous memory block. The stored procedure data block in memory must observe the same rules as the resultset data block in memory. The stored procedure memory block has an additional optimization to indicate which SQL stored procedure parameters are input values and which are output values.

The column entries (the COLUMN_ENTRY lines) define the stored procedure parameters. When the SET_PARAM_TYPE macro is used, all stored procedure parameters after the MACRO declaration have the same direction attributes. For example, the first parameter in the preceding code, m_RETURNVALUE, is an output. The second parameter, m_var1, is an input. The third parameter does not have any declaration, which means it uses the last parameter type declaration, which is input. If there are no parameter declarations in the column declaration, the default of input is assumed.

The last part of the structure, the DEFINE_COMMAND macro, is the definition of a default command that is executed when the CdboaddAndReturn1.Open method is called. The macro can be used to define any type of database command. In our example, it calls a stored procedure, but it also could have been an SQL SELECT command.

Executing the Command

Now let's look at how the CdboaddAndReturn1Accessor class is used in a sample client. You will notice that it is very similar to the CTable example presented earlier in the "Opening the Table" section. The difference is that when the CdboaddAndReturn1.Open method is called, the parameters of the CdboaddAndReturn1Accessor class must be set. Consider the following implementation:

```
CoInitialize( NULL);
try {
CdboaddAndReturn1 var;

var.m_var1 = 2;
var.m_var2 = 3;
_com_util::CheckError( var.Open());

printf("The answer of adding %ld and %ld is %ld\n", var.m_var1, var.m_var2,
var.m_value);

var.Close();
} catch( _com_error err) {
printf(" Oooops an error happened.... %s\n", err.ErrorMessage());
}
CoUninitialize();
```

Using Multiple Accessors

We have seen two types of column maps: parameter maps and resultset maps.
Now I want to do examine some details of the resultset maps. Remember the
music example. In that example, I said that with OLE DB consumer templates
you have the capability to do resultset binding on demand. The examples thus far
are all autobinding. By examining some of the details of resultset maps, you will
learn how to bind the data manually.

OPENING STATIC ACCESSORS

Now recall the CdbousersAccessor class, which is a C++ data class. In the second
half of the class declaration, there was a BEGIN_COLUMN_MAP macro declaration.
That macro expands to the following:

```
#define BEGIN_COLUMN_MAP(x) \
BEGIN_ACCESSOR_MAP(x, 1) \
    BEGIN_ACCESSOR(0, true)
```

The BEGIN_COLUM_MAP macro is used to define a single accessor map, and the
BEGIN_ACCESSOR_MAP macro opens the multiple accessor map. The first parameter
of BEGIN_ACCESSOR_MAP is the name of the class that contains the various data
members that will be used to bind the resultset to the memory block. The
second parameter of BEGIN_ACCESSOR_MAP defines how many accessors will be
present in the map.

The BEGIN_ACCESSOR macro defines the starting point of an accessor, and the
first parameter of BEGIN_ACCESSOR defines the ID of the accessor. This ID is used
when the resultset is bound to the memory block defined by the C++ data class. The
second parameter of BEGIN_ACCESSOR defines whether or not autobinding is used.

When using an accessor, the accessor binds the data to the consumer. When
a command is executed, a resultset is created on the database server, and OLE

DB receives a reference to that server-side resultset. The next step is to move the data from the database server to the consumer. This is referred to as binding the resultset to a local memory block. The consumer determines how the data is bound to the memory block. With OLE DB consumer templates, the second step can be delayed and defined manually. If the autobinding is set to FALSE, then the resultset remains as a reference. When the C++ data class is bound to the resultset, the accessor defines which data fields in the resultset are bound.

DEFINING A SIMPLE MULTIPLE ACCESSOR

Now let's implement the music selection application. Consider the following music table definition:

```
CREATE TABLE [dbo].[Music] (
[id] [int] IDENTITY (1, 1) NOT NULL ,
[song_name] [varchar] (255) NOT NULL ,
[description] [varchar] (512) NOT NULL ,
[song] [binary] (10) NULL ,
[genre] [varchar] (64) NOT NULL ,
[artist] [varchar] (64) NOT NULL)
```

The table will store the full MP3 song file in the song data field, which is of the type binary. However, what we want to do is create two accessors: the first to retrieve the song details and the second to actually retrieve the song. The song can be retrieved using either a SELECT statement or a stored procedure.

Because we have already seen how to call a stored procedure using the CCommand object, let's use a parameterized SELECT statement. You use this method when querying a SQL view. The C++ data class is implemented as follows:

```
class CMusicAccessor {
public:
LONG m_id;
TCHAR m_songname[ 255];
TCHAR m_description[ 64];
TCHAR m_genre[ 64];
TCHAR m_artist[ 64];
ISequentialStream*      pSong;

BEGIN_ACCESSOR_MAP(CMusicAccessor, 2)
BEGIN_ACCESSOR( 0, true)
    COLUMN_ENTRY(1, m_id)
    COLUMN_ENTRY(2, m_songname)
    COLUMN_ENTRY(3, m_description)
    COLUMN_ENTRY(4, m_genre)
    COLUMN_ENTRY(5, m_artist)
END_ACCESSOR()
BEGIN_ACCESSOR( 1, false)
```

```
    BLOB_ENTRY(6, IID_ISequentialStream, STGM_READ, pSong)
END_ACCESSOR()
END_ACCESSOR_MAP()

BEGIN_PARAM_MAP(CMusicAccessor)
COLUMN_ENTRY(1, m_genre)
END_PARAM_MAP()

DEFINE_COMMAND(CMusicAccessor, _T(" \
SELECT id, song_name, description, genre, artist, song \
FROM Music WHERE genre = ?"))
};
```

This class demonstrates how to combine a parameter map with a resultset map. The SQL command is defined in the DEFINE_COMMAND macro, and this SELECT statement includes a SQL WHERE statement that performs a parameterization. In the case of the CMusicAccessor class, the parameter selects the genre of music as defined by the question mark. When the CMusicAccessor class is bound to an execution class, the SELECT statement generates a six-column resultset. However, to generate that resultset, a parameter is sent to the server specifying the genre of music. The parameter map is defined by the BEGIN_PARAM_MAP macro and only needs one column entry to represent the genre parameter. This data member is going to be shared with both the parameter map and the column map, which is okay because the parameter map specifies that the genre is an input-only parameter. Had genre been an output parameter, an additional data member would need to be declared—if it were not declared, it would not cause an error, but it would overwrite the memory when the resultset was bound to the data members.

Now let's consider the resultset map (BEGIN_ACCESSOR_MAP). There are two accessors, with IDs of 0 and 1. The 0 accessor binds the resultset data automatically. This accessor contains the data fields m_id (Music.id), m_songname (Music.song_name), m_description (Music.description), m_genre (Music.genre), and m_artist (Music.artist). The resultset contains also the song data field, which is a binary, but because it is part of the second accessor, it is not bound until requested. The 1 accessor contains only one data field: pSong (Music.song). The difference between the two accessors is that the data field index (the second parameter of COLUMN_ENTRY) is based on the location of the resultset of the SQL command.

The CMusicAccessor is bound to the CCommand-based CMusic class. Because it is identical in functionality to previous CCommand-based execution classes, the implementation of CMusic is not shown. When a consumer instantiates CMusic and calls CMusic.Open, the 0 accessor is automatically bound to the resultset. To retrieve the 1 accessor, you need to call the CMusic.GetData method with the ID of the accessor that should be bound. An example implementation is as follows:

```
CMusic music;

strcpy( music.m_genre, "Techno");
```

```
music.Open();

music.MoveFirst();
do {
    printf( "Music song is %s, %s\n", music.m_artist, music.m_songname);
    if( music.m_id > 0) {
        music.GetData( 1);
        // Do something with the accessor
    }
} while (music.MoveNext() == S_OK);
}
```

When iterating through the resultset, the Music.GetData method has to be called whenever the record is changed. This is because the contents are not automatically updated as the iteration moves the cursor from one record to the next.

The only step that we haven't looked at here is how to manipulate the binary data. We'll look at that later in the chapter, when we discuss BLOB (binary large objects) data.

More on COLUMN_ENTRY

To this point, the defined columns are simple columns that contain straight memory variables. The default COLUMN_ENTRY macros have the capability to automatically map the C++ data types to the SQL data types. However, there are instances where you need to control how the SQL data is managed in memory or how it is converted to C++ data types. Column macros can be used for this purpose, and we will look at a few of them.

COLUMN_ENTRY_EX

There are situations when an SQL data type needs to be explicitly mapped to a specific C++ data type. For example, you may want to map an SQL numeric data type to a C++ char string data type. The column entries need to have an explicit data-type mapping, and the macro that does this is as follows:

```
COLUMN_ENTRY_EX(nOrdinal, wType, nLength, nPrecision, nScale, data, length,
status)
```

The macro defines the consumer column properties. For example, when the length is specified, it is in reference to the C++ data-class member.

The nOrdinal parameter defines the location of the field in the resultset or the parameter set, which starts at 1.

The wType parameter defines the type of the variable that is being bound. The binding could be string, date, globally unique identifier (GUID), or real numbers, and it is based on the OLE DB data-type enumerator DBTYPEENUM. You can define COM interfaces (DBTYPE_IUNKNOWN and DBTYPE_IDISPATCH) as data fields, but if you do, check the database documentation for which COM interfaces are being exposed.

The nLength parameter is used to define the length of the string the C++ data class is exposing. The nScale and nPrecision parameters are used when you want to define your own view for an SQL numeric data type. The length parameter specifies the actual length of the data that was bound. The status parameter is explained later, under the "COLUMN_ENTRY_STATUS" heading.

COLUMN_ENTRY_TYPE

This column entry is like the regular COLUMN_ENTRY macro except that the specific data type is clarified. For example, if your data type is a redefinition of another base type, the C++ template compiler may generate an error indicating that it can- not do a safe typecast. Because you know what the base type actually is, though, you can specify the typecast that should be used. The macro is defined as follows:

COLUMN_ENTRY_TYPE(nOrdinal, wType, data)

The wType parameter specifies what the data member variable is. The wType parameter is a declaration of type DBTYPEENUM.

COLUMN_ENTRY_LENGTH

There are situations in which you do not know the length of the C++ data type. Typically, this is because the C++ template compiler cannot figure it out, or you are specifying the boundaries of a generic buffer. To explicitly specify the length of a C++ data type, the following macro is used:

COLUMN_ENTRY_LENGTH(nOrdinal, data, length)

The length parameter specifies the length of the C++ data member.

COLUMN_ENTRY_TYPE_SIZE

COLUMN_ENTRY_TYPE_SIZE(nOrdinal, wType, nLength, data)

This macro combines both COLUMN_ENTRY_TYPE and COLUMN_ENTRY_LENGTH so that the type and the length can be specified. It is easier to use than the COLUMN_ENTRY_EX macro because it does not require that you specify every detail of the column or parameter.

COLUMN_ENTRY_STATUS

When retrieving data from a resultset, there may be times when the retrieval is not successful. This may have something to do with a specific field. For example, the binary retrieval in the music application described earlier in the chapter might fail. Or perhaps the data field conversion truncated some significant digits. If you use generic errors, it is not possible to identify which fields caused the error. With OLE DB consumer templates, it is possible to add a status flag to the COLUMN_ENTRY map entry.

The status flag determines whether the data-field retrieval was a success, a partial failure, or a complete failure. An example of a status-enabled column-entry macro is as follows:

```
COLUMN_ENTRY_STATUS(nOrdinal, data, status)
```

The status parameter is of type DBSTATUSENUM, and it is most useful when doing conversions of data types.

This is just one example of the status-enabled column-entry macro. There are many other column-entry macros that are status enabled (for example, COLUMN_ENTRY_LENGTH_STATUS). The naming pattern is to take your column-entry macro name, append _STATUS to it, and then append the status flag.

BOOKMARK_ENTRY

When working with a resultset, you are likely to want to navigate forward and backward, and you are likely to want to be able to move your cursor back to a previous location. The way to move a cursor to a specific location is to use a bookmark. A bookmark is a column entry added to the resultset parameter map. The macro is defined as follows:

```
BOOKMARK_ENTRY(variable)
```

The bookmark variable parameter is a template of the type CBookmark. When defining the template you need to specify the buffer size of the bookmark, which is dependent on your database. Or, if you decide that you want it allocated dynamically, you can pass in a buffer size of 0 and CBookmark will figure it out for you.

Let's extend the music application to accept bookmarks so that the user can return later and select a bookmarked song to listen to. The modified C++ data class is as follows:

```
class CMusicAccessor {
public:
LONG m_id;                    TCHAR m_songname[ 255];
TCHAR m_description[ 64];     TCHAR m_genre[ 64];
TCHAR m_artist[ 64];         ISequentialStream*    pSong;
CBookmark< 4> m_bookmark;

BEGIN_ACCESSOR_MAP(CMusicAccessor, 2)
BEGIN_ACCESSOR( 0, true)
    BOOKMARK_ENTRY( m_bookmark)
    COLUMN_ENTRY(1, m_id)
    COLUMN_ENTRY(2, m_songname)
    COLUMN_ENTRY(3, m_description)
    COLUMN_ENTRY(4, m_genre)
    COLUMN_ENTRY(5, m_artist)
END_ACCESSOR()
```

```
BEGIN_ACCESSOR( 1, false)
    BLOB_ENTRY( 6, IID_ISequentialStream, STGM_READ, pSong)
END_ACCESSOR()
END_ACCESSOR_MAP()

BEGIN_PARAM_MAP(CMusicAccessor)
COLUMN_ENTRY(1, m_genre)
END_PARAM_MAP()

DEFINE_COMMAND(CMusicAccessor, _T(" \
SELECT id, song_name, description, genre, artist, song FROM Music WHERE
genre = ?"))
};
```

The bookmark macro is added to the 0 accessor, so that any movement to
that location causes an automatic binding of the 0 accessor. In this example,
CBookmark is declared to be 4 bytes because the Microsoft SQL Server bookmark
is 4 bytes, and in this book, we are using Microsoft SQL Server. If you do not
know the length, then just use the zero-length default.

By default, when a resultset is created, bookmark references are not defined.
The capability to create bookmarks has to be added to the resultset in the form
of an OLE DB property. In terms of the OLE DB consumer template-generated
class, the properties are added to the OpenRowset of the execution class. An example of doing this is as follows:

```
class CTestBookmark : public CCommand<CAccessor<CTestBookmarkAccessor> >
{
public:
HRESULT OpenRowset() {
    CDBPropSet    propset(DBPROPSET_ROWSET);
    propset.AddProperty(DBPROP_BOOKMARKS, true);
    propset.AddProperty(DBPROP_IRowsetLocate, true);

    return CCommand<CAccessor<CTestBookmarkAccessor
        > >::Open(m_session, NULL, &propset);
}
CSession    m_session;
};
```

The two properties DBPROP_BOOKMARKS and DBPROP_IRowsetLocate must be set
to TRUE. The DBPROP_IRowsetLocate property needs to be enabled because it enables navigation in a forward and reverse direction.

To actually use this class in a consumer, you store a bookmark locally in the
client program. The C++ data-class bookmark changes every time the cursor location changes, so you need to store the bookmark value. To store a bookmark,

you need to declare a variable of the type CBookmark. To move the cursor to a stored bookmark, you call the CCommand.MoveToBookmark method.

If we modify the music application, we would end up with the following code. I've left out some of the code here for brevity, but the full source is in the source code for the book.

```
CMusic music;
CBookmark< 4> bookmark;

strcpy( music.m_genre, "Techno");
music.Open();

// Clear the C++ data class and open the resultset
do {
    // Iterate through the various songs
    if( music.m_id == 2) {
        // We want to store the current bookmark
        bookmark = music.m_bookmark;
    }
} while (music.MoveNext() == S_OK);
music.MoveToBookmark( bookmark);
}
```

One last note about bookmarks. The values stored within them are only valid for the life of the resultset. If you close the resultset, all of the bookmarks are invalidated.

Working with BLOB Data

The last part of our music application that needs to be defined is the part that retrieves the song itself. We cannot use a standard text field and hope that it all fits in one block of memory, because some songs are long and some are short. What we need to do is stream the contents of the field. The streaming is handled by a COM interface that can be used to retrieve chunks of information from the buffer. The BLOB column-entry macro references a COM interface pointer that is used to retrieve the contents of an SQL BLOB data field. The macro is defined as follows:

```
BLOB_ENTRY(nOrdinal, IID, flags, data)
```

The second parameter is defined as IID, and this means that your data field is not a piece of memory but a COM interface pointer. OLE DB streams data using COM interfaces, and in most cases, you will use the ISequentialStream COM interface.

The flags parameter specifies how the data will be manipulated. There are three options: to read data you can use STGM_READ; to write data you can use STGM_WRITE; and to both read and write data you can use STGM_READWRITE.

So, let's look at our CMusicAccessor class and see how the BLOB_ENTRY macro was implemented. Once again, some pieces of code have been left out for brevity, but the full source is available with the rest of the source code for this book.

```
class CMusicAccessor {
public:
ISequentialStream*    pSong;

BEGIN_ACCESSOR_MAP(CMusicAccessor, 2)
BEGIN_ACCESSOR( 1, false)
    BLOB_ENTRY( 6, IID_ISequentialStream, STGM_READ, pSong)
END_ACCESSOR()
END_ACCESSOR_MAP()
};
```

To iterate through the resultset, the data is bound to the 1 accessor. The accessor does not bind to the data in the database, but instantiates an ISequentialStream interface and indicates that it will be read-only (STGM_READ). This COM interface has a method that enables the client code to retrieve the contents of the data field in chunks of data. The data is retrieved as follows:

```
if( music.m_id > 0) {
BYTE myBuffer[ 65536];
ULONG cb;

music.GetData( 1);
if( music.pSong != NULL) {
    music.pSong->Read(myBuffer, 65536, &cb);
    music.pSong->Release();
}
}
```

Because the data field for the song is a COM interface, the streaming interface is reference counted like every COM object. This means that you need to release the COM interface after you are done with it by using the standard COM Release method. Failure to do so will result in peculiar bugs that will depend on the database provider.

Another way of releasing the COM interface pointers is to call CMusic.FreeRecordMemory. It is a bit cleaner because it also checks whether there any referenced BSTR's that need to be freed.

Retrieving Bulk Records

When data is being read, it is read using one handle at a time. It is possible to retrieve multiple sets of data to work on them in bulk. To use this class there are two changes to be made. The first is to declare the CCommand template, as follows:

```
CCommand<CManualAccessor, CBulkRowset> accessor;
```

In contrast to what we have done so far, the second parameter of the CCommand template uses CBulkRowset. It derives from and is used much like CRowset. The only exception is that you can specify the number of rows that should be fetched in one call. By default, the number is 10, but it can be changed as follows:

```
accessor.SetRows( 30);
```

This example loads 30 rows whenever it is required to load a set of records. The client code still uses the same navigation method calls (MoveFirst, MoveNext, and so on). What changes is the rowset behavior. Moving the cursor to the first location loads records 1 to 30. If we navigate to record 30 and then to record 31, then a new data set of 30 records is loaded.

This means the user can iterate through a page-set size and it will seem very fast. The catch is that this only works if you do not iterate between the records 30 and 31. When you navigate past the rowset boundaries, you load new data sets in memory—there is no solution to this problem.

Putting It in Perspective

A friend of mine was responsible for the OLE DB consumer template classes, and I learned from him how he structured everything. One thing that I learned was that OLE DB consumer templates are simple, yet powerful.

OLE DB consumer templates can be bent to do anything that you want. This flexibility exists because a very large Web site that was serving multimedia content required OLE DB consumer templates. Using ADO was not fast enough.

As a Visual C++ developer, I use OLE DB consumer templates, but I have modified them to my own specific functionality. This is because in the architecture I define, which is very stored-procedure intensive, some optimizations can be introduced. For example, instead of having a single default SQL command in the execution class, my optimizations allow for multiple SQL commands. Also an accessor was written that could work directly with COM objects and not individual data structures. These solutions did not break OLE DB consumer templates. They extended them. They show how powerful and flexible the OLE DB consumer templates truly are.

Does this mean that the first thing you should do in your projects is create custom OLE DB Consumer template extensions? The answer is no. First use the templates as is and get some experience. Once you have done that, then write the extensions that you require.

Chapter 18

Directory Services

A directory service is used to locate information in a distributed computing environment. Most companies have either a single page or a full book for their telephone directory. Now suppose your company regularly communicates with another company that has its own telephone directory. The two companies would probably exchange public versions of their corporate telephone books. And suppose another company wants to share its telephone book, too. The amount of data could quickly become unmanageable. So how can all this be managed? What you need is a directory service. This directory does not store all of the telephone numbers for all of the companies, but only a single company's telephone book. That directory is then instructed to communicate with another corporation, and the two directories are combined to create a bigger directory. However, each corporation is only responsible for maintaining its own data.

A directory service handles the details of where the information is and how it is combined in a bigger directory service. In Windows 2000, Microsoft created Microsoft Active Directory to manage information for us. This chapter explains what the Microsoft Active Directory is and how to program code to use it.

Architecture of Microsoft Active Directory

The Microsoft Active Directory is a hierarchical data store. It is optimized for reading data frequently. Within the data store are a number of objects that have a one-parent to many-child relationship. There are a number of standard programming interfaces that can be used to manipulate the objects within the data store, including LDAP (Lightweight Directory Access Protocol) and ADSI (Active Directory Service Interfaces).

The data within the Active Directory can be replicated in various directory stores on different computers. It is a loosely coupled architecture, which means that when there are two data stores, either can be updated without requiring an immediate update of the other. When the data is replicated from one data store to another data store, Active Directory automatically handles the convergence of the data.

Active Directory Object

There are two basic items in Active Directory: the class and the attribute. Everything is based on these two items.

The *attribute* is like a key-value pair. For example, you may have an attribute called *name*, which represents the name of a user, computer, or product. At this point, it does not mean anything. The attribute has an associated resource foot-print, which may be a string data type or a numeric data type, but it is always an Active Directory data type. If desired, the attribute can also have maximum and minimum values, which have different meanings depending on the attribute's data type. For example, a string maximum and minimum value specifies the string's length. A maximum and minimum value for a numeric field specifies the maximum and minimum numeric values that the field can contain.

The *class* is a grouping of attributes. An Active Directory class is not like a programming language class—an Active Directory class references attributes but the attributes are not declared within the class itself. This means multiple classes can reference an Active Directory attribute, as is shown in Figure 18–1.

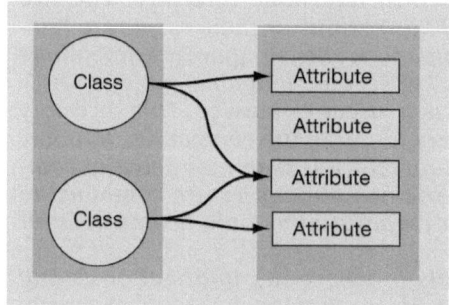

Figure 18–1: Relationship between classes and attributes

When a class is instantiated, it is called an Active Directory object. Every Active Directory object must represent some class and attribute definition. Active Directory objects cannot be created without type information. Information about the classes, attributes, and their characteristics is stored in the Active Directory schema. The schema is split into two parts: the defined attributes and the defined classes.

THE DETAILS OF AN ACTIVE DIRECTORY OBJECT

When attributes are added to an Active Directory class definition, they can have a value status. For example, attributes can be required, meaning that when the Active Directory class is instantiated, the attributes must contain values. Optional attributes can, but need not, have values when the Active Directory class is instantiated.

Active Directory attributes are indexed for faster retrieval times but objects are not. However, before you decide to index all attributes, you have to consider what the ramifications will be. Active Directory uses a modified version of the B-star indexing algorithm, which means that every new entry added to the data store requires time to be indexed. As the index becomes larger, it requires a longer time to index the new entry. And if an object has ten different indexed attributes, then inserting the new entry could take quite a bit of time.

An attribute can be single-valued or multivalued. A single-valued attribute looks like the following:

```
key = value
```

A multivalued attribute looks like this:

```
key = value1, value2, ... , valueN
```

In a multivalued attribute, there is no guarantee of the order of the individual values. This means that when you iterate through the individual values, you cannot rely on a value being in a specific location. An attribute can, however, be constrained by defining an upper range and a lower range.

Active Directory classes support inheritance. Let's consider this in the context of the conference registration application. In that application, there are two sorts of users: simple users and registered users. With Active Directory inheritance, the base class would be user, and the RegisteredUser class would inherit from user. All Active Directory classes must derive from top, which is the base class of the Active Directory, somewhere in the inheritance chain.

There are three different class types:

- **Structural:** Structural classes are the only classes that can be instantiated in Active Directory. Structural classes may derive from any of the three techniques possible in Active Directory.
- **Abstract:** Abstract classes are templates used to derive new abstract and structural classes. An auxiliary class can only be a subclass of an abstract class. Abstract classes cannot be instantiated in Active Directory.
- **Auxiliary:** Auxiliary classes are similar to C++ include files; an auxiliary class contains a list of attributes. Adding the auxiliary class to the definition of a structural or abstract class adds the auxiliary class's optional and required attributes to the definition. An auxiliary class cannot be instantiated in the directory. New auxiliary classes can be derived from existing auxiliary or abstract classes.

ACTIVE DIRECTORY CONTAINER

Active Directory has a special class called the container. A container class is very different from the usual Active Directory class because it may contain other Active Directory objects, as shown in Figure 18–2.

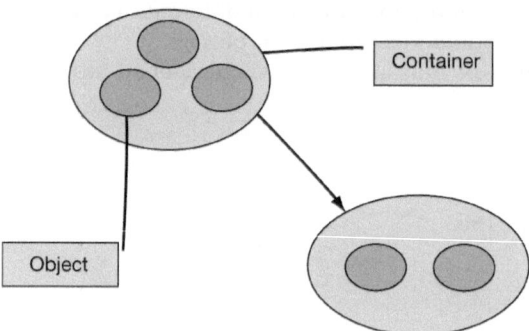

Figure 18–2: Active Directory container object

The container object contains three other objects, one of which is a container itself that contains two other objects. Using this technique, it is possible to build a hierarchical repository. The container object and class are just like other Active Directory classes. They can reference multiple Active Directory attributes and may be subclassed by other Active Directory classes.

HOW DATA IS REPLICATED AND RETRIEVED

Active Directory objects are systematically replicated by Active Directory. When an object is first instantiated on a specific server, the object resides on that server. When a server is added to a network of Active Directory servers, the information that is stored in the local server's global catalogue is replicated to the other servers. The global catalogue contains all the attributes that are defined as replication capable, and some of the root attributes that have to be replicated, such as the name of the object. When Active Directory objects are replicated, only the attributes are replicated, which could mean that half of an object exists on the network while the other half exists only on the original server.

When users search the Active Directory, they are searching their local global catalogue. If there is an object that interests them, then all attributes of that object are retrieved from the local global catalogue and presented. If the user is interested in a specific attribute that has been replicated, Active Directory seeks the original location of the object and retrieves the full contents of the object.

This brings us to the next point, which is how you define attributes and classes. Many people say that you should make sure that the object is small, but that rule doesn't make sense to me. When considering what size to make the individual attributes, there are three important factors: replication frequency, retrieval frequency, and the size of the attribute. Those three factors need to be considered together such that network traffic is minimized. It may be useful to put a large picture attribute into the global catalogue if the picture changes only once every two years and the attribute is constantly retrieved because the number of times that that data will be replicated is minimal.

A Practical Active Directory Example

Now that we have a basic understanding of what the Active Directory is, let's browse an Active Directory installation and create a user by using some administrative tools.

When Active Directory is installed, specific containers are created. The ones that interest us are the different users registered in the domain, as shown in Figure 18–3.

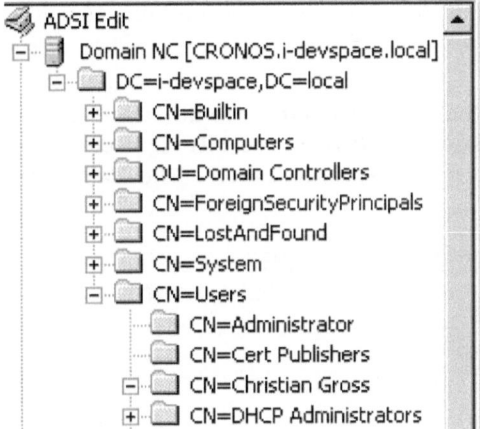

Figure 18–3: Hierarchy of a user

In Figure 18–3, there are a number of DCs and CNs. When they are combined, these make up a distinguished name, and they were originally specified by the X.500 standard. DC stands for Domain Container and CN stands for Common Name. Active Directory makes very heavy use of both the X.500 open standard and the LDAP standard, which is used to provide directory services.

If you are not familiar with the X.500 notation, consider the following directory specification:

```
c:\directory1\directory2\myfile.txt
```

Translated into X.500, this directory would be identified as follows:

```
FILE=myfile.txt,DIRECTORY=directory2,DIRECTORY=directory1,DISK=c
```

X.500 notation defines keys to be used in key value pairs to identify the various attributes in the string. With X.500 you can define any resource or location, and because it is a key value pair system the system can figure out what the individual keys are referring to. When using Active Directory, the most common X.500 keys used are CN and DC.

UNDERSTANDING DISTINGUISHED NAMES

In X.500, a Uniform Resource Locator (URL) is called a *distinguished name*, and it represents all items uniquely in the directory service. The distinguished name notation orders the location of the object, starting with the least significant item. For example, in Figure 18–3, the distinguished name for the object CN=Christian Gross is as follows:

CN=Christian Gross,CN=Users,DC=i-devspace,DC=local

The comma is used as a separator, but the semicolon is acceptable, as well.

ADDING A NAME MANUALLY

It is possible to manually add a user to the Active Directory. To do this using the ADSI editor (distributed with the Windows 2000 resource kit) right-click the CN=Users node and select the new object from the context menu. The dialog box shown in Figure 18–4 will appear:

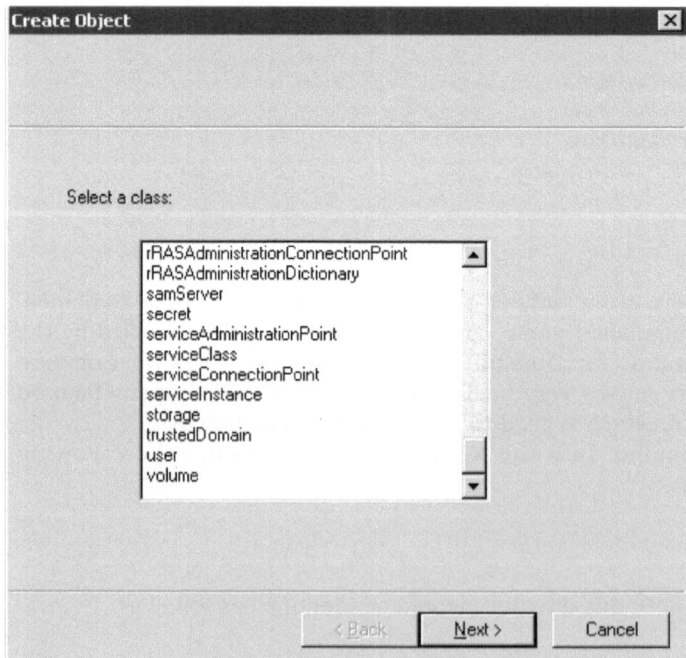

Figure 18–4: Creating a user object manually

From the list box, select the user class. Then click Next. You will be asked for the CN value. Type in An administrator and click Next. Now you will be asked for a value for the sAMAccountName, so, again, type in An administrator. Click Finish.

Now look at the directory and you will see another entry: An administrator. This entry is a user. If you open the management console to manage users, the list box shown in Figure 18–5 displays.

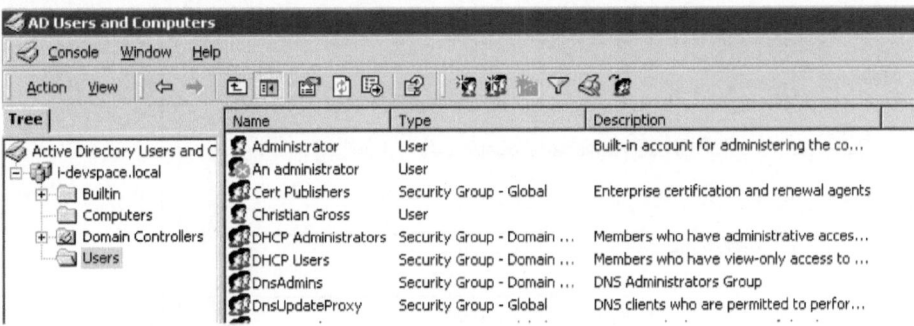

Figure 18–5: Modified user list

As you can see, the user An administrator was added to the list. However, there is a problem. Associated with the user is a little red . This means that although the user was added to the Active Directory, it is not a valid user. The problem is that creating a user with the Active Directory ADSI editor does not set all of the user attributes properly. Only the Windows 2000 user administrative tool can do this properly.

LOOKING AT THE USER ATTRIBUTES

The Active Directory user object is an instance of the Person object. Use the ADSI editor to find the user that we just added (An administrator) in the user's container. Then right-click that user and select Properties from the pop-up menu. From the dialog box that appears, select the Mandatory property objectCategory, as shown in Figure 18–6.

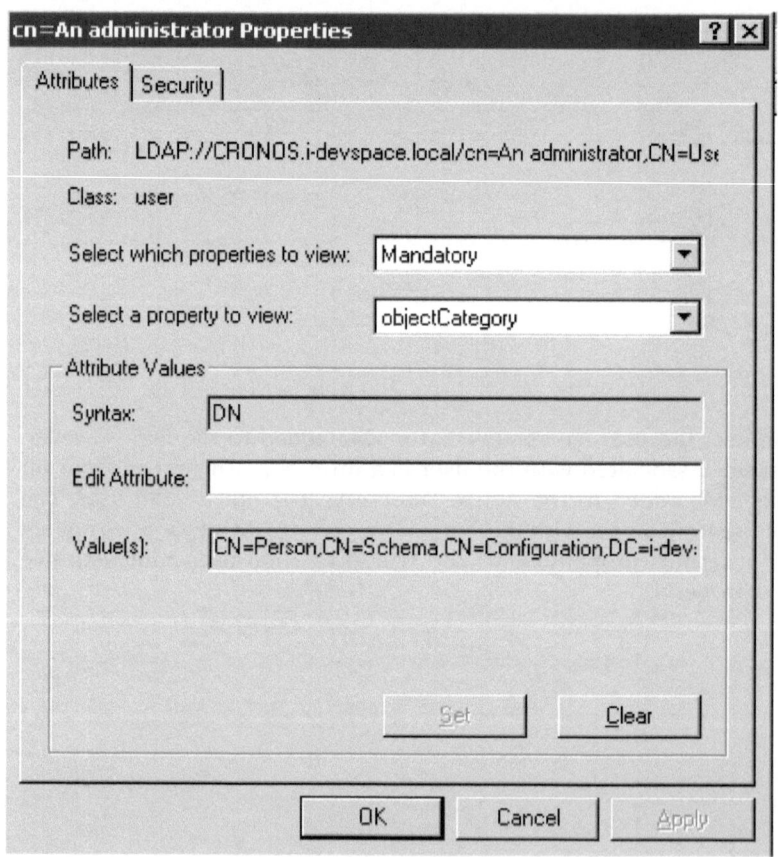

Figure 18–6: Contents of objectCategory property

What you are looking at is the name of the Person schema class that the administrator object is an instance of. In the ADSI editor, this is called a property, but in fact it is an Active Directory attribute.

Accessing the User with ADSI

I will not go into any more administrative details because those issues are best left to an administrative book. Instead, what I'll concentrate on is writing programs that manipulate the Active Directory objects.

To access Active Directory, you could use the ADSI COM interfaces, but these are not your only choices. It is possible to use the LDAP client Software Developer's Kit (SDK) and communicate with Active Directory. Keep in mind that ADSI is not exclusively used for Active Directory. ADSI is used to administer Microsoft Internet Information Server (IIS) and Microsoft Exchange Server. Our focus, however, is on using ADSI to manage an Active Directory.

CONNECTING TO THE ROOTDSE

When writing an Active Directory application, you need to know what the domain for the server is. We cannot simply write a specific domain in the code. However, LDAP specifies that the current domain must be dynamically retrievable. This is something like TCP/IP (Transmission Control Protocol/Internet Protocol), where the localhost specifies the local machine.

When building an LDAP connection, you will want to query for the rootDSE object. Using the rootDSE, it is possible to figure out where the schema and global catalogue are located. For example, to retrieve the name of the domain, the defaultNamingContext attribute can be queried. Or to retrieve the schema, the schemaNamingContext attribute can be queried.

The application that we will build is one in which we query for a specific user and then retrieve some information about that user. To connect to the LDAP server, the new LDAP COM moniker is used. Here is an example of connecting to the rootDSE object in Visual Basic:

```
Set rootDSE = GetObject("LDAP://rootDSE")
```

Normally, I would not show the Visual C++ code because it is almost identical to Visual Basic when using COM. However, I want to show how Visual C++ code instantiates the rootDSE object.

When using Visual C++, you have the option of using the MIDL (Microsoft IDL)-generated ADSI header files or the COM compiler output of the activeDS.tlb file. However, I prefer the COM-compiler-generated classes. As in Visual Basic, you need to use the LDAP COM moniker to retrieve the rootDSE COM object. In Visual C++, the code implementation is as follows:

```
_com_util::CheckError( CoGetObject( L"LDAP://rootDSE", NULL,
__uuidof( ActiveDs::IADs), (void **)&ptr));
```

Those who have been reading the Microsoft Platform SDK documentation will notice that there are a series of ADSI helper functions. For the most part, I do not suggest that you use them because they are not necessary.

From this point on, I will be using Visual Basic as source code examples, but there are some very good Visual C++ demos in the source code for this book.

IADS: THE ROOT COM INTERFACE

Just as the attribute and class are the basis of Active Directory, the IADs COM interface is the root of all ADSI objects. The IADs COM interface is supported by all ADSI-instantiated objects and can be used to retrieve or set all of the object attributes. In Interface Definition Language (IDL), the IADS COM interface is defined as follows (some methods and properties have been removed for simplicity):

```
interface IADs : IDispatch {
[id(0x00000002), propget]HRESULT Name([out, retval] BSTR* retval);
[id(0x00000003), propget]HRESULT Class([out, retval] BSTR* retval);
[id(0x00000004), propget]HRESULT GUID([out, retval] BSTR* retval);
[id(0x00000005), propget]HRESULT ADsPath([out, retval] BSTR* retval);
[id(0x00000006), propget]HRESULT Parent([out, retval] BSTR* retval);
[id(0x00000007), propget]HRESULT Schema([out, retval] BSTR* retval);
[id(0x00000008)]HRESULT GetInfo();
[id(0x00000009)]HRESULT SetInfo();
};
```

Using these properties, it is possible to dynamically quiz the attribute names and values:

- **IADs::Name**   The common name (CN) of the object
- **IADs::Parent**   The location of the object
- **IADs::AdsPath**   The combination of the name and parent properties
- **IADs::Class**   The class type in the schema database
- **IADs::Schema**   The full distinguished name of the class type

All of these properties are formatted using the distinguished name format.

The methods IADs::GetInfo and IADs::SetInfo are used to move data from the directory to the cache. Remember that the object is found in the global catalogue, and calling these methods retrieves all of the information associated with the individual object. By calling these methods, the entire object state is moved from the global directory to the cache or vice versa. These methods are also useful when you want the to refresh the local cache.

For example, when debugging an application, the alterations performed may not be available. Calling IADs::GetInfo refreshes the cache. This action may cause a delay and require some bandwidth. If only some specific properties are to be loaded, the IADs::GetInfoEx method should be used.

The other operation that you will want to perform on this base interface is the retrieving or setting of the attributes. This can be done using the following methods exposed in the IADs COM interface as represented in IDL (some methods and properties have been removed for simplicity):

```
interface IADs : IDispatch {
[id(0x0000000a)]HRESULT Get(
        [in] BSTR bstrName, [out, retval] VARIANT* pvProp);
[id(0x0000000b)]HRESULT Put(
```

```
            [in] BSTR bstrName, [in] VARIANT vProp);
[id(0x0000000c)]HRESULT GetEx(
            [in] BSTR bstrName, [out, retval] VARIANT* pvProp);
[id(0x0000000d)]HRESULT PutEx( [in] long lnControlCode,
            [in] BSTR bstrName, [in] VARIANT vProp);
};
```

The `IADs::Put` and `IADs::Get` methods manipulate single-value attributes.
The `IADs::PutEx` and `IADs::GetEx` methods manipulate multivalue attributes.

In the previous example, we created a user. Let's query that same branch of
the Active Directory for the user Christian Gross, and retrieve that person's
e-mail address. The code to do that is as follows:

```
Set findObj = GetObject("LDAP://CN=Christian Gross;CN=Users, DC=ldevspace,
DC=local")
Debug.Print "Name is :" & findObj.Get("mail")
```

Notice that the `mail` attribute represents the e-mail address. When dealing
with the multi-value attributes, `VARIANT` values represent arrays of the data.

IADSCONTAINER: MANAGING COLLECTIONS

It is not directly possible to expose an Active Directory container in COM. A better solution is to expose the container as a COM collection.

The COM interface that manages containers is `IADsContainer`. To retrieve a
container object, retrieve it as you would retrieve a normal object, except that
the distinguished name should reference a container. To add a user, use the
following code:

```
Dim contObj As IADsContainer
Dim usr As IADs

Set contObj = GetObject("LDAP://CN=Users,DC=ldevspace, DC=local")
Set usr = contObj.Create("user", "CN=SimpleUser")
```

In this code sample, when the object is retrieved using the `GetObject` call, the
interface `IADsContainer` is queried for. Because `IADsContainer` collection represents
a container, that interface is retrieved. This interface contains a series of container
manipulation routines, such as one that permits the creation of an object.

To create an object, the method `IAdsContainer::Create` is called. The first
parameter (`user`) of this method specifies the class type, and this type must exist
in the schema catalogue. (We discuss the schema on page 467.) The second parameter (`CN=SimpleUser`) specifies the common name (`CN`) of the object. It must be
specified in the X.500 notation, because the original query used the X.500 notation. (I mention this because many of the older ADSI examples use the `WinNT://`
notation, which does not require a distinguished name.)

When the object is created, it exists only in the ADSI cache. It is a valid object of that class type with all the attributes. To save it to the directory data store, the IADs::SetInfo method must be called, as in the following example:

```
usr.Put "sAMAccountName", "example3"
usr.SetInfo
```

The user that has just been created can also be deleted as follows:

```
[id(0x00000007)]HRESULT Delete(
        [in] BSTR bstrClassName, [in] BSTR bstrRelativeName);
```

The parameters are identical to those used when creating the object. This means that the first parameter (bstrClassName) specifies the class, and the second parameter (bstrRelativeName) defines the name of the class. Again, because we are using X.500 notation, the name must be in that notation.

If you want to move or copy an object, the following methods are available:

```
[id(0x00000008)]HRESULT CopyHere(
        [in] BSTR SourceName, [in] BSTR NewName,
        [out, retval] IDispatch** ppObject);
[id(0x00000009)]HRESULT MoveHere( [in] BSTR SourceName,
        [in] BSTR NewName, [out, retval] IDispatch** ppObject);
```

In both cases, the parameters are distinguished names. The first parameter (SourceName) is a full distinguished name that specifies an object located somewhere in the Active Directory. It is then copied to the local container and given the common name, as specified by the second parameter (NewName). If the operation is successful, then the new object is returned.

By default, when the container is opened, all elements that are in the Active Directory container are transferred to the IADsContainer collection. It is possible to filter out a subset of objects based on some criterion of an attribute. In the users collection that we have been referencing, there are objects that are of the user and group class types. If we want to iterate only through the users, the following code could be written:

```
Dim users As IADsContainer
Dim usr As IADs

Set users = GetObject("LDAP://CN=Users, DC=ldevspace, DC=local")
users.Filter = Array("User")

For Each usr In users
Debug.Print "Distinguished name :(" & usr.ADsPath & ") Class is :(" &
usr.Class & ")"
Next
```

OPTIMIZING ACCESS

The object that has been manipulated so far is of the class type user. To simplify some of the user class-type operations, there is a series of COM interfaces that represent the individual Active Directory objects. For the user class type, the COM interface is IADsUser. An example of using it is as follows:

```
Dim findObj As IADs
Dim userObj As IADsUser

Set findObj = GetObject("LDAP://CN=Christian Gross;CN=Users, DC=ldevspace,
DC=local")
Set userObj = findObj
Debug.Print "Email is :" & userObj.EmailAddress
```

Looking back to our IADs definition, you will see that it is derived from the IDispatch COM interface. This means that when you retrieve an Active Directory object, the IDispatch COM interface exposes all Active Directory attributes as COM properties. This approach works well in Visual Basic or scripting because the IDispatch interface can be dynamically queried without writing mounds of code.

Languages such as Visual C++ and Visual J++ can call IDispatch interfaces, but it requires more work. Both languages prefer a custom COM interface. Hence the advantage of using IADsUser with its predefined methods and properties. There are other COM interfaces to manage things such as computers (IADsComputer), domains (IADsDomain), and groups (IADsGroup). The specifications of the various interfaces are defined in the Active Directory subsection of the Platform SDK.

Creating Custom Objects

The power in Active Directory is not in just being able to use the default Active Directory class definitions. Instead, what you will want to do is create a repository of custom-defined objects. This makes it possible to create custom objects and then exchange them with your business partners.

To add a custom class, you need to extend the schema, and this is a one-time operation—once it has been done, there is no turning back. Schema extensions cannot be deleted, only disabled. There are two ways to extend the schema: by using the Schema Manager tool or by writing a program. In this book, I use the Schema Manager tool, which is distributed as part of the Windows 2000 resource kit.

It is also possible to modify the schema using ADSI objects. If you do that, I highly recommend that you write some scripting files that use COM automation. Using any other programming language is too difficult and not worth the time. Remember that extending the schema is something that you do once, and it is never done by end users. Hence, there is no need for a fancy graphical user interface (GUI).

AN EXAMPLE OF USING THE ACTIVE DIRECTORY

One example of using Active Directory custom objects is to move the conference registration users from the database to the Active Directory. This offers the advantage of having the user information replicated across various registration applications and communities automatically without the intervention of a program.

We will define a custom user because you do not want the user to be part of your domain. The conference user is only required for a conference application and is not required to log on to any computer in your domain. Also, the custom user will not be located in the users container. We will create a new container that will contain all of the conference users.

ADDING THE ATTRIBUTES

Earlier we looked at how Active Directory classes are defined. Now, the first step in creating our new custom Active Directory user class is to define the various attributes that will be part of the class. One attribute is userRegistrationLevel, which will be added to the global catalogue.

Using the Schema management tool, right-click on the Attributes node and select Create Attribute from the context menu. A dialog box will warn you about the consequences of adding an attribute. Click Continue, and the dialog box shown in Figure 18–7 will appear.

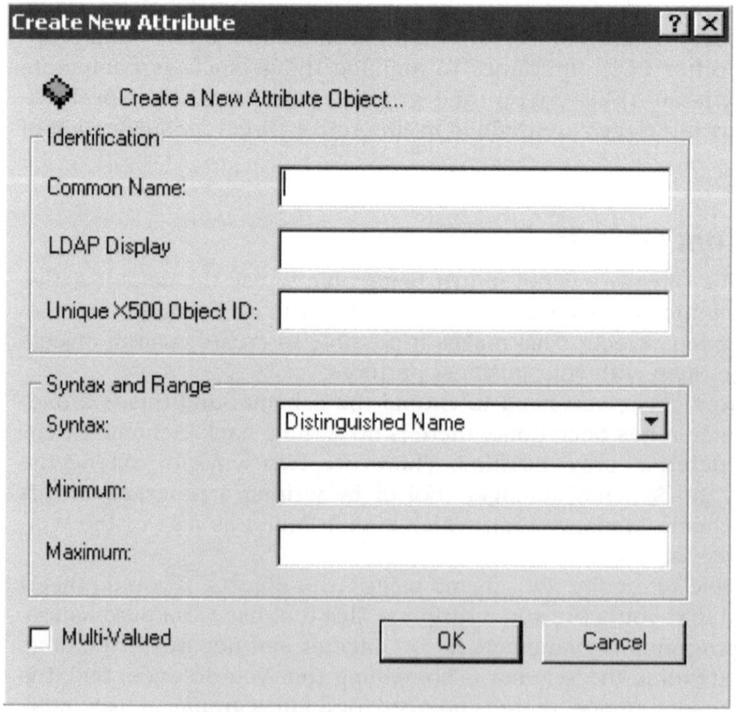

Figure 18–7: Attribute properties

In the dialog box, the Common Name text box identifies the CN of the object being created. Enter userRegistrationLevel as the name. The LDAP Display text box defines the name that will be displayed for this attribute when an LDAP client communicates with Active Directory. By default, you should keep this the same as the common name.

The Unique X.500 Object ID text box identifies the attribute in terms of a numeric address. This is identical in functionality to a Globally Unique Identifier (GUID), but it uses a different format. The Object Identifiers (OIDs) use the X.500 format specification. OIDs are unique numeric values issued by various authorities to uniquely identify data elements, syntaxes, and other parts of distributed applications. OIDs are found in Open Systems Interconnection (OSI) applications, X.500 Directories, Simple Network Management Protocol (SNMP), and other applications where uniqueness is important. OIDs are based on a tree structure, in which a superior issuing authority (such as ISO) allocates a "branch" of the tree to a subauthority, which can, in turn, allocate subbranches. The LDAP protocol requires a directory service to identify object classes, attributes, and syntaxes with OIDs. This is part of the LDAP X.500 legacy.

The OIDs in Active Directory include some issued by the International Standards Organization (ISO) for X.500 classes and attributes, and some issued by Microsoft and other issuing authorities. OID notation is a dotted string of numbers, for example, 1.2.840.113556.1.5.4, which breaks down as shown in the following table:

VALUE	DESCRIPTION
1	ISO, the "root authority"—issued "1.2" to ANSI
2	ANSI—issued "1.2.840" to USA
840	USA—issued "1.2.840.113556" to Microsoft
113556	Microsoft
1	Microsoft—Active Directory Service
5	Microsoft—Active Directory Service: Classes
4	Microsoft—Active Directory Service: Classes: Built-in Domain

There are several ways of generating OIDs. The first is to request one from the ISO Name Registration Authority. This is a one-time action; once you have obtained a root OID, the OID space it defines is yours and you can administer it yourself.

The second way of generating an OID is to use the OIDGEN.EXE command-line utility, which generates valid OIDs. The OIDs are generated using a base OID from Microsoft's branch of the ISO OID tree, generating a GUID each time the program is run.

The last way to generate an OID is to request one from Microsoft by sending e-mail to oids@microsoft.com.

The Syntax text box specifies the Active Directory data type. For our example, we need an integer. It has a single value, meaning that the Multivalued checkbox does not need to be checked. The text box's Maximum and Minimum fields do not need to be filled out. Finally, click OK and the attribute will be added.

ADDING THE CLASS

Using the Schema management tool, right-click on the Classes node. From the context menu select Create Class. The dialog box shown in Figure 18–8 will appear:

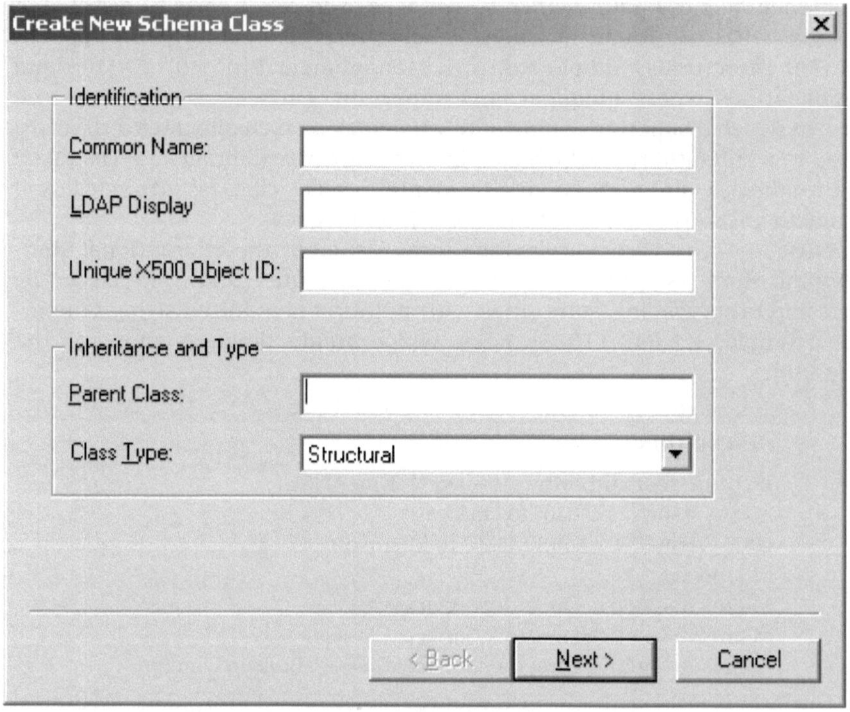

Figure 18–8: Class definition

The first three text boxes—Common Name, LDAP Display, and Unique X500 Object ID—are identical to what we saw when we added an attribute to the schema. The Common Name of the class is webUser. However, when you define a class, it needs to inherit from some other class. In our example, the class inherits from the user class. What is new in this dialog box is the Parent Class and Class Type text boxes. The webUser class will have the user class as a Parent Class. The Class Type defines how the class will be defined in the schema; in our case, it is structural. Click Next to get to the dialog box shown in Figure 18–9.

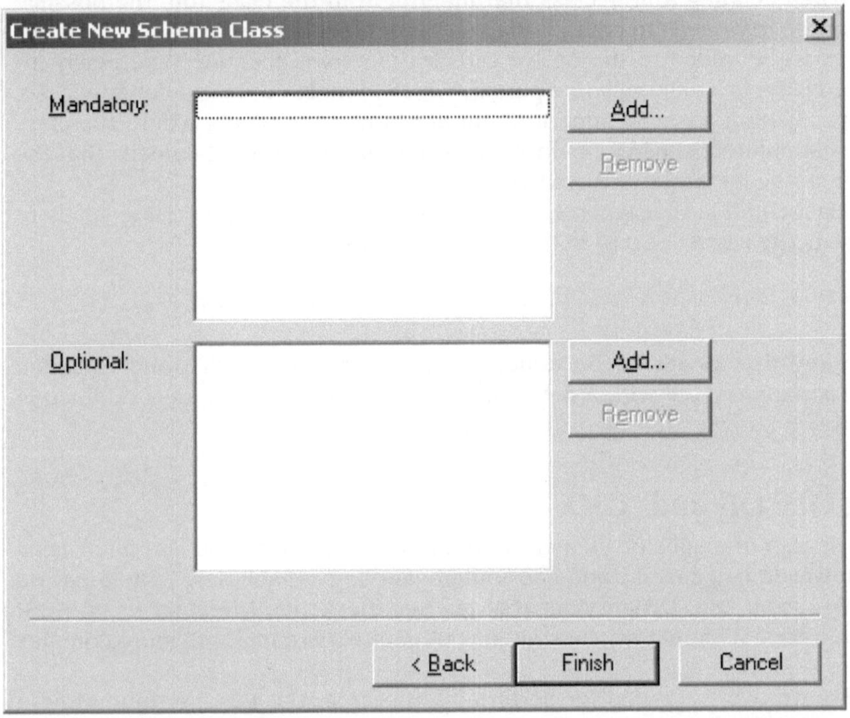

Figure 18–9: Class attributes definition

This dialog box enables you to define which attributes are mandatory and which are optional. Mandatory attributes are those that need to be filled out before they can be persisted to the data store. Optional attributes are those that can be empty and may be filled in later.

In this case, the only attribute that needs to be added is considered optional. Click Add to get to another dialog box, and find the userRegistrationLevel attribute in the list box of available attributes. Then click OK. Click OK again to save this class definition to the schema. Remember that inheritance adds all of the other attributes defined in the base user class to an instance of webUser.

Working with a Custom Active Directory Object

Working with a custom object is not much different from working with a "regular" object, except that there are more attributes and it is not possible to use any of the optimized interfaces because it is a different object. If you want to create an optimized interface to access the object, you need to write it. The implementation of the optimized object will use the core ADSI interfaces.

There is a catch to using custom data objects. When instantiating an Active Directory object and adding to a container, the parent of the object is a container. When defining a new class that inherits from the class top, the possible superior property needs to contain the container object. When a class is instantiated, it must be added to the Active Directory in some location. The newly instantiated class is a child of some parent, which in most cases is a container. So, when specifying a possible superior, you are in fact specifying where the class may be instantiated. Having an empty possible superior property means that the class cannot be instantiated anywhere.

The last catch is that when extending the schema, the update flag needs to be toggled. The key is located in the following Registry location:

```
HKEY LOCAL MACHINE\System\Current Control Set\Services\NTDS\Parameters
```

The key that needs to be added is of the type REG_DWORD and is called Schema Updates Allowed with a data value of 1. This entire process is outlined in the Microsoft knowledgebase article Q216060.

Using OLE DB and ADO

To do a search of a specific element in the Active Directory, you can filter using ADSI. However, it is specific and has limited querying capabilities. With Windows 2000 there is an OLE DB provider that queries the Active Directory using ADSI COM interfaces; it should be used when you require a broader and more complex search.

There are two notations for performing a search: the LDAP notation and a SQL-type notation. The LDAP notation takes a bit of getting used to. If you are familiar with SQL, that is a simpler notation to use.

Querying Using the LDAP Notation

An LDAP query is made up of four individual parts:

```
Root; Filter; Attributes; Scope
```

The Root is a distinguished name indicating where the search will start. Using our example Active Directory, you could search within the Users tree using the following distinguished name:

```
<LDAP://CN=Users, DC=ldevspace, DC=local>
```

Note the angled brackets. These are required when a search is being performed.

When searching, you define the elements that you are interested in. This is referred to as setting the `Filter` property. The filter notation is defined by RFC 2254. (The Platform SDK references RFC 960, which is incorrect. It should have read RFC 1960, which was replaced with RFC 2254.)

The filter is a series of key value pairs that are combined with different operators. The key in the filter is any attribute of the object, such as `objectcategory` and `mail address`. For example, to search for all classes of a specific type, the attribute `objectcategory` would be used, as follows:

```
(objectcategory=user)
```

The operator used in the previous notations is the equality operator (=). It is also possible to use the less than (<=), greater than (>=), and other operators. If you want to search for all items except a specific one, a NOT (!) can be put in front of the attribute.

To perform a search that tests multiple criteria, combine them using filter operators such as `AND (&)`, `OR (|)`, `NOT (!)`, and so on. An example of searching for multiple items is as follows:

```
(|(objectCategory=user)(objectCategory=group)(mail=cgross@devspace.com))
```

You can use as many items as needed. The combination can be nested, as shown in the following example:

```
(&(mail=*devspace.com)(|(objectCategory=user)(objectCategory=group)))
```

This search uses the wildcard character (*) to find `user` and `group` objects that have an e-mail address ending with `devspace.com`.

When a resultset is found, the specific attributes that are displayed in the resultset are defined by the `attributes` part of the LDAP query.

The last part of the LDAP query, `scope`, specifies how the search will be performed. There are three different types of searches:

- **Base:** This performs a search on the object specified in the distinguished name. Remember that the distinguished name is an object—usually it is a container object that contains children.
- **One level:** This performs a search on the items within the container of the object, but it does not include the container itself.
- **Subtree:** This performs search on the items in the container of the object, but it does not include the container itself. If the objects within the container are containers themselves, the search is continued within those containers.

A complete LDAP query would look something like this:

```
<LDAP://CN=Users, DC=ldevspace, DC=local>;(objectCategory=*);name,mail;Base
```

Querying Using the SQL Notation

The SQL query notation is very similar to the SQL that we looked at in Chapter 15. The difference is that here we are querying Active Directory objects instead of tables. Here the table is a container and the SELECT statement is executed on the contents of the container. Consider this example:

```
SELECT name FROM 'LDAP://CN=Users, DC=ldevspace, DC=local' WHERE
objectCategory='user' ORDER BY name
```

The distinguished name (LDAP://...) defines a specific container, and from that container we are selecting all objects that have the objectCategory attribute equal to "user". The resultset will be ordered by the name field.

Using ADO

Regardless of whether you use the LDAP query notation or the SQL query notation, the command is executed as if it were another resource. Remember that this was the point of the Universal Data Access (UDA), where everything is some kind of data. The details of using Active Data Objects (ADO) are outlined in Chapter 16. The change from an SQL database is that the ADO Command.CommandText contains the query string that we have just defined. The resultset that is generated is manipulated as explained in Chapter 16.

Putting It in Perspective

The Active Directory is an application that behaves quite a bit like a database. The marketing explanations for Active Directory say it is a directory service, but a directory service is really just a specialized database geared to the replication and distribution of data. Everything that a directory service can do can be done with an SQL database. However, with a directory service everything has been optimized.

Should you use a directory service in your application? The answer is yes, because it will be extremely important for applications in the future. You may be able to avoid using a directory service for another year or two, but after that you will need to use it. Better to take the time to learn and experiment with it now, rather than wait and try to learn under the pressure of project deadlines. A directory service makes it possible to store information about your application on a network. This makes the maintenance of your application simpler because there are no local files or settings to move.

Microsoft has often created technology that only Microsoft supported, but Active Directory is different. The programmers who wrote Active Directory understood that while Microsoft is big, it is not the only game in town. Active Directory supports LDAP standard completely, and I have used it successfully on UNIX clients. The only major difference is that the layout of the hierarchy is slightly different from some traditional UNIX hierarchies.

Chapter 19

The Quality Control Process

Quality control in the software industry is something that many people have problems with. Very often there are system crashes and the end user is left hanging without recourse. The question that must be answered is this: How do we develop an effective quality control process? The quality control process should not start after the component is developed. It should be a continuous part of the full development process.

In this chapter, three concepts are discussed. The first is why a quality control process is necessary. The second is how to achieve quality by testing the application. And the third is how to achieve quality by testing the performance of the application and hardware. Only when all three concepts are combined is resulting application acceptable to the end user.

Defining the Quality Control Process

Quality control in the software industry has not generally been approached or handled properly. Microsoft has a large, developed quality-control staff, but you might not guess that by its software's reputation. In contrast, I worked on a project where only one person handled the quality control process, but he knew exactly what he was doing. The result was a stable product that people were happy with. I also consulted at an Indian software house where they used a brute-force technique to ensure quality. The result was a stable product, albeit at a high labor cost, which is only thinkable where the cost of labor is low.

What I present here is a model for a practical quality control process. Often, a quality control process includes steps that make sense, but that are not done. For example, code reviews, documentation, and setting up coding standards are preached as ways of improving quality, and they do that, but they cost too much time. The trick is to introduce a quality control process that is efficient and that does not cost too much time.

When defining a quality control process, do not miss the obvious quality control helpers. My experience is that you can introduce "foolproof" quality control techniques, but if the development team is not happy, bugs and problems will appear anyway. Team harmony is extremely important. I am not going to preach about team management and team morale because they are beyond the scope of this book, but teams that are happy produce better code. Often, just focusing on this issue makes a huge amount of difference.

Another good quality improvement is to ensure that proper program designs are created. Good designs will reduce bug counts and help you produce a shipping product more quickly, which is the primary purpose of this book.

Defining a Metric

Now, let's say you have a good team and you did a proper design, but you still have some bugs—what are you to do? The answer is to develop a metric. Software developers generally do not like metrics because it means that their productivity can be measured. However, that is not necessarily bad. Metrics are bad when the metric is used to quantify whether the developer is good or bad. This leads to seeing only one aspect of a developer and to bad team morale.

I use metrics to estimate when parts of projects will be completed. For example, when I wrote this book I tracked the time I spent on each chapter. I guessed when I started this book that I would be able to write a chapter in about four days, but I was wrong. My chart indicated that even though some chapters were written in less time, the average was about 5.8 days. The danger in using this metric would be to ask me to write faster, which would result in lower quality and a shorter book.

THE INTERFACE METRIC

I like to use an interface-based metric, in which each and every interface is tracked as an individual entity. Other people like to use design-point-based metrics, but exactly what qualifies as a design point is open to discussion. Using a Unified Modeling Language (UML)-diagram-based metric can be too vague, because some elements may not have been thought about, and the diagrams and metric require constant updating. The classic metric of measuring lines of code is really bad because it leads people to write bloated code.

In an interface-based metric, it might make sense to track the number of methods of the interface, but that would lead away from the main theme of having one metric. Counting methods is not something that should be started, because it takes time and is too volatile—interfaces will change during the development process. We will assume that your interfaces are well designed, and that there are no interfaces with 300 methods. (Incidentally, I am not talking about Component Object Model (COM) interfaces here, because there are other types of interfaces. For example, we may have Structured Query Language (SQL) stored-procedure interfaces.) For those interfaces that cannot be grouped into objects, a naming convention must be used. In Chapter 15, a naming convention was developed that makes it possible to group SQL stored procedures.

THE PROBLEM AREAS

An interesting study done by IBM found that 57 percent of the errors were bundled in 7 percent of the modules. This is an example of the 80/20 rule, which states that 80 percent of the problems are concentrated in 20 percent of the areas. This study suggests that the key to developing a product with fewer bugs is to identify the problem areas and focus on them.

By defining your metric as based on interfaces, you can locate the problem areas. Whenever there is a bug or a change in the interface, it can be marked on a chart as a change. Keeping track of these marks is useful in locating the problem interfaces. There are five general dynamics to measure.

- **Number of versions of interfaces**: When implementing an interface, there is always a need to change the interface. This is okay so long as the interface was not made public. However, when an interface is public and changed, the consumer may need to be changed, as well. If the version changes are numerous, this could indicate a badly designed interface, or an interface that needs to be split into different functionalities. If there are no version changes for the interface, that could indicate an interface that has not yet been consumed or fully utilized. It is like a ticking time bomb, and when the interface is actually used it may become problematic. At that stage, you may be too far into the development to do anything about it.
- **Implementation size of interface**: This metric is not always a good indicator of whether or not there is a problem. However, in the extreme case of code bloat, it may indicate a problem.
- **Number of interfaces consumed by implementation**: Counting the number of interfaces that are consumed makes it possible to figure out the complexity of the implementation. If the count is high, there must be a fairly high level of complexity. In that case, it would make sense to inspect the implementation and attempt to simplify the code. Another potential problem in such an implementation is that it may be constantly affected by interface changes. This will require constant attention, which may lead to being sloppy when applying a fix.
- **Number of implementations that consume an interface:** If the interface is used by many different implementations, a change in the interface will require changes of all the consumers. This means the stability of the application could be compromised. It is crucial to make sure that there is adequate granularity.
- **Bugs per interface**: The bugs-per-interface indicator points out what interfaces really need attention immediately.

Let's say that you have a project, and that you have identified all of the interfaces and measured all the dynamics we just defined. What you do with those dynamics next is build a picture of what could happen and what is happening. All of the dynamics, except the bug count, are indicators of potential problems, and those dynamics can be evaluated in the design process.

You do not want to build a series of numeric values that say that if the implementation is above a certain size, it must be changed. That is too simplistic. What you want to be able to do is say, "interface Y seems to be a bit complicated. Let's look at it and see if it can be simplified. Or if it can't be simplified, let's make sure that the implementation of the interface works before anything else is tested."

Tracking Bugs

An important task in developing software is to track the bugs. You can track them with a paper-based method or use a software-based method. It doesn't matter. What does matter is that they are tracked.

A BUG-TRACKING SYSTEM

There are many ways to track bugs, but regardless of the system used, you should record the following attributes about the bug:

- **Problem**: This describes the bug. It should be a short paragraph describing the problem and what should have occurred.
- **Steps to reproduce the problem**: This is a list of the steps that caused the bug. (I discuss this in more detail in the "Testing the Application" section of this chapter.)
- **System module or interface**: This defines in which section of the application the bug occurred.
- **Stage of bug fixing**: This indicates what has been done about the bug so far. Possible stages include bug recognition, bug fixing started, bug fixing ended, bug retest completed, bug solved.
- **Priority**: This specifies the importance of the bug. It could be critical (that is, it causes application shutdown or is embarrassing), major (it is a bad bug, but allows some functionality), minor (it impairs application functionality), cosmetic (the user interface does not correspond to the actions), or nice to have (it is a feature that should be there, but is not critical).

ORGANIZING THE BUG PROCESS

Your beta testers will be the ones who generate the various bug reports. Hence, your beta testers are your crucial testers of application stability. From experience, I can say that the best beta testers are the ones within the company who are hired to do the testing. Do not solely rely on end users or customers to do the testing. Most people do not have the time or know how to do proper testing. Thus, the common practice of giving out a beta version to the public is a bad process. While it may be interesting to give customers a look at your product, do not expect to create a stable product based on the public beta.

Once you have bugs, you will need to organize them for individual attention. The person who organizes the bugs should be someone who has good knowledge of the product and has an interest in its success. Typically, a project leader organizes the bugs. The project leader knows what the product does and knows how best to solve a bug. A project leader is also able to assess the ramifications of the bug fix.

Here is an example of how *not* to organize bugs. One big company has decided that the best way to organize bugs is to create a special help desk that does nothing but look at bugs and organize them. Because it is a corporation, this is an easy thing to manage. But the problem is that the people doing the organization do not have experience with the product, so they are not able to consider what the bug submitter is trying to accomplish. As a result, I have frequently submitted a bug report only to be told that it is not reproducible. Only when I send in a bitmap image showing the bug, or say that a developer team member has also seen the bug, is it passed on.

WHEN A PRODUCT CAN SHIP

It is always difficult to predict when a product will be ready to ship, but I once worked with a quality assurance manager who really knew his business. He was able to predict when a product could be shipped by creating a chart of bugs raised to bugs solved.

This chart is not simple and cannot be represented using a single chart. Let's look at charts of the bugs raised over time, bugs solved over time, bugs outstanding, and the bug bars that many companies use.

Bugs Raised

The bugs-raised graph typically looks similar to the one in Figure 19–1.

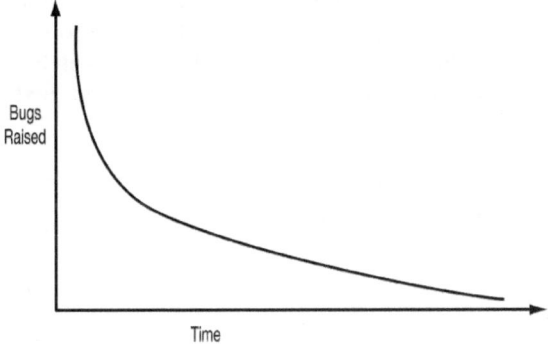

Figure 19–1: Typical example of a bugs-raised graph

This graphs tracks the number of bugs raised per unit of time. It assumes that as time goes on there will be fewer bugs to find or that they will be more difficult to find. Either way, there will be fewer bugs raised per week. I generally compare this curve to an inverse exponential curve, but in reality, the curve has a jigsaw pattern to it, as in Figure 19–2.

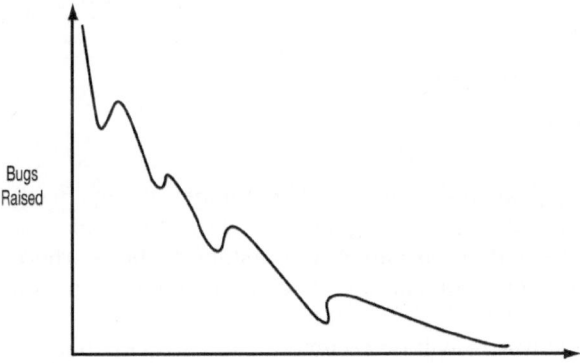

Figure 19–2: Jigsaw pattern in bugs-raised graph

The jigsaw pattern appears because with each new beta release, there is a spike of new bugs found. If the version being released is not a feature-freeze version, then the spikes could be substantially larger, and the graph is drawn out. To predict approximately when the number of bugs found will stabilize, you can do an approximate curve fit. Under all circumstances, you want to see an inverse exponential curve.

Bugs Solved

The most difficult graph to generate is the bugs solved per time graph. This is because the rate of solving bugs depends on the team solving the bugs. What you want to know is how many bugs can be solved per week. To keep calculations simple, assume that the number of bugs solved per week is a constant and that the constant is a running average of the number of bugs solved per week. While this may not be the best indicator, it is the simplest. The possible exception in which this will need to be adjusted is if there is a definite trend toward solving more or fewer bugs. In my experience, though, there hasn't been any trend, just some good days and some bad days.

Bugs Outstanding

When the bugs-raised curve is combined with the bugs-solved curve, the curve in Figure 19–3 results.

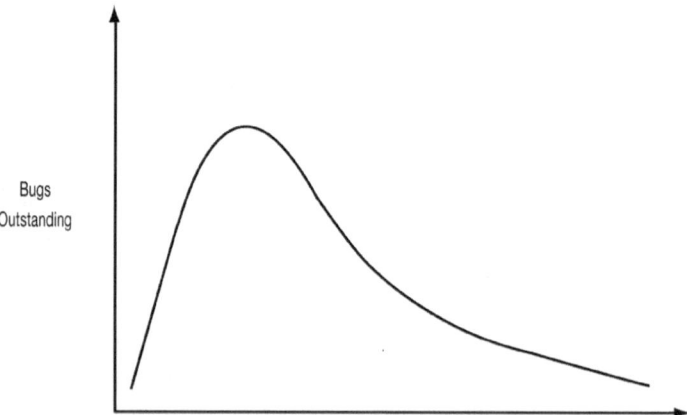

Figure 19–3: A bugs-outstanding curve

The curve will have a definite peak, indicating that the number of bugs being solved is greater than the number of bugs being generated. After the peak, the curve will keep dropping until finally there are no more outstanding bugs. There may be a jigsaw pattern, reflecting variations in the rate at which bugs are raised and solved.

The prediction of when the software will be complete can be tricky, but according to the bugs-outstanding curve, there is a point at which the graph peaks.

You need to find this peak and make sure that the descent has started. From there you can use curve fitting to figure out when the application will contain a given number of bugs.

Bug Bars

Many companies implement something called a *bug bar*. When shipping a product, it is not always possible to fix all bugs. Companies want to fix as many bugs as possible, but there is almost always a lack of time. As a result, decisions must be made about which bugs are solved and when. This is handled using a mathematical equation that factors in the priority of the bugs, the time required to fix the bugs, and the cost of fixing the bugs. Those bugs that bring the most benefit for the least cost are attacked first. As time allows, the other bugs are fixed.

This solution is not ideal, because it results in a release of buggy software. However, it is not always possible to avoid this. Again, I must stress that these situations can largely be avoided by properly thinking out the design before starting coding.

I have outlined some very basic graphs and you may think, "I know this already." But the question is whether you are actually applying it. In the one project where the quality assurance manager knew how to apply the graphs, his results were quite impressive. The team leaders knew when they needed to work overtime and when they did not. In the end, the product was shipped on time, unlike our competitors' products. Being on time was absolutely crucial, because this application was required to be available by government mandate, and without it the company could no longer do business.

Testing the Application

Testing an application is not simple. The biggest challenge in testing is being able to set up a testing scenario, and this is typically not easy. There are tools that can be bought to simplify testing—they make it possible to write scripts and capture output. Then the tester must go through the tests and see what happened or did not happen. However, these tools do not simplify testing considerably.

You should use testing tools to help you to organize and repeat a testing scenario that you created. This would typically involve writing some COM objects, scripting code, and some Microsoft Office Visual Basic for Applications (VBA).

Defining a Testing Strategy

What we are going to do now is define a testing strategy based on the conference registration application. The conference registration application has a Web site that communicates with the Active Server Page (ASP) library. The ASP scripts execute and communicate with the database directly, or communicate with a series of business objects. The business objects have the option of sending messages, or they can call other business objects or the database directly.

Based on this application, there are three different types of tests that will be applied. The simplest is the unit test, which will test individual interfaces and their implementations. Then, when several implementations are combined, an integration test is carried out. And, finally, a system test that tests all of the pieces together is carried out. It is important that this order of testing be followed because not following it wastes time and money.

UNIT TESTING

The application is nothing more than a series of objects that communicate with each other. (I am using the term *object* very loosely to denote two pieces of code talking to each other.) The objects are arranged in a layered hierarchy, and when one object is taken out of the hierarchy to be tested, this is called *unit testing*. What you want is to test the object in isolation to determine the number of bugs in the object itself. Figure 19–4 illustrates unit testing.

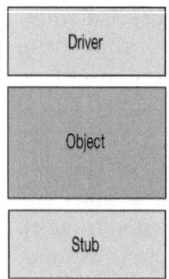

Figure 19–4: Layer being tested by a driver and a stub

A driver is a program that controls the object. The driver calls the methods and then records the output of the results. Then the outputs are studied to determine what worked correctly and what went wrong.

The stub represents the objects that the object calls. The stub is a simple COM object that returns an answer, in accordance with the definition of the COM object that it implements. The stub makes it possible to isolate a bug in a specific object so that you can fix it before putting it back into the application. You use stubs because the underlying objects may not be perfect and fully tested. Testing an object that relies on other buggy objects complicates the debugging process, because you cannot be sure if the object that is being isolated is at fault or if the underlying object is at fault.

Determining When a Stub Is Needed

Sometimes a stub must be written. An example is when you are testing a callback object, as shown in Figure 19–5. In this situation, object A is being tested. It calls object B, which is tied to object A using a callback. To do proper unit testing, it must be assumed that object B does everything correctly while you test object A. This, however, requires that object B has been correctly tested, which would require assuming that object A is functioning correctly. This callback cycle makes this a never-ending situation. To test either object, a stub must be written to take the place of the other object.

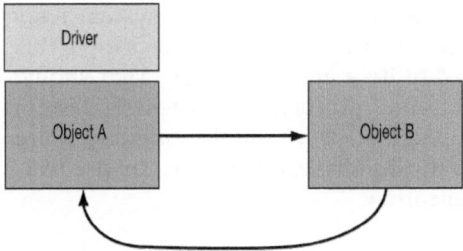

Figure 19–5: Callback objects

Another situation where a stub is vital is when a specific program area is very problematic. Perhaps it has the highest proportion of errors, and every fix causes another problem. What you need to do is isolate the object from the rest of the system, and then perform a full test to see what does work and what does not work.

INTEGRATION TESTING

If proper unit testing were run for every object, then each object would have a driver and a stub. However, to create a stub for every object is a lot of extra work, and sometimes it is not possible to write an effective stub because a real stub requires too much programming effort. Integration testing is a testing method that can be used in these cases. In integration testing, some of the stubs can be eliminated because of the layered nature of the application.

In a layered application architecture there is always a base layer that does not need a stub because it is the core of the application. Therefore, if a testing scenario were to start at the lowest layer and move upward, a stub is not necessary. This testing model assumes that the layers do not call upward, that all calls move downward from untested layers to tested layers.

In Chapter 4, we looked at a layered architecture where lower layers do not call upper layers. This is why I said there that creating a good layered design results in a less-buggy system.

There are situations in which multiple companies or departments are implementing an application and full integration testing is not possible because some systems have not yet been implemented. In that case, writing a stub becomes very important. It also makes testing simpler, because the different companies or departments can fix their own bugs before figuring out what bugs result from integration.

SYSTEM TESTING

System testing is the last step in testing. This is when all of the objects are put together in one grand application and are tested together. This is the stage at which you involve beta testers or end users. They will be able to see what the system is doing and check whether things are visually correct.

In system testing, the focus is not the same as in integration or unit testing. Integration and unit testing are based on specifications, whereas system tests are used to make sure that the business problem is being solved properly. This does not mean that the system test is used to do a major redesign. That should have been handled earlier in the designing and prototyping stages. In system testing, functional issues should be addressed, such as whether messages are being sent properly, data is being saved to the database, and so on. You are testing issues that only arise in a working application.

When to System Test

With the release of Visual Studio, Microsoft has made it possible to debug an application from the beginning to the end in one action. While this is neat to look at, it should never be attempted when you are debugging during a system test, which is like attempting to find a needle in a haystack. In a system test, there are so many objects working together that it is almost impossible to find a bug and determine its ramifications.

A system test uses a user interface, and when a bug arises, a workaround has to be developed so that the tester can test other functionality. However, using a workaround is a bad habit because there is not full coverage in the testing. As a result, the system test cannot replace the unit test or the integration test.

REGRESSION TESTING

There are some other issues to be considered before a test is set up. For example, when a bug is found it needs to be fixed, and once it is fixed it needs to be tested again. This is when a regression test must be performed. The tests that have worked before must be done again to make sure that they will work again. Regression testing is extremely boring. Many people cut corners at this stage, but this is an extremely important part of testing. It is vital that automation tools be employed to do the regression testing systematically.

COVERAGE TESTING

How many tests are enough to ensure that an application is fully tested? This is an interesting question. Traditionally the approach has been to test every aspect of the application, and if all tests prove successful, then the application is bug free. However, this approach is also the most time-intensive. It requires you to think of all the possibilities and then manually go through each one.

The problem is that as the complexity of the system increases, the cost of the system increases exponentially and that extra cost of testing must be accounted for. Testing in complex situations, such as when a computer system controls a nuclear power plant, is beyond the scope of this book.

How can coverage testing be accomplished efficiently in Windows DNA? First, you cannot do a full coverage test because there are so many subsystems within Windows 2000 that have not been fully tested. You have to assume that Windows 2000 is without bugs.

What you can do is write unit, integration, and system tests for your application and hope for the best. That is what it boils down to. I agree that this is not a good answer, but it is the best that can be offered.

WHO OWNS THE TEST SCRIPTS?

Writing an application to do testing is something that is typically left to the quality assurance team, but that is not the best approach. The quality assurance team may understand what the application is trying to do, but it will not understand the design. The architectural team understands the design, so it should be responsible for creating the testing applications. The architectural team will not have to carry out the tests or process the test results, but by making it write its own tests, the architectural team will see the advantages or problems in its own design. This creates a feedback loop that can be used to improve the next application. Also, during the testing phase the architectural team has nothing else to do.

WHEN TO BUILD THE PROJECT

Depending on whom you talk to, people have different opinions about whether a daily build is a good idea. The difference of opinion is a result of the different scopes of various projects. One consultant friend says that doing a daily build eats up development time. A friend at Microsoft said that daily builds of Windows NT/2000 were necessary because of the size of the application.

What you need are builds that are frequent enough. Frequent does not mean that each person checks in his or her sources every night. That only leads to a development process that is out of control. People cannot write code in each day that is perfect and without bugs. What you want to build with is checked-in code that has been unit tested. The Windows 2000 daily build process used this strategy. And because the scope of Windows 2000 was so large, there were always changes in the integration and system tests.

Building a Test Framework

A test framework makes it possible to perform unit, integration, and system testing. A framework is necessary because it makes tracing bugs much easier. UNIX programmers have a really poor debugger, but they more than make up for that with run-time debugging support in the form of libraries and utilities. Here I review the various things that you can do to improve the quality of your code.

SOURCE CODE INSPECTION

The source code should normally be inspected in code review, but code reviews often fail to find many bugs because people use code reviews to ensure that general coding practices are followed. This is one role of a code review.

You can use automated tools to optimize a source code review. These tools will go through your source code and point out typical errors. NUMEGA makes extremely good tools of this sort, and it has source code analysis tools for all of the Visual Studio development environments.

There are many freeware tools on the Internet that do the same thing for C++. These tools are a bit more difficult to use, but they come with the source, which makes it possible for you to tweak the tool to suit your company's programming policies.

After these tools have gone through the code, you need to inspect the code yourself for any coding problems. This means looking at the design and then looking at the implementation. It is a lengthy, but necessary, process. Instead of a code review, you could call it a project audit.

PREPARING YOUR APPLICATION FOR TESTING

The problem with debugging large distributed applications is in replicating the bugs. Some bugs only appear once in every ten times, and to debug nine extra times to see the one error is very expensive. It is vital that the application be capable of capturing the state at the time errors occur.

Writing Logging Code

Most of our implementations are COM objects, and the COM objects reside in the business tier, which is the central place that all data has to pass through. Hence, the COM objects are the place to add logging programming logic. The logging programming logic makes it possible to trace the problem when something goes wrong.

Just logging any type of information is not very useful. What you want to log is the state of the object. There are a couple of things that we are already doing in our code that will help with this scenario. First, we are writing our code using exceptions. The exceptions capture state information and then write it to a log file. Second, the exception is propagated and more state is captured.

Let's look at a logging example implemented in Visual C++:

```
STDMETHODIMP CAGTProject::execute() {
try {
    TNINTERFACELib::IImplResolverPtr ptrResolve( "TNInterface.ImplRe-
solver.1");
    TNINTERFACELib::IResolverPtr ptrFile = ptrResolve->getDefaultImpl();
    ...
    if( checkoutStatus != FALSE) {
        // Push the file back up the tree
        char tmpPath[ MAX_PATH];
        if( getStringValue( SEC_ROOT, KEY_FTPDIRECTORY, tmpPath) == false) {
            GenError( "Cache directory key does not exist");
        }
    }
} catch( _com_error err) {
    TraceCOM();
    return err.Error();
```

```
}
return S_OK;
}
```

All of the code in this example is contained in an exception block. That is nothing new. What is new is the GenError function call. This function is a macro that logs the error that has occurred. It notes the file line number and the file that the error is located in. The error is then converted to a COM error.

The COM error is then caught in the exception block, and the TraceCOM function is called, which again logs the error. This second logging is necessary, because with COM compiler support, not all errors are a result of the GenError function call. The err.Error() method returns the error as an external COM error, which is then received by the caller and handled. If the caller does the same thing again, we will have a chain of events and state. This helps in figuring out what the COM object was doing and why it failed.

Logging Code within a Scripting Context

The preceding example applies to Visual C++ and any other programming language, and in a scripting context things are similar. Because the logging routines use COM objects to log the error, the scripting language can do the same thing. The only difference is that in a scripting context, you do not have a file and line number and the error can be propagated using exceptions.

Why Write a Custom Logging Object?

You may question why we are writing custom COM logging objects. You might think that it is more efficient to write to the Windows 2000 event service.

When I originally built systems for clients, logging to the event system was not feasible—the client wanted remote diagnosis. By using a custom error-logging facility, it was possible for the system to write a log file and then send it to me automatically—the client did not have to do anything special to send us the error information. As well, large amounts of logging data are sometimes generated, and the event service is not always happy when a few megabytes of data are streamed to it.

WRITING A STUB

Writing a stub is not complicated. The stub is an implementation of a COM interface, and the COM interface has a series of parameters and methods. How they are called depends on the design document, because the stub simply implements the design document. You are basically implementing a truth table. This means that if the parameter is X and the method is Y, then the result should be Z.

Writing a Driver

When you write a driver, you need to go through the design document, call the various scenarios, and test to see whether the results match the design document. This can be complicated, because generating the various test conditions requires a permutations and combinations approach. Additionally, figuring out whether everything actually went correctly is complicated.

What we are going to do is write a driver to do unit testing for a COM interface and implementation that we have already discussed—the operations object that is responsible for adding a user to the conference registration application. If you are unsure how the COM interface and implementation work, you may want to revisit them in Chapters 8 and 9.

DEFINING A TEST CONDITION CATALOGUE

For every interface that is to be tested, regardless of its type, a condition catalogue needs to be defined. The condition catalogue defines the various conditions of the method parameters to be used. It is important to identify the conditions because they will be used to build a testing plan. If there are not enough conditions, then the plan will be weak and bugs will appear.

I am not going to illustrate the testing of the entire operations object, just a single method. The method that we will write a condition catalogue for is the following one:

```
HRESULT ISimpleOperations::addUser( [out,retval]long *userId);
```

There are no input conditions for the method, itself. There is only an output parameter. At this point, you might think that writing the condition catalogue will be simple. If the method is called, then the output must be greater than 1. However, that is not entirely correct, because the parameters for this method are stored on the ISimpleData interface. Therefore, the condition catalogue has to consider both the method and the ISimpleData COM interface, which is defined as follows:

```
interface ISimpleData : IDispatch {
[propget, id(1)] HRESULT username([out, retval] BSTR *pVal);
[propput, id(1)] HRESULT username([in] BSTR newVal);
[propget, id(2)] HRESULT password([out, retval] BSTR *pVal);
[propput, id(2)] HRESULT password([in] BSTR newVal);
[propget, id(3)] HRESULT userId([out, retval] long *pVal);
[propput, id(3)] HRESULT userId([in] long newVal);
};
```

When adding a parameter to the condition catalogue, you need to specify a valid value and an invalid value. This is called equivalence partitioning. In the condition catalogue, you only want to define the values that are valid. In our situation, the condition catalogue for the method addUser is as follows:

VARIABLE	CONDITION
username	8 < length < 255
username	value != existing value
password	8 < length < 255
userid	generated

According to our equivalence partitioning concept there are three conditions to test for the password: a string length less than 9 characters, a string of 9 to 254 characters, and a string greater than 254 characters. Testing any more conditions is a waste of processing cycles. However, of these three conditions, two are negative conditions and one is positive: negative conditions test specific situations in which the method should fail; positive conditions test a successful method call.

It is tempting to do more tests, because how can three tests be enough? Let's consider the case of searching for a user based on a userId. Theoretically, any number assigned to userId can represent some user. Hence, there is only one test required, where the UserId is assigned. And if it works, then everything should be okay. This, of course, is not true, because the user may or may not exist, and both situations have to be played out. The problem here is that the test conditions are being mixed up with the implementation test scenarios. The test catalogue defines the minimum number of tests that need to be executed to test all possibilities in terms of parameters. What we forgot to add in the search for a user condition catalogue is the business process.

Let's go back to the original condition catalogue for the adduser method. The condition that says the username must not already exist. This test condition is a condition that is based on business logic and can only be realized by the implementation of the method.

With positive conditions, there is an additional situation where bugs may occur, called the boundary condition. A boundary condition is when the test condition is executed on the limit of acceptance. For example, a boundary condition is when the password string has a length of eight. The value is valid, but many programmers have a habit of confusing eight for nine or for seven. This may seem like a silly test, but it occurs as often as not.

With the inclusion of boundary testing, the number of test conditions for password is four (two negative and two positive conditions that are boundary conditions). The different test string lengths are 7 and 8, and 254 and 255. This is the maximum required number of test scenarios for the password. Some people feel uneasy about this and recommend that more tests be performed. To put those people at ease, two additional tests can be introduced, a random valid condition and a random invalid condition. This then puts the number of test conditions up to six. More test conditions only waste time and money.

An exception in which you may require more test conditions, is when you are testing a mathematical algorithm. This is because when a math calculation is improperly implemented, a small test condition catalogue may be correct, but a bigger test condition catalogue may expose incorrect calculations.

DEFINING TEST CASES

After the individual test conditions are defined, it is necessary to define the individual test cases. The test cases are defined as being either negative or positive. A positive test case means that everything is okay and stable. A negative test case means that something went wrong and needs to be logged.

The driver uses the test cases to call the interface. Combining the various parameters with a test condition creates a test case. For each parameter and each test condition, a test case must be generated. The task really becomes a matter of permutations of the different parameters and test conditions. The simplest way to organize this is to create a test matrix.

The following table defines all the test cases for our example COM interface. It includes boundary tests, but no random or iterative test conditions.

NUMBER	TYPE OF TEST CASE	TEST CASES
1	Negative test	**username** length = 9, **password** length = 8
2	Negative test	**username** length = 8, **password** length = 9
3	Negative test	**username** length = 9, **password** length = 255
4	Negative test	**username** length = 255, **password** length = 9
5	Positive test	**username** length = 9, **password** length = 254
6	Positive test	**username** length = 254, **password** length = 9
7	Negative test	**username** exists length = 254, **password** length = 9

I have not done a full permutation of the test conditions. This is not because I trust the person who wrote the code or that I am lazy. It is because I am optimizing the testing conditions. For example, look at test cases 1 and 2. They are both negative tests. The first negative test case is a result of one test condition being positive and the other being negative. The second is the opposite scenario. The missing negative test is when both test conditions are negative. That test is unnecessary because each parameter will have been tested for negativity, and combining the two will not execute a different code path. Notice, however, that this optimization can only be applied some of the time. It works for simple test conditions, but it may not work in a mathematical formula, because two negatives may make a positive.

The two positive tests are based on the boundary test conditions. Note that when writing the driver, the two positive tests must not use the same username test condition. Suppose you are adding a user and the driver uses the same username for test cases 5 or 6. In test 5, which is the first positive test case, it would work. But if you use the same username test condition in test 6, the second positive case, it will fail. Suppose you then submit a bug report, the developer tests the code, and it works. The tester tests the "fixed" code and it fails again. Now the tester and developer are at odds. Who is correct? The answer is that the developer is correct, because the supposed positive test case 6 is actually negative test case 7. The driver has the wrong data and it needs to be fixed.

WRITING A SCRIPT DRIVER

The simplest way to drive a series of COM objects is to write a series of scripts using the Windows Scripting Host. By default, Windows 2000 installs the VB-Script and Jscript (Microsoft's version of JavaScript) scripting languages. But it is also possible to use scripting languages such as Perl, Rexx, or Python.

My samples are written using JavaScript script. An example driver using JavaScript that executes test case 1 follows:

```
var tstObject;
var logObject;
logObject = WScript.CreateObject("Tester.logging");
logObject.startTestCases("SimpleOperations::addUser method test");
tstObject = WScript.CreateObject( "SimpleProject.ImplOperations");
tstObject.simpleData.username = "A valid name";
tstObject.simpleData.password = "invalid";
try {
tstObject.addUser();
logObject.failedNegativeTest( 1);
} catch( e) {
    logObject.successfulNegativeTest( 1);
}
...
logObject.endTestCases();
```

I expect this script to be a negative test and to fail. A logging object is added so that I can track what happened. This also helps me when doing regression testing. For example, in this test case, the method addUser is tested. The startTestCases log object method opens a file that will record the outcome of the various test cases. Then the various test conditions are assigned and the tstObject.addUser method is called.

The Windows 2000 release of JavaScript introduces exception handling. The exception-handling mechanism will capture COM errors. Thus, using the error-generation scheme, the script will capture the error if anything goes wrong. Because the test is a negative test, an exception should be generated, which means that the successfulNegativeTest log object method with the test case id should be recorded. If an exception is not thrown, it needs to be recorded as a failed test using the failedNegativeTest method.

You may wonder why the state is not saved when the test fails. It might seem that saving the state would make it easier to debug the interface, but this is not true. With this type of unit and integration test, the test case can easily be identified and replicated so that the bug can be found in the debugging session. Remember that the integration tests are performed layer by layer, which results in less complexity.

WRITING OTHER DRIVERS

There are other types of drivers that need to be written, such as Web drivers and database drivers. Each of these drivers is developed in the same fashion. First, the test conditions are determined; second, the test cases are defined; and finally, the test cases are implemented using a programming language. When testing a database, the programming language that is used may not be a script, but perhaps a Visual Basic or Visual C++ program. The tools and environments may vary, but the process of testing is the same.

Writing a User Interface Driver

When doing system testing, you use the user interface. This is where testing becomes difficult. Although there are scripting tools to take snapshots resulting from a test case, they are really difficult for a computer to decipher. Automation tools can help by making it possible to capture images and compare them. This is very powerful and useful.

What is indispensable as a user interface driver is a utility that makes it possible to record keyboard and mouse actions. When regression testing needs to be performed, the tester can just activate a recorded session and see whether everything went well. This not only reduces boredom, it also ensures consistency of the tester. Recording programs, such as Macro Magic, can be bought for less than $50.

The same process of defining the test cases applies to user interface testing. The exception is that the test conditions may not be based on numbers or letters—they may be based on actions performed. Remember that you should not be performing unit or integration testing during system testing. That should have occurred before.

Performance Testing

When an application is being designed, prototyped, and tested, there is always the question of how to achieve good performance. What people end up doing is creating a design that should perform optimally, and if the implementation has unacceptable performance, the decision is made to get bigger hardware. If the performance needs tweaking, then the developer will attempt to find the problems and change a few things.

But let's consider the situation of building a distributed application. In this scenario, it is possible to buy faster hardware, but much hardware will need to be bought. Performance cannot simply be designed into the application because you generally cannot specify where the application will be distributed. What you want to do is make performance another quantifiable parameter in your design process. To do this, the performance testing must be split into two categories: testing the performance of the hardware and testing the performance of the application and the infrastructure.

Testing the Hardware

In my consulting experience, very few clients take the time to do a performance test of hardware. People just buy bigger machines because that solves the problem. Very few people actually calculate a ROI (return on investment) for a piece of hardware.

By testing the hardware, a set of benchmarks is established, based on your environment and conditions. But the tests are controlled in such a manner that two different machines will execute the same application using the same context. The Application Performance Explorer (APE) tool in Microsoft Visual Studio provides a controlled environment to carry out distributed processing tasks. Be forewarned, however, that the benchmarks created with this tool do not serve as general benchmarks. They only serve as relative benchmarks for assessing the performance of a machine. This test can then be used to compare which piece of hardware is the most cost effective.

THE APPLICATION PERFORMANCE EXPLORER

Visual Studio Enterprise Edition has a very useful and simple utility called APE. This utility, shown in Figure 19–6, makes it possible to provide a controlled environment for testing the performance of the hardware.

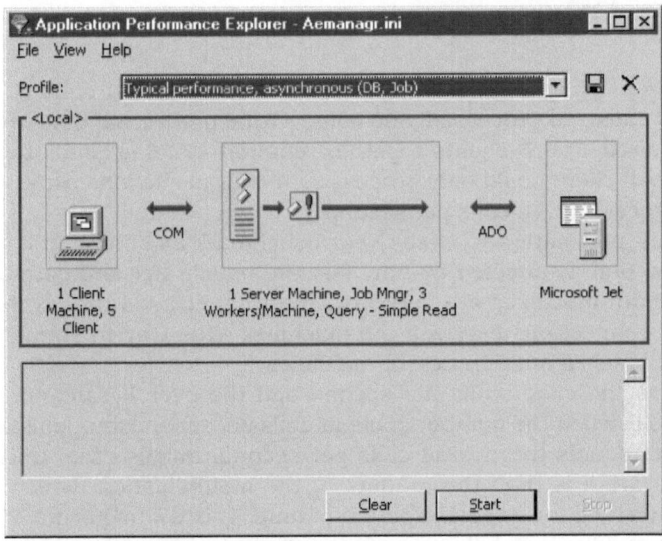

Figure 19–6: APE window

APE is a dialog-based application. Look at the diagram in the middle of Figure 19–6—there is a client box communicating with a middle-tier box using COM, which talks to a data-services box using Active Data Objects (ADO). This is an example of a distributed Windows DNA application.

What it is telling us is that we should test the scenario where there is one client machine executing five worker tasks. The client will call a single server that has a maximum number of three worker objects handling the client requests. The middle-tier server action is based on a selection using a simple read select on a Jet (Microsoft Access) database.

This APE scenario is a defined and controlled scenario that can be executed on different hardware that can be benchmarked. By comparing the benchmarks from different hardware, the performance of the two machines can be quantified for use in an ROI calculation.

Make sure that no other applications are running on the hardware to be tested and click Start. After a little while, some output will be displayed in the box below the diagram, such as the following:

```
Click graphical button images to configure APE test scenarios.
All requested clients were successfully created.
All requested workers were successfully created.
Test Started.
Collecting and writing log records ...
Total Calls = 500
Elapsed Time = 11.65 seconds (47.85 seconds in clients)
Client Calls Per Second = 8.94
Overall Calls Per Second = 42.48
```

The output is telling us that the scenario involved is making 500 calls (5 clients each making 100 calls). To process all 500 calls, a total processing time of 11.65 seconds was required. The 5 clients together required 47.85 seconds to process the 500 calls. Each client could only process 8.94 calls per second. However, the server could process 42.48 calls per second.

How can you use this information to tweak your benchmark and find bottlenecks? The total elapsed time is affected by how fast the middle tier and database server are. When both machines are very fast, the total elapsed time will depend on the network connections between the machines. One way to shrink the total elapsed time is to use a multiprocessor machine.

You want to increase the client calls per second and the overall calls per second. The perfect ratio is when the number of client calls per second multiplied by the number of clients equals the overall calls per second. In this case, the overall calls per second are less than the product of the multiplication, which means that the client is waiting for a specific period of time. This waiting is not a result of the database or middleware, but is because of the network used to communicate between the various layers.

USING APE

To understand the simulation that APE runs, you have to first understand the different deployment models supported by APE. APE can simulate three different remote deployment models:

- Synchronous communication model
- Asynchronous communication model
- Queued objects communication model with callbacks

Figure 19–7 shows a workflow model that illustrates the architecture of APE's simulations.

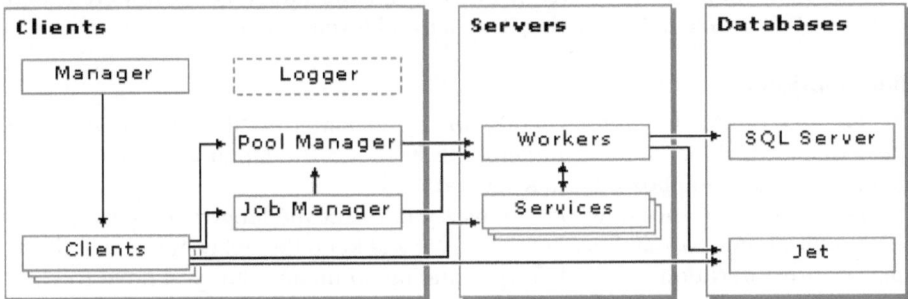

Figure 19–7: APE Workflow

In synchronous communication mode, the client waits for the call to be completed and cannot do anything until the server returns. In Figure 19–7, the client creates a worker via the job manager. The worker then creates a service that does the work and returns the value to the logger. After the task is completed, both the worker and the service are destroyed. This is a very inefficient architecture, but it is a useful simulation when trying to determine the throughput of a network.

In asynchronous communication mode, workers are not destroyed after use—they are reused. This saves the time required to create them. In this model, the client uses the Pool Manager to invoke a free worker, which then creates a service that does the work. There are no return values in this model. If queuing were used, the client would go through the job manager, which would then communicate with the pool manager to invoke a free worker. This keeps the number of workers under control; clients are queued until a worker from the pool is available.

In the queued object communication with callbacks mode, a return value is passed back to the client via callbacks. The use of callbacks frees the client to perform other tasks while waiting for a return value from the server, as opposed to being blocked, as is the case with synchronous communication mode.

Selecting a Profile

The first step in using APE is to select a profile. A list of predefined profiles appears in the Profile combo box shown in Figure 19–6.

When you start a simulation, the client creates a service. How it goes about creating this service is determined by the profile you selected. For example, if you selected the synchronous mode, then the client will create a service directly;

if you selected asynchronous mode, the client will go to the job manager to create the service. With the pooling option, the client uses the pool manager to simulate the use of pooled objects to perform a task.

All parameters of the predefined profiles are configurable via dialog boxes. These profiles are just there to help you get started. Once you understand how APE works, you can start defining your own profile to suit your system.

For our example, we will select the profile called Typical performance, asynchronous (DB, Job). Then we will work through the individual parameters and customize this profile before saving it under a different name.

Client Options

You can open the Client Options dialog box by clicking the Client button (the one with 1 Client Machine, 5 Client underneath it) or via the menu item View/Client Options.... This dialog box contains several tabs.

The first tab is General, which enables you to set the length of your test and the amount of time to wait between calls. We will keep the delay between calls at 0 ms. The test duration can be left open (doing so means that you have to click Stop to stop it), or you can have the test go through a fixed number of calls, or you can have it run for a fixed length of time. Bear in mind that the longer your test is, the more accurate it will be. For this example, set the test to go through 50 calls.

The second tab is Concurrency, which enables you to set which machines will act as clients and how many processes will run on each machine. By default, the local machine is used as the client. You can add remote machines if you want to test performance using processes from different machines. This is a very good idea for distributed applications, because it makes use of the network.

For this example, leave the number of processes per machine at 5. We will use two client machines, which will create a total of ten processes. Selecting the checkbox beside Use Remote Client Machines enables the Configure... button. Click this button to display the Configure Remote Client Machines dialog box shown in Figure 19–8.

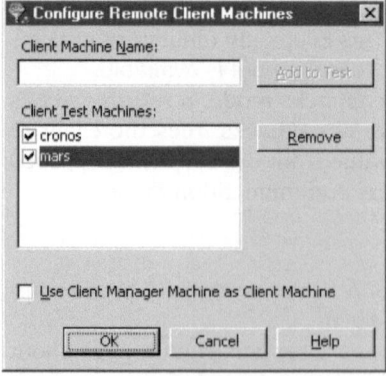

Figure 19–8: APE Remote client

Before you can select the client test machines, you have to make sure they are properly configured:

- Make sure all remote client machines are running Windows NT 4 or Windows 2000.
- Set the security settings on the machines so that processes can be created remotely. You can change this setting by using the RA Connection Manager. Just select Run from the Start menu and type in Racmgr32.exe before clicking OK. In the Client Access tab of the Remote Automation Connection Manager, select the system security policy to Allow All Remote Creates, and then close the dialog box via the File/Exit menu.
- Start the Automation Manager, which is available in your Visual Studio menu under the Enterprise tools. You need to do this on all machines that are to be used remotely in your APE test.

After your client machines are configured, you can add them to your test. For this example, I used two remote clients and no local machine. (You can set this by unchecking the Use Client Manager Machine as Client Machine checkbox in the Configure Remote Client Machine dialog box, which is accessed when you are adding the remote machines.)

You are now ready to specify what type and amount of data will be sent from the client to the server services. This is set in the Send Data tab. The type of data should always be set to variant array, because passing a variant collection is too costly to be a plausible option. Then you can set the size of the data—for this test I decided to pass 20+/–5 Bytes/Row and 6+/0 Rows of data.

The Return Data tab allows you the same type of selection as the Send Data tab, but it specifies the data being passed from the server services to the client. I selected the same values as in the Send Data specifications.

Finally, you need to specify the callback options in the Callback tab. This tab is only relevant if you are using the job manager. Because we selected an asynchronous method in this example, the job manager will be used, and so the type of callback should be set. There are three choices:

- To have the client pass the callback object only once
- To have the client pass a callback object for every service request
- To not pass a callback object but have results returned to the client by activating events on the client

For this example, let's select the first option.

Now that you have finished defining the client options, you should save the profile via the File/Save Profile As... menu. Give the new profile a meaningful name, because you will want to refer back to this profile in the future to reproduce this performance test. Typically, you will run multiple tests to narrow down the designs when deciding on the best architecture for your application.

Service Connection Options

When you want to control the remote server, you need to set the service options. To do this, open the Application Service Connection Options dialog box with the

View/Service Connection Options... menu item or by clicking the double-arrow button that links the client to the server machine. For this example test, we will keep all the default values. However, I'll run through the different options here so that you know what to select in your future tests.

The connection type enables you to define the type of connection used to connect to remote clients and/or the remote server machine. Your choices are Distributed COM or Remote Automation. We have already configured our remote client machines to use Remote Automation, so that's what we should select here.

You can also specify the server location to be used for your test from the current dialog box. If you select a remote server, make sure that it is configured to enable the remote creation of processes and that it is running the automation manager as described for the use of remote clients.

If you selected Distributed COM as the connection type and you want to use a remote server, then you need to configure your server machine. There are quite a few steps involved in doing this, and they are well described in the MSDN Library help file, so I will not repeat them here. Look in the chapter titled "Application Performance Explorer Common Tasks," under the section "Installing Application Performance Explorer," to find the task "Configuring DCOM Access Permissions Using DCOMCNFG." If you follow the instructions, you should be able to use Distributed COM as your type of connection.

Service Options

You can bring up the service options dialog box with the View/Service Options... menu or by clicking the button above the server machine description. In this dialog box, you can specify what types of tasks your server should perform during the test, and how these tasks should be processed.

The DB Task tab enables you to specify the database workload. Two types of tasks are available: distributed Microsoft Transaction Server (MTS) Transactions and database query. You can select distributed MTS transactions only if an SQL Server database is selected in the database option (described in the "Database Options" section, later in this chapter). For this example test, specify a database query to be used.

Four different queries are available for testing. When selecting them, you can see the SQL code they execute, but you cannot modify it. For this example, specify the Simple Transaction query.

The CPU Task tab is used to specify the details of simulating CPU-based workloads on the server machine. You can specify the task duration and the sleep period for that task. Note that the task duration is how long the task will take to execute and is not the same as the CPU task duration because there might be break periods during the execution of a single task, depending on CPU availability. For this test, we only test the performance of the database query, so leave the Simulate CPU Based Task checkbox unchecked.

You can now specify pooling options in the Pooling tab. By using preexisting, pooled resources, the client can benefit from picking from a pool of workers when it needs one, instead of having to create a new one every time. The workers are automatically be made available when they are free and are recycled by the APE after use. Selecting to use the job manager means that both job pooling and job queuing are used; selecting to use the pool manager only makes use of job pooling. Either way, the number of pooled workers can be specified. For this test, use both job pooling and job queuing with a pool of three workers per machine.

Another setting that you can specify in this dialog box is the use of remote machines to run the workers. Note that the remote server machine used to run workers needs to have DCOM configured as described in the help-file chapter "Application Performance Explorer Common Tasks," section "Installing Application Performance Explorer," task "Configuring DCOM Access Permissions Using DCOMCNFG."

Finally, in the Service Binding tab, you can specify what type of binding will be used for service objects. COM early binding will definitely give performance improvements, but you can find out just how much by comparing the two. You may often want to use late binding for design reasons, but you always have a trade-off with performance. Using APE enables you to learn how big this trade-off is and whether making it is worthwhile. Checking the Retain Service References checkbox enables you to specify that services should be created only once and that a reference to them be kept once they are created. Checking the Preload Services checkbox keeps the creation of the services objects from being part of the performance test if the Retain Service References checkbox was checked. For this example test, check the three checkboxes.

At this stage, you should save the profile by clicking the floppy disk icon next to the drop-down combo box containing the names of the profiles. Note that a little star appears to the left of the profile name in the Profile combo box after it has been changed.

Database Connection

The next setting you have to specify is the database access method. You can invoke the Database Connection Options dialog box by clicking the double arrow that links the server to the database, or by selecting the View/Database Connection Options... menu item.

The only parameter that needs to be set is the access method. You have the choice between ADO, RDO (Remote Data Objects), DAO (Data Access Objects), and ODBC (Open Database Connectivity) API (Application Programming Interface). Try different ones and compare their performance. Bear in mind, though, that ADO is now the preferred Microsoft database access method and that DAO is still supported but only for backward compatibility. When selecting an access method, as with other architectural issues, performance is not the only criteria that should motivate your choice.

For our test, select ADO as the access method.

Database Options

Finally, you can select which database to use via the Database Options dialog box. This dialog box is opened by clicking the button at top of the database description or by selecting the View/Database Options... menu option.

Two databases are supported: Microsoft Access (Jet) or SQL Server. If you select Microsoft SQL Server as your database for the first time, the APE Database Setup Wizard will guide you through selecting your SQL Server database.

The first choice the wizard gives is to connect to an existing APE SQL Server database or to install a new one. If you have never installed the APETEST database, select the option to install a new database, and the APE Database Setup Wizard will guide you through the process.

You have to use the APETEST database to perform your test, because the queries are designed to use that database. If you want to use a different database, you could write your own queries for the APE source code, which is available in

```
..\Program Files\Microsoft Visual Studio\Common\Tools\Ape\Source\
```

Having the source code gives you total flexibility to customize APE to suit your project.

The APE Database Setup Wizard creates an ODBC User Data Source Name on your machine with the name APEDB_SQLServer pointing to the database you specified. Then, if you elected to install a new database, it installs the database on the server of your choice. If you would like to run the APE Database Setup Wizard again, you will have to delete the User DSN that it created. Alternatively, if you just want to change the database it points to, you can modify the DSN yourself.

After your APETEST database is created, you are ready to run your first performance test.

Testing Results

I ran the earlier test in this chapter on two different machines. One machine is a dual-processor machine and the other is a single-processor machine. We'll now figure out which machine offers the better bang for the buck. Following are the results of the two tests. (You will not get the same results on your own hardware, because these results are hardware specific.)

DUAL-CPU MACHINE	SINGLE-CPU MACHINE
Total Calls=500	Total Calls=500
Elapsed Time=20.88 seconds (152.63 seconds in clients)	Elapsed Time=38.24 seconds (266.86 seconds in clients)
Client Calls Per Second=3.28	Client Calls Per Second=1.87
Overall Calls Per Second=23.95	Overall Calls Per Second=13.08

The results show very clearly that the dual-processor machine performed better than the single-processor machine for this test scenario. In fact, it is almost twice as fast: with the dual-processor machine, an average of 24 calls could be performed every second, whereas only 13 calls could be performed using the single-processor machine.

Now let's calculate a simple ROI. Let's say that the single-processor machine costs $1,000 and the dual–processor machine costs $3,000. Theoretically, I can buy two single-processor machines to get the performance of a dual-processor machine. Whether or not I could actually do this depends on the load-balancing functionality. This is, yet again, another controlled scenario to test, and based on that test, a ROI could be calculated.

Testing the Application with Visual Studio Analyzer

Visual Studio Analyzer is a tool from Microsoft that traps events from your live distributed application. It gives you an overall view of the communication occurring between the different components that make up your application, even if they are running on different machines. It lets you see the interaction between the different building blocks of your application without going into the details of how those building blocks are constructed. Unlike APE, Visual Studio Analyzer (VSA) shows you how your application performs in a real environment, not in a simulated environment.

VSA traps events only from technologies that are enhanced to have the capability to give information to Visual Studio Analyzer. COM, ADO, and COM+ are such technologies. You can also customize your application to give information to Visual Studio Analyzer, but that is beyond the scope of this book. More information can be found in the VSA section of the MSDN Library.

USING VSA

To use Visual Studio Analyzer, you need an application that can be monitored. We will monitor the process of adding a user to the database in the conference registration application—the same one that we wrote the test cases for.

Now that you have an application to profile, you have to create a Visual Studio Analyzer project. There are a number of steps involved in recording events from an application:

1. Create or open a VSA project.
2. Connect to the machines that you want to profile in the project.
3. Create or open a collection filter and mark it as the recording filter.
4. Create a new event log and begin collection. An event log can only be used to collect events once.
5. Run your application and VSA will start recording events.

Fortunately, Microsoft provides a wizard to take you through most of these steps. To create a new VSA project via the wizard, open up the Visual Studio development environment and select the File/New Project menu item. This brings up a dialog box that enables you to create different types of Visual Studio projects. Select Visual Studio Analyzer Project and then click the Analyzer Wizard icon that appears on the right side of the dialog box. You just need to specify a name and path for your location, and you are ready to create your first VSA project. The VSA wizard guides you through the different steps required to create your project.

Your first option is whether or not to let the wizard scan your network to create a list of machines. You can go ahead with this, but in my case, the only machine appearing in the list was my local machine. I had to manually add the other machines I wanted to be part of the test.

You are then prompted for the components for which you would like to see events on each machine you selected to monitor.

Finally, you can select, from a list, the filters you would like to include in your application. The filters make it possible to catch specific subsystem events. For the time being, it's a good idea to include them all.

While the wizard is setting up your project to start recording, you will see a list of tasks to be done. After the wizard finishes its tasks, the recording begins immediately. If you stop the recording, you cannot record again in the same event log—you have to create a new one. Instead of stopping the recording, you should just pause it.

To view what is happening, double-click the event log that is currently recording. This will bring up the event list view, and you can watch as events are being trapped. Start your application, and the recording of the events will start. Only the events specified in the recording filter are trapped and displayed in the event log, as shown in Figure 19–9.

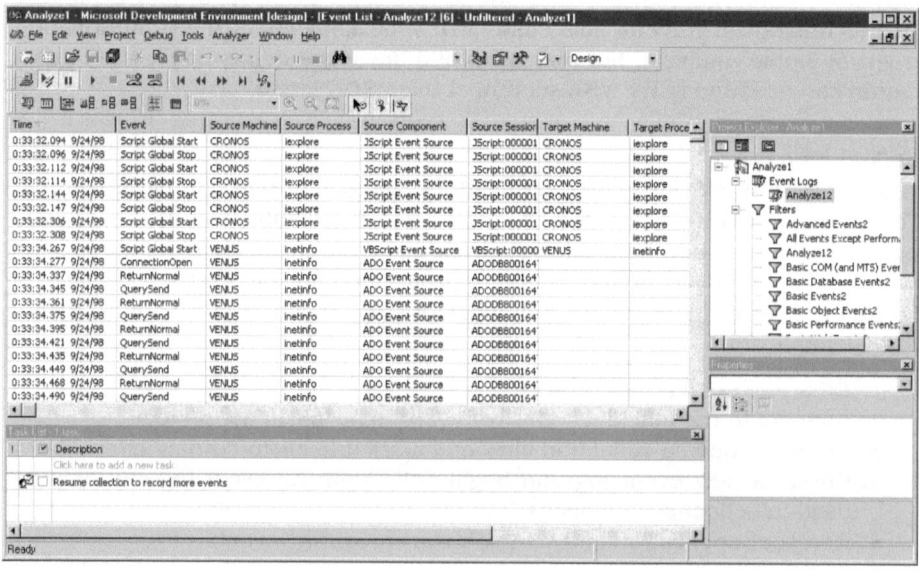

Figure 19–9: VSA event example

The event list displays a sequential list of all the events that were trapped while your application was running. This view can be overwhelming, but you can refine it. Even though you can only have one filter that specifies the events that will be recorded in the event log, you can apply different filters to the views of the event log, narrowing down the displayed data.

To apply a filter to a view, right-click the filter and select Apply Filter to View from the pop-up menu. To see what types of events a filter is covering, just double-click the filter, and the Edit Filter dialog box will display This dialog box enables you to see which events will be trapped and to modify this filter.

The most useful view for checking the performance of your application is the chart view, shown in Figure 19–10. Right-click your event log and select Chart from the pop-up menu to display that view.

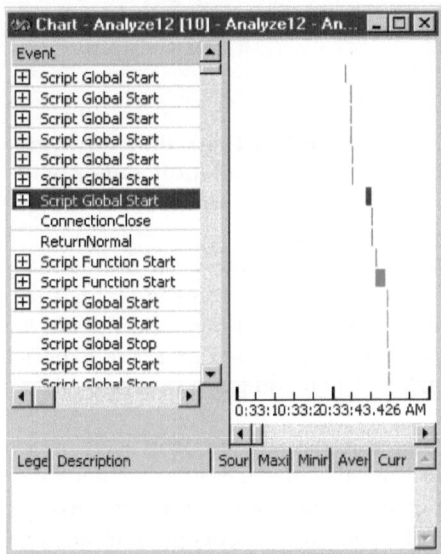

Figure 19–10: VSA application performance

The chart view lets you easily pinpoint those tasks that required more time to execute. To get a detailed view of those events, just double-click the area on the chart you are interested in. A view containing a detailed description of the event pops up. In this way, you can find out which parts of your application took longer to execute.

In the case of our sample application, the performance is quite uniform. The only thing you will notice is that some Jscript (Microsoft's version of JavaScript) events executed in the browser sometimes take longer to execute.

To further help your analysis, you can display a line graph of data recorded by the Windows NT Performance Monitor. This is done by right-clicking the graph and selecting Add Graph from the pop-up menu. You can only view data that your recording filter was capturing. The data recorded by the Windows NT Performance Monitor appears in the category All Measured Events, subcategory PerfMon events. This data can help you find areas of slow performance that are due to activities on the machine, rather than to an internal application task or setting.

A NOTE ABOUT VSA

I discussed VSA rather briefly because VSA is an idea that is semicomplete. VSA makes it possible to track events, but figuring out the events that you are tracking is even more difficult than using a UNIX command line. The descriptions are very terse, and it is difficult for someone who does not understand the application to do a performance analysis.

What can be interesting is adding your custom events to the VSA and then tracking them in the application architecture. In this way, it is possible to tune the application and find problem areas. When you use the VSA in this context you are creating a sort of superprofiler.

Putting It in Perspective

Ensuring quality control is not easy. Some people tend to think that throwing more resources at a problem will solve it, but that is not the solution. Other people add more complexity. I have found that quality is based on keeping things simple. This includes the design and implementation process.

I get two types of comments about the topics in this chapter. The first is that the bug graphs cannot be as simple as I've made them seem. But the fact is that they really are that simple. What is not simple is figuring out how to do the curve fitting. The curve fit is not purely mathematical—it is also based on some experience. For example, mathematics will not help you when you learn that one of the managers is being an idiot.

The other comment is that more test cases must be needed. However, more aren't needed. In that situation, you need to trust the mathematics, which says that you only need a specific number of test cases. If you need more comforting, I suggest you read a statistical quality control book. Many concepts will not directly apply, but you can learn the mathematics of understanding defects.

Chapter 20

Creating Services

We have considered many different aspects of developing an application, but there is one thing that we neglected to discuss: How are tasks that are not under the control of a user executed? For example, in Chapter 12, we talked about messaging, and we just assumed that the message at the other end would be automatically read and executed. But how was this done? The answer is "by a service."

This chapter focuses on wrapping up these loose ends of writing a distributed application. There are two types of services: 24☐7 and periodic. A periodic service can also be called a batch process.

Running a 24☐7 Process

The main reason for having a 24☐7 process is to monitor the system and then provide feedback. In Chapter 12, where we discussed messaging, this kind of process is used to pull Microsoft Message Queue (MSMQ) messages from an MSMQ queue. The MSMQ message is then processed, and another message may be generated and sent on its way.

You might also use a service for a Component Object Model (COM)+ event publisher. For example, there is a COM+ event for indicating when a stock price goes below a specific level. The service could monitor the stock price, and when the stock price changes, an event is sent to the COM+ event system.

A COM service is also appropriate when a COM object exposes COM connection-based events. These events cannot be processed if you are using a typical COM+ application, but because the service is a persistent process, it can be a receiver of the connection point-based event. This makes an application more efficient than if it were constantly polling for an answer.

The point is that it is sometimes necessary to have a dedicated process, and on Windows 2000 the only sensible way of creating a dedicated process is to write a Windows 2000 service. A Windows 2000 service is a faceless process that is loaded when Windows 2000 is started. A service is like a console program—it is an executable program and it does not need to support COM, but it can call COM objects and Windows Application Programming Interfaces (APIs).

Controlling a Service

A service is controlled through the Service Control Manager (SCM), which is responsible for maintaining the individual services and the database of services. SCM enables you to start or stop a service using the dialog box shown in

Figure 20–1. In this figure, the service that is being controlled is the Web server (W3SVC).

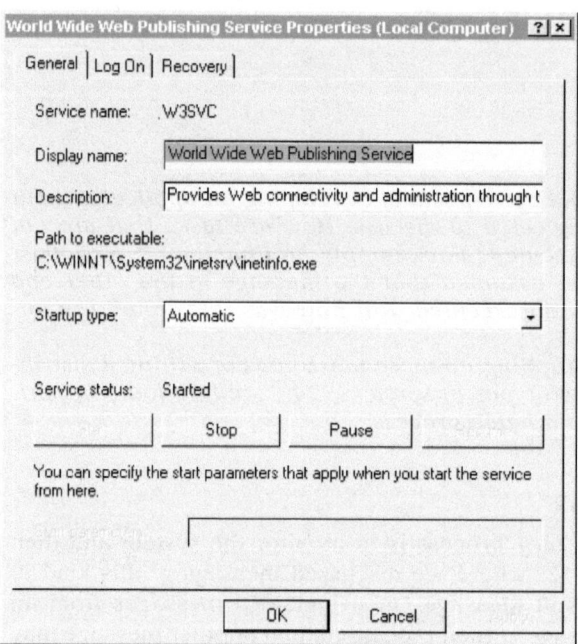

Figure 20–1: Service Properties dialog box

When a service is added to the SCM database, a Startup type must be specified. The Startup type defines how the service will be started when Windows 2000 is booting up. You can select from among these Startup types:

- Automatic: When the computer starts, the service is automatically started.
- Manual: When the computer starts, the service is not started, but it can be started using the SCM.
- Disabled: When the computer is started, the service is not started, nor can it be started using the SCM.

Depending on the Startup type, the Service status will reflect the current execution state of the service. In the case of Figure 20–1, the Startup Type is automatic, so the Service status is Started.

There are three service execution states:

- Started: The process is active, and it responds to events and processes requests.
- Stopped: The process is not active and it does not do anything. It effectively ends itself and "exits."
- Paused: The process is active, but it does not accept new tasks or events. It finishes whatever it was doing. This can also be called a graceful shutdown.

DETAILS OF SERVICES

Our next step is to write a Windows 2000 service. When writing a service, the most complex part is multithreading concepts.

A service is similar to a console application. When a console program is started, the main function is called first. The same thing happens with a service, except that the thread that calls main is called the *main entry thread*.

The main entry thread is responsible for initializing the service status, and when the main entry thread is starting, the service is considered to be in an unstable state. The SCM waits while the main entry thread initializes and defines the ServiceMain entry point. The last function that the main entry thread calls is StartServiceCtrlDispatcher, which accepts the ServiceMain entry point as input. If this function works, the call will not return until the service has ended.

After the SCM has the ServiceMain information, the SCM starts another thread and calls the ServiceMain function, which has multiple responsibilities. The first responsibility is to register a service control handler. The SCM has the capability to start, stop, and pause the service that we are currently writing. When the service is started, stopped, or paused, the SCM calls the service control handler function. This call occurs on a thread that is separate from the ServiceMain thread, which means that this call is made at the same time as the service is processing data. Hence, it is up to the service to react to the service control handler function. Failure to do so in a timely manner will result in the SCM doing a hard exit.

When the ServiceMain thread starts, the service is still in an unstable state. It is up to the ServiceMain thread to indicate the status of the thread, indicating whether the service is starting, stopping, or running.

Building a Service

Services are generally written with C++ because of the multithreading and control issues. There are add-ons and libraries that let you write services in other languages, but it is still best to use C++. But don't worry that the entire application needs to be written using C++. A service has the capability to call COM+ applications, such as the conference registration application.

There is also a free Visual C++ add-on utility (the CodeGuru NT Service Wizard) that does a very good job of creating service applications, so that you don't have to write the C code yourself. The generated service application handles all of the lower-level details of communicating with the SCM. The wizard written by Joerg Konig can be found at the CodeGuru site (www.codeguru.com). It is included with the source code accompanying this book in the *util/ntservice* directory.

USING THE CODEGURU NT SERVICE WIZARD

The utility is written as a wizard—when it is installed, it is used as a project wizard. When you start Visual C++ Developer Studio and generate a new application, you are presented with a project wizard selection list, similar to the one in Figure 20–2.

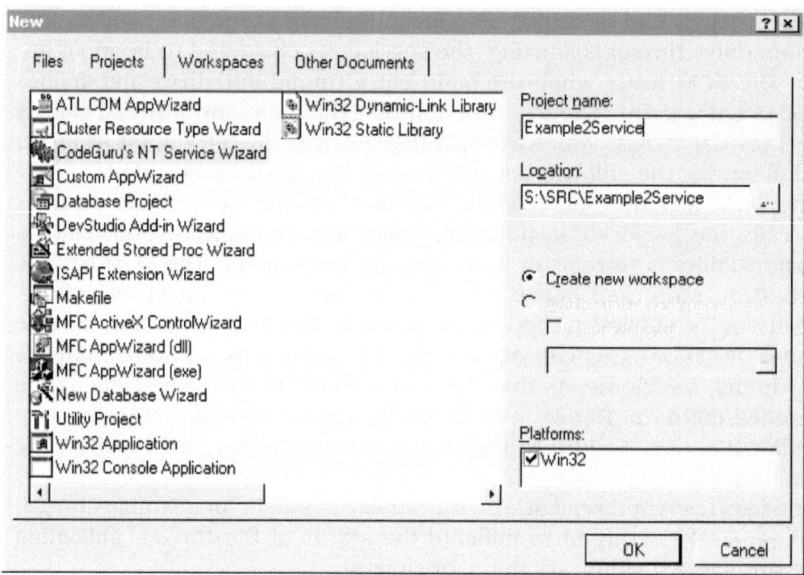

Figure 20–2: Project wizard selection

The name of the project can be anything that you want. In Figure 20–2 the Project Name is Example2Service. Click OK to move to the next page of the wizard, which is shown in Figure 20–3.

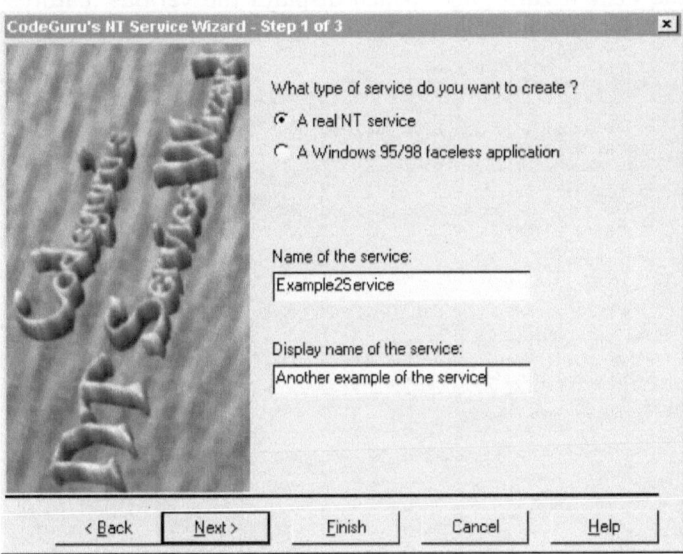

Figure 20–3: Service definition

On this page of the wizard, you choose to create A Real NT Service or A Windows 95/98 Faceless Application. The default option is to create an NT service, which also means that the service is Windows 2000. Because the future of corporate server development involves Windows 2000, this is the selection that you will most commonly make.

The text entered in the `Name of the Service` text box is used when an event is logged in the event services. The text entered in the Display Name of the Service text box is used when the service is displayed in the Service Control MMC. Click Next to move on to the next wizard page, which displays the various features that the service supports, as shown in Figure 20–4.

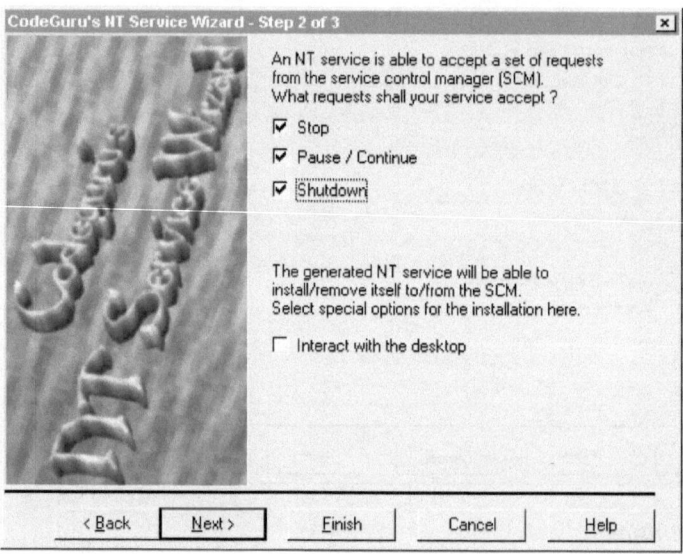

Figure 20–4: Service feature support

There are three checkboxes that can be set in this wizard page. These checkboxes correlate with the messages that can be sent to the service control handler function: stopping, pausing, and shutting down. If you do not check anything, the SCM will consider the service to be hostile and will shut it down abruptly. To be considered a good service, the bare minimum of checkboxes that need to be set are the Stop and Shutdown checkboxes.

The wizard page shown in Figure 20–4 might lead you to think that the SCM or service control handler function has the capability to filter messages. However, that is not what happens. By default, all messages are sent to the service control handler function, and the Service Wizard generates a stub that either implements or skips the message. This means it is possible to add message functionality after the service source code has been generated.

By default, a service is like a console program, and a console program does not have the capability to manage windows and other client areas. In normal situations, a service has the same constraint. If your service requires the capability to create windows and other client areas, then it must have the capability to interact with the desktop. To allow this, check the Interact with the Desktop checkbox.

As a warning, though, do not attempt to raise dialog boxes to indicate errors. This will only frustrate administrators. Instead, write to the Windows 2000 event log to indicate errors, or send an e-mail to the administrator.

Click Next to get to the next wizard page, which enables you to specify the username and password that the service will use for security rights when it is executing. While this may seem useful, it is not. The wizard stores the username and password in the source code, and this is just asking for security problems. Click Finish to generate the source code.

LOOKING THROUGH THE SOURCE CODE

To understand how the service works, let's inspect the source code. The source code does not depend on any headers, except those from Windows—it is intended to be lean and mean. This means it does not rely on a specific library, so you can integrate MFC (Microsoft Foundation Classes) or ATL (Active Template Libraries) or your own library.

The class view is shown in Figure 20-5. The project contains two classes: CExampleService and CNTService. The CExampleService class subclasses CNTService. The way that the project is set up is that the CNTService class handles all of the SCM requests and service details, such as the registration and event management of the service. When required, CNTService delegates functionality to CExampleService using C++ virtual methods. The CExampleService class implements the service functionality and the service control handler functions.

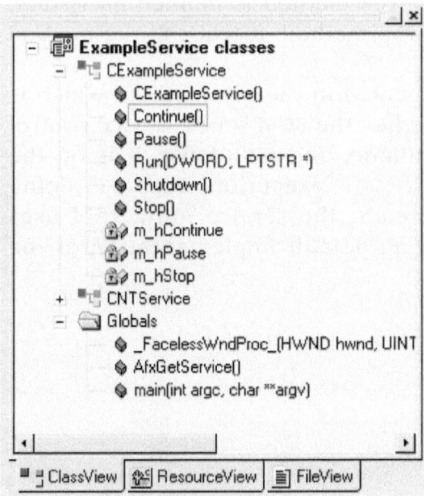

Figure 20-5: Example service class view

Within the `CNTService` class are several static methods:

```
static void WINAPI    ServiceCtrl(DWORD CtrlCode);
static void WINAPI    ServiceMain(DWORD argc, LPTSTR * argv);
static BOOL WINAPI    ControlHandler(DWORD CtrlType);
```

These methods are called by the SCM, but because they are static, they do not have a reference to the `CExampleService` class. Instead, the sources define a global variable: gpTheService. When the SCM wants to control the service, it calls the `ControlHandler` method. The method then decides which action is desired, such as starting or stopping the service. These actions are delegated to the `CNTService` method's implementations of the actions, which are defined as follows:

```
virtual void    Stop();
virtual void    Pause();
virtual void    Continue();
virtual void    Shutdown();
```

In the wizard screen shown in Figure 20–4, we specified which SCM service control messages we wanted to be informed of. The wizard implements the appropriate methods in the `CExampleService` class. Suppose the Stop checkbox in Figure 20–4 is checked. In that case, the Codeguru NT Service Wizard generates a stop method in `CExampleService`, which has the same method signature as the `CNTService::Stop`. Because the `CNTService::Stop` method is defined as virtual, when the `ControlHandler` method calls the Stop method, it will call the method declared in `CExampleService`.

The main service functionality is implemented in the `Run` method, which is called by the `ServiceMain` method. However, when the SCM sends service control messages to the methods Stop, Pause, Continue, and Shutdown, it is on the service control handler thread. The `ServiceMain` execution thread is doing something else. To synchronize the two threads, the service Appwizard uses a Windows API event. Consider the following default implementation of the `CExampleService::Run` method:

```
void CExampleService::Run(DWORD dwArgc, LPTSTR * ppszArgv) {
ReportStatus(SERVICE_START_PENDING);
m_hStop = ::CreateEvent(0, TRUE, FALSE, 0);
m_hPause = ::CreateEvent(0, TRUE, FALSE, 0);
m_hContinue = ::CreateEvent(0, TRUE, FALSE, 0);
ReportStatus(SERVICE_RUNNING);
while( ::WaitForSingleObject(m_hStop, 10) != WAIT_OBJECT_0 ) {
    if(::WaitForSingleObject(m_hPause, 5) == WAIT_OBJECT_0) {
        while(::WaitForSingleObject(m_hContinue, 50) != WAIT_OBJECT_0)
            if(::WaitForSingleObject(m_hPause, 50) == WAIT_OBJECT_0)
                goto Stop;
        ::ResetEvent(m_hPause);
```

```
        ::ResetEvent(m_hContinue);
    }

    // TODO: Enter your service's real functionality here
}
Stop:
if( m_hStop )
    ::CloseHandle(m_hStop);
if(m_hPause)
    ::CloseHandle(m_hPause);
if(m_hContinue)
    ::CloseHandle(m_hContinue);
}
```

At the beginning of the Run method, the ReportStatus method is called. This is an important method call—the ReportStatus method must be called every 20 seconds from the time ServiceMain is called to indicate that the service is alive and reacting to the actions being put to it. If the 20 seconds pass and the ReportStatus method is not called, the service manager will think that the process has died. In the first ReportStatus call, the SERVICE_START_PENDING constant is passed in as a parameter.

Next, the event objects stop (m_hStop), pause (m_hPause), and continue (m_hContinue) are created using CreateEvent. After those function calls, you can add your own initialization routines, but remember that if they take longer than 20 seconds, you need to call ReportStatus. After everything is initialized, ReportStatus is called, and the SERVICE_RUNNING constant is passed in as a parameter.

In the wizard-generated code, a generic while loop is started to periodically check whether an event to stop or pause was triggered. Those events are triggered by the implementations of the CExampleService service control methods. If nothing was triggered, the service is allowed to do some work, but this does not mean the work can take over the thread. You must periodically check whether the SCM has sent a request for the service to change execution status.

ADDING THE COM+ APPLICATION CODE

The execution code that you add to the service is the same code that you would use to consume a COM+ component in Visual C++. This means that you write code using the COM compiler and adding exception handling to handle errors.

In the CExampleService::Run method, where it says *TODO*, you could add the following code:

```
try {
SIMPLECOMLib::ITestInterfacePtr ptr( "SimpleCOM.TestInterface.1");

ptr->delayMethod( 10000);

} catch( _com_error err) {
;
}
```

Remember that in the initialization of the CExampleService::Run method, you need to add a CoInitialize function call.

STOPPING THE SERVICE

When the SCM sends a message to stop the service, the CExampleService::Stop method is called. The default implementation is as follows:

```
void CExampleService::Stop() {
ReportStatus(SERVICE_STOP_PENDING, 5000);
if( m_hStop )
    ::SetEvent(m_hStop);
}
```

The implementation sends back a message that the service is about to stop (ReportStatus) and that it should take five seconds. Of course, this value can be changed, but the problem is actually determining how long it will take for a service to stop. Windows 2000 is not a real-time operating system in which interrupts force a process to stop and change focus. Instead, the Stop method has put the service into a state of pending stop and the SCM will wait for the service to finish or wait for further events. If the ServiceMain thread has run wild and is not responding, there is a problem. The only way to kill the process is to use the Windows 2000 tlist and kill utilities, which are found in the Windows 2000 resource kit and which will kill any process. This saves you from having to reboot the machine.

This isn't the only way to deal with a badly behaving service. In the implementation of Stop, you can wait for a confirmation of the stop event. While the method is waiting, it can keep sending a pending stop using the ReportStatus method. If the confirmation does not come within a defined period of time, then the ServiceMain thread can be killed. The advantage of using this approach is that if there are any outstanding resources, the Stop method can release them.

HANDLING COM OBJECTS IN CONCURRENT THREADS

Our service is currently doing all of its work in a single thread. There is no concurrency. This means that if the computer has four processors, only one processor will be used. What we want is to have the ServiceMain thread spawn other threads to handle more processing.

Achieving Scalability by Using Multiple Threads

When using multiple threads in a service application, there are two problems: COM objects calling other COM objects executing in different threads, and providing synchronization. To solve these two problems and provide scalability, we will create a method call that will be almost identical to the CExampleService::Run method, except that it will be executed multiple times. We need a separate method because the CExampleService::Run (ServiceMain) thread and the spawned threads initially have differing functions. The CExampleService::Run thread is responsible for spawning and managing the threads. But when CExampleService::Run has completed that work, it is free to do something else, and in this case it will run the same code as the spawned threads.

The method that will perform the work is defined as follows:

```
void RunInThread( void *reference) {
long refId = (long)reference;
while( ::WaitForSingleObject(m_hStop[ refId], 10) != WAIT_OBJECT_0 ) {
    if(::WaitForSingleObject(m_hPause[ refId], 5) == WAIT_OBJECT_0) {
        while(::WaitForSingleObject(m_hContinue[ refId], 50) != WAIT_OBJECT_0)
            if(::WaitForSingleObject(m_hPause[refId], 50) == WAIT_OBJECT_0)
                goto Stop;
        ::ResetEvent(m_hPause[ refId]);
        ::ResetEvent(m_hContinue[refId]);
    }
    CoInitialize( NULL);
    try {
        SIMPLECOMLib::ITestInterfacePtr ptr( "SimpleCOM.TestInterface.1");

        ptr->delayMethod( 10000);

    } catch( _com_error err) {
        ;
    }
    CoUninitialize();
}
}
```

In this case, the code looks very similar to the code snippets shown previously. The difference is that the pause, continue, and stop event objects are part of an array. Each thread is assigned an ID that indexes this array. When a thread needs to be stopped or paused, it checks its own event.

Giving each thread its own event may seem a bit more complicated than using some other global type of synchronization. However, the problem with global synchronization is that it requires more code than is actually necessary. The data is stored in a thread local structure and is defined as follows:

```
struct _threadData {
    HANDLE      m_hStop;
    HANDLE      m_hPause;
    HANDLE      m_hContinue;
};
```

When one thread needs to call another, it simply retrieves the ID of the thread to be called, which corresponds to an index in the _threadData array. By using SCM or another administrative tool, it is possible to put all threads on pause, or to only start some threads. If more threads are needed, then more threads are started, and each has its own ID, which is an index to the _threadData array.

Multiple Threads Calling Each Other

Now that our application is multithreaded with proper synchronization, the next task is to describe how the individual COM objects in the different threads can communicate with each other. When running multithreaded COM applications, you cannot just create a global COM object and then reference it in every thread because you may conflict with COM threading.

In COM threading, there are three different models: free-threading (MTA), apartment-threading (STA), and neutral-threading (NTA). All of the COM and COM+ consumer-object examples were STA-based applications.

The difference between the different models is how the COM objects are synchronized when a client is consuming them. In STA, when a client makes a method call on a COM object, that client is guaranteed to be the only client making a method call on that COM object. Any other client attempting to make a method call is put on hold until the first client has finished the method call. In MTA, when a client makes a method call on a COM object, another client can make a concurrent method call. In NTA, the COM object automatically switches into STA or MTA mode depending on the client. This makes the COM method calls faster, because there is no thread context switch.

How does all of this apply to the multithreaded service? Using the STA model makes writing synchronization simpler because COM will handle the details regardless of the threading model that the COM+ object uses. Because of how COM+ works, it is better for COM+ to manage the details of synchronization. When the thread uses the MTA COM threading and there is a COM object that says it can handle both, bugs may appear because COM threading is almost like black magic—very few people understand it. Some programming languages, such as Visual Basic, cannot handle MTAs, so using an MTA will not provide a huge advantage. A stable and robust service is the goal, even if it is a bit slower.

So, assuming that we are using STA, when one thread calls a COM object executing in another thread, it needs a safe COM handle—otherwise the application will crash. To retrieve a safe COM handle, the COM interface pointer needs to be passed from one thread to another using the CoMarshalInterThreadInterfaceInStream function. It essentially saves the interface pointer to a stream, which is then read by the other thread. When the interface pointer is read from the stream, it is automatically marshaled. The marshaling process ensures that the COM and COM+ context and attributes are not bypassed.

The following example shows a thread that previously instantiated a COM interface pointer and is about to save it to the IStream stream.

```
IStream *gStream;
void thread1( void *param) {
...
CoMarshalInterThreadInterfaceInStream( IID_ISimpleInterface, pInterface,
&gStream);
// Signal an event that the interface has been marshaled
}
```

To read the saved COM interface pointer, the other thread would use this code:

```
void thread2( void *param) {
...
CoGetInterfaceAndReleaseStream( gStream, IID_ISimpleInterface,
pLocalInterface);
}
```

The CoGetInterfaceAndReleaseStream function reads the interface pointer and then releases the stream. Now the second thread can call the COM interface pointer and proceed as normal.

While using this method may seem like more work, it is less work than writing your own synchronization code, which may not be COM+ compliant. COM+ can provide synchronization for the life of the transaction, and this information cannot be deciphered in the service.

Running a Batch Process

Sometimes you need to generate reports every week or every month in a batch process. The easiest way of running a batch process is to use the Windows 2000 scheduled tasks to execute a script that communicates with your COM+ application.

Using the Windows Scripting Host

In the previous chapter on debugging, the scripting host was used as a driver, but I did not explain how it worked. A scripting file is written in a script-based language, and the scripting host can execute this file and process the language commands. A scripting file is like a batch file in that it can carry out complex tasks. The advantage of using the scripting host is that it is a COM-based scripting environment. The script can call other COM objects and the scripting host is exposed as a COM object to the script being executed.

To start the scripting host, execute the command cscript or wscript. Both commands can execute either a JavaScript file (.js) or a VB script file (.vbs).

The `cscript` command is a console-based program and `wscript` is a Windows-based program. For the purpose of running tasks on the server, console mode is more appropriate.

USING WSCRIPT

Using the scripting object there are three main COM objects: `WScript`, `WshShell`, and `WshNetwork`. For most tasks, you only use `WScript`.

When the script starts, you can execute some functions that are inherent in the scripting language. However, your main task will most likely be to create other COM or COM+ objects and then manipulate them. To do that you need to reference the `WScript` COM object. It is the COM object that is used to create other COM objects. For example, to create another COM object and then call a method on the created COM object, the following JavaScript code could be executed:

```
var tempObject;
tempObject = WScript.CreateObject("SimpleObject.SimpleInterface")
temp.delayMethod( 1000);
```

The `WScript.CreateObject` method accepts as a parameter the PROG ID of the COM object. When the object is instantiated, it retrieves the `IDispatch` interface so that it can access the individual methods. Make sure that your COM and COM+ object supports `IDispatch`.

To release the object, the `WScript.DisconnectObject` method is called, as follows:

```
WScript.DisconnectObject( tempObject);
```

If it is necessary to send some information to the desktop, the `WScript.Echo` method is used, as follows:

```
WScript.Echo("Hello world");
```

Finally, you either exit the script when the script ends or you call the `WScript.Quit` method.

KEEPING TRACK OF PAST ACTIONS

When you are running a batch process multiple times, it is often useful to keep track of what has happened in the past. This is typically done by using a file or a database. A simple way to do this is to use the Registry.

The `WshShell` COM object has three methods: `WshShell.RegRead`, which reads a Registry key, `WshShell.RegWrite`, which writes a Registry key, and `WshShell.RegDelete`, which deletes a Registry key. The following example shows them in use:

```
tempObject = WScript.CreateObject( "WScript.Shell");
tempObject.RegWrite( "HKEY_CURRENT_USER\\Value", "Some string value");
WScript.Echo( tempObject.RegRead( "HKEY_CURRENT_USER\\Value"));
```

RUNNING ANOTHER PROGRAM

Sometimes a batch file needs to start another batch process or another console program. The WshShell.Run method can be used for that purpose. An example implementation is as follows:

```
tempObject = WScript.CreateObject( "WScript.Shell");
tempObject.Run( "secondprocess.exe", 0, FALSE);
```

The first parameter of the tempObject.Run method specifies the process to be started. The second parameter specifies what the window state will be when it is started. Because this is a server-side process, the window state will be 0. The last parameter specifies whether or not the scripting host will wait until the process is done. A value of FALSE means that the scripting host will not wait, and TRUE means that it will wait and return the error code as a return value.

Adding a Scheduled Task

To add a scheduled task to the task scheduler, it is possible to use a series of COM interfaces and write a program that will add the task for you. Instead, we will use the task wizard to add a task to the task scheduler.

First, from the Explorer window, expand the MyComputer -> Control Panel node, and then select the Scheduled Tasks node. On the right side, double-click the Add Scheduled Task option. The starting dialog box will appear. Click Next, and the dialog box shown in Figure 20–6 appears.

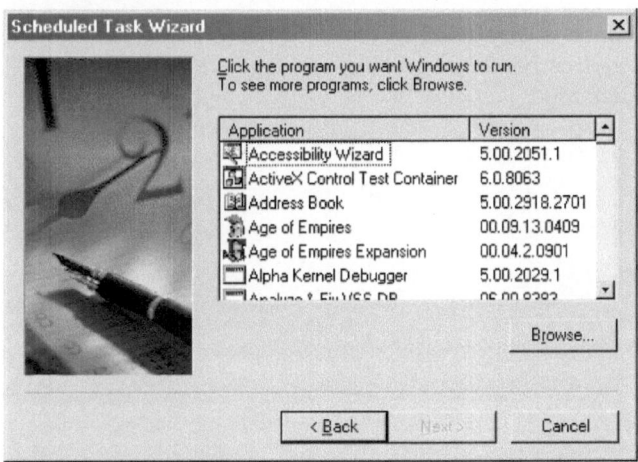

Figure 20–6: Program selection

The list of applications contains all of the applications that can be started by the task scheduler. The cscript.exe application is not found in this list. To add this application, click the Browse button and search for the cscript.exe from the common open dialog. Usually it is found in the windows\system32 directory.

Click OK and then Next. The dialog box in Figure 20–7 will appear, and in this dialog box you can define the name of the task and when it should be performed. There is a variety of possibilities, such as daily, weekly, monthly, and so on. For the time being, select daily and click Next.

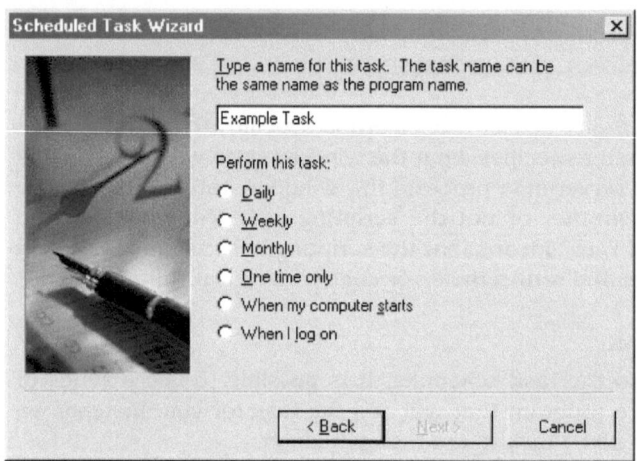

Figure 20–7: Scheduled task definition

The next dialog box controls the properties of the time selection. Leave it set as is and click Next.

The next step defines which user is used when the process is started. Select this carefully, because it requires batch-processing privileges. Type in the username and password, and click Next.

The next dialog box, shown in Figure 20–8, describes the task that you just defined. Check the Open advanced properties for this task when I click Finish checkbox, and click Finish.

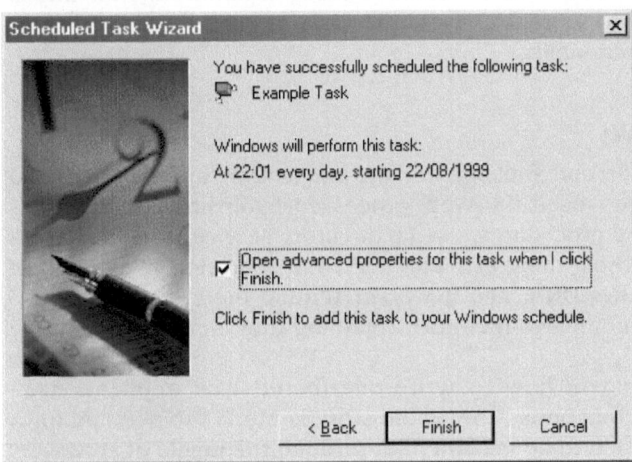

Figure 20–8: Task description

Finally, in the Advanced Task Properties dialog box shown in Figure 20–9, look at the Run text box. It contains only the name of the file that contains the script to be executed, as shown here:

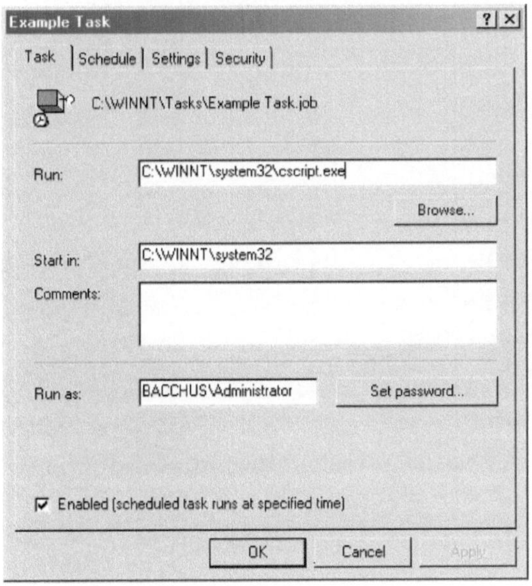

Figure 20–9: Advanced task properties

```
C:\WINNT\system32\cscript.exe s:\src\script\example.js
```

Now, the dialog box can be closed by clicking OK.

This is all you need to do to create a batch process. If richer functionality is required, it may be better to write a console program or some additional COM objects to provide that functionality.

The Final Perspective

We have now designed, built, and implemented the application, and we have used transactions, sent messages, used the Web, processed Extensible Markup Language (XML), written stored procedures, used a directory service, connected to a database, and made the whole thing available for 24□7 operation. We did all of this in the name of Windows DNA, and it works! Writing big systems that use many different systems is complex—it is not something that can be done in one step.

This book has shown you how to write distributed Web applications. I haven't said everything in this book—the whole story is much too detailed for a single book. What I have tried to do is cut a path through the jungle of acronyms and provide you with a guide on how you can cut your own path in the jungle.

If you have any comments about this book, good or bad, please send them to me at cgross@devspace.com. And remember to visit the Web site (www.devspace.com/windna) for the latest information about this book.

Appendix A
Patterns Used in This Book

This appendix lists the patterns used in this book. If this pattern was originally described in another book, then the reference to it is given.

Bridge Pattern

See *Design Patterns: Elements of Reusable Object-Oriented Software*; Gamma et al., Addison-Wesley, 1997; ISBN 0-201-63361-2.

PROBLEM

The point of object-oriented development of a system is to abstract the design and then develop multiple implementations. The traditional example is of defining a generic shape class and from that deriving square, circle, and other classes. Doing this is fine, but there is a side effect. When the abstraction is bound to the implementation, the client is bound to the implementation. This makes the entire architecture difficult to extend and change because all of the classes are too tightly bound.

SOLUTION

The solution to this problem is to create an interface that defines a specific functionality, and then have a class implement that interface. The advantage of this solution is that it has the ability to not define a permanent binding—the client binds to an interface and not a specific implementation.

An example of an interface is as follows:

```
class MyInterface {
public:
virtual void myMethod( long param1) = 0;
}
```

And a sample implementation would be defined as follows:

```
class MyImplementation : public MyInterface {
public:
virtual myMethod( long param) { }
};
```

CONSEQUENCES

- **Decouples interface and implementation**: An interface is not bound to any specific implementation. When an interface is associated with an implementation, it is not permanent and it can alter the binding of the interface at runtime.
- **Improved extensibility**: Both the interface and implementation can be extended independently.
- **Hiding implementation details**: Because the client only sees the interface, it does not need to know anything about the details of the implementation. The implementation could be one class, or ten thousand classes. It does not matter.

Command Pattern

See *Design Patterns: Elements of Reusable Object-Oriented Software*; Gamma et al., Addison-Wesley, 1997; ISBN 0-201-63361-2.

PROBLEM

In most application designs, the architecture is limited to a single computer. Or, if it is distributed on several machines, it is a synchronous communication (such as DCOM). Reliable and robust applications can be developed using messaging applications. However, the problem with messaging is that a message needs to be explicitly defined and the data must be explicitly serialized. In a messaging environment, the sending and receiving processes must also be explicitly programmed. All of these extra steps make programming more complicated.

SOLUTION

The solution is to create a class definition that has a method that is called by a container. The method is then implemented by an object that executes its own actions. This is the most flexible arrangement because it uncouples the functionality from the container and the object.

The class is defined as follows:

```
class Command {
public:
virtual void execute( IUnknown *pUnk) = 0;
};
```

CONSEQUENCES

This pattern has these consequences:

- It uncouples the design, such that the object that invokes the operation does not need to know how to perform the operation.
- Command objects can be extended, manipulated, and built to specification, so long as they implement the **MSMQCommand** interface.

- Commands can be embedded, combined with other commands, or combined as composite commands.
- Creating new command objects is simple, because the container that executes the command does not need to know what it does. It only needs to know about the **MSMQCommand** interface. This means the number of commands is limitless.

Data Abstraction Pattern

See *Pattern Languages of Program Design*; Vlissides et al.; Addison Wesley, 1996; ISBN 0-201-89527-7.

PROBLEM

When developing applications or components, there is the problem of persisting the data. When creating a persistence solution, you need to determine how to convert the natural format of the data, which could be a database, to some specific language, which could be Visual Basic. After the data is converted, you need to figure out how to save it back to the native format.

Other questions that you also need to ask are these: How does the solution scale? How stable is the solution? How coherent is the solution in a multiuser scenario? These questions are typical in the development of an enterprise system.

SOLUTION

The solution to this problem is to abstract the native data format into the language-specific data format. A data-abstraction class is used to store the data, and there is another class, called an operations class, that will operate directly on the data class.

Because there are no resources attached to the language-specific data format classes, the operations class does not care where the data comes from. The language-specific data format classes will form the core of the layered application.

CONSEQUENCES

- **Scalable**: The solution can be made more scalable because there is one storage location, the central repository.
- **Centralized storage**: There is only one copy of the data throughout the entire network. The performance and cache capabilities are a responsibility of the resource and not of the operations manipulating the data structure.
- **Resource independence**: The language-specific data format class is a representation of some underlying native data format. It represents a specific format because data abstraction does not define the operations used to gain access to the native data format.
- **Encapsulation through interfaces**: The data abstraction represents a native data structure, so the consumer does not need to explicitly know what the native data format is.

Façade Pattern

See *Design Patterns: Elements of Reusable Object-Oriented Software*; Gamma et-al., Addison-Wesley, 1997; ISBN 0-201-63361-2.

PROBLEM

When a system is developed, the design initially starts with a group of well-designed objects, and the interaction between the objects is also well defined. However, both time deadlines and bug fixes require that some shortcuts be taken and that some objects that were not foreseen in the original design be created. As a result, the object count increases and the design begins to fragment.

Or, perhaps a system is developed with a fine granular design. Even though the design is good, the client must manipulate many different objects to accomplish any given task, as shown in Figure A1-1.

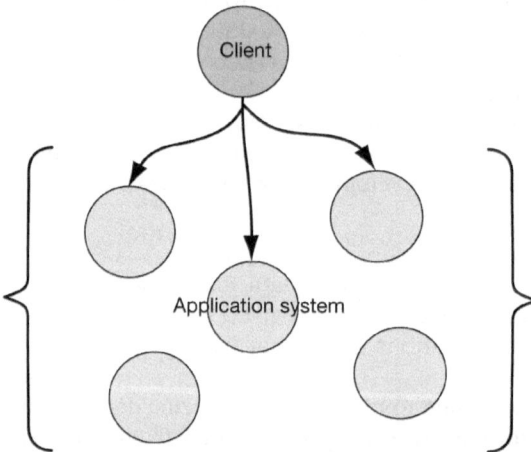

Figure A1-1: Fine granular object architecture

Or, in this architecture, a client may need to manipulate a low-level object. This increases the object-dependency count and the number of clients that may need to be modified if the object is modified.

SOLUTION

The solution is to create an object that encapsulates the functionality of several lower-level objects. The newly encapsulated object becomes a sort of superobject that does not contain any logic other than the encapsulation of the lower-level tiers. Typically, these objects are specialized to solve a specific problem.

The design is shown in Figure A1-2.

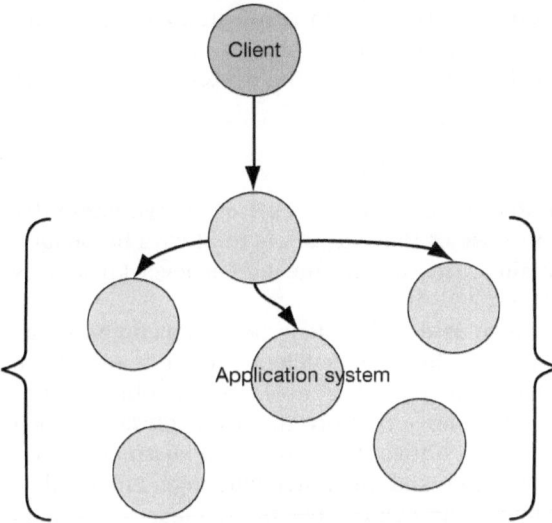

Figure A1-2: Façade object architecture

CONSEQUENCES

This architecture shields the client from the underlying subsystem, making it easier to understand what the architecture is doing, without having to understand all of the details. The client only needs to understand the details of one object. Façade users are purely application programmers who really do not care what the lower level is doing or why.

This architecture promotes the weak coupling of the client and the underlying subsystem. Because the façade interface definition resembles a known business process, the entire implementation can change without requiring any changes to the client.

Layered Pattern

See *Pattern Languages of Program Design*; Vlissides et al.; Addison Wesley, 1996; ISBN 0-201-89527-7.

PROBLEM

In large systems, objects are often developed to access specific functionality. That functionality can be accessing a resource, interfacing with a consumer, or something else. But those components access other components without a properly defined abstraction and protocol. The word *protocol* here refers to a calling sequence and not a data stream.

Consider the example of a consumer calling a predefined data component. Suppose to create a quick bug fix, that data component were bypassed and the consumer accessed the resource directly. This would result in chaos. As more quick fixes are added, the system would become unstable because the ramifications of each fix are unknown. In the extreme case, the system becomes one huge patch.

SOLUTION

To avoid this situation, the proper strategy is to create a series of layers that defines a specific functionality. The purpose of these layers is to always be opaque to the layer that uses its functionality. This means the higher-level layer uses only functionality from the lower layer.

In Figure A1-3, the layers are drawn as a series of circles. Let's compare this to the conference registration application that was developed in the book. At the center of the system is the core, which can be a set of tables or core objects. Typically, it is a view of the data. One level above that are the utility classes, which could be stored procedures or SQL views. Above that is the data abstraction that forms the connection between the resource and the native language. Encapsulating that layer is the helper object layer. The helper objects are classes that help perform specific actions, but are not application related. And finally, above the helper classes are the application classes. At this level there may be many other levels, but that is totally dependent on the application being developed.

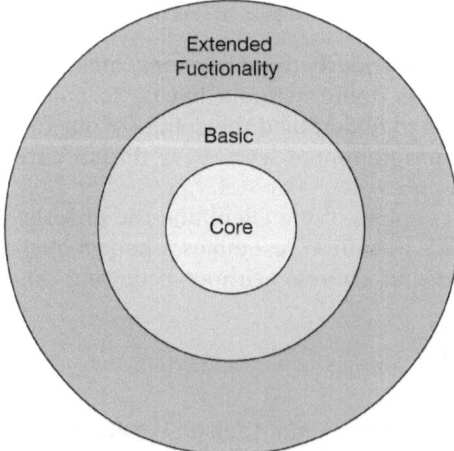

Figure A1-3: Layered architecture

CONSEQUENCES

- **Organization**: The entire system is organized. When one layer is altered, the ramifications are easy to identify and fix. This is does not mean that the design is monolithic, because within the layers certain entry points can be defined.

- **Dependence**: Because one layer depends on another, a change to one layer will directly affect only the layer above.
- **Single thread**: It is assumed that when one layer is accessed, only a single thread of action is executing.

Remote Control Pattern

See Chapter 14 of this book.

PROBLEM

Most applications written for the Web present client applications that don't offer shortcuts for the power user. On the Web, things generally are made self-explanatory, but for a power user this extra information slows down productivity. The power user understands the application and wants to move through the steps quickly. The power user does not want to click 50 hyperlinks before finding the desired Web page. However, maintaining two code bases for two users would be silly. Doing so would double the costs of distribution, training, and development.

SOLUTION

The remote control pattern takes its name from its conceptual similarity to remote controls for TVs, VCRs, and other electronic devices. On those remote controls, there are simple buttons and complex buttons. The simple buttons that let you change the volume and channel are for all users. These buttons tend to be big and easy to read.

The power user will want more control, perhaps to adjust the Surround Sound or to tape the latest movie from satellite. The power user will use the little buttons that offer more complex features on the remote control. The steps involved are more complex and involve reading messages on the TV to validate the programming. The power user is not influencing the content, but is making the content more accessible for his or her needs.

The remote control pattern uses this concept for the user interface. With Microsoft Internet Explorer, it is possible to embed the Web browser control in an application and then program the control. Using this technique, it is possible to command the browser to retrieve and manipulate pages according to the power user's requirements. The functionality of the Web is not changed, nor does this change how the Web application works. This simply offers power users a technique to make them more productive when surfing a specific Web application.

CONSEQUENCES

- **The client application is de-coupled from the Web content**: The features added at the presentation layer do not influence the overall Web application flow because Internet Explorer is embedded as a control. Any power user proficient in a programming language can program the browser to his or her tastes. It fulfills the needs for all users, even though they are using the same Web application.

- **Centralized Web content**: The end solution still uses the Web to retrieve the content and display it to the user. The main Web application can be updated on the server, without requiring an update of the remote control pattern application. Traditional applications would need updating on the client side.
- **Browser dependent**: This solution does require the functionality of the Microsoft Internet Explorer Web browser control. It cannot be replaced with a competitor's component because there is no browser control component specification.

Separating Format from Logic Pattern

See White Paper in the MSDN library; Christian Gross; 1998. This White Paper is included with the source code for this book, in the *demo/pattern* directory.

PROBLEM

Consider a traditional user interface with buttons, tables, and radio buttons. When a button is clicked, some action happens on a table or list box. The buttons are user interface elements and the action is user interface logic. In a traditional application the user interface elements and logic are tightly coupled. This is part of RAD (Rapid Application Development) and its ease of creating user interfaces. The user interface is constructed using a series of controls that encapsulate logic that can be programmed. This type of approach is considered to be the only successful reusable technology.

Although the preceding statement is true, there are some ramifications. The tight integration of elements and logic has forced the code to be nonreusable. It is not possible to easily extend or remove pieces of the user interface without adversely affecting the logic or elements. In fact, it is not possible to make the user interface controls display data using your specific format. It is a situation in which you either accept the user interface as it stands or reject the entire user interface.

One of the solutions is to create a thin client that has only user interface elements and minimal user interface logic. Although this solves the problem of nonreusability of user interfaces, there is a cost to moving all of the processing to the server. Bigger servers and faster and bigger networks are required to handle the extra processing.

An optimal client should only contain user interface elements and user interface logic. The user interface elements are used to move data from the user interface logic to the backend server. User interface logic is the presentation of data in a specific format that requires conversion from another format.

Graphing is an example of a more advanced client and is a big client in byte terms. Generating graphs that revolve or try out various scenarios requires quite a bit of programming logic, and all of this programming logic is dedicated to the user interface. At no point do the graphing routines attempt to manipulate data on the resource. The user interface elements can be controls or base elements native to the development environment, but user interface elements, such as the logic, must not modify data on the server side, bypassing the architecture. If they do bypass the architecture, system state and maintainability will be sacrificed.

SOLUTION

The solution is to dynamically associate user interface elements with the user interface logic. This is a typical approach for JavaScript, but not for user interface logic embedded within components. The user interface logic is defined by an application controller, and if necessary, by individual application implementations. The purpose of the application controller is to abstract the task of the application to something generic, such as buying, selling, and organizing. The controller is the connection to the script interface. The controller must be generic so that it can be implemented in an situation that the application specifies.

The application implementations implement specific tasks, working with the parameters of buying a stock, punching in a vacation time slot, and so on. The implementations depend on the controller, not vice versa. The implementations register themselves with the controller and it implements an interface that the controller expects to see. Once registered with the controller, the implementations plays a passive role where the controller manages its actions.

The user interface elements are registered with the components. This way, the user interface can be updated while still using all of parts of the components. All of these associations are based on the layered-pattern approach. The implementations are dependent on the controller, and the controller is dependent on the user interface elements. However, in the other direction there is no dependency. A user interface element does not need the application controller, and the application controller does not need an implementation. This makes it easier to substitute new components.

CONSEQUENCES

- **Language neutral**: The architecture is defined as a series of layers that interacts with components. This means it is possible update any of the layers without adversely affecting the entire architecture. The components can be written in any language.
- **Controller dependent**: If the controller was badly designed and did not reflect the business practices, the controller will become obsolete. A good controller forces the definition of the process in generic terms.
- **Implementation details hiding**: At each level, the individual components do not care how things are implemented. Instead, the focus is on how to communicate using the interfaces required at each level.
- **Simple**: The design cleanly separates the format of the user interface from the logic of the user interface.
- **Extensibility**: The association of one level to the next is done in a run-time dynamic mechanism. Therefore, it is possible to update it at run-time, making changes simpler and updates less costly.

Appendix B

Source Code Description

What follows is an explanation of what is contained in the various directories of the Windows DNA source code.
www.apress.com/titles/1-893115-17-8

/ActiveDirectory

Associated chapter: 18

In this directory are the Visual Basic and Visual C++ samples that show how to write an Active Directory application using the ADSI COM interfaces.

/appConference

Associated chapters: 9, 10, 11

In this directory are the various versions of the conference registration application. The last two letters of the subdirectory names within this directory indicate the programming language used to implement the conference registration application.

subdirectory: /interfaces

This directory contains the various COM interface definitions for the conference registration application.

subdirectory: /receiver

This contains the Visual C++ application used to test the asynchronous receiver.

/appMSGermany

Associated chapters: 8, 9, 10

In this directory are the various versions of the Web registration application. The last two letters of the subdirectory names indicate the programming language used to implement the user registration application.

subdirectory: /interfaces

This directory contains the various COM interface definitions for the user registration application.

/ASPIntegration

Associated chapter: 13

In this directory are a Visual Basic application and a Visual C++ application that show how ASP and the associated language can be integrated.

/COMEvents

Associated chapter: 12

In this directory are projects that show how to write a COM+ event application.

/common

In this directory are several header files that a Visual C++ developer will find of interest. They are used throughout the demos in this book. The headers make it simpler to write enterprise applications.

/demos

subdirectory: /cppcomponents

In this directory are various samples that were distributed with the Microsoft VC++ e-commerce CD. They were included with this source code because I wrote the Visual C++ e-commerce components. For more information, please refer to the readme.doc file in this directory.

subdirectory: /DataAccess

Associated chapter: 16

In this directory are various ADO examples that show how to use ADO, data shaping, and ADO 2.5 record navigation.

subdirectory: /OLEDBExamples

Associated chapter: 17

In this directory are various examples of how to use the OLE DB consumer templates in a Visual C++ application.

subdirectory: /pattern

In this directory is an application and associated white paper that I wrote, which show how to apply patterns in the development of client HTML applications.

subdirectory: /persistence

Associated chapter: 11

In this directory are various applications that show how to persist COM objects using the MSMQ COM components.

subdirectory: /VIWeb

Associated chapters: 4, 5, 6

In this directory are the various HTML demos that show how to manipulate ASP, DHTML, and XML.

/errors

Associated chapter: 9

This directory contains the Visual C++ error-handling component that can be used to log errors in a log file using a generic COM object.

/IEIntegration

Associated chapter: 14

In this directory are the various applications used to demonstrate how the hybrid client application can be built using Visual Basic and Visual C++.

/interfaces

Associated chapters: 8, 9

In this directory are various applications that demonstrate how to consume and create COM objects in the three different languages: Visual Basic, Visual C++, and Visual J++. Also shown is how to create the different IDL files.

/queued

Associated chapter: 12

In this directory is a sample application that shows how to write a COM+ queued component.

/SQL

Associated chapter: 15

In this directory are the various SQL scripts that are used in the conference registration application.

/util

subdirectory: /devaids

Associated chapter: 19

In this directory are two sample applications that track bugs and track test cases using Access 97. The applications are of very good quality.

subdirectory: /ntservice

Associated chapter: 20

In this directory is the CodeGuru Service wizard that can be used to generate source code for an NT or Windows 2000 service.

subdirectory: /RegInterface

In this directory is a very simple application, which, when compiled, makes it possible to register type libraries in the Registry.

subdirectory: /UML models

Associated chapters: Throughout the book

In this directory are the various UML diagrams used to build the conference registration applications. Rational Rose is required to read the UML diagrams.

subdirectory: /XMLango

In this directory is a time-limited edition of XMLango, which is a very comprehensive framework to build XML and Web-based e-commerce applications.

/XML

Associated chapter: 14

In this directory are the various XML samples used to build the hybrid client application.

Index